The Official Guide to

America's
National Parks

TWELFTH EDITION

Fodor's Travel Publications
New York • Toronto • London • Sydney • Auckland
www.fodors.com/

Fodor's

The Official Guide to America's National Parks

Editor: Emmanuelle Morgen
Design: Guido Caroti
Contributors: Pat Hadley-Miller, Alicia Muñoz, Erica Rex, Holly Smith, and Pamela Wiesen
Production Editor: David Downing
Research Assistance: Research assistance provided by the National Park Service: Office of Communications; Office of Public Affairs; Division of Park Planning and Protection; Harpers Ferry Center Publications Division
Photography: Tim Davis/Stone/Getty, cover; PhotoDisc, xvii, xli, 413, 445; PictureQuest, iii

Copyright

Twelfth Edition
ISBN 1-4000-1375-5
ISSN 1532-9771

Special Sales

CONTENTS

THE NATIONAL PARK FOUNDATION

Every year millions of Americans travel to national parks like Yosemite and Yellowstone, which incorporate some of the most stunning landscapes on Earth. The National Park Service, which preserves and protects these areas, also cares for several hundred other areas, including not only forestlands studded with unique natural features but also coastal areas and historic sites and landmarks.

Chartered by Congress in 1967, the National Park Foundation is the official nonprofit partner of the National Park Service. The National Park Foundation honors, enriches, and expands the legacy of private philanthropy that helped create and continues to sustain America's National Parks.

This book, as the official guide, helps support the national parks. So when you take it home, you'll be helping to preserve and protect some of the most fascinating and most beautiful parts of the United States.

Another way to help the parks is by purchasing a National Parks Pass. The National Parks Pass costs $50 and is valid for one full year from the time you first use it for admission to all National Parks that charge an entrance fee. The Pass comes with a special National Park Pop-Out map, a Proud Partner vehicle decal, and an offer for a free *GoParks* newsletter.

The image on the National Parks Pass is chosen through an annual nationwide photo contest. The National Parks Pass *Experience Your America* Photo Contest is sponsored by the National Park Foundation and the National Park Service with Kodak, a Proud Partner of America's National Parks. For more information, please visit www.nationalparks.org, home of the National Park Foundation.

Officers

Chairman
The Honorable Gale A. Norton
U.S. Secretary of the Interior

Vice Chair
David Rockefeller Jr.
Director, Rockefeller & Co., Inc.

Secretary
Fran P. Mainella
Director, National Park Service

President
Jim Maddy

HOW TO USE THIS BOOK

The national parks are the focus of this guide, and you'll find a thumbnail sketch of each along with information about what you'll see and do there. It should help you immeasurably as you plan your travels.

In these pages the alphabet rules. Parks are grouped by states, and both the states and the parks they contain are arranged in alphabetical order. Some parks straddle state lines, or have units in more than one state; you'll find the text for these in the chapter devoted to the state in which the headquarters are found. Affiliated areas, which are not federally owned or administered by the National Park Service but that draw on technical or financial aid from the Park Service, are listed in the Other National Parklands section at the end of the book, along with the couple of dozen national trails, national heritage areas, and national rivers that are not administered by the park service. At the end of each chapter are cross-references to all affiliated areas and multistate parks found within the boundaries of the state covered by the chapter. Regional maps at the front of the book pinpoint locations of the parks (or, in the case of multistate entities, that of their headquarters).

What to See & Do

The activities and pastimes offered by the park begin this section, followed by a list of park **Facilities,** such as visitor centers, contact and ranger stations, museums, hiking trails, book and gift stores, etc. Often the best place to start your visit is at the visitor center, where you can pick up maps of the park, see interpretive exhibits, and obtain in-depth information about attractions.

In addition to opportunities for outdoor or cultural pastimes, many parks also sponsor special programs, which operate either year-round or seasonally. In the **Programs & Events** section we've spelled out those you'll find year in and year out and noted when others are available. These are orchestrated when demand warrants and when peoplepower and funding permit.

Sometimes programs are cut and hours scaled back at short notice. So, although you can rest assured that all information in this book was checked thoroughly by the park rangers themselves at press time, it's always a good idea to confirm information when it matters—especially if you're making a detour to visit a specific place.

The **Tips & Hints** section helps you plan a safe and enjoyable visit. If a park is very remote, you'll want to prepare in advance by packing lunch or supplies. Of course, you'll need to check for park-specific rules, regulations, and advisories before you go and once you're there.

Food, Lodging & Supplies

The **Camping** section lets you know where to put up a tent or park your RV in or near the park. We provide you with information on the number of sites at a campground, the price range for one night, and the facilities you can expect to find—flush, vault, or pit toilets; hot or cold showers; and RV hook-ups. Most drive-in campsites in the national parks are run on a first-come, first-served basis. If you're traveling during peak summer months, arrive as early as possible or have standby reservations at a nearby public or private campground. For more than 30 of the most popular parks, you can make reservations in advance through the National Parks Reservation Service (tel. 800/365–2267 or http://reservations.nps.gov); these include Acadia, Assateague, Big South Fork, Cape Hatteras, Carlsbad Caverns, Channel Islands, Death Valley, Everglades, Fort Hunt, Frederick Douglas, Glacier, Grand Canyon, Great Smoky, Greenbelt, Golden Gate, Gulf Islands, Independence, Joshua Tree, Katmai, Mammoth Cave, Mount Rainier, Olympic, Rocky Mountain, Sequoia and Kings Canyon, Shenandoah, Sleeping Bear, Whiskeytown, Wright Brothers and Zion. For 12 others—Arches, Big Bend, Black Canyon of the Gunnison, Blue Ridge Parkway, Bryce Canyon, Buffalo National River, Chickasaw, Curecanti, Lake Roosevelt, Lassen Volcanic, North Cascades, and Ozark Riverways—you can make reservations through the National Recreation Reservation Service (tel. 877/444–6777 or www.reserveusa.com). A separate telephone number (tel. 800/436–7275) takes reservations for Yosemite. Reservations are available up to five months in advance; not all campgrounds may be available.

Most national park campgrounds are can accommodate RVs, although you will usually find only basic facilities. Electrical hook-ups, water pumps, and disposal stations are available only at a handful of locations.

In the **Hotels** and **Restaurants** sections, we list lodging and dining establishments in the park, or near to it. Accommodations in and near national parks range from chain hotels and motels with modern appliances to rough and rugged wilderness camps with kerosene lamps instead of electricity. Cabins with housekeeping facilities are popular, as are small, family-owned bed-and-breakfasts and the occasional grand old hotel. If you're traveling in high season—roughly between Memorial Day and Labor Day—make reservations three or four months in advance or more, if you can. At some of the most famous hostelries, some people reserve for the next summer as they check out. Hotel prices listed in this book are for two people in a standard room in high season. Prices drop as much as 25% in low season. For a complete list of hotel chains and their toll-free phone numbers and Web sites, *see* Lodging Contact Information at the back of the book.

Restaurants were chosen for proximity to the parks and convenience for the traveler, with lunch service the priority; prices reflect the range in cost for main courses at lunch. Remember, prices are likely to be higher for dinner.

Fees, Hours & Regulations

This section includes the entry fee to the park, if any, and the cost of special services, like tours; the hours of operation for the park and all its visitor centers; and information about permits and park regulations. For example, in many parks where backcountry camping is allowed, you are required to register at the visitor center and obtain a permit before embarking, and sometimes a fee is charged.

Types of Parks

There are a variety of parks, and each type is indicated by an icon, as follows:

 National Parks contain a variety of resources protected by large areas of land or water. **National Preserves** also protect specific resources but allow activities not permissible in national parks, such as hunting, fishing, and the extraction of minerals and fuels, so long as they do not jeopardize natural values. **National Reserves** are like National Preserves, but are managed not by the Park Service proper but instead by local or state authorities.

National Memorials are primarily commemorative of a historical subject or person.

National Monuments, usually smaller than national parks and lacking their diversity, preserve at least one nationally significant resource.

Parks designated as **National Historic Sites** preserve places and commemorate persons, events, and activities important in the nation's history. **National Historical Parks** are similar but are larger and more complex.

National Military Parks, National Battlefield Parks, National Battlefield Sites, and **National Battlefields** are all associated with American military history.

National Recreation Areas are set aside purely for recreational use. **National Lakeshores and National Seashores** preserve shorelines and islands while providing water-oriented recreation. **National Rivers and Wild and Scenic Riverways** protect ribbons of land bordering streams that have not been dammed, channelized, or otherwise altered. Besides preserving rivers in their natural state, these areas provide opportunities for outdoor activities. **National Scenic Trails** are long-distance footpaths that wind through areas of natural beauty. **National Parkways** include a roadway and the ribbons of land flanking them, offering leisurely drives through areas of scenic interest.

OTHER TERMS USED IN THIS BOOK

The section of the guide entitled "Other National Parklands" also discusses Affiliated Areas and National Heritage Areas. An **Affiliated Area** is a significant property preserved in the United States or Canada that has not been designated by Congress as one of the 388 units of the National Park System but that draws on the financial or technical expertise of the National Park Service. Some of these sites have been recognized by Acts of Congress; others have been designated National Historic Sites by the Secretary of Interior. (Some National Historic Sites are part of the park system proper, while some are Affiliated Areas.) There are also a number of **National Heritage Areas** around the country, which conserve the nation's natural and cultural heritage and make it accessible to visitors. These regions, mainly private property, are managed by partnerships among federal, state, and local governments and private nonprofit organizations.

National park areas may also have additional designations assigned by the United Nations Educational, Scientific, and Cultural Organization (UNESCO) in accordance with the World Heritage Convention. **World Heritage Sites** are irreplaceable properties of outstanding international significance; **Biosphere Reserves,** exemplifying some of the world's varied ecosystems, provide a field for research and education, serve as repositories of genetic diversity, and provide baseline data for monitoring global environmental change.

ABOUT YOUR VISIT

More than ever, our national parks are being discovered and rediscovered by travelers who want to spend their vacations appreciating nature, watching wildlife, and taking adventure trips. But as the number of visitors to the parks increases, so does stress on wildlife and plant life. Tourism can drum up concern for the environment, but it can also cause great physical damage to parks. As you visit the parks, please keep in mind that these lands will not thrive without your care, nor will they last without your support. And use common sense to keep your visit as safe as it will be enjoyable.

Entrance Fees

The entrance fees charged by many national park areas are noted in the text. If your travels will take you to many national parks, consider purchasing the **National Parks Pass** ($50), which admits you and your companions to all parks that charge entrance fees for one year at no additional charge. (Camping and parking cost extra.) A percentage of  the proceeds from sales of the pass helps to fund important projects in the park. The **Golden Age Passport** ($10), for those 62 and older, and the **Golden Access Passport** (free), for travelers with disabilities, both entitle holders to free entry to all national parks, plus 50% off fees for the use of many park facilities and services. You must show proof of age and of U.S. citizenship or permanent residency (such as a U.S. passport, driver's license, or birth certificate) and, if requesting Golden Access, proof of your disability. You must get your Golden Access or Golden Age passport in person; the former is available at all federal recreation areas, the latter at federal recreation areas that charge fees. You may purchase the National Parks Pass by mail or on the Internet. For information, contact the National Park Service (Department of the Interior, 1849 C St. NW, Washington, DC 20240-0001, 202/208–4747, www.nps.gov). To buy the National Parks Pass, write to the National Park Foundation, Attention: Park Pass, Box 34108, Washington, DC 20043-4108, call 888/467–2757 (888/GO–PARKS), or visit www.nationalparks.org.

Staying Safe

Motor-vehicle accidents, drownings, and falls are among the leading causes of death in the national parks. These are accidents that common sense can help you avoid. If you find yourself in an emergency situation, call 911 and the park rangers; there are telephone booths at the visitor centers and other locations throughout the parks. Some parks have their own emergency numbers as well.

Before you go, be sure to pack a first-aid kit, including a first-aid manual. Keep in mind that even in summer the weather can change unexpectedly—especially in mountainous parks. Temperatures can rise into the 90s during the day and drop into the teens or lower at night. Always have warm clothing and rain gear handy, no matter how promising the day.

WILD ANIMAL ENCOUNTERS

As human development shrinks wildlife habitats, animal encounters are increasingly common in national parks. To avoid attracting bears, raccoons, and other scavengers, be sure to animal-proof your food supplies. At many developed campsites, animal-proof containers are available; in the backcountry, hang food in a bag or container at least 15 feet above ground and as far away from the trunk of the tree as possible. Stay away from bears and their cubs, and try not to hike at dawn or dusk, when encounters with mountain lions are most common. If you do see one, inch away steadily without turning your back or bending down.

Staying Healthy

ALTITUDE SICKNESS

One of the most common problems for hikers is altitude sickness, which results when you ascend above 8,500 feet without proper acclimatization. To help prevent altitude sickness, spend a night or two at a higher elevation before attempting any strenuous physical activity, and if you have a history of heart or circulatory problems, talk to your doctor before planning a visit to areas at high altitudes.

Symptoms of altitude sickness include headache, nausea, vomiting, shortness of breath, weakness, and sleep disturbance. If any of these occur, retreat to a lower altitude. Altitude sickness can develop into high-altitude pulmonary edema (HAPE) and high-altitude cerebral edema (HACE), both of which can be permanently debilitating or fatal.

ANIMAL & SNAKE BITES

Some animals, especially rodents, carry dangerous diseases. If you are bitten by a wild animal, see a doctor as soon as possible. Many animal bites require a tetanus shot and, if the animal could be rabid, a rabies shot.

Snakes do everything to avoid you, but in the event that you have a run-in and are bitten, act quickly. If it's a harmless snake, treat as you would any other puncture wound. If it's poisonous, have the victim lie down and remain as still as possible so as to minimize the spread of venom through the body. Keep the wound below the rest of the body, and have another person seek medical help immediately.

GIARDIA

You can't see giardia, but these tiny water-borne organisms can turn your stomach inside out. Carry bottled water for day trips; drinking water is available at many campgrounds. If you're hiking into the backcountry and can't carry enough water, you must purify all spring or stream water, no matter how clear. The easiest way to purify water is to drop in a water-purification tablet, or eight drops of chlorine bleach or 20 drops of iodine per gallon of water. You can also filter it through a water-purification pump, available at camping equipment stores. Boiling water, another method, takes time and uses fuel. But if it is the only method available, allow the water to boil for at least 10 minutes, longer at high altitudes.

HAZARDS OF HIKING, PRECAUTIONS TO TAKE

Always choose hiking trails suitable to your physical condition and the amount of weight you plan to carry. Consider the length of the trail, its steepness, and how acclimated you are to the altitude at the start and finish. Always be aware of the possibility of altitude sickness. Every hiker planning multiday backcountry trips, particularly those traveling solo, should leave their intended route, planned length of trip, and return date with a park ranger before setting out.

Proper clothing is essential, especially on more rigorous hikes. Hiking boots should be well broken in and sturdy, with good traction and ankle support. On less demanding trails, athletic shoes are fine. Wear thick wool socks, and always bring a second pair in case one gets wet. Rain gear is a good idea, since the weather in most of the national parks can change drastically within moments. Always carry at least two quarts of water per person per day, even more if you are staying overnight or are hiking in hot weather.

HYPOTHERMIA & FROSTBITE

It does not have to be below freezing for hypothermia to strike: This potentially fatal decrease in body temperature occurs even in relatively mild weather. Symptoms are chilliness and fatigue, followed by shivering and mental confusion. The minute you spot these signs, seek shelter, remove wet clothing, and wrap the victim in warm blankets or a sleeping bag—if possible get into the sleeping bag with him or her. High-energy food and hot drinks also aid recovery.

Frostbite is caused by exposure to extreme cold for a prolonged period of time. Symptoms include the numbing of ears, nose, fingers, or toes; white or grayish yellow skin is a sure sign. Take frostbite victims into a warm place as soon as possible, and remove wet clothing. Then immerse the affected area in water that's warm—not hot—or wrap the area in a warm blanket. Do not rub, as this may permanently damage tissues. When thawing begins, have the victim exercise the area to stimulate blood circulation. If bleeding or other complications develop, get to a doctor as soon as possible.

LYME DISEASE

This potentially debilitating illness is caused by a virus carried by deer ticks, which thrive in dry, brush-covered areas. Before walking in woods, brush, or through fields in areas where Lyme disease has been found, spray yourself thoroughly with tick repellent and wear pants tucked into socks, and long sleeves. When you undress, search your body for ticks and remove them with rubbing alcohol and tweezers.

Watch the area for several weeks. Some people develop a rash or flulike symptoms; if this happens, see your physician immediately. Lyme disease is treated with antibiotics.

PLANT POISONS

Learn to recognize poison ivy, poison oak, and poison sumac, and avoid them. If you accidentally step into a patch, wash exposed skin immediately with soap and water, and do not touch clothing that has been in contact with the plants. If a rash and blisters develop, use calamine lotion or cortisone cream to relieve itching.

SUNBURN & HEAT STROKE

Always protect yourself from the sun. At higher altitudes, where the air is thinner, the ultraviolet rays are stronger. Sun reflected off snow, sand, or water can do special damage, even on overcast days. Liberally apply a sunscreen of SPF 15 or higher before you go out, and wear a wide-brimmed hat and sunglasses.

If you are exposed to extreme heat for a prolonged period, you run the risk of heat stroke (also known as sunstroke), a serious medical condition. It begins quite suddenly with a headache, dizziness, and fatigue but can quickly lead to convulsions and unconsciousness or even death. If someone in your party develops any of the symptoms, have one person go for help, move the victim to a shady place, wrap him or her in wet clothing or bedding, and try to cool him or her down with water or ice.

Leave No Trace

FIRE PRECAUTIONS

When it comes to fire, never take a chance. Always build them in a safe place (away from tinder of any kind) and use a fireplace or fire grate if one is available. Clear the ground in the immediate area so wind cannot blow sparks into dry leaves or grass, keep your fire small, and never leave it unattended. Throw used matches into the fire, and always have a pot of water or sand next to your campfire or stove. Don't build fires when you're alone. When you are finished with your fire, be sure it is out cold—you should be able to touch it with your bare hands. Never cook in your tent or a poorly ventilated space.

MINIMUM-IMPACT CAMPING & HIKING

The little extra effort it takes to use the parks responsibly goes a long way toward ensuring the future of North America's natural beauty. Do not leave garbage on trails or in campgrounds. If you hike in the backcountry, carry out what you've carried in, including all your trash. Bury human waste at least 100 feet from any trail, campsite, or water source in a hole at least 8 inches deep; some parks and many environmental organizations advocate packing out even human waste. Do not wash dishes or clothing in lakes and streams. If you must use soap, make sure it is biodegradable, and carry water in clean containers 100 feet away from its source before using it for cleaning.

In national parks that include dunes and barrier islands, walk on marked pedestrian paths. Over time, climbing on the dunes causes erosion and weakens the primary dune system. Never pick dune grasses, which also help ensure the preservation of the dunes.

PETS IN THE PARKS

Generally, pets are allowed only in parks' developed areas, including drive-in campgrounds and picnic areas, but they must be kept on a leash at all times. With the exception of guide or service dogs, pets are not allowed inside buildings, on most trails, on beaches, or in the backcountry. They also may be prohibited in areas controlled by concessionaires. Some parks have kennels, which charge a small daily fee. Be sure to inquire about restrictions on pets before leaving home.

RESPECTING WILDLIFE

Have respect for the creatures you encounter: Never sneak up on them, don't disturb nests and other habitats, and don't touch animals or try to remove them from their habitat, even for the sake of a photograph. Never stand between animal parents and their young, and never surround an animal or group of animals. To help protect endangered species, report any sightings.

VOLUNTEERING

Air pollution, acid rain, wildlife poaching, and encroaching development are among the threats to America's national parks. These problems are being addressed by the National Park Service, but you can help by donating time or money. The National Park Service's Volunteers in the Parks program welcomes volunteers to do anything from paperwork to lecturing on environmental issues. To participate, you must apply to the park where you would like to work, or visit the Web site at www.nps.gov/volunteer. To contribute money, contact the National Park Foundation, the official nonprofit partner of the National Park Service (11 Dupont Circle NW, Suite 600, Washington DC, 20036, tel. 202/238–4200, fax 202/234–3103, www.nationalparks.org).

On the Web

The Web site of the National Park Service, **www.nps.gov,** has complete information about each park. The National Park Foundation's site, **www.nationalparks.org,** can also greatly enhance your experience. You can add a photo to the National Park Foundation's Photo Quilt, send a National Park postcard, contribute your park story to the NPF Park Journal, or enter the National Parks Pass *Experience Your America* Photo Contest. You can also learn about National Park Foundation programs, find out how you can give something back to the parks, and buy an annual parks pass on-line. In addition, in the site's Insider Opinions section, you can trade park tips with other travelers.

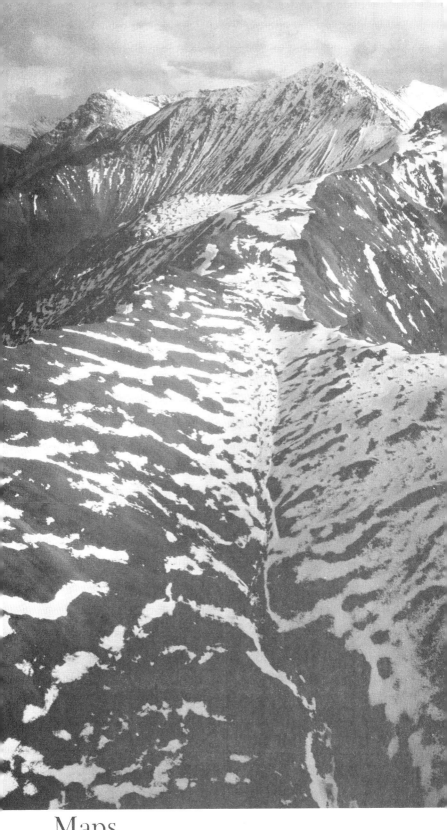

Maps

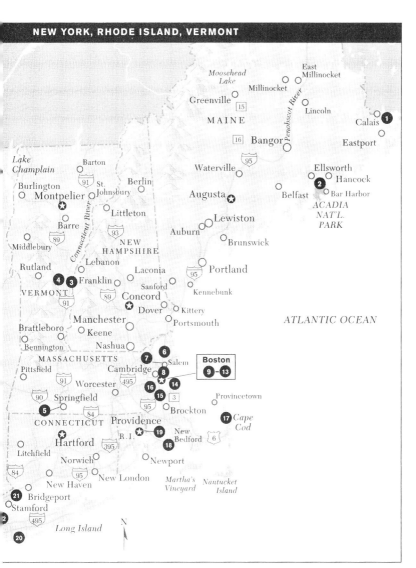

MAP 2: DELAWARE, MARYLAND, NEW

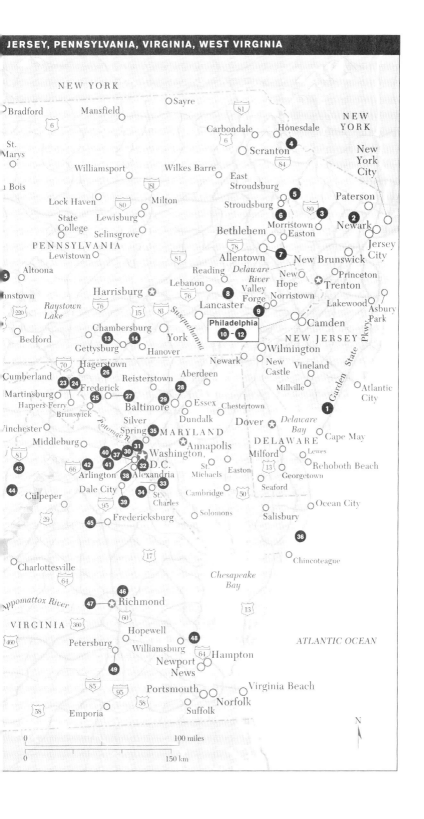

MAP 3: ALABAMA, FLORIDA, GEORGIA,

Gulf of Mexico

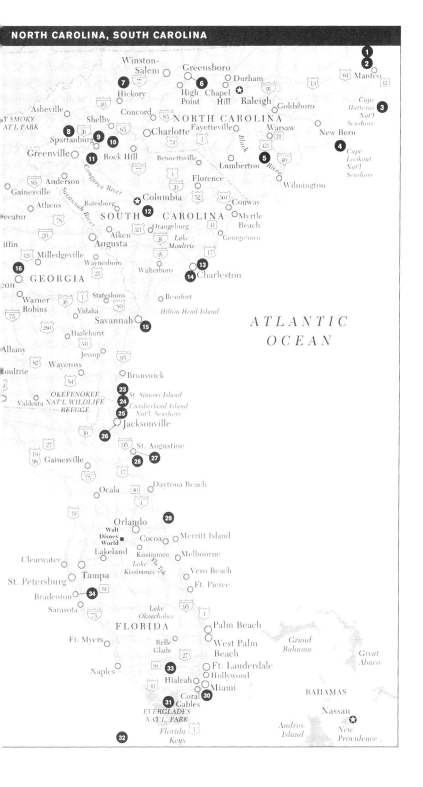

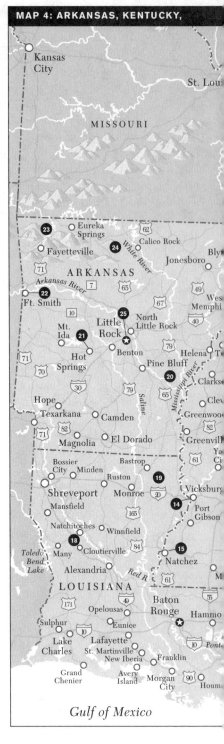

MAP 4: ARKANSAS, KENTUCKY,

MAP 5: ILLINOIS, INDIANA, MICHIGAN,

CANADA

①

ortage

⑦ Isle Royale
Nat'l Park

*Lake
Superior*

ls

Keweenaw
Peninsula **⑧** ○ Copper
Harbor

○ Houghton

○ Sudbury

○ Ironwood

○ Marquette

Sault
Ste. Marie ○

⑨

*Mackinac
Island*

Iron
Mountain

MICHIGAN

NSIN

○ Escanaba

*Beaver
Island*

○ Mackinaw
City

*Manitoulin
Island*

*Georgian
Bay*

Petoskey 【75】

○ Alpena

Wausau ○

Marinette ○

○ Northport

Green
Bay

Sturgeon
○ Bay

⑩

○ Traverse
City

MICHIGAN 〔23〕

*Lake
Huron*

ns Point ○

apids ○

Appleton ○

Manitowoc ○

○ Cadillac

*Lake
Winnebago*

Bay
City ○

〔25〕

N

isconsin 〔51〕
Dells
sse ○

Oshkosh ○
Fond ○
du Lac

○ Sheboygan 〔31〕

〔131〕

Saginaw ○

reen ○ Baraboo

〔43〕

*Lake
Michigan*

Grand
Rapids

Flint 〔69〕

〔75〕

Port
Huron

g ○

Madison 〔94〕
✪

Waukesha

○ Milwaukee

〔96〕

✪ Lansing

○ Detroit

⑪

*Lake
Erie*

en Blue
Mounds ○ New
Glarus

○ Racine
○ Kenosha

Battle
Creek ○ 〔196〕

○ Jackson 〔94〕

Ann

Ashtabula ○

○ Galena Rockford

○ Waukegan

Kalamazoo ○

Arbor

Port

Cleveland 〔90〕

Stockton ○ Arlington
Heights ○ Evanston

South
Bend 〔69〕

○ Clinton

⑫

○ Savanna Elmhurst ○ ○ Chicago

〔80〕
〔90〕

Toledo

〔80〕
〔90〕

⑬

Sterling ○

Aurora ○

○ Angola

Sandusky ○

Akron

〔50〕
○
La Salle

Joliet ○

⑳

Gary La
Porte

○ Auburn

Mansfield ○

Canton

⑭

〔55〕

Kankakee

Huntington ○

○ Ft.
Wayne

Lima ○

OHIO

○

○ Peoria

Logansport 〔57〕

〔24〕 〔69〕

Marion ○

〔71〕

nton ○

INDIANA

Wapakoneta ○

Zanesville

Bloomington 〔74〕

Danville Lafayette
○

Muncie ○

Dayton 〔70〕

✪ Columbus

ngfield
✪

Champaign ○

Crawfordsville **✪**

Anderson ○ ○

○ Zionsville

〔71〕

Marietta ○

ville ○ Decatur
㉑

〔36〕

Indianapolis

⑯

⑮ ○ Chillicothe

〔55〕 〔51〕

〔70〕

○ Terre
Haute

Columbus 〔74〕

Cincinnati

〔36〕

ILLINOIS

Bloomington 〔65〕 Madison
○

〔50〕

E.St.
is ○ Louis 〔57〕

Vincennes ○

⑰

Belleville ○

○ Centralia

⑲

New
Albany ○

○

Mount
Vernon 〔64〕

Gentryville ○

Corydon ○

Louisville

KENTUCKY

○ Carbondale

Evansville

Ohio R.

⑱

0				150 miles
0				225 km

MAP 6: IOWA, KANSAS, MISSOURI,

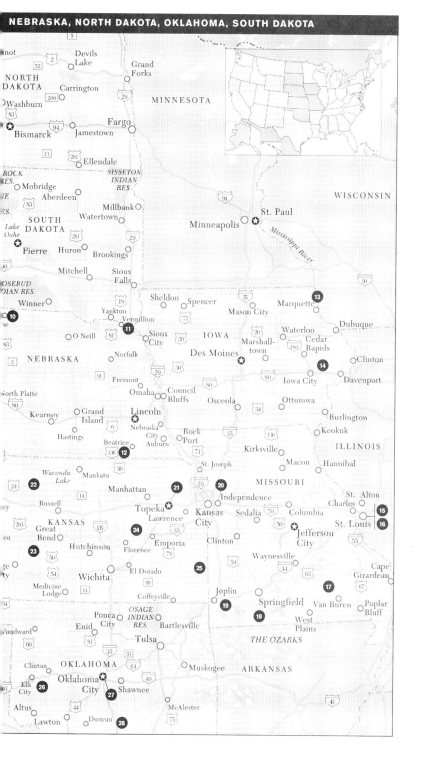

MAP 7: ARIZONA, NEVADA, NEW MEXICO

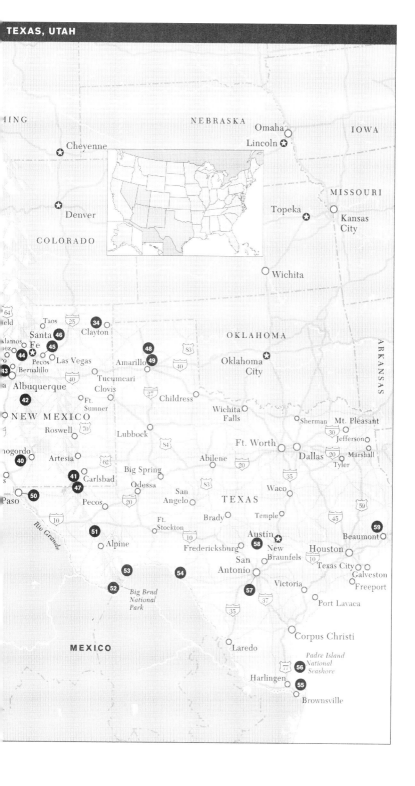

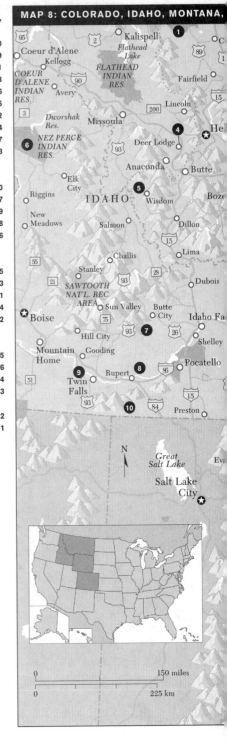

MAP 9: CALIFORNIA, OREGON, WASHINGTO

See Continuation at right

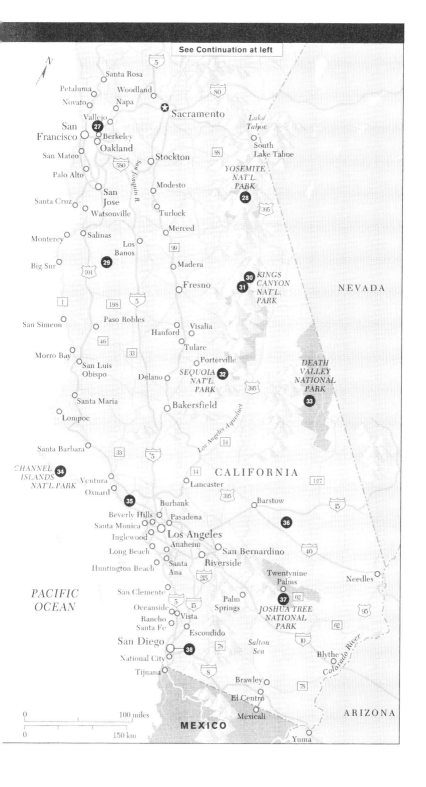

See Continuation at left

N

Santa Rosa

Petaluma
Novato
Napa
Woodland

⭐ Sacramento

Lake
Tahoe

Vallejo
San
Francisco
27
Berkeley
Oakland

South
Lake Tahoe

San Mateo
580
Stockton

Palo Alto

Modesto

YOSEMITE
NAT'L.
PARK
28

Santa Cruz
San
Jose
Watsonville

Turlock

Monterey
Salinas

Merced

Los
Banos

Big Sur
29
101

Madera

Fresno

KINGS
CANYON
NAT'L.
PARK
30
31

NEVADA

1
198
5

Paso Robles

Visalia
Hanford

San Simeon

46
33

Tulare

Porterville

Morro Bay
San Luis
Obispo

Delano

SEQUOIA
NAT'L.
PARK
32

DEATH
VALLEY
NATIONAL
PARK
33

Santa Maria

Bakersfield

Lompoc

Los Angeles Aqueduct

Santa Barbara
33
5

14

CALIFORNIA

CHANNEL
ISLANDS
NAT'L.PARK
34
Ventura
Oxnard
35

14
Lancaster
395

127

Barstow

15

Burbank
Beverly Hills
Santa Monica
Inglewood
Pasadena
Los Angeles
Anaheim

36

Long Beach
Huntington Beach
Santa
Ana
215
Riverside
San Bernardino

40

Twentynine
Palms

Needles

PACIFIC
OCEAN

San Clemente
5
Oceanside
Vista
Rancho
Santa Fe
San Diego
Escondido
National City
Tijuana

Palm
Springs
37
62

JOSHUA TREE
NATIONAL
PARK

95

62

10

38
78

Salton
Sea

8

Blythe

Colorado River

Brawley

El Centro

ARIZONA

0   100 miles

0   150 km

MEXICO
Mexicali

Yuma

XXXV

MAP 10: ALASKA AND HAWAII

Barrow

KAUAI
Wailua
Lihue
Waimea   Poipu
Kauai Channel
NIIHAU
OAHU   Waikiki
Honolulu
Kaiwi
HAWAII
Channel
MOLOKAI
Lahaina
MAUI
Kahului
Lanai City   Kihei   Hana
LANAI
Wailea
Alenuihaha Channel
PACIFIC OCEAN
Waimea
Volcanoes
National Park
Mauna
Kea   Hilo
Kailua-Kona
Mauna
Loa
Kilauea
Crater
Naalehu
HAWAII
(The Big Island)

0   50 miles   N
0   50 km

KS

RANGE

tes of the Arctic
National Park
and Preserve
8

Kanuti Flats
National
Wildlife
Refuge

kon River
Baker   Livengood
Chena
Hot Springs
Yukon
Yukon-
Charley Rivers
National
Preserve
18

na National
dlife Refuge
Fairbanks

Boundary
Dawson
City

CANADA

Denali
National Park
and Preserve
17
Delta Jct
Tok

MOUNTAINS
Mt. McKinley
Cantwell
RANGE
Paxson
Slano   Tetlin
National
Wildlife
Refuge
Wrangell-
St. Elias
20
National Park
and Preserve
Mt. St. Elias

GEORGE PARKS
HWY

ALASKA

Willow   Palmer
Glennallen

16
Anchorage
ke Clark   Tyonek
onal Park   Whittier
Preserve   Kenai
Valdez
Chugach
National Forest
Prince
William
Sound   Cordova

Whitehorse

Seward
19
Kenai
Fjords
National
Park

YUKON TERR
BRITISH COLUMBIA
Skagway

Homer
Cook Inlet
Haines
21
Juneau

Kenai National
Wildlife Refuge

Glacier Bay
National Park
and Preserve
22

us
Kodiak
Chugach
National
Forest

Gulf of Alaska

Hoonah

23
Sitka
Tongass
National
Forest

mal

PACIFIC OCEAN

N
0   100 miles
0   150 km

MAP 11: AMERICAN SAMOA, NORTH

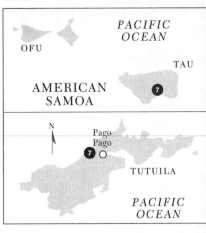

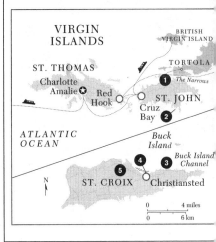

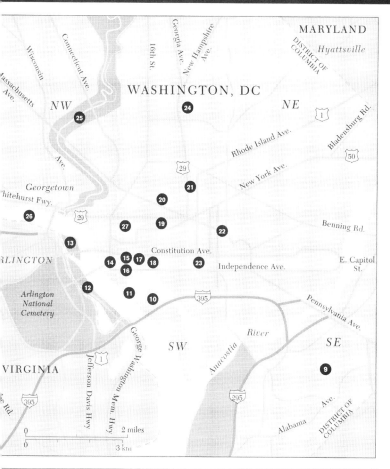

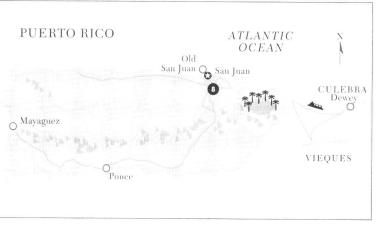

America's National Parks

ALABAMA

Horseshoe Bend National Military Park

In east-central Alabama, near Dadeville

On March 27, 1814, General Andrew Jackson's Tennessee Army of 3,000 regulars, militia, and allied warriors defeated 1,000 Red Stick Creek natives led by Chief Menawa. The bloody battle ended the Creek Indian War, broke the tribe's power in the Southeast, and added Creek lands comprising three-fifths of present-day Alabama and one-fifth of Georgia to the United States. The park was authorized in 1956.

WHAT TO SEE & DO

Fishing (permit required), picnicking, touring museum and battlefield, watching video program and electric map presentations. **Facilities:** Visitor center, sales outlet, 2.8-mi nature trail, 3-mi tour road, boat ramp, picnic area with grills, tables and pavilions, soda vending machine. **Programs & Events:** Living-history programs (monthly), including firing demonstrations, Horseshoe Bend audio-cassette tours, evening campfire and lantern programs, musket drill (monthly, Sat.). Battle anniversary encampment (last weekend, Mar.), park anniversary program (Aug.). **Tips & Hints:** Go Mar.–June or Sept.–Nov. for better weather and more living-history programs. Busiest in May and June, least crowded Dec. and Jan.

FOOD, LODGING & SUPPLIES

Camping: None in park. In Wind Creek State Park: Wind Creek Campground (4325 Rte. 128, 7 mi southeast of Alexander City, tel. 256/329–0845; 640 sites; $14; flush toilets, hook-ups). **Hotels:** None in park. In Alexander City: Horseshoe Inn (3146 U.S. 280, tel. 256/234–6311; 64 rooms; $50–$70), Jameson Inn (4335 U.S. 280, tel. 256/234–7099 or 800/541–3268; 52 rooms; $53). **Restaurants:** None in park. In Alexander City: Cecil's Public House (243 Green St., tel. 256/329–0732; $11–$25; no lunch Sat., closed Sun.). **Groceries & Gear**: None in park. In Wind Creek State Park: The Country Store (4325 Rte. 128, Alexander City, tel. 256/329–0845).

FEES, HOURS & REGULATIONS

Free. Audio-cassette tours $2. No hunting or firearms. Leashed pets only. Pedestrian traffic only on trails. Park scenic road open daily 8–5. Visitor center open daily 8–4:30. Fishing permit required and available at the Country Store in Wind Creek State Park.

HOW TO GET THERE

12 mi north of Dadeville on Rte. 49. Closest airport: Birmingham International Airport (85 mi).

CONTACTS

Horseshoe Bend National Military Park (11288 Horseshoe Bend Rd., Daviston, AL 36256, tel. 256/234–7111, www.nps.gov/hobe). Wind Creek State Park (4325 Rte. 128, Alexander City, tel. 256/329–0845, www.alapark.com). Dadeville Chamber of Commerce (185 S. Tallahassee St., Dadeville, AL 36853, tel. 256/825–4019).

Little River Canyon National Preserve

In northeastern Alabama, near Fort Payne

The nation's longest mountaintop river and the Southeast's deepest canyon create an awe-inspiring backdrop for the preserve. Formed by river waters that are among the nation's purest, the canyon's cliffs tower up to 600 feet and enclose vast biodiversity, including rare and endangered species. Recreational opportunities abound, including hiking, rock climbing, hunting, and fishing. The preserve was authorized on October 24, 1992.

WHAT TO SEE & DO

Canoeing, fishing, hiking, horseback riding, hunting, mountain biking, picnicking, rock climbing, wading, walking. **Facilities:** DeSoto State Park, Canyon Rim Drive, overlooks. Gift shop, grills, pavilion and picnic tables. **Tips & Hints:** Be prepared for challenging rapids and rock climbing. Watch footing on scenic bluffs and cliffs. Go late Oct.–early Nov. for fall colors, Mar.–June for wildflowers.

FOOD, LODGING & SUPPLIES

Camping: In the park: DeSoto State Park Campground (13883 Rte. 89, tel. 256/845–5075 or 800/760–4089; 78 sites; $15–$18; flush toilets, showers, hook-ups). **Hotels:** In the park: DeSoto State Park Lodge (265 Rte. 951, off Rte. 35; tel. 256/845–5380 or 800/568–8840; 25 rooms; $70). In Fort Payne: Fort Payne Inn (1828 Gault Ave. N, tel. 256/845–0481; 69 rooms; $50). **Restaurants:** In the park: DeSoto State Park Lodge (265 Rte. 951, Fort Payne, off U.S. 35, tel. 256/845–5380; $5–$6), Little River Café (4608 De Soto Pkwy., tel. 256/997–0707; $5–$8). **Gear:** In the park: DeSoto State Park Country Store & Information Center (2922 Rte. 618, Fort Payne, tel. 256/845–5075).

FEES, HOURS & REGULATIONS

$2 per vehicle at Canyon Mount Day Use Area. Alabama state fishing and hunting licenses required. Permit required for rock climbers to add or remove bolts. Leashed pets only. Hunting restricted to wildlife management area in season only. No vehicles off roads. No bikes in DeSoto State Park. No collecting rocks or plants. No weapons, alcohol, or fireworks. Park open daily. Canyon Mouth Park open daily 8–8.

HOW TO GET THERE

From Chattanooga, TN, take I–24 west to I–59 south to Fort Payne Exit 222 and follow signs to the preserve. From Birmingham, AL, take I–59 north to Fort Payne Exit 215 (Rte. 35). Take Rte. 35 to the preserve. Closest airports: Chattanooga (45 mi), Birmingham (100 mi), Atlanta (100 mi).

CONTACTS

Little River Canyon National Preserve (2141 Gault Ave. N, Fort Payne, AL 35967, tel. 256/845–9605, fax 256/997–9129, www.nps.gov/liri). DeKalb County Tourist Association (1503 Glenn Blvd. SW, Fort Payne, AL 35968, tel. 256/845–3957, fax 256/845–3946). Fort Payne Chamber of Commerce (Box 680125, Fort Payne, AL 35968, tel. 256/845–2741). De Soto State Park Camping Reservations & Information Center (13883 Rte. 89, Fort Payne, AL 35967, tel. 256/845–5075).

Russell Cave National Monument

In northeastern Alabama, near Bridgeport

Russell Cave was inhabited for almost 10,000 years, from at least 7000 BC to AD 1650. Virtually no other place in the region offers so many clues to how the "First Americans" fed, clothed, and protected themselves. The monument was proclaimed on May 11, 1961.

WHAT TO SEE & DO

Touring cave, watching film. **Facilities:** Information center, museum, trail. Bookstore. **Programs & Events:** Conducted programs and guided cave walks, demonstrations of prehistoric tools and weapons (daily by request). **Tips & Hints:** Plan to spend at least one hour in the museum area and cave mouth. Add one hour for conducted programs. Busiest July and Oct., least crowded Dec. and Jan.

FOOD, LODGING & SUPPLIES

🏕 **Camping:** None at monument. Near Scottsboro: Jackson County Park (2302 County Park Rd., tel. 256/574–4719; 144 sites; $15; flush toilets, showers, hook-ups). 🏨 **Hotels:** None at monument. In Stevenson: Budget Host Inn (U.S. 72 E, tel. 256/437–2215 or 800/283–4678; 30 rooms; $30–$40). ✗ **Restaurants:** None at monument. In Stevenson; River Bend Bistro (104 Adams St., tel. 256/437–0010; $5–$10; no dinner Sun.–Wed.). ♿ **Groceries & Gear:** None at monument. In Bridgeport: Big Daddy's Outdoors (52680U.S. 72, tel. 256/495–9225; closed Sun. Aug.–Feb.).

FEES & HOURS

Free. Monument open Apr.–Oct., daily 8:30–5; Nov.–Mar., daily 8–4:30.

HOW TO GET THERE

7 mi northwest of Bridgeport via Rtes. 75 and 98. Closest airport: Chattanooga, TN (45 mi).

CONTACTS

Russell Cave National Monument (3729 Rte. 98, Bridgeport, AL 35740, tel. 256/495–2672, www.nps.gov/ruca). Jackson County Chamber of

Commerce (407 E. Willow St., tel. 256/259–5500 or 800/259–5508). Jackson County Park (2302 County Park, Scottsboro, tel. 256/574–4719).

Tuskegee Airmen National Historic Site

In east-central Alabama, in Tuskegee

This site commemorates and interprets the actions of the Tuskegee Airmen during World War II. The Airmen included African-American pilots, navigators, bombardiers, and others trained by the Army Air Corps program to fly and maintain combat aircraft. The Tuskegee Airmen overcame segregation and prejudice to become one of the most highly respected fighter groups during the war. Their achievements, together with those of the men and women who supported them, paved the way for full integration of the U.S. military. The site was authorized on November 6, 1998.

WHAT TO SEE & DO

Touring historic site, watching video. **Facilities:** Museum with exhibits. Bookstore. **Tips & Hints:** At this writing, the park is still under development.

FEES & HOURS

Free. Site open daily 9–4:30.

HOW TO GET THERE

Headquarters is on the campus of Tuskegee University in Tuskegee. The University is on Old Montgomery Rd., 1½ mi northwest of downtown Tuskegee, 35 mi east of Montgomery, and 20 mi west of Auburn. From I–85, take Exit 38 and travel north on Rte. 81 for 6 mi to Tuskegee. Follow signs to site. Closest airport: Dannelly Field (Montgomery, 50 mi).

CONTACTS

Tuskegee Airmen National Historic Site (Drawer 10, Tuskegee Institute, AL 36087, tel. 334/727–3200, www.nps.gov/tuai). Tuskegee Area Chamber of Commerce (121 Main St., Tuskegee 36083, tel. 334/727–6619). Chewacla State Park (124 Shelltoomer Pkwy., Auburn, AL 36830, tel. 334/887–5621). Tuskegee National Forest (125 National Forest Rd. 949, Tuskegee, AL 36083, tel. 334/727–2652).

Tuskegee Institute National Historic Site

In east-central Alabama, inTuskegee

In 1881, at the age of 26, Booker T. Washington became the first principal of the newly formed Normal School for Negroes in Tuskegee. George Washington Carver joined the faculty in 1896 and revolutionized agricultural development in the South in the early 20th century. Preserved here are the brick buildings the students constructed, Washington's home, and the George Washington Carver Museum. The site was authorized on October 26, 1974.

WHAT TO SEE & DO

Touring the Historic Campus District, touring the Chappie James University Exhibit (by appointment), visiting Carver Museum and The Oaks. **Facilities:** Carver Museum; The Oaks, home of Booker T. Washington; Chappie James University Museum; walking trail through Historic Campus District. Bookstore. **Programs & Events:** Ranger-led tours of The Oaks. Black History Month Program and Exhibit (Feb.), Annual Carver Crafts Festival (May), Annual Carver Sweet Potato Festival (Oct.), Open House (Dec.). **Tips & Hints:** Plan to spend at least two hours at the Carver Museum and the Oaks. Busiest Feb.–May, least crowded Sept.–Dec.

FEES & HOURS

Free. Site and George Washington Carver Museum open daily 9–4:30. The Oaks open by tour reservation only.

HOW TO GET THERE

The site is on the campus of Tuskegee University in Tuskegee. The University is on Old Montgomery Rd., 1½ mi northwest of downtown Tuskegee, 35 mi east of Montgomery, and 20 mi west of Auburn. From I–85, take Exit 38 and travel north on Rte. 81 for 6 mi to Tuskegee. Follow signs to site. Closest airport: Dannely Field (Montgomery, 50 mi).

CONTACTS

Tuskegee Institute National Historic Site (1212 W. Montgomery Rd., Tuskegee Institute, Tuskegee, AL 36087, tel. 334/727–3200, www.nps. gov/tuin). Tuskegee Area Chamber of Commerce (121 Main St., Tuskegee, AL 36083, tel. 334/727–6619). Chewacla State Park (124 Shelltoomer Pkwy., Auburn, AL 36830, tel. 334/887–5621). Tuskegee National Forest (125 National Forest Rd. 949, Tuskegee, AL 36083, tel. 334/727–2652).

See Also

Natchez Trace Parkway, Mississippi. *Natchez Trace National Scenic Trail,* Mississippi. *Selma to Montgomery National Historic Trail* and *Trail of Tears National Historic Trail,* in Other National Parklands.

Alagnak Wild River

On Aleutian Range, near King Salmon

The 69 mi of federally designated Alagnak Wild River runs out of Kukaklek Lake in the Katmai National Preserve. It offers outstanding white-water floating, as well as abundant wildlife and sportfishing for five species of salmon. The wild river was established on December 2, 1980.

WHAT TO SEE & DO

Fishing, float trips, wildlife watching. **Facilities:** King Salmon Visitor Center. **Tips & Hints:** Bring rain gear, waterproof footgear, and wool clothing. Busiest July and Aug., least crowded Dec. and Jan.

FOOD, LODGING & SUPPLIES

Camping: In the park: Brooks Camp (Brooks River area, tel. 800/365–2267; 17 sites; $8; flush toilets, showers, no hook-ups). Backcountry camping allowed. **Hotels:** None in park. In East Anchorage: Merrill Field Inn (420 Sitka St., tel. 907/276–4547 or 800/898–4547; 39 rooms; $65–$136). In King Salmon: Quinnat Landing Hotel (1 Eskimo Creek Pkwy., tel. 907/246–3000; 48 rooms; $234–$259). ✗ **Restaurants:** None in park. In Anchorage: Gwennie's Old Alaskan Restaurant (4333 Spenard Rd., tel. 907/243–2090; $16–$23). In Kind Salmon: Eddie's Fireplace Inn (1 Main St., tel. 907/246–3435; $8–$30). **Groceries:** None in park. In King Salmon: Alaska Commercial Co. (100 Southside Eskimo Creek, tel. 907/246–6109).

FEES, HOURS & REGULATIONS

Free. Permits (free) recommended for all primitive camping. Alaska state fishing license required. Park open daily.

HOW TO GET THERE

Via boat from King Salmon. Charter flights are available from Anchorage and King Salmon.

CONTACTS

Katmai National Park & Preserve (Box 7, King Salmon, AK 99613, tel. 907/246–3305, www.nps.gov/alag). Alaska Public Lands Information & Visitors Center (605 W. 4th Ave., Suite 105, Anchorage, AK 99501, tel. 907/271–2737).

Aniakchak National Monument & Preserve

On Alaska Peninsula, near Port Heiden

The Aniakchak Caldera covers 10 square mi and is one of the great dry calderas in the world. Located in the volcanically active Aleutian Mountains, the Aniakchak last erupted in 1931. Inside the crater are lava flows, cinder cones, and explosion pits, as well as Surprise Lake, the source of the Aniakchak River, which cascades through a 1,500-foot gash in the crater wall. The site also contains the Aniakchak Wild River. The site was proclaimed a national monument in 1978 and established as a national monument and preserve in 1980.

WHAT TO SEE & DO

Fishing, float trips, wildlife watching. **Tips & Hints:** Bring wool clothing, rubber boots, and good rain gear. Bring all food if camping, and be sure tents can withstand bad weather: the caldera is subject to violent windstorms. Busiest Aug. and Sept., least crowded Jan. and Feb.

LODGING & SUPPLIES

🔺 **Camping:** Backcountry camping only. 🏨 **Hotels:** None in park. In Port Heiden: Carlson's Lodge (2739 Seaview Dr., tel. 907/837–2233; 2 rooms; $100–$120), Carol's Bed & Breakfast (6 Upper Meshik Heights, tel. 907/837–2203; 4 rooms; $120). ♿ **Groceries**: None in park. In Port Heiden: Jack's Store (New Meshik Mall, tel. 907/837–2217).

FEES, HOURS & REGULATIONS

Free. Backcountry permits available from Aniakchak office in King Salmon. Alaska state fishing license required. Park open daily.

HOW TO GET THERE

Regular flights are available from Anchorage to King Salmon. Regular and charter flights are available from King Salmon to Port Heiden, a 10-mi hike over open tundra from the monument. Closest airport: Port Heiden.

CONTACTS

Aniakchak National Monument & Preserve (Box 7, King Salmon, AK 99613, tel. 907/246–3305, www.nps.gov/ania). Alaska Public Lands Information Center (605 W. 4th Ave., Suite 105, Anchorage, AK 99501, tel. 907/271–2737).

Bering Land Bridge National Preserve

In the west, on Seward Peninsula, near Nome

The preserve is a remnant of the land bridge that connected Asia to North America more than 13,000 years ago. The land bridge is now beneath the Chukchi Sea and the Bering Sea. During the glacial epoch, whenever ocean levels fell enough to expose the land bridge, people and animals migrated into the area. Archaeologists agree that it was across this Bering Land Bridge, also called Beringia, that humans first passed between Asia and northwestern Alaska. The preserve is home to paleontological and archaeological resources, large populations of migratory birds, wildlife (including brown bear, moose, caribou, and reindeer), and ash explosion craters and lava flows. The park was proclaimed a national monument in 1978 and a preserve in 1980.

WHAT TO SEE & DO

Arts and crafts, backpacking, bird-watching, canoeing, coastal boating, cross-country skiing, dogsledding, exploring ancient Eskimo and gold rush–era remains, fishing, hiking, hunting, observing Eskimo reindeer herding, river floating, snowmobiling. **Facilities:** Visitor center (240 Front St., Nome). **Programs & Events:** Interpretive talks, demonstrations, Junior Ranger Program (all June–Aug.). **Tips & Hints:** Be prepared to be self-sufficient. Exposure and hypothermia are threats throughout the year. Temperatures in summer are usually around 50°F on the coast and 65°F–75°F inland. Snow, freezing temperatures, and long periods of clouds, rain, and wind are possible year-round. Summer days are long, almost without darkness. Average Jan. lows are -15°F on the coast and -50°F in the interior. Winds average 8–12 mph but can reach 70 mph in storms. Winter days are short, with only a few hours of light. Go May–June for rare migratory bird viewing. Busiest June–Aug., least crowded Jan. and Feb.

FOOD, LODGING & SUPPLIES

Camping: In the park: Serpentine Hot Springs (west side of park near Taylor; primitive cabin with 20 bunk beds; free). 6 primitive cabins scattered elsewhere in park. Backcountry camping allowed. Nearby: Salmon Lake Park Campground (north end of Salmon Lake, 38 mi north of Nome, tel. 907/443–2177; 9 sites; free). **Hotels:** None in park. In Nome: Nome Nugget Inn (315 W. Front St., tel. 907/443–2323 or 877/443–2323; 47 rooms; $90–$100), Aurora Inn (302 E. Front St., tel. 907/443–3838 or 800/354–4606; 68 rooms; $139–$225). **Restaurants:** None in park. In Nome: Fat Freddies Restaurant (100 Front St., tel. 907/443–5899; $7–$13), Fort Davis Roadhouse (224 Front St., tel. 907/443–5191; $10–$15). **Groceries & Gear:** None in park. In Nome: The Country Store (1008 E. Front St., tel. 907/443–5666 or 800/478–3297).

FEES, HOURS & REGULATIONS

Free. Alaska hunting and fishing licenses required. No helicopters or all-terrain vehicles. Preserve open daily.

HOW TO GET THERE

Accessible only by foot travel, small aircraft, and boats in summer and fall, by snowmobile, dogsled, cross-country skis, or small plane on skis in winter and spring. Closest airports: Kotzebue, Nome.

CONTACTS

Bering Land Bridge National Preserve (Box 220, Nome, AK 99762, tel. 907/443–2522, www.nps.gov/bela). Western Arctic National Parkland

(Box 1029, Kotzebue, AK 99752, tel. 800/478–7252). Nome Convention & Visitors Bureau (Box 240, Nome, AK 99762, tel. 907/443–6624, fax 907/443–5832, www.nomealaska.org).

Cape Krusenstern National Monument

In northwestern Alaska, near Kotzebue

Archaeological sites along a succession of 114 lateral beach ridges illustrate every known Eskimo cultural period in Alaska over 4,000 years. Older sites are located inland along the foothills. The monument includes a representative example of the Arctic coastline along the Chukchi Sea. The monument was proclaimed on December 1, 1978.

WHAT TO SEE & DO

Backpacking, beach walking, bird-watching, hiking, kayaking, wildlife viewing. **Facilities:** Park Headquarters (Kotzebue), Innaigvik Education and Information Center. **Tips & Hints:** Be prepared to be self-sufficient. Rugged terrain is subject to high winds, rain, and snow. Guard against hypothermia, giardiasis, wild animals, mosquitoes, and biting flies. Don't interfere with subsistence camps, fishnets, or other equipment. Respect property and privacy. Go in summer for wildflowers and migrating birds. Busiest July and Aug., least crowded Sept.–Nov.

FOOD, LODGING & SUPPLIES

Camping: Backcountry camping only. **Hotels:** None in park. In Kotzebue: Nullagvik Hotel (308 Shore Ave., tel. 907/442–3331; 73 rooms; $125–$149). **Restaurants:** None in park. In Kotzebue: Kotzebue Pizza House (543 Bison St., tel. 907/442–3432; $5–$15). **Groceries & Gear:** None in park. In Kotzebue: Hansons Eagle Quality Center (305 Front St., tel. 907/442–3101).

FEES, HOURS & REGULATIONS

Free. Reservations recommended for most visitor services from commercial vendors. Open daily. Park Headquarters (Kotzebue) open weekdays 8–5. Kotzebue Public Lands Information Center hours mid-May–mid-Sept., daily 8–6.

HOW TO GET THERE

Accessible by plane from Fairbanks or Anchorage to Kotzebue; scheduled flights available from Kotzebue to the villages of Noatak, Kivalina, Shungnak, Ambler, Kobuk, Kiana, and Noorvik; summer access to and through the monument via motorized and nonmotorized watercraft and aircraft and on foot; air taxis and snowmobiles can be used in winter.

CONTACTS

Cape Krusenstern National Monument (Box 1029, Kotzebue, AK 99752, tel. 907/442–3890, www.nps.gov/cakr). Western Arctic National Parkland (Box 1029, Kotzebue, AK 99752, tel. 800/478–7252).

Denali
National Park & Preserve

In south-central Alaska

Denali, the "High One," is the name the Athabascan people gave to Mt. McKinley (20,320 feet), the massive peak that crowns the 600-mi Alaska Range. The park's 6.1 million acres include countless other spectacular mountains and large glaciers. Denali encompasses a complete subarctic ecosystem, which is populated with grizzly bears, wolves, Dall sheep, caribou, and moose. Mt. McKinley National Park was established in 1917 and designated an international biosphere reserve in 1976. The park's name was changed to Denali and it was tripled in size with the addition of new park and preserve lands in 1980.

WHAT TO SEE & DO

Backpacking, bicycling, bus touring, cross-country skiing (backcountry permit required; *see below*), dog mushing, hiking (backcountry permit required, *see below*), mountaineering (permit required, *see below*), snowmobiling, snowshoeing, stargazing, wildlife viewing. **Facilities:** 2 visitor centers: Denali (mile 237, George Parks Hwy.), Eielson (mile 66, Denali Park Rd.); Talkeetna Mountaineering Center ranger station. Bookstores. **Programs & Events:** Ranger and naturalist programs (mostly June–Aug.). **Tips & Hints:** Main visitor season and best weather late May–early Sept. Plan to spend at least one day to tour the park road by shuttle or tour bus, several days for hiking. Get reservations for camping and shuttle to avoid one- to two-day wait for bus availability during peak season. Bring rain gear and hiking boots in summer when weather is cool and damp. Bring specialized cold-weather gear for winter visits, when temperatures drop to -40°F or lower. Read *Mountaineering: Denali National Park and Preserve* to begin planning mountain climbs in the park. Busiest July and Aug., least crowded Jan. and Feb.

FOOD, LODGING & SUPPLIES

🏕 **Camping:** 6 campgrounds in the park: Igloo Creek (mile 34, Park Rd.; 7 sites; $13; pit toilets), Riley Creek (park entrance; 100 sites; $12–$18; flush toilets), Sanctuary River (mile 23, Park Rd.; 7 sites; $13; pit toilets), Savage River (mile 13, Park Rd.; 36 sites; $18; flush toilets), Teklanika River (mile 29, Park Rd.; 53 sites; $20; flush toilets), Wonder Lake (mile 85, Park Rd.; 28 sites; $20; flush toilets). Backcountry camping available (permit required, *see below*). In Healy: McKinley RV Park & Campground (mile 248.5, George Parks Hwy., tel. 907/683–2379 or 800/478–2562; 89 sites; $24–$29; flush toilets, showers, hook-ups). 🏨 **Hotels:** In the park: Camp Denali (mile 89, Park Rd., tel. 907/683–2290; 17 cabins; $1,200–$1,600 for 3 days, including meals, transportation, and guided outings; closed mid-Sept.–June), Denali Backcountry Lodge (mile 89, Park Rd., tel. 907/783–1342 or 800/841–0692; 30 cabins; $290–$510, including meals and transportation; closed mid-Sept.–early June), North Face Lodge (mile 89, Park Rd., tel. 907/683–2290; 15 rooms; $1,200 for 3 days, including meals, transportation, and guided outings; closed mid-Sept.–June). Nearby: Denali Princess Wilderness

Lodge (1 mi north of park entrance, tel. 907/683–2283 or 800/462–0500; 353 rooms; $179; closed mid-Sept.–mid-May), Perch Cabins (mile 224, George Parks Hwy., tel. 888/322–2523; 20 cabins; $65–$95). In Healy: Motel Nord Haven (mile 249.5, George Parks Hwy., tel. 907/683–4500 or 800/683–4501; 28 rooms; $65–$140). ✗ **Restaurants:** None in park. Nearby: The Perch Restaurant (mile 224 on George Parks Hwy., tel. 907/683–2523; $10–$15), McKinley–Denali Salmon Bake (1 mi north of park entrance, tel. 907/683–2733; $8–$13; closed Oct.–Apr.). In Healy: Totem Inn (mile 248.7, George Parks Hwy., tel. 907/683–2420; $5–$10). ⬧ **Groceries & Gear:** In the park: Riley Creek Mercantile (park entrance, tel. 907/683–9246). In Healy: Lynx Creek General Store (mile 238, George Parks Hwy., tel. 907/683–2548).

FEES, HOURS & REGULATIONS

Entrance fee: $10 per family, $5 per person. Fees vary for shuttle (reservations available, tel. 907/272–7275 or 800/622–7275, fax 907/264–4684) and tour bus service (tel. 800/276–7234). Backcountry permits required (free). Camper bus pass ($22.50) needed to reach most backcountry sites. Mountaineering permit registration packets must be submitted 60 days in advance ($150). No snowmobiling in wilderness core area of park and preserve. Park open daily. Denali Visitor Center open late May–mid-Sept., daily 7 AM–8 PM. Winter headquarters open mid-Sept.–early May, daily 8–4:30. Eielson Visitor Center open June–mid-Sept., daily 9–7.

HOW TO GET THERE

Denali is accessible by car or the Alaska Railroad (tel. 907/265–2494 or 800/544–0552) from Anchorage and Fairbanks. In summer, a variety of private bus and van services and the railroad operate daily from Anchorage and Fairbanks. The park and preserve is on Rte. 3 (George Parks Hwy.), 240 mi north of Anchorage, 125 mi south of Fairbanks, and 12 mi south of Healy. The Denali Park Rd. is accessible by private vehicle for 15 mi to the Savage River Bridge. Shuttles and tour buses travel farther into the park. Mountaineering headquarters is in Talkeetna, 100 mi north of Anchorage. Closest airport: Fairbanks.

CONTACTS

Denali National Park & Preserve (Box 9, Denali Park, AK 99755, tel. 907/683–2294, fax 907/683–9612, www.nps.gov/dena). Talkeetna Mountaineering Center (Box 588, Talkeetna, AK 99676, tel. 907/733–2231). Healy Chamber of Commerce (Box 437, Healy, AK 99743, tel. 907/683–4636, www.denalichamber.com).

Gates of the Arctic National Park & Preserve

In central Brooks Range, near Bettles, in the north

This park and preserve may be Alaska's ultimate wilderness park. The National Park Service manages this 8.4-million-acre park and preserve and maintains the land's wild and undeveloped character. There are no roads, trails, or visitor services here. In this, the park system's northernmost park, visitors experience the natural world much as it was when wilderness advocate Robert Marshall visited it more than 60 years ago. The area was proclaimed a national monument in 1978 and established as a park and preserve in 1980.

WHAT TO SEE & DO

Dogsledding, fishing, hiking, hunting, kayaking, mountain climbing, rafting, snowmobiling. **Facilities:** Ranger Station at Anaktuvuk Pass (periodically unstaffed, call to schedule appointment, *see below*). Visitor contact station (Bettles); interagency visitor center (June–Sept., Coldfoot). Book sales outlet (Bettles, Coldfoot). **Programs & Events:** Backcountry orientation and limited interpretive programs available at a park ranger station in Bettles. Interpretive programs (Bettles: by request; Coldfoot: June–Sept., daily). **Tips & Hints:** Plan to be self-sufficient in the park, where contact with other visitors is rare. Be knowledgeable about camping and hiking in bear country. Contact park staff in Anaktuvuk Pass, Bettles, or Coldfoot for updated information before going into the park or preserve. Bring plenty of insect repellent and head nets. Biting mosquitoes and gnats in summer can make a stay unbearable. Insect numbers decline by late Aug. Go May–Sept. to avoid snow. Winter temperatures (Oct.–Mar.) usually are subzero and can drop to as low as -60°F. Busiest July and Aug., least crowded Oct.–Jan.

FOOD, LODGING & SUPPLIES

⚠ **Camping:** Backcountry camping only (orientation required for camping in the park). 🛏 **Hotels:** In the park: Peace of Selby (Manley Hot Springs, tel. 907/672–3206; 1 lodge, 4 cabins; $300 lodge, $150 cabins). In Bettles: Sourdough Outfitters Lodge (6 Hickel Hwy., tel. 907/692–5252; 3 cabins, 2 apartments; $80 cabins, $100 apartments). ✗ **Restaurants:** None in park. In Bettles: Sourdough Outfitters Café (6 Hickel Hwy., tel. 907/692–5252; $9–$20). ⚮ **Groceries & Gear:** None in park. In Bettles: Sourdough Outfitters Store (6 Hickel Hwy., tel. 907/692–5252).

FEES, HOURS & REGULATIONS

Free. Alaska state fishing, hunting, or trapping licenses required. Commercial guide required for nonresidents hunting in preserves for certain species of wildlife. Hunting in preserve areas only. No motorized vehicles. Pets must be under control at all times. No rest rooms. Park and preserve open daily. Visitor center in Bettles open daily 8–5; in Coldfoot, May–Sept., daily 8–5.

HOW TO GET THERE

The park and preserve are accessible on foot, by small aircraft, or by boat. Bettles and Anaktuvuk Pass, 160 mi and 240 mi north of Fairbanks, are nearest to the center of the park. Neither has road access. Scheduled air service from Fairbanks is available daily. Coldfoot, which provides access to the east section of the park and preserve, is 250 mi north of Fairbanks via the Elliot and Dalton highways.

CONTACTS

National Park Service (Box 26030, Bettles, AK 99726, tel. 907/692–5494, www.nps.gov/gaar). Anaktuvuk Pass Ranger Station (tel. 907/661–3520). City of Bettles (General Delivery, Bettles, AK 99726, tel. 907/692–5191).

Glacier Bay
National Park & Preserve

In southeastern Alaska, near Gustavus

Glacier Bay is a 3.2-million-acre wilderness park accessible only by boat or plane. Just 200 years ago a solid sheet of ice covered what is now the bay. In two centuries, the glacial ice has retreated 65 mi and left a newly barren landscape to be recolonized by plant and animal life. You can travel by boat from a lush green rain forest up to the impressive tidewater glaciers and, perhaps, see wildlife along the way, including bears, mountain goats, whales, seals, eagles, and puffins. The site was created as a national monument in 1925 and designated a national park in 1980. The park was designated a Biosphere Reserve in 1986 and a World Heritage Site in 1992.

WHAT TO SEE & DO

Fishing, hiking, kayaking (rentals, Bartlett Cove, Gustavus), viewing glaciers by boat. **Facilities:** Glacier Bay Visitor Center (Bartlett Cove). Book and map sale area. **Programs & Events:** Ranger-guided hikes, walks, evening programs (mid-May–mid-Sept.). **Tips & Hints:** Bring rain gear: Glacier Bay gets more than 75 inches per year. Busiest June and July, least crowded Nov. and Dec.

FOOD, LODGING & SUPPLIES

⚑ **Camping:** In the park: Bartlett Cove (walk-in tent camping; free; permit required, *see below*). ☗ **Hotels:** In the park: Glacier Bay Lodge (Bartlett Cove, tel. 907/697–2226 or 800/820–2628; 56 rooms; $149–$219; closed mid-Sept.–mid-May). In Gustavus: Gustavus Inn (Gustavus Rd., tel. 907/697–2254 or 800/649–5220; 13 rooms; $300). ✕ **Restaurants:** In the park: meals at Glacier Bay Lodge (Bartlett Cove, tel. 907/697–2226; $20–$25; closed mid-Sept.–mid-May). In Gustavus: Bear Track Inn (Rink Creek Rd., Gustavus, tel. 907/697–3017 or 888/697–2284; $35; closed Oct.–Apr.). ⚑ **Groceries & Gear:** None in park: In Gustavus: Gustavus Building Supply (25 Dock Rd., tel. 907/697–2297), Bear Track Mercantile (Dock Rd., tel. 907/697–2358).

FEES, HOURS & REGULATIONS

Free. Glacier Bay Lodge offers daily boat trips to the glaciers. Backcountry permits (free) and camper orientation required. Permit required for pleasure boat operators to enter Glacier Bay or dock at Bartlett Cove (June–Aug.). Permit applications are available from park Web site and should be returned no earlier than 60 days prior to the proposed date of entry. Because the number of permits is limited, planning ahead is strongly advised. Permits can be issued for up to seven days. Alaska state fishing and hunting license required. No firearms in park. Hunting in preserve only. No pets onshore except in Bartlett Cove. Leashed pets in restricted areas only in cove. Park open daily. Visitor center open mid-May–mid-Sept., daily 12:30–9.

HOW TO GET THERE

60 mi northwest of Juneau. Flights are available from Juneau, Skagway, or Haines to Gustavus, which is 10 mi by road from Bartlett Cove, the park headquarters.

CONTACTS

Glacier Bay National Park & Preserve (Box 140, Gustavus, AK 99826, tel. 907/697–2230, fax 907/697–2654, www.nps.gov/glba). Gustavus Visitor Association (Box 167, Gustavus, AK 99826, tel. 907/697–2475).

Katmai
National Park & Preserve

In southeastern Alaska, near King Salmon

Variety marks this vast land, where lakes, forests, mountains, and marshlands abound in wildlife. The Alaska brown bear—the world's largest carnivore—thrives here, feeding upon red salmon that spawn in the many lakes and streams. Wild rivers and renowned sportfishing add to the attractions of this subarctic environment. In 1912 Novarupta Volcano erupted violently here, forming the ash-filled "Valley of Ten Thousand Smokes" where steam rose from countless fumaroles. Today only a few active vents remain. The park also contains part of the Alagnak Wild River. The site was proclaimed as Katmai National Monument in 1918 and established as a national park and preserve in 1980.

WHAT TO SEE & DO

Backcountry camping, bear viewing, boat touring, bus touring, fishing, hiking. **Facilities:** 2 visitor centers: King Salmon (next to the airport terminal), Brooks Camp (open June–mid-Sept.). Bear viewing platforms, bookstore. **Programs & Events:** Ranger-led cultural walks, interpretive programs, evening slide programs (June–mid-Sept., Brooks Camp). **Tips & Hints:** Be prepared for cold, windy, rainy weather as well as some warm, sunny days in summer. Temperatures usually hover around 60°F. Winters days receive six hours of sunlight. Get bear-resistant canisters at visitor centers. Be prepared for bears in vicinity of Brooks Camp. Very close encounters with bears are common and require visitors to move briskly. Go in July and Sept. for best bear viewing. Expect waits and time limits on bear viewing platforms in July. Busiest in July, least crowded in Jan. and Feb.

FOOD, LODGING & SUPPLIES

Camping: In the park: Brooks Camp (17 sites; $8; flush toilets, showers). Backcountry camping allowed. **Hotels:** In the park: Brooks Lodge (tel. 907/243–5448 or 800/544–0551; 16 rooms; $144–$455;

closed Oct.–May), Grosvenor Lodge (tel. 907/243–5448 or 800/544–0551; 3 cabins; $2,125 for 3 days, including meals, lodging, guided outings, and gear; closed Oct.–May), Kulik Lodge (tel. 907/243–5448 or 800/544–0551; 12 cabins; $2,150 for 3 days, including meals, lodging, guided outings, and gear; closed Oct.–May). *See Alagnak Wild River.* ✕ **Restaurants:** In the park: Brooks Lodge (tel. 907/243–5448; $12–$26). *See Alagnak Wild River.* ⚖ **Groceries & Gear:** In the park: Brooks Lodge Trading Post (tel. 907/243–5448). *See Alagnak Wild River.*

FEES, HOURS & REGULATIONS

Free. Reservations recommended for daily bus tour ($79) from Brooks Lodge (tel. 907/243–5448 or 800/544–0551) to the Valley of Ten Thousand Smokes. The trip starts at Brooks Camp and includes a day hike to Ukak Falls. Backcountry permits (recommended) available at Brooks Camp and King Salmon. No capsicum bear spray allowed on commercial flights. Park open daily. Park Service and concession services offered at Brooks Camp early June–mid-Sept.

HOW TO GET THERE

290 mi southwest of Anchorage on the Alaska Peninsula, just west of King Salmon; no road access. Daily commercial flights run between Anchorage and King Salmon. Charters, air taxis, and boat tours available from King Salmon, Anchorage, Homer, and Kodiak. Scheduled service into Brooks Camp available from King Salmon by floatplane and boat. Many area lodges provide their own transportation to the park.

CONTACTS

Katmai National Park & Preserve (Box 7, King Salmon, AK 99613, tel. 907/246–3305, www.nps.gov/katm). Katmailand (concessionnaire, www.katmailand.com). Alaska Public Lands Information Center (605 W. 4th Ave., Suite 105, Anchorage, AK 99501, tel. 907/271–2737).

Kenai Fjords National Park

In south-central Alaska, near Seward

Harding Icefield—300 square mi in size and one of four major ice caps in the United States—is one of the attractions in this coastal mountain park. Tens of thousands of birds breed in the park's rich, varied rain forest, and sea lions, otters, and seals inhabit the park's waters. The 669,500-acre site was proclaimed a national monument in 1978 and established as a national park in 1980.

WHAT TO SEE & DO

Bird and wildlife viewing, boat touring, fishing, flightseeing, hiking, kayaking. **Facilities:** Visitor center (Seward), trails. Bookstore. **Programs & Events:** Ranger-led walks (Memorial Day–Labor Day). **Tips & Hints:** Weather is usually overcast and cool in this maritime climate, and it rains often. May is the driest month, following months see increasing precipitation, and the wet, stormy fall begins in Sept. Expect summer daytime temperatures between 45°F and 70°F. Bring wool or synthetic clothing and sturdy rain gear, including pants, coat, and a hat. Stay on the glacier trail and off the ice. Commercial guides provide camping, fishing, and kayaking services. Get bear-resistant canisters at visitor center. Air charters provide flightseeing and fjord access. Boat tours and charters are available in Seward. In summer, boat tours ply the coast, observing calving glaciers, sea birds, and marine mammals. Boat charters offer overnight fjord trips and fishing trips to the fjords and Resurrection Bay. Busiest July and Aug., least crowded Nov.–Jan.

FOOD, LODGING & SUPPLIES

⚠ **Camping:** In the Park: Exit Glacier (Exit Glacier Rd., 3 mi out of Seward; 12 sites, 1 cabin; free), 3 backcountry coastline cabins ($35) in the fjords of Holgate Arm, Aialik Bay, and North Arm, accessible by boat, kayak, or small plane. 🛏 **Hotels:** None in park: In Seward: Hotel Seward (221 5th Ave., tel. 907/224–2378 or 800/528–1234; 38 rooms; $12–$26). ✕ **Restaurants:** None in park. In Seward: Harbor Dinner Club & Lounge (220 5th Ave., tel. 907/224–3012; $6–$45), Ray's Waterfront (4th St. on the harbor, tel. 907/224–5606; $6–$40). 🛒 **Groceries & Gear:** None in park. In Seward: Eagle Quality Center (mile 1.5, Seward Hwy., tel. 907/224–3698).

FEES & HOURS

$5 vehicle fee at Exit Glacier. Park open daily. Visitor center open Apr.–Sept., daily 9–5. Park headquarters open weekdays 8–5.

HOW TO GET THERE

The park is 130 mi south of Anchorage on Seward Hwy. The park's headquarters and visitor center are in Seward's small harbor. Bus and commuter flight service link Seward and Anchorage. The Alaska Marine Hwy. (ferry) System connects Seward with Homer and Seldovia via Kodiak and provides service to Valdez and Cordova. The Alaska Railroad serves Seward from Anchorage mid-May–mid-Sept. Exit Glacier can be reached in summer by car on an 8-mi paved road and a short trail. The Harding Icefield is accessible by air or trail. Air and boat charters provide access to the fjords.

CONTACTS

Park Headquarters, Kenai Fjords National Park (Box 1727, Seward, AK 99664-1727, tel. 907/224–3175, fax 907/224–2144, www.nps.gov/kefj). Seward Chamber of Commerce (Box 749, Seward, AK 99664, tel. 907/224–8051 or 907/224–3094).

Klondike Gold Rush National Historical Park

In Skagway and in Seattle, WA

The park has two units: one in Skagway, Alaska, and the other in Seattle, Washington. The Skagway unit includes 15 buildings in Skagway, plus the Chilkoot and White Pass trails. Miners used the trails in 1897 and 1898 to reach the rich Yukon gold fields. Hikers can retrace the miners' footsteps on the Chilkoot Trail. The White Pass and Yukon

Route Railway, constructed between 1898 and 1900, runs a train through the pass to Fraser, British Columbia, each summer. News of the gold strike in Canada's Yukon Territory spread from Seattle across the country, and most prospectors left for the northern gold fields from Seattle. Today, the Seattle unit has a visitor center in the Pioneer Square Historic District, the center of gold rush activity. The park was established on June 30, 1976.

WHAT TO SEE & DO

In Skagway: Attending slide programs, fishing, hiking (backcountry permit required, *see below*), touring the historic districts and museums. In Seattle: Touring Pioneer Sq., watching movie and slide show and gold-panning demonstration. **Facilities:** In Skagway: visitor center (2nd Ave. and Broadway), hiker information center (Trail Center across from visitor center), exhibit area in the Railroad Bldg. (2nd Ave.), Mascot Saloon (Broadway and 4th Ave.), Moore House (5th Ave. and Spring St.), interpretive displays (town of Dyea), wayside exhibits (Alaska Marine Hwy. Ferry Terminal, Broadway), and Klondike Hwy. In Seattle: visitor center, historic district. Bookstores at both units. **Programs & Events:** In Skagway: gold rush film (by request); film (May–Sept., hourly), guided walking tours of historic district (May–Sept., twice daily), ranger-led tours of Dyea (June–Aug.), tours of Moore House (May–Sept.), reading of poetry by Robert Service (June–Aug., Mon. and Tues. evenings); presentations and special events subject to staffing. In Seattle: movie and slide program; Pioneer Sq. walking tour and gold-panning demonstration (summer). **Tips & Hints:** In Skagway: Tours and buses pick up and drop off hikers at both ends of Chilkoot Trail. Go May and June for best weather, mid-July for blooms, Aug. for salmon run. In Seattle: Allow 2½ hours for exhibits, movies, and gold-panning demonstration in summer. Busiest June and July, least crowded Dec. and Jan.

FOOD, LODGING & SUPPLIES

🏕 **Camping:** In the park: Dyea Campground (10 mi north of Skagway, tel. 907/983–9234; 22 sites; pit toilets). 🏨 **Hotels:** None in park. In Skagway: Golden Rush Lodge (607 Alaska St., tel. 907/983–2831; 12 rooms; $105–$115). ✗ **Restaurants:** None in park: In Skagway: Skagway Fish Co. (on the waterfront, tel. 907/983–3474; $7–$36). ⛟ **Groceries & Gear:** None in park. In Skagway: Skagway Hardware (400 Broadway, tel. 907/983–2233), Mountain Shop (355 4th St., tel. 907/983–2544).

FEES, HOURS & REGULATIONS

Skagway: free. Moore House tour fee: $2 adults, $1 ages 15 and under and 62 and over. Backcountry permits required to hike the Chilkoot Trail (free on U.S. side, available from Trail Center, June–Aug.; call 800/661–0486 for Canadian-side fees and permits). Alaska state fishing license required. No hunting on Chilkoot Trail. No motorized or mechanized equipment on trail. No pets on trails. Visitor center open May–Sept., daily 8–6; June–Aug., daily 8–8. Trail Center open daily 7:30–4:30. Moore House open May–Sept., daily 10–noon, 1–5. Mascot Saloon exhibit open May–Sept., daily 9–5. Seattle: free. Visitor center open daily 9–5.

HOW TO GET THERE

Skagway: 80 mi north of Juneau by air or water and 110 mi south of Whitehorse, Yukon (Canada), by road. Closest airport: Skagway. Seattle: From I–5 or I–90, exit on 4th Ave., make a left on Main St. to 117 S. Main St. Closest airport: SeaTac.

CONTACTS

Skagway: Klondike Gold Rush National Historical Park (Box 517, Skagway, AK 99840, tel. 907/983–2921, fax 907/983–9249, www.nps.gov/klgo). Skagway Convention & Visitors Bureau (Box 415, Skagway, AK 99840, tel. 907/983–2854, fax 907/983–3854, www.skagway.org). Seattle: Klondike Gold Rush National Historical Park (117 S. Main St., Seattle, WA 98104, tel. 206/553–7220, fax 206/553–0614, www.nps.gov/klgo).

Kobuk Valley National Park

In northwestern Alaska, near Kotzebue

Located 26 mi above the Arctic Circle, this 1.8-million-acre park preserves the central Kobuk River valley, the Great Kobuk Sand Dunes, and the Little Kobuk and Hunt rivers. Here are the northernmost limits of the boreal forest, as well as caribou, wolf, fox, and grizzly and black bear. The site was proclaimed a national monument in 1978 and redesignated in 1980.

WHAT TO SEE & DO

Backpacking, boating, canoeing, hiking, kayaking, rafting, wildlife watching. **Facilities:** Information center and park headquarters in Kotzebue. No facilities in park. Sales area. **Programs & Events:** Interpretive talks and demonstrations (Kotzebue; June–Aug.). Junior Ranger Program (June–Aug.). **Tips & Hints:** Prepare to be self-sufficient. Wear sturdy hiking boots and waders for wet terrain. Expect high winds throughout the year and short, cool, and sunny summers with 24 hours of daylight in June. Winters are long, dark, and extremely cold. Guard against hypothermia, giardiasis, wild animals, mosquitoes, and biting flies. Don't interfere with subsistence camps, fishnets, or other equipment. Respect property and privacy. Busiest July and Aug., least crowded Dec. and Jan.

FOOD, LODGING & SUPPLIES

None in park. *See Cape Krusenstern National Monument.*

FEES & HOURS

Free. Park open daily. Information center open mid-May–mid-Sept., daily 8–6.

HOW TO GET THERE

Kotzebue is 26 mi north of the Arctic Circle in northwest Alaska. Access to Kotzebue (headquarters and information center) is by Alaska Airlines. To reach the park, air taxis and scheduled and charter flights are available. In summer, access is by motorized and nonmotorized watercraft, aircraft, and foot. In winter, access is by snowmobile and aircraft.

CONTACTS

Park Headquarters (Box 1029, Kotzebue, AK 99752, tel. 907/442–3890 headquarters; 907/442–3760 Innaigvik Education and Information Center, www.nps.gov/kova). Western Arctic National Parkland (Box 1029, Kotzebue, AK 99752, tel. 800/478–7252).

Lake Clark
National Park & Preserve

In southwestern Alaska, near Port Alsworth

Covering 4 million acres, this spectacular park and preserve stretches from the shores of Cook Inlet across the Chigmit Mountains to the tundra-covered hills of the western interior. The Chigmits, the junction of the Alaska and Aleutian ranges, are an awe-inspiring array of jagged mountains and glaciers that include Mt. Redoubt and Mt. Iliamna, two active volcanoes. The 50-mi-long Lake Clark and other waters in the park are vital salmon habitats for the Bristol Bay salmon fishery, one of the world's largest sockeye salmon fishing grounds. Anglers find trophy fish; hikers explore high tundra slopes; river runners thrill to the Tlikakila, Mulchatna, or Chilikadrotna wild rivers; and campers find lakeshore sites inspirational. The site was proclaimed a national monument in 1978 and established as a national park and preserve in 1980.

WHAT TO SEE & DO

Backpacking, bird- and wildlife watching, fishing, flightseeing (charters, Port Alsworth, Kenai, Anchorage), hiking, hunting (preserve), kayaking, mountaineering, river running (rentals, Anchorage, Kenai, Port Alsworth). **Facilities:** Visitor center (Port Alsworth), backcountry patrol cabins (Telaquana Lake, Twin Lakes, Crescent Lake, and Chinitna Bay), trails. Book sales area, post office. **Programs & Events:** Slide shows and presentations (on request as staffing permits). Slide presentations (June–Sept.), guided hikes (on request). **Tips & Hints:** Go in summer for best fishing, Sept. for fall colors. Prepare to be self-sufficient for backcountry travel. Stay away from game trails and fresh signs of bears. Bring extra food and cooking fuel. Expect 50–65°F temperatures June–Aug., with considerable precipitation. Plan for frost and snow as early as Aug. Plan for strong winds any time and winter temperatures to -40°F. Respect private property within park boundaries. Weather changes can delay scheduled pickup by aircraft by several days. Busiest June–Sept., least crowded Jan. and Feb.

FOOD, LODGING & SUPPLIES

🏕 **Camping:** Backcountry camping only. 🏨 **Hotels:** None in park. In Port Alsworth: Farm Lodge (on the lake, tel. 907/781–2208 or 888/440–2281; 5 cabins; $244), Lake Clark Inn (1 Lang La., tel. 907/781–2224; 4 cabins; $145). ✕ **Restaurants:** None in park. In Port Alsworth: Homestead Café (1 Willow Rd., tel. 907/781–2256; closed Oct. 15–May 15). ⚲ **Groceries & Gear:** None in park. In Port Alsworth: The Tanalian Country Store (tel. 907/781–2224).

FEES, HOURS & REGULATIONS

Free. Alaska state fish and hunting licenses required. Hunting and trapping in preserve only. No gathering of plants or live trees. Leashed pets only. No rest rooms available. Park and preserve open daily. Visitor center open summer 8–5.

HOW TO GET THERE

150 mi southwest of Anchorage on the west side of the Cook Inlet and the north end of the Alaska Peninsula. Access to the Lake Clark region is by air only. A one- to two-hour flight from Anchorage, Kenai, or Homer provides access to most points within the park and preserve. Scheduled commercial flights between Anchorage and Iliamna, 30 mi outside the boundary, also provide access. Floatplanes may land on lakes. Wheeled planes land on open beaches, gravel bars, or private airstrips in or near the park.

CONTACT

Lake Clark National Park & Preserve (1 Park Pl., Port Alsworth, AK 99653, tel. 907/781–2218, www.nps.gov/lacl).

Noatak National Preserve

In northwestern Alaska, near Kotzebue

One of North America's largest mountain-ringed river basins with an unaltered ecosystem, the Noatak is home to many Arctic plants and animals and offers superlative wilderness float-trip opportunities. The 6.6-million-acre preserve also includes the 65-mi-long Grand Canyon of the Noatak. The Noatak was proclaimed a national monument in 1978, established as a national preserve in 1980, and designated a Biosphere Reserve in 1976.

WHAT TO SEE & DO

Backpacking, boating, canoeing, hiking, hunting, rafting, wildlife watching. **Facilities:** Information center and park headquarters in Kotzebue. No facilities in park. **Programs & Events:** Interpretive talks and demonstrations (Kotzebue; June–Aug.). Junior Ranger Program (June–Aug.). **Tips & Hints:** Prepare to be self-sufficient. Wear sturdy hiking boots and waders for wet terrain. Expect high winds throughout the year; short, mild, cool, and sunny summers with 24 hours of daylight for one month; and long, severe, harsh, extremely cold winters with one hour of daylight by Dec. 1. Guard against hypothermia, giardia lamblia, wild animals, mosquitoes, and biting flies. Don't interfere with subsistence camps, fishnets, or other equipment. Respect property and privacy. Busiest July and Aug., least crowded Nov. and Dec.

FOOD, LODGING & SUPPLIES

None in park. *See Cape Krusenstern National Monument.*

FEES & HOURS

Park open daily. Kotzebue information center open mid-May–Sept. 30, daily 8–6.

HOW TO GET THERE

Kotzebue is 26 mi north of the Arctic Circle in northwest Alaska. Access to Kotzebue (headquarters and information center) is by Alaska Airlines. To reach the park, air taxis and scheduled and charter flights are available. In summer, access is by motorized and nonmotorized watercraft, aircraft, and foot. In winter, access is by snowmobiles and aircraft.

CONTACTS

Park Headquarters (Box 1029, Kotzebue, AK 99752, tel. 907/442–3890, www.nps.gov/noat). Kotzebue Public Lands Information Center (Box 1029, Kotzebue, AK 99752, tel. 907/442–3760). Western Arctic National Parkland (Box 1029, Kotzebue, AK 99752, tel. 800/478–7252).

Sitka
National Historical Park

In southeastern Alaska, near Sitka

Sitka was the cultural and political hub of Russian America in the early 19th century. In 1867, Russia ended its 126-year New World enterprise with the sale of Alaska to the United States for $7.2 million. In addition to commemorating the battle of 1804 between the local Tlingits and the Russians, the park's 107 acres were set aside in 1890 to preserve and interpret numerous totem poles in the park as well as the Russian Bishop's House and czarist Russia's exploration and colonization of Alaska. The park was placed into the National Park System in 1910, making it the oldest and smallest national park in Alaska. The temperate rain-forest park consists of the fort site, a sizable totem-pole collection, the Southeast Alaska Indian Cultural Center (housed in the visitor center), and the restored Russian Bishop's House, which was built in 1842. The site was proclaimed in 1910 and designated a national historical park in 1972.

WHAT TO SEE & DO

Bird- and wildlife watching, picnicking, touring the restored living quarters in the Russian Bishop's House, viewing exhibits and salmon-spawning stream, walking, watching film and local artisans at work in the cultural center. **Facilities:** Visitor center, Russian Bishop's House, cultural center, trails, interpretive signs. Bookstore, picnic area. **Programs & Events:** Russian Bishop's House tours (mid-May–Sept. 30, daily; rest of year, by appointment), film (upon request). Tours of the Bishop's House and battle walks (June–Sept.), other programs (depending on staff availability). **Tips & Hints:** Bring rain gear and rubber boots. Visit June–Aug. Busiest July and Aug., least crowded Dec. and Jan.

FOOD, LODGING & SUPPLIES

Camping: None in park. In Sitka: Starrigavin Campgrounds (204 Siginaka Way, tel. 877/444–6777; 22 sites; pit toilets). **Hotels:** None in park. In Sitka: Westmark Shee Atika (330 Seward St., tel. 907/747–

6241 or 800/544–0970; 101 rooms; $139–$159). ✗ **Restaurants:** None in park. In Sitka: Channel Club (mile 3.5, 2906 Halibut Point Rd., tel. 907/747–9916; $15–$25). ♿ **Gear:** None in park. In Sitka: The Work & Rugged Gear Store (407 Lincoln St., tel. 907/747–6238).

FEES, HOURS & REGULATIONS

Entrance fee: $3 for Russian Bishop's House and $3 for visitor center. Fishing restricted to Dolly Vardens only. Alaska state fishing license required. Leashed pets only. No bike riding. No camping. No fires, outside grills. No motorized vehicles on trails. Park grounds open summer, daily 6 AM–10 PM; fall–spring, daily 7 AM–8 PM. Visitor center open mid-May–Sept., Mon.–Sat. 8–5; Nov.–mid-May, weekdays 8–5. Russian Bishop's House open late May–Sept., daily 9–5; rest of year, by appointment.

HOW TO GET THERE

0.3 mi from downtown Sitka. The Bishop's House is downtown. Closest airport: Sitka (1[1//2] mi).

CONTACTS

Sitka National Historical Park (103 Monastery St., Sitka, AK 99835, tel. 907/747–0110, fax 907/747–5938, www.nps.gov/sitk). Sitka Convention & Visitors Bureau (303 Lincoln St., Box 1226, Sitka, AK 99835, tel. 907/747–5940, fax 907/747–3739, www.sitka.org).

Wrangell–St. Elias National Park & Preserve

In southeastern Alaska

This 13.2-million-acre park and preserve, the largest in the United States and the largest protected roadless wilderness in the world, encompasses towering mountains, glaciers, meandering rivers, and volcanoes. Here the Chugach, Wrangell, St. Elias, and Alaska mountain ranges converge to form what is considered the "mountain kingdom of North America." The park and preserve contains the continent's largest assemblage of glaciers and greatest collection of peaks above 16,000 feet. Mt. St. Elias (18,008 feet) is the second highest peak in the United States. The site was proclaimed a national monument in 1978, a World Heritage Site in 1979, and a park and preserve in 1980.

WHAT TO SEE & DO

Backpacking, fishing, flightseeing, hiking, hunting, kayaking, mountain biking, mountaineering, river floating, sea kayaking, wildlife viewing. **Facilities:** Visitor center (Copper Center); ranger stations at Yakutat, Slana, and Chitina; trails. Bookstore. **Programs & Events:** Slide program. Interpretive talks (June–Aug.). **Tips & Hints:** Thoroughly research your visit to the Wrangells. This is a vast expanse of rugged wilderness with few services. Develop map- and compass-reading skills for backcountry travel. Be prepared for unpredictable weather, dangerous stream crossings, and grizzly and black bear encounters. Road access to park is via Nabesna and McCarthy roads, both gravel-surfaced. Take an air taxi to view the park's mountain wilderness. Visit mid-May–Oct. for best weather. Busiest July and Aug., least crowded Dec. and Jan.

FOOD, LODGING & SUPPLIES

Camping: 2 campgrounds in the park: Glacier View (½ mi west of Kennicott River Bridge, tel. 907/554–4490; 20 sites; $10–$12; vault toilets; closed Oct.–Apr.), West McCarthy Wayside park (end of McCarthy Rd., tel. 907/746–0606; tent camping area; $10–$15; closed Oct.–Apr.). Backcountry camping available is Nabesna District. **Hotels:** In the park: Kennicott Glacier Lodge (tel. 907/554–4402; 35 rooms; $179–$229; closed mid-Sept.–May), McCarthy Lodge–Ma Johnson's Hotel (tel. 907/554–4402; 20 rooms; $159; open mid-May–mid-Sept.). **Restaurants:** In the park: meals at Kennicott Glacier Lodge (tel. 907/554–4477; $8–$12; closed mid-Sept.–mid-May), McCarthy Lodge Restaurant & Saloon (tel. 907/554–4402; $9–$12; closed mid-Sept.–mid-May), Taylor Made Pizza (tel. 907/554–1155; $9–$26; closed Oct.–mid-May). **Groceries & Gear:** None in park. In Glennallen: Sparks General Store (mile 189, Glenn Hwy., tel. 907/822–5990), Parks Place (mile 188, Glenn Hwy., tel. 907/822–3334), The Sports Page (mile 187, Glenn Hwy., tel. 907/822–5833).

FEES, HOURS & REGULATIONS

Free. Alaska state fishing and hunting license required. ATVs in designated areas only, permit required. Park open daily. Visitor center open Labor Day–Memorial Day, weekdays 8–4:30; Memorial Day–Labor Day, daily 8–6. Ranger stations open Memorial Day–Labor Day, daily hours vary.

HOW TO GET THERE

The park visitor center is 199 mi east of Anchorage via Rte. 1, about 260 mi southeast of Fairbanks via Rtes. 2 and 4, and 105 mi north of Valdez via Rte. 4. Air service available between Glennallen and Anchorage.

CONTACTS

Wrangell–St. Elias National Park & Preserve (Box 439, Copper Center, AK 99573, tel. 907/822–5234, fax 907/822–7216, www.nps.gov/wrst). Greater Copper Valley Chamber of Commerce (Box 469, Glenallen, AK 99588, tel. 907/822–5555).

Yukon-Charley Rivers National Preserve

In east-central Alaska, near Eagle

On the Canadian border in central Alaska, the 2.5-million-acre preserve protects 115 mi of the 1,800-mi Yukon River and the entire Charley River basin. Numerous rustic cabins and historic sites are reminders of the importance of the Yukon River during the 1898 gold rush. Peregrine falcons nest in bluffs overlooking the river, and the preserve's rolling hills are home to an array of wildlife. The Charley, an 88-mi wild river, is considered to be the most spectacular river in Alaska. The site was proclaimed a national monument in 1978 and established as a national preserve in 1980.

WHAT TO SEE & DO

Bird- and wildlife watching, exploring historic trapping, mining, and woodcutter sites, fishing, hunting, river running. **Facilities:** Eagle Visitor Center. Book and map sale area. **Programs & Events:** Video presentations. Yukon Quest dogsled race (Feb.). **Tips & Hints:** Be prepared to be self-sufficient. Winter temperatures are as low as -60°F, and summer highs can reach 90°F. Busiest in June and Aug., least crowded Nov. and Dec.

FOOD, LODGING & SUPPLIES

Camping: In the park: 7 cabins along the Yukon River corridor at Nation Bluff, Glenn Creek, Washington Creek, Kandik River mouth, and historic Slaven's Roadhouse at the mouth of Coal Creek. Backcountry camping allowed. In Eagle City: Eagle Trading Co. RV Par (36 Front St., tel. 907/547–2220; 4 RV sites; $20; flush toilets, showers, hook-ups). **Hotels:** None in park. In Eagle City: Falcon Inn Bed & Breakfast (220 Front St., tel. 907/547–2254; 5 rooms; $60–$75). **Restaurants:** None in park. In Eagle City: Eagle Trading Co. Café (36 Front St., tel. 907/547–2220; $7–$12). **Groceries & Gear:** None in park. In Eagle City: Eagle Trading Co. (36 Front St., tel. 907/547–2220).

FEES, HOURS & REGULATIONS

Free. Alaska state hunting and fishing license required. No artifact collecting. Preserve open daily. Eagle field office open year-round. Visitor center open mid-May–mid-Sept., daily 8–4:30; mid-Sept.–mid-May, weekdays 8–4:30.

HOW TO GET THERE

The preserve is in east interior Alaska, 150 mi east of Fairbanks. Air taxis serve Eagle, located upriver, and Circle, downriver of the preserve. Eagle is at the end of Taylor Hwy., and Circle is on Steese Hwy. The preserve is reached by either river or air travel along the Yukon or by flying in to upper Charley River.

CONTACTS

Yukon-Charley Rivers National Preserve Headquarters (Box 74718, Fairbanks, AK 99707, tel. 907/547–2233, www.nps.gov/yuch). Yukon-Charley Rivers National Preserve Field Office (Box 167, Eagle, AK 99738-0167, tel. 907/547–2233).

See Also

Alatna Wild River, Aleutian World War II National Historic Area, Aniachak Wild River, Charley Wild River, Chilikadrotna Wild River, Iditarod National Historic Trail, John Wild River, Kobuk Wild River, Mulchatna Wild River, Noatak Wild River, North Fork of the Koyukuk Wild River, Salmon Wild River, Tinayguk Wild River, and *Tlikakila Wild River,* in Other National Parklands.

ARIZONA

Canyon de Chelly National Monument

In northeastern Arizona, near Chinle

At the base of sheer red cliffs and in caves inside canyon walls are ruins of Native American villages built between AD 350 and 1300. The monument presents southwestern Native American history from the earliest Pueblos to the Navajo who currently live and farm here. The monument was designated on April 1, 1931.

WHAT TO SEE & DO

Auto touring (permit required in canyon, *see below*), hiking (permit required in canyon, *see below*), horseback riding (rentals), Jeep touring (rentals, Chinle), picnicking, pictograph viewing. **Facilities:** Visitor center, auto and hiking trails. **Programs & Events:** Guided tours of ruins, Oct.–Apr. **Tips & Hints:** Beware of quicksand, deep dry sand, cliffs, loose rocks, and flash floods. Inner canyons impassable in winter and during and after heavy rains. Busiest May and Aug., least crowded Dec. and Jan.

FOOD, LODGING & SUPPLIES

Camping: In the park: Cottonwood Campground (tel. 928/674–5500; 95 sites; donations suggested; flush toilets). **Hotels:** In the park: Thunderbird Lodge (U.S. 191, and Rte. 7, tel. 928/674–5841 or 928/674–5842; 73 rooms; $97–$114). In Chinle: Holiday Inn (Rte. 7, tel. 928/674–5875; 107 rooms; $89–$109). **Restaurants:** In the park: Thunderbird Lodge (U.S. 191 and Rte. 7, tel. 928/674–5841 or 928/674–5842; $15–$25). **Groceries:** None in park. In Chinle: Bashas' Market (U.S. 191 and Rte. 7, tel. 928/674–3464).

FEES, HOURS & REGULATIONS

Free. Driving along the canyon bottom and hiking within the canyon both require a Park Service permit (free) and an authorized Navajo guide ($15 per hour), except for hikes along the 2.5-mi White House Ruins Trail. Drive on paved roads only. No vehicles over 40 feet at park campground. Visitor center open Oct.–Apr., daily 8–5; May–Sept., daily 8–6.

HOW TO GET THERE

3 mi east of U.S. 191, near Chinle, via Exit 333 off I–40. Closest airports: Albuquerque, NM (180 mi), Gallup, NM (98 mi).

CONTACT

Superintendent, Canyon de Chelly National Monument (Box 588, Chinle, AZ 86503, tel. 928/674–5500, www.nps.gov/cach).

Casa Grande Ruins National Monument

In south-central Arizona, in Coolidge

Among the 60 prehistoric Native American sites preserved at Casa Grande Ruins National Monument, Casa Grande, the four-story caliche building built 650 years ago, is the most prominent. Its purpose in the Hohokam culture, which flourished for 1,000 years in the Sonoran Desert, never has been determined. The site was established as a federal reservation in 1892 and a national monument in 1918.

WHAT TO SEE & DO

Picnicking, touring the archaeological sites. **Facilities:** Visitor center, museum, self-guided trail, observation platform. Bookstore, covered picnic tables. **Programs & Events:** Slide presentations. Interpretive programs (Nov.–Apr.). Archaeology tours for Arizona State Archaeology month (Mar.), special events for Native American month (Nov.). **Tips & Hints:** Summer temperatures can reach 115°F, and there's little shade. Go from mid-Oct–early May for mild weather. Busiest Jan.–Mar., least crowded July and Aug.

FOOD, LODGING & SUPPLIES

Camping: None at site. Nearby: Picacho Peak State Park (Exit 219 off I–10, tel. 520/466–3183; 88 sites; $12–$21; flush toilets, showers, hook-ups). **Hotels:** None in park. In Coolidge: Grande Vista Motel (1211 N. Arizona Blvd., tel. 520/723–7793; 25 rooms; $40–$45). **Restaurants:** None in park. In Florence: Old Pueblo Restaurant (505 Main St., tel. 520/868–4784; $5–$15). **Groceries & Gear:** None in park. In Coolidge: Wal-Mart Supercenter (1695 N. Arizona Blvd., tel. 520/723–0945).

FEES, HOURS & REGULATIONS

Entrance fee: $3 adults; free ages 16 and under. Only Compound A (Casa Grande ruin) and picnic area (with observation platform) open to the public. Monument and visitor center open daily 8–5.

HOW TO GET THERE

On the north edge of the city of Coolidge, 60 mi southeast of Phoenix and 70 mi northwest of Tucson. Closest airport: Phoenix.

CONTACTS

Casa Grande Ruins National Monument (1100 Ruins Dr., Coolidge, AZ 85228, tel. 520/723–3172, fax 520/723–7209, www.nps.gov/cagr). Coolidge Chamber of Commerce (Box 943, Coolidge, AZ 85228, tel. 520/723–3009).

Chiricahua National Monument

In southeastern Arizona, near Willcox

A volcanic eruption 27 million years ago, 1,000 times greater than the eruption at Mt. St. Helens, laid down 2,000 feet of ash and pumice that fused into rock and later eroded into the huge balanced rocks, towering spires, and massive stone columns present in the monument today. Now the intersection of two deserts and two mountain ranges, Chiricahua's 12,000 acres represent one of the premier areas of biological diversity in the Northern Hemisphere. Also on site is the Faraway Ranch, originally the homestead of Swedish immigrants and later a working cattle and guest ranch. The monument was proclaimed in 1924 and transferred to the Park Service in 1933.

WHAT TO SEE & DO

Auto touring, bird-watching, hiking, picnicking, touring historic ranch, wildlife watching. **Facilities:** Visitor center, hiking trails. **Programs & Events:** Interpretive walks, talks, evening programs, tours of the Faraway Ranch house (Jan.–May, Sept.–Dec., days and times vary). **Tips & Hints:** Get gas in Willcox. Watch for rattlesnakes. Drive carefully on winding scenic road. Avoid rainy season (July–Sept.). Bring light clothing that you can layer in summer, when temperatures range from 50°F to 95°F each day, and warm clothing in winter, when temperatures range from 10°F to 60°F each day, with wind chills possibly below zero. Busiest Mar. and Apr., least crowded June and July.

FOOD, LODGING & SUPPLIES

Camping: In the park: Bonita Canyon (24 sites; $12; flush toilets). **Hotels:** None in park. In Pearce: Sunglow Guest Ranch (14066 S. Sunglow Rd., tel. 520/824–3334 or 866/786–4569; 9 rooms; $130–$400, including meals). In Bisbee: Inn at Castle Rock (112 Tombstone Canyon Rd., tel. 520/432–4449 or 800/566–4449; 15 rooms; $47–$87). **Restaurants:** None in park. In Willcox: Desert Rose Café (706 S. Haskell Ave., tel. 520/384–0514; $5–$36). **Groceries & Gear:** None in park. In Willcox: Safeway (650 N. Bisbee Ave., tel. 520/384–3952), Bob's IGA (900 W. Rex Allen Dr., tel. 520/384–2502), Alco (510 N. Bisbee Ave., tel. 520/384–0159).

FEES & HOURS

Entrance fee: $5 adults; free ages 16 and under. Visitor center open daily 8–5.

HOW TO GET THERE

120 mi east of Tucson via Exit 340 (Willcox) off I–10, Rtes. 186 and 181. Closest airports: Phoenix (235 mi), Tucson (120 mi).

CONTACTS

Superintendent, Chiricahua National Monument (13063 E. Bonita Canyon Rd., Willcox, AZ 85643, tel. 520/824–3560, Ext. 113 campground information). Willcox Chamber of Commerce & Agriculture

(1500 N. Circle I Rd., Willcox, AZ 85643, tel. 520/384–2272, www. willcoxchamber.com).

Coronado National Memorial

On United States–Mexico border, east of Nogales

The 4,750-acre memorial commemorates the first major exploration of the American southwest by Europeans. The scenic overlook at Montezuma Pass offers sweeping views of the San Pedro River Valley, which is believed to have been the expedition route of Vasquez de Coronado in 1540. The natural environment typifies the "Sky Island" mountains of southeast Arizona, with desert grasslands and oak woodlands. Near the visitor center is a large limestone cave with stalactites, stalagmites, and flowstones; this is open to the public. The site was authorized as an International Memorial on August 18, 1941, and redesignated on November 5, 1952.

WHAT TO SEE & DO

Caving, hiking, picnicking. **Facilities:** Visitor center, outdoor interpretive exhibits, hiking trails. Book and map sales, picnic tables. **Programs & Events:** Interpretive talks and walks (Feb. and Mar., weekly). **Tips & Hints:** Go in spring and fall for best hiking, bird migrations. Busiest Feb. and Mar., least crowded Nov. and Dec.

FOOD, LODGING & SUPPLIES

Camping: None at site. In Hereford: Reef Townsite Campground (5990 W. Rte. 92, tel. 520/378–0311; 24 sites; $10; pit toilets). **Hotels:** None in park. In Sierra Vista: The Windameer Hotel & Conference Center (2047 S. Rte. 92, tel. 520/459–5900 or 800/825–4656; 149 rooms; $55–$195). **Restaurants:** None in park. In Sierra Vista: Mesquite Tree Restaurant (S. Rte. 92 at Carr Canyon Rd., tel. 520/378–2758; $10–$18). **Groceries & Gear:** None in park. In Sierra Vista: Big Five Sporting Goods (135 S. Rte. 92, tel. 520/459–1801). In Hereford: Canyon General Minimart (S. Rte. 92, tel. 520/378–0223).

FEES, HOURS & REGULATIONS

Free. Flashlights (one per person, two if traveling alone) and permit required (free) to visit Coronado Cave. No hunting. No pets on trails or backcountry. No bikes or motorized vehicles on trails. Memorial open daily dawn–dusk. Visitor center open daily 8–5.

HOW TO GET THERE

50 mi south of I–10 off Rte. 92. The turnoff from Rte. 92 onto Coronado Memorial Rd., which leads to E. Montezuma Canyon Rd., is 16 mi south of Sierra Vista and 21 mi west of Bisbee. Closest airports: In Sierra Vista–Fort Huachuca (20 mi), Phoenix (210 mi), Tucson (95 mi).

CONTACTS

Coronado National Memorial (4101 E. Montezuma Canyon Rd., Hereford, AZ 85615, tel. 520/366–5515 Ext. 23, fax 520/366–5705, www.nps.gov/coro). Sierra Vista Convention & Visitors Bureau (21 E. Wilcox Dr., Sierra Vista, AZ 85635, tel. 520/458–6940 or 800/288–3861, fax 520/452–0878, www.arizonaguide.com/sierravista).

Fort Bowie National Historic Site

In southeastern Arizona, near Bowie and Willcox

Fort Bowie commemorates the bitter conflict between the Chiricahua Apaches and the U.S. military. For more than 30 years Fort Bowie and Apache Pass were the focal points of military operations that culminated in the surrender of Geronimo in 1886 and the banishment of the Chiricahuas to Florida and Alabama. It was the site of the Bascom Affair, a wagon train massacre; and the Battle of Apache Pass, where a large force of Chiricahua Apaches under Mangus Colorados and Cochise fought the California Volunteers. The remains of Fort Bowie, the adobe walls of post buildings, and the ruins of a Butterfield Stage Station are carefully preserved. The site was authorized in 1964 and established in 1972.

WHAT TO SEE & DO

Bird-watching, hiking, picnicking, touring fort ruins. **Facilities:** Visitor center, hiking trails. Bookstore, picnic tables. **Tips & Hints:** Plan at least a two-hour hike to fort and back. Busiest Mar. and Apr., least crowded June–Aug.

FOOD, LODGING & SUPPLIES

🏕 **Camping:** None at site. In Bowie: Mountain View RV Park (off Exit 362 at I–10, tel. 520/847–2510; 35 sites; $10; flush toilets, showers, hook-ups). 🏨 **Hotels:** None in park. In Willcox: Muleshoe Ranch (6502 N. Muleshoe Ranch Rd., R.R. 1, Box 1542, tel. 520/212–4295; 5 units; $100–$155), Days Inn (724 N. Bisbee Ave., tel. 520/384–4222; 73 rooms; $44–$54). ✗ **Restaurants:** None in park. In Willcox: Desert Rose Café (706 S. Haskell Ave, tel. 520/384–0514; $5–$12). ⚙ **Gear:** None in park. In Willcox: Ace Hardware (914 W. Rex Allen Dr., tel. 520/384–4446).

FEES & HOURS

Free. Visitor center open daily 8–5. Ruins Trail open daily sunrise–sunset.

HOW TO GET THERE

116 mi east of Tucson and 227 mi southeast of Phoenix via I–10. From Willcox, off I–10, take Rte. 186 to the Fort Bowie turnoff, then drive 8 mi on unpaved road to Fort Bowie Trailhead. Closest airports: Phoenix (227 mi), Tucson (116 mi).

CONTACTS

Fort Bowie National Historic Site (Box 158, Bowie, AZ 85605, tel. 520/847–2500, www.nps.gov/fobo).

Glen Canyon
National Recreation Area

In northern Arizona, near Page, and southern Utah

The 1.2-million-acre recreation area lies in the midst of the country's most rugged canyon country and some of the most scenic backpacking country on the Colorado Plateau. Lake Powell, the second largest man-made lake in the United States, stretches for 186 mi along the old Colorado River channel with a shoreline of 1,960 mi. The construction of the Glen Canyon Dam and the creation of Lake Powell were flashpoints for environmental preservation groups. The park is now a major draw for water sports and camping. It contains the world's largest natural bridge (Rainbow Bridge National Monument, *see* Utah); Lees Ferry, which contains two historic district properties; and the Orange Cliffs unit next to Canyonlands National Park in Utah. At this writing, new plans were in the works for the use of personal watercraft; contact the visitor centers for more information. The recreation area is administered under cooperative agreements with the Bureau of Reclamation, U.S. Dept. of the Interior, signed April 18, 1958, and September 17, 1965, and was established on October 27, 1972.

WHAT TO SEE & DO

Backpacking, boating (rentals at park marinas, Page, AZ; Big Water and Ticaboo, UT; tours at Bullfrog, Halls Crossing, Wahweap), fishing, four-wheel driving, hiking, hunting, mountain biking, picnicking, swimming, waterskiing. **Facilities:** 3 visitor centers: Carl Hayden (Glen Canyon Dam on U.S. 89), Bullfrog (Rte. 276), and Navajo Bridge Interpretive Center (U.S. 89A, near Lees Ferry); beaches, outdoor interpretive exhibits, hiking trails, marinas. Book and map sales, gift shops, picnic tables. **Programs & Events:** Interpretive programs (on request). Ranger programs (Memorial Day–Labor Day). **Tips & Hints:** Know and follow all boating-safety and water-quality regulations. Use of portable toilets is a must. Bring a hat and be prepared for little, if any, shade. Check park Web site or call to find out about the lake's water level. Busiest July and Aug., least crowded Jan. and Feb.

FOOD, LODGING & SUPPLIES

⚠ **Camping:** 4 campgrounds in the park: Bullfrog (78 sites; $18; flush toilets, hook-ups), Halls Crossing (64 sites; $18; flush toilets, hook-ups), Lees Ferry (30 sites; $10; pit toilets), Wahweap (group site; $18; pit toilets, hook-ups). 2 primitive camping areas ($6; pit toilets; permit required for some sites), Lake Powell shoreline camping (free). ⊤ **Hotels:** In the park: Wahweap Lodge (100 Lake Shore Dr., Page, tel. 800/528–6154; 350 rooms; $101–$159), Uncle Bill's Place (117 8th Ave., Page, tel. 928/645–1224; 12 rooms; $33–$59). ✗ **Restaurants:** In the park: Wahweap Lodge Restaurant (100 Lake Shore Dr., Page, tel. 800/528–6154), Dam Bar & Grille (644 N. Navajo, Page, tel. 928/645–2161; $6–$23). ⛏ **Groceries & Gear:** None in park. In Page: Lake Powell Waterworld (920 Hemlock, tel. 928/645–8845), Safeway (Safeway Plaza, Lake Powell Blvd., tel. 928/645–2064), Sticks Bait & Tackle (5 S. Lake Powell Blvd., tel. 928/645–2891).

FEES, HOURS & REGULATIONS

Entrance fee: $10 per vehicle or $3 per pedestrian, bicyclist, or motorcyclist. Boat launch fee: $10 for first vessel, $4 for each additional vessel. Backcountry camping permit required for Orange Cliffs district (available from Canyonlands National Park, *see* Utah), recommended for Escalante district (available from Escalante Interagency Visitor Center). Arizona or Utah state fishing or hunting license required. Leashed pets only in developed areas. No pets at Rainbow Bridge. Mountain bikes on established roads only. Hunting allowed in restricted areas. Park and roads open daily, except the Chains and Sunset Hill overlooks, which are open daylight hours only. Carl Hayden Visitor Center open daily 8–5. Bullfrog visitor center open intermittently in Mar.; Apr.–Oct, daily 8–5. Navajo Bridge Interpretive Center open mid-Apr.–Oct., daily 9–5, Nov.–early Apr., weekends 10–4.

HOW TO GET THERE

Glen Canyon Dam and the Wahweap Marina are near Page, AZ on U.S. 89. North sections of the area, Bullfrog, Halls Crossing, and Hite and the Orange Cliffs may be reached from U.S. 95 and Rte. 276. Lees Ferry and the Navajo Bridge Interpretive Center are off U.S. 89A near Marble Canyon. Closest airports: Page (3 mi), Phoenix (275 mi).

CONTACTS

Glen Canyon National Recreation Area (Box 1507, Page, AZ 86040, tel. 520/608–6404, www.nps.gov/glca). Escalante Interagency Visitor Center (755 W. Main St., Escalante, UT 84726, tel. 435/826–5499).

Grand Canyon
National Park

In northern Arizona, north of Flagstaff

One of the most spectacular examples of erosion anywhere in the world is the Grand Canyon, where the incomparable vistas have dazzled visitors for centuries. As it carves through the earth, the Colorado River opens an incomparable geologic record, from the 260-million-year-old limestone on the canyon rims to the metamorphic rock at the bottom of the gorge, estimated at 1.8 billion years old. The striated rock and towering buttes and mesas become saturated with color at sunrise and sunset. The canyon reaches a depth of nearly 6,000 feet and the distance from the North Rim to the South Rim varies from about half a mile to 18 mi. Among the best hiking trails are Bright Angel, the Rim trail, and the North and South Kaibab trails. In addition to the awesome canyon and rock formations, the park encompasses ancient Native American ruins, a vintage railway between the town of Williams and the South Rim, an IMAX theater, photography studios, old copper mines, and plenty of designated lookout points. Grand Canyon Village, on the South Rim, has the fullest concentration of facilities, with a bank and ATM, post office, groceries, and supplies. The Grand Canyon was proclaimed as a forest preserve in 1893 and a game preserve in 1906, a national monument in 1908, transferred to the National Park Service and established as a national park in 1919, and declared a World Heritage Site in 1979.

WHAT TO SEE & DO

Air, auto, and bus touring (rentals); fishing; hiking; horseback riding (rentals); mountain biking; mule riding (rentals); rafting (rentals). **Facilities:** Canyon View Information Plaza (South Rim, south of Mather Point), Yavapai Observation Station (5 mi south of South Rim park entrance), Desert View Visitor Center (eastern park entrance at South Rim), and North Rim Visitor Center (Bright Angel Peninsula, North Rim). North Rim Wilderness Information Center (at ranger station) and South Rim Wilderness Information Center (near Parking Lot E). Tusayan Museum of Pueblo life (Desert View Dr., South Rim), guided tours, hiking trails, IMAX movie theater (Tusayan). Bookstores, gift shops, photo shop. **Programs & Events:** Ranger-led walks, talks, and evening programs; air tours; mule trips; horse rides; Kolb Studio art exhibits. Grand Canyon Field Institute seminars, backpacking trips, and river trips (Mar.–Nov.). Grand Canyon Music Festival (Sept.). Check the *Guide* on arrival for schedule of additional seasonal activities and events. **Tips & Hints:** Plan several months ahead for lodging, backcountry permits, rafting trips, and mule trips. Write the park in advance to request a *Trip Planner* or *Backcountry Trip Planner*. Bring an extra set of car keys. Always carry water in your car. Keep your gas tank full. Use shuttle transportation within the park. Never feed animals. Don't hike alone and avoid hiking in direct sunlight. When hiking, pack light and always stay on the trail. Remember that hiking at high altitudes is exceptionally tiring. Do not try to hike down to the bottom of the canyon and back in one day. Do not attempt to swim in the Colorado River. Drink and eat frequently during outdoor activities. If you are going into the backcountry, you must follow the "leave no trace" principles. For the best photos, take pictures in the morning or late afternoon. Watch carefully for changing weather conditions. Be prepared for a variety of climates. Expect snow in winter and cool nights in summer at the South Rim (elevation approximately 7,000 feet) and snow almost any time of year at North Rim (elevation approximately 8,000 feet). In summer, inner canyon temperatures can reach 120°F on canyon floor. Avoid crowds by making a very early start. Expect crowds during winter holiday weekends, spring break, and all summer. Busiest July and Aug., least crowded Nov.–Jan.

FOOD, LODGING & SUPPLIES

Camping: 4 campgrounds in the park: Desert View (South Rim; 50 sites; $10; flush toilets; closed mid-Oct.–mid-May), Mather (South Rim; 313 sites; $15–$40; flush toilets, showers), North Rim (72 sites; $15;

flush toilets, showers; closed mid-Oct.–mid-May), Trailer Village (South Rim, tel. 303/297–2757 or 888/297–2757; 80 sites; $25; flush toilets, showers, hook-ups). Backcountry camping allowed (permit required, *see below*). ⊞ **Hotels:** On the South Rim: Bright Angel Lodge (Grand Canyon Village; 30 rooms, 42 cabins; $49–$67, $84–$127 cabins), El Tovar Hotel (Grand Canyon Village; 78 rooms; $123–$286), Kachina Lodge (Grand Canyon Village; 49 rooms; $115–$125), Maswik Lodge (Grand Canyon Village; 250 rooms, 28 cabins; $77–$119, $64 cabins), Phantom Ranch (Canyon floor; 4 dorms, 2 cabins; $26, $72–$94 cabins), Thunderbird Lodge (Grand Canyon Village; 55 rooms; $115–$125), Yavapai Lodge (Grand Canyon Village; 358 rooms; $91–$103). On the North Rim: Grand Canyon Lodge (44 rooms, 157 cabins; $91–$116; closed mid-Oct.–mid-May). ✕ **Restaurants:** On the South Rim: Arizona Room (Grand Canyon Village, tel. 928/638–2631; $12–$22, no lunch), Bright Angel Restaurant (Grand Canyon Village, tel. 928/638–2631; $6–$14), El Tovar Dining Room (Grand Canyon Village, tel. 928/638–2631; $17–$25). ⌂ **Groceries & Gear:** On the South Rim: Canyon Village Marketplace. On the North Rim: Camper store near visitor center.

FEES, HOURS & REGULATIONS

Entrance fee: $20 per vehicle; $10 per bicyclist or walk-in. Free shuttle service in Grand Canyon Village. Mule trips into canyon: $130 (tel. 928/638–2631, 888/297–2757 reservations). Permit required for all backcountry camping ($10 for permit plus $5 per person per day, available from Backcountry Information Center (tel. 928/638–7875). No bikes on trails except for Greenway system on the South Rim. Arizona State fishing license required (Canyon Village Marketplace, South Rim). Pets must be leashed at all times and are not allowed below the canyon rim, in park lodgings, or on park buses. South Rim open year-round, daily. North Rim Rd. open mid-May–mid-Oct., daily. Canyon View Information Plaza and Yavapai Observation Station open daily 8–5. Desert View information center open daily 9–5. North Rim visitor center open mid-May–mid-Oct., daily 8–6. North Rim Backcountry Information Center open mid-May–mid-Oct., 8–noon and 1–5. South Rim Backcountry Information Center open daily 8–noon and 1–5.

HOW TO GET THERE

Grand Canyon Village on the South Rim is 60 mi north of I–40 at Williams via U.S. 64 and 80 mi northwest of Flagstaff via U.S. 180. The North Rim is 44 mi south of Jacob Lake via Rte. 67. Train service (tel. 800/843–8724) available from Williams. Shuttles (tel. 928/638–0871 or 928/638–0821) run from Tusayan to Grand Canyon Village. Taxis available from Grand Canyon National Park Lodges, tel. 928/638–2631 Ext. 6563. Closest airports: Tusayan (8 mi), Flagstaff (80 mi), Phoenix (220 mi), Las Vegas, NV (291 mi).

CONTACTS

Grand Canyon National Park (Box 129, Grand Canyon, AZ 86023, tel. 928/638–7888, 800/365–2267 campground reservations, www.nps.gov/grca). Grand Canyon (Tusayan) Chamber of Commerce (Box 3007, Grand Canyon, AZ 86023, tel. 928/638–2901). Flagstaff Convention & Visitors Bureau (211 W. Aspen Ave., Flagstaff, AZ 86001, tel. 928/779–

7611, fax 928/556–1305, www.flagstaffarizona.org). Flagstaff Visitor Center (1 E. Rte. 66, Flagstaff, AZ 86001, tel. 928/774–9541 or 800/842–7293). Arizona Office of Tourism (2702 N. 3rd St., Suite 4015, Phoenix, AZ 85004, tel. 800/842–8257). Kane County (Utah) Chamber of Commerce (78 E. 100 S, Kanab, UT 84741, tel. 435/644–5033). Kingman Chamber of Commerce (120 W. Andy Devine, Kingman, AZ 86401, tel. 928/753–6106). Page Chamber of Commerce (Box 727, Page, AZ 86040, tel. 520/645–2741). Williams Chamber of Commerce (200 W. Railroad Ave., Williams, AZ 86046, tel. 928/635–4061). Xanterra Parks & Resorts (14001 E. Iliff, Suite 600, Aurora, CO 80014, tel. 303/338–6000 or 888/297–2757, fax 303/297–3175, www.xanterra.com).

Hohokam Pima National Monument

In south-central Arizona, south of Phoenix

Preserved here are the archaeological remains of a Hohokam village that was occupied between AD 300 and AD 1100. Hohokam is a Pima Indian word meaning "those who have gone."

WHAT TO SEE & DO
The site is closed to the public.

CONTACT
Hohokam Pima National Monument (c/o Casa Grande Ruins National Monument, 1100 Ruins Dr., Coolidge, AZ 85228, tel. 520/723–3172, www.nps.gov/pima).

Hubbell Trading Post National Historic Site

In northeastern Arizona, near Ganado

This site in the Navajo Nation commemorates the distinctive role of the Native American trader in the American Southwest. The post has a preeminent place in the history and ethnography of the Navajo people. It still functions much the way John Lorenzo Hubbell operated it in the late 1800s and is internationally renowned for authentic and high-quality Native American arts. The site was designated a National Historic Site in 1965 and transferred to the National Park Service in 1967.

WHAT TO SEE & DO
Buying arts and crafts, jewelry, and rugs; picnicking; touring the post and Hubbell homestead; watching Navajo weavers. **Facilities:** Visitor center with Navajo weavers, trading post, Hubbell homestead. Bookstore, picnic tables. **Programs & Events:** Homestead walks, Navajo culture talks, tours of the Hubbell family home. Pueblo Colorado Wash walking tour (May–Sept.), Native American Arts Auction (Apr. and

Aug.), Old Time Trading Days (one weekend, Aug.), Luminaria Night (Dec.). **Tips & Hints:** Navajo Nation time is one hour later than time in the State of Arizona Apr.–Oct., because the Navajo Nation observes daylight saving time but the State of Arizona does not. Busiest June and July, least crowded Dec. and Jan.

FOOD, LODGING & SUPPLIES

Camping: None in park. Available in Canyon de Chelly National Monument (*see separate entry*). **Hotels:** None in park. In Chinle: Best Western Canyon de Chelly Inn (Indian Rte. 7, tel. 928/674–5875 or 800/327–0354; 102 rooms; $89–$99). **Restaurants:** None in park. In Ganado: Ramones (Rte. 264, tel. 928/755–3404; $6–$13). **Groceries & Gear:** In the park: Hubbell Trading Post. In Ganado: Mustang Convenience Store (Rte. 264, tel. 928/755–3261).

FEES & HOURS

Free. Site and visitor center open Oct.–Apr., daily 8–5; May–Sept., daily 8–6.

HOW TO GET THERE

On Rte. 264, ½ mi west of Ganado. Closest airports: Albuquerque, NM (180 mi), Gallup, NM (60 mi), Phoenix (320 mi).

CONTACTS

Hubbell Trading Post National Historic Site (Box 150, Ganado, AZ 86505, tel. 928/755–3475, fax 928/755–3405, www.nps.gov/hutr). Gallup Convention & Visitors Bureau (Box 600, Gallup, NM 87301, tel. 505/863–3841 or 800/242–4282, fax 505/863–2280, www.gallupnm.org). Gallup Chamber of Commerce (103 W. U.S. 66, Gallup, NM 87301, tel. 505/722–2228, www.gallupchamber.com).

Montezuma Castle National Monument

In central Arizona, near Camp Verde

Montezuma Castle is one of the best-preserved prehistoric structures in the Southwest. Despite the romantic name, it has no actual connection to Montezuma; it was dubbed this by early Western settlers who thought that the building was associated with the Aztec emperor. In fact, Sinagua farmers began building the five-story, 20-room dwelling in the 12th century. A detached unit of the monument, known as Montezuma Well, is a blue-green pool, a limestone sink that measures more than 400 feet across and supplied irrigation water to the prehistoric people. The monument was proclaimed in 1906.

WHAT TO SEE & DO

Hiking, picnicking, viewing the ancient dwelling and well. **Facilities:** Visitor center, interpretive trails. Book and map sales, picnic tables. **Programs & Events:** Ranger talks. **Tips & Hints:** Avoid summer heat. Go in spring or fall. Busiest Mar. and Apr., least crowded Dec. and Jan.

FOOD, LODGING & SUPPLIES

Camping: None at site. Near Cottonwood: Dead Horse Ranch State Park (Off Rte. 89A, tel. 928/634–5283; 127 sites; $12–$19; flush toilets, showers, hook-ups). **Hotels:** None in park. In Camp Verde: The Lodge at Cliff Castle (333 Middle Verde Rd., tel. 800/524–6343; 82 rooms; $74–$79). **Restaurants:** None in park. In Camp Verde: The Gathering (The Lodge at Cliff Castle, 333 Middle Verde Rd., tel. 800/524–6343; $13–$16). **Groceries & Gear:** None in park. In Camp Verde: Bashas' Market (650 W. Finnie Flat Rd., tel. 928/567–4585), Fort Verde Gas (328 Main St., tel. 928/567–3152).

FEES, HOURS & REGULATIONS

Entrance fee: $3 per person. Leashed pets only. Monument and visitor center open Sept.–May, daily 8–5; June–Aug., daily 8–7.

HOW TO GET THERE

3 mi north of Camp Verde on Montezuma Castle Hwy., off I–17. Closest airports: Flagstaff (50 mi), Phoenix (95 mi).

CONTACTS

Montezuma Castle National Monument (Box 219, Camp Verde, AZ 86322, tel. 928/567–3322, www.nps.gov/moca). Camp Verde Chamber of Commerce (Box 3520, Camp Verde, AZ 86322, tel. 928/567–9294).

Navajo National Monument

In northeastern Arizona, near Kayenta

Well-preserved ruins of villages abandoned around AD 1300 by Pueblo peoples are the attractions in this park. Built and occupied for only 50 years, the ruins represent the final settlement of farmers who adapted to the area's scarce rainfall to grow crops, build houses, and raise families. Betatakin, Keet Seel, and Inscription House (closed since 1968 because of its fragility) are three cliff dwellings at the site. There's a terrific view from a designated overlook at the ruddy sandstone dwellings of Betatakin. There are limited hiking opportunities to see Betatakin and Keet Seel close up. You can watch Navajo artisans at work in the visitor center. The monument was proclaimed on March 20, 1909.

WHAT TO SEE & DO

Hiking, picnicking, viewing ruins. **Facilities:** Visitor center, guided and self-guided tours, hiking trails. Arts and crafts store, bookstore, picnic tables. **Programs & Events:** Ranger-led tours (Memorial Day–Labor Day), evening campfire programs. **Tips & Hints:** Bring plenty of water. Get gas and food in Black Mesa. Busiest July and Aug., least crowded Jan. and Feb.

FOOD & LODGING

Camping: In the park: Navajo Campground (31 sites; free; flush toilets). Backcountry camping available at Keet Seel (permit required, *see below*). **Hotels:** None in park. In Kayenta: Hampton Inn (U.S. 160, tel. 928/697–3170; 73 rooms; $60–$119). In Tuba City: Quality Inn (Main St., tel. 928/283–4545 or 800/644–8383; 80 rooms; $74–$89). ✗ **Restaurants:** None in park. In Kayenta: Golden Sands (U.S. 163, tel. 928/697–3684; $7–$15). In Tuba City: Kate's Café (Main and Edgewater Sts., tel. 928/283–6773; $5–$15).

FEES, HOURS & REGULATIONS

Free. Access to Betatakin ruins by ranger-guided tour only. Backcountry permits (free) required for hike to Keet Seel; permit covers overnight stay. Advance reservations required for Keet Seel (tel. 520/672–2366). Surrounding backcountry land is Navajo property and off limits to visitors. No collecting. No wood or charcoal fires. Camp stoves only. Visitor center open Mar.–Nov., daily 8–5; Dec.–Feb., daily 8–4:30.

HOW TO GET THERE

The visitor center turnoff at Black Mesa on Rte. 564 is 50 mi northeast of Tuba City and 19 mi southwest of Kayenta off U.S. 160. Turn north on Rte. 564 and travel 9 mi to the visitor center. Closest airports: Page (88 mi), Phoenix (250 mi).

CONTACT

Navajo National Monument (HC-71, Box 3, Tonalea, AZ 86044-9704, tel. 928/672–2366/2367, fax 928/672–2345, www.nps.gov/nava).

Organg Pipe Cactus National Monument

In southwestern Arizona, near Ajo

This monument gives you a rare chance to see the extraordinary plants and animals that can survive the extreme climate of the Sonoran Desert—including the namesake organ pipe cactus, a large cactus rarely found in the United States. These multi-armed cacti tend to grow on south-facing slopes, and you can see them from one of the scenic roads that loop through the park. Gila monsters, rattlesnakes, and scorpions are among the creatures that have adapted to the region's extreme temperatures, intense sunlight, and infrequent rainfall. The monument was proclaimed in 1937 and designated a Biosphere Reserve in 1976.

WHAT TO SEE & DO

Auto touring, backpacking, bird- and wildlife watching, hiking, mountain biking, picnicking. **Facilities:** Visitor center, self-guided nature trail. Bookstore, picnic tables. **Programs & Events:** Guided hikes, interpretive talks and evening programs (Jan.–Mar., daily). O'Odham Day Celebration (mid-Mar.). **Tips & Hints:** Beware of the cactus and six varieties of rattlesnakes, as well as Gila monsters and scorpions. Be prepared for desert walking. Carry a minimum of one gallon of drinking water per person per day. Best time to camp and hike is mid-Nov.–mid-Mar. Go mid-Mar.–mid-Apr. for flowers and Apr.–Sept. for migrating birds. Busiest Jan.–Mar., least crowded July and Aug.

FOOD, LODGING & SUPPLIES

Camping: 2 campgrounds in the park: Alamo (4 sites; $6; pit toilets), Twin Peaks (208 sites; $10; flush toilets). Backcountry camping allowed (permit required, *see below*). **Hotels:** None in park. In Ajo: Guest House Inn Bed & Breakfast (700 Guest House Rd., tel. 520/387–6133; 4 rooms; $69–$89). In Lukeville: Gringo Pass Motel & RV Park (S. Rte. 85, tel. 520/387–5507; 12 rooms; $53–$72). **Restaurants:** None in park. In Ajo: Marcella's Restaurant (1117 W. Dorsey St., tel. 520/387–4139; $5–$10). **Groceries:** None in park. In Ajo: Olsen's Market (601 N. 2nd Ave., tel. 520/387–5641).

FEES, HOURS & REGULATIONS

Entrance fee: $3 per person on bike or foot; $5 per vehicle. Backcountry and primitive camping permit ($5) required. No collecting. No hunting. No off-road vehicles. No pets in backcountry; leashed pets elsewhere. Special trails marked for pet use. Mountain bikes on maintained roads only. Monument open daily. Visitor center open daily 8–5.

HOW TO GET THERE

Monument headquarters is 22 mi south of Why via Rte. 85. Closest airports: Phoenix (115 mi), Tucson (150 mi).

CONTACTS

Organ Pipe Cactus National Monument (10 Organ Pipe Dr., Ajo, AZ 85321, tel. 520/387–6849, fax 520/387–7144, www.nps.gov/orpi). Ajo Chamber of Commerce (400 Taludro St., Ajo, AZ 85321, tel. 520/387–7742, www.ajoinaz.com).

Petrified Forest National Park

In eastern Arizona, near Holbrook

Petrified Forest has one of the world's largest and most colorful concentrations of petrified wood. The wood was fossilized by mineral deposits so it's now brightly colored: pink, deep red, yellow, orange, white, even green. It's scattered in logs and chunks; there's even a structure, the Agate House, built with it. The park's 93,533 acres also include the multihued badlands of the Painted Desert, archaeological sites, and displays of 225-million-year-old fossils. This tableland is also one of the last pristine vestiges of "shortgrass prairie" and its inhabitants. The park was designated a national monument in 1906 and a national park in 1962.

WHAT TO SEE & DO

Backpacking, hiking, viewing film, walking, wildlife watching. **Facilities:** Painted Desert Visitor Center (Exit 311 off I–40); Painted Desert Inn National Historic Landmark with archaeology displays, Rainbow Forest Museum, hiking trails, interpretive signs. Covered picnic tables, gift shops. **Programs & Events:** Ranger-led interpretive talks, walks, and hike. Summer Solstice at Puerco Pueblo, a prehistoric solar calendar at work (a two-week period around June 21, 8–10 AM). **Tips & Hints:**

Watch out for rattlesnakes and kingsnakes. Prepare for summer temperatures near 90°F, high elevation (5,100–6,235 feet), and high winds, particularly in spring. Avoid rainy season, often accompanied by lightning storms, mid-July–early Sept. Visit in spring and fall. Busiest July and Aug., least crowded Dec. and Jan.

FOOD, LODGING & SUPPLIES

⚠ **Camping:** Backcountry camping only (permit required, *see below*). ⛺ **Hotels:** None in park. In Holbrook: Best Western Adobe Inn (615 W. Hopi Dr., tel. 928/524–3948 or 877/524–3948; 54 rooms; $45–$54). ✗ **Restaurants:** None in park. In Holbrook: El Rancho (867 Navajo Blvd., tel. 928/524–3332; $5–$10). ⛓ **Groceries:** In the park: Painted Desert Oasis (North entrance, tel. 928/524–3756), snack bar–soda fountain (South entrance, tel. 928/524–3138).

FEES, HOURS & REGULATIONS

Entrance fee: $10 per private vehicle or $5 for walk-ins and bicyclists. Backcountry permits required for overnight trips (free, visitor center or Rainbow Forest Museum). Collecting strictly forbidden. Gift shops sell petrified wood that has been legally obtained from private land outside the park boundaries. Motorized vehicles and bicycles on paved roads only. No four-wheel-drive vehicles or mountain biking. No pets in buildings, in backcountry, or on Giant Logs Trail; leashed pets permitted elsewhere. Park, visitor center, and museum open mid-May–early Sept., daily 7–7; Sept.–May, daily 8–5. Park gates are locked at night.

HOW TO GET THERE

The park stretches between I–40 and U.S. 180 (Exit 285 at Holbrook). From the west, enter the south end of the park off U.S. 180. Travel through the park and exit at I–40 E. From the east, enter at Exit 311 of I–40. Travel through the park to U.S. 180 on to Holbrook and I–40 W. The north entrance is 25 mi east of Holbrook on I–40. The south entrance is 19 mi east of Holbrook on U.S. 180. Closest airports: Albuquerque, NM (180 mi), Holbrook or Flagstaff (125 mi), Gallup, NM (60 mi).

CONTACTS

Superintendent, Petrified Forest National Park (Box 2217, Petrified Forest, AZ 86028, tel. 928/524–6228, www.nps.gov/pefo). Holbrook Chamber of Commerce (100 E. Arizona St., Holbrook, AZ 86025, tel. 928/524–6558 or 800/524–2459, www.ci.holbrook.az.us).

Pipe Spring
National Monument

In northern Arizona, near Fredonia

Pipe Spring's waters allow plant and animal life to thrive in this desert region north of the Grand Canyon. Beginning at least 1,000 years ago, ancestral Puebloans and later Paiutes raised crops in the area. In 1871, Mormon pioneers built a fort, called Windsor Castle, over the main spring and established a cattle-ranching operation. The monument commemorates western pioneer settlement and American Indian–pioneer interactions on the frontier. Its museum, revamped in 2003, includes exhibits on the history of the Kaibab Paiutes. The monument was proclaimed on May 31, 1923.

WHAT TO SEE & DO

Hiking ½-mi trail, touring the fort and grounds, and visiting museum. **Facilities:** Visitor center and museum, audio stations on grounds, hiking trail. Bookstore and gift shop. **Programs & Events:** Ranger-guided tours of fort. Ranger talks (June–Sept., 2–3 times a day), cultural demonstrations (June–Sept., 3–6 times a week). **Tips & Hints:** Services in the area are scarce, so fill your gas tank as often as possible and carry water in your car. Watch for rattlesnakes in summer. Stay on sidewalks. Go Mar. and Apr. or Sept. and Oct. for bird migrations, May and Sept. for flower blooms. Busiest July and Aug., least crowded Dec. and Jan.

FOOD, LODGING & SUPPLIES

Camping: None at site. Nearby: Kaibab Band of Paiute Indians Campground (Off Rte. 389, tel. 928/643–7245; 40 sites; $5–$10; flush toilets, showers, hook-ups). **Hotels:** None at site. In Kanab, UT: Shilo Inn (296 W. 100 N on U.S. 89, tel. 435/644–2562 or 800/222–2244; 118 rooms; $66–$136). **Restaurants:** None at site. In Kanab, UT: Rocking V Café (97 Center St., tel. 435/644–8001; $10–$25). **Groceries & Gear:** None at site. In Kanab, UT: Food Town Deli (264 S. 100 E, tel. 435/644–5029), Willow Canyon Outdoor Company (263 S. 100 E, tel. 435/644–8884).

FEES, HOURS & REGULATIONS

Entrance fee: $4 per person, free for those age 16 and under. No bikes or motorized vehicles. No pets in historic buildings. Leashed pets only on trails. Monument and visitor center open June–Sept., daily 7–5; Sept.–May, daily 8–5.

HOW TO GET THERE

15 mi west of Fredonia, AZ, via Rte. 389; 60 mi east of Hurricane, UT, via Rte. 59 and Rte. 389. Closest airports: Phoenix (350 mi), St. George, UT (65 mi).

CONTACTS

Pipe Spring National Monument (HC 65, Box 5, Fredonia, AZ 86022, tel. 928/643–7105, fax 928/643–7583, www.nps.gov/pisp). Kane County Travel Council (78 S. 100 E, Kanab, UT 84741, tel. 435/644–5033).

Saguaro National Park

In south-central Arizona, near Tucson

The saguaro cactus, which can grow 50 feet tall in a 200-year life span, was the primary reason for creating the park, which has districts on the west and east sides of Tucson. (The west side is smaller but more heavily visited.) But the park is home to many other wonders as well. More than 1,000 species of plant life dot the lower elevations of the 91,453-acre park. Douglas fir and Ponderosa pine are common in forests at 8,000 feet. Nearly 200 mi of hiking trails challenge visitors; you can also visit cactus gardens and drive or cycle along scenic loop routes. Numerous historic structures blend into the vistas, and ancient Hohokam petroglyphs abound in this predominantly wilderness park. The site was proclaimed a national monument in 1933 and redesignated a national park in 1994.

WHAT TO SEE & DO

Auto touring, bicycling, hiking. **Facilities:** 2 visitor centers: East District (Old Spanish Trail at Freeman Rd., east of Tucson), Red Hills West District (Kinney Rd., west of Tucson); hiking trails. Bookstore, covered picnic tables. **Programs & Events:** Interpretive walks and talks. **Tips & Hints:** Bring plenty of water and sunscreen. Go late Mar.–early Apr. (usually) for desert plant blooms, Mar.–May for saguaro blooms. Busiest Nov.–Mar., least crowded June and July.

FOOD, LODGING & SUPPLIES

⚠ **Camping:** Backcountry camping area in Rincon Mountain District (permit required, *see below*). Nearby: Colossal Cave Mountain Park (16721 E. Old Spanish Trail, tel. 520/647–7275; 57 sites; $3; pit toilets), Tucson Mountain Park (Kinney Loop Rd., between Gate Pass Rd. and Arizona Sonora Desert Museum, tel. 520/877–6000; 146 sites; $7–$12; flush toilets, hook-ups). 🛏 **Hotels:** None in park. In Tucson: Westward Look Resort (245 E. Ina Rd., tel. 520/297–1151 or 800/722–2500; 244 rooms; $79–$300), White Stallion Ranch (9251 Twin Peaks Rd., tel. 520/297–0252 or 888/977–2624; 24 rooms, 17 suites; $125, $175 suites; closed June–Aug.). ✘ **Restaurants:** None in park. In Tucson: Wildflower Grill (7037 N. Oracle Rd., tel. 520/219–4230; $10–$23), Vivace (4310 N. Campbell Ave., tel. 520/795–7221; $10–$30). ⚘ **Gear:** None in park. In Tucson: Popular Outdoor Outfitters For Less (6315 E. Broadway Blvd., tel. 520/290–1644).

FEES, HOURS & REGULATIONS

Entrance fee: $6 per vehicle for scenic loop drive in East District only; $3 for pedestrians and bicyclists. Backcountry permit required and available at East District Visitor Center. No pets on trails; leashed pets on roads. Both district roads open daily 7 AM–sunset. Visitor centers open daily 8:30–5.

HOW TO GET THERE

Reach East District and park headquarters from Tucson by driving east on Speedway, Broadway, or Old Spanish Trail; reach West District via Speedway Blvd. W. Closest airports: Tucson, Phoenix (115 mi).

CONTACTS

Saguaro National Park (3693 S. Old Spanish Trail, Tucson, AZ 85710, tel. 520/733–5153, fax 520/733–5183, www.nps.gov/sagu). Tucson Chamber of Commerce (465 W. St. Mary's Rd., Tucson, AZ 85701, tel. 520/792–1212, www.tucsonchamber.org).

Sunset Crater Volcano National Monument

In north-central Arizona, near Flagstaff

A volcano that erupted in the winter of 1064–65, when molten rock sprayed high into the air out of a crack in the ground, is protected here. Periodic eruptions formed a cinder cone 1,000 feet high, a dramatic black shape with a reddish rim. Lava that flowed from the base of the volcano appears now as a stark, jagged landscape. You can't hike into the crater, but you can follow a trail around the base, take a scenic loop drive, or climb another, smaller volcano nearby. The site was proclaimed a national monument in 1930 and transferred from the Forest Service in 1933.

WHAT TO SEE & DO

Auto touring, hiking, picnicking, touring museum, walking. **Facilities:** Visitor center and movie (2 mi east of U.S. 89 on Forest Rd. 545), outdoor interpretive exhibits, hiking trails, self-guided walks. Book and map sales area, picnic tables. **Programs & Events:** Ranger-guided walks in morning and afternoon (June–Aug.), evening programs (Fri., Sat., and some weekdays, June–Aug.). **Tips & Hints:** Watch for deep, narrow cracks in the earth and razor-sharp lava when hiking. Wear closed, sturdy shoes. Drink water and reduce activity at high elevation (7,000 feet). Use caution on unpaved roads because vehicles can become stuck in soft cinders (in dry weather) or mud (during flash floods). Come June–Oct. for best weather. Busiest June and July, least crowded Jan. and Feb.

FOOD, LODGING & SUPPLIES

Camping: None at site. In Coconino National Forest: Bonito Campground (Rte. 545, off U.S. 89, 12 mi north of Flagstaff, tel. 928/526–0866; 40 sites; flush toilets, pit toilets; closed Oct. 15–Apr.). **Hotels:** None in park. In Flagstaff: Hotel Monte Vista (100 N. San Francisco St., tel. 928/779–6971 or 800/545–3068; 48 rooms; $60–$120), Little America at Flagstaff (2515 E. Butler Ave., tel. 928/779–2741 or 800/352–4386; 248 rooms; $89–$275), Radisson Woodlands Plaza Hotel (1175 W. Rte. 66, tel. 928/773–8888 or 800/333–3333; 183 rooms; $79–$179). **Restaurants:** None at site. In Flagstaff: Buster's Restaurant (1800 S. Milton Rd., tel. 928/774–5155; $10–$23), Café Express (16 N. San Francisco St., tel. 928/774–0541; $5–$9), Cottage Place (126 W. Cottage Ave., tel. 928/774–8431; $10–$18), Down Under New Zealand Restaurant (6 E. Aspen Ave., tel. 928/774–8431; $12–$23). **Groceries & Gear:** None at site. In Flagstaff: Fry's Food & Drug Store (201 N. Switzer Dr., tel. 928/774–2719), Hank's Trading Post (U.S. 89 N, tel. 928/679–2357), Peace Surplus (14 W. Rte. 66, tel. 928/779–4521).

FEES, HOURS & REGULATIONS

Entrance fee: $5 adults, free ages 16 and under. Sunset Crater Volcano closed to hiking but other nearby volcanoes can be climbed. No pets on trails; leashed pets only in parking lots and picnic areas. No bicycles or motorized equipment on hiking trails. No hunting. Park open daily sunrise–sunset. Visitor center open Mar.–May and Sept.–Nov., daily 8–5; June–Aug., daily 8–6; Dec.–Feb., daily 9–5.

HOW TO GET THERE

Reach park from Flagstaff via U.S. 89 for 13 mi and Forest Rd. 545 for 2 mi. Closest airports: Flagstaff (15 mi), Phoenix (155 mi).

CONTACTS

Sunset Crater Volcano National Monument (Rte. 3, Box 149, Flagstaff, AZ 86004, tel. 928/526–0502, fax 928/714–0565, www.nps.gov/sucr). Flagstaff Convention & Visitors Bureau (211 W. Aspen Ave., Flagstaff, AZ 86001, tel. 928/779–7611, fax 928/556–1305, www.flagstaffarizona. org). Flagstaff Visitor Center (1 E. Rte. 66, Flagstaff, AZ 86001, tel. 928/774–9541 or 800/842–7293).

Tonto National Monument

In south-central Arizona, near Globe

Well-preserved cliff dwellings here were occupied during the 13th and 14th centuries by the Salado culture, which farmed the Tonto Basin Valley. It's the only Salado site in the park system. The monument was proclaimed in 1907.

WHAT TO SEE & DO

Hiking to Lower and Upper Cliff Dwellings (permit required for Upper Cliff Dwellings, *see below*), picnicking, touring museum, watching video program. **Facilities:** Visitor center (1 mi off Rte. 88), hiking trails. Bookstore, covered picnic tables. **Programs & Events:** Upper Cliff Dwelling tours and guided hikes (Nov.–Apr.); Lower Cliff Dwelling interpretive talks, self-guided tours (on request). Open House to Upper Cliff Dwelling (1st weekend, Nov. and mid- Mar.). **Tips & Hints:** Make reservations in advance for Upper Cliff Dwelling tour. Watch out for snakes and cactus. Stay on trail. Visit Nov.–Apr. Busiest Jan.–Mar., least crowded June–Aug.

FOOD, LODGING & SUPPLIES

Camping: None at site. Spring Creek Inn & RV Resort (Rte. 188, 18½ mi from Globe, tel. 928/467–2888; 81 sites; $20; flush toilets, showers, hook-ups). **Hotels:** None at site. In Globe: El Rey Motel (1201 E. Ash St., tel. 928/425–4427; 23 rooms; $26–$32). **Restaurants:** None at monument. In Globe: Chalo's (902 E. Ash St., tel. 928/425–0515; $5–$8). **Groceries & Gear:** None at site. In Payson: Bashas' Market (142 E. U.S. 260, tel. 928/474–4495).

FEES, HOURS & REGULATIONS

Entrance fee: $3 per person. No hunting. No resource gathering. Leashed pets only at Visitor Center and Lower Cliffdwelling trail. No pets on Upper Cliffdwelling trail. No fires. Park and visitor center open daily 8–5, Lower Cliff Dwelling trail open daily 8–4.

HOW TO GET THERE

65 mi northeast of Phoenix via U.S. 60 and Rte. 88; 30 mi northwest of Globe via Rte. 188; and 55 mi south of Payson via Rte. 188. Closest airport: Phoenix.

CONTACTS

Tonto National Monument (HC02, Box 4602, Roosevelt, AZ 85545, tel. 928/467–2241, fax 928/467–2225, www.nps.gov/tont). Greater Globe–Miami Chamber of Commerce (1360 N. Broad St., Globe, AZ 85501, tel. 928/425–4495, www.globemiamichamber.com). Payson Chamber of Commerce (100 W. Main St., Payson, AZ 85541, tel. 928/474–4515).

Tumacácori National Historical Park

In southern Arizona, near Nogales

Tumacácori was first visited by a missionary, Father Eusebio Francisco Kino, in 1691; in 1751 the Jesuits built a church here. At that time, Tumacácori was the northern frontier of the Spanish colonial empire. The Jesuits, and later the Franciscans, attempted to convert the native population to Christianity and incorporate them into Spanish society. The conversion of these native people, known as the Pima, was only partly successful. The settlement was abandoned in 1848; now you will find the stabilized ruins of the Franciscan church, a garden, a cemetery, and other outbuildings. Tumacácori is also one of the ends of the 4.5-mi Juan Bautista de Anza National Historic Trail, which links with Tubac on the route taken by the conquistadors. The park was proclaimed a national monument in 1908 and redesignated in 1990.

WHAT TO SEE & DO

Picnicking, self-guided and ranger-led tours of the museum, church, and other historic structures. **Facilities:** Visitor center, hiking trail, outdoor interpretive signs. Bookstore, picnic tables. **Programs & Events:** Ranger-led tours (Oct.–Apr., generally at 11 and 2 daily and by special arrangement); crafts demonstrations such as tortilla, paper-flower, and pottery making (Oct.–Jan., Apr., and May, weekends; Feb. and Mar., daily). Fiesta (1st weekend, Dec.); Latin High Mass (twice yearly, usually May and Oct.); Full Moon and special night tours with musicians and crafts demonstrations (occasionally); Photo Scavenger Hunt for children (on request). **Tips & Hints:** Allow two hours to see the park. Prepare for 100°F temperatures in summer and below-freezing temperatures on winter nights. Bring rain gear if visiting June–Sept. Busiest Jan.–Mar., least crowded June–Sept.

FOOD, LODGING & SUPPLIES

🏨 **Hotels:** None in park. In Amado: Amado Territory Inn (3001 Frontage St., tel. 520/398–8684 or 888/398–8684; 11 rooms; $95–$135). In Tubac: Burro Inn (70 W. El Burro La., tel. 520/398–2281; 4 rooms; $89–$124). ✕ **Restaurants:** None in park. In Tumacácori: Wisdoms

(1931 E. Frontage Rd., tel. 520/398–2397; $5–$8; closed Sun.–Tues. and Aug.). In Rio Rico: Rio Rico Resort (1069 Camino Caralampi, tel. 520/281–1901 or 800/288–4746; $20–$30). ♿ **Groceries & Gear:** None in park. In Tubac: Tubac Country Market (2261 E. Frontage Rd., tel. 520/398–2695 or 520/398–8381). In Carmen: The Carmen Store (2035 E. Frontage Rd., tel. 520/398–2760).

FEES, HOURS & REGULATIONS

Entrance fee: $3 adults, free ages 16 and under. No hunting, bicycling, or collecting historic or natural artifacts. Park open daily 8–5.

HOW TO GET THERE

Tumacácori is 45 mi south of Tucson and 18 mi north of the Mexican border in Nogales via Exits 29 or 34 off I–19. Closest airport: Tucson.

CONTACT

Tumacácori National Historical Park (Box 67, Tumacacori, AZ 85640, tel. 520/398–2341, fax 520/398–9271, www.nps.gov/tuma).

Tuzigoot
National Monument

In central Arizona, near Cottonwood

Tuzigoot, an Apache word meaning "crooked water," is the remnant of a Sinaguan village built between AD 1100 and AD 1400. The original pueblo was two stories high in places and had 77 ground-floor rooms. Although this site is not as well preserved as the dwellings at Montezuma Castle (*see separate listing*), it's larger in scope. Exhibits in the visitor center display Sinaguan artifacts such as agricultural and household tools. Designated hiking trails get you very close to the ruins. The monument was proclaimed on July 25, 1939.

WHAT TO SEE & DO

Bird-watching, hiking, viewing ruins. **Facilities:** Visitor center, ruins, hiking trails. Book sale area. **Programs & Events:** Interpretive programs. **Tips & Hints:** Visit in spring and fall. Busiest Mar. and Apr., least crowded Dec. and Jan.

FOOD, LODGING & SUPPLIES

▲ **Camping:** None at site. *See Montezuma Castle National Monument.* 🏨 **Hotels:** None at monument. In Cottonwood: Pines Motel (920 S. Camino Real, tel. 928/634–9975; 14 rooms; $44–$64). ✕ **Restaurants:** None at monument. In Cottonwood: Nic's Italian Steak & Crab House (925 N. Main St., tel. 928/634–9626; $10–$25) ♿ **Groceries:** None at monument. In Cottonwood: Safeway (635 E. Cottonwood St., tel. 928/634–3711), Bashas' Market (1501 E. U.S. 89A, tel. 928/634–4281).

FEES, HOURS & REGULATIONS

Entrance fee: $3 adults, free ages 16 and under. Leashed pets only. Visitor center and monument open Labor Day–Memorial Day, daily 8–5; Memorial Day–Labor Day, daily 8–7.

HOW TO GET THERE

2 mi east of Clarkdale along Rte. 89A and 50 mi south of Flagstaff via Rte. 89A. Closest airports: Flagstaff (50 mi), Phoenix (110 mi).

CONTACTS

Tuzigoot National Monument (Box 219, Camp Verde, AZ 86322, tel. 928/634–5564, www.nps.gov/tuzi). Cottonwood Chamber of Commerce (1010 S. Main St., Cottonwood, AZ 86326, tel. 928/634–7593, http://cottonwood.verdevalley.com).

Walnut Canyon National Monument

In north-central Arizona, near Flagstaff

Cliff dwellings built by the Sinagua people between 1100 and 1250 are preserved in this monument. Using existing limestone alcoves, the Native Americans built side and front walls and nature provided the roof overhang. At this site, you can enter some of the ruins, getting an incomparable feel for life centuries ago. The presence of water at the time the Sinaguans lived in the canyon probably made this a very desirable place to live. The Sinagua (Spanish for "without water") were dry-land farmers who grew crops on the canyon rims and supplemented their diet by hunting and gathering. Their departure around 1250 is a subject for speculation, but archaeologists think that Hopi people who live on mesas in northern Arizona today are probably the descendants of the Sinagua. The park was proclaimed on November 30, 1915.

WHAT TO SEE & DO

Hiking, picnicking, touring cliff dwellings. **Facilities:** Visitor center, self-guided 0.75-mi and 0.9-mi interpretive trails, interpretive display boards. Bookstore, picnic tables. **Programs & Events:** Ranger-guided hikes, interpretive talks (June–Sept.). **Tips & Hints:** The Island Trail may be strenuous; it descends 240 steps at an elevation of 6,800 feet. Borrow baby backpacks from visitor center for Island Trail hikes because strollers aren't allowed. Limited parking space for large vehicles. Busiest June and July, least crowded Dec. and Jan.

FOOD, LODGING & SUPPLIES

None at monument. *See Sunset Crater Volcano National Monument* for Flagstaff listings.

FEES, HOURS & REGULATIONS

Entrance fee: $5 adults, free ages 16 and under. No pets on trails or in visitor center. Reservations required for ranger-guided tours. No hunting or firearms. No open fires. Gas stoves only. No collecting potsherds, rocks, pinecones, flowers. Park and visitor center open Dec.–Feb., daily 9–5; Mar.–May and Sept.–Nov., daily 8–5; June–Aug., daily 8–6.

HOW TO GET THERE

10 mi east of Flagstaff, off I–40 via Exit 204. Closest airports: Flagstaff (10 mi), Phoenix (155 mi).

CONTACTS

Walnut Canyon National Monument (3 Walnut Canyon Rd., Flagstaff, AZ 86004, tel. 928/526–3367, fax 928/527–0246, www.nps.gov/waca). Flagstaff Convention & Visitors Bureau (211 W. Aspen Ave., Flagstaff, AZ 86001, tel. 928/779–7611, fax 928/556–1305, www.flagstaffarizona. org). Flagstaff Visitor Center (1 E. Rte. 66, Flagstaff, AZ 86001, tel. 928/774–9541 or 800/842–7293).

Wupatki National Monument

In north-central Arizona, near Flagstaff

The monument preserves the ruins of red sandstone pueblos built about 1100 by farming Sinagua and Anasazi people—including the largest and most influential pueblo in the region at the time, Wupatki. Wupatki had nearly 100 rooms and was originally three stories tall. Next to this main pueblo is a blowhole, a fissure where air is forced up by underground pressure; this may have had spiritual significance for the early inhabitants. Near Wupatki are a few smaller pueblos: Lumaki, Wukoki, and Citadel, easily reached by walking. Made from slabs of sandstone, limestone, and basalt and held together with clay-based mortar, the dwellings were inhabited until about 1225. The modern Hopi are believed to be partly descended from these people. The monument was proclaimed on December 9, 1924.

WHAT TO SEE & DO

Picnicking, self-guided walking to four sites. **Facilities:** Visitor center, interpretive signboards. Book and map sale area, picnic tables. **Programs & Events:** Discovery hikes (June–Aug., Sat. for 3–4 hrs). **Tips & Hints:** Busiest June and July, least crowded Dec. and Jan.

FOOD, LODGING & SUPPLIES

None at site. *See Sunset Crater Volcano National Monument* for Flagstaff listings.

FEES, HOURS & REGULATIONS

Entrance fee: $5 adults, free ages 16 and under. No pets or bikes on trails. No off-trail hiking. Monument open daily sunrise–sunset. Visitor center open Mar.–May and Sept.–Nov., daily 8–5; June–Aug., daily 8–6; Dec.–Feb., daily 9–5.

HOW TO GET THERE

40 mi north of Flagstaff via U.S. 89 and Forest Rd. 545, a 35-mi loop road that connects Wupatki with Sunset Crater Volcano National Monument (*see separate entry*). Closest airport: Flagstaff (46 mi), Phoenix (190 mi).

CONTACTS

Wupatki National Monument (HC 33, Box 444A, Flagstaff, AZ 86004, tel. 928/679–2365, fax 928/679–2349, www.nps.gov/wupa). Flagstaff Convention & Visitors Bureau (211 W. Aspen Ave., Flagstaff, AZ 86001, tel. 928/779–7611, fax 928/556–1305, www.flagstaffarizona.org). Flagstaff Visitor Center (1 E. Rte. 66, Flagstaff, AZ 86001, tel. 928/774–9541 or 800/842–7293).

See Also

Lake Mead National Recreation Area, Nevada. *Juan Bautista de Anza National Historic Trail,* in Other National Parklands.

ARKANSAS

Arkansas Post National Memorial

In southeastern Arkansas, near Gillett

This memorial on the banks of the Arkansas River commemorates the site's complex history as the earliest semi-permanent French settlement in the Lower Mississippi River valley, which began when Henri de Tonti established the "Poste de Arkansea" in 1686 at a Quapaw village near the confluence of the Mississippi and Arkansas rivers. After a century of struggle among the French, Spanish, and English for control of interior North America, the United States bought the area in 1803 from the French as part of the Louisiana Purchase. The post thrived in the first half of the 19th century, serving as territorial capital of Arkansas from 1819 to 1821. Following the relocation of the Capital to Little Rock in 1821, the Post community fell into decline. Many of the remaining structures were destroyed by the U.S. Army and Navy attack on the Confederate fort on January 11, 1863. Activities include fishing, watching wildlife, and exploring remnants of the town site and Civil War earthworks. The memorial was authorized on July 6, 1960.

WHAT TO SEE & DO

Fishing, hiking, picnicking, touring museum, watching film. **Facilities:** Visitor center, orientation film, hiking trails, outdoor interpretive exhibits, self-guided tour. Bookstore, picnic tables with fire grills. **Programs & Events:** Self-guided tours of town site and nature trails. Special events, living-history programs and demonstrations. **Tips & Hints:** Watch for alligators. The park is extremely hot and humid in summer; drink plenty of water and wear insect repellent. Busiest May and June, least crowded Nov. and Dec.

FOOD, LODGING & SUPPLIES

Camping: None at memorial. In Dumas: Pendleton Bend Campground (426 Rte. 212, tel. 877/444–6777; 31 sites; $13–$16; flush toilets, showers, hook-ups), Wilber Mills Campground (599 Rte. 212, tel. 877/444–6777; 21 sites; $14; flush toilets, showers, hook-ups). In Tichnor: Merrisach Lake Campground (148 Merrisach La., tel. 877/444–6777; 65 sites; $9–$16; flush toilets, showers, hook-ups). **Hotels:** None at memorial. In Dumas: Days Inn (501 U.S. 65 S, tel. 870/382–4449; 53 rooms; $45–$65). **Restaurants:** None at memorial. In Gillett: Rice Paddy (4379 U.S. 165 S, tel. 870/548–2223; $5–$10). **Groceries & Gear:** None at memorial. In Dumas: Channel View Marina (173 Pendleton La., off U.S. 165, tel. 870/382–0009).

FEES, HOURS & REGULATIONS

Free. Arkansas state fishing license required (available at Channel View Marina). No hunting or firearms. Fires in grills only. Leashed pets only. Park open daily 8–dark. Visitor center open daily 8–5.

HOW TO GET THERE

On Rte. 169 9 mi south of Gillett via U.S. 165 (Great River Rd.); 17 mi northeast of Dumas via U.S. 165. Closest airport: Little Rock (100 mi).

CONTACT

Arkansas Post National Memorial (1741 Old Post Rd., Gillett, AR 72055, tel. 870/548–2207, fax 870/548–2431, www.nps.gov/arpo).

Buffalo National River

In north-central Arkansas, near Harrison

Totaling about 95,700 acres, this free-flowing, unpolluted river—one of the few left in the United States—encompasses 135 mi of the 150-mi-long Buffalo River, which begins as a trickle in the Boston Mountains, 15 mi above the park boundary. Following what is likely an ancient riverbed, the Buffalo cuts its way through massive limestone bluffs and travels east through the Ozarks and into the White River. It's a terrific place to go canoeing. The national river has three designated wilderness areas totaling 36,000 acres within its boundaries. The national river was authorized on March 1, 1972.

WHAT TO SEE & DO

Canoeing (rentals), fishing, hiking, horseback riding, picnicking, swimming. **Facilities:** Tyler Bend visitor center (Middle District, 11 mi north of Marshall on U.S. 65); 2 ranger stations: Pruitt Upper District Ranger Station (5 mi north of Jasper on Rte. 7) and Buffalo Point Ranger Station (17 mi south of Yellville on Rtes. 14–268); more than 100 mi of trails. Bookstores, picnic tables. **Programs & Events:** Ranger-led hikes, canoe trips, and evening programs (Memorial Day–Labor Day). **Tips & Hints:** Allow an hour for visitor center. Bring a wet suit if you plan to canoe Dec.–Feb., rain gear Mar.–May, shorts and T-shirts June–Aug. For best floating, go to Upper District Mar.–May, to Middle District May and June, and to Lower District June–Aug. Check river conditions with visitor center before canoeing. Park busiest June and July, least crowded Jan. and Feb.

FOOD, LODGING & SUPPLIES

⚠ **Camping:** 13 campgrounds in the park (310 sites; $10–$17 charged Apr.–Oct.; some flush toilets, some vault toilets, some showers, some hook-ups). 🏨 **Hotels:** In the park: Buffalo Point Cabins (tel. 870/439–2812; 12 cabins; $75–$100). In Harrison: Comfort Inn (1210 U.S. 62/65 N, tel. 870/741–7676; 93 rooms; $70–$75). In Jasper: Cliff House Inn & Restaurant (Rte. 31, tel. 870/446–2292; 5 rooms; $50–$60). In Yellville: Eagle's Nest Resort (Rte. 235, tel. 870/449–5050; 22 rooms; $40–$90). ✗ **Restaurants:** None in park. In Jasper: Ozarks Cliff House Inn (Rte.

31, tel. 870/446–2292; $5–$8; no dinner). ♿ **Groceries & Gear**: None in park. In Jasper: Bob's Supermarket (Rte. 7 S, tel. 870/446–2381).

FEES, HOURS & REGULATIONS

Free. Park open daily. Tyler Bend visitor center open Memorial Day–Labor Day, daily 8–5; Labor Day–Memorial Day, Thurs.–Mon. 8:30–4:30. Park headquarters open weekdays 8–4:30. Pruitt Ranger Station open Memorial Day–Labor Day, hours vary. Buffalo Point Upper Ranger Station open daily 8:30–4:30.

HOW TO GET THERE

Middle District: U.S. 65 south from Harrison for 31 mi; Upper District: Rte. 7 or 43 from Harrison; Lower District: U.S. 65 south out of Harrison 5 mi, then U.S. 62/412 east and Rte. 14 south. Closest airports: Harrison (31 mi), Fayetteville (80 mi), or Little Rock, AR (150 mi); Springfield, MO (80 mi).

CONTACTS

Buffalo National River Headquarters (407 N. Walnut St., Suite 136, Harrison, AR 72601, tel. 870/741–5443, www.nps.gov/buff). Tyler Bend Visitor Center (U.S. 65, Marshall, tel. 870/439–2502). Harrison Chamber of Commerce (621 E. Rush, Harrison, AR 72601, tel. 870/741–2659, www.harrison-chamber.com). Jasper Chamber of Commerce (Box 250, Jasper, AR 72641, tel. 870/446–2455, www.theozarkmountains.com). Yellville Chamber of Commerce (Box 369, Yellville, AR 72687, tel. 800/832–1414, www.yellville.com).

Central High School National Historic Site

In central Arkansas, in Little Rock

Little Rock High School, now Central High School National Historic Site, is a national emblem of the often-violent struggle over school de-segregation and represents the federal government's commitment to eliminating separate systems of education for blacks and whites. The site honors nine black students, known as the Little Rock Nine, who were the first African-Americans to attend this high school, initiating public school integration in 1957. The governor of Arkansas tried to stymie integration; federal troops had to be posted at the school to enforce the law and protect the Nine, who endured continual harassment. Central is the only operating high school in the nation to be designated a national historic site; it has a commemorative sculpture garden. The site was designated on November 6, 1998.

WHAT TO SEE & DO

Touring the school, viewing videos and exhibits. **Facilities:** Central High Museum Visitor Center, audiovisual presentations. Book-and-gift shop. **Programs & Events:** Guided tours of visitor center and high school (reservations required).

FOOD, LODGING & SUPPLIES

🛏 **Hotels:** None at site. In Little Rock: Doubletree Hotel (424 W. Markham, tel. 800/222–8733; 287 rooms; $79–$121), Peabody Hotel (No. 3 Statehouse Plaza, tel. 800/732–2639; 480 rooms; $189–$199).
✕ **Restaurants:** None at site. In Little Rock: Sonny's Steak House (500 President Clinton Ave., Suite 100, tel. 501/324–2999; $16–$40; closed Sun.).

FEES, HOURS & REGULATIONS

Free. No pets. Site open Mon.–Sat. 10–4, Sun. 1–4.

HOW TO GET THERE

Take I–630 to Martin Luther King Dr. exit, left on Martin Luther King Dr., right on Daisy L. Gatson Bates Dr. Site is at the intersection of Daisy L. Gatson Bates Dr. and Park St. Closest airport: Little Rock (7 mi).

CONTACTS

Central High School National Historic Site (2125 Daisy L. Gatson Bates Dr., Little Rock, AR 72205, tel. 501/374–1957; www.nps.gov/cehi and http://home.swbell.net/chmuseum). Little Rock Convention & Visitors Bureau (426 W. Markham, No. 7 Statehouse Plaza, AR 72201, tel. 501/376–4781, www.littlerock.com).

Fort Smith National Historic Site

In downtown Fort Smith, in western Arkansas, on the Oklahoma border

The site commemorates a significant phase of America's westward expansion and stands as a reminder of 80 turbulent years in the history of Federal Indian policy. It includes the remains of two frontier forts and the 19th-century Federal Court of the Western District of Arkansas. Its visitor center is in a former barracks, courthouse, and jail. The first Fort Smith was established at the end of 1817, as the U.S. Army fortified the line of American territory against Native American tribes. The second version, which stood from 1838 to 1871, was a focal point of regional Civil War operations; afterward, it became the seat of a federal court. Judge Isaac Parker, known as the "Hanging Judge," was appointed here; he was given the name for putting more than 80 men to death during his tenure. You can see the restored courtroom, jail cells, and gallows, as well as a commissary storehouse. Fort Smith is also tied to the Trail of Tears, as it supplied both the forcibly dislocated Native Americans and the federal posts in what was then known as Indian Territory, west of the Mississippi River. The site was authorized on September 13, 1961.

WHAT TO SEE & DO

Bird-watching, touring renovated historic buildings and grounds, viewing video, walking river trail with wayside exhibits. **Facilities:** Visitor center, hiking trails, indoor and outdoor interpretive exhibits. Bookstore. **Programs & Events:** Guided tours (by appointment) of courtroom, jail, gallows, and grounds. Living-history programs, Civil War encampments, artillery demonstrations (June–Aug.). Frontier Fest (late Oct.), historic re-enactment for fort's anniversary (Apr. 22–23), ranger talks on executions (anniversaries of hangings carried out here 1873–1896). **Tips & Hints:** Nooses are hung on the gallows on the anniversaries of the executions done here 1873–1896. Busiest June and July, least crowded Dec. and Jan.

FOOD, LODGING & SUPPLIES

Hotels: None at site. In Fort Smith: Holiday Inn (700 Rogers Ave., tel. 479/783–1000; 255 rooms; $59–$109). **Restaurants:** None at site. In Fort Smith: Hamburger Barn (317 Garrison Ave., tel. 479/782–0233; $6–$12), Varsity Restaurant (318 Garrison Ave., tel. 479/494–7173; $7–$20). **Groceries & Gear:** None at site. In Fort Smith: Point Liquor & Convenience Store (1116 Grand Ave., tel. 479/783–1600), Harps Grocery Store (3100 Grand Ave., tel. 479/783–3690).

FEES & HOURS

Entrance fee: $3 adults, free ages 16 and under, $6 family rate. Site open daily 9–5.

HOW TO GET THERE

From Garrison St. (U.S. 64) turn south on 4th St., west on Garland Ave. to Rogers Ave. Closest airport: Fort Smith (8 mi).

CONTACTS

Fort Smith National Historic Site (Box 1406, Fort Smith, AR 72902, tel. 479/783–3961, fax 479/783–5307, www.nps.gov/fosm). Fort Smith Convention & Visitors Bureau (2 North B St., Fort Smith, AR 72901, tel. 800/637–1477, www.fortsmith.org).

Hot Springs National Park

In west-central Arkansas, in Hot Springs

The park's 47 hot springs, which lack the sulfur odor and taste of many hot springs, are at the heart of a great social and medical resort. In its heyday, between 1890 and 1920, the park's monumental bathhouses catered to crowds of health seekers. Today the park preserves the finest collection of historic bathhouses in the United States. Approximately 850,000 gallons of natural thermal water still flow out of the mountainside and into the beautifully landscaped Bathhouse Row area each day. Much of the water is still supplied to traditional bathhouses and jug fountains for bathing and drinking. At this writing, six vacant historic bathhouses were closed for stabilization; they are due to reopen in 2005. Hot Springs Reservation was set aside on April 20, 1832; dedicated to public use as a park on June 16, 1880; and redesignated a national park March 4, 1921.

WHAT TO SEE & DO

Auto touring, bicycling (rentals in Hot Springs), fishing, going up observation tower, hiking, picnicking, taking thermal baths, touring the visitor center in the historic Fordyce Bathhouse, viewing springs. **Facilities:** Visitor center, (Fordyce Bathhouse, Bathhouse Row, 300 block of Central Ave.), film, hiking trails, interpretive signs. Book-and-gift shop, picnic tables with fire grills. **Programs & Events:** Guided tours of Fordyce Bathhouse. Thermal features tours (Apr.–Nov.), special programs and hikes (occasionally). Constitution Week (Sept. 17–23), Volksmarsch–Oktoberfest (one week in Oct., Hot Springs). **Tips & Hints:** Go in Apr. for dogwood blooms and spring warbler migration, May–July for southern magnolias, Oct. and Nov. for fall colors. Busiest June and July, least crowded Jan. and Feb.

FOOD, LODGING & SUPPLIES

⚠ **Camping:** In the park: Gulpha Gorge (43 sites; $10; flush toilets). ⊤ **Hotels:** None in park. In Hot Springs: Arlington Hotel (239 Central St., tel. 501/623–7771; 460 rooms; $75–$90), Austin Hotel (305 Malvern Ave., tel. 501/623–6600; 200 rooms; $85–$230). ✗ **Restaurants:** None in park. In Hot Springs: Faded Rose (210 Central Ave., tel. 501/624–3200; $5–$10). ⌣ **Groceries & Gear:** Wal-Mart (4019 Central Ave., tel. 501/525–3457).

FEES, HOURS & REGULATIONS

Free. Thermal water bathing prices $42–$51. Tickets are available at the bathhouses: Buckstaff Bathhouse (509 Central Ave., tel. 501/623–2308), Hot Springs Health Spa (tel. 501/321–9664). Physical therapy using hot spring water available at Libbey Memorial Physical Medicine Center (inside park, tel. 501/321–9664) and Levi Hospital (outside park, tel. 501/624–1281). Hot Springs Mountain Tower, $6. Arkansas state fishing license required (available at local Wal-Marts). No vehicles or bicycles on sidewalks and trails. No vehicles over 30 feet on Hot Springs Mountain Dr. No hunting. Do not remove or disturb any plant, animal, rock, or other object. Leashed pets only. No pets in visitor center. Park open daily. Visitor center open early Aug.–mid-May, daily 9–5; late May–early Aug., daily 9–6.

HOW TO GET THERE

From I–30, take U.S. 70 o, U.S. 270 to the city of Hot Springs, which adjoins the park. Park visitor center is on Rte. 7, along Bathhouse Row. Closest airports: Hot Springs, Little Rock (55 mi).

CONTACTS

Hot Springs National Park (Box 1860, Hot Springs, AR 71902, tel. 501/624–3383 Ext. 640, fax 501/624–3458, www.nps.gov/hosp). Hot Springs Convention & Visitors Bureau (134 Convention Blvd., Hot Springs, AR 79101, tel. 800/772–2489, www.hotsprings.org).

Pea Ridge
National Military Park

In northwestern Arkansas, near Rogers

The 4,300-acre park represents one of the best-preserved Civil War battlefields in the country. The March 7–8, 1862, battle, which pitted Major General Earl Van Dorn's 13,000 Confederates against 10,250 Union soldiers under Brigadier General Samuel Curtis, saved Missouri for the Union. The Confederate force included 800 Cherokees, and one-third of the Union army were German immigrants recruited near St. Louis. The park includes a reconstruction of the Elkhorn Tavern, site of bitter fighting on both days. The park also includes a 2½-mi segment of the Trail of Tears, the route used by the Cherokees between 1838 and 1839 when they were forcibly moved from their homeland in the South to the Indian Territories of Oklahoma and Arkansas. The site was authorized on July 20, 1956.

WHAT TO SEE & DO

Auto touring of battlefield, hiking, horseback riding, picnicking, touring museum, watching slide show, wildlife viewing. **Facilities:** Visitor center, 7-mi tour road, 11-mi horse trail, 10-mi hiking trail. Bookstore, picnic tables. **Programs & Events:** Living-history demonstrations and education programs (summer, weekends as staffing permits), tours of Elkhorn Tavern (Memorial Day–3rd week in Oct. as staffing permits). Battle anniversary (weekend nearest Mar. 7–8), Memorial Day remembrance. **Tips & Hints:** Busiest May–July, least crowded Jan. and Feb.

FOOD, LODGING & SUPPLIES

Camping: None at site. In Rogers: Beaver Lake Hide-A-Way Campground (8369 Campground Circle, tel. 479/925–1333; 89 sites; $16–$18; flush toilets, showers, hook-ups). **Hotels:** None in park. In Eureka Springs: Alpen-Dorf (6554 U.S. 62, tel. 479/253–9475 or 800/771–9876; 30 rooms; $28–$125). In Rogers: Beaver Lake Lodge (14733 Dutchman Dr., tel. 479/925–2313; 23 rooms; $59). **Restaurants:** None in park. In Eureka Springs: Bubba's (60 Kings Hwy., tel. 479/253–7706; $4–$19; closed Sun.), Forest Hill Restaurant (3016 Van Buren St., tel. 479/253–2422; $8–$16). Near Rogers: Bean Palace (11045 War Eagle Rd., tel. 479/789–5343 Ext. 307; $3–$6; no dinner, closed Jan. and weekdays in Feb.). **Groceries & Gear:** Wal-Mart (406 S. Walton Blvd., tel. 479/273–0060).

FEES, HOURS & REGULATIONS

Entrance fee: $2 adults, free ages 16 and under. No recreational sports. No hunting or trapping. Park and visitor center open daily 8–5. Tour road open daily 8–4:30.

HOW TO GET THERE

80 mi southwest of Springfield, MO, via U.S. 60, Rte. 37, and U.S. 62; 90 mi northeast of Fort Smith, AR, via I–44, I–540, U.S. 71, and U.S.

62 east; and 120 mi east of Tulsa, OK, via the Cherokee Turnpike and U.S. 412, U.S. 71, and U.S. 62 east. Closest airports: Bentonville, AR(25 mi), Springfield, MO (82 mi).

CONTACTS

Pea Ridge National Military Park (Box 700, Pea Ridge, AR 72751, tel. 479/451–8122, fax 479/451–8635, www.nps.gov/peri). Rogers–Lowell Area Chamber of Commerce (317 W. Walnut St., Rogers, AR 72756, tel. 479/636–1240). Eureka Springs Chamber of Commerce & Visitor Information Center (137 W. Van Buren, Eureka Springs AR 72632, tel. 479/253–8737, www.eurekaspringschamber.com).

See Also

Trail of Tears National Historic Trail, in Other National Parklands.

CALIFORNIA

Cabrillo National Monument

In southwestern California, in San Diego

The site commemorates Juan Rodríguez Cabrillo's 1542 expedition, the first European exploration of the west coast of the United States. The park is home to the Old Point Loma Lighthouse, one of the first lighthouses built on the West Coast, and remnants of coastal defense structures from World War II. It also preserves a beautiful landscape of tide pools and coastal sage scrub (among the most endangered in the world). The view of San Diego from the site is said to be the finest harbor view in the nation. It's a great place to whale-watch, too. There are several permanent exhibits to see, including the reconstructed interior of the 1880s lighthouse, photos and film footage shot during World War II displayed in a former Army radio building, and a multimedia show on Cabrillo in the visitor center. At this writing, a new lighthouse exhibit was slated to open in spring 2004. The site was established on October 14, 1913.

WHAT TO SEE & DO

Attending ranger programs, bird-watching, hiking, visiting tide pools, watching film presentations, whale-watching. **Facilities:** Visitor center with outdoor interpretive signs, beach, movies, hiking trail. Bookstore. **Programs & Events:** Ranger-guided tours and programs and frequent costumed interpretive programs available year-round. Gray whale talks and watching (Dec.–Feb.), wildflower walks (Feb.–Apr.), tide pool walks (Nov.–May). Cabrillo Festival with traditional dances, food, costumed interpretation (Sun. closest to Sept. 28), lighthouse programs, costumed interpreters, tower and catwalk open to public (Aug. 25 and Nov. 15), Whale Watch Weekend with speakers, whale programs, children's programs (3rd weekend in Jan.). **Tips & Hints:** Go in winter for clearest weather, Dec.–Feb. for whale migration. Bring binoculars for whale-watching. For the best look at tide pools, go on winter afternoons during full and new moon periods for extreme low tides. Wear shoes with good traction, particularly on the tide pools. Stay on the hiking trail and beware of rattlesnakes. Keep away from the cliff edges as they are very unstable. Busiest Mar.–Aug., least crowded Oct.–Jan.

FEES, HOURS & REGULATIONS

Entrance fee: $5 per vehicle; $3 per pedestrian, motorcyclist, and bicyclist, ages 16 and under free with paying adult. Pets may be taken to tide pools only, and then only when leashed. No bikes on trails or sidewalks. No swimming, surfing, or diving. Park and visitor center open July 4–September 1, daily 9–6:15; Sept. 2–July 3, daily 9–5:15.

HOW TO GET THERE

10 mi from downtown San Diego; from I–8 or I–5, take the Rosecrans Ave. exit. Drive south on Rosecrans to Cañon St., go west on Cañon to Catalina Blvd., then go south on Catalina Blvd to the end. Closest airport: San Diego (8 mi).

CONTACTS

Cabrillo National Monument (1800 Cabrillo Memorial Dr., San Diego, CA 92106, tel. 619/557–5450, fax 619/557–5469, www.nps.gov/cabr). San Diego Convention & Visitors Bureau (401 B St., Suite 1400, San Diego, CA 92101-4237, tel. 619/232–3101, fax 619/696–9371, www. sandiego.org). San Diego Visitor Information Center (11 Horton Pl., at 1st Ave. and F St., tel. 619/236–1212).

Channel Islands National Park

Off the southern coast, in the Santa Barbara Channel

In this park are five islands (Anacapa, Santa Barbara, Santa Cruz, Santa Rosa, and San Miguel) and 125,000 acres of submerged lands that provide habitat for marine life from microscopic plankton to Earth's largest creature—the blue whale. Like the Galapagos Islands, the Channel Islands have nurtured unique plant and animal species. It's an exceptional place for kayaking, bird-watching, and diving; you can also see the remains of Chumash villages and visit the largest known sea cave, known as the Painted Cave for its colorful lichen and algae. But you can also get a taste of the islands without even leaving the mainland by stopping by the visitor center in Ventura, which has exhibits, an observation tower, and a tide pool. The park was proclaimed a national monument April 26, 1938, and designated a Biosphere Reserve in 1976 and a national park on March 5, 1980.

WHAT TO SEE & DO

Bird-watching, boating (permit required, *see below*), camping, diving, fishing, hiking, kayaking, picnicking, snorkeling, swimming, whale-watching. **Facilities:** 3 visitor centers—Ventura (1901 Spinnaker Dr.), Anacapa, and Santa Barbara islands, beaches, hiking trails. Book and map sales (Ventura), picnic tables (Anacapa and Santa Barbara). **Programs & Events:** Ranger programs (Ventura, weekends 11 and 3) and guided walks (islands, daily) available. Underwater video program (Memorial Day–Labor Day, Tues. and Thurs. at 2). **Tips & Hints:** Be prepared for high winds; wear shoes with sturdy, nonslip soles. Bring binoculars for whale- or bird-watching. Visit Jan.–Mar. to see migrating gray whales, in spring to see wildflowers. Busiest July and Aug., least crowded Oct.–Dec.

FOOD, LODGING & SUPPLIES

Camping: 6 campgrounds in the park: Anacapa Island (7 sites; $10; pit toilets), Del Norte (Santa Cruz Island; 4 sites; $10; pit toilets), San

Miguel Island (9 sites; $10; pit toilets), Santa Barbara Island (8 sites; $10; pit toilets), Santa Rosa Island (15 sites; $10; pit toilets), Scorpion Valley (Santa Cruz Island; 40 sites; $10; pit toilets). 🏨 **Hotels:** None in park. In Ventura: Clocktower Inn (181 E. Santa Clara St., tel. 805/652–0141; 50 rooms; $89–$109). ✕ **Restaurants:** None in park. In Ventura: Jonathon's at Peirano's (204 E. Main St., tel. 805/648–4853; $8–$16). ⚁ **Groceries:** None in park. In Ventura: Vons Market (2433 E. Harper Blvd., tel. 805/642–6761), Village Market at the Marina (1559 Spinnaker Dr., tel. 805/644–2970).

FEES, HOURS & REGULATIONS

Free. Boating permits required (free) and available from the Nature Conservancy (tel. 805/898–1642). No pets. No mountain bikes. Park open daily. Visitor centers open daily 8:30–5.

HOW TO GET THERE

The park is in the Santa Barbara Channel. Closest park island is 14 mi and farthest is 55 mi from Ventura harbor. Main visitor center is in Ventura harbor. Transportation available through boat and airplane concessionaires, information available from park. Private boats permitted. Closest airports: Los Angeles (70 mi), Oxnard (5 mi), Santa Barbara (30 mi).

CONTACTS

Channel Islands National Park (1901 Spinnaker Dr., Ventura, CA 93001, tel. 805/658–5700, fax 805/658–5799, www.nps.gov/chis). Ventura Visitors & Convention Bureau (89 S. California St., Suite C, Ventura, CA 93001, tel. 805/648–2075, www.ventura-usa.com).

Death Valley National Park

In eastern California, in Death Valley

Despite the severity of Death Valley's geology and desert climate, more than 1,000 species of plants and 98 species of animals live within the park's boundaries. Also in the park, which gets hotter temperatures than any other place in North America, are snow-covered peaks, rugged canyons, and beautiful sand dunes. In extremely wet years, perhaps once in a decade, wildflowers come into bloom, a striking sight in such a landscape. This is the country's largest national park outside Alaska; you can only reach some of the most spectacular areas by taking a four-wheel-drive vehicle. Badwater Basin is the lowest point in the Western Hemisphere, at 282 feet below sea level. In addition to the incredible natural sights—the volcanic deposits of Artists Palette, the salt flats and giant sand dunes, Ubehebe Crater, the salt pinnacles of the Devil's Golf Course—there are some man-made sights, such as the Harmony Borax Works and the 1920s Moorish mansion called Scotty's Castle. The center of activity in the park is Furnace Creek Village, where you'll find the visitor center; the other town within the park boundaries is Stovepipe Wells Village. Despite the punishing temperatures, the park draws a wave of mostly European travelers in July and

August. The park was proclaimed a national monument in 1933 and redesignated a national park in 1994. It was designated a part of the Colorado and Mojave Desert Biosphere Reserve in 1984.

WHAT TO SEE & DO

Auto touring, bicycling, bird-watching, hiking, horseback riding, Jeep riding, picnicking. **Facilities:** Visitor center (Furnace Creek, Rte. 190), ranger station (Stovepipe Wells), Borax Museum (Furnace Creek Ranch), hiking trails, wayside exhibits. Book and map sales area, gift shop, picnic tables. **Programs & Events:** Guided tours of Scotty's Castle (year-round). Ranger-guided talks, interpretive talks, and evening slide programs (Nov.–Apr.). 49ers Encampment (2nd week, Nov.). **Tips & Hints:** Always check on weather conditions before hiking or driving. Be prepared for extremely hot temperatures Apr.–Oct. Flash floods are a risk; watch for water running in washes and across road dips. Do not hike in lower elevations in hot weather. Always carry plenty of water in the car and on hikes. When no trail is available, hike on the hardest, most durable surfaces. Beware of rattlesnakes, scorpions, and black widow spiders. Do not enter any mines. Note that cell phones do not work in all areas of the park. Dress warmly when visiting the mountains in winter. Best time to visit: Oct.–Apr. Visit Mar. and Apr. for wildflowers, May–Oct. to hike Telescope Peak. Busiest Feb.–mid-Apr. and Nov., least crowded Dec. and Jan.

FOOD, LODGING & SUPPLIES

🚿 **Camping:** 9 campgrounds in the park: Emigrant (10 sites; free; flush toilets), Furnace Creek (136 sites; $10–$16; flush toilets), Mahogany Flat (10 sites; free; pit toilets; closed Dec.–Feb.), Mesquite Spring (30 sites; $10; flush toilets), Stovepipe Wells (190 sites; $10; flush toilets; closed late Apr.–mid-Oct.), Sunset (1,000 sites; $10; flush toilets; closed late Apr.–mid-Oct.), Texas Spring (92 sites; $12; flush toilets; closed late Apr.–mid-Oct.), Thorndike (6 sites; free; pit toilets; closed Dec.–Feb.), Wildrose (23 sites; free; flush toilets). Backcountry camping (permit required, *see below*). 🏨 **Hotels:** In the park: Furnace Creek Inn (Rte. 190, tel. 760/786–2361; 66 rooms; $240–$370; closed May–mid-Oct.), Furnace Creek Ranch (Rte. 190, tel. 760/786–2345; 224 rooms; $85–$174), Panamint Springs Resort (Rte. 190, tel. 775/482–7680; 15 rooms; $65–$139), Stovepipe Wells Village (Rte. 190, tel. 760/786–2387; 83 rooms; $86–$107). ✗ **Restaurants:** In the park: Furnace Creek Inn Restaurant (tel. 760/786–2361 Ext. 150; $6–$12), Furnace Creek Ranch Coffee Shop (tel. 760/786–2345 Ext. 253; $7–$10), Panamint Springs Restaurant (tel. 775/482–7680; $8–$12), Stovepipe Wells Village Restaurant (tel. 760/786–2604; $10–$20). In Shoshone: Crowbar Café & Saloon (Rte. 127, tel. 760/852–4180; $6–$18). 🛒 **Groceries:** In the park: Furnace Creek Ranch General Store (Rte. 190, tel. 760/786–2381).

FEES, HOURS & REGULATIONS

Entrance fee: $5 per person on foot, bicycle, or motorcycle; $10 per vehicle. Guided tours of Scotty's Castle tours, $9 adults; $7 ages 62 and older; $5 ages 6–15, free ages 5 and under. Permits required for backcountry camping (free). No collecting or disturbing natural, historical, or archaeological features. Don't feed or disturb wildlife. All vehicles, including motorcycles, trail bikes, bicycles, and four-wheel drives, must remain on established roads. No hunting or firearm use. Leashed pets only. No pets on trails or in wilderness. Park open daily. Visitor center open daily 8–6.

HOW TO GET THERE

From U.S. 395, take Rte. 190, 136, or 178. From U.S. 95, take Rte. 267, 373, or 374. From I–15, take Rte. 127 at Baker to Rte. 178 or 190. Closest airport: Las Vegas, NV (120 mi).

CONTACTS

Death Valley National Park (Box 579, Death Valley, CA 92328–0579, tel. 760/786–2300, fax 760/786–3283, www.nps.gov/deva). Stovepipe Wells Ranger Station (tel. 760/786–2342).

Devils Postpile National Monument

In east-central California, near Mammoth Lakes

Hot lava cooled and cracked to form fractured basalt columns 40 feet to 60 feet high that resemble a giant rock pipe organ. The 798-acre monument high in the Sierra Nevada also protects the 101-foot Rainbow Falls and Soda Springs, carbonated mineralized springs. It's accessible in summer only by shuttle bus, which begins operation when the roads are cleared of snow, usually June or early July, and runs through Labor Day. The John Muir and Pacific Coast trails cross the monument. It was proclaimed in 1911 and transferred to the Park Service in 1933.

WHAT TO SEE & DO

Fishing, hiking to springs and falls. **Facilities:** Ranger station, trails. **Programs & Events:** Ranger-led interpretive programs, campfire programs (July–Labor Day). **Tips & Hints:** Stay back from cliff edges. Store food properly to avoid bears. Busiest July and Aug., least crowded Oct.–June.

FOOD, LODGING & SUPPLIES

Camping: In the park: Devils Postpile (21 sites; $14; flush toilets). **Hotels:** None in park. In Mammoth Lakes: Tamarack Lodge Resort (take Lake Mary Rd. off Rte. 203, tel. 760/934–2442 or 800/626–6684; 11 rooms, 29 cabins; $150). **Restaurants:** None in park. Near Mammoth Lakes: The Restaurant at Convict Lake (2 mi south of U.S. 395, 2000 Convict Lake Rd., tel. 760/934–3803; $15–$30). **Groceries & Gear:** None in park. In Mammoth Lakes: General Store (in Red Meadows Resort & Café, at the end of Rte. 203, tel. 800/292–7758).

FEES, HOURS & REGULATIONS

Entrance fee: $7 adults, $4 ages 16 and under. Day-use visitors must use shuttle bus late June–Labor Day, between 7:30 and 5:30, at Mammoth Mountain Inn to reach park. California fishing license required. No hunting. Leashed pets only. No bikes off road. Monument open mid-June–Oct.

HOW TO GET THERE

10 mi west from U.S. 395 on Rte. 203 to Minaret Summit, then 7 mi on a paved narrow mountain road. Closest airports: Mammoth (22 mi), Reno, NV (181 mi).

CONTACT

Devils Postpile National Monument (Box 3999, Mammoth Lakes, CA 93546, tel. 760/934–2289, www.nps.gov/depo).

Eugene O'Neill National Historic Site

Near San Francisco, in Danville

Eugene O'Neill, the architect of modern American theater and the only Nobel Prize–winning playwright from the United States, lived at Tao House from 1937 to 1944. Here he wrote his final and most successful plays: *The Iceman Cometh*, *Long Days Journey Into Night*, and *A Moon for the Misbegotten*. Since 1980, the National Park Service has been restoring Tao House and its courtyard and orchards. Reservations are required for park visits, including free transportation to the park and a free guided tour of the home and courtyard. The site was authorized on October 12, 1976.

WHAT TO SEE & DO

Facilities: Visitor center, bookstore. **Programs & Events:** On-site plays in May, June, and Sept. **Tips & Hints:** Best time to visit is Mar.–May and Sept. and Oct. Busiest Apr.–June, least crowded in Dec. Stairs only to second floor.

FOOD, LODGING & SUPPLIES

⚠ **Camping:** None at site. In Mount Diablo State Park: Juniper (2 mi below the summit on Summit Rd., tel. 800/444–7275; 36 sites; $12–$15; flush toilets, showers), Live Oak (1 mi above Southgate entrance station, off Southgate Rd., tel. 800/444–7275; 22 sites; $12–$15; flush toilets, showers), Junction (intersection of Southgate and Northgate Rds.; 6 sites; $12–$15; flush toilets, showers). 🛏 **Hotels:** None at site. In Walnut Creek: Marriott Hotel (2355 N. Main St., tel. 925/934–2000 or 800/228–9290; 338 rooms; $180–$380). ✕ **Restaurants:** None at site. In Danville: Basil Leaf (501 Hartz Ave., tel. 925/831–2828; $12–$21). 🛒 **Groceries & Gear:** None at site. In Danville: Longs (650 San Ramon Valley Blvd., tel. 925/820–1446), Andronico's (345 Railroad Ave., tel. 925/855–8920).

FEES, HOURS & REGULATIONS

Free. Reservations required to visit the park (tel. 925/838–0249). Visits available Wed.–Sun. 10 AM and 12:30 PM.

HOW TO GET THERE

Danville is 26 mi east of San Francisco off I–680 in San Ramon Valley. Directions to the park shuttle pick-up site are when making reservations. Closest airport: Oakland (20 mi).

CONTACTS

Eugene O'Neill National Historic Site (Box 280, Danville, CA 94526-0280, tel. 925/838–0249, fax 925/838–9471, www.nps.gov/euon). Danville Area Chamber of Commerce (117 E. Town and Country Dr., Danville, CA 94526, tel. 925/837–4400, www.danvillecachamber.com). Mount Diablo State Park (Clayton; take I–680 to Danville, Diablo Rd. Exit, then 3 mi east to Mt. Diablo Scenic Blvd., tel. 925/837–2525).

Fort Point National Historic Site

In the Presidio, San Francisco

Situated beneath the Golden Gate Bridge, Fort Point is a classic example of the coastal fortifications constructed by the U.S. Army Corps of Engineers during the mid-19th century. Built prior to the beginning of the Civil War, the brick-and-granite fort embodies the commercial and strategic military importance of San Francisco. Between 1933 and 1937 the fort was used as a base of operations for the construction of the Golden Gate Bridge. During World War II, Fort Point was occupied by 100 soldiers with searchlights and rapid-fire cannon as part of the protection of a submarine net strung across the bay entrance. The site was established on October 16, 1970.

WHAT TO SEE & DO

Touring fort, viewing photography and history exhibits, watching videos. **Facilities:** Ranger station, museum. Bookstore. **Programs & Events:** Ranger-guided tours (daily), cannon drill demonstrations (daily), education programs. Crabbing program (Mar.–Oct.), Candlelight tours (Oct.–Feb.). Special events available. **Tips & Hints:** Allow at least one hour for your visit. Be careful when walking around front of building, as ground can be slippery. Weather at Fort Point is cool and windy. Summer months can be cold, with fog rolling into San Francisco Bay. Winters are generally cold with variable precipitation. Go in spring and fall for best weather. Busiest June–Aug., least crowded Dec. and Jan.

FEES, HOURS & REGULATIONS

Free. Audio tour rental: $2.50 adults, $1 ages 16 and under. Fort open Fri.–Sun. 10–5.

HOW TO GET THERE

Beneath the south end of the Golden Gate Bridge. Turn off U.S. 101 at the bridge and turn left on Lincoln Blvd. Closest airport: San Francisco (15 mi).

CONTACTS

Fort Point National Historic Site (Box 29333, Presidio of San Francisco, San Francisco, CA 94129, tel. 415/556–1693, www.nps.gov/fopo). San Francisco Convention & Visitors Bureau (201 3rd St., Suite 900, San Francisco, CA 94103, tel. 415/974–6900, www.sfvisitor.org).

Golden Gate National Recreation Area

In San Francisco area

This recreation area is the largest national park adjacent to an urban area in the world. The 76,500-acre park encompasses 28 mi of shoreline in San Francisco, Marin, and San Mateo counties, including ocean beaches, redwood forest, lagoons, marshes, former military properties, a cultural center at Fort Mason, and Alcatraz Island. The area also includes *Fort Point National Historic Site* and *Muir Woods National Monument (see separate entries for each)*. The park was established in 1972 and designated a Biosphere Reserve in 1988.

WHAT TO SEE & DO

Attending cultural programs, bicycling, bird-watching, board sailing, golfing, hiking, off-road biking, picnicking, sailing, swimming, visiting museum, walking. **Facilities:** 7 visitor centers: Fort Mason, Presidio, Muir Woods *(see separate listing)*, Alcatraz, Marin Headlands, Cliff House, Fort Point *(see separate listing)*; hiking trails, museum. Picnic tables. **Programs & Events:** Year-round programs available. **Tips & Hints:** Allow two or three days to see all areas of the recreation area. Expect windy, cool temperatures, fog in summer, and best weather in spring and fall. Busiest July and Aug., least crowded Dec.–Feb.

LODGING

Camping: 4 campgrounds in the park: Bicentennial (Battery Wallace; 3 walk-in tent sites; free), Hawkcamp (Bobcat Trail, 4 mi from Marin Headlands Visitor Center; 3 hike-to tent sites; free; pit toilets), Haypress (¼ mi from Tennessee Valley parking lot; 5 walk-in tent sites; free), Kirby Cove (near Golden Gate Bridge; 4 walk-in tent sites; $25; pit toilets; closed Nov.–Mar.).

FEES, HOURS & REGULATIONS

Entrance fee: $1 day-use fee for Alcatraz Island (plus ferry transportation). Reservation required for Alcatraz (tel. 415/705–5555). Ferry transportation fee: $9.50 round-trip adults, $4.75 ages 64 and over, $4.75 ages 6–12. Audiotape tour: $3.50 adults, $1.50 ages 5–11. Permit required for backcountry camping at Marin Headlands. Cliff House Visitor Center open daily 10–5. Marin Headlands Visitor Center open daily 9:30–4:30. Presidio Visitor Center open daily 9–5. Fort Mason and Alcatraz open daily 9:30–5. Nike Missile Site open at Marin Headlands weekdays and 1st Sun. of the month 12:30–3:30.

HOW TO GET THERE

Much of the recreation area is within walking distance of San Francisco, with other areas up to an hour's drive away. The recreation area follows the city's north and west shoreline, extending down the peninsula. Across Golden Gate Bridge in Marin County, follow access roads off U.S. 101, including Alexander Ave., Shoreline Rte., and Sir Francis Drake Blvd., to the recreation area. The Municipal Railway (MUNI) bus system serves Rodeo Beach in Marin on Sun. Recreation area lands in San Mateo County are accessible via Skyline Blvd. In San Francisco, MUNI provides frequent service from downtown to shoreline destinations, especially Aquatic Park, the Cliff House, Ocean Beach, and Fort Mason. Limited MUNI transportation is available to the Presidio. Because traffic is sometimes heavy and parking is limited, public transportation is recommended. MUNI also connects from San Francisco to other Bay Area transit systems: Golden Gate Transit (GGT) in Marin County; Bay Area Rapid Transit (BART) and Alameda–Contra Costa Transit (AC TRANSIT) in the East Bay; and San Mateo Transit (SAM TRANS) in the peninsula area. The Blue & Gold Fleet ferries provide transportation to Alcatraz. Closest airports: San Francisco and Oakland.

CONTACTS

Golden Gate National Recreation Area Headquarters (Fort Mason, Bldg. 201, San Francisco, CA 94123, tel. 415/561–4700, www.nps.gov/goga). Other visitor information centers: Presidio (Presidio, Bldg. 102, San Francisco, CA 94129, tel. 415/561–4323); Alcatraz (Fort Mason, Bldg. 201, San Francisco, CA 94123, tel. 415/556–0560); Marin Headlands (National Park Service, Marin Headlands Visitor Center, Bldg. 948, Fort Barry, Sausalito, CA 94965, tel. 415/331–1540); Cliff House (Golden Gate National Park Association, Point Lobos Ave., San Francisco, CA 94121, tel. 415/556–8642). San Francisco Convention & Visitors Bureau (201 3rd St., Suite 900, San Francisco, CA 94103, tel. 415/974–6900, www.sfvisitor.org). *See also Fort Point National Historic Site and Muir Woods National Monument.*

John Muir National Historic Site

In San Francisco Bay area, in Martinez

Naturalist John Muir lived in this 14-room Victorian home from 1890 until his death in 1914. Also preserved are 325 acres of open space and 8½ acres of the fruit ranch. Muir served as first president of the Sierra Club and advocated the creation of Yosemite, Sequoia, Mount Rainier, and Grand Canyon national parks. He popularized the idea of preserving wild lands not for their commodities (timber, grazing, and water resources) but for their wildness, openness, and natural splendor. The site was authorized on August 31, 1964.

WHAT TO SEE & DO

Hiking, picnicking, touring the house and grounds, viewing film. **Facilities:** Visitor center, hiking trail. Bookstore, picnic tables. **Programs & Events:** Guided tours, bird-watching, wildflower walks. Full-moon walks (June and July, Sept.), Perseid Meteor Shower viewing (Aug.). Muir's Birthday (early May), Ranch Days (Sept.), Victorian Christmas and Las Posadas (Dec.). **Tips & Hints:** Busiest May and June, least crowded Sept. and Jan.

FOOD, LODGING & SUPPLIES

⚠ **Camping:** None at site. *See Eugene O'Neill National Historic Site.* ☈ **Hotels:** None at site. In Martinez: Best Western John Muir Inn (445 Muir Station Rd., tel. 925/229–1010; 115 rooms; $104–$129). ✗ **Restaurants:** None at site. In Martinez: Carrows (500 Center Ave., tel. 925/228–0600; $7–$10). ☌ **Groceries & Gear:** None at site. In Martinez: Safeway Supermarket (2 mi north of the site, 3334 Alhambra Ave., tel. 925/229–0212), Rite Aid Pharmacy (3800 Alhambra Ave., tel. 925/228–1740).

FEES, HOURS & REGULATIONS

Entrance fee: $3 adults, free ages 16 and under. Leashed pets only. No smoking. No food in house. No mountain bikes on nature trail. Park and visitor center open Wed.–Sun. 10–5.

HOW TO GET THERE

In the San Francisco metro area, on the East Bay in Martinez. Take Alhambra Ave. exit off Rte. 4 between I–80 and I–680. Closest airport: Oakland (30 mi).

CONTACTS

John Muir National Historic Site (4202 Alhambra Ave., Martinez, CA 94553, tel. 925/228–8860, fax 925/228–8192, www.nps.gov/jomu). Martinez Chamber of Commerce (620 Las Juntas St., Martinez, CA 94553, tel. 925/228–2345). Mount Diablo State Park (Clayton; take I–680 to Danville, Diablo Rd. exit, then 3 mi east to Mt. Diablo Scenic Blvd., tel. 925/837–2525, for campground reservations call 800/444–7275).

Joshua Tree National Park

In southeastern California, near Twentynine Palms

A beautiful and strange Joshua Tree forest, rugged geological formations, a handful of palm oases, mining history, homesteading history, and peace and quiet are the attractions at this 792,750-acre park. It's a prime spot for rock climbing and hiking. Two different deserts meet at Joshua Tree: in the north and west portions is the Mojave Desert; and in the south and east portions is the Colorado Desert, a subsystem of the Sonoran Desert. The site was designated a national monument in 1936, redesignated a national park in 1994, and designated a Biosphere Reserve in 1984.

WHAT TO SEE & DO

Backpacking, boulder hopping, hiking, mountain biking, rock climbing (rentals, town of Joshua Tree), picnicking. **Facilities:** 3 visitor centers: Twentynine Palms (Rte. 62), Cottonwood (off I–10), Black Rock Nature Center (Yucca Valley), hiking trails. Bookstore and sales areas, picnic tables. **Programs & Events:** Ranger-led hikes, interpretive talks, and campfire programs (mid-Oct.–May). **Tips & Hints:** Be prepared for all types of weather. Temperatures can reach 110°F June–Sept. Bring plenty of water, at least one gallon per person per day. Go Feb.–mid-May for flowers, Feb.–Apr. and in fall for bird migrations; and in spring, fall, and winter for best weather. Busiest Mar. and Apr., least crowded July and Aug.

FOOD, LODGING & SUPPLIES

⚠ **Camping:** 9 campgrounds in the park: Belle (18 sites; free), Black Rock (100 sites; $10; flush toilets), Cottonwood (62 sites; $10; flush toilets), Hidden Valley (sites; free), Indian Cove (101 sites; $10), Jumbo Rocks (125 sites; free), Ryan (31 sites; free), Sheep Pass (tel. 800/365–2267; 6 sites; $20–$35), White Tank (15 sites; free). 🏨 **Hotels:** None in park. In Twentynine Palms: 29 Palms Inn (73950 Inn Ave., tel. 760/367–3505; 15 rooms, 4 suites; $75–$100), Roughley Manor (74744 Joe Davis Rd., tel. 760/367–3238; 6 suites; $135–$150). ✘ **Restaurants:** None in park. In Yucca Valley: Edchadas (56805 Rte. 62, tel. 760/365–7655; $5–$9). ♿ **Groceries & Gear:** None in park. In Twentynine Palms: Circle K (5687 Adobe Rd., tel. 760/367–6116).

FEES, HOURS & REGULATIONS

Entrance fee: $5 per person on foot, $10 per vehicle. No hunting. Leashed pets only. Pets may not be left alone and are restricted to campgrounds and dirt road areas. Mountain bikes only on designated trails and roads open to motorized vehicles. Park open daily. Visitor centers open daily 8–5.

HOW TO GET THERE

50 mi north of Palm Springs. From I–10, take Rte. 62 north to the town of Joshua Tree and turn south on Park Blvd. to reach west entrance. Park entrances also at Twentynine Palms (15 mi east of Joshua Tree) and off I–10 (47 mi east of Palm Springs). Closest airport: Palm Springs.

CONTACTS

Joshua Tree National Park (74485 National Park Dr., Twentynine Palms, CA 92277, tel. 760/367–5500; 800/365–2267 campground reservations, fax 760/367–6392, www.nps.gov/jotr). Twentynine Palms Chamber of Commerce (6455A Mesquite Ave., Twentynine Palms, CA 92277, tel. 760/367–3445, www.29chamber.com). Joshua Tree Chamber of Commerce (Box 600, Joshua Tree, CA 92252, tel. 760/366–3723, www.joshuatreechamber.org). Yucca Valley Chamber of Commerce (55569 Rte. 62, Yucca Valley, CA 92284, tel. 760/365–6323, www.yuccavalley.org).

Kings Canyon National Park

See Sequoia and Kings Canyon National Parks.

Lassen Volcanic National Park

In northeastern California, near Mineral

All four types of volcanoes in the world are found in Lassen Volcanic National Park. Lassen Peak, possibly the world's largest plug dome volcano, erupted in May 1914 and was active through 1921. Today the park has bubbling mud pots and steaming fumaroles, great lava pinnacles, lava flows, and jagged craters. Two great mountain ranges, the Sierra Nevada and Cascades, intersect with the Great Basin lava flows at the park, and flora and fauna from both ranges intermingle here. Much of the park is inaccessible from late fall to mid-spring because of heavy snow. At this writing, a new visitor center was under construction, due to open in fall 2006. The new center will have interpretive exhibits, space for films and lectures, a restaurant, and more. The park was established on August 9, 1916.

WHAT TO SEE & DO

Auto touring, cross-country skiing, fishing, hiking, horseback riding, picnicking, viewing volcanic landscape and thermal features. **Facilities:** Visitor center (Park Headquarters, Mineral); Loomis Museum (near Manzanita Lake), wayside interpretive signs, hiking trails. Book and map sale areas, gift shop, picnic tables with fire grills. **Programs & Events:** Talks, walks, and evening programs (late June–Labor Day, daily), snowshoe walks (Jan.–Mar.). **Tips & Hints:** Buy park road guide. Ground around thermal areas is dangerously thin; stay on boardwalks and supervise children closely when near thermal areas. Watch for lightning. Wear layers of clothing. Temperatures may vary from freezing to 90°F. Go late July–mid-Aug. for flowers, and Aug. and Sept. for best hiking and car touring. Busiest July and Aug., least crowded Dec. and Jan.

FOOD, LODGING & SUPPLIES

🏕 **Camping:** In the park: Butte Lake (98 sites; $14–$50; flush toilets), Crags (45 sites; $12; vault toilets), Juniper Lake (18 sites; $10–$30; pit toilets), Lost Creek (8 group sites; $50; vault toilets), Manzanita Lake (179 sites; $10–$16; flush toilets), Southwest (21 walk-in sites; $10–$14; flush toilets), Summit Lake North (46 sites; $16; flush toilets), Summit Lake South (48 sites; $10–$14; pit toilets), Warner Valley (18 sites; $10–$14; vault toilets). Backcountry camping allowed (permit required, *see below*). 🛏 **Hotels:** In the park: Drakesbad Guest Ranch (tel. 530/529–1512; 19 rooms; $143, including three meals per day; closed Oct.–May). ✕ **Restaurants:** In the park: Drakesbad Guest Ranch (tel. 530/529–1512; reservations essential; closed Oct.–May). Near Chester: St. Bernard Lodge (44801 Rte. 36, 10 mi west of Chester, tel. 530/258–3382; $5–$10). 🛒 **Groceries:** None in park. In Mineral: Lassen Mineral Lodge Store (Rte. 36, tel. 530/595–4422), Mineral Gas Mart & Deli (Rte. 36, tel. 530/595–3222).

FEES, HOURS & REGULATIONS

Entrance fee: $5 per person on foot, bicycle, horse, or motorcycle; $10 per vehicle. Backcountry permits (free) required for all backcountry camping. California state fishing license required. No hunting. Bikes on paved roads and campgrounds only. No motorized or mechanized equipment on trails. No pets beyond roads or campgrounds. Leashed pets only. Park open daily. Park road may close between late Oct. and mid-June because of snow. Park headquarters open weekdays 8–4:30. Southwest Information Station open mid-June–Labor Day, daily 9–4, when staffing permits. Loomis Museum open mid-June–late Sept., daily 9–5; late May–mid-June, weekends 9–5.

HOW TO GET THERE

52 mi east of Red Bluff via Rte. 36, and 48 mi east of Redding via Rte. 44. Closest airport: Redding (48 mi).

CONTACTS

Lassen Volcanic National Park (Box 100, Mineral, CA 96063-0100, tel. 530/595–4444, fax 530/595–3262, www.nps.gov/lavo). Shasta Cascade Wonderland Association (1699 Rte. 273, Anderson, CA 96007, tel. 800/326–6944, fax 530/365–1258, www.shastacascade.org). Chester–Lake Almanor Chamber of Commerce (529 Main St., Box 1198, Chester, CA 96020, tel. 530/258–2426, fax 530/258–2760, www.chester-lakealmanor.com).

Lava Beds
National Monument

In northern California, near Tulelake

Lava Beds National Monument is on the north face of the Medicine Lake shield volcano, the largest in the Cascade Range. Numerous cinder cones, spatter cones, and lava flows cover the landscape, as well as more than 450 lava-tube caves. The monument also contains sites associated with the Modoc War of 1872–73, including Captain Jack's Stronghold, a natural fortress used by Modoc Indians for four months to withstand a siege by the U.S. Army. A separate site—Petroglyph Point—contains an outstanding collection of Native American rock art. The site was proclaimed in 1925 and transferred from the Forest Service in 1933.

WHAT TO SEE & DO

Bird-watching, cave exploration, picnicking, walking. **Facilities:** Visitor center (Indian Well), Mushpot Cave interpretive trail. Book sale area, picnic tables. **Programs & Events:** Fern Cave tour (year-round on Sat.; June–Sept. on Tues.; reservations required). Guided walks, cave tours, evening programs, living-history programs (mid-May–mid-Sept.); Crystal Cave tours (Dec.–Mar., Sat. only; reservations required). Modoc Reunion–Gathering (annually). **Tips & Hints:** Watch for low ceilings, steep trails and stairways, and uneven footing in lava-tube caves. Carry more than one light source (free at visitor center). Wear hard-sole shoes and protective headgear (nominal charge at visitor center). Notify ranger if exploring caves not listed in park brochure or if using own lighting equipment. Watch for rattlesnakes. Busiest July and Aug., least crowded Jan. and Feb.

FOOD, LODGING & SUPPLIES

⛺ **Camping:** In the park: Indian Wells (40 sites; $10; flush toilets). Backcountry camping allowed. 🏨 **Hotels:** None in park. In Tulelake: Fey's Bed & Breakfast (660 Main St., tel. 530/667–5145; 7 rooms; $50–$60). ✗ **Restaurants:** None in park. In Tulelake: Mike & Wanda's (423 Modock Ave., tel. 530/667–3226; $8–$17). ⚒ **Groceries & Gear:** None in park. In Tulelake: Jock's Supermarket (395 Modock Ave., tel. 530/667–2612).

FEES, HOURS & REGULATIONS

Entrance fee: $3 for pedestrians, bicycles, motorcycles; $5 per vehicle. No hunting, gathering of specimens, or collecting souvenirs. No pets in caves or on trails. No trail bikes, motorized vehicles on trails. No backcountry fires. Park grounds open year-round. Visitor center open Memorial Day–Labor Day, daily 8–6; Labor Day–Memorial Day, daily 8–5.

HOW TO GET THERE

24 mi from Tulelake and 58 mi from Klamath Falls, OR, off Rte. 139. Closest airport: Klamath Falls.

CONTACT

Lava Beds National Monument (Box 867, Tulelake, CA 96134, tel. 530/667–2282, fax 530/667–2737, www.nps.gov/labe).

Manzanar
National Historic Site

In eastern California, near Independence

A reminder of an ugly episode in U.S. history, the remains of the Manzanar War Relocation Center have been designated a Historic Site. Manzanar was one of 10 camps at which Japanese-American citizens and resident aliens were forcibly interned after the attack on Pearl Harbor, for the duration of World War II. In the process, most Japanese-Americans lost their homes and businesses. Located at the foot of the imposing Sierra Nevada in eastern California's Owens Valley, Manzanar is one of the best preserved of these camps. The camp auditorium is being restored, a guard tower is being reconstructed, and a mess hall has been returned to the site. An interpretive center is due to open in the auditorium in fall 2004. The site was authorized on March 3, 1992.

WHAT TO SEE & DO

Auto touring, guided tours. **Facilities:** Visitor center due to open in fall 2004. **Programs & Events:** Guided tours (June–Aug.). Manzanar Pilgrimage (last Sat. in Apr., tel. 323/662–5102). **Tips & Hints:** Plan for a one- to two-hour walking tour of camp. Self-guided tour brochures available on site. Be prepared for strong winds and blowing dust at any time of year. Wear sturdy walking shoes. Busiest Apr.–Sept., least crowded Nov.–Feb.

FOOD, LODGING & SUPPLIES

⚠ **Camping:** None in park. In Independence: Lower Graze Campground (Onion Valley Rd., tel. 877/444–6777; 17 sites; $11; pit toilets), Upper Graze Campground (Onion Valley Rd., tel. 877/444–6777; 35 sites; $11; pit toilets). ⛺ **Hotels:** None at site. In Independence: Winnedumah Hotel Bed & Breakfast (211 N. Edwards St., tel. 760/878–2040; 24 rooms; $50–$80), Mt. Williamson Hotel (515 S. Edwards

St., tel. 760/878–2121; 8 rooms; $49–$66). ✗ **Restaurants:** None at site. In Lone Pine: Seasons Restaurant (206 S. Main St., tel. 760/876–8927; $10–$23). ⛁ **Groceries & Gear:** None in park. In Independence: Austin's General Store (130 S. Edwards St., tel. 760/878–2242), Mairs Market (149 S. Edwards St., tel. 760/878—2169).

FEES & HOURS

Free. Site open daily during daylight hours.

HOW TO GET THERE

12 mi north of Lone Pine, off U.S. 395, and 5 mi south of Independence. Closest airport: Bishop (40 mi), Lone Pine, Independence.

CONTACT

Manzanar National Historic Site (Box 426, Independence, CA 93526-0426, tel. 760/878–2932, fax 760/878–2949, www.nps.gov/manz).

Mojave National Preserve

In southeastern California, near Baker

Largely untouched by modern development, this 1.6-million-acre preserve is the meeting place of the Mojave, Great Basin, and Sonoran deserts, and it has a remarkable scenic diversity. In the southern section of the preserve are Joshua trees, cinder cones, and the huge, shimmering Kelso Dunes. In the Mitchell Caverns Natural Preserve you can see all three kinds of cave formations: dripstone, flowstone, and erratics. Hole in the Wall, meanwhile, is an aptly named geologic formation, which offers a challenging climb down a vertical chute (with metal handholds) into the pock-marked Banshee Canyon. There's one small settlement, Cima, within the preserve boundaries. A visitor center in the Kelso Depot is due to open in fall 2004. The preserve was established on October 1, 1994.

WHAT TO SEE & DO

Auto and four-wheel-drive touring (rentals, Barstow, CA, and Las Vegas, NV), hiking, hunting. **Facilities:** 2 information centers: Baker (72157 Baker Rd.), Hole-in-the-Wall (intersection of Essex and Black Canyon Rds.). Zzyzx Desert Studies Consortium, a California State University field center within the park. Book and map sales areas. Hole-in-the-Wall: picnic tables. **Programs & Events:** Interpretive talks (on request). Campfire programs (Oct.–Apr.). **Tips & Hints:** Carry and drink plenty of water, at least one gallon per person per day. Fill gas tank and check fluids and tires before entering preserve. There are privately owned lands within the preserve; respect NO TRESPASSING signs. Be cautious of cattle in the road because of open-range grazing: approach slowly and pass quietly. Watch out for snakes, including rattlesnakes, and tarantulas (most commonly seen in fall mating season). Be prepared for strong winds in fall and late winter–early spring. Best times to visit are winter and spring, when temperatures are moderate. Go Mar.–May for wildflower blooms.

FOOD, LODGING & SUPPLIES

Camping: In the park: Black Canyon (equestrian/group site; $25; pit toilets), Hole-in-the-Wall (35 sites; $12; pit toilets), Mid Hills (26 sites; $12; pit toilets). Backcountry camping allowed. **Hotels:** None in park. In Baker: Wills Fargo Motel (72252 Baker Blvd., tel. 760/733–4477; 31 rooms; $37–$68). **Restaurants:** None in preserve. In Baker: The Mad Greek (Baker Blvd. at I–15, tel. 760/733–4354; $5–$11). **Groceries & Gear:** None in park. In Nipton: Nipton Trading Post (107–355 Nipton Rd., tel. 760/856–2335).

FEES, HOURS & REGULATIONS

Free. California state hunting license required. No target shooting. Confined or leashed pets only. Don't leave pets unattended or in closed vehicles or trailers in extreme heat. No bicycles or motorized vehicles allowed in wilderness areas. No collecting firewood. Preserve open daily. Baker information center open daily 9–5. Hole-in-the-Wall information center weekends 10–2, as staffing permits.

HOW TO GET THERE

60 mi southwest of Las Vegas, NV, and 60 mi northeast of Barstow, CA, between I–15 and I–40. Closest airports: Las Vegas, NV and Ontario, CA (150 mi).

CONTACTS

Headquarters, Mojave National Preserve (222 E. Main St., Suite 202, Barstow, CA 92311, tel. 760/255–8801, fax 760/255–8809, www.nps.gov/moja). Baker Information Center (Box 241, Baker, CA 92309, tel. 760/733–4040, fax 760/733-4027). Baker Area Chamber of Commerce (Box 131, Baker, CA 92309, tel. 760/733–4469). Barstow Area Chamber of Commerce (222 E. Main St., Suite 216, Barstow, CA 92312, tel. 760/256–8617, www.barstowchamber.com). Needles Area Chamber of Commerce (Box 705, Needles, CA 92363, tel. 760/326–2050). Zzyzx Desert Studies Consortium (write c/o California State University, Box 6850, Fullerton, CA 92834-6850, tel. 741/278–2428).

Muir Woods National Monument

Near San Francisco

"This is the best tree-lovers monument that could possibly be found in all the forests of the world," declared conservationist John Muir when describing this grove of majestic coastal redwoods. The forest of towering trees and canyon ferns is a wonderfully tranquil place. Other park attractions are the redwood forest, Redwood Creek, wildflowers, and forest wildlife. The site was proclaimed on January 9, 1908.

WHAT TO SEE & DO

Hiking, viewing wildlife, walking. **Facilities:** Visitor center, trails. **Programs & Events:** Ranger talks. Seasonal activities available. Earth Day (Jan.), Summer Solstice Celebration (June), Winter Solstice Celebration (Dec.). **Tips & Hints:** Park is cool, shaded, and moist year-round. Visit early or late in the day to avoid peak crowd times. Busiest June–Aug., least crowded Dec. and Jan.

FOOD, LODGING & SUPPLIES

⚠ **Camping:** None in park. In Mill Valley: Pantoll Campground (Mount Talmapais State Park, 801 Panoramic Hwy., tel. 415/388–2070; 16 sites; $12; flush toilets). 🏨 **Hotels:** None in park. In Muir Beach: Pelican Inn (10 Pacific Way, at Rte. 1, tel. 415/383–6000; 7 rooms; $201–$240). ✗ **Restaurants:** In the park: Aramark Café (tel. 415/388–7059; $5–$10). In Mill Valley: Mountain Home Inn Restaurant (810 Panoramic Hwy., tel. 415/382–9000; $8–$38). ⛶ **Groceries & Gear:** None in park. In Mill Valley: Bell Market (207 Flamingo Rd., tel. 415/383–6242).

FEES, HOURS & REGULATIONS

Entrance fee: $3 adults, free ages 16 and under. No pets on trails. No bikes. No picnicking. No portable radios. No RV parking. No vehicles over 35 feet long on steep, winding road leading to monument. Park open daily 8–sunset.

HOW TO GET THERE

12 mi north of the Golden Gate Bridge via U.S. 101 and Rte. 1. Closest airport: San Francisco.

CONTACTS

Muir Woods National Monument (Mill Valley, CA 94941, tel. 415/388–2595, fax 415/389–6957, www.nps.gov/muwo). *See also Golden Gate National Recreation Area.*

Pinnacles National Monument

In central California, entrances near Soledad and Hollister

The monument preserves the rock formations known as "The Pinnacles," talus caves, and wilderness areas. The spires and crags that inspired the park name are remnants of ancient volcanic activity that is part of the long geologic history of the San Andreas Rift Zone. Pinnacles is on the Pacific Plate. Its sister rock, the other part of the same volcanic activity, is on the North American Plate. Pinnacles has moved 195 mi northwest as the plates have shifted over millions of years. The monument was established on January 16, 1908.

WHAT TO SEE & DO

Bird-watching, caving, hiking, rock climbing, viewing wildflowers. **Facilities:** Bear Gulch Visitor Center (east entrance on Rte. 146 via Rte. 25), Chaparral Ranger Station (west entrance via Rte. 146 from Soledad), outdoor interpretive exhibits, hiking trails. Book and map sale areas, picnic tables. **Programs & Events:** Guided hikes and interpretive talks (Mar.–May). Night hikes and bat viewings (fall). **Tips & Hints:** Prepare for temperatures of 110°F in summer. Carry plenty of water. Wear sturdy footwear. Trail elevations range from 800 feet to 3,300 feet. Bring flashlights to visit caves (open seasonally). If you want to visit caves, enter from the west side of the park for easy access to the Balconies Cave trail. Go between Feb. and May for wildflowers. Go during the week in spring to avoid crowds (and consequently limited parking). Busiest Mar.–May, least crowded July and Aug.

FOOD, LODGING & SUPPLIES

Camping: None in park. At east entrance: Pinnacles (tel. 831/389–4462; 128 sites; $7–$28; flush toilets, showers, hook-ups). **Hotels:** None in park. In Hollister: Best Western San Benito Inn (660 San Felipe Rd., tel. 831/637–9248; 42 rooms; $99–$120). **Restaurants:** None in park. In King City: Guadalajara Restaurant (211 Broadway St., tel. 831/385–4606; $6–$8). **Groceries:** None in park. In Paicines: General Store (12261 Airline Rte., tel. 831/628–3293), Pinnacles Convenience Store (2400 Rte. 146, tel. 831/389–4462.)

FEES, HOURS & REGULATIONS

Entrance fee: $5 per vehicle; $2 per person on foot, bicycle, or motorcycle, free ages 15 and under. No pets, bikes, or strollers on trails. No pets beyond parking and picnic areas. Leashed pets only. Charcoal fires only. No firewood gathering. No hunting. Watch out for tarantulas (especially in autumn, the mating season), black widow spiders, and rattlesnakes. Be wary of poison oak in shaded areas of woodlands. Park open daily at 7:30 AM, closing hours change seasonally. Visitor center open daily 9–5. Chaparral Ranger Station open weekends 9–5, intermittent weekdays.

HOW TO GET THERE

The monument's east entrance is 33 mi south of Hollister via Rte. 25 and Rte. 146. The west entrance is 13 mi east of Soledad via Rte. 146. No connecting road through the monument. Closest airport: San Jose (75 mi).

CONTACTS

Pinnacles National Monument (5000 Rte. 146, Paicines, CA 95043, tel. 831/389–4485, fax 831/389–4489, www.nps.gov/pinn). King City Chamber of Commerce (203 Broadway St., King City, CA 93930, tel. 831/385–3814). San Benito County Chamber of Commerce (tel. 831/637–5315).

Point Reyes
National Seashore

On the northern coast, near Point Reyes Station

This peninsula north of San Francisco is noted for long beaches backed by tall cliffs and lagoons; forested ridges; and offshore bird and sea lion colonies. Highlights include the short Earthquake Trail, which passes by what was likely the epicenter of the devastating 1906 quake, and the late 19th-century Point Reyes Lighthouse, a good spot to watch for whales. There's also a bird observatory (most easily reached via Bolinas). The small towns of Olema, Point Reyes Station, and Inverness are in or border on the park. The seashore was authorized in 1962, established in 1972, and designated a Biosphere Reserve in 1988.

WHAT TO SEE & DO

Beachcombing, bicycling (rentals, Olema), bird-watching, fishing, hiking, horseback riding (rentals, Fivebrooks, tel. 415/663–1570), kayaking, tide-pooling, whale-watching. **Facilities:** 3 visitor centers: Bear Valley (Bear Valley Rd., Olema), Lighthouse (Sir Francis Drake Blvd., 23 mi from Bear Valley), and Ken Patrick (Drakes Beach, off Sir Francis Drake Blvd.); 140 mi of hiking trails, beaches, outdoor exhibit panels. **Programs & Events:** Programs on lighthouses and lifeboat stations, gray whales, seals and sea lions, wildflowers, birds, geology, Native Americans, tide pools (throughout the year). Native American Big Time Festival (4th Sat., July), Sand Sculpture Contest (Sun. of Labor Day weekend). **Tips & Hints:** The lighthouse can be reached only by climbing 300 stairs. It's occasionally closed due to high winds. Check tide tables before walking on the beaches; high tides can trap you. Stay away from the cliff edges and do not walk below the cliffs; the cliffs are unstable and there may be falling rocks. Not all beaches have lifeguards on duty. After hiking, carefully check your body for ticks, as ticks carrying Lyme disease have been found in the area. Go Feb.–May for flowers, Dec.–Apr. for migrating gray whales, Nov.–Apr. for breeding elephant seals, Aug.–Feb. for migrating birds. Busiest in Aug. and Dec., least crowded in Feb. and Apr.

FOOD, LODGING & SUPPLIES

Camping: 5 campgrounds (permit required) in the park: Tomales Bay (boat-in beach camping area; $12–$35; pit toilets), Coast Camp ($12–$35; pit toilets), Glen Camp ($12–$35; pit toilets), Sky Camp ($12–$35; pit toilets), Wildcat Camp ($12–$35; pit toilets). **Hotels:** In the park: Point Reyes Hostel (tel. 415/663–8811; 44 beds; $10–$16). In Inverness Park: Blackthorne Inn (266 Vallejo Ave., tel. 415/663–8621; 5 rooms; $225–$325). **Restaurants:** In the park: Drakes Beach café (tel. 415/669–1297; $4–$12). In Inverness: Priscilla's (12781 Sir Francis Drake Blvd., tel. 415/669–1244; $6–$20).

FEES, HOURS & REGULATIONS

Free. Shuttle fee for whale viewing ($4). Camping permits required (available at Bear Valley Visitor Center). California fishing license required. No hunting. No pets or bikes in wilderness. No car camping. Seashore open daily sunrise–sunset. Bear Valley Visitor Center weekdays 9–5, weekends 8–5. Lighthouse Visitor Center Thurs.–Mon. 10–4:30. Ken Patrick weekends and holidays 10–5.

HOW TO GET THERE

45 mi north of San Francisco via U.S. 101 and Sir Francis Drake Blvd. or via Rte. 1. Closest airport: San Francisco.

CONTACTS

Bear Valley Visitor Center (Point Reyes National Seashore, Point Reyes, CA 94956, tel. 415/464–5100). Administrative office: Point Reyes National Seashore (Point Reyes Station, CA 94956, tel. 415/464–5100, fax 415/663–8132, www.nps.gov/pore).

Redwood National & State Parks

In northwestern California, near Orick

The park, which runs for 40 mi along the Pacific Coast, is best known for its magnificent old-growth redwoods, some of the world's tallest trees. Redwoods can live more than 2,000 years and grow to over 300 feet tall. Less well known are the park's prairies, oak woodlands, and coastal and marine ecosystems. The area encompasses three state parks: Prairie Creek Redwoods, Del Norte Coast Redwoods, and Jedediah Smith Redwoods. The park was established in 1968 and designated a World Heritage Site in 1980 and an International Biosphere Reserve in 1983.

WHAT TO SEE & DO

Auto touring, backpacking, bicycling, bird-, elk-, and whale-watching, hiking, horseback riding and tours, picnicking. **Facilities:** 2 information centers: Crescent City (1111 2nd St.) and Hiouchi (Rte. 199) 3 visitor centers: Jedediah Smith (U.S. 101, Hiouchi), Prairie Creek (Newton Drury Scenic Pkwy., off U.S. 101), Thomas H. Kuchel (U.S. 101, Orick); hiking trails, outdoor interpretive exhibits. Bookstores, picnic tables. **Programs & Events:** Ranger-led programs (mid-June–Labor Day), environmental education programs (Mar.–May, Oct. and Nov.), children's program (mid-June–Labor Day). Wildflower walks (spring), Founders Day (Aug. 25). **Tips & Hints:** Wear layers of clothing to handle varying temperatures between coastal and inland sections. Bring rain gear and good walking shoes. After hiking, carefully check your body for ticks, as ticks carrying Lyme disease have been found in the area. Do not hike alone. Both cougars and bears inhabit the parklands; if you see either, do not run away; wave your arms to scare it off. Borrow animal-proof food canisters at Redwood Information Center. Busiest July and Aug., least crowded in Dec. and Jan.

FOOD, LODGING & SUPPLIES

⚠ **Camping:** In the parks: Mill Creek (Del Norte Coast Redwoods State Park; 145 sites; $12–$15; flush toilets, showers; closed Oct.–Apr.), Jedediah Smith Redwoods State Park (106 sites; $12–$15; flush toilets, showers), Elk Prairie (Prairie Creek Redwoods State Park; 75 sites; flush toilets, showers), Gold Bluffs Beach (Prairie Creek Redwoods State Park; 29 sites; $12–$15; flush toilets, showers). Backcountry camping allowed (permit required, *see below*). ⛺ **Hotels:** In the parks: De Martin Redwood Youth Hostel (Wilson Creek Rd., 14480 U.S. 101, Klamath, tel. 707/482–8265 or 800/909–4776 Ext. 733; 28 dorm beds,

1 private room; $16 per person). In Crescent City: Hampton Inn & Suites (100 A St., tel. 707/465–5400; 53 rooms; $89–$149). ✗ **Restaurants:** None in parks. In Crescent City: Harbor View Grotto (150 Starfish Way, tel. 707/464–3815; $5–$15). ⚥ **Groceries:** None in park. In Orick: Orick Market (121175 U.S. 101, tel. 707/488–3225). In Klamath: Woodland Villa Grocery Store (15870 U.S. 101, tel. 707/482–2081).

FEES, HOURS & REGULATIONS
Free. Permit required for backcountry camping (tel. 707/464–6101). Tall Tree Outfitters offers guided day and overnight horseback rides (tel. 707/488–5785). Redwood Creek Trail is impassable during high water. California state fishing license required. No pets on any trails. Leashed pets only. Park open daily. Information center hours: Crescent City daily 9–5. Hiouchi mid-June–mid-Sept. daily 9–5.

HOW TO GET THERE
The park runs along U.S. 101 from Hiouchi (Rte. 199) to Crescent City and down to Orick. Park headquarters and information center is in Crescent City. Redwood information center is 335 mi north of San Francisco on U.S. 101 about 2 mi west of Orick. Closest airport: Eureka–Arcata and Crescent City.

CONTACTS
Redwood National Park (1111 2nd St., Crescent City, CA 95531, tel. 707/464–6101, www.nps.gov/redw). Orick Chamber of Commerce (Box 234, Orick, CA 95555, tel. 707/488–2885, www.orick.net). Crescent City Chamber of Commerce (1001 Front St., Crescent City, CA 95531, tel. 707/464–3174 or 800/343–8300, www.northerncalifornia.net).

Rosie the Riveter/ World War II Home Front National Historical Park

Near San Francisco Bay, in Richmond

Several historic sites, including a waterfront shipyard, a hospital, child-development centers, and fire stations, comprise this park, which commemorates the homebound workforce and its contributions during World War II. The shipyards, one of 56 war industries in Richmond, were the most productive in the country in the early 1940s. The park especially honors the women, called "Rosies," who joined the wartime effort in great numbers. Minorities and other groups are also recognized. The park was established on October 24, 2000.

WHAT TO SEE & DO
Auto-touring, touring World War II cargo ship, viewing exhibits. **Facilities:** Exhibits in Richmond City Hall South and in Barbara & Jay Vincent Park, memorial in Marina Bay Park, S.S. *Red Oak Victory,* observation point. **Tips & Hints:** This park is under development. Some

sites are not open to the public. A temporary visitor center in Richmond City Hall South has exhibits and auto-touring maps.

FEES, HOURS & REGULATIONS

Free. S.S. *Red Oak Victory* suggested donation $5; tours Tues.–Sun., 11–4. Richmond City Hall open weekdays 9–5. Rosie the Riveter Memorial in Marina Bay Park open dawn–dusk. Barbara & Jay Vincent Park open dawn–dusk. At this writing the following park sites are on private property and closed to the public: Atchison Village, Ford Assembly Building, Kaiser Field Hospital, Maritime and Powers Child Development Centers, Shipyard No. 3.

GETTING THERE

To get to the Rosie Memorial from I–80, take I–580 toward Richmond/San Rafael, then the Marina Bay/S. 23rd St. exit. Turn left onto Marina Bay Pkwy, right onto Regatta Blvd., and left at Melville Sq. to Marina Bay Park.

To get to Richmond City Hall South from I–80, take I–580 toward Richmond/San Rafael, then take the Harbour Way exit. Turn left onto Hall Avenue, then right onto Marina Way South. Closest airports: Oakland (12 mi), San Francisco (17 mi).

CONTACTS

Rosie the Riveter/World War II Home Front National Historical Park (c/o Richmond City Hall, 1401 Marina Way S, Richmond, CA 94804, tel. 510/232–5050, www.nps.gov/rori). S.S. *Red Oak Victory* (c/o Richmond Museum of History, Box 1276, Richmond, CA 94802, tel. 510/235–7387 or 510/237–2933 tours).

San Francisco Maritime National Historical Park

In San Francisco

Included in this park are a fleet of historic ships, a maritime museum, and a maritime library. The fleet includes the 1886 square-rigger *Balclutha;* the 1895 schooner *C.A. Thayer;* the 1891 scow schooner *Alma;* the 1890 ferryboat *Eureka;* the 1914 paddlewheel tug *Eppleton Hall;* and the 1907 steam tugboat *Hercules.* The *Hercules* and *Alma* have been restored and steam (and sail) to ports around the bay. The museum, in a streamline modern building, displays models, huge ships' parts, figureheads, and fine arts, and includes the Steamship Room, which presents the history of West Coast steam. The Maritime Library houses books, periodicals, and oral histories, and provides access to more than 250,000 photographs, 120,000 sheets of ships' plans, and other historic documents. The park's extensive artifact collections include oils and watercolors, scrimshaw, delicate fancywork, carvings, tools, and navigational instruments. The park was established in 1988.

WHAT TO SEE & DO

Attending boatbuilding classes, doing library research, picnicking, touring historic vessels, viewing exhibits, visiting museum. **Facilities:** Visitor center, museum, library. Bookstore and gift shop. **Programs & Events:** Steam-engine and living-history demonstrations, boatbuilding and woodworking classes. Heritage month programs (Women's History, Asian–Pacific, Black History, etc.); Festival of the Sea (usually in Sept.), Sea Music Concert Series (fall), Christmas at Sea (winter). **Tips & Hints:** Use public transportation to get to the park. The best time to visit is in fall. Busiest July and Aug., least crowded Dec. and Jan.

FEES & HOURS

Entrance fee: Hyde St. Pier (historic vessels): $5 adults, $2 ages 12–17 and 64 and over, free ages 11 and under. Museum and library free. Visitor center open Memorial Day–Oct. 1, daily 9:30–7; Oct. 2–Memorial Day, daily 9:30–5. Hyde St. Pier open daily 9:30–5:30. Maritime Museum open daily 10–5. Library open Tues. 5–7, Wed.–Fri. 1–5, Sat. 10–5.

HOW TO GET THERE

West end of Fisherman's Wharf, at the Hyde Street cable-car terminus. Closest airport: San Francisco (15 mi).

CONTACTS

San Francisco Maritime National Historical Park (Bldg. E, Room 265, Fort Mason Center, San Francisco, CA 94123, tel. 415/561–7000, fax 415/556–1624, www.nps.gov/safr). San Francisco Convention & Visitors Bureau (201 3rd St., Suite 900, San Francisco, CA 94103, tel. 415/974–6900, www.sfvisitor.org)..

Santa Monica Mountains National Recreation Area

Near Los Angeles

The Santa Monica Mountains rise above Los Angeles, widen to meet the curve of Santa Monica Bay, and reach their greatest height facing the ocean, forming a beautiful and multifaceted landscape. Residents use "L.A.'s backyard" for mountain biking and hiking. For sensational views, drive along Mulholland Drive, which cuts through the park. The recreation area is a cooperative effort that joins federal, state, and local park agencies with private preserves and landowners to protect the natural and cultural resources of this transverse mountain range and seashore. Encompassed within this recreation area are Topanga, Leo Carrillo, Point Mugu, and Malibu Creek state parks. The area was established on November 10, 1978.

WHAT TO SEE & DO

Attending festivals and cultural workshops and events, bird- and whale-watching, hiking, horseback riding (rentals), mountain biking, picnicking, surfing, swimming, walking. **Facilities:** Visitor center (401 W. Hillcrest Dr., Thousand Oaks); Satwiwa Native American Indian

Culture Center (Via Goleta, off Lynn Rd.), 580 mi of trails, beaches. Bookstore. **Programs & Events:** Ranger-led walking tours, cultural programs, natural history talks. Seasonal activities and special events include nature walks, guided tours of Historic Paramount Ranch western movie set, Silent Films under the Stars. **Tips & Hints:** Expect hot, dry summers (80°F–100°F) and relatively cool, wet winters (40°F–70°F). Plan for coastal side of the mountains to be 10–15 degrees cooler than inland side during summer (in winter this pattern is reversed). Bikers must yield to hikers; hikers must yield to equestrians. Watch out for poison oak and rattlesnakes. Bring plenty of water. Busiest May and June, least crowded Dec. and Jan. Contact park for copy of "Outdoors" calendar of events.

FEES, HOURS & REGULATIONS

Free. Parking fees charged at most state parks and some local parks within recreation area. Some special events charge fees. Horse rentals available at Dos Vientos Stables (tel. 805/498–9222) and Adventures on Horseback (tel. 818/706–0888). Park open daily. Visitor center open daily 9–5.

HOW TO GET THERE

West of Griffith Park in Los Angeles County and east of Oxnard Plain in Ventura County. U.S. 101 (Ventura Freeway) borders the mountains on the north, and Rte. 1 (Pacific Coast Hwy.) and the Pacific Ocean form the southern boundary. Access is via many roads that cross the mountains between these two highways. Part of the park stretches into the Simi Hills north of U.S. 101. To reach the visitor center from U.S. 101, take Lynn Rd. exit, travel north on Lynn Rd., turn east (right) on Hillcrest Dr., turn left onto McCloud Ave. The driveway to the visitor center will be on the right-hand side. Closest airports: Burbank (20 mi), Los Angeles International (15 mi).

CONTACTS

Santa Monica Mountains National Recreation Area (National Park Service, 401 W. Hillcrest Dr., Thousand Oaks, CA 91360, tel. 805/370–2301, www.nps.gov/samo). Santa Monica Convention & Visitors Bureau (520 Broadway, Santa Monica, CA 90401, tel. 310/319–6263 or 800/544–5319, www.santamonica.com).

Sequoia & Kings Canyon National Parks

In east-central California, near Three Rivers

Sequoia, the second-oldest national park in the United States, was established in 1890 to protect the Big Trees in Giant Forest, including the General Sherman Tree, the world's largest living tree. There's an excellent Giant Forest Museum that traces the ecology of sequoias. Sequoia also contains Crystal Cave, filled with marble stalactites and stalagmites, and Mt. Whitney, the highest mountain in the lower 48 states.

(However, you can't easily access Whitney from the park itself.) A small portion of what is now Kings Canyon was set aside in 1890 as General Grant National Park. In 1940, General Grant was absorbed into the new and larger Kings Canyon National Park, which eventually grew to include the South Fork of the Kings River and 456,552 acres of backcountry wilderness. Together, Sequoia and Kings Canyon have a total wilderness area of 736,980 acres. There are a few small developed areas within and abutting the park, including Grant Grove Village and Cedar Grove Village in Kings Canyon, Wuksachi Village, the northern gateway to Sequoia, and Lodgepole in Sequoia. Sequoia National Park was established on September 25, 1890, and Kings Canyon National Park was established on March 4, 1940.

WHAT TO SEE & DO

Auto touring, backpacking, cross-country skiing, fishing, hiking, horseback riding, snowshoeing, viewing sequoias, visiting museum and cave. **Facilities:** 4 visitor centers: Cedar Grove (end of Rte. 180, Kings Canyon National Park), Foothills (Generals Rte., Sequoia National Park), Grant Grove (Rte. 180, Kings Canyon National Park), Lodgepole (Lodgepole Rd., just off Generals Rte., Sequoia National Park); ranger station (Mineral King, Sequoia National Park); outdoor interpretive exhibits and signs, 140 mi of scenic roads, 800 mi of hiking trails, museum. Book and map sales. **Programs & Events:** Ranger-led walks, talks, and evening programs; field seminars. Horseback rides (June–Sept.), Crystal Cave tours (May–Sept.), snowshoe walks (Dec.–Feb., depending on snowfall). Nation's Christmas Tree Ceremony (2nd Sun. of Dec., General Grant Tree in Kings Canyon). **Tips & Hints:** Plan on a two-hour drive from Ash Mountain entrance on Rte. 198 to Grant Grove at Rte. 180 entrance. Add two to three hours for side trip from Grant Grove into Kings Canyon. Bring rain gear and layered clothing for hiking. Use extra caution when driving as many park roads are steep and narrow. Rent or buy bear-resistant food storage containers. Black bears inhabit the parklands; if you see one, make plenty of noise and wave your arms to scare it away, but do not run. Never approach a bear or a cub. Parks busiest June–Aug., least crowded Jan. and Feb.

FOOD, LODGING & SUPPLIES

🏕 **Camping:** 14 campgrounds in park (1,295 sites; $12–$20; some flush toilets, some pit toilets, some showers). Backcountry camping allowed (permit required, *see below*). 🏨 **Hotels:** In the parks: John Muir Lodge (Grant Grove Village, tel. 866/522–6966; 30 rooms, 6 suites; $89–$140), Cedar Grove Lodge (bottom of Kings Canyon, tel. 866/522–6966; 21 rooms, $99–$110; closed Oct.–May), Wuksachi Village (tel. 888/252–5757; 102 rooms; $177–$219). In Three Rivers: Lazy J Ranch Motel (39625 Sierra Dr., tel. 559/561–4449 or 888/315–2378; 18 rooms; $105). ✗ **Restaurants:** In the parks: Grant Grove Village Restaurant (tel. 866/522–6966; $7–$15), Wuksachi Village Dining Room (tel. 599/565–4070; $5–$30). In Three Rivers: Gateway Restaurant & Lodge (45978 Sierra Dr., tel. 559/561–4133; $15–$32). ⛄ **Groceries & Gear:** In the parks: Grant Grove Village General Market (tel. 866/522–6966), Lodgepole Market (tel. 559/565–3301), Wuksachi Village Market (tel. 559/565–4070).

FEES, HOURS & REGULATIONS

Entrance fee: $10 per vehicle or $5 per person on foot, bicycle, or motorcycle. Backcountry permit (free) required for all backcountry camping. Hiking permit (free) required for all hiking to Mt. Whitney. California state fishing license required. No bikes on trails. Bear-proof storage required for food, trash, toiletries, baby wipes, and any other such scented items. Road to Mineral King in Sequoia National Park open Memorial Day–Oct., weather permitting. Vehicles longer than 22 feet not advised on Generals Rte. between Potwisha Campground and Giant Forest in Sequoia. Rte. 180 to Cedar Grove in Kings Canyon open mid-Apr.–mid-Nov. Park open daily. Foothills Visitor Center open June–Aug., daily 8–5; Sept.–May, daily 8–4:30. Grant Grove Visitor Center open June–Aug., daily 8–6; Sept.–Nov. and Mar.–May, daily 8–5; Dec.–Feb., daily 9–4:40. Lodgepole Visitor Center open June–Aug., daily 8–6; Sept.–Nov. and Mar.–May, daily 9–5; Dec.–Feb., Fri.–Mon. 9–4:30. Mineral King Visitor Center open May–Oct., daily 8–4:30.

HOW TO GET THERE

There are no roads into the parks from the east. From the west, take Rte. 180 from Fresno to enter Kings Canyon and Rte. 198 from Visalia to enter Sequoia. Generals Rte. connects the two roads, making loop trips possible. In winter, the Generals Rte. between Lodgepole and Grant Grove may be closed by snow. Closest airport: Fresno (53 mi).

CONTACTS

Sequoia & Kings Canyon National Parks (Visitor information, 47050 Generals Rte., Three Rivers, CA 93271, tel. 559/565–3341, www.nps. gov/seki).

Whiskeytown-Shasta-Trinity National Recreation Area

In northern California, near Redding

Nestled in the rugged Klamath Mountains watershed, Whiskeytown preserves much of the colorful history of the California gold rush and has a wealth of water-oriented and backcountry opportunities. Although Whiskeytown Lake is smaller than Shasta or Trinity lakes, which are administered by the Forest Service rather than the National Park service, its clear, blue water and full pool level in summer attract many recreationists to its shores. The recreation area was authorized in 1965 and established in 1972.

WHAT TO SEE & DO

Backpacking (permit required, *see below*), boating (rentals, Oak Bottom Marina and in Redding), canoeing, fishing, gold-panning (permit required, *see below*), hiking, horseback riding, hunting, kayaking, mountain biking, picnicking, sailing, scuba diving, swimming, waterskiing. **Facilities:** Visitor information center (junction of Rte. 299 and Kennedy Memorial Dr., 8 mi west of Redding); beaches, 50 mi of backcountry roads and trails, outdoor interpretive exhibits and signs. Book and map sales, picnic tables. **Programs & Events:** Guided walks, evening programs, demonstrations and talks pertaining to natural and cultural resources of the area, tours through Tower House Historic District. National Park Week Celebration and Pick Up Lake Litter Volunteer Cleanup (both in Apr.). **Tips & Hints:** Bears and mountain lions inhabit the park. If you see a bear or mountain lion, do not run; make noise and wave your arms to scare it off. Keep all scented items (food, toiletries, and other such items) in airtight, bear-proof containers. Dispose of all trash in bear-proof garbage cans. Watch out for Western diamondback rattlesnakes. Beware of abandoned mine shafts. Go in spring for wildflowers and hiking, although trails may be too wet for mountain biking and horseback riding. Go in summer for water activities, camping, and fishing; fall for foliage, hiking, mountain biking, and horseback riding before beginning of rainy season. Busiest June and July, least crowded Dec. and Jan.

FOOD, LODGING & SUPPLIES

Camping: 3 campgrounds in park: Brandy Creek (tel. 530/246–1225; 36 sites; $14), Dry Creek (tel. 800/356–2267; 2 group sites; $75; pit toilets), Oak Bottom (tel. 800/365–2267; 120 sites; $14–$18; flush toilets, showers). Backcountry camping available (permit required, *see below*). **Hotels:** None in park. In Redding: Red Lion Inn (1830 Hilltop Dr., tel. 530/221–8700; 194 rooms; $114–$250). **Restaurants:** None in park. In Redding: Jack's Grill (1743 California St., tel. 530/241–9705; $10–$25; closed Sun.). **Groceries & Gear:** In the park: limited supplies and groceries at Oak Bottom Marina.

FEES, HOURS & REGULATIONS

Entrance fee: $5 per vehicle. Fee charged for Whiskey Creek Group Picnic Area (reservations required, tel. 800/365–2267). Permits required (free) for backpacking and backcountry camping. Permits for gold panning ($1) and wood collecting ($10 for 2 cords of wood) required. California hunting and fishing license required. No motorized vehicles on trails. Horses and mountain bikes restricted to certain trails. No dogs at Oak Bottom and Brandy Creek beaches. Leashed dogs elsewhere. Recreation area open daily. Certain areas (some rest rooms and several backcountry roads) closed in winter. Visitor center open Memorial Day–Labor Day, daily 9–6; Labor Day–Memorial Day, daily 10–4.

HOW TO GET THERE

8 mi west of Redding on Rte. 299. Closest airports: Redding and Sacramento (165 mi).

CONTACTS

Whiskeytown National Recreation Area (Box 188, Whiskeytown, CA 96095-0188, tel. 530/242–3400, fax 530/246–5154, www.nps.gov/whis). Redding Chamber of Commerce (747 Auditorium Dr., Redding CA 96001, tel. 530/225–4433). Redding Convention & Visitors Bureau (777 Auditorium Dr., Redding, CA 96001, tel. 530/225–4100 or 800/874–7562, fax 530/225–4354, www.visitredding.org).

Yosemite National Park

In east-central California,
surrounding Yosemite Village

Yosemite Valley is the heart of the magnificent 1,200-square-mi park that spurred conservationist John Muir and photographer Ansel Adams to some of their best achievements. The park is so large that it can be grouped into several different areas. Yosemite Valley is famed for its waterfalls, such as the 2,425-foot Yosemite Falls, highest in North America, and the granite monoliths of El Capitan and Half Dome. Some of the best views of this valley can be seen from Glacier Point. The Wawona area, near the south entrance, has a cluster of historic buildings and the Mariposa Grove of giant sequoias. Both Wawona and Yosemite Valley are open year-round. The Hetch Hetchy reservoir area and the subalpine Tuolumne Meadows, on the other hand, stay open only as long as snowfall allows. There are a few developed areas within the park, including Wawona and Yosemite Village in Yosemite Valley, which has lodges, restaurants, the Ansel Adams photography gallery, a medical center, and other services. Yosemite Valley and Mariposa Big Tree Grove were granted to the State of California in 1864. The national park was established in 1890. The federal government accepted lands returned by the state in 1906. The El Portal site was authorized in 1958. The park was designated a World Heritage Site in 1984.

WHAT TO SEE & DO

Auto and bus touring, backpacking, bicycling (rentals), bird- and wildlife watching, cross-country skiing, fishing, hiking, horseback riding, ice-skating, rafting, rock climbing, skiing, swimming, viewing geological features and waterfalls. **Facilities:** 4 visitor centers: Valley (Yosemite Valley), Big Oak Flat, Wawona, and Tuolumne; 196 mi of scenic roads, 800 mi of hiking trails, museum. Bookstores. **Programs & Events:** Ranger-led walks, talks, and evening programs; bus tours; horseback rides; theatrical events; tram tours. **Tips & Hints:** Plan to spend at least four hours touring Yosemite Valley and two days to visit entire park. Drive slowly and with extra caution in case of wildlife on the roads. Use turnouts to pull completely off the road to look at views, take photographs, etc. Do not enter the water near the brim of a waterfall. Check water conditions with park staff and swim only when the water is low. Dress in layers and bring rain gear to accommodate weather changes. Expect warm, dry summers; most moisture falls Jan.– Mar. Busiest July and Aug., least crowded Nov. and Jan.

FOOD, LODGING & SUPPLIES

Camping: 13 campgrounds in park (1,445 sites; $8–$40; some flush toilets, some vault toilets). Backcountry camping allowed (permit required, *see below*). **Hotels:** In the park: Ahwahnee Hotel (99 rooms, 24 cottages; $357), Curry Village (18 rooms, 183 cabins; $76–$110), Redwoods Guest Cottages (tel. 209/375–6666; 120 units; $88–$500), Wawona Hotel (104 rooms; $96–$161), White Wolf Lodge (4 cabins; $84), Yosemite Lodge (239 rooms; $103–$146). **Restaurants:** In the park: Ahwahnee Hotel Dining Room (tel. 209/372–1489; $15–$30), Mountain Room Restaurant (tel. 209/372–1281; $18–$30), Wawona Hotel (tel. 209/375–1425; $11–$24), White Wolf Lodge (tel. 209/372–8416; $12–$17). In Oakhurst: Castillo's Mexican Restaurant (49271 Golden Oak Loop, tel. 209/683–8000; $6–$12), Kyoto Kafe (40423 Rte. 41, tel. 209/692–2400; $5–$14), the Mountain House (Rte. 41 at Rd. 222, tel. 209/683–5191; $5–$11). ⚬ **Groceries & Gear:** In the park: The Village Store (9012 Village Dr.; tel. 209/372–1253).

FEES, HOURS & REGULATIONS

Entrance fee: $20 per vehicle or $10 per bus passenger, bicyclist, or walk-in. Free shuttle bus in east end of Yosemite Valley (year-round) and between Wawona and the Mariposa Grove of Giant Sequoias and from Tuolumne Meadows to Tenaya Lake (June–Sept.). California fishing license required. Wilderness permit (free in person; $5 for telephone reservations) required for any backcountry camping (tel. 209/372–0740). No pets on trails or beaches or in backcountry or public buildings. Leashed pets restricted to specific campgrounds. No hunting. No discharging weapons. Don't deface or remove natural historic features. The Tioga Pass entrance is closed Nov.–early June because of snow. Park open daily. Yosemite Valley Visitor Center open June 15–Sept. 15, daily 8–7; Sept. 16–June 14, daily 8–5. Tuolumne Meadows Visitor Center open June–Sept, daily 9–5.

HOW TO GET THERE

There are four entrances to the park: the south entrance on Rte. 41 north from Fresno, the Arch Rock entrance on Rte. 140 east from Merced, the Big Oak Flat entrance on Rte. 120 east from Modesto and Manteca, and the Tioga Pass entrance on Rte. 120 west from Lee Vining and U.S. 395. Closest airports: Merced (80 mi), Fresno (94 mi), San Francisco (200 mi).

CONTACTS

Public Information Office, Yosemite National Park (Box 577, Yosemite, CA 95389, tel. 209/372–0200, www.nps.gov/yose). Mariposa Visitors Bureau (Box 425, Mariposa, CA 95338, tel. 209/966–2456 or 800/208–2434, www.visitmariposa.net). Yosemite Sierra Visitors Bureau (41969 Rte. 41, Oakhurst, CA 93644, tel. 559/683–4636, www.go2yosemite. net). Lee Vining Chamber of Commerce (Box 130, Lee Vining, CA 93541, tel. 760/647–6629 or 760/647–6595, www.leevining.com).

See Also

AIDS Memorial Grove National Memorial, California National Historic Trail, Port Chicago Naval Magazine National Memorial, Juan Bautista de Anza National Historic Trail, Kern River, Kings River, Klamath River, Merced River, Pacific Crest National Scenic Trail, Pony Express National Historic Trail, and *Tuolumne River,* in Other National Parklands.

COLORADO

Bent's Old Fort National Historic Site

*In southeastern Colorado,
between La Junta and Las Animas*

Preserved here is a reconstructed adobe trading post on the old Santa Fe Trail. In its heyday (1833–49), the fort was the largest American-owned commercial center in the 700 mi between Independence, Missouri, and Santa Fe, New Mexico. The park was established on June 3, 1960.

WHAT TO SEE & DO

Touring the fort, visiting the sales area in the trade room and bookstore. **Facilities:** Fort and fort furnishings. Audiovisual program, bookstore, sales area with trade room. **Programs & Events:** One-hour ranger-guided tours (June–Aug., daily; Sept.–May, by appointment). Historic lifestyle demonstrations (June–Aug.). Kid's Quarters (June), Santa Fe Trail Encampment (late July or early Aug.), Holiday Celebration (Dec.) **Tips & Hints:** Busiest Apr.–Aug., least crowded Jan. and Feb.

FOOD, LODGING & SUPPLIES

Camping: None in park. In John Martin Reservoir State Park (Rte. 24, south of U.S. 50, tel. 800/678–2267): Lake Hasty Campground (109 sites; $12–$16; flush toilets, showers, hook-ups), The Point (104 sites; $8–$12; pit toilets). **Hotels:** None in park. In La Junta: Holiday Inn Express (27994 Frontage Rd., tel. 719/384–2900; 59 rooms; $79–$89). **Restaurants:** None in park. In La Junta: Hog's Breath Saloon (808 E. 3rd St., tel. 719/384–7879; $10–$25). In Las Animas: Best Western Bent's Fort Inn (U.S. 50, ¼ mi east of Las Animas, tel. 719/456–0011; $5–$7). **Groceries & Gear:** None in park. In La Junta: Loaf & Jug Store (101 N. Main St., tel. 719/384–8360).

FEES, HOURS & REGULATIONS

Tour fee: $3 adults, $2 ages 6–12, free ages 5 and under. Permits required in advance for commercial filming. No pets in allowed in fort rooms. Park open June–Aug., daily 8–5:30; Sept.–May, daily 9–4.

HOW TO GET THERE

6 mi east of La Junta and 13 mi west of Las Animas on Rte. 194; 75 mi east of Pueblo and 140 mi west of Garden City, KS, via U.S. 50. Closest airport: Pueblo (75 mi).

CONTACTS

Bent's Old Fort National Historic Site (35110 Rte. 194 E, La Junta, CO 81050-9523, tel. 719/383–5010, fax 719/383–5031, www.nps.gov/beol). La Junta Chamber of Commerce (110 Santa Fe Ave., La Junta, CO

81050, tel 719/384–7411). John Martin Reservoir State Park (30703 Rte. 24, Hasty, CO 81044, tel. 719/829–1801; 800/678–2267 campground reservations).

Black Canyon of the Gunnison National Park

In southwestern Colorado, east of Montrose

Carved by the Gunnison River, the walls of schist and gneiss in Black Canyon are some of the most imposing in North America. The canyon and its rims are home to black bear, mule deer, golden eagles, and peregrine falcon. The site was proclaimed a monument on March 2, 1933, and was redesignated a national park on October 21, 1999.

WHAT TO SEE & DO

Camping, cross-country skiing, fishing, hiking, kayaking (expert only), picnicking, rock climbing, snowshoeing, wildlife viewing. **Facilities:** Visitor center (Gunnison Point, south rim), trails, amphitheater, auditorium, interpretive signs. Book sale area. **Programs & Events:** Ranger-guided and evening programs (Memorial day–Labor Day); ranger-guided snowshoe walks (free snowshoes provided), full-moon ranger-guided cross-country ski programs along the rim (weekends only, mid-Jan.–early Mar., reservations required, tel. 970/641–2337). **Tips & Hints:** Hiking in the canyon is strenuous and a permit is required. Go mid-May–mid-June for wildflowers, late Sept. for fall foliage. Busiest July and Aug., least crowded Dec. and Jan.

FOOD, LODGING & SUPPLIES

Camping: In the park: North Rim (13 sites; $5; pit toilets), South Rim (9 sites; $10–$15; pit toilets). Backcountry camping allowed (permit required, *see below*). In Montrose: Cedar Creek RV Park (126 Rose La., tel. 970/249–3884 or 877/425–3884; 47 sites; $20–$24; flush toilet, showers, hook-ups), Montrose RV Resort (200 N. Cedar Ave., tel. 888/ 249–9554; 43 sites; $16–$23; flush toilet, showers, hook-ups). **Hotels:** None in park. In Montrose: Best Western Red Arrow Motor Inn (1702 E. Main St., tel. 970/249–9641 or 800/468–9323; 60 rooms; $69–$109). In Crawford: Crawford Country Store & Motel (313 Rte. 92, tel. 970/921–5040; 10 rooms; $40–$65). **Restaurants:** None in park. In Montrose: Red Barn Restaurant (1413 E. Main St., tel. 970/249–9202; $4–$14). **Groceries & Gear:** None in park. In Montrose: Black Canyon Corner Store (U.S. 50 and Rte. 347, tel. 970/249–5113).

FEES, HOURS & REGULATIONS

Entrance fee: $7 per vehicle. Backcountry permits (free) required to go into inner canyon. Colorado state fishing license required. No vehicles or bicycles off roads. No pets in wilderness, leashed pets elsewhere. Fires only in campground grates. South rim open year-round, north rim closed in winter when snowfall is over 4 inches. Gunnison Point Visitor Center open June–Sept., daily 8–6; Oct.–May, 8:30–4.

HOW TO GET THERE

South rim is 15 mi east of Montrose via U.S. 50 and Rte. 347, north rim is 11 mi south of Crawford, off Rte. 92 (6 mi unpaved). Closest airport: Montrose (15 mi).

CONTACTS

Black Canyon of the Gunnison National Park (102 Elk Creek, Gunnison, CO 81230, tel. 970/641–2337, fax 970/249–3127, www.nps.gov/blca). Montrose Chamber of Commerce (1519 E. Main St., Montrose, CO 81401, tel. 970/249–5000, fax 970/249–2907).

Colorado National Monument

In west-central Colorado, near Grand Junction

The towering red monolithic, sheer-walled canyons here reflect the environment and history of this colorful sandstone country. Residents include bighorn sheep, golden eagles, mule deer, and mountain lions. The monument was proclaimed on May 24, 1911.

WHAT TO SEE & DO

Auto touring, bicycling, bird-watching, hiking, picnicking, rock climbing. **Facilities:** Visitor center, scenic drive, overlooks, trails. Bookstore, picnic area. **Programs & Events:** Audiovisual program. **Tips & Hints:** Plan to spend two to five hours at the monument. Busiest May and June, least crowded Dec. and Jan.

FOOD, LODGING & SUPPLIES

Camping: In the park: Saddlehorn (80 sites; $10; flush toilets). Backcountry camping allowed (permit required, *see below*). **Hotels:** None in park. In Grand Junction: Adams Mark (743 Horizon Dr., tel. 970/241–8888; 246 rooms, 14 suites; $79). ✗ **Restaurants:** None in park. In Grand Junction: Dolce Vita (336 Main St., tel. 970/242–8482; $9–15).

FEES, HOURS & REGULATIONS

Entrance fee: $5 per car, $3 per person. Permit required (free) for backcountry camping. Leashed pets only. No pets in backcountry. Park open daily. Visitor center open Memorial Day–Labor Day, daily 8–6; Labor Day–Memorial Day, daily 9–5.

HOW TO GET THERE

From the east, exit I–70 at Horizon Dr. for east entrance. From the west, take Exit 19 to west entrance. Closest airport: Grand Junction (15 mi).

CONTACT

Colorado National Monument (Fruita, CO 81521, tel. 970/858–3617, fax 970/858–0372, www.nps.gov/colm).

Curecanti
National Recreation Area

In southwestern Colorado, west of Gunnison

Three reservoirs, extending for almost 40 mi between the towns of Gunnison and Montrose, form the heart of Curecanti. Blue Mesa Reservoir, stocked with trout and salmon, is a mecca for anglers and water-sports enthusiasts. Bald eagles, and sandhill and whooping cranes, migrate through the area in spring and fall. The area is named after Curecanti, a subchief of the Ute Indians, who lived here when European settlers arrived in the 1800s. The park is administered under a February 11, 1965, cooperative agreement with the Bureau of Reclamation.

WHAT TO SEE & DO

Boating (rentals, Elk Creek and Lake Fork marinas), camping, cross-country skiing, fishing (rentals, Elk Creek and Lake Fork marinas), hiking, ice fishing, picnicking, snowmobiling, snowshoeing, swimming, waterskiing, windsurfing. **Facilities:** 3 visitor centers: Elk Creek, Lake Fork, and Cimarron. Bookstores, fire grates, picnic tables. **Programs & Events:** Ranger-led evening programs and boat tours (Memorial Day–Labor Day). Ranger-led snowshoe walks, hikes, cross-country ski tours (Jan.–Mar., weekends). **Tips & Hints:** You have to hike down 232 stairs to get to the boat dock. Bring water and a jacket. Go May–Aug. for wildflowers, May and Sept. for bird migrations, all year for fishing. Busiest July and Aug., least crowded in Dec. and Mar.

FOOD, LODGING & SUPPLIES

Camping: 10 campgrounds in the park: Cimarron (U.S. 50, 20 mi east of Montrose, tel. 970/249–4074; 22 sites; $10; flush toilets; closed Oct.–mid-May), Dry Gulch (U.S. 50, 17 mi west of Gunnison, tel. 970/641–2337; 10 sites; $10; vault toilets; closed Oct.–mid-May), East Elk Creek (U.S. 50, 16 mi west of Gunnison, tel. 970/641–2337; group site; $30–$50; vault toilets, showers; closed Oct.–mid-May), East Portal (East Portal Rd., below Crystal Dam at bottom of canyon, tel. 970/641–2337; 15 tent sites; $10; vault toilets; closed Oct.–mid-May), Elk Creek (U.S. 50, 16 mi west of Gunnison, tel. 970/641–2337 Ext. 205; 179 sites; $10; flush toilets, showers), Gateview (Off unpaved road off Rte. 149, at extreme southern end of Lake Fork Arm, tel. 970/641–2337; 7 sites; free; vault toilets; closed Oct.–mid-May), Lake Fork (U.S. 50, 27 mi west of Gunnison, tel. 970/641–2337; 87 sites; $10; flush toilets, showers; closed Oct.–mid-May), Ponderosa (Soap Creek Rd., tel. 970/641–2337; 29 sites; $10; vault toilets; closed Oct.–mid-May), Red Creek (Off U.S. 50, 19 mi west of Gunnison, tel. 970/641–2337; 2 sites, group site; $10, $20 group site; vault toilets; closed Oct.–mid-May), Stevens Creek (U.S. 50, 12 mi west of Gunnison, tel. 970/641–2337; 54 sites; $10; vault toilets; closed Oct.–mid-May). Backcountry camping allowed. **Hotels:** None in park. In Gunnison: Mary Lawrence Inn (601 N. Taylor St., tel. 970/641–3343; 7 rooms; $85–$135). **Restaurants:** In the park: Pappy's Restaurant (near Elk Creek Marina, tel. 970/641–0403; $7–$13;

closed Oct.–mid-May). ♿ **Groceries & Gear:** In the park: Gunnison Lakeside Resort Store (28357 W. U.S. 50, tel. 970/641–0477). Elk Creek Marina Store (at Elk Creek Marina, tel. 970/641–0707).

FEES, HOURS & REGULATIONS

Free. Boat permit required ($4 for 2 days, $10 for 14 days, $30 per year) on Blue Mesa Reservoir. Boat tours Memorial Day–Labor Day, daily at 9:30 and 11:30. Colorado fishing license required. Leashed pets only. No bikes or motorized vehicles on trails. Park open daily. Elk Creek Visitor Center open Memorial Day–Sept., daily 8–4:30; Oct.–Apr., hrs vary. Lake Fork and Cimarron visitor centers open Memorial Day–Labor Day, daily 9–4.

HOW TO GET THERE

Park headquarters is 15 mi west of Gunnison on U.S. 50. Closest airport: Gunnison.

CONTACTS

Curecanti National Recreation Area (102 Elk Creek, Gunnison, CO 81230, tel. 970/641–2337, fax 970/641–3127, www.nps.gov/cure). Gunnison County Chamber of Commerce (500 E. Tomichi Ave., Gunnison, CO 81230, tel. 970/641–1501). Montrose Chamber of Commerce (1519 E. Main St., Montrose, CO 81401, tel. 970/249–5515).

Dinosaur National Monument

In northwestern Colorado and northeastern Utah

The memorial is the only park that protects a dinosaur quarry: the Douglass Quarry. The fossil site represents one of the best windows scientists have into the world of upper Jurassic (150-million-year-old) dinosaurs. Archaeological sites in the park represent one of the most complete records of human occupation and development in North America. The site's Green and Yampa river canyons are of great scenic and recreational value. The park was established on October 4, 1915.

WHAT TO SEE & DO

Auto touring, fishing, hiking, rafting, visiting Dinosaur Quarry, whitewater boating. **Facilities:** 2 visitor centers: Dinosaur Quarry (7 mi north of Jensen, UT) and Monument Headquarters (2 mi east of Dinosaur, CO). Self-guided auto tours: Tour of the Tilted Rocks (22 mi, 2 hours, near Dinosaur Quarry), Journey Through Time (31 mi, 4 hours, Monument Headquarters); self-guided nature trails. Bookstores, picnic areas. **Programs & Events:** Quarry and nature talks, guided walks, evening campground talks (June–Aug., daily). **Tips & Hints:** Plan to hike, auto tour, and see the Dinosaur Quarry. Go even in winter to see quarry and do Tour of the Tilted Rocks. Visit in fall for smallest crowds and nicest weather. Busiest June and July, least crowded Dec. and Jan.

FOOD, LODGING & SUPPLIES

Camping: 6 campgrounds in the park: Deerlodge (Off U.S. 40, 53 mi northeast of headquarters; 8 tent sites; free; vault toilets), Echo Park (Harpers Corner Dr., 38 mi north of headquarters; 22 tent sites; $6; vault toilets), Gates of Lodore (Off 318, far north corner of park; 17 sites; $5; vault toilets), Green River (Club Creek Rd., 5 mi east of Dinosaur Quarry; 88 sites; $12; flush toilets; closed Nov.–mid-Apr.), Rainbow Park (Island Park Rd.; 2 tent sites; free; vault toilet), Split Mountain (Club Creek Rd., 4 mi east of Dinosaur Quarry; 4 group sites; $35; flush toilets). Backcountry camping allowed (permit required, *see below*). **Hotels:** None in park. In Craig: Holiday Inn (300 Rte. 13 S, tel. 970/824–4000; 152 rooms, 19 suites; $89). In Vernal, UT: Landmark Inn Bed & Breakfast (288 E. 100 S, tel. 435/781–1800 or 888/738–1800; 7 rooms, 3 suites; $55), Weston Lamplighter (120 E. Main St., Vernal, tel. 435/789–0312; 94 rooms; $39–$95). **✕ Restaurants:** None in park. In Craig: Golden Cavvy (538 Yampa Ave., Craig, tel. 970/824–6038; $10–$20). In Vernal, UT: Stockman's (Weston Plaza, 1684 W. U.S. 40, tel. 435/781–3030; $7–$10). **Groceries & Gear:** None in park. In Vernal, UT: Davis Jubilee (575 W. Main St., tel. 435/789–2001), True Value Hardware (280 W. Main St., tel. 435/781–1556).

FEES, HOURS & REGULATIONS

Entrance fee: $10 per vehicle, $5 for walk-in, bike, motorcycle. Utah or Colorado state fishing license required. White-water boating permit required (tel. 970/374–2468), backcountry camping permit required (free). Park open daily. Dinosaur Quarry Visitor Center open Memorial Day–Labor Day, daily 8–7; Labor Day–Memorial Day, daily 8–4:30. Monument Headquarters Visitor Center open Memorial Day–Labor Day, daily 8–6; Labor Day–Memorial Day, weekdays 8–4:30.

HOW TO GET THERE

The main access points to the park are Dinosaur Quarry, 7 mi north of Jensen, UT, on Rte. 149, and Monument Headquarters, 2 mi east of Dinosaur, CO, on U.S. 40.

CONTACT

Dinosaur National Monument (4545 E. U.S. 40, Dinosaur, CO 81610-9724, tel. 970/374–3000, fax 435/781–7714, www.nps.gov/dino). Vernal Area Chamber of Commerce (134 W. Main St., Vernal, UT, 84078, tel. 435/789–1352, www.dinoland.com).

Florissant Fossil Beds National Monument

In central Colorado, 40 mi west of Colorado Springs

The 6,000-acre monument preserves one of the world's most comprehensive fossil sites of late Eocene life. Some 35 million years ago, a volcanic field erupted and buried a redwood forest at the site in volcanic mud. The ash and mudflows sealed the Florissant lake bottom sediments. Trapped within these sediment layers are thousands of insect species and 140 different plants, along with fish, birds, and mammals. The monument was established on August 25, 1969.

WHAT TO SEE & DO

Cross-country skiing (rentals, Colorado Springs, Woodland Park), hiking, picnicking, snowshoeing (free, park), taking interpretive walks, touring 1878 homestead and petrified redwood forest. **Facilities:** Visitor center, 13 mi of trails, outdoor exhibits, trails, amphitheater, Hornbek Homestead. Book and map sales area, picnic areas. **Programs & Events:** Ranger-led interpretive programs (mid-June–Sept., daily 10–4 on the hour), guided walks (June–Sept.), wildflower walks (mid-June–mid-Aug., Fri. 10:30 AM); special programs on fossils, elk watches, etc. (mid-June–Oct., weekends). Hornbek Homestead Open House (last weekend in July, 2nd weekend in Dec.). **Tips & Hints:** Be prepared for high-altitude (8,400 feet) conditions, rapidly changing weather, and moderate physical activity. Go June and July for wildflowers, Sept. and Oct. for fall colors, fewer people, and elk activity. Busiest July and August, least crowded Dec. and Jan.

FOOD, LODGING & SUPPLIES

🚐 **Camping:** None in park. Near Divide: Mueller State Park (Rte. 67, off U.S. 24, tel. 800/678–2267; $12–$16; 132 sites; flush toilets, showers, hook-ups). 🏨 **Hotels:** None in park. In Cripple Creek: Victor Hotel (4th and Victor Sts., tel. 719/689–3553; 30 rooms; $49–$79). In Lake George: Eleven Mile Motel (38122 U.S. 24, tel. 719/748–3931; 10 cabins; $43–$80). In Woodland Park: The Country Inn (723 W. U.S. 24, tel. 719/687–6277; 60 rooms; $65–$95). ✗ **Restaurants:** None in park. In Florissant: Fossil Inn (2651 U.S. 24, tel. 719/748–1114; $4–$9). 🛒 **Groceries & Gear:** In Florissant: St. Clair Convenience Store (2839 W. U.S. 24, tel. 719/748–8080). In Woodland Park: City Market (Gold Hill Sq. S, tel. 719/687–3592).

FEES, HOURS & REGULATIONS

Entrance fee: $3 adults, free ages 16 and under. Reservations required (tel. 719/748–3253) for four-hour summer programs on wildlife, ecology, and history. No fossil collecting, hunting, off-road vehicle travel. No firearms. No pets in backcountry. No pets, horses, bicycles, or motorized vehicles on trails. Park and visitor center open June–Aug., daily 8–7; Sept.–May, daily 8–4:30.

HOW TO GET THERE

Teller County Rd. 1½ mi south of Florissant, 35 mi west of Colorado Springs on U.S. 24. Closest airport: Colorado Springs.

CONTACTS

Florissant Fossil Beds National Monument (Box 185, Florissant, CO 80816, tel. 719/748–3253, fax 719/748–3164, www.nps.gov/flfo). Woodland Park Chamber of Commerce (200 E. Midland Ave., Woodland Park, CO 80863, tel. 719/687–9885).

Great Sand Dunes National Monument & Preserve

In south-central Colorado, near Alamosa

In a corner of the remote San Luis Valley in the Colorado Rockies, the Great Sand Dunes rise to heights of nearly 750 feet, forming the tallest sand dunes in North America. Covering 30 square mi, the monument provides opportunities for hiking, wilderness camping, and exploring. The monument was proclaimed in 1932.

WHAT TO SEE & DO

Cross-country skiing, dune climbing, four-wheel-drive touring (reservations, tel. 719/378–2222), hiking, horseback riding (rentals, tel. 719/589–4186), picnicking, snowshoeing, walking. **Facilities:** Visitor center, self-guided interpretive trails, outdoor amphitheater. Grills, picnic tables. **Programs & Events:** Self-guided trails, ranger-guided hikes, evening slide programs, interpretive talk (Memorial Day–Labor Day), summer concerts (Sun., July and Aug.). Sand Castle Building–Kite Flying Day (last Sat., June). **Tips & Hints:** Hike dunes with shoes on early or late on summer days. Summer temperatures of 80°F cause sand temperature to rise to 140°F. Go in spring or early summer to visit Medano Creek, which flows at the base of the dunes. Go in July for wildflowers, Aug. and Sept. for prairie sunflowers. Busiest July and Aug., least crowded in Dec. and Jan.

FOOD, LODGING & SUPPLIES

Camping: In the park: Piñon Flats (88 sites; $12; flush toilets). Backcountry camping allowed (permit required, *see below*). Nearby: Great Sand Dunes Oasis (at park entrance, tel. 719/378–2222; 100 sites, 4 cabins; $12–$19, $33 cabins; flush toilets, showers, hook-ups; closed Oct.–Apr.). **Hotels:** None in park. Nearby: Great Sand Dune Lodge (7900 Rte. 150 N, tel. 719/378–2900; 10 rooms; $85; closed Nov.–Apr.) In Alamosa: Best Western Alamosa Inn (2005 Main St., tel. 719/589–2567 or 800/459–5123; 120 rooms; $89). **Restaurants:** None in park. Nearby: Great Sand Dunes Oasis Restaurant (5400 Rte. 150 N, tel. 719/378–2222; $6–$13; closed Nov.–Mar., no dinner Mon.–Thurs.). **Groceries & Gear:** None in park. Nearby: Great Sand Dunes Oasis Store (5400 Rte. 150 N, tel. 719/378–2222; closed Nov.–Mar).

FEES, HOURS & REGULATIONS

Entrance fee: $3 adults, free ages 16 and under. Backcountry permits required (free). Colorado state fishing license required. Leashed pets only. Pets not recommended on hot dunes. Mountain bikes, motor vehicles on established roads only. No mechanical equipment on dunes. No all-terrain vehicles, hunting, firewood gathering. Monument open daily. Visitor center open May–Sept., daily 9–7; Oct.–Apr., daily 9–4:30.

HOW TO GET THERE

34 mi northeast of Alamosa on Rte. 150. Closest airport: Alamosa.

CONTACTS

Great Sand Dunes National Monument & Preserve (11999 Rte. 150, Mosca, CO 81146, tel. 719/378–6300, fax 719/378–6310, www.nps.gov/grsa). Alamosa Chamber of Commerce (Cole Park, Alamosa, CO 81101, tel. 719/589–3681).

Hovenweep
National Monument

In southwestern Colorado, near Cortez,
and in southeast Utah

Hovenweep protects some of the finest examples of ancient stone architecture. The inhabitants of Hovenweep were part of the large farming culture that lived in the area from 500 BC until AD 1300, and their well-preserved stone towers and pueblo-style buildings perch on large boulders and slickrock canyon rims. The monument is noted for its solitude, clear skies, and undeveloped natural character and was proclaimed on March 2, 1923.

WHAT TO SEE & DO

Guided and self-guided tours of cliff dwellings, towers, and pueblos; picnicking. **Facilities:** Ranger station, trails. Bookstore, picnic tables. **Programs & Events:** Ranger-led and self-guided tours. Evening programs (late-May–early-Sept.). **Tips & Hints:** Plan to spend one to two hours visiting ranger station, Square Tower Group area trails, and archaeological sites. Go in spring and fall for best hiking. Bring insect repellent in late May when biting piñon gnats are out. Go before 10 AM in summer to avoid heat. Avoid late-afternoon winter visits because of remote location and possible storms. Gravel roads may become impassable during and after storms. Busiest July and Aug., least crowded Dec. and Jan.

FOOD, LODGING & SUPPLIES

Camping: In the park: Hovenweep Campground (near visitor center; 31 sites; $10; flush toilets). No backcountry camping. **Hotels:** None in park. In Cortez: Anasazi Motor Inn (640 S. Broadway, tel. 970/565–3773 or 800/972–6232; 89 rooms; $57–$71). **Restaurants:** None in park. In Cortez: M&M Family Restaurant & Truck Stop (7006 U.S. 160 S., tel. 970/565–6511; $6–$14). **Groceries:** None in park. In Blanding: Clark's Market (820 S. Main St., tel. 435/678–2721).

FEES, HOURS & REGULATIONS

Free. No climbing on ancient walls or collecting artifacts. Hiking on established trails only. Mountain bikes on roadways only. Ranger Station open 8–5. Trail open sunrise–sunset.

HOW TO GET THERE

From Cortez, CO, the monument can be reached via U.S. 666/160 south and Rte. 6 (Airport Rd.) west. Follow Hovenweep signs. Route includes 12 mi of graded gravel road. From Blanding or Bluff, UT, turn east off U.S. 191 on Rte. 262 to the Hatch Trading Post. Follow Hovenweep signs. Closest airports: Cortez (20 mi), Durango (45 mi).

CONTACTS

Superintendent, Hovenweep National Monument (McElmo Rte., Cortez, CO 81321, tel. 970/562–4282, fax 970/562–4284, www.nps. gov/hove).

Mesa Verde National Park

In southwestern Colorado, near Cortez

Covered mostly by piñon and juniper forest, this 52,080-acre park preserves the cliff dwellings and surface sites of the Anasazi, or Ancestral Puebloan people, who lived in the area between 500 and 1300. Elevations range from 6,400 feet in the deep canyons to 8,500 feet at Park Point. The park was established in 1906 and designated a World Heritage Site in 1978.

WHAT TO SEE & DO

Hiking, touring cliff dwellings, visiting museum. **Facilities:** Far View Visitor Center with ticket sales desk and interpretive exhibits, Chapin Mesa Museum, Morefield Ranger Station (May–Sept.), amphitheaters, kiosk. Gas station, gift shops (Morefield, Fair View, Chapin Mesa), laundry, picnic areas with grates, post office. **Programs & Events:** Tours of Balcony House, Cliff Palace, Long House, and Spruce Tree House; Junior Ranger Program. Interpretive talks at Cliff Palace Overlook, evening campfire programs at Morefield Campground, Far View Lodge Multi-Media Presentation, and Far View Sites Walk (Memorial Day–Labor Day). Luminaria Ceremony (Christmas). **Tips & Hints:** Plan ahead for guided tours, which require tickets from Far View Visitor Center. Take it slow at 7,000 feet elevation. The park's best weather is in May, Sept., and Oct. Go in late May for flowers and late Sept. for fall colors. Busiest June–Aug., least crowded Jan. and Feb.

FOOD, LODGING & SUPPLIES

Camping: In the park: Morefield (tel. 970/533–7731 or 800/449–2288; 435 sites; $19–$55; flush toilets, showers, hook-ups; closed late Nov.–mid-Apr.). No backcountry camping. Group campsites available (reservations required, tel. 970/533–7731). **Hotels:** In the park: Far View Lodge (tel. 970/533–7731 or 800/449–2288; 150 rooms; $93–$101; closed Nov.–Mar.). **Restaurants:** In the park: Far View Terrace (tel. 970/529–4444; $4–$8; closed late-Oct.–early Apr.), Knife's Edge Café (tel. 970/529–4421, $17–$20; closed late-Oct.–early Apr.), Metate Room (tel. 970/529–4422; $6–$25; closed late-Oct.–early Apr.), Spruce Tree Terrace (tel. 970/529–4521; $3–$8), Wetherill Mesa snack bar ($4–$7; closed Labor Day–Memorial Day). **Groceries:** In the park: Spruce Tree Terrace Shop (tel. 970529–4521). In Cortez: Safeway (1580 E. Main St., tel. 970/564–9590). In Hesperus: One Stop Convenience Store (10868 U.S. 160, tel. 970/259–0572).

FEES, HOURS & REGULATIONS

Entrance fee: $10 per private noncommercial vehicle or $5 per person. Balcony House, Cliff Palace, and Long House are accessible only by ranger- or concessionaire-led tour. No hunting. No pets in cliff dwellings, park buildings, or on trails. Leashed pets elsewhere. No mountain biking or trails for bicycles. Bicycling discouraged because of narrow roads. No motorized vehicles on trails. Entrance road open daily. Mesa Top Loop Drive open daily 8–sunset. Wetherill Mesa Road open Memorial Day–Labor Day, daily 9–6. Cliff Palace and Balcony House loop open only for cross-country skiing or walking in winter. Cliff Palace generally open Apr.–Oct., daily. Balcony House open mid-May–mid-Oct., daily. Visitor center open Apr.–Oct., daily 8–5. Chapin Mesa Museum open mid-Apr.–mid-Oct., daily 8–6:30; mid-Oct.–mid-Apr., daily 8–5.

HOW TO GET THERE

36 mi west of Durango and 8 mi east of Cortez via U.S. 160. Closest airports: Cortez (8 mi), Durango (36 mi).

CONTACTS

National Park Service (Box 8, Mesa Verde, CO 81330, tel. 970/529–4465, fax 970/529–4637, www.nps.gov/meve). Cortez Chamber of Commerce (928 E. Main, Cortez, CO 81321, tel. 970/565–3414, fax 970/565–8373). Durango Chamber of Commerce (Box 2587, Durango, CO 81302, tel. 970/247–0312, fax 970/385–7884).

Rocky Mountain National Park

In north-central Colorado, near Estes Park

Spectacular snow-mantled peaks overlooking verdant subalpine valleys and glistening lakes are the draw at this park. Tundra predominates in one-third of the park above the tree line and is a major reason why these peaks and valleys have been protected. More than one-quarter of the plants found here are also native to the Arctic. As elevation rises, ponderosa pine and juniper, Douglas fir, blue spruce, lodgepole pine, and aspen can be found. Wildflowers dot meadows and glades. Englemann spruce and subalpine fir take over in the subalpine ecosystem. Openings in these cool, dark forests produce wildflower gardens where the blue Colorado columbine reigns. At the upper edges of this zone, twisted, grotesque trees hug the ground. Then the trees disappear and you enter fragile alpine tundra. The park was established in 1915 and designated an International Biosphere Reserve in 1976.

WHAT TO SEE & DO

Auto touring, backpacking, cross-country skiing, fishing, hiking, horseback riding, picnicking, snowshoeing, wildlife watching. **Facilities:** 5 visitor centers: Beaver Meadows–park headquarters (2½ mi west of Estes Park on U.S. 36), Kawuneeche (north of Grand Lake on U.S. 34),

Alpine (23 mi west of park headquarters), Fall River (U.S. 34, in Horseshoe Ranch west of Estes Park and east of Fall River entrance station), Lily Lake (7 mi south of Estes Park on Rte. 7). Sheeps Lake information station (2 mi west of Fall River entrance), Moraine Park Museum (Bear Lake Rd. near Beaver Meadows entrance on U.S. 36), Never Summer Ranch (7 mi north of Kawuneechee visitor center on U.S. 34); amphitheaters, auditoriums, roadside pullouts with wayside interpretive exhibits, trails. Book and map sales areas, picnic areas. **Programs & Events:** Junior Ranger Program; ranger-led programs including talks, tours, and hikes. **Tips & Hints:** Watch for signs of altitude sickness (nausea, dizziness, headache, insomnia, rapid heartbeat, and shortness of breath). Park roads are 7,500–12,183 feet above sea level. Get below tree line by early afternoon to avoid lightning. Go June and July to see bighorn sheep, late June and July for wildflowers, mid-July–early Sept. for nontechnical climb up Longs Peak, and Sept–early Oct. for elk-mating season. Busiest July and Aug., least crowded Jan. and Feb.

FOOD, LODGING & SUPPLIES

Camping: 5 campgrounds in the park: Aspenglen (Off U.S. 34, ½ mi south of Fall River entrance, tel. 970/586–1206; 54 sites; $18; flush toilets; closed late Sept.–mid-May), Glacier Basin (Off Bear Lake Rd., tel. 800/365–2267; 150 sites; $18; flush toilets; closed mid-Sept.–mid-May), Longs Peak (Off Rte. 7, tel. 970/586–1206; 26 sites; $18; flush toilets), Moraine Park (Off Bear Lake Rd., tel. 800/365–2267; 225 sites; $18; flush toilets), Timber Creek (Off Trail Ridge Rd., tel. 970/586–1206; 100 sites; $18; flush toilets). Backcountry camping allowed (permit required, *see below*). **Hotels:** None in park. In Estes Park: Apenzell Inn (1100 Big Thompson Ave., tel. 970/586–2023 or 800/475–1125; 28 suites; $95–$175; Nov.–Apr., groups only), Lake Estes Inn & Suites (1650 Big Thompson Ave., tel. 970/586–3386; 47 rooms, 4 suites; $59–$149). In Grand Lake: Gateway Inn (U.S. 34, tel. 970/627–2400 or 877/627–1352; 31 rooms; $76–$150), Mountain Lake Lodge (10480 U.S. 34, tel. 970/627–8448; 10 cabins; $75–$145; closed in Apr. and Nov.). **Restaurants:** In the park: Trail Ridge Store snack bar, next to Alpine Visitor Center. In Estes Park: Nicky's Cattleman Restaurant (1350 U.S. 34, tel. 970/586–5376; $15–$27), Notchtop Bakery & Café (Upper Stanley Village, tel. 970/586–0272; $5–$15). In Grand Lake: The Rapids (209 Rapids La., tel. 970/627–3707; $16–$30). **Groceries & Gear:** None in park. In Estes Park: Rocky Mountain Gateway (3450 Fall River Rd., tel. 970/577–0043), B&B Food Mart (1110 Woodstock Dr., tel. 970/586–5749).

FEES, HOURS & REGULATIONS

Entrance fee: $15 per private vehicle, $5 per hiker, bicyclist, motorcyclist. Free ages 16 and under. Colorado state fishing license required. Backcountry permits required (tel. 970/586–1242 or write Backcountry Office, Rocky Mountain National Park, Estes Park, CO 80517, no telephone reservations May 15–Sept. 30; free Oct.–Apr., $15 May–Sept.). No hunting. No pets beyond roadsides, picnic areas, or campgrounds. Leashed pets only. Bicycles on roads only. No motorized vehicles permitted off-road. Park open daily. Trail Ridge Rd. (U.S. 34) usually closed mid-Oct.–Memorial Day weekend. Beaver Meadows Visitor Center open mid-June–Labor Day, daily 8 AM–9 PM; Labor Day–mid-June, daily 8–5. Kawuneeche Visitor Center open June–Labor Day, daily 7–7; Labor Day–Oct., daily 8–5; Nov.–May, daily 8–4:30. Alpine Visitor Center open late May–mid-Oct. Lily Lake Visitor Center open late June–Aug., daily 8–4:30; May and Sept., weekends only. Fall River Visitor Center open daily 8 AM–9 PM. Moraine Park Museum open May–mid-Oct. Sheep Lakes Information Station open May 15–Aug. 15, daily 9–4:30. Never Summer Ranch open June–Sept., daily 8–5.

HOW TO GET THERE

From the east via U.S. 34, U.S. 36, and Rte. 7; from the west via U.S. 40 and U.S. 34. Closest airports: Denver, CO (70 mi), Cheyenne, WY (91 mi).

CONTACTS

Rocky Mountain National Park (Estes Park, CO 80517, tel. 970/586–1206, www.nps.gov/romo). Estes Park Chamber of Commerce (500 Big Thompson Ave., Estes Park, CO 80517, tel. 800/443–7837 or 970/586–4431, www.rockymtntrav.com/estes). Grand Lake Chamber of Commerce (14700 U.S. 34, Grand Lake, CO 80447, tel. 800/531–1019 or 970/627–3402, www.grandlakechamber.com).

Yucca House National Monument

In southwestern Colorado, near Cortez

This large prehistoric Indian pueblo site west of Mesa Verde is as yet unexcavated. There are no public facilities or services. The monument was proclaimed on December 19, 1919.

CONTACT

Yucca House National Monument (c/o Box 8, Mesa Verde National Park, CO 81330, tel. 970/529–4465, fax 970/529–4637, www.nps.gov/yuho).

See Also

Cache la Poudre River, Continental Divide National Scenic Trail, Pony Express National Historic Trail, Santa Fe National Historic Trail, in Other National Parklands.

CONNECTICUT

Weir Farm National Historic Site

In southwestern Connecticut, in Wilton and Ridgefield

Weir Farm preserves and interprets the farm, summer home, and studio of J. Alden Weir (1852–1919), one of the founders of the impressionist tradition in American art. The site also includes the studio of the sculptor Mahonri Young (1877–1957). The site was authorized on October 31, 1990.

WHAT TO SEE & DO

Fishing, painting, picnicking, touring art studios, walking trails. **Facilities:** Visitor center, studio, trails. Gift shop. **Programs & Events:** Guided tours of historic art studios (year-round, contact park for tour times), self-guided walking tours. Artist-in-Residence and Visiting Artists Programs available through Weir Farm Trust. Children's art classes (July and Aug.). "Jazz in the Garden" (early Sept.), Junior Ranger Program. **Tips & Hints:** Expect to see structures and landscapes that inspired artists to paint rather than an art gallery, which is planned for the future. Wear comfortable walking shoes for hikes. Visit in spring and fall. Busiest in Aug. and Oct., least crowded Jan. and Feb.

FOOD, LODGING & SUPPLIES

Camping: None in park. In Southbury: Kettletown State Park (1400 Georges Hill Rd., tel. 860/283–8088; 68 sites; $13; flush toilets). **Hotels:** None in park. In Danbury: Marriott Residence Inn (22 Segar St., tel. 203/797–1256; 79 rooms; $109–$169). **Restaurants:** None in park. In Ridgefield: Gail's Station House (378 Main St., tel. 203/438–9775; $13–$26). **Groceries:** None in park. In Ridgefield: Ancona's Market (720 Branchville Rd., tel. 203/544–8883).

FEES, HOURS & REGULATIONS

Free. Connecticut state fishing license required. No buses, RVs, or large vehicles in parking lot. No hunting. Dogs on leashes permitted. No mountain or trail bikes, motorized or mechanized equipment on trails. Grounds open daily dawn–dusk. Visitor center open Wed.–Sun. 8:30–5.

HOW TO GET THERE

From I–95 or I–84 take U.S. 7 to Rte. 102 west make a left at Old Branchville Rd., and a left at Nod Hill Rd; go 0.7 mi to visitor center on right. Closest airports: La Guardia in New York City (55 mi), Westchester–White Plains, NY (30 mi).

CONTACTS

Weir Farm National Historic Site (735 Nod Hill Rd., Wilton, CT 06897, tel. 203/834–1896, fax 203/834–2421, www.nps.gov/wefa). Weir Farm Trust (tel. 203/761–9945). Coastal Fairfield County Convention & Visitors Bureau (20 Marshall St., Suite 102, South Norwalk, CT 06854, tel. 203/840–0770 or 800/866–7925, www.coastalct.com).

See Also

Appalachian National Scenic Trail, West Virginia. *Farmington River (west branch)* and *Quinebaug & Shetucket Rivers Valley National Heritage Corridor,* in Other National Parklands.

DISTRICT OF COLUMBIA

Constitution Gardens

On the National Mall

The 50-acre garden, built during the U.S. Bicentennial in 1976, is a tribute to the founding of the nation with a memorial to the 56 signers of the Declaration of Independence. Included in the gardens are a 6½-acre lake and a 1-acre island. The site was authorized in 1974 and dedicated in 1978.

WHAT TO SEE & DO

Touring garden. **Facilities:** Trails, memorial. Bookstores at nearby Lincoln Memorial, Washington Monument, and Jefferson Memorial, benches. **Programs & Events:** Ranger-led interpretive programs and talks, walking tours (various sites around the Mall). Constitution Day Naturalization Ceremony (Sept. 17). Special events available. **Tips & Hints:** Plan to spend a day or more visiting the Mall. Busiest Apr. and May, least crowded Jan. and Feb.

FEES & HOURS

Free. Tourmobile stops at 25 sites along the Mall and Arlington National Cemetery. Tourmobile fee: $16 adults, $7 ages 3–11. Gardens open daily.

HOW TO GET THERE

Between the Washington Monument and the Lincoln Memorial, bordered by Constitution Ave., 17th St., and the Reflecting Pool; nearest Metro subway stations: Foggy Bottom or Farragut West on the Blue and Orange lines. Closest airport: Reagan Washington National.

CONTACTS

National Capital Parks–Central (The National Mall, 900 Ohio Dr. SW, Washington, DC 20242, tel. 202/426–6841, www.nps.gov/coga). Arlington National Cemetery (tel. 202/554–5100 or 888/868–7707, www.arlingtoncemetery.org). Tourmobile (tel. 202/554–5100 or 888/868–7707, www.tourmobile.com).

Ford's Theatre National Historic Site

In Washington, D.C.

On the night of April 14, 1865, President Abraham Lincoln was shot in Ford's Theatre by John Wilkes Booth. The president died in the early hours of April 15 in the small back bedroom of a boardinghouse across the street. An act of April 7, 1866, provided for purchase of Ford's Theatre by the Federal Government. It was redesignated as Lincoln Museum in 1932 and Ford's Theatre (Lincoln Museum) in 1965. The house where Lincoln died was authorized in 1896. Both were transferred to the Park Service in 1933 and combined as an historic site in 1970.

WHAT TO SEE & DO

Touring theater, museum, and boardinghouse. **Facilities:** Theater, museum, House Where Lincoln Died (Petersen's House). Bookstore. **Programs & Events:** 15-minute narratives (daily at 9:15, 10:15, 11:15, 2:15, 3:15, and 4:15). Theatrical productions (Sept.–June, Tues.–Sun. 7:30 PM; matinees Thurs. 1:30; Sun. 2:30). **Tips & Hints:** Busiest Apr. and May, least crowded Jan. and Feb.

FEES & HOURS

Free. Site open daily 9–5. Theater closes during matinees (Thurs. and Sun. afternoons) and rehearsals; museum and Petersen House remain open.

HOW TO GET THERE

In downtown Washington, DC, at 511 10th St. NW, between E and F Sts. Nearest Metro subway station is Metro Center at 11th and G Sts.

CONTACT

Ford's Theatre National Historic Site (511 10th St. NW, Washington, DC 20004, tel. 202/426–6924, www.nps.gov/foth).

Franklin Delano Roosevelt Memorial

Along the Potomac River

The outdoor memorial to the nation's 32nd president is divided into four outdoor galleries, or rooms, one for each of FDR's terms in office. The granite memorial includes sculptures that depict the launching of the New Deal, a fireside chat, an urban breadline, FDR and his dog Fala, and Eleanor Roosevelt's role as First Lady and human-rights advocate. An FDR Memorial Commission was established in 1955, and the memorial was dedicated in 1997.

WHAT TO SEE & DO

Touring memorial. **Facilities:** Memorial, ranger office with interpretive panels. Bookstore. **Programs & Events:** Ranger-led interpretive programs. **Tips & Hints:** Take Metrorail or Tourmobile to avoid street parking. Go in early spring or fall for best weather, early to mid-April for cherry blossoms.

FEES, HOURS & REGULATIONS

Free. Tourmobile fee: $16 adults, $7 ages 3–11; access points throughout National Mall or Arlington National Cemetery. Leashed pets only.

No food or drink. No smoking, bicycling, skating, jogging, picnicking, or sports activity. Rangers on duty daily 8 AM–midnight. Parking access open daily 8 AM–1 AM. Bookstore open daily 8 AM–10 PM.

HOW TO GET THERE

At the junction of Ohio and W. Basin Drs., in W. Potomac Park, midway between the Lincoln and Jefferson memorials. Nearest Metro subway stations: Smithsonian Institution, Arlington National Cemetery, Foggy Bottom (all 1¼ mi). Closest airport: Reagan Washington National.

CONTACTS

National Capital Parks–Central (The National Mall, 900 Ohio Dr. SW, Washington, DC 20242, tel. 202/426–6841, www.nps.gov/fdrm). Washington Convention and Visitors Association (1212 New York Ave. NW, Suite 600, Washington, DC 20005-3992, tel. 202/789–7000). Tourmobile (tel. 202/554–5100 or 888/868–7707, www.tourmobile.com).

Frederick Douglass National Historic Site

In the southeast part of the city

Frederick Douglass, the nation's leading 19th-century African-American spokesman, made his home here from 1877 to 1895. The site outlines Douglass's efforts to abolish slavery and his struggle for human rights, equal rights, and civil rights for all oppressed people. Among his achievements, Douglass was U.S. minister to Haiti in 1889. Cedar Hill, his 21-room mansion on 8½ acres, has been preserved with 90% of its original furnishings. The site was authorized as the Frederick Douglass Home in 1962 and redesignated in 1988.

WHAT TO SEE & DO

Touring house, watching film. **Facilities:** Visitor center, house. Bookstore. **Programs & Events:** Film (every ½ hour), interpretive talks, guided house tours (throughout day, reservations available, tel. 800/967–2283). **Tips & Hints:** Busiest Jan.–June, least crowded July–Sept.

FEES & HOURS

Home tours: $2 per person. Site open mid-Oct.–mid-Apr., daily 9–4; mid-Apr.–mid-Oct., daily 9–5.

HOW TO GET THERE

Take the 11th St. Bridge (toward Anacostia) to Martin Luther King Ave. Go 3 blocks, turn left on W St. Follow W St. for 4 blocks to the visitor center parking lot on right.

CONTACT

Frederick Douglass National Historic Site (1411 W St. SE, Washington, DC 20020-4813, tel. 202/426–5961, www.nps.gov/frdo).

Korean War Veterans Memorial

On the National Mall

The garden memorial to the veterans of the Korean War (1950–54) includes a black granite wall with murals by Louis Nelson of New York City, a reflecting pool, and 19 statues of infantrymen by sculptor Frank C. Gaylord. The memorial was authorized in 1986 and dedicated in 1995.

WHAT TO SEE & DO

Viewing memorial. **Facilities:** Information kiosk with computer to look up and print out information on soldiers killed or missing in action during Korean War. Bookstore in Lincoln Memorial. **Programs & Events:** Ranger-led interpretive talks and programs. **Tips & Hints:** Plan to spend a day or more touring the National Mall. Take the Tourmobile, a narrated shuttle tour of 25 Mall sites and Arlington National Cemetery.

FEES, HOURS & REGULATIONS

Free. No biking or in-line skating at memorial. Memorial open daily 8 AM–midnight. Bookstore at the Lincoln Memorial open daily 8:30 AM–10 PM. Tourmobile fee: $16 adults, $7 ages 3–11; access points throughout National Mall or Arlington National Cemetery.

HOW TO GET THERE

Off Independence Ave. and Daniel French Dr., across from the Lincoln Memorial. Nearest Metro subway station: Foggy Bottom, at 23rd and I Sts. NW, on the Blue and Orange lines. Limited parking available on Ohio Dr. SW, off Independence Ave.

CONTACTS

National Capital Parks–Central (The National Mall, 900 Ohio Dr. SW, Washington, DC 20242, tel. 202/426–6841, www.nps.gov/kwvm). Tourmobile (tel. 202/554–5100 or 888/868–7707, www.tourmobile.com).

Lincoln Memorial

On the National Mall

Constructed as a tribute to the president who led the country through its greatest trial—the Civil War—the Lincoln Memorial houses the famous statue that is 19 feet tall, 19 feet wide, and carved from 28 blocks of white Georgia marble. The memorial was authorized in 1911, dedicated in 1922, and transferred to the Park Service in 1933.

WHAT TO SEE & DO

Viewing memorial. **Facilities:** Memorial. Bookstore. **Programs & Events:** Ranger-led talks and interpretive programs. Ranger-led walking tours (June–Aug.). **Tips & Hints:** Plan to spend a day or more visiting the Mall. Ride Tourmobile for narrated shuttle tour of 25 Mall sites and Arlington National Cemetery. Busiest Apr. and May, least crowded Jan. and Feb.

FEES, HOURS & REGULATIONS

Free. No biking or in-line skating in memorial. Memorial open daily 8 AM–midnight. Bookstore hours daily 8:30 AM–10 PM. Tourmobile fee: $16 adults, $7 ages 3–11; access points throughout National Mall or Arlington National Cemetery.

HOW TO GET THERE

Off Constitution Ave. and 23rd St. NW. Nearest Metro subway station: Foggy Bottom, 23rd St., and I St. NW, on the Blue and Orange lines.

CONTACTS

National Capital Parks–Central (The National Mall, 900 Ohio Dr. SW, Washington, DC 20242, tel. 202/426–6841, www.nps.gov/linc). Tourmobile (tel. 202/554–5100 or 888/868–7707, www.tourmobile.com).

Lyndon Baines Johnson Memorial Grove on the Potomac

Along the Potomac River

This memorial to the nation's 36th president, in Lady Bird Johnson Park, consists of a serpentine pattern of walks and trails leading to a granite monolith. The trails are shaded by hundreds of white pine and dogwood trees and framed by azalea and rhododendron bushes. Thousands of yellow daffodils bloom in season. The focal point of the grove is a tall, rugged monolith of sunset-red granite that stands 19 feet high and weighs 43 tons. Spaced along the walkway surrounding the stone, four granite markers bear quotations from Lyndon B. Johnson's speeches. The site was authorized in 1973 and dedicated in 1976.

WHAT TO SEE & DO

Fishing, picnicking, strolling. **Facilities:** Grove, granite memorial. Picnic tables. **Programs & Events:** Ranger-led talks and guided tours. **Tips & Hints:** Busiest June and July, least crowded Nov.–Jan.

FEES, HOURS & REGULATIONS

Free. Washington, DC, fishing license required. Grove open daily during daylight hours.

HOW TO GET THERE

In Lady Bird Johnson Park, on the George Washington Memorial Pkwy. west of I–95 and the 14th St. Bridge. Parking at nearby Columbia Island Marina. Closest airport: Reagan Washington National.

CONTACT

Lyndon Baines Johnson Memorial Grove on the Potomac (c/o George Washington Memorial Pkwy., Turkey Run Park, McLean, VA 22101-1717, tel. 703/289–2500, www.nps.gov/gwmp).

Mary McLeod Bethune Council House National Historic Site

In Washington, DC

Commemorated here are the life of Mary McLeod Bethune (1875–1955) and the organization she founded, the National Council of Negro Women. The site includes her three-story Victorian home, which housed the council, and a two-story carriage house in which the National Archives for Black Women's History is located. Bethune founded Bethune-Cookman College in Daytona Beach, Florida, and served as an adviser on African-American affairs to four presidents. The site was authorized in 1991.

WHAT TO SEE & DO

Touring home. **Facilities:** Visitor center, home, carriage house (by appointment only). Bookstore, research facility (by appointment only). **Programs & Events:** Ranger-guided tours. Black History Month (Feb.), Women's History Month (Mar.), Annual Open House for Dupont-Kalorama Museum Walk Weekend (1st full weekend, June). Martin Luther King, Jr. Birthday Commemoration (Jan. 19), Bethune Birthday Celebration (July 10). Other special programs. **Tips & Hints:** Busiest June and July, least crowded Oct. and Nov.

FEES & HOURS

Free. Site and visitor center open Mon.–Sat. 10–4.

HOW TO GET THERE

In northwest Washington, DC, on Vermont Ave. Nearest metro stations: McPherson Sq. on the Blue and Orange lines; U St. Cardozo on the Green line.

CONTACT

The National Park Service, Mary McLeod Bethune Council House National Historic Site (1318 Vermont Ave. NW, Washington, DC 20005, tel. 202/673–2402, fax 202/673–2414, www.nps.gov/mamc).

National Capital Parks

In Washington, DC

The District of Columbia has more than 300 parks, parkways, and reservations, including Battleground National Cemetery, the President's Park (Lafayette Park north of the White House and the Ellipse south of the White House), and a variety of military fortifications and green areas. The park was authorized in 1790 and transferred to the Park Service in 1933.

WHAT TO SEE & DO

Bicycling, fishing, golfing, ice-skating, jogging, picnicking, playing team sports, paddleboating, sightseeing, swimming. **Facilities:** More than 300 parks, parkways, and reserved lands around the capital. **Programs & Events:** Outdoor ice-skating at National Gallery of Art Sculpture Garden Ice Rink (7th St. and Constitution Ave., tel. 202/289–3360) and Pershing Park Ice Rink (14th St. and Pennsylvania Ave., tel. 202/737–6938). Hispanic Heritage Month (Sept. 15–Oct. 15), Annual Civil Rights Film Festival (mid-Jan.). **Tips & Hints:** Busiest in July and Oct., least crowded Jan. and Feb. Use Tourmobile to visit 25 major parks and sites in central Washington, DC.

FEES, HOURS & REGULATIONS

National Gallery of Art Sculpture Garden Ice Rink: $6 adults, $5 ages 12 and under, $2.50 for skate rentals; open Mon.–Thurs. 10 AM–11 PM, Fri. and Sat. 10 AM–midnight, Sun. 11 AM–9 PM. Pershing Park Ice Rink: $6 adults, $5 ages 12 and under, $2.50 for skate rentals; open daily 3 PM–11 PM. Tourmobile fee: $16 adults, $7 ages 3–11; access points throughout National Mall or Arlington National Cemetery.

HOW TO GET THERE

The 300 parks are located throughout the District of Columbia. Closest airport: Reagan Washington National.

CONTACTS

National Capital Region (1100 Ohio Dr. SW, Washington, DC 20242-0001, tel. 202/619–7222, www.nps.gov/nacc or www.nps.gov/nace). Washington Convention & Visitors Association (1212 New York Ave. NW, Suite 600, Washington, DC 20005-3992, tel. 202/789–7000). Tourmobile (tel. 202/554–5100 or 888/868–7707, www.tourmobile.com).

National Mall

In Washington, DC

This tree-lined, 146-acre park stretches from the Capitol to the Lincoln Memorial and is a principal axis in the plan developed by French engineer Pierre L'Enfant in 1790. The Mall was authorized in 1790 and transferred to the Park Service in 1933.

WHAT TO SEE & DO

Attending outdoor events, jogging, picnicking, playing sports, strolling. **Facilities:** Mall. Bookstores. **Programs & Events:** Ranger-led interpretive programs, walks, talks at surrounding monuments and memorials. **Tips & Hints:** Plan to spend a day or more to visit the Mall, monuments, memorials, and museums. Consider taking Tourmobile, a narrated shuttle tour to 25 sites on the Mall. Busiest June and July, least crowded Jan. and Feb.

FEES & HOURS

Free. Mall open daily. Memorials and monuments on Mall open daily 8 AM–midnight. Tourmobile fee: $16 adults, $7 ages 3–11; access points throughout National Mall or Arlington National Cemetery.

HOW TO GET THERE

The Mall is in downtown Washington, DC, between Constitution and Independence Aves. The Smithsonian Metro stop comes out on the National Mall.

CONTACTS

National Capital Parks–Central (The National Mall, 900 Ohio Dr. SW, Washington, DC 20242, tel. 202/426–6841, www.nps.gov/nama). Tourmobile (tel. 202/554–5100 or 888/868–7707, www.tourmobile.com).

Pennsylvania Avenue National Historic Site

Between the White House and U.S. Capitol

The nation celebrates the election of a president every four years with a parade on the world-famous 1¼-mi stretch of Pennsylvania Avenue. Other national heroes and foreign leaders have been honored with parades and motorcades here as well. Known as "America's Main Street," the site also encompasses Ford's Theatre National Historic Site, several blocks of the Washington commercial district—including the Old Post Office—and a number of federal structures. The site was authorized on September 30, 1965.

WHAT TO SEE & DO

Attending theatrical performances, ice-skating, shopping, sightseeing, touring National Archives, FBI, National Museum of American Art, and National Gallery. **Facilities:** Museums, theaters, and stores. **Programs & Events:** Ranger-led tours of the Old Post Office Tower. **Tips & Hints:** Consider riding Tourmobile for narrated shuttle tour of 25 Mall sites and Arlington National Cemetery. Busiest in July and Aug., least crowded Jan. and Feb.

FEES & HOURS

Free. Site open daily. Tourmobile fee: $16 adults, $7 ages 3–11; access points throughout National Mall or Arlington National Cemetery.

HOW TO GET THERE

The site is in downtown Washington, between the Capitol and the White House, and includes the architecturally and historically significant areas in the Pennsylvania Ave. area. There are Metro stations at Federal Triangle and Metro Center.

CONTACTS

National Capital Parks–Central (The National Mall, 900 Ohio Dr. SW, Washington, DC 20242, tel. 202/426–6841, www.nps.gov/paav). Tourmobile (tel. 202/554–5100 or 888/868–7707, www.tourmobile.com).

Potomac Heritage
National Scenic Trail

Along the Potomac River between Virginia and Maryland; in Washington, DC; and in southern Pennsylvania.

The Potomac Heritage National Scenic Trail, one of 23 national historic and scenic trails in the National Trails System, is a developing network of existing, planned, and proposed routes for nonmotorized travel, on water as well as land, between the Chesapeake Bay and the Laurel Highlands of western Pennsylvania—a corridor of approximately 425 mi. The trail includes the 17-mi Mount Vernon Trail, managed by George Washington Memorial Parkway; the 184.5-mi C&O Canal Towpath, managed by C&O Canal National Historical Park; and the 70-mi Laurel Highlands Hiking Trail, managed by the Pennsylvania Dept. of Conservation and Recreation. In addition, the Great Allegheny Passage, a National Recreation Trail between Cumberland, Maryland, and Pittsburgh, Pennsylvania, connects the Towpath with the Laurel Highlands Trail. The Potomac River Water Trail is becoming a major feature of Potomac Heritage Trail corridor. The trail system was established on March 28, 1983.

WHAT TO SEE & DO

Bicycling, boating, cross-country skiing, hiking, horseback riding, visiting historic sites. **Facilities:** Visitor Information Center (Harpers Ferry). **Programs & Events:** Potomac River sojourn, guided hikes, bicycle tours. **Tips & Hints:** Occasional trail flooding—check local weather conditions.

CONTACTS

Potomac Heritage National Scenic Trail (c/o Potomac Heritage National Scenic Trail Office, National Park Service, Box B, Harpers Ferry, WV 25425, tel. 304/535–4014, www.nps.gov/pohe). Potomac Heritage Trail Association (c/o Potomac Appalachian Trail Club, 118 Park St. SE, Vienna, VA, tel. 703/242–0693).

Rock Creek Park

In the northwest part of the city

One of the nation's oldest national parks, Rock Creek is home to more than 1,700 acres of hardwood forest, meadows, and streams that form a ribbon of green through the nation's capital. The park offers hiking, bicycling, horseback riding, picnicking, and boating. A nature center and planetarium, historic Pierce Mill, 18th-century Old Stone House, and the remains of Civil War forts round out the area's natural and cultural attractions. The park was authorized in 1890 and transferred to the Park Service in 1933.

WHAT TO SEE & DO

Attending concerts, bicycling (rentals, Thompson's Boat House and in city), bird-watching, boating (rentals, Thompson's Boat House), exercise trails and recreational fields, fishing, golfing (rentals, Rock Creek Golf Course), hiking, horseback riding (rentals, Rock Creek Horse Center), jogging, kite flying, painting and sketching, picnicking, playing tennis, touring the forts, Carter Barron Amphitheatre, Old Stone House, Pierce Mill, and the Pierce Barn (weekends, noon–4). **Facilities:** Nature Center and Planetarium with exhibits, children's nature discovery room, and auditorium (5200 Glover Rd. NW), Pierce Mill (Tilden St. and Beach Dr. NW), Old Stone House (3051 M St. NW, Georgetown), forts, trails, golf course, recreation fields, amphitheater, tennis courts. Book sales areas, picnic pavilions, tables, grills. **Programs & Events:** Ranger-guided nature walks and planetarium shows (Nature Center); ranger-guided tours (Pierce Mill and Old Stone House). **Tips & Hints:** The best seasons to visit are spring and fall. Busiest July and Aug., least crowded Dec. and Jan.

FEES, HOURS & REGULATIONS

Free. Washington, DC, fishing license required. Leashed pets only. Bikes on paved bike trails and roads only. No collecting rocks, firewood, animals, plants, natural or cultural objects. Park open daily during daylight hours. Traffic permitted all the time. No trucks or buses. Nature Center open Wed.–Sun. 9–5.

HOW TO GET THERE

In Washington, DC, at Military Rd. NW and Glover Rd. NW, about 1 mi east of Connecticut Ave. NW and ½ mi west of 16th St. NW. The Friendship Heights Metro station is nearest the Nature Center, the Van Ness Metro station is nearest the Pierce Mill, and the Foggy Bottom Metro station is nearest the Old Stone House.

CONTACTS

Rock Creek Park (3545 Williamsburg La. NW, Washington, DC 20008-1207, tel. 202/895–6000; 202/895–6239 recorded events line, fax 202/282–7612, www.nps.gov/rocr).

Theodore Roosevelt Island

On the Potomac River

This 89-acre wooded island is a memorial to the outdoorsman, naturalist, and visionary who was the 26th president. The outdoor memorial captures the spirit of this energetic president. Trails lead through the marsh, swamp, and forest on the island. The site was authorized in 1932 and transferred to the Park Service in 1933. The memorial was dedicated on October 27, 1967.

WHAT TO SEE & DO

Bird-watching, fishing, hiking, touring memorial, jogging, walking. **Facilities:** Kiosk, memorial, wayside exhibits, trails, 2,800-foot boardwalk through swamp. **Programs & Events:** Guided tours (reservations required). Ranger-led programs and tours. Roosevelt Birthday Celebration (Oct.). **Tips & Hints:** Busiest July and Aug., least crowded Nov.–Jan.

FEES, HOURS & REGULATIONS

Free. Washington, DC, fishing permit required. Island open during daylight hours.

HOW TO GET THERE

The parking area is reached via the northbound lane of the George Washington Memorial Pkwy. on the Virginia side of the Potomac River in Rosslyn. A footbridge connects the island to the Virginia shore. Visitors may also exit the Metro at Rosslyn, take a 20-minute walk to the Key Bridge, and join the Mount Vernon Trail to the island. Closest airport: Reagan Washington National.

CONTACT

Theodore Roosevelt Island (c/o George Washington Memorial Pkwy., Turkey Run Park, McLean, VA 22101-1717, tel. 703/289–2500, www. nps.gov/this).

Thomas Jefferson Memorial

Near the Potomac River

Thomas Jefferson, author of the Declaration of Independence and third U.S. president, is memorialized here. The interior walls present inscriptions from his writings. Rudolph Evans sculpted the statue. John Russell Pope and his associates Otto Eggers and Daniel Higgins designed the memorial. The memorial was authorized in 1934 and dedicated in 1943.

WHAT TO SEE & DO

Attending ranger interpretive programs and talks, viewing memorial. **Facilities:** Bookstore. **Programs & Events:** Ranger-led interpretive talks (daily). Ranger-led walking tours of National Mall (Memorial Day–Labor Day). Cherry Blossom Festival (early Apr.). **Tips & Hints:** Consider taking Tourmobile, a daily narrated shuttle tour to 25 major sites on the National Mall and in Arlington National Cemetery. Busiest Apr.–July, least crowded Jan. and Feb.

FEES, HOURS & REGULATIONS

Free. No in-line skating or bicycling in memorial. Memorial open daily 8 AM–midnight. Tourmobile fee: $16 adults, $7 ages 3–11; access points throughout National Mall or Arlington National Cemetery.

HOW TO GET THERE

The memorial is on the south bank of the Tidal Basin south of the National Mall. A parking lot at the memorial provides two-hour parking. The Smithsonian Metro stop comes out on the National Mall.

CONTACTS

National Capital Parks–Central (The National Mall, 900 Ohio Dr. SW, Washington, DC 20242, tel. 202/426–6841, www.nps.gov/thje). Tourmobile (tel. 202/554–5100 or 888/868–7707, www.tourmobile.com).

Vietnam Veterans Memorial

On the National Mall

The names of more than 58,000 soldiers who were killed in the Vietnam War or are missing are engraved in the black granite walls of the memorial. The memorial's mirrorlike surface reflects the surrounding trees, lawns, monuments, and people, creating a quiet place to remember and honor all Vietnam veterans. The memorial also includes the Statue of Three Servicemen and the Vietnam Women's Memorial. The memorial was authorized in 1980 and dedicated in 1982.

WHAT TO SEE & DO

Viewing and finding names on memorial. **Facilities:** Memorials, statue. Bookstore in Lincoln Memorial. **Programs & Events:** Ranger-led talks and programs. **Tips & Hints:** Plan to spend a day or more visiting all the sites on the National Mall. Consider taking Tourmobile, a daily narrated shuttle tour to 25 major sites on the National Mall and in Arlington National Cemetery. Busiest Apr. and May, least crowded Jan. and Feb.

FEES, HOURS & REGULATIONS

Free. No bicycling or in-line skating at memorial. Memorial open daily 8 AM–midnight. Tourmobile fee: $16 adults, $7 ages 3–11; access points throughout National Mall or Arlington National Cemetery.

HOW TO GET THERE

Off Constitution Ave. and 23rd St. NW. Nearest metro subway station: Foggy Bottom, 23rd and I St. NW, on the Blue and Orange lines.

CONTACTS

National Capital Parks–Central (The National Mall, 900 Ohio Dr. SW, Washington, DC 20242, tel. 202/426–6841, www.nps.gov/vive). Tourmobile (tel. 202/554–5100 or 888/868–7707, www.tourmobile.com).

Washington Monument

On the National Mall

The graceful, delicate obelisk rises 555 feet to dominate the capital skyline and serves as a memorial to the nation's first president and leader of the American Revolution, George Washington. The monument was authorized in 1848, dedicated in 1885, and transferred to the Park Service in 1933.

WHAT TO SEE & DO

Taking elevator to top of monument. **Facilities:** Monument and grounds. Bookstore. **Programs & Events:** Elevator rides to top of monument, ranger-led interpretive programs and talks (Apr.–Labor Day, daily 8 AM–midnight; Labor Day–Mar., daily 8–5). **Tips & Hints:** Plan to spend a day or more visiting sites on the Mall. Consider taking

Tourmobile, a daily narrated shuttle tour to 25 major sites on the National Mall and in Arlington National Cemetery. Busiest June and July, least crowded Jan.–Mar.

FEES & HOURS

Free. Advance reservations for elevator ride available (tel. 800/505–5040 or pick up at ticket kiosk on 15th St., at base of monument). Monument open 1st Sun. in Apr.–Labor Day, daily 8 AM–midnight (last trip up 11:45); Labor Day–1st Sun. in Apr., daily 9–5 (last trip up 4:45). Tourmobile fee: $16 adults, $7 ages 3–11; access points throughout National Mall or Arlington National Cemetery.

HOW TO GET THERE

In downtown Washington, DC, on the National Mall, midway between the U.S. Capitol and the Lincoln Memorial. The Metro stops at the Smithsonian on the Mall, and there's a parking lot at the monument.

CONTACTS

National Capital Parks–Central (The National Mall, 900 Ohio Dr. SW, Washington, DC 20042, tel. 202/426–6841, www.nps.gov/wamo). Arlington National Cemetery (tel. 202/554–5100 or 888/868–7707, www. arlingtoncemetery.org). Tourmobile (tel. 202/554–5100 or 888/868–7707, www.tourmobile.com).

White House

North of the Washington Monument

Every president except George Washington has lived, entertained, and conducted the nation's business at the White House. The White House was transferred to the National Park Service on August 10, 1933.

WHAT TO SEE & DO

Touring White House. **Facilities:** Visitor center, White House. **Programs & Events:** Self-guided tours of White House grounds only, guided garden tours, limited guided tours of interior, living-history programs, military concert series. **Tips & Hints:** Call in advance to find out updated tour information. Busiest Apr.–Aug., least crowded Jan. and Feb.

FEES, HOURS & REGULATIONS

Free. Due to heightened security, tours of the White House have been restricted. Call 202/619–7222 for tour information. No photos or videotaping. No strollers (strollers stored at visitor center). No animals, oversize backpacks, balloons, food or beverages, chewing gum, electric stun guns, fireworks or firecrackers, guns or ammunition, knives with blades longer than 3 inches, mace, smoking, or suitcases. White House Visitor Center open daily 7:30–4. Tourmobile fee: $16 adults, $7 ages 3–11; access points throughout National Mall or Arlington National Cemetery.

HOW TO GET THERE

The White House is at 1600 Pennsylvania Ave. NW, in downtown Washington, DC. Closest Metro station: Federal Triangle on Blue and Orange lines.

CONTACTS

The White House (c/o National Capital Region, 1100 Ohio Dr. SW, Room 344, Washington, DC 20242, tel. 202/208–1631, www.nps.gov/whho or www.whitehouse.gov). Tourmobile (tel. 202/554–5100 or 888/868–7707, www.tourmobile.com).

See Also

Sewall-Belmont House National Historic Site, in Other National Parklands.

FLORIDA

Big Cypress National Preserve

In the southern part of the state, near Ochopee

The preserve conserves and protects the natural scenic, floral and faunal, and recreational values of the Big Cypress Watershed. The importance of this watershed to the *Everglades National Park* (*see separate entry*) was a major consideration for its establishment. The name Big Cypress does not refer to the size of the trees, but to the vast number of cypress that covers about one-third of the 729,000-acre preserve. The preserve is also home to the endangered Florida panther and red-cockaded woodpecker. The preserve was authorized on October 11, 1974.

WHAT TO SEE & DO

Bicycling, bird-watching, fishing, hiking, hunting, off-road-vehicle driving (permit required, *see below*), picnicking, scenic driving, wildlife viewing. **Facilities:** Visitor center, scenic loop roads, trails. Bookstore, picnic areas. **Programs & Events:** Ranger-led wet walks, biking, canoeing excursions, campfire programs (Dec.–Mar.). **Tips & Hints:** The preserve's climate is subtropical, with mild winters and hot, wet summers. Wear long sleeves, pants, sturdy shoes, and bug repellent when hiking. Allow at least two hours to drive the Loop Rd., an hour for the Turner River–Birdon Rd. loop. Go to visitor center for information on closing of areas to off-road vehicles, hunting, and road conditions. Go in winter (dry season) for best hiking conditions along Florida Trail. Busiest Feb.–Dec., least crowded in June and Sept.

FOOD, LODGING & SUPPLIES

Camping: 5 campgrounds in the park: Bear Island (40 sites; $14; no water), Midway (26 sites; $14; no water), Mitchell's Landing (15 sites; $14; no water), Monument (26 sites; $14; flush toilets, cold showers), Pinecrest (10 sites; $14; no water). Backcountry camping allowed. **Hotels:** None in park. In Everglades City: Ivey House (107 Camellia St., tel. 239/695–3299; 27 rooms, 1 cottage; $50–$125). **Restaurants:** None in park. In Everglades City: Oar House Restaurant (305 Collier Ave., tel. 239/695–3535; $9–$18). **Groceries:** None in park. In Everglades City: Gator Express (203 Collier Ave., tel. 239/695–3937), Subway Everglades Convenience Store (31990 Tamiami Trail E, tel. 239/695–3340).

FEES, HOURS & REGULATIONS

Free. ORV permits: $50 a year, vehicle inspection required. Florida state fishing and hunting license required. Park open daily. Visitor center open daily 8:30–4:30.

HOW TO GET THERE

The visitor center is on Tamiami Trail (U.S. 41), halfway between Naples and Miami. Closest airports: Miami International (75 mi), Ft. Myers International (70 mi).

CONTACTS

Big Cypress National Preserve (HCR61, Box 110, Ochopee, FL 34141, tel. 239/695–4111, www.nps.gov/bicy). Everglades City Chamber of Commerce (Box 130, at corner of Rte. 29 and U.S. 41, Everglades City, tel. 800/914–6355 or 239/695–3941).

Biscayne National Park

In the southeast part of the state, near Homestead

The 180,000-acre park, 95% of which is water, is a wonderful place to boat, sail, fish, snorkel, dive, and camp. The park protects a deep green forest of mangroves, and its water provides habitat for the Florida spiny lobster, shrimp, fish, sea turtles, and manatees. Its stunning emerald islands, fringed with mangroves, contain tropical hardwood forests, and its coral reefs support a kaleidoscope of fish, plants, and other animals. The park was established as a national monument in 1968 and redesignated a park in 1980.

WHAT TO SEE & DO

Boating (rentals, Miami and Key Largo), canoeing (Convoy Point), diving, fishing, sailing, snorkeling. **Facilities:** Visitor center and 3 videos in English and Spanish (Convoy Point, 9 mi east of Homestead on S.W. 328th St.), nature trails on keys. Book sales area, grills, picnic tables. **Programs & Events:** Glass-bottom boat trips to islands and reefs, snorkel trips, scuba diving. **Tips & Hints:** To see the park, either bring your own boat, or make reservations with Biscayne National Underwater Park, Inc. (tel. 305/230–1100) to go on boat tours or snorkel or dive trips, or take water taxi service to the islands (campers). Bring your own water. Only Elliott Key has drinking water. Busiest Nov.–Apr., least crowded May–Oct.

FOOD, LODGING & SUPPLIES

⚠ **Camping:** 2 campgrounds in the park: Boca Chita (accessible by boat only; tent camping area; $10; pit toilets), Elliott Key (waterside and forested camping areas on a 7-mi-long island accessible by boat only; tel. 305/230–7275; 20 sites; $10; flush toilets, cold showers). 🏨 **Hotels:** None in park. In Homestead: Redland Hotel (5 S. Flagler Ave., tel. 305/246–1904; 13 rooms; $69–$99). ✗ **Restaurants:** None in park. In Homestead: El Toro Taco (1 S. Krome Ave., tel. 305/245–8182; $10–$20). ⛽ **Groceries & Gear:** None in park. In Florida City: The Wal-Mart Supercenter (33501 S. Dixie Hwy., tel. 305/242–4447).

FEES, HOURS & REGULATIONS

Free. Glass-bottom boat trips: $24.45 adults, $16.45 ages 12 and under, $19.45 ages 62 and over. Snorkel trips: $35 per person. Canoe rentals: $9 per hour. Kayak rentals: $16 per hour. For scuba trips and island shuttles, call Biscayne National Underwater Park, Inc. (tel. 305/230–1100). Overnight docking fee at Boca Chita and Elliot keys $15 per night. Florida state fishing license required. Leashed pets only in the developed areas of Convoy Point and Elliott Key. No pets on all other islands or mainland, on boats moored to the islands, or in the shallow waters around the islands. No guns. No skateboards, roller skates, or in-line skates. Visitor center open daily 9–5. Adams Key open daily sunrise–sunset. Elliott Key, Boca Chita Key, and all park waters open daily.

HOW TO GET THERE

9 mi east of Homestead on S.W. 328th St. (N. Canal Dr.). Closest airport: Miami International Airport (35 mi).

CONTACTS

Biscayne National Park (9700 S.W. 328th St., Homestead, FL 33033, tel. 305/230–7275, fax 305/230–1190, www.nps.gov/bisc). Tropical Everglades Visitor Association (160 U.S. 1, Florida City, FL 33034, tel. 800/388–9669). Greater Homestead–Florida City Chamber of Commerce (43 N. Krome Ave., Historic Old Town Hall, Homestead, FL 33030-6014, tel. 305/247–2332). The Greater Miami Convention & Visitors Bureau (701 Brickell Ave., Suite 2700, Miami, FL 33131, tel. 305/539–3000).

Canaveral
National Seashore

In the east-central part of the state, near Titusville

The longest stretch of preserved coastline on the east coast of Florida is at this seashore. Besides its recreational appeal, the 24 mi seashore is situated on a barrier island and protects 57,662 acres of undeveloped beach and wetlands. The park offers sanctuary to 1,000 species of plants and 300 species of birds, including 14 threatened or endangered species. The seashore was established on January 3, 1975.

WHAT TO SEE & DO

Beachcombing, bird- and wildlife watching, boating, canoeing (rentals, outside North District), fishing, hiking, surfing, swimming, visiting Eldora State House, Turtle Mound and Seminole Rest Trail historical sites. **Facilities:** Information center (North District New Smyrna Beach), Eldora State House. Bookstore. **Programs & Events:** Ranger-led walks, talks, canoe, and pontoon boat tours. Sea Turtle Watch programs (June and July). **Tips & Hints:** Visit Oct.–Mar. for best island camping. Beaches busiest Apr.–Aug., least crowded in Oct. and Jan.

FOOD, LODGING & SUPPLIES

Camping: Backcountry beach and island camping allowed (permit required, *see below*). Near Titusville: Manatee Campground (7275 S. U.S. 1, tel. 321/264–5083; 183 sites; $18–$20; flush toilets, showers, hook-ups). **Hotels:** None in park. In Titusville: Holiday Inn (4951 S. Washington Ave., tel. 321/269–2121; 117 rooms; $74–$200). **Restaurants:** None in park. In Titusville: Dixie Crossroads (1475 Garden St., tel. 321/268–5000; $8–$28). ♿ **Groceries & Supplies:** None in park. In Titusville: Publix (3265 Garden St., tel. 321/383–0511).

FEES, HOURS & REGULATIONS

Entrance fee: $5 per car or motorcycle, $3 per bicyclist or walk-in. Backcountry permit required ($10–$20 per night; tel. 386/428–3384 Ext. 10). Reservations required (tel. 386/428–3384) for ranger-led canoe trips, pontoon boat rides, and Turtle Watch programs. Lifeguards on duty Memorial Day–Labor Day, daily 10–4. No beach camping in summer. Park closes when parking lots are full, which occurs during most summer weekends at the North District. Seashore open Nov.–Mar., daily 6–6; Apr.–Oct., daily 6 AM–8 PM. Information center open daily 9–4:30. South District (Titusville) closes three days prior to a shuttle launch at Kennedy Space Center and reopens the day following a successful launch.

HOW TO GET THERE

North District: Take I–95, Exit 84 on Rte. 44 to Rte. A1A in New Smyrna Beach. South District: Take I–95, Exit 80 on Rte. 406–402. Closest airports: Orlando International Airport (50 mi), Daytona Airport (50 mi).

CONTACTS

Canaveral National Seashore (Park Headquarters, 308 Julia St., Titusville, FL 32796, tel. 321/267–1110, www.nps.gov/cana). Titusville Chamber of Commerce (2000 S. Washington St., Titusville, 32780, tel. 321/267–3036).

Castillo de San Marcos National Monument

In the northeast part of the state, in St. Augustine

Castillo de San Marcos was for many years the northernmost outpost of Spain's vast New World empire. Begun in 1672 and completed in 1695, it's the oldest masonry fort and the best-preserved example of a Spanish colonial fortification in the continental United States. The site was proclaimed a national monument on October 15, 1924.

WHAT TO SEE & DO

Attending ranger presentations, living-history reenactments, and cannon-firing demonstrations, self-guided tours. **Facilities:** Interpretive exhibits inside rooms within the fort. Bookstore, gift shop. **Programs & Events:** Ranger presentations (daily). Cannon-firing demonstrations (summer weekends at 11, 1:30, 2:30, 3:30). Confederate encampment (Jan.); Union encampment (Mar.); Spanish "Nightwatch" (June); Change of Flags ceremony (July); Siege of 1702 reenactment (Nov.); British "Nightwatch," Christmas open house (Dec.). **Tips & Hints:** Busiest Apr.–July, least crowded Oct.–Jan.

FEES, HOURS & REGULATIONS

Entrance fee: $5 adults, $2 ages 6–16. Leashed dogs only on grounds. No pets in fort. No alcohol. Grounds are open 5:30 AM–midnight; fort interior is open 8:45–4:45.

HOW TO GET THERE

The monument is in the center of St. Augustine, on Matanzas Bay. Nearest airport: Jacksonville (40 mi).

CONTACTS

Castillo de San Marcos National Monument (1 S. Castillo Dr., St. Augustine, FL 32084, tel. 904/829–6506, fax 904/823–9388, www.nps.gov/casa). St. Augustine Visitor & Convention Bureau (88 Riberia St., Suite 400, St. Augustine, FL 32084, tel. 904/829–1711, fax 904/829–6149, www.visitoldcity.com).

De Soto National Memorial

On Tampa Bay south shore, in Bradenton

The memorial pays tribute to the remarkable expedition led by Hernando de Soto, who reached Florida's Gulf Coast in May 1539. This was the first large-scale European expedition into what is now the interior southern United States. De Soto traveled 4,000 mi during his four-year mission and had a significant impact on the course of North American history. The memorial was authorized on March 11, 1948.

WHAT TO SEE & DO

Participating in living-history presentations, viewing movie, walking. **Facilities:** Visitor center, 20-minute orientation film, self-guided trail through mangrove swamp, outdoor exhibit. Bookstore. **Programs & Events:** *Hernando de Soto in America* (hourly, 9–4). Costumed ranger-led living-history programs (late Dec.–mid-Apr., daily), crossbow and musket firing (late Dec.–mid-Apr.). Other special programs and scheduled events. **Tips & Hints:** Busiest Mar. and Apr., least crowded Aug.–Sept.

FEES, HOURS & REGULATIONS

Free. Leashed pets only. No bikes on trail. Park grounds open daily sunrise–sunset. Parking lots close at 5 PM. Visitor center open daily 9–5.

HOW TO GET THERE

2½ mi north of Manatee Ave. (Rte. 64) on 75th St. NW in Bradenton. Closest airports: Sarasota–Bradenton International (12 mi), Tampa International (55 mi).

CONTACTS

De Soto National Memorial (Box 15390, Bradenton, FL 34280, tel. 941/792–0458, fax 941/792–5094, www.nps.gov/deso). Manatee County Tourist Information Center (5030 U.S. 301N, Ellenton, FL 34222, tel. 941/729–7040).

Dry Tortugas National Park

In the south, 70 nautical mi west of Key West, FL

Known for its famous marine and bird life and its legends of pirates and sunken treasure, the park includes a cluster of seven islands or "keys" amid 100 square mi of shoals, water, and coral gardens. Fort Jefferson, its main cultural feature, is the largest 19th-century American coastal fort. The park was proclaimed as Fort Jefferson National Monument in 1935 and redesignated as Dry Tortugas National Park in 1992.

WHAT TO SEE & DO

Fishing, picnicking, sailing, scuba diving, snorkeling, touring historic structures. **Facilities:** Visitor center (Fort Jefferson). Book and chart sale areas, grates, picnic tables. **Programs & Events:** Occasional ranger-led tours, campfire talks, moat walks, living-history programs. **Tips & Hints:** Go mid-Apr.–mid-May for migrating birds, June–Aug. for best weather. Busiest Mar.–May, least crowded Sept.–Nov.

FOOD & LODGING

Camping: In the park: Garden Key Campground (10 sites; $3; flush toilets). No backcountry camping. **Hotels:** None in park. In Key West: Ambrosia House (615, 618, and 622 Fleming St., tel. 305/296–9838 or 800/535–9838; 19 rooms; $129–$549). **Restaurants:** None in park. In Key West: Pepe's Café & Steak House (806 Caroline St., tel. 305/294–7192; $12–$21).

FEES, HOURS & REGULATIONS

Free. Florida saltwater fishing license required. Fort Jefferson open daily dawn–dusk. Grounds outside fort open daily. Bush Key closed to visitors Feb.–Sept. to protect nesting sooty and noddy terns. Visitor center open daily 8–5.

HOW TO GET THERE

70 mi west of Key West, FL. Several boat and air-taxi services offer trips to the park. Closest airport: Key West International.

CONTACTS

Dry Tortugas National Park (Box 6208, Key West, FL 33041, tel. 305/242–7700, fax 305/242–7728, www.nps.gov/drto). Key West Chamber of Commerce (Mallory Sq., Key West, FL 33041, tel. 305/294–2587).

Everglades National Park

In the southern part of the state, west of Homestead

The 1.5-million-acre park is the largest subtropical wilderness in the continental United States. It has extensive fresh, estuarine, and saltwater areas, open Everglades prairies, hardwood tree islands, cypress domes, pinelands, and mangrove forests. It's the only place in the world where alligators and crocodiles coexist. The park was authorized on May 30, 1934; dedicated on December 6, 1947; designated an International Biosphere Reserve on October 26, 1976; a World Heritage Site on October 26, 1979; and designated a Wetland of International Importance on June 4, 1987.

WHAT TO SEE & DO

Bicycling (rentals, Flamingo, Shark Valley), boating, boat touring (Flamingo, Gulf Coast), canoeing (rentals, Flamingo, Gulf Coast), fishing, hiking, kayaking (rentals, Flamingo, Gulf Coast), picnicking, tram touring (Shark Valley). **Facilities:** 5 visitor centers: Ernest F. Coe (main entrance, west of Homestead–Florida City), Royal Palm (4 mi west of Coe), Flamingo (38 mi southwest of main entrance), Shark Valley (U.S. 41, north side of park), and Gulf Coast (Everglades City); interpretive displays, trails, roadside interpretive exhibits, amphitheaters, boat-launch areas. Book sale areas, gift shops, fire pits, gasoline (daytime only, Flamingo), picnic areas, religious services (winter only). **Programs & Events:** Guided walks, talks (Royal Palm), boat tours (Flamingo, Gulf Coast), tram tours (Shark Valley). Guided walks, talks, evening programs (Long Pine Key, Flamingo campgrounds), bicycle tours (Shark Valley), canoe tours (Flamingo, Gulf Coast), slough slogs (Shark Valley). All late Dec.–early Apr. **Tips & Hints:** Go Dec.–Apr. for best wildlife viewing. Busiest Dec.–Apr., least crowded May–Nov.

FOOD, LODGING & SUPPLIES

Camping: 2 campgrounds in the park: Flamingo (end of main park road; 278 sites; $14; flush toilets, cold showers), Long Pine Key (7 mi from the main entrance off main road; 108 sites; $14; flush toilets). Backcountry camping allowed (permit required, *see below*). **Hotels:** In the park: Flamingo Lodge (tel. 239/695–3101 or 800/600–3813; 74 rooms, 24 cottages; $65–$135). **Restaurants:** In the park: Flamingo Lodge Restaurant (tel. 239/695–3101 or 800/600–3813; $10–$35). **Groceries & Gear:** In the park: The Marina Store (1 Flamingo Lodge Rd., tel. 239/695–3101 Ext. 304).

FEES, HOURS & REGULATIONS

Entrance fee: $10 per vehicle or $5 per person on foot or bicycle (main entrance), $8 per vehicle or $4 per person on foot or bicycle (Shark Valley). This rate may be applied toward the higher entrance fee at the main entrance. Backcountry camping permits ($10–$30) available at Flamingo, Gulf Coast visitor centers. Boat-launch fees are $5 ($3 for nonmotorized). Boat tours at Flamingo and Gulf Coast vary in price (Flamingo Lodge & Marina, tel. 941/695–3101; Everglades City Boat Tours, tel. 941/695–2591). Shark Valley tram tours: $9.30 adults, $5.15 ages 12 and under (tel. 305/221–8455). Reservations recommended for all tours Dec.–Apr. Florida state fishing license required. No hunting. No pets on trails or in backcountry. Leashed pets only in campgrounds. Bicycles on selected trails only. No motorized vehicles on trails. Motorized boat use restricted. No airboats. Main park entrance open all the time. Shark Valley open daily 8:30–6. Ernest Coe Visitor Center open daily 8–5; Royal Palm Visitor Center open daily 8–4:15. Flamingo Visitor Center open Dec.–Apr., daily 7:30–5; May–Nov. intermittently. Shark Valley Visitor Center open daily 8:30–5:15. Gulf Coast Visitor Center open Nov.–Apr., daily 7:30–5:30; May–Oct., daily 8:30–4:30.

HOW TO GET THERE

The park is in south Florida, southwest of Miami. Access points are Gulf Coast, in the northwest corner of the park, reached via U.S. 41 south of Naples and Fort Myers; Shark Valley, on the north side of the park, reached via U.S. 41 west of Miami or south of Naples–Fort Myers; and the main park entrance, reached via Rte. 9336 west of Homestead and Florida City. Closest airports: Miami (45 mi northeast of main entrance), Fort Myers (70 mi northwest of Gulf Coast).

CONTACTS

Everglades National Park (40001 Rte. 9336, Homestead, FL 33034-6733, tel. 305/242–7700, www.nps.gov/ever). Tropical Everglades Visitor Association (160 U.S. 1, Florida City, FL 33034, tel. 800/388–9669). Homestead and Florida City Chamber of Commerce (43 N. Krome Ave., Homestead, FL 33030, tel. 305/247–2332). Greater Miami Convention & Visitor Bureau (701 Brickell Ave., Suite 2700, Miami, FL 33131, tel. 305/539–3000 or 800/283–2707). Everglades Area Chamber of Commerce (Box 130, Everglades City, FL 34139, tel. 239/695–3941).

Fort Caroline National Memorial

In the northeast part of the state, near Jacksonville

The memorial pays tribute to the colony the French tried to establish near the mouth of the St. Johns River in 1564. The colony was plagued with hardship and conflicts with the Spanish, who were uneasy about a French settlement that was near the routes used by their treasure ships. The memorial was authorized on September 21, 1950.

WHAT TO SEE & DO

Hiking, picnicking, walking to Fort Caroline exhibit. **Facilities:** Visitor center, fort exhibit, trail, Spanish Pond area, Ribault Column. Bookstore, picnic area. **Programs & Events:** Ranger programs (weekdays 1 PM and 3 PM, weekends 3 PM). **Tips & Hints:** Bring insect repellent. Visit in spring and fall. Busiest Jan. and Feb., least crowded Dec. and July.

FEES, HOURS & REGULATIONS

Free. No hunting or fishing. Leashed pets only on trails. No bicycles on trails. Visitor center and memorial open daily 9–5.

HOW TO GET THERE

13 mi east of downtown Jacksonville. Closest airport: In Jacksonville (25 mi).

CONTACTS

Fort Caroline National Memorial (12713 Ft. Caroline Rd., Jacksonville, FL 32225, tel. 904/641–7155, fax 904/641–3798, www.nps.gov/foca). Jacksonville and the Beaches Florida Convention & Visitors Bureau (201 E. Adam St., Jacksonville, FL 32202, tel. 904/798–9111, fax 904/

798–9103). Huguenot Memorial State Park (10980 Heckscher Dr., Jacksonville 32226, tel. 904/251–3335).

Fort Matanzas National Monument

In the northeast part of the state, south of St. Augustine

Fort Matanzas ("slaughter" in English) marks the site where, on September 29 and October 12, 1565, almost 300 soldiers from the nearby French Fort Caroline were killed by the Spaniards in a battle for supremacy in the New World. The fort itself is a masonry fortification built by the Spanish between 1740 and 1742 to guard the "back door" to St. Augustine at the south end of Matanzas Inlet. The site was proclaimed a national monument in 1924.

WHAT TO SEE & DO

Riding ferry to fort, touring fort, walking on boardwalk trails. **Facilities:** Visitor center, fort, interpretive exhibits, boardwalk. Bookstore–gift shop. **Programs & Events:** Year-round ferry boat rides, ranger presentations (every hour on the half hour 9:30–4:30), living-history reenactments. **Tips & Hints:** Busiest Apr.–Aug., least crowded Sept. and Jan.

FOOD, LODGING & SUPPLIES

Camping: None in park. In St. Augustine: Ocean Grove RV Resort (4225 A1A S, tel. 800/342–4007; 195 sites; $41; flush toilets, showers, hook-ups). **Hotels:** None in park. In St. Augustine: Sheraton's Vistana Resort at World Golf Village (100 Front 9 Dr., tel. 904/940–2000 or 800/477–3340; 134 rooms, $129–$219). **Restaurants:** None in park. In St. Augustine: Zaharias (3945 Rte. A1A S, tel. 904/471–4799; $9–$18). **Groceries:** L'il Champ Convenience Store (8880 A1A S, St. Augustine, tel. 904/471–6501.)

FEES, HOURS & REGULATIONS

Free. Leashed pets only. No alcohol. No driving or walking on sand dunes. Park open daily 9–5:30; visitor center open daily 9–4:30. Ferry runs 9:30–4:30, weather permitting.

HOW TO GET THERE

The park is on Anastasia Island, 14 mi south of St. Augustine on Rte. A1A. Closest airports: Daytona (60 mi), Jacksonville (50 mi), and Orlando (100 mi).

CONTACTS

Fort Matanzas National Monument (8635 A1A S, St. Augustine, FL 32080, tel. 904/471–0116, fax 904/471–7605, www.nps.gov/foma). St. Augustine Visitor & Convention Bureau (88 Riberia St., Suite 400, St. Augustine, FL 32084, tel. 904/829–1711, fax 904/829–6149).

Gulf Islands National Seashore

In the northwest part of the state, near Pensacola, and in southeast Mississippi, near Ocean Springs

These offshore islands offer sparkling white-sand beaches, historic forts and structures, nature trails, and adjacent open waters. On the mainland are salt marshes and bayous in the Mississippi District; and there are a Naval Live Oak Reservation and military forts in the Florida District. Research, monitoring, and mitigation programs preserve, protect, and restore the natural and cultural resources within the park. The seashore was authorized on January 8, 1971.

WHAT TO SEE & DO

Bird-watching, bicycling (rentals, Gulf Breeze, Pensacola Beach), boating (rentals, Gulf Breeze, Pensacola Beach, Perdido Key), fishing, picnicking, swimming, touring forts, walking. **Facilities:** 4 visitor centers: Naval Live Oaks (U.S. 98 east of Gulf Breeze, FL), Fort Pickens (Santa Rosa Island west of Pensacola Beach), Fort Barrancas (on Pensacola Naval Air Station), William M. Colmer (Ocean Springs, MS); beaches, forts, auditorium, nature trails, interpretive display boards. Ball field, boat launch, book and map sale areas, picnic areas, and shelters. **Programs & Events:** Tours at Fort Pickens (daily at 2) and Fort Barrancas (daily at 2), Advanced Redoubt (Sat. at 11). Guided tours of Fort Massachusetts on West Ship Island, MS (late Mar.–Oct., daily 10:30 and 1:30), candlelight tours. Beach cleanup (Sept., FL; May and Sept., MS), Earth Day (Apr.). **Tips & Hints:** Don't swim alone in unguarded waters. Be cautious about rip currents, jellyfish, Portuguese men-of-war, and barnacle-covered rocks. Be alert for sudden storms and seek shelter during thunderstorms. Watch your step while exploring the forts and batteries. Go Apr.–Oct. for good weather and blooms, late Mar.–mid-May and Sept. and Oct. for migrating birds. Busiest May–July, least crowded Jan. and Feb.

FOOD, LODGING & SUPPLIES

Camping: 3 campgrounds in the park: Davis Bayou (south of Ocean Springs; tel. 228/875–3962; 52 sites; $14–$16; flush toilets, showers, hook-ups), Fort Pickens (west end of Santa Rosa Island, south of Pensacola, tel. 228/875–3962, 800/365–2267 reservations; 200 sites; $20; flush toilets, showers, hook-ups), Naval Live Oak (tel. 850/934–2622; group site; $20–$30; flush toilets, cold showers). Primitive camping allowed on East Ship, Horn, and Petit Bois islands in MS and Perdido Key, FL (permit required, *see below*). **Hotels:** None in park. In Ocean Springs, MS: Days Inn (7305 Washington Ave., tel. 228/872–8255; $50–$70). In Pensacola Beach: Clarion Suites Resort & Convention Center (20 Via de Luna, tel. 850/492–2755 or 800/934–3301; 86 suites; $184–$199). **Restaurants:** In the park: snack bars and stores. In Ocean Springs, MS: Catch of the Day (2114 Bienville Blvd., tel. 228/872–7003; $6–$10). In Pensacola: Bay Breeze Restaurant (7601 Scenic Hwy., tel. 850/477–7155; $11–$20).

👍 **Groceries & Gear:** In the park: Fort Pickens campground store (1400 Fort Pickens Rd., tel. 850/934–2622).

FEES, HOURS & REGULATIONS

Entrance fee: $8 per vehicle, $3 for walk-ins. Florida or Mississippi state fishing license required. Primitive camping permit required (free, must apply in person) for Perdido Key (tel. 850/492–7278). No glass containers on beaches. No motor vehicles off roads. No metal detectors. No pets on beaches in Florida, in swimming area of Ship Island, on tour boats, and in historic structures or buildings. Leashed pets elsewhere. Don't feed or disturb wildlife. Seashore open daily 8–sunset. Fort Barrancas Visitor Center open Nov.–Feb., daily 8:30–3:45; Mar.–Oct., daily 9:30–4:45. Fort Pickens Visitor Center open daily 8:30–4. Davis Bayou Visitor Center open Nov.–Feb., daily 8–4:30; Mar.–Oct., daily 8:30–5.

HOW TO GET THERE

Mississippi District: the offshore access to Ship Island is provided by concession boats from Gulfport, MS (Mar.–Oct.). Private boats may dock near Ft. Massachusetts on W. Ship Island during the day. NPS-licensed or private boats provide access to Horn, Petit Bois, Cat, and E. Ship islands. Follow the signs on U.S. 90 for the seashore to Davis Bayou, MS. Florida District, Johnson Beach (Perdido Key): take Rte. 292 southwest from Pensacola; for historic mainland forts and Naval Museum: use the main entrance of Pensacola Naval Air Station off Barrancas (Rte. 295); for Naval Live Oaks and the Fort Pickens and Santa Rosa areas: take U.S. 98 from downtown Pensacola across the Pensacola Bay Bridge. Closest airports: Florida District—Pensacola (20 mi), Mississippi District—Gulfport (30 mi).

CONTACTS

For the Mississippi District: Superintendent, Gulf Islands National Seashore (3500 Park Rd., Ocean Springs, MS 39564; tel. 228/875–0821; 228/875–3962 campgrounds, fax 228/872–2954). For the Florida District: Superintendent, Gulf Islands National Seashore (1801 Gulf Breeze Pkwy., Gulf Breeze, FL 32563, tel. 850/934–2600, fax 850/932–9654, www.nps.gov/guis). Pensacola Visitors Information Center (1401 E. Gregory St., Pensacola, FL 32501, tel. 800/874–1234). Pensacola Beach Visitors Information Center (735 Pensacola Beach Blvd., Pensacola Beach, FL 32561, tel. 800/635–4803). Emerald Coast Convention & Visitors Bureau (Box 609, Fort Walton Beach, FL 32549-0609, tel. 800/322–3319). Navarre Beach Area Chamber of Commerce (8543 Navarre Pkwy., Navarre, FL 32566, tel. 850/939–2691). Biloxi Visitors Center (710 Beach Blvd., Biloxi, MS 39530, tel. 228/374–3105). Ocean Springs Area Chamber of Commerce (1000 Washington Ave., Ocean Springs, MS 39564, tel. 228/875–4424).

Timucuan Ecological & Historic Preserve

In the northeast part of the state, in Jacksonville

The preserve protects 46,000 acres of estuarine natural resources and historic and prehistoric sites between the Lower St. Johns and Nassau rivers. The site includes four areas: Fort Caroline National Memorial (*see separate entry*), Kingsley Plantation, the Theodore Roosevelt area, and Cedar Point. The Kingsley Plantation includes the oldest remaining plantation house in Florida. The 18th- and 19th-century structures include the planter's home, kitchen house, barn, and 23 of the original 32 slave quarters. The Theodore Roosevelt area preserves a maritime hammock forest and evidence of the Timucuan Indians who once inhabited northeast Florida. The Cedar Point area is undeveloped but has informal hiking trails. The preserve was authorized on February 16, 1988.

WHAT TO SEE & DO

Bird- and wildlife watching, boating, hiking, picnicking, touring Kingsley Plantation and Fort Caroline. *See Fort Caroline National Memorial.* **Facilities:** Visitor centers and bookstores at Fort Caroline and Kingsley Plantation. Fort Caroline includes a near full-scale rendering of the original fort, a 1-mi nature trail, and picnic area. The Theodore Roosevelt area offers an observation tower located at the marsh's edge, plus 3.5 mi of trails. **Programs & Events:** Ranger talks at Kingsley Plantation, occasional ranger programs at Theodore Roosevelt area and Fort Caroline. **Tips & Hints:** Busiest Feb. and Mar., least crowded Aug. and Sept.

FEES, HOURS & REGULATIONS

Free. No hunting. Leashed pets only. No pets in buildings. No bicycles on trails. Fort Caroline National Memorial and visitor center open daily 9–5. Kingsley Plantation open daily 9–5. Theodore Roosevelt Area open Oct.–Apr., daily 6 AM–6 PM; Oct.–Apr., daily 6 AM–8 PM.

HOW TO GET THERE

The preserve is in northeast Jacksonville. From I–95, exit on Heckscher Dr. (Rte. 105). Follow Heckscher east to Rte. 9A. For Kingsley Plantation, continue on Heckscher Dr. for 9 mi, turn left at the park sign onto Fort George Island, and follow signs to plantation; for Theodore Roosevelt area and Fort Caroline National Memorial, turn right onto 9A heading south, take the next exit, and at the traffic light, turn left and follow the signs to Fort Caroline National Memorial and Theodore Roosevelt; for Cedar Point, go ¼ mi to the next light (New Berlin Rd.), turn left at the light and follow New Berlin Rd. to the intersection with Cedar Point Rd. (a triangleular intersection), turn right on Cedar Point Rd. and follow it to the end. The four sites are about 35 minutes driving time apart. Closest airport: Jacksonville International.

CONTACT
Timucuan Ecological and Historic Preserve (12713 Ft. Caroline Rd., Jacksonville, FL 32225, tel. 904/641–7155, fax 904/641–3798, www.nps. gov/timu).

See Also

Florida National Scenic Trail and *Wekiva River,* in Other National Parklands.

Andersonville National Historic Site

In central Georgia, in Andersonville

Andersonville, or Camp Sumter, was the largest Confederate military prison established during the Civil War. More than 45,000 Union soldiers were confined in the camp during 14 months, and nearly 13,000 died from disease, poor sanitation, malnutrition, overcrowding, and exposure. The site is the only park that serves as a memorial to all Americans ever held as prisoners of war. The 495 acres include the national cemetery, with 18,000 interments, and the partially reconstructed prison site. The historic site was authorized on October 16, 1970.

WHAT TO SEE & DO

Auto touring, hiking, picnicking, researching, touring cemetery and prison, walking. **Facilities:** National Prisoner of War Museum, visitor center, cemetery, prison, monuments. Bookstore, picnic area. **Programs & Events:** Ranger-guided cemetery walks and prison-site talks (daily at 11 and 2). Andersonville Revisited "Living History Weekend" (2nd weekend in Mar.), Memorial Day ceremony (last Sun., May). **Tips & Hints:** Plan to stay at least two hours. Wear comfortable clothing and walking shoes. Summers are hot and humid, winters are mild and rainy. Busiest in Mar. and July, least crowded Dec. and Jan.

FOOD, LODGING & SUPPLIES

Camping: None in park. In Andersonville: Andersonville Campground (114 E. Church St., tel. 229/924–2558; 27 sites; flush toilets, showers, hook-ups). **Hotels:** None in park. In Americus: Windsor Hotel (125 W. Lamar St., tel. 229/924–1555 or 888/297–9567; 41 rooms, 12 suites; $101). **Restaurants:** None in park. In Andersonville: Andersonville Restaurant (Church St., tel. 229/928–8480; $7–$9; closed Mon. and Sat.). **Groceries:** None in park. In Andersonville: One Stop Store (211 Ellaville St., tel. 229/924–3070).

FEES & HOURS

Free; donations accepted. Driving tour audio: $1 rental. Park grounds open daily 8–5. Visitor center–museum open daily 8:30–5.

HOW TO GET THERE

From I–75 northbound, exit at Cordele, take U.S. 280 west to Americus and Rte. 49 north for 10 mi to park entrance on right. Closest airports: Columbus (60 mi), Macon (60 mi), Atlanta (175 mi).

CONTACTS

Andersonville National Historic Site (496 Cemetery Rd., Andersonville, GA 31711, tel. 229/924–0343, fax 229/928–9640, www.nps.gov/ande).

The Americus-Sumter Chamber of Commerce (400 Lamar St., tel 229/924–2646).

Chattahoochee River National Recreation Area

Near Atlanta

The recreation area has 16 units along a 48-mi stretch of the Chattahoochee River. In addition to fishing, hiking, picnicking, and boating, the park contains a wide variety of natural habitats, flora and fauna, 19th-century historic sites, and Native American archaeological sites. The site was established on August 15, 1978.

WHAT TO SEE & DO

Boating, canoeing (rentals, May–Labor Day; Johnson Ferry, Paces Mill, Powers Island), fishing, hiking, picnicking, rafting (rentals, May–Labor Day; Johnson Ferry, Paces Mill, Powers Island). **Facilities:** Visitor contact station (Island Ford), more than 60 mi of hiking trails, stocked trout stream. Bookstores, picnic areas, and pavilion (reservations tel. 770/395–6851). **Programs & Events:** Ranger-led interpretive talks. **Tips & Hints:** Busiest in June and Aug., least crowded in Nov. and Jan.

FOOD & LODGING

Camping: None in park. Near Buford: U.S. Army Corps of Engineers Sawnee Campground (1050 Buford Dam Rd., Lake Lanier, tel. 770/887–0592 or 877/444–6777; 56 sites; flush toilets, showers, hookups). **Hotels:** None in park. In Roswell: Country Inn & Suites (2950 Mansell Rd., tel. 770/552–0006 or 800/456–4000; 65 suites; $89–$99). **Restaurants:** None in park. In Roswell: Fratelli di Napoli (928 Canton St., tel. 770/642–9917; $10–$20).

FEES, HOURS & REGULATIONS

Free. Shuttle bus (tel. 770/395–6851) runs among Johnson Ferry, Powers Island, and Paces Mill (May–Labor Day). Parking fee ($2 daily, $25 annual). Georgia fishing license and trout stamp required for ages 16 and over. Park open dawn to dusk year-round. Visitor contact station open daily 8–6.

HOW TO GET THERE

Visitor contact station: From I–285, take Rte. 400 north to Exit 6 (Northridge Rd.). Stay in right lane and follow signs. Closest airport: Atlanta (22 mi).

CONTACT

Chattahoochee River National Recreation Area (1978 Island Ford Pkwy., Atlanta, GA 30350, tel. 678/538–1200, fax 770/399–8087, www.nps.gov/chat).Atlanta Convention & Visitors Bureau (233 Peachtree St. NE, Suite 100, Atlanta, GA 30303, tel. 404/521–6600 or 800/285–6282, fax 404/577–3293, www.atlanta.net).

Chickamauga & Chattanooga National Military Park

In northwestern Georgia,
and in southeastern Tennessee, near Chattanooga

On the fields of this park in the fall of 1863, more than 150,000 Union and Confederate soldiers clashed in a series of battles remembered as some of the hardest fighting of the Civil War. The fighting ended with the Union Seizure of Chattanooga, the gateway to the deep South. The park was established on August 19, 1890, and transferred from the War Department on August 10, 1933.

WHAT TO SEE & DO

Auto touring, walking, watching film. **Facilities:** 2 visitor centers: Chickamauga Battlefield (Fort Oglethorpe, GA) and Lookout Mountain Battlefield (Lookout Mountain, TN). Cravens House and Ochs Museum (both at Lookout Mountain, TN), trails. Bookstores, picnic areas. **Programs & Events:** Chickamauga Battlefield: 26-minute movie (shown hourly 9–4); car caravan tours (June–Sept., daily at 10:30, 12:30, and 2); living-history demonstrations (June–Sept., hourly 10–4). Lookout Mountain: *The Walker Painting*, a short movie on the "Battle Above the Clouds", shown on request; guided walks (June–Sept.); living-history demonstrations (June–Sept.); Cravens House tours (June–Aug.), Cravens House Christmas programs. **Tips & Hints:** Visit in spring and fall. Busiest July and Aug., least crowded Jan. and Feb.

FOOD, LODGING & SUPPLIES

Camping: None in park. In Trenton: Lookout Mountain KOA (930 Mountain Shadows Dr., tel. 706/657–6815; 114 sites, 14 cabins; $15–$50; flush toilets, showers, hook-ups). **Hotels:** None in park. In Chattanooga, TN: Read House Hotel & Suites (827 Broad St., tel. 423/266–4121 or 800/333–3333; 140 rooms, 100 suites; $99–$109). In Fort Oglethorpe: Best Western Battlefield Inn (2120 Lafayette Rd., tel. 706/866–0222; 39 rooms; $69–$89). **Restaurants:** None in park. In Chattanooga, TN: Southside Grill (1400 Coward St., tel. 423/266–9211; $16–$25; closed Sun.). In Fort Oglethorpe: O'Charley's (2542 Battlefield Pkwy., tel. 706/861–5520; $6–$11). **Groceries & Gear:** In Fort Oglethorpe: K-Mart (526 Battlefield Pkwy., tel. 706/866–1337).

FEES, HOURS & REGULATIONS

Chickamauga Battlefield: free; multimedia presentations $3 adults, $1.50 ages 63 and over. Point Park at Lookout Mountain: $3 adults, $1.50 ages 63 and over; Cravens House tours (June–Aug.) $2 per person. No bicycles on trails. No hunting. No in-line skating, roller-skating, or skateboarding. No metal detecting. Park open daily 8–dark. Visitor centers open Sept.–May, daily 8–4:45; June–Aug., daily 8–5:45.

HOW TO GET THERE

The Chickamauga Battlefield Visitor Center is in Fort Oglethorpe, on the Lafayette Rd., off I–75 south of Chattanooga, TN. The Lookout

Mountain Battlefield Visitor Center is at the entrance to Point Park, which may be reached from downtown Chattanooga via the Scenic or Ochs highways. Closest airport: Chattanooga (10 mi).

CONTACT

Chickamauga & Chattanooga National Military Park (Box 2128, Fort Oglethorpe, GA 30742, tel. 706/866–9241, fax 423/752–5215, www.nps. gov/chch). Catoosa County Chamber of Commerce (Box 52, Ringgold, GA 30736, tel. 706/965–5201, www.gatewaytogeorgia.com).

Cumberland Island National Seashore

In southeastern Georgia, near St. Marys

The seashore offers outstanding opportunities for relaxation and solitude in an undisturbed island paradise. One of the largest undeveloped barrier islands in the world, the seashore contains federally designated wilderness and one of the largest maritime forests remaining in the United States. It also preserves a mansion built by Thomas Carnegie, the American industrialist who once owned most of the island. The seashore was established in 1972 and designated a Biosphere Reserve in 1986.

WHAT TO SEE & DO

Nature walking, swimming. **Facilities:** Visitor center–park headquarters, Sea Camp Ranger Station (exhibits), Ice House at Dungeness Dock, Plum Orchard mansion, trails. Bookstore. **Programs & Events:** Ranger-guided tours (twice daily, Dungeness Dock), naturalist program (Sea Camp Ranger Station), mansion tour (2nd and 4th Sun. of month, Plum Orchard). Beach and marsh ecology program (intermittently), deer and hog hunts (Oct.–Feb., application required, *see below*). **Tips & Hints:** Access by boat and ferry only. Watch for ticks. Best time to visit: spring and fall. Busiest Apr. and May, least crowded Dec. and Jan.

FOOD, LODGING & SUPPLIES

Camping: In the park: Sea Camp (tel. 888/817–3421; 18 sites; $4; flush toilets, cold showers), 4 backcountry sites (permit required, *see below*). **Hotels:** None in park. In St. Marys: Spencer House Inn (200 Osborne St., tel. 912/882–1872 or 888/840–1872; 14 rooms; $100–$175). **Restaurants:** None in park. In St. Marys: Pauly's Café (102 Osborne St., tel. 912/882–3944; $5–$12), El Potro Mexican Restaurant (1923 Osborne St., tel. 912/882–0900; $6–$13). **Groceries & Gear:** None in park. In St. Marys: Wal-Mart (6586 Rte. 40 E, tel. 912/882–3096).

FEES, HOURS & REGULATIONS

User fee: $4 per person. Deer and hog hunts July and Aug. by application only; selection is by lottery and there's a $35 fee for those selected. Roundtrip ferry fee (reservations required, tel. 912/882–4335): $12 adults, $7 ages 12 and under, $9 ages 65 and over. Backcountry permits

($2) available on island. No motorized vehicles allowed. No bicycles in wilderness area or trails. Park open daily 8:15–4:30. Ferry doesn't operate Dec.–Feb., Tues. and Wed.

HOW TO GET THERE

Seashore access at St. Marys, 10 mi east of I–95. Closest airport: Jacksonville, FL (34 mi).

CONTACTS

Cumberland Island National Seashore (Box 806, St. Marys, GA 31558, tel. 912/882–4336, fax 912/882–6284, www.nps.gov/cuis). St. Marys Tourism Council (Box 1191, 414 Osbourne St., St. Marys, GA 31558, tel. 800/868–8687). Kingsland Tourist & Convention Bureau (Box 1928, Kingsland, GA 31548, tel. 800/433–0225, fax 912/729–7618).

Fort Frederica National Monument

On St. Simons Island

Fort Frederica's ruins are a reminder of the struggle for empire between Spain and Great Britain. James Edward Oglethorpe founded the Georgia colony and built the fort on St. Simons Island, where it flourished in the 1740s. The southernmost post of the British colonies in North America, the fort protected Georgia and South Carolina from the Spanish in Florida. The park is known for its exceptional beauty and the antiquity of the tabby sugar mill ruins. Stately oaks, exceptionally large grapevines, and Spanish moss lend an air of antiquity that is unequaled on the coast. The park was authorized on May 26, 1936.

WHAT TO SEE & DO

Ranger-led or self-guided walking tour of town ruins, viewing film. **Facilities:** Visitor center, 25-minute film *This Is Frederica,* trail, wayside exhibits. Museum store. **Programs & Events:** Ranger-led tours, costumed interpretive programs. Frederica Festival (2nd Sat. in Feb.), National Park Day (Aug. 25), Holiday Open House (1st weekend after Christmas). **Tips & Hints:** Plan to spend two hours at the monument. Sand gnats and mosquitoes are present year-round. Biting flies are worst in May and Sept. Busiest Feb. and Mar., least crowded Dec. and Jan.

FOOD & LODGING

⛺ **Camping:** None in park. On Jekyll Island: Jekyll Island Campground (1197 Riverview Dr., tel. 912/635–3021; 206 sites; $25–$27; flush toilets, showers, hook-ups). 🛏 **Hotels:** None in park. On Jekyll Island: Days Inn (60 Beach View Dr., tel. 912/635–9800; 124 rooms; $60–$130). On St. Simons Island: Best Western Island Inn (301 Main St., Plantation Village, tel. 912/638–7805 or 800/673–6323). ✕ **Restaurants:** None in park. On St. Simons Island: Putter's (1701 Frederica Rd., Suite 101, tel. 912/638–9454; $4–$10).

FEES, HOURS & REGULATIONS

Entrance fee: $5 per vehicle or $3 per bicyclist. No vehicles or bikes allowed in town site. Monument open daily 8–5. Visitor center open 9–5.

HOW TO GET THERE

On St. Simons Island, 12 mi from Brunswick, accessible from I–95 and U.S. 17 via the F.J. Torras (Brunswick–St. Simons) Causeway. Directional signs to the park are located on all major roads to the island. The fort is on Frederica Rd. near Christ Church Episcopal Church.

CONTACTS

Superintendent, Fort Frederica National Monument (Rte. 9, Box 286-C, St. Simons Island, GA 31522-9710, tel. 912/638–3639, www.nps.gov/fofr).

Fort Pulaski National Monument

Near Savannah

On April 11, 1862, defense strategy changed forever when a Union-rifled cannon overcame a masonry fortification after only 30 hours of bombardment. Named for Revolutionary War hero Count Casimir Pulaski, the fort took 18 years to build. Constructing this fort was Robert E. Lee's first military assignment. This remarkably intact example of 19th-century military architecture, with its estimated 25 million bricks and 7½-foot-thick walls, is preserved for future generations as a reminder of the elusiveness of invincibility. The monument contains 5,365 acres, including some of the most pristine and scenic marshland on the Georgia coast. The monument was proclaimed in 1924 and transferred to the Park Service in 1933.

WHAT TO SEE & DO

Biking; bird-, wildlife, and ship watching; boating; fishing; hiking; picnicking; self-guided touring of fort and nature trail. **Facilities:** Visitor center, fort, nature trail, lighthouse. Bookstore, picnic areas. **Programs & Events:** Ranger-led talks and demonstrations; *The Battle for Fort Pulaski*, a 20-minute film. Troop encampments, special programs, and demonstrations (holiday weekends). **Tips & Hints:** Plan to spend at least two hours. Busiest Apr.–Aug., least crowded Dec. and Jan.

FOOD & LODGING

⚑ **Camping:** None in park. On Tybee Island: River's End Campground (915 Polk St., tel. 912/786–5518; 100 sites; $34; flush toilets, showers, hook-ups). 🏨 **Hotels:** None in park. On Tybee Island: Beachside Colony (404 Butler Ave., tel. 912/786–4535; 67 condos; $150–$300). ✕ **Restaurants:** None in park. On Tybee Island: Crab Shack (40-A Estille Hammock Rd., tel. 912/786–9857; $7–$15), George's of Tybee (1105 U.S. 80 E, tel. 912/786–9730; $18–$28; no lunch). ⛏ **Gear:** None in park. On Tybee Island: T.S. Chu Hardware (No. 6 Tybrisa St., tel. 912/786–4561).

FEES, HOURS & REGULATIONS

Entrance fee: $3 adults, free ages 16 and under. Permit required (free) for recreational shellfish harvesting in park waters. Cockspur Island Lighthouse (1857) accessible by private boat only. No bikes on trails leading to fort. Monument open Memorial Day–Labor Day, daily 8:30–6:45; Labor Day–Memorial Day, daily 8–5:30. Visitor center open Memorial Day–Labor Day, daily 9–6:30; Labor Day–Memorial Day, daily 9–5.

HOW TO GET THERE

15 mi east of Savannah on U.S. 80. Follow signs for Fort Pulaski, Tybee Island, and beaches. Closest airport: Savannah (30 mi).

CONTACT

Fort Pulaski National Monument (Box 30757, U.S. 80E, Savannah, GA 31410-0757, tel. 912/786–5787, www.nps.gov/fopu). Savannah Convention & Visitors Bureau (101 E. Bay St., Savannah, GA 31401, tel. 877/728–6624, www.savcb.com).

Jimmy Carter National Historic Site

In central Georgia, in Plains

The rural southern culture of Plains revolves around farming, church, and school and molded the character of the 39th U.S. president. The site includes President Carter's residence, boyhood home, school, and the railroad depot, which served as his campaign headquarters during the 1976 election. The area surrounding the residence is under the protection of the Secret Service and is not open to the public. The site was authorized on December 23, 1987.

WHAT TO SEE & DO

Touring Plains by car or bicycle, visiting boyhood farm and 1976 campaign headquarters, watching film. **Facilities:** Visitor center (Plains High School), historic farm and home. Bookstore, picnic area in town park. **Programs & Events:** 27-minute film, audio tour. Plains Peanut Festival (last Sat. in Sept.) **Tips & Hints:** Plan to spend two to three hours visiting places associated with the Carters. Busiest Mar. and Apr., least crowded Dec. and Jan.

FOOD, LODGING & SUPPLIES

Camping: None in park. In Plains: M&W Campground (120 Buena Vista Rd., tel. 229/824–5775; 16 RV sites; $10–$18; hook-ups). **Hotels:** None in park. In Plains: Plains Inn (106 Main St., tel. 229/824–4517; 7 rooms; $85–$140). **✗ Restaurants:** None in park. In Plains: Old Bank Café (118 Main St., tel. 229/824–4520; $3–$5). **Groceries:** None in park. In Plains: Peanut Gallery (205 Church St., tel. 229/824–7734).

FEES & HOURS

Free. Visitor center open daily 9–5.

HOW TO GET THERE

From I–75 northbound, take Exit 33 (Cordele) and U.S. 280 west to Plains. From Columbus, take U.S. 280 east to Plains. Boyhood farm is 2 mi west of Plains on U.S. 280. Closest airport: Columbus (55 mi).

CONTACT

Park Headquarters, Jimmy Carter National Historic Site (300 N. Bond St., Plains, GA 31780, tel. 229/824–4104, www.nps.gov/jica).

Kennesaw Mountain National Battlefield Park

Between Kennesaw and Marietta, near Atlanta

Eleven miles of earthworks are preserved within the 2,884-acre park, which commemorates two Civil War battles where, during Sherman's 1864 Atlanta Campaign, Union General William T. Sherman met Confederate General Joseph E. Johnston. The site was authorized as a national battlefield in 1917, transferred to the Park Service in 1933, and redesignated in 1935.

WHAT TO SEE & DO

Auto touring to mountaintop or Cheatham Hill (main battlefield), hiking, picnicking, viewing exhibits and film. **Facilities:** Visitor center, battlefield and earthworks, auto tour roads, 16 mi of trails. Bookstore, grills. **Programs & Events:** 19-minute film: *Kennesaw Mountain and the Atlanta Campaign.* Ranger program, living-history programs (June–Aug., weekends). **Tips & Hints:** Allow two to three hours for visit. Take shuttle bus to mountaintop on weekends and major holidays. Stay on trails. Busiest in Oct. and Apr., least crowded Jan. and Feb.

FEES, HOURS & REGULATIONS

Free. Leashed pets only. No bicycles on trails. Park open daily 7:30–dusk. Visitor center open Mar.–Oct., weekdays 8:30–5, weekends 8:30–6; Nov.–Feb., daily 8:30–5.

HOW TO GET THERE

3 mi north of Marietta. From I–75, take Exit 269 and follow the brown-and-white park signs. Closest airport: Atlanta (35 mi).

CONTACTS

Kennesaw Mountain National Battlefield Park (900 Kennesaw Mountain Dr., Kennesaw, GA 30152, tel. 770/427–4686, fax 770/528–8399, www.nps.gov/kemo).

Martin Luther King Jr. National Historic Site

In Atlanta

In this two-block area, Atlanta honors the life, legacy, and teachings of Martin Luther King, Jr., the civil rights leader who was assassinated on April 4, 1968, at age 39. The site contains the home where King was born, Ebenezer Baptist Church, Martin Luther King Jr. Center for Nonviolent Social Change, King's gravesite, Fire Station #6 Museum, and the residential and commercial districts of the "Sweet Auburn" community. The site was established in 1980.

WHAT TO SEE & DO

Touring the site, watching films and puppet shows. **Facilities:** Visitor center (450 Auburn Ave. NE), videos, Birth Home of Martin Luther King Jr., Ebenezer Baptist Church (407 Auburn Ave. NE), King Center Freedom Hall exhibits and King gravesite (449 Auburn Ave. NE), Fire Station #6 Museum, wayside exhibits in neighborhood. Bookstores and gift shops. **Programs & Events:** Ranger-led tours of King's birth home, talks on historic role of black churches, puppet shows for children (tel. 404/331–6922 Ext. 3606 reservations). Gospel concerts, arts programs (monthly). King Week Celebration (Jan.), Black History Month (Feb.), King Remembrance Day (Apr. 4), March on Washington Anniversary (Aug.), National Historic Site Birthday (Oct. 10), Candlelight Tour of Birth Home (Dec.). **Tips & Hints:** The best months to visit are Oct.–Dec. Busiest Jan. and Feb., least crowded in Mar. and Dec.

FEES & HOURS

Free. Site and visitor center open Memorial Day–Labor Day, daily 9–6; Labor Day–Memorial Day, daily 9–5.

HOW TO GET THERE

1½ mi east of downtown Atlanta. Closest airport: Atlanta.

CONTACTS

Martin Luther King Jr. National Historic Site (450 Auburn Ave. NE, Atlanta, GA 30312, tel. 404/331–5190, fax 404/730–3112, www.nps.gov/malu). Atlanta Convention & Visitors Bureau (233 Peachtree St. NE, Suite 100, Atlanta, GA 30303, tel. 404/521–6600 or 800/285–6282, fax 404/577–3293, www.atlanta.net).

Ocmulgee National Monument

In Macon

Twelve thousand years of human habitation, from Ice Age "Paleo" hunters to the Muscogee (Creek) Confederacy of historic times, are on display at this monument. People of the Early Mississippian Period

Macon Plateau culture 1,000 years ago built a large town, which is now protected here. Huge earthen mounds and a unique ceremonial earth lodge, reconstructed over the original hand-molded clay floor, are reminders of this ancient agricultural society. One of two temple mounds at the Lamar site is the only remaining "spiral" mound. The British built a trading post at the site in the late 1600s. The Dunlap House and an earthen gun emplacement date from the Civil War battle that was fought here. The monument was authorized in 1936.

WHAT TO SEE & DO

Bird-watching, fishing, hiking, jogging, picnicking, touring the museum, viewing 17-minute movie, walking to earth lodge and mounds. **Facilities:** Visitor center with archaeological museum, theater, audio programs at two sites, 6-mi trail. Gift shop. **Programs & Events:** Lantern Light Tours (Mar.); Field Trip to Lamar Mounds and Village, Artifact Identification Day (May and Nov.); Children's Summer Workshops (July); Ocmulgee Indian Celebration (3rd weekend, Sept.). **Tips & Hints:** Visit in spring and fall. Busiest Sept.–Nov., least crowded Dec. and Jan.

FEES, HOURS & REGULATIONS

Free. Permits required to visit Lamar Mounds unit. Georgia state fishing license required. Stay on trails. No bikes on trails. No climbing on mounds. No hunting. No kite flying. Leashed pets only. Park and visitor center open daily 9–5.

HOW TO GET THERE

On the east edge of Macon, off I–16 Exit 2. Closest airports: Macon (12 mi), Atlanta (90 mi).

CONTACTS

Ocmulgee National Monument (1207 Emery Hwy., Macon, GA 31217, tel. 478/752–8257, fax 478/752–8259, www.nps.gov/ocmu). Macon–Bibb County Convention & Visitors Bureau (200 Cherry St., Macon, GA 31201, tel. 912/743–3401).

See Also

Appalachian National Scenic Trail, West Virginia. *Augusta Canal National Heritage Area, Overmountain Victory National Historic Trail*, and *Trail of Tears National Historic Trail*, in Other National Parklands.

Haleakala National Park

In east Maui

The park preserves the outstanding volcanic landscape of the upper slopes of Haleakala (10,023 feet) and protects the fragile ecosystems of Kipahulu Valley, the scenic pools along Oheò Gulch, and many rare and endangered species. Hike through rain forests or a cinder desert or picnic at the foot of a 400-foot waterfall in this park of extremes. Haleakala originally was one of two units of Hawaii National Park (along with Hawaii Volcanoes National Park, *see separate entry*). It was redesignated as a separate park in 1961 and designated a Biosphere Reserve in 1980.

WHAT TO SEE & DO

Bird-watching, bicycling, hiking, picnicking, stargazing, sunrise and sunset watching, swimming, walking, whale-watching. **Facilities:** 3 visitor centers: Park Headquarters (mile 11, Crater Rd.), Haleakala (mile 21, Crater Rd.), and Kipahulu (mile 42, Rte. 31). Trails, interpretive exhibits, pre-contact Hawaiian structures (prior to 1778), historic walls, Sugar Mill dam ruins. Bookstores. **Programs & Events:** Guided walks and programs on geological, natural, and cultural history (Summit Bldg., daily at 9:30, 10:30, 11:30; Kipahulu Visitor Center, daily at 12:30, 1:30, 2:30, 3:30), guided cinder desert hike (Tues. and Fri. at 9; Haleakala visitor center), guided cloud forest hike (Mon. and Thurs. at 9; Hosmer Grove, just inside park entrance), bamboo forest hike (Sun.–Fri. at 9:30), Star programs (May–Aug.). **Tips & Hints:** Wear sturdy, comfortable shoes and lightweight, layered clothing that will keep you warm in wet weather at the summit. Temperatures range from 40°F to 65°F but can be below freezing with wind chill year-round. At Summit, watch for altitude sickness, hypothermia, and black ice on roads in winter. At Kipahulu, watch for flash floods, strong ocean currents, rockfalls, hypothermia, and mosquitoes. Bring binoculars to stargaze. Go to Halemauu Trail and the Summit for sunsets. Busy year-round, but least crowded mid-Jan. and Feb.

FOOD, LODGING & SUPPLIES

⚠ **Camping:** 2 campgrounds in the park: Hosmer Grove (Summit area; tent camping area; free; pit toilets), Kipahulu Campground (near Kipahulu Visitor Center; tent camping area; free; pit toilets). 3 cabins and 2 tent sites in the backcountry (permit required, *see below*). 🏠 **Hotels:** None in park. In Hāna: Hotel Hāna-Maui (Hāna Hwy., tel. 808/ 248–8211 or 800/321–4262; 19 rooms, 47 cottages; $295–$375). ✗ **Restaurants:** None in park. In Hāna: Pauwela Café (375 W. Kuiaha Rd., off Hāna Hwy., tel. 808/575–9242; $6–$20). 🛒 **Groceries:** In Pukalani: Pukalani Superette (15 Makawao Ave., tel. 808/572–7616).

FEES, HOURS & REGULATIONS

Entrance fee: $10 per vehicle, $5 for walk-ins and bicyclists. Back-country permits (free) required. To enter wilderness cabin reservation lottery, write the park, "Attention Cabins," at least 90 days before arrival. Include alternate dates and avoid weekends to increase chances of obtaining slot. Call park at 808/572–4400 Ext. 0 daily between 1 and 3 to check on filling last-minute cancellations. Fishing at Kipahulu must be done in accordance with state fishing regulations. Bicycling restricted to roads. No skateboarding, skating, or hang gliding. No pets on trails. Leashed pets allowed in campground only. Park open daily. Park headquarters open daily 7:30–4. Haleakala Visitor Center open daily sunrise–3. Kipahulu Visitor Center open daily 9–5.

HOW TO GET THERE

The park's summit area is a 1½-hour drive (38 mi) from Kahului via Rtes. 37, 377, and 378. Kipahulu is a three- to four-hour drive (61 mi) from Kahului via Rtes. 36, 360, and 31. Closest airport: Kahului.

CONTACTS

Haleakala National Park (Box 369, Makawao, HI 96768, tel. 808/572–4400, fax 808/572–1304, www.nps.gov/hale). Hawaii Visitor Bureau (Box 1738, Kahului, HI 96732, tel. 808/244–3530).

Hawaii Volcanoes
National Park

On the south end of the island of Hawaii

The park preserves the natural setting of Mauna Loa (13,677 feet), the world's most massive volcano, and Kilauea (the world's most active). It contains lush rain forests, raw craters, acid deserts, and great areas covered by lava flows. The park was established in 1916 and designated a Biosphere Reserve in 1980 and a World Heritage Site in 1987.

WHAT TO SEE & DO

Hiking, scenic driving. **Facilities:** Kilauea Visitor Center, museum, art center, 11-mi loop road, trails, overlook. Book and map sale areas, gift shop. **Programs & Events:** Ranger talks and walks (daily), evening programs (Tues., 2 to 3 times a month). Kilauea Cultural Heritage (2nd weekend, July). **Tips & Hints:** Be prepared for anything from snow and high winds to heat exhaustion. Bring rain gear, light sweaters, and windbreakers, sturdy shoes, hats, water bottles, sunglasses, and sunscreen with a high UV factor. Call 808/935–8555 for weather forecasts. Stay on trails and don't enter lava tubes (except Thurston Lava Tube). Avoid volcanic fumes. Campers can shower for a fee at Volcano House. Busiest July and Aug., least crowded in Apr. and Sept.

FOOD, LODGING & SUPPLIES

Camping: 2 campgrounds in park: Namakami Paio (Off Rte. 11, near summit; tent camping area; free; flush toilets), Kulanaokuaiki (Hilina Pali Rd.; 3 sites; free; vault toilets). Backcountry camping allowed (permit required, *see below*). ☂ **Hotels:** In the park: Volcano House (Off Rte. 11, near summit, tel. 808/967–7321; 42 rooms, 10 cabins; $45–$195), Kilauea Military Camp (tel. 808/967–7315; active-duty and retired military personnel and Defense Department employees only). In Maunaloa Estates: Carson's Volcano Cottage (11-3920 6th St., across from Volcano Village, tel. 808/967–7683; 6 rooms, 5 cottages; $110–$165). ✗ **Restaurants:** In the park: Volcano House Restaurant (tel. 808/967–7321; $13). In Volcano Village: Volcano's Lava Rock Café (Old Volcano Hwy., tel. 808/967–8526; $5–$8). ☖ **Groceries:** In Volcano Village: Kilauea General Store (Old Volcano Hwy., tel. 808/985–9995).

FEES, HOURS & REGULATIONS

Entrance fee: $10 per vehicle, $5 for walk-ins or bicyclists. Backcountry camping permit required for all backcountry (free). Park open daily. Visitor center open daily 7:45–5. Jagger Museum open daily 8:30–5.

HOW TO GET THERE

From Hilo, go 30 mi southwest on Rte. 11; from Kailua-Kona, travel 96 mi southeast on Rte. 11 or 125 mi through Waimea and Hilo via Rtes. 19 and 11. Closest airport: Hilo.

CONTACTS

Hawaii Volcanoes National Park (Box 52, Hawaii National Park, HI 96718-0052, tel. 808/985–6000 [Ext. 1 for eruption information], fax 808/967–8186, www.nps.gov/havo). Big Island Visitors Bureau (250 Keawe St., Hilo, HI 96720, tel. 808/961–5797).

Kalaupapa National Historical Park

On north shore of Molokai

Kalaupapa and Kalawao, the historic Hansen's disease (leprosy) settlements, are preserved in this park. Kalaupapa is still home for many surviving patients. Although Hansen's disease is contagious, it is very unlikely visitors would contract the disease from anyone in Kalaupapa, because all the patients have been cured by drug therapies introduced after World War II. In Kalawao are the churches of Siloama, established in 1866, and St. Philomena, associated with the work of Joseph De Veuster (Father Damien). Kalaupapa peninsula was inhabited by Hawaiian people prior to the establishment of the quarantine settlement at Kalawao in 1866. Evidence of this occupation in four *ahupuaa* (land divisions) is relatively undisturbed and represents one of the richest archaeological preserves in Hawaii. The 10,700-acre park contains spectacular sea cliffs, narrow valleys, a volcanic crater, a rain forest, lava tubes and caves, and offshore islands and waters. The park was authorized on December 22, 1980.

WHAT TO SEE & DO

Touring Kalaupapa and Kalawao settlements. **Facilities:** Wayside exhibits. Bookstore and sales shop. **Programs & Events:** Tours of Kalaupapa and Kalawao (Mon.–Sat.). **Tips & Hints:** Make reservations for commercial tours of the settlement, for mule rides on the Pali trail, and for flights to Kalaupapa from Oahu or Molokai (Molokai Shuttle, tel. 808/567–6847; Pacific Wings, tel. 888/575–4546). Go Nov.–Mar. to see whales and migratory birds from Alaska.

FOOD, LODGING & SUPPLIES

⚠ **Camping:** None in park. Near Kualapu'u: Pala'au State Park (End of Kalae Rd. [Rte. 47], tel. 808/984–8109 or 808/587–0300; tent camping area; $5; flush toilets; permit required). Near Mauna Loa: Papohaku Beach Park (Kaluakoi Rd., off Rte. 460, tel. 808/553–3204; tent camping area; $3; flush toilets, showers; permit required). 🏨 **Hotels:** None in park. In Kaunakakai: Hotel Molokai (Kamehameha Hwy., tel. 808/553–5347; 45 rooms; $70–$140). ✗ **Restaurants:** None in park. In Kaunakakai: Kanemitsu Bakery & Restaurant (79 Ala Malama St., tel. 808/553–5855; $2–$5; closed Tues.). ⚲ **Groceries:** None in park. In Kaunakakai: Friendly Market Center (90 Ala Malama Str., tel. 808/553–5595).

FEES, HOURS & REGULATIONS

Free. Reservations and fees required for commercial tours, mule rides, and air flights. Contact Molokai Mule Rides, Inc. (tel. 808/567–6088 or 800/567–7550) for mule ride reservations, Damien Tours (tel. 808/567–6171) for tour reservations. Visitation limited to scheduled tour or personal guests of residents. No one under 16 allowed. No hunting or firearms. No pets. No photographs of patients without their written permission. Park open daily. Commercial tours operate Mon.–Sat.

HOW TO GET THERE

The Kalaupapa Peninsula is at the base of a 2,000-foot cliff. There's no road access from the rest of Molokai. Visitors must hike or ride a trail down the cliff or fly into the airport in the park. Visitors will be picked up by the tour bus at the trailhead or airport. Closest airport: Kalaupapa (2 mi).

CONTACTS

Kalaupapa National Historical Park (National Park Service, Box 2222, Kalaupapa, HI 96742, tel. 808/567–6802, fax 808/567–6729, www.nps.gov/kala). Molokai Business Association (130 Kamehameha V-Hwy., Suite 210, Molokai, HI 96748, tel. 808/553–3034).

Kaloko-Honokohau National Historical Park

On west coast of island of Hawaii, near Kailua Kona

Kaloko-Honokohau preserves traditional native Hawaiian activities and culture. It's the site of an ancient Hawaiian settlement with four different *ahupuaa,* or traditional sea-to-mountain land divisions. Resources include fishponds, house-site platforms, petroglyphs, a stone slide, and a religious site. The park was established on November 10, 1978.

WHAT TO SEE & DO

Bird-watching, fishing, hiking, picnicking, snorkeling, surfing, swimming. **Facilities:** Contact station (Honokohau, off Rte. 19). **Programs & Events:** Interpretive programs (occasionally). **Tips & Hints:** Busiest June and July, least crowded Sept. and Oct.

FOOD, LODGING & SUPPLIES

⚠ **Camping**: None in park. Near Kawaihae: Samuel M. Spencer Beach Park (Rte. 270, tel. 808/961–8311; tent camping area; $5; flush toilets, showers; permit required). ⊞ **Hotels**: None in park. In Kailua-Kona: Kanaloa at Kona (78–261 Manukai St., tel. 808/322–9625, 808/322–2272, or 800/688–7444; 166 units; $205–$305), Kona Magic Sands (77-6452 Alii Dr., tel. 808/329–9393 or 800/622–5348; 37 rooms; $95–$125). ✕ **Restaurants:** None in park. In Kailua-Kona: Jameson's by the Sea (6452 Ali'i Dr., tel. 808/329–3195; $18–$32), Kona Inn Restaurant (75-5744 Ali'i Dr. in the Kona Inn Shopping Village, tel. 808/329–4455; $16–$28). ⛁ **Groceries & Gear:** In Kawaihae: Kawaihae Market & Deli (613665 Akoni Pule Hwy., tel. 808/880–1611).

FEES, HOURS & REGULATIONS

Free. No collecting artifacts, plants, rocks, or coral. Kaloko road gate open daily 8–3:30. Visitors are welcome in the park after 3:30, but vehicles need to be out before gate closes. Headquarters open weekdays 8–4.

HOW TO GET THERE

At the base of Hualalai Volcano along the Kona coast, 3 mi north of Kailua-Kona and south of the airport on Rte. 19 (Queen Kaahumanu Hwy.). The Kaloko gate is across the highway from the Kaloko New Industrial Park across from Kona Trade Center building. The park can also be accessed from the south end, by way of the Honokohau small boat harbor. Park headquarters is in the Kaloko New Industrial Park on Rte. 19. From the highway, turn toward the mountain on Hina Lani St. and make a right on Kanalani St. Turn right into the fourth driveway on your right. Headquarters is at the end. Closest airport: Keahole-Kona (3 mi).

CONTACTS

Kaloko-Honokohau National Historical Park (73–4786 Kanalani St., #14, Kailua-Kona, HI 96740, tel. 808/329–6881, www.nps.gov/kaho). Big Island Visitors Bureau (250 Keawe, Hilo, HI, 96720, tel. 808/961–5797).

Pu'uhonua o Honaunau National Historical Park

In southwest of the island of Hawaii, near Ho'naunau

Until 1819 this park was a sanctuary for vanquished Hawaiian warriors, noncombatants, and kapu breakers. The park includes prehistoric house sites, royal fishponds, coconut groves, and spectacular shore scenery. The 182-acre park was authorized as City of Refuge National Historical Park in 1955 and renamed in 1978.

WHAT TO SEE & DO

Fishing, hiking, picnicking, self-guided tours, watching crafts demonstrations. **Facilities:** Visitor center, restored temple, trail. Picnic area. **Programs & Events:** Hawaiian Cultural Festival (June). **Tips & Hints:** Be alert for unexpected high waves. Watch for falling coconuts and coconut fronds off the trail. Busiest in Feb. and July, least crowded Dec. and Jan.

FOOD, LODGING & SUPPLIES

Camping: None in park. *See* Kaloko-Honokohau National Historical Park. **Hotels:** None in park. In Captain Cook: Manago Hotel (826155 Mamalahoa Hwy., tel. 808/323–2642; 64 rooms; $26–$52). **Restaurants:** None in park. In Captain Cook: Manago Hotel Restaurant (826155 Mamalahoa Hwy., tel. 808/323–2642; $4–$13). **Groceries:** None in park. In Captain Cook: Choice Mart (Kealakekua Ranch Center, tel. 808/323–3994).

FEES & HOURS

Entrance fee: $5 per person. Park open Mon.–Thurs. 6 AM–8 PM, Fri.–Sun. and holidays 6 AM–11 PM. Visitor center open daily 8–4:30.

HOW TO GET THERE

From the airport, take Rte. 19 to Kailua, then Rte. 11 to Honaunau, then Rte. 160 to the park. Closest airport: Kona (30 mi).

CONTACTS

Pu'uhonua o Ho'naunau National Historical Park (Box 129, Honaunau, HI 96726, tel. 808/328–2326, www.nps.gov/puho). Kona-Kohala Chamber of Commerce (75–5737 Kuakini Hwy., Suite 208, Kailua-Kona, HI 96740, tel. 808/261–2727 or 808/329–1758).

Pu'ukohola Heiau National Historic Site

In northwest of island of Hawaii, near Kawaihae

High on a hill above the Pacific Ocean sits Pu'ukohola Heiau, the last major religious structure of the ancient Hawaiian culture. Kamehameha I built the "Temple on the Hill of the Whale" between 1790 and 1791 during his rise to power and dedicated it to his family war god, Kuka'ilimoku. The 85-acre site was authorized on August 17, 1972.

WHAT TO SEE & DO

Bird-watching, guided and self-guided tours of historical sites, hiking, shark- and whale-watching. **Facilities:** Visitor center, trails. **Programs & Events:** Interpretive talks, guided tours, Hawaiian programs. Arts-and-crafts demonstrations (once weekly, Jan.–Sept.). Pacific Islander Day (May). Hawaiian Cultural Festival (Aug.). **Tips & Hints:** Hike only if you are prepared for a long and rugged trail. Make guided-tour reservations two weeks in advance (tel. 808/882–7218). Busiest in May and Aug., least crowded Dec. and Jan.

FOOD, LODGING & SUPPLIES

None in park. *See Kaloko-Honokohau National Historical Park.*

FEES & HOURS

Free. Park gate closes at 4. Visitor center open daily 7:30–4.

HOW TO GET THERE

On the northwest shore of the island of Hawaii in the district of South Kohala. The visitor center is off Rte. 270, ¼ mi north of Rte. 19 intersection. Closest airport: Kailua-Kona (32 mi).

CONTACTS

Pu'ukohola Heiau National Historic Site (Box 44340, Kawaihae, HI 96743, tel. 808/882–7218, fax 808/882–1215, www.nps.gov/puhe). Kona-Kohala Chamber of Commerce (75–5737 Kuakini Hwy., Suite 208, Kailua-Kona, HI 96740, tel. 808/329–1758, fax 808/329–8564).

USS *Arizona* Memorial

In Hawaii, at Pearl Harbor

The USS *Arizona* Memorial grew out of a wartime desire to honor those who died in the December 7, 1941, attack. The memorial is the final resting place for many of the *Arizona*'s 1,177 crewmen who lost their lives that day. Their names are inscribed on the memorial. The park was established on September 9, 1980.

WHAT TO SEE & DO

Taking shuttle boat to memorial, touring memorial and museum, watching 23-minute film. **Facilities:** Visitor center, theaters, memorial. Bookstore. **Programs & Events:** Tours (June–Aug., daily 7:45–3; Sept.–May, daily 8–3). Local, military, and cultural history tours (Memorial Day, July 4, Veterans Day, Dec. 7). **Tips & Hints:** Plan for a two-hour visit. Secure all valuables in hotels or on person because the visitor center is in a high-theft area. Go early in day to avoid a long wait. Busiest June–Aug., least crowded Dec.–Feb. Due to security regulations, backpacks, fanny packs, purses, diaper bags, shopping bags, large camera bags, luggage and any other item that offers concealment are not allowed. Bags can be checked in the parking lot for $2.

FEES, HOURS & REGULATIONS

Free; donations encouraged. Audio guides ($4) available in English, Japanese, Mandarin Chinese, German, and Spanish. No baby strollers, carriages, or baby backpacks in the theaters or on the boats. No beach or swimwear. No pets. The memorial is open daily 7:30–5.

HOW TO GET THERE

The memorial is a half-hour drive from Waikiki. Take Rte. 1 west to Arizona Memorial–Stadium Exit 15A, then Rte. 99 to the visitor center. Access is also available via a one-hour ride on Bus 20 or Bus 42 from Waikiki. Closest airport: Honolulu International (3 mi).

CONTACTS

Superintendent, USS *Arizona* Memorial (1 Arizona Memorial Pl., Honolulu, HI 96818-3145, tel. 808/422–2771, www.nps.gov/usar). Hawaii Visitor & Convention Bureau (2270 Kalakaua Ave., Suite 801, Honolulu, HI 96815, tel. 808/923–1811).

City of Rocks
National Reserve

In southern Idaho, 45 mi south of Burley

In this reserve are historic pioneer trails in the midst of geologic grandeur. The name "City of Rocks" refers to massive granite rock formations—up to 2.5 billion years old and 600 feet high—that reminded California-bound emigrants in the 1800s of city buildings. The park also has world-class rock climbing and a diversity of habitat, wildlife, and vegetation. City of Rocks, which is cooperatively managed by the National Park Service and the State of Idaho, was designated on November 18, 1988.

WHAT TO SEE & DO

Bicycling, cross-country skiing, hiking, horseback riding (rentals, Almo), hunting, picnicking, rock climbing, snowmobiling, snowshoeing. **Facilities:** Visitor center (Almo), trails, wayside exhibits, kiosk. Gift shop, grills, picnic tables. **Programs & Events:** Interpretive talks, guided hikes, cultural demonstrations (Memorial Day–Labor Day, Fri. and Sat. nights). Stargazing (May–Oct.), City of Rocks Trail Ride (Sept.). **Tips & Hints:** Go late May–early June for wildflowers, May–June for birds, late Sept.–early Oct. for fall colors. Busiest May–June, least crowded Jan. and Feb.

FOOD, LODGING & SUPPLIES

Camping: In the park: City of Rocks Campground (tent camping area; $7; vault toilets). 75 backcountry sites scattered throughout park (free; permit required, *see below*). **Hotels:** None in park. In Almo: Almo Creek Outpost Cabins (3020 Elba Almo Rd., tel. 208/824–5577; 3 cabins; $65). In Burley: Best Western Burley Inn (800 N. Overland Ave., Exit 208 off I–84, tel. 208/678–3501; 126 rooms; $60–$80). **Restaurants:** None in park. In Almo: Almo Creek Outpost Restaurant (3020 Elba Almo Rd., tel. 208/824–5577; $5–$12). In Burley: Charlie's Café (615 E. Main St., tel. 208/678–0112; $6–$12). **Groceries & Gear:** None in park. In Almo: Tracy Merc Store (3001 Elba-Almo Rd., tel. 208/824–5570).

FEES, HOURS & REGULATIONS

Free. Permit required (free) for backcountry camping and backpacking. Leashed dogs only. Hunting in designated areas only. Idaho state hunting license required. Bikes and horses on designated trails only. No motorized vehicles or equipment on trails. Reserve is open year-round but in winter (Dec.–Mar.) is not accessible by car; you can hike, ski, snowmobile, or snowshoe in. Visitor center open Apr.–Oct., daily 8–4:30; Nov.–Mar., weekdays 8–4:30.

HOW TO GET THERE

In Almo, ID, on the Idaho–Utah border. From Boise and west, take I–84 to Declo, Exit 216 (Rte. 77) to Almo. Closest airport: Twin Falls (85 mi).

CONTACTS

City of Rocks National Reserve (Box 169, Almo, ID 83312, tel. 208/824-5519, fax 208/824-5563, www.nps.gov/ciro).

Craters of the Moon National Monument & Preserve

In south-central Idaho, southwest of Arco

The monument preserves approximately 1,100 square mi of land encompassing almost all of the volcanic rift zone known as the Great Rift. It includes three lava fields: Craters of the Moon, Wapi, and Kings Bowl. There are more than 25 cones and 60 lava flows that range in age from 15,000 to 2,000 years old. The park contains one of the largest basaltic cinder cones in the world (Big Cinder Butte) and some of the best examples of spatter cones in the world. The north end of the monument contains a portion of Goodale's Cutoff, which is part of the Oregon Trail. The monument was proclaimed on May 2, 1924.

WHAT TO SEE & DO

Bird-watching, bicycling, caving, driving loop road, hiking, skiing, snowshoeing, telemarking. **Facilities:** Visitor center, overlooks, trails, wayside exhibits, amphitheater. Bookstore, picnic tables. **Programs & Events:** Guided walks, evening programs (mid-June–Labor Day). Guided snowshoe hikes (Jan. and Feb., weekends, reservations required). **Tips & Hints:** Bring sturdy ground cloth to protect tent bottoms. Go in mid-June for peak flower display, in late summer and fall for most ice-free caving. Busiest July and Aug., least crowded Dec. and Jan.

FOOD, LODGING & SUPPLIES

🏕 **Camping:** In the park: Craters of the Moon Lava Flow Campground (51 sites; free; flush toilets). Backcountry camping allowed (free; permit required, *see below*). In Arco: Landing Zone RV Park (2424 N. 3000 W, tel. 208/527-8513; 44 sites; $18–$23; flush toilets, showers, hook-ups), Mountain View (705 W. Grand Ave., tel. 208/527-3707; 34 sites; $17–$23; flush toilets, showers, hook-ups; closed Nov.–Apr.). 🏨 **Hotels:** None in park. In Arco: DK Motel (316 S. Front St., tel. 208/527-8282 or 800/231-0134; 25 rooms, 6 suites; $45). ✗ **Restaurants:** In the park: snacks at visitor center. In Arco: The Golden West Café (U.S. 20/26, tel. 208/527-8551; $5–$7). 🛒 **Groceries:** None in park. In Arco: Cindy's Craters Edge Chevron (967 W. Grand St., tel. 208/527-9944).

FEES, HOURS & REGULATIONS

Entrance fee: $5 per car, $3 per person on bicycle or on foot. Backcountry camping permit and permit to enter north section of monument required (free). No bikes except on Goodale's Cutoff. No hunting within original boundaries of monument; hunting permitted in expanded portions. No off-road vehicle travel. No pets on trails. Park road closed in winter. Park open daily. Visitor center open mid-June–Labor Day, daily 8–6; Labor Day–mid-June, daily 8–4:30.

HOW TO GET THERE

18 mi southwest of Arco on U.S. 20/26/93. Closest airport: Sun Valley (60 mi).

CONTACTS

Craters of the Moon National Monument & Preserve (Box 29, Arco, ID 83213, tel. 208/527–3257, fax 208/527–3073, www.nps.gov/crmo). Lost River Chamber of Commerce (Box 46, Arco, ID 82313, tel. 208/527–8977).

Hagerman Fossil Beds National Monument

In south-central Idaho, in Hagerman

Here are the world's richest known deposits from the late Pliocene era, roughly 3.5 million years ago. The collection includes the largest concentration of fossil horses in North America and more than 100 other animal species. The monument provides a glimpse of life that existed before the Ice Age and the earliest appearance of modern flora and fauna. The site was authorized in 1988.

WHAT TO SEE & DO

Auto touring, hiking. **Facilities:** Temporary visitor center, self-guided driving tour, trails. Bookstore, overlooks. **Programs & Events:** Junior Ranger Program. Tours (Memorial Day–Aug., weekends). Hagerman Fossil Days Celebration (Memorial Day weekend). **Tips & Hints:** Best time to visit is June–Sept. Go in Dec. to see migratory waterfowl.

FOOD, LODGING & SUPPLIES

Camping: None in park. In Hagerman: Hagerman RV Village (18049 U.S. 30, tel. 208/837–4906; 68 sites; $20; flush toilets, showers, hook-ups). **Hotels:** None in park. In Hagerman: Hagerman Valley Inn (661 Frogs Landing, tel. 208/837–6196; 16 rooms; $46). **Restaurants:** None in park. In Hagerman: Snake River Grill (State St. and Hagerman Ave., tel. 208/837–6227; $7–$25). **Groceries & Gear:** None in park. In Hagerman: Fossil Fuels (361 S. State St., tel. 208/837–4025), Trader Jack's (441 S. State St., tel. 208/837–6044).

FEES, HOURS & REGULATIONS

Free. Many areas closed to public. Monument open daily. Visitor center open Memorial Day–Labor Day, daily 9–5; Labor Day–Memorial Day, Thurs.–Mon. 9–5.

HOW TO GET THERE

Visitor center is in Hagerman, on U.S. 30 across from the high school. Closest airport: Twin Falls (45 mi).

Hagerman Fossil Beds National Monument (221 N. State St., Box 570, Hagerman, ID 83332, tel. 208/837–4793, fax 208/837–4857, www.nps. gov/hafo). Hagerman Valley Chamber of Commerce (Box 599 Hagerman, ID 83332, tel. 208/837–9131). Hagerman Valley Historical Society (100 S. State St., Hagerman, ID 83332, tel. 208/837–6288).

Minidoka Internment National Monument

In south-central Idaho, near Jerome

The monument commemorates the hardships and sacrifices of Japanese Americans interned on-site here during World War II. Hunt Camp, as it was called during the war, operated from August 1942 until October 1945. It comprised 33,000 acres with 600 buildings. About 13,000 internees from Washington, Oregon, and Alaska were held here. The monument preserves a portion of the camp's original acreage and buildings. It was authorized on January 17, 2001.

WHAT TO SEE & DO

Touring site; viewing spud cellar, foundations, ornamental rock garden, entrance station. **Tips & Hints:** The park is under development. There's no visitor center, and some of the camp buildings are on private property. Call 208/837–4793 before visiting. Summer temperatures average at about 87°F. Visit in spring or fall for best weather.

FOOD, LODGING & SUPPLIES

Camping: None in park. In Jerome: Jerome-Twin Falls KOA (5431 U.S. 93, tel. 208/324–4169; 96 sites; $18–$30; flush toilets, showers, hook-ups). **Hotels:** None in park. In Twin Falls: Shadow Inn Suites (1586 Blue Lake Blvd. N, tel. 208/733–7545; 40 suites; $80). **Restaurants:** None in park. In Twin Falls: Jakers (1598 Blue Lakes Blvd. N, tel. 208/733–8400; $6–$11). **Groceries & Gear:** None in park. In Twin Falls: Fred Meyer (705 Blue Lakes Blvd. N, tel. 208/736–5340).

FEES, HOURS & REGULATIONS

Free. Monument open daily dawn–dusk. Collection of artifacts, rocks, plants, animals, or any other object within the National Monument is prohibited.

HOW TO GET THERE

From Boise take I–84 southwest for about 120 mi to Exit 173 at the intersection of I–84 and U.S. 93. Go north on U.S. 93 for 5 mi, then head east on Rte. 25 for 9½ mi, then north on Hunt Rd. for about 2 mi. The park is 21 mi east of Jerome and 17 mi northeast of Twin Falls. Closest airports: Twin Falls and Boise.

CONTACTS

Superintendent, Minidoka Internment National Monument (Box 570, Hagerman, ID 83332, tel. 208/837–4793, fax 208/837–4857, www,nps.

gov/miin). Jerome Chamber of Commerce (1731 S. Lincoln St., Jerome, ID 83338, tel. 208/324–2711, fax 208/324–6881).

Nez Perce
National Historical Park

In north-central Idaho, near Lewiston;
and in Washington, Oregon, and Montana

Nez Perce culture, traditions, and history are commemorated and celebrated in this park's 38 sites, which are located in four states. Sites range from small roadside pullouts to village sites and battlefields. The Nez Perce National Historic Trail follows the route the Nez Perce took in the 1877 War and runs from the Wallowa Valley of northeast Oregon to Bear Paw Battlefield in north-central Montana. The park was authorized on May 15, 1965.

WHAT TO SEE & DO

Fishing, picnicking, walking, watching film, wildlife viewing. **Facilities:** 2 visitor centers: in Spalding, ID, and at Big Hole National Battlefield (*see separate entry*), near Wisdom, MT; trails, museums, interpretive display boards. Book and map sales areas, picnic tables. **Programs & Events:** Tours and walks (by reservation, tel. 208/843–2261 Ext. 199). Guided hikes, interpretive talks, cultural demonstrations (mid-May–Sept., weekends). Commemorations of Nez Perce War of 1877 (White Bird, June 17; Big Hole, Aug. 6; Bear Paw, Oct. 5). **Tips & Hints:** Allow plenty of time to visit 38 sites that stretch 1,500 mi. Be prepared for extreme changes in climate and elevation. Busiest in May and Aug., least crowded in Nov. and Feb.

FOOD, LODGING & SUPPLIES

Camping: None in park. In Harpster: Harpster Riverside RV Park (Off Rte. 13, 13 mi north of Grangeville, tel. 208/983–2312 or 800/983–1918; 25 sites; $22; flush toilets, showers, hook-ups), **Hotels:** None in park. In Lewiston: Red Lion Hotel (621 21st St., tel. 208/799–1000; 136 rooms; $66–$99). **Restaurants:** None in park. In Lapwai: Donald's Family Dining (U.S. 95, tel. 208/843–7273; $5–$8). In Lewiston: Bojack's Broiler Pit (311 Main St., tel. 208/746–9532; $9–$17; closed Sun.). **Groceries & Gear:** None in park. In Lapwai: Valley Foods (204 U.S. 95 N, tel. 208/843–2070).

FEES, HOURS & REGULATIONS

Free. Idaho state fishing license required. Nez Perce Reservation permit required for steelhead fishing. Leashed pets only. No hunting. Spalding unit open during daylight. Spalding visitor center open June–Sept., daily 8–5:30; Oct.–May, daily 8–4:30.

HOW TO GET THERE

Spalding visitor center is 10 mi east of Lewiston on U.S. 12/95. Closest airport: Lewiston.

CONTACTS

Nez Perce National Historical Park (39063 U.S. 95 Spalding, ID, 83540, tel. 208/843–2261, fax 208/843–2001, www.nps.gov/nepe). Lewiston Chamber of Commerce (111 Main St., Suite 120, Lewiston, ID 83501, tel. 208/743–3531).

See Also

Yellowstone National Park, Wyoming. *California National Historic Trail, Continental Divide National Scenic Trail, Lewis & Clark National Historic Trail, Nez Perce National Historic Trail,* and *Oregon National Scenic Trail,* in Other National Parklands.

Lincoln Home
National Historic Site

In Springfield

Abraham Lincoln bought this house in the spring of 1844 for his wife and son, and it was the only home the family ever owned. They lived in it for 17 years, during which time Lincoln built his law practice and began a political career that would lead him to the presidency in 1861. The house has been restored to its 1860s appearance. It stands in the midst of a four-block historic neighborhood that the National Park Service is restoring so the neighborhood, like the house, will appear much as Lincoln would have remembered it. The site was authorized in 1971 and established in 1972.

WHAT TO SEE & DO

Touring the home and neighborhood. **Facilities:** Visitor center (426 S. 7th St.), sculptures, film, home, neighborhood. Bookstore. **Programs & Events:** Guided home tours, interpretive programs, walks. Lincoln's Birthday (Feb.), Lincoln Colloquium (Sept.), Christmas in Mr. Lincoln's Neighborhood (Dec.). **Tips & Hints:** Watch your footing on slippery boardwalks. Busiest in May and July, least crowded Dec. and Jan.

FEES, HOURS & REGULATIONS

Free. Visitor parking lot fee ($2 per hour). No vehicles in the site's four city blocks. Leashed pets only. Park grounds open daily to pedestrians. Visitor center open daily 8:30–5.

HOW TO GET THERE

In downtown Springfield, at the intersection of 7th and Jackson Sts. Closest airport: Springfield (5 mi).

CONTACTS

Lincoln Home National Historic Site (413 S. 8th St., Springfield, IL 62704, tel. 217/492–4241 Ext. 221, fax 217/492–4648, www.nps.gov/liho). Springfield Convention & Visitors Bureau (109 N. 7th St., Springfield, IL 62701, tel. 800/545–7300).

See Also

Lewis and Clark National Historic Trail, Mormon Pioneer National Historic Trail, and *Trail of Tears National Historic Trail,* in Other National Parklands.

INDIANA

George Rogers Clark National Historical Park

In southwestern Indiana, in Vincennes

The park, including a classic memorial building, is on the site of the Revolutionary War Battle of Fort Sackville. The memorial commemorates the capture of the fort from the British by Lieutenant Colonel George Rogers Clark and his men on February 25, 1779, and the subsequent settlement of the region north of the Ohio River. The site was authorized in 1966.

WHAT TO SEE & DO

Picnicking, touring Clark Memorial and surrounding 26 acres of landscaped lawns. **Facilities:** Visitor center, memorial building, grounds. Book and gift shop sales area, picnic table area. **Programs & Events:** Reenactor Gathering (3rd Sun. of month, Apr.–Nov.). Spirit of Vincennes Rendezvous (Memorial Day weekend), July 4 fireworks. **Tips & Hints:** Busiest in May and July, least crowded Jan. and Feb.

FOOD, LODGING & SUPPLIES

Camping: None in park. In Vincennes: Ouabache Trails Park (3500 N. Lower Fort Knox Rd., tel. 812/882–4316; 35 sites; $13; flush toilets, showers, hook-ups). **Hotels:** None in park. In Vincennes: Executive Inn (1 Executive Blvd., off the 6th St. Exit from U.S. 41, tel. 812/886–5000 or 800/457–9154; 167 rooms; $65). **Restaurants:** None in park. In Vincennes: Old Thyme Diner (331 Main St., tel. 812/886–0333; $4–$7; no dinner Mon.–Thurs. and Sat., closed Sun.). **Groceries:** None in park. In Vincennes: Cash n' Dash (512 Willow St., Vincennes, tel. 812/882–6102), Wal-Mart (650 Kimmel Rd., tel. 812/886–0312).

FEES, HOURS & REGULATIONS

Entrance fee: $3 adults, free ages 16 and under, $4 per family. Leashed pets only. Park and visitor center open daily 9–5.

HOW TO GET THERE

In downtown Vincennes. Take Willow or 6th St. Exit off U.S. 41 or 6th St. Exit off U.S. 50. Closest airport: Evansville (60 mi).

CONTACTS

George Rogers Clark National Historic Park (401 S. 2nd St., Vincennes, IN 47591, tel. 812/882–1776, fax 812/882–7270, www.nps.gov/gero). Vincennes–Knox County Convention & Visitors Bureau (Box 602, Vincennes, IN 47591, tel. 812/886–0400 or 800/886–6443). Knox County Chamber of Commerce (Box 553, Vincennes, IN 47591, tel. 812/882–6440, www.accessknoxcounty.com).

Indiana Dunes National Lakeshore

Between Gary and Michigan City, along Lake Michigan

The 15,000-acre park preserves three main dune ridges that run parallel to Lake Michigan's shoreline. The younger dunes, which rise 180 feet, are still open and sandy but the 8,000- to 12,000-year-old dune ridges are covered with oak and maple forests. Beaches, bogs, marshes, swamps, prairie remnants, and a farm and homestead dating to 19th-century fur trading and pioneer agriculture are also open to the public. The lakeshore was authorized on November 5, 1966.

WHAT TO SEE & DO

Bicycling (rentals, Chesterton), bird-watching, boating, cross-country skiing, fishing, hiking, horseback riding, picnicking, swimming. **Facilities:** 2 visitor centers: Dorothy Buell (U.S. 12 and Kemil Rd.) and Bailly-Chellberg (Mineral Spring Rd. and U.S. 20, Porter). Paul H. Douglas Center for Environmental Education, beaches, biking and hiking trails, amphitheater. Bookstores, bathhouse, picnic pavilions, and shelters. **Programs & Events:** Ranger-guided hikes and programs, farm feeding programs (weekends), musicals (3rd Fri. of the month). Ranger-guided Pinhook Bog tours (May–Oct., weekends; reservations required, tel. 219/926–7561 Ext. 225), day and night hikes (May–Oct., daily), Chellberg Farm and Bailly Homestead house tours and historic demonstrations (May–Oct., Sun. 1–4), campfire programs (May–Oct., weekend evening). Maple Sugar Time Festival (1st 2 weekends, Mar.), Walpurgis Night (4th Sat., Apr.), Duneland Harvest Festival (3rd weekend, Sept.), Duneland Christmas (Dec.). **Tips & Hints:** Watch for rip currents. Don't walk on shoreline shelf ice. Go in spring for migrating birds and wildflowers, summer for swimming and wildflowers, fall for fall colors and prairie wildflowers. Busiest June–Aug., least crowded Dec. and Jan.

FOOD, LODGING & SUPPLIES

Camping: In the park: Dunewood Campground (79 sites; $15; flush toilets, showers). **Hotels:** None in park. In The Pines: Al and Sally's (3221 W. Dunes Hwy., tel. 219/872–9131; 16 rooms; $65). **Restaurants:** None in park. In Chesterton: Lakeshore Café (475 Sandcreek Dr., tel. 219/921–1488; $5–$15). **Groceries:** None in park. In Beverly Shores: The Dunes Mart (U.S. 12 and Broadway, tel. 219/879–8048).

FEES, HOURS & REGULATIONS

Parking fee: $6 per vehicle for day use at West Beach (Memorial Day–Labor Day). Indiana state fishing license required. Smelt fishing permit required. No dune buggies or snowmobiles. No hunting. No open fires except in campground. No pets on some beaches (May–Oct.). Park open daily dawn–dusk. Visitor centers open Memorial Day–Labor Day, daily 8–6; Labor Day–Memorial Day, daily 8–5.

HOW TO GET THERE

Take I–80, I–90, or I–94 to Rte. 49 in Chesterton or Rte. 249 in Portage at Burns Harbor. From Chesterton, take Rte. 49 north and then either U.S. 20 or U.S. 12 to park. From Portage, take Rte. 249 to U.S. 12 east to park. Closest airports: Chicago's Midway (45 mi), Gary Airport (10 mi).

CONTACTS

Indiana Dunes National Lakeshore (1100 N. Mineral Springs Rd., Porter, IN 46304, tel. 219/926–7561, fax 219/926–7561 Ext. 557, www. nps.gov/indu). Duneland Chamber of Commerce (303 Broadway, Chestertown, IN 46304, tel. 219/926–5513, fax 219/926–7593). Porter County Tourism (800 Indian Boundary Rd., Chestertown, IN 46304, tel. 219/926–2255 or 800/283–8687, fax 219/929–5395).

Lincoln Boyhood National Memorial

In southwestern Indiana, in Lincoln City

On this Southern Indiana farm, Abraham Lincoln spent 14 years, from the ages of 7 to 21. He worked the land with his father, developed his love of reading and his curiosity for knowledge, and experienced the death of his mother, Nancy Hanks Lincoln, when he was nine years old. The memorial was authorized in 1962.

WHAT TO SEE & DO

Picnicking, touring living historical farm, visiting Nancy Hanks Lincoln's grave, and Cabin Site Memorial. **Facilities:** Visitor center with 2 Memorial Halls, living historical farm, museum, auditorium, gravesite, cabin site, trail. Bookstore, picnic tables, post office. **Programs & Events:** Interpretive programs (June–Aug.). Dec. Holidays (1st weekend, Dec.), Lincoln Day (Sun. preceding Feb. 12). **Tips & Hints:** Visit May–Sept., when living historical farm is open. Busiest July and Aug., least crowded Jan. and Feb.

FOOD, LODGING & SUPPLIES

Camping: None in park. In Lincoln City: Lincoln State Park (Rte. 162 off U.S. 231, tel. 866/622–6746; 150 sites; $24; flush toilets, showers, hook-ups). **Hotels:** None in park. In Dale: Baymont Inn & Suites (I–64 and U.S. 231, tel. 812/937–7000; 71 rooms, 3 suites; $70–$130). **Restaurants:** None in park. In Dale: Windell's Café (6 W. Medcalf St., tel. 812/937–4253; $6–$8). **Groceries & Gear:** None in park. In Dale: Circle S (2 N. Washington St., tel. 812/937–2964).

FEES, HOURS & REGULATIONS

Entrance fee: $3 adults, free ages 16 and under, $5 per family. Leashed pets only. No bicycles or motorized equipment on trails. Visitor center open daily 8–5. Grounds open daily 8–dusk. Farm open May–Sept., daily 8–5.

HOW TO GET THERE

In Lincoln City, 8 mi south of I–64 via U.S. 231 and Rte. 162. Closest airports: Evansville, IN (40 mi), Louisville, KY (80 mi).

CONTACTS

Lincoln Boyhood National Memorial (Box 1816, Lincoln City, IN 47552, tel. 812/937–4541, fax 812/937–9929, www.nps.gov/libo). Spencer County Visitors Bureau (Box 202, Santa Claus, IN 47579, tel. 812/937–2848 Ext. 209 or 888/444–9252, www.legendaryplaces.org).

IOWA

Effigy Mounds National Monument

In northeastern Iowa, near Marquette

Two hundred and six prehistoric burial and ceremonial mounds, some in the shapes of bears and birds, are preserved here. Woodland Native Americans built the mounds between 500 BC and AD 1300. The land was untouched by the glaciers of the Ice Age, so it provides a rugged terrain that includes bluffs towering 300 feet to 400 feet above the Mississippi River. Located where the eastern hardwood forest meets the midwestern prairie, the monument includes forests, prairies, rivers, and ponds. It was established on October 25, 1949.

WHAT TO SEE & DO

Hiking, skiing, viewing mounds. **Facilities:** Visitor center, museum, and auditorium (3 mi north of Marquette), wayside exhibits, trails. Bookstore. **Programs & Events:** Ranger-guided walks (Memorial Day–Labor Day), moonlight hikes (June–Aug.), bird walks (June–Sept., once each month), film festival (Jan.–Mar., weekends). Iowa Archaeology Month (Sept.), Hawk Watch (last weekend of Sept.). **Tips & Hints:** Go in spring and late Sept. for bird migrations, in winter to see bald eagles. Busiest in Aug. and Oct., least crowded in Dec. and Jan.

FOOD, LODGING & SUPPLIES

Camping: None in park. In Prairie du Chien, WI: Big River Campground (106 W. Parquette, tel. 608/326–2712; 108 sites; $16–$20; flush toilets, showers, hook-ups). **Hotels:** None in park. In McGregor: Alexander Hotel (213 Main St., tel. 563/873–3454; 11 rooms, 1 suite; $50–$95 rooms). **Restaurants:** None in park. In McGregor: Riverview Inn (Main St., tel. 563/873–9667; $8–$12). **Groceries:** None in park. In McGregor: Kwik Star Convenience Store (125 Main St., tel. 563/873–3825).

FEES, HOURS & REGULATIONS

Entrance fee: $3 adults, free ages 16 and under, or $5 per vehicle. No bicycles or motorized vehicles on trails. Leashed pets only. Visitor center open Memorial Day–Labor Day, 8–6; Labor Day–Memorial Day, 8–4:30. Trails open daily 8–dark.

HOW TO GET THERE

3 mi north of Marquette, IA, on Rte. 76. Closest airports: Prairie du Chien, WI (8 mi), La Crosse, WI (70 mi), Dubuque, IA (60 mi).

CONTACTS

Effigy Mounds National Monument (151 Rte. 76, Harpers Ferry, IA 52146, tel. 563/873–3491, fax 563/873–3743, www.nps.gov/efmo).

McGregor–Marquette Chamber of Commerce (Box 105, McGregor, IA 52157, tel. 563/873–2186).

Herbert Hoover National Historic Site

In east-central Iowa, in West Branch

In this 187-acre park are the birthplace, Friends Meetinghouse, and boyhood neighborhood of the 31st president, the gravesite of President and Mrs. Hoover, and the Hoover Presidential Library and Museum. A replica of a typical blacksmith shop, similar to the one operated by Herbert Hoover's father, is near the Birthplace Cottage and the first schoolhouse built in West Branch. Seventy-six acres of restored tallgrass prairie flank the south and west sides of the park. The Library-Museum is administered by the National Archives and Records Administration. The site was authorized on August 12, 1965.

WHAT TO SEE & DO

Cross-country skiing, hiking, picnicking, touring buildings and library-museum. **Facilities:** Visitor center (Parkside Dr.–Main St. intersection), library-museum, birthplace cottage and other buildings, gravesite, wayside exhibits. Fire grate, gift shop, picnic shelters, post office. **Programs & Events:** Ranger-guided tours, prairie walks. Hooverfest (1st weekend, Aug.), "Harvest Home" (1st weekend, Oct.), Christmas Past (1st weekend, Dec.), library-museum exhibits (occasionally, all year). **Tips & Hints:** Be careful on slippery boardwalks during frosty or wet weather. Busiest July and Aug., least crowded Jan. and Feb.

FOOD, LODGING & SUPPLIES

Camping: None in park. In West Liberty: KOA Campground (1961 Garfield Ave., tel. 319/627–2676; 58 sites; $23–$25; flush toilets, showers, hook-ups). **Hotels:** None in park. In West Branch: Presidential Motor Inn (711 S. Downey Rd., Exit 264 off I–80, tel. 319/643–2526; 47 rooms; $46–$56). **Restaurants:** None in park. In West Branch: The Hoover House (102 W. Main St., tel. 319/643–5420; $5–$20). **Groceries:** None in park. In West Branch: Dewey's Jack & Jill (115 E. Main St., tel. 319/643–2611).

FEES, HOURS & REGULATIONS

Entrance fee: $3 adults, $1 ages 62 and over. Picnic shelter reservations available ($25, tel. 319/643–2541). Leashed pets only. No skateboarding. Bikes in designated areas only. Park and visitor center open daily 9–5.

HOW TO GET THERE

The visitor center is at the intersection of Parkside Dr. and Main St., 0.4 mi north of Exit 254 off I–80. Closest airport: Cedar Rapids (28 mi).

CONTACTS

Superintendent, Herbert Hoover National Historic Site (Box 607, West Branch, IA 52358, tel. 319/643–2541, www.nps.gov/heho). West Branch Chamber of Commerce (Box 365, West Branch, IA 52358, tel. 319/643–2111).

See Also

California National Historic Trail, Lewis and Clark National Historic Trail and *Mormon Pioneer National Historic Trail,* in Other National Parklands.

KANSAS

Brown v. Board of Education National Historic Site

In Topeka, 61 mi west of Kansas City

In the former Monroe Elementary School building, once a segregated school for African-American children, this site commemorates the landmark Supreme Court decision that made segregation in public schools illegal. On May 17, 1954, the U.S. Supreme Court unanimously declared that, "separate but equal educational facilities are inherently unequal." Such facilities violate the 14th Amendment to the U.S. Constitution, which guarantees all citizens "equal protection of the laws," the court said. The lead plaintiff's daughter attended Monroe Elementary School when *Brown v. Board of Education of Topeka* was initially filed in 1951. The site was established on October 26, 1992.

WHAT TO SEE & DO

Touring former courtroom, watching orientation video. **Facilities:** Visitor center with interpretive displays. **Tips & Hints:** Busiest July and Aug., least crowded Sept.–Feb.

FEES & HOURS

Free. Visitor center open weekdays 8–4.

HOW TO GET THERE

The park office (424 S. Kansas Ave.) and Monroe School (1515 Monroe St.) are in downtown Topeka. Closest airport: Kansas City (70 mi).

CONTACTS

Brown v. Board of Education National Historic Site (424 S. Kansas Ave., Suite 220, Topeka, KS 66603-3441, tel. 785/354–4273, fax 785/354–7213, www.nps.gov/brvb). Greater Topeka Chamber of Commerce (120 S.E. 6th Ave., Suite 110, Topeka, KS 66603-3515, tel. 785/234–2644, www.topekachamber.org).

Fort Larned National Historic Site

In west-central Kansas, west of Larned

Fort Larned was built in 1859 to protect travelers on the Santa Fe Trail from conflicts with Native Americans. In the 1860s the fort served as an agency of the Indian Bureau. Nine original buildings dating from 1866 still exist in a relatively undisturbed setting at a bend in the Pawnee River. Now that the parade ground, the flag pole, and most of the buildings have been restored or reconstructed, Fort Larned is one of the best surviving examples of an Indian Wars–era fort. A separate unit of the park contains a 44-acre plot of virgin prairie where you can see wagon ruts from the Santa Fe Trail and a prairie-dog town. The site was authorized in 1964 and established in 1966.

WHAT TO SEE & DO

Hiking, picnicking, touring buildings and grounds. **Facilities:** Visitor center, slide show, museum, 1.5-mi nature trail, wayside exhibits. Bookstore, picnic tables with fire grills. **Programs & Events:** Guided tours by appointment. Living-history programs (Memorial Day–Labor Day). Fort Larned Old Guard Roll Call (1st weekend, May), Candlelight Tour (2nd Sat., Oct., reservations essential), Christmas Open House (2nd Sat., Dec.). **Tips & Hints:** The best living-history programs take place on Memorial Day, July 4th, and Labor Day weekends. Busiest June and July, least crowded Dec. and Jan.

FOOD & LODGING

Hotels: None at site. In Larned: Best Western Townsman Inn (123 E. 14th St., tel. 620/285–3114; 44 rooms; $48–$59), Country Inn (135 E. 14th St., tel. 620/285–3216; 16 rooms; $25–$40). **Restaurants**: None at site. In Larned: Burgerteria (417 W. 14th St., tel. 620/285–3135; $4–$8), Peking Garden (621 Edwards St., tel. 620/285-2263, $5–$9), Walkers Steak House (718 Fort Larned Ave., tel. 620/285–6226; $5–$8).

FEES, HOURS & REGULATIONS

Entrance fee: $3 adults, free 16 and under, $5 per family. Leashed pets only. No hunting or relic hunting. Park and visitor center open Labor Day–Memorial Day, daily 8–6; Memorial Day–Labor Day, daily 8:30–5.

HOW TO GET THERE

6 mi west of Larned, Kansas via Rte. 156. Closest airports: Great Bend (28 mi), Wichita (136 mi).

CONTACTS

Fort Larned National Historic Site (Rte. 3, Larned, KS 67550-9321, tel. 620/285–6911, fax 620/285–3571, www.nps.gov/fols). Larned Area Chamber of Commerce (Box 240, Larned, KS 67550, tel. 620/285–6916 or 800/747–6919, www.larned.org/chamber).

Fort Scott
National Historic Site

In southeastern Kansas, in Fort Scott

Established in 1842, Fort Scott guarded the Permanent Indian Frontier and kept settlers and Native Americans out of each other's territory. As the frontier was pushed westward, Fort Scott became obsolete. Abandoned in 1853, the fort then became a town and was drawn into the violence of "Bleeding Kansas" and the Civil War. Today, the site has been restored to its 1840s appearance. It contains 20 major historic structures in which 33 rooms are furnished with original and reproduction 19th-century items, plus a parade ground, and 5 acres of restored tallgrass prairie. The site was authorized in 1978.

WHAT TO SEE & DO

Touring buildings, walking trail. **Facilities:** Visitor center, museum. Bookstore, picnic tables. **Programs & Events:** Self-guided tours year-round. Guided tours (Memorial Day–Labor Day, daily at 1). Living-history programs, reenactments, and demonstrations (Memorial Day, July 4, and Labor Day weekends). Civil War Encampment (Apr.). Good Ol' Days (June). American Indian Heritage Weekend (Sept.). Candlelight Tour (Dec., reservations essential). **Tips & Hints:** Watch footing on uneven walkways and steep stairs. Allow 1–2 hours to see audio-visual program and tour site. Busiest May and June, least crowded Jan. and Feb.

FOOD, LODGING & SUPPLIES

Camping: None in park. In Fort Scott: Gunn RV Park (Park Ave., south of 9th and Burke Sts., tel. 620/223–0550; 14 RV sites, grassy area for tents; $4–$8; flush and portable toilets, hook-ups), Fort Scott RV Park (2162 Native Rd., tel. 620/223–3440 or 800/538–0216; 64 sites; $12–$19; flush toilets, showers, hook-ups). **Hotels:** None in park. In Fort Scott: Best Western Fort Scott Inn (101 State St., tel. 620/223–0100; 76 rooms; $52–$64), Chenault Mansion Bed & Breakfast (820 S. National St., tel. 620/223–6800; 5 rooms; $89–$99). **Restaurant:** None in park. In Fort Scott: Papa Don's (22 N. Main St., tel. 620/223–4171; $4–$6; no dinner Sun.). **Groceries:** None in park. In Fort Scott: Gene's IGA (911 E. 6th St., tel. 620/223–3710).

FEES, HOURS & REGULATIONS

Entrance fee: $3 adults, free 16 and under. No pets indoors; no unleashed pets outdoors. No plant or artifact collecting. No metal detecting. Site and visitor center open Apr.–Oct., daily 8–5; Nov.–Mar., daily 9–5.

HOW TO GET THERE

Near the intersection of U.S. 54 and U.S. 69, in downtown Fort Scott, 90 mi south of Kansas City via U.S. 69, 60 mi from Joplin via Rte. 43 north to U.S. 54. Closest airports: Fort Scott, Joplin, Kansas City.

CONTACTS

Fort Scott National Historic Site (Old Fort Blvd., Box 918, Fort Scott, KS 66701, tel. 620/223–0310, fax 620/223–0188, www.nps.gov/fosc). Fort Scott Area Chamber of Commerce (231 East Wall, Fort Scott, KS 66701, tel. 620/223–3566 or 800/245–3678, www.fortscott.com).

Nicodemus National Historic Site

In northwestern Kansas, in Nicodemus

Nicodemus was established in 1877 and settled by African-Americans during Reconstruction after the Civil War. It's the site of one of the oldest reported post offices supervised by African-Americans in the United States. Five historic buildings are within the 161-acre site: the First Baptist Church, built in 1907; the African-Methodist-Episcopal Church, built between 1885 and 1907; Township Hall, built in 1939; St. Francis Hotel, built in 1881; and Nicodemus District No. 1 School, built in 1918. The site was established as a National Historic Landmark in 1976 and as a National Historic Site in 1996.

WHAT TO SEE & DO

Auto or bike touring, touring Township Hall, walking around grounds. **Facilities:** Visitor center, Historical Society museum. Bookstore, picnic tables. **Programs & Events:** Ranger-led guided tours year-round. Emancipation Day–Homecoming (last weekend, July), Pioneer Days (2nd weekend, Oct.). **Tips & Hints:** As of this writing, the park essentially consists of Township Hall, which is the visitor center. The other historic buildings on site are privately owned.

FOOD, LODGING & SUPPLIES

Camping: None in park. In Stockton: Webster State Park (1210 9 Rd., tel. 785/425–6775; 166 sites; $8–$15 plus $6 per vehicle; flush and pit toilets, showers, hook-ups). **Hotel:** None in park. In Stockton: Midwest Motel (1401 Main St., tel. 785/425–6706; 13 rooms; $36). **Restaurant:** None in park. In Stockton: Home Cookin' (1203 Main St., tel. 785/425–6494; $3–$5). **Groceries:** None in park. In Hill City: Hill City IGA (113 E. Main St., tel. 785/421–2051).

FEES & HOURS

Free. Park, visitor center, Township Hall, and bookstore open daily 8:30–5, though hours may vary.

HOW TO GET THERE

Nicodemus is 11 mi east of Hill City and 19 mi west of Stockton on U.S. 24. From Hays, take U.S. 183 north to Stockton. Closest airports: Hill City, Hays (50 mi).

CONTACTS

Nicodemus National Historic Site (304 Washington Ave., Bogue, KS 67625, tel. 785/839–4233, fax 785/839–4325, www.nps.gov/nico). Hill City Chamber of Commerce (104 W. Main St., Hill City, KS 67642, tel. 785/421–5621, www.discoverhillcity.com).

Tallgrass Prairie National Preserve

In east-central Kansas, near Strong City

This site in the Flint Hills region of Kansas protects 17 square mi of the once vast tallgrass prairie ecosystem that once covered much of North America. Several 19th-century buildings listed as National Historic Landmarks, including a ranch house, limestone barn, and one-room schoolhouse, plus the cultural resources of the Spring Hill–Z Bar

Ranch, are also part of the preserve. The National Park Trust—a non-profit organization that bought the property in 1994—owns most of the land but shares in the management of it with the National Park Service. The site was authorized on November 12, 1996.

WHAT TO SEE & DO

Hiking trails, touring historic buildings in groups, touring preserve by bus, touring ranch headquarters. **Facilities:** Visitor center (in historic barn May–Oct., on back porch of ranch house Nov.–Apr.), information kiosks, interpretive wayside exhibits, orientation video, 1.75-mi Southwind Nature Trail. Bookstore–gift shop. **Programs & Events:** Self-guided tours of ranch headquarters and nature trail. Guided tours of ranch house (May–Oct., hourly 9:30–3:30; Nov.–Apr. by appointment). Bus tours of tallgrass prairie (end of Apr.–Oct., daily at 11, 1, and 3), living-history programs (June–Oct., weekends). **Tips & Hints:** Watch for poisonous snakes, poison ivy, biting insects, ticks, and uneven terrain. Go mid-Apr. to June or late Aug. and Sept. for wildflowers, early fall to see the tallgrass at peak height. Reservations advised for bus tours. Busiest June–Oct., least crowded Jan.–Mar.

FOOD, LODGING & SUPPLIES

⚠ **Camping:** None in park. In Cottonwood Falls: Swope Park (Walnut and County Rd., tel. 620/273–6666; 6 RV sites; $5; hook-ups). 🛏 **Hotels:** None in park. In Emporia: Best Western Hospitality House (3021 W. U.S. 50, tel. 620/342–7587; 143 rooms; $55–$65), Days Inn (3032 W. U.S. 50 Business, tel. 620/342–1787; 39 rooms; $64). ✗ **Restaurants:** None in park. In Emporia: Bruff's Bar & Grill (22 E. 6th St., tel. 620/342–1223; $5–$13). In Cottonwood Falls: Emma Chase Café (317 Broadway, tel. 620/273–6020; $5–$7; no dinner Sat.–Tues. and Thurs., closed Mon.), Grand Central Hotel & Grill (215 Broadway, tel. 620/273-6763; $5–$15; closed Sun.). ♦ **Groceries & Gear:** In Strong City: Clarks Farm & Home Store (4th and Cottonwood Sts., tel. 620/273–6656), Strong City Grocery (322 Cottonwood St., tel. 620/273–8639).

FEES, HOURS & REGULATIONS

House tours free. Prairie bus tours $5 adults, $3 ages 5–18, and free ages 4 and under. Combination bus–house tours $7 adults, $4 ages 5–18, and free ages 4 and under. No visitors beyond ranch headquarters except on ranger-led bus tours. Leashed pets only. No horses or bicycles on nature trails. Preserve open daily 9–4:30; one-room schoolhouse open May–Oct., weekends noon–4.

HOW TO GET THERE

The ranch headquarters area is 2 mi north of Strong City on Rte. 177. Closest airports: Emporia (18 mi), Kansas City (100 mi), Wichita (80 mi).

CONTACTS

Tallgrass Prairie National Preserve (Attn: Park Rangers, Box 14, Rte. 177, Strong City, KS 66869, tel. 620/273–8494, fax 620/273–8950, www.nps.gov/tapr). Chase County Chamber of Commerce (318 Broadway, Cottonwood Falls, KS 66845, tel. 620/273–8469 or 800/

431–6344). Emporia Convention & Visitors Bureau (719 Commercial St., Emporia, KS 66801, tel. 800/279–3730 or 620/342–1803, fax 620/342–3223, www.emporiakschamber.org).

See Also

California National Historic Trail, Lewis & Clark National Historic Trail, Oregon National Historic Trail, Pony Express National Historic Trail, and *Santa Fe National Historic Trail,* in Other National Parklands.

Abraham Lincoln Birthplace
National Historic Site

In southern Kentucky, south of Louisville

Abraham Lincoln, the 16th president of the United States, was born on Sinking Spring Farm on February 12, 1809, and today nearly one-third of the farm is preserved at this National Historic Site. The memorial overlooks Sinking Spring, the water source for the original 348-acre property. In 1911 the Lincoln Farm Association added a neoclassical-style shrine for the symbolic birthplace cabin, and in 2001 the park added the Abraham Lincoln Boyhood Home at Knob Creek, which preserves the site of Lincoln's home from ages 2 to 7. The park was authorized July 17, 1916 and designated as a national historical site on September 8, 1959.

WHAT TO SEE & DO

Hiking, picnicking, touring the grounds, viewing 18-minute video. **Facilities:** Visitor center, outdoor interpretive exhibits and signs, movie, self-guided tours, hiking trails. Bookstore, covered picnic tables with fire grills, picnic tables. **Programs & Events:** Self-guided tours, daily interpretive talks. Musical tribute to Dr. Martin Luther King, Jr. (Sun. before holiday in Jan. at 2), wreath-laying ceremony at symbolic birthplace cabin (Feb. 12, 1:30), founding of the National Park Service (Aug. 25), U.S. Constitution Week (Sept. 17). **Tips & Hints:** Go July–Aug. for the best weather; visit Dec. and Jan. to avoid crowds.

FOOD, LODGING & SUPPLIES

Camping: None at site. In Elizabethtown: KOA (209 Tunnel Hill Rd., tel. 270/737–7600; 800/562–7605 reservations; 70 sites, 3 cabins; $15–$27, $40 cabins; flush toilets, showers, hook-ups). **Hotels:** None in park. In Elizabethtown: Best Western Cardinal Inn (642 E. Dixie Ave., at Exit 91, off I–65, tel. 270/765–6139; 47 rooms; $75). **Restaurants:** None in park. In Hodgenville: Joel Ray's (2579 Lincoln Farm Rd./U.S. 31 E, tel. 270/358–3545; $5). **Groceries:** None in park. In Hodgenville: Save-A-Lot Foodstore (102 S. Lincoln Dr., tel. 270/358–3108).

FEES, HOURS, & REGULATIONS

Entrance fee: Free. No unleashed pets. No bikes, horses, or motorized equipment on trails. No hunting. Park and visitor center open Memorial Day–Labor Day, daily 8–6:45; Labor Day–Memorial Day, daily 8–4:45. Knob Creek open Apr.–Oct., daily 8:30–4:30.

HOW TO GET THERE

3 mi south of Hodgenville, on U.S. 31 E via Rte. 61. Closest airport: Louisville (55 mi).

CONTACTS
Abraham Lincoln Birthplace National Historic Site (2995 Lincoln Farm Rd., Hodgenville, KY 42748, tel. 270/358–3137, fax 270/358–3874, www.nps.gov/abli). LaRue County Chamber of Commerce (58 Lincoln Sq., Box 176, Hodgenville, KY 42748, tel. 270/358–3411, fax 270/358—8978, www.laruecountychamber.org).

Cumberland Gap
National Historical Park

Junction of Kentucky, Virginia,
and Tennessee, near Middlesboro, KY

This natural passageway across the Appalachian Mountains opened the west to 18th-century travelers and explorers. Native Americans first discovered the gap by following buffalo herds as they headed into the verdant hills of what is now Kentucky. Around 300,000 settlers later passed through here from 1775 through 1810, expanding American settlements and opening new routes across the continent. Today you'll find wayside exhibits, a museum, and the abandoned old cabins of the former Hensley settlement, all with signage noting the area's historic significance. The park was authorized in 1940.

WHAT TO SEE & DO

Auto touring, hiking, picnicking. **Facilities:** Visitor center, museum, hiking trails. Book-and-gift store, covered picnic tables with fire grills, picnic tables (reservations and fee, *see below*). **Programs & Events:** Ranger-led walking tours (May–Aug.; reservations required), Gap (Cudjo's) Cave tours (Jan.–Mar., weekends 10 and 2; Apr.–May and Sept.–Dec. daily at 10, weekends at 2; Memorial Day–Aug., daily 9, 11:30, 3; reservations required). **Tips & Hints:** Go Apr.–May for wildflowers, in Sept. for great hiking, and in mid-Oct. for peak foliage. Busiest July–Oct., least crowded Jan. and Feb. Come prepared for variable weather all year. Pinnacle Overlook may close in winter due to bad weather.

FOOD, LODGING & SUPPLIES

⚠ **Camping:** In the park: Wilderness Road Campground (160 sites; $10–$15; flush toilets, showers, hook-ups). Backcountry camping (permit required, *see below*). 🏨 **Hotels:** None in park. In Middlesboro: Best Western Inn (1623 E. Cumberland Ave., tel. 606/248–5630; 100 rooms; $48–$63), Holiday Inn Express (1252 N. 12th St./U.S. 25 E, tel. 606/248–6860 or 800/465–4329; 60 rooms; $79). ✗ **Restaurants:** None in park. In Middlesboro: J. Milton's Steak House (910 N. 12th St./U.S. 25 E, tel. 606/248–0458; $7–$15). In Pineville: Pine Mountain State Park Resort Dining Room (1050 State Park Rd., tel. 606/337–3066; $7–$14). ⛽ **Groceries & Gear:** None in park. In Cumberland Gap: Zoe's (719 Pennylane Ave., tel. 423/869–0705). In Gibson Station, VA: Montgomery's Grocery (Noetown Rd., tel. 606/248–2772).

FEES, HOURS & REGULATIONS

Free. Pinnacle Overlook shuttle: $3. Hensley Settlement tour: $12 adults, $6 ages 12 and under. Gap (Cudjo's) Cave tour: $7 adults, $3.50 ages 12 and under and Golden Age Passport holders. Picnic pavilions $20 per day, reservations required. Backcountry permits required (free). No vehicles over 20 feet on Pinnacle Rd. No unleashed pets, skateboards, or in-line skates. Bikes on paved roads and designated trails only. Do not feed animals. Park open daily dawn–dusk. Visitor center open Memorial Day–Oct., daily 8–6; Nov.–Memorial Day, daily 8–5.

HOW TO GET THERE

Via U.S. 25 east in Tennessee and Kentucky, and via U.S. 58 in Virginia. Closest airports: Middlesboro (3 mi), Knoxville (90 mi).

CONTACTS

Cumberland Gap National Historic Park (Box 1848, Middlesboro, KY 40965, tel. 606/248–2817; 606/246–1075 activity reservations, fax 606/248–2818, www.nps.gov/cuga). Claiborne County Chamber of Commerce and Tourism (3222 U.S. 25, Tazewell, TN 37879, tel. 423/626–4149 or 800/332–8164, fax 423/626–1611, www.claibornecounty.com). Bell County Tourism Commission (2215 Cumberland Ave., Middlesboro, KY 40965, tel. 606/248–2482 or 800/988–1075, fax 606/248–0011, www.mountaingateway.com). Town of Cumberland Gap (330 Colwin, Box 78, Cumberland Gap, TN 37724, tel. 423/869–3860, fax 423/869–8534).

Mammoth Cave National Park

In south-central Kentucky, northeast of Bowling Green

The Mammoth Cave network is the world's longest, extending for more than 360 mi beneath the mountains of southern Kentucky. This incredible maze of underground passages, endless vertical shafts, and cold, black rivers also hides many unusual nocturnal creatures: eyeless fish, cave spiders, white crayfish, and rare beetles, among many others. Above ground the park has 70 mi of backcountry hiking and horseback riding trails, plus 31 mi of scenic shorelines along the Green and Nolin rivers. The site was established in 1941, designated a World Heritage Site in 1981, and declared an International Biosphere Reserve in 1990.

WHAT TO SEE & DO

Bird-watching, canoeing (rentals Brownsville), cave touring, fishing, hiking, horseback riding (rentals nearby), kayaking, picnicking. **Facilities:** Visitor center, hiking trails. Book-and-gift shop, covered picnic tables, picnic tables with fire grills. **Programs & Events:** Daily ranger-led cave tours, talks, and slide presentations. Ranger-led nature walks, evening programs (May–Oct.). Wildflower Day (Apr.), Roots in the

Cave (Oct.). **Tips & Hints:** Wear comfortable walking shoes and bring a jacket for inside the cave. Go in spring for dogwood blooms, Aug. for wildflower peak. Busiest July and Aug., least crowded Dec. and Jan. Winter visits yield gorgeous icicle formations along the rivers.

FOOD, LODGING & SUPPLIES

⚠ **Camping:** 3 campgrounds in the park: Headquarters (109 sites; $16; flush toilets; closed Dec.–Feb.), Houchins Ferry (12 sites; $12; pit toilets), Maple Springs (7 group sites; $25; pit toilets). Backcountry camping available (permit required, *see below*). ⛺ **Hotels:** In the park: Mammoth Cave Hotel (Rte. 70, tel. 270/758–2225; 62 rooms, 20 cottages, 10 cabins; $35–$75; cottages closed Oct.–mid-May, cabins closed Nov.–mid-Mar.). In Horse Cave: Budget Host Inn (Rte. 218 at I–65, tel. 270/786–2165; 80 rooms; $30–$47), Hampton Inn Horse Cave (750 Flint Ridge Rd., tel. 270/786–5000 or 800/426–7866; 101 rooms; $74–$79). ✕ **Restaurants:** In the park: Mammoth Cave Hotel (Rte. 70, tel. 270/758–2225; $2–$8). In Cave City: Sahara Steak House (413 E. Happy Valley Rd., tel. 270/773–3450; $9–$30). ⛏ **Groceries & Gear:** In the park: Service Center–Caver's Camp Store (near Headquarters Campground, tel. 270/758–2232).

FEES, HOURS & REGULATIONS

Free. Scenic cave tours $5–$12, Introduction to Caving tour $22, Wild Cave Tour $45; children ages 6 or under or less than 42 inches tall not allowed on some tours. Other restrictions apply. Backcountry camping permits (free) required. No pets on cave tours or off leash. Mountain bikes and in-line skates in designated areas only. No fireworks. No Jet Skis on river. No off-road motorized equipment. Park open year-round, with daily cave tours. Visitor center open Jan.–Feb., daily 9–5; Mar.–mid-June and Labor Day–Dec., daily 8–5; mid-June–Labor Day, daily 7:30–7.

HOW TO GET THERE

Via I–65 to Cave City or Park City exits, then head west on Rte. 70 or Mammoth Cave Parkway. Closest airports: Louisville, KY (90 mi), Nashville, TN (100 mi).

CONTACTS

Mammoth Cave National Park (Box 7, Mammoth Cave, KY 42259, tel. 270/758–2178; 800/967–2283 for activities requiring reservations or online at reservations.nps.gov, fax 270/758–2349, www.nps.gov/maca). Cave City Chamber of Commerce and Welcome Center (Box 460, 502 Mammoth Cave St., Cave City, KY 42127, tel./fax 270/773–5159). Edmonson County Tourist Commission (Box 628, Brownsville, KY 42210, tel. 800/624–8687, www.cavesandlakes.com).

See Also

Big South Fork National River and Recreation Area, Tennessee. *Trail of Tears National Historic Trail,* in Other National Parklands.

Cane River Creole
National Historical Park

In west-central Louisiana, near Natchitoches

Two sprawling plantations are joined in this historic park area: Oakland Plantation, founded in 1785, and Magnolia Plantation, settled in 1735 and founded in 1835. Both sites represent the gradual continuum from 18th-century land grants to mid-20th-century occupation and use by the same families who owned the plantations—as well as by many of the families who worked for them, first as slaves and later as tenants and sharecroppers. The Oakland unit includes the 1820s "Main House" and most of the original outbuildings. The Magnolia unit has eight brick cabins from the 1830s, plus wooden and steam cotton ginning and pressing equipment. The park was authorized on November 2, 1994.

WHAT TO SEE & DO

Touring plantations. **Facilities:** Visitor center. **Programs & Events:** Daily guided tours of Oakland (9, 11, 1, and 3) and Magnolia (24-hour advance reservations required, tel. 318/356–8441). **Tips & Hints**: Expect to spend about one hour on each tour. Busiest May–Sept., least crowded July and Aug.

FOOD, LODGING & SUPPLIES

Hotels: None in park. In Natchitoches: Comfort Inn (5362 Rte. 6 W, tel. 318/352–7500 or 800/228–5150; 59 rooms; $60–$68), Hampton Inn (5300 Rte. 6 W, tel. 318/354–0010 or 800/426–7866; 74 rooms; $64–$74). ✕ **Restaurants:** None in park. In Natchitoches: Almost Home (Rte. 1 Bypass, tel. 318/352–2431; $7–$11; no dinner Sun.–Thurs., closed Sat.), The Landing Restaurant (530 Front St., tel. 318/352–1579; $6–$10; closed Mon.). ♻ **Groceries:** None in park. In Natchitoches: Brookshires (318 Dixie Plaza, tel. 318/352–4000).

FEES, HOURS & REGULATIONS

Free. Park open via guided tour only. Office open weekdays 8–4:30.

HOW TO GET THERE

Oakland Plantation: 8 mi south of Natchitoches on Rte. 119; Magnolia Plantation: 10 mi farther south on Rte. 119. Closest airports: Alexandria (45 mi), Shreveport (75 mi).

CONTACTS

Cane River Creole National Historical Park (mailing address: 400 Rapides Dr., Natchitoches, LA 71457; location: 4386 Rte. 494, Natchez, LA 71456, tel. 318/352–0383, fax 318/352–4549, www.nps.gov/cari). Natchitoches Parish Tourist Commission (781 Front St., Natchitoches, LA 71457, tel. 318/352–8072 or 800/259–1714, www.natchitoches.net).

Jean Lafitte National Historical Park & Preserve

In southern Louisiana, between Eunice and New Orleans

The rich history of Louisiana's Mississippi River Delta is the focus of this diverse park's many sectors. Relics of Acadian history and culture are on exhibit at the Lafayette, Thibodaux, and Eunice sites, while boardwalks meander through the forest, swampland, and marshy environments of the Barataria Preserve near Crown Point, just south of New Orleans. Chalmette Battlefield was the site of the 1815 Battle of New Orleans, and Chalmette National Cemetery holds the graves of veterans from the Civil to the Vietnam wars. The visitor center, smack in the New Orleans French Quarter, follows the history and culture of the city and the Mississippi Delta. The Chalmette Monument and Grounds, established in 1907, was transferred to the Park Service in 1933, renamed a national historical park in 1939, and incorporated into Jean Lafitte National Historical Park & Preserve in 1978.

WHAT TO SEE & DO

Attending cultural demonstrations and educational programs, canoeing, hiking, touring grounds, battlefields, and cemetery. **Facilities:** 6 visitor centers: Acadian (501 Fisher Rd., Lafayette), Prairie Acadian (250 W. Park Ave., Eunice), Wetlands Acadian (314 St. Mary St., Thibodaux), Barataria (on Rte. 45, near Crown Point, 17 mi south of New Orleans), Chalmette (St. Bernard Hwy., Chalmette), and French Quarter (419 Decatur St., New Orleans); movies, self-guided tours, hiking trails. Bookstores at each site. **Programs & Events:** Acadian: film 9–4, hourly; Prairie Acadian: demonstrations Sat. 3–6, live music Sat. 6 PM–8 PM; Wetlands Acadian: music Mon. 5:30 PM–7 PM; Barataria: natural-history walks daily at 2, group walks (reservation only), canoe trips Sat. 9:30 AM (reservation only), full-moon canoe trips (reservation only); Chalmette: battle talks daily 11:15 and 2:45, living-history demonstrations (Mar.–May and Oct. and Nov., Sat. 10–3), Battle of New Orleans anniversary (2nd Sat., Jan.); French Quarter: walking tours (daily at 9:30), folklife demonstrations (Sat. 11–3). All sites have films shown on request. **Tips & Hints:** Visit in spring and fall for best weather; summer is hot and humid. Watch for fire ants at Chalmette Battlefield, snakes and alligators at Barataria Preserve. Busiest Mar., Apr., and Oct.; least crowded July–Sept. and Dec. and Jan.

LODGING

Camping: None in park. Near Barataria Preserve: Bayou Segnette State Park (7777 Westbank Expressway, Westwego, tel. 504/736–7140; 98 sites; $12; flush toilets, showers, hook-ups). Near Chalmette Battlefield: St. Bernard State Park (St. Bernard's Pkwy., Braithwaite, tel. 504/682–2101; 51 sites; $12; flush toilets, showers, hook-ups). **Hotels:** None in park. In Eunice: Best Western (1531 W. Laurel Ave., tel. 337/457–2800 or 800/962–8423; 35 rooms; $69–$79).

FEES & HOURS

Free. Acadian open daily 8–5; Prairie open Tues.–Fri. 8–5, Sat. 8–6; Wetlands open Fri.–Sun. 9–5, Mon. 9–8, Tues.–Thurs. 9–6; Barataria, Chalmette, and French Quarter open daily 9–5. All sites except Prairie Acadian Cultural Center closed Mardi Gras.

HOW TO GET THERE

Between Eunice and New Orleans via 210 mi of I–10 and U.S. 90. Closest airports: Lafayette (½ mi from Acadian Cultural Center), New Orleans (10 mi from French Quarter Visitor Center).

CONTACTS

Jean Lafitte National Historical Park and Preserve (419 Decatur St., New Orleans, LA 70130, tel. 504/589–3882, fax 504/589–3851, www. nps.gov/jela). Acadian Cultural Center (501 Fisher Rd., Lafayette, LA 70508-2033, tel. 337/232–0789); Barataria Preserve (6588 Barataria Blvd., Marrero, LA 70072, tel. 504/589–2330); Chalmette Battlefield (8606 St. Bernard Hwy., Chalmette, LA 70043, tel. 504/281–0510); New Orleans Metropolitan Convention & Visitors Bureau (2020 St. Charles Ave., New Orleans, LA 70130, tel. 800/672–6124 or 504/566–5011, www.neworleanscvb.com); French Quarter Visitor Center (419 Decatur St., New Orleans, LA 70130, tel. 504/589–2636); Prairie Acadian Cultural Center (250 W. Park Ave., Eunice, LA 70535, tel. 337/457-8499); Wetlands Acadian Cultural Center (314 St. Mary St., Thibodaux, LA 70301, tel. 504/448–1375).

New Orleans Jazz National Historical Park

In southeast Louisiana, in New Orleans

This fascinating, musically oriented park serves up the sights, sounds, and settings from where jazz first evolved in America. Elaborate exhibits on the origins, early history, development, and progression of jazz are found throughout the site. Indoor and outdoor stages host a range of live performances, and visitors are invited to participate in interpretive music programs. The park was authorized on October 31, 1994.

WHAT TO SEE & DO

Attending concerts, participating in music programs, watching parades, demonstrations, videos. **Facilities:** Visitor center, movies, guided tours. Book-and-gift shop. **Programs & Events:** Jazz workshops, conferences, guest lectures, live concerts, jazz-theme walking tours of the French Quarter. **Tips & Hints:** In late 2003, construction began on the park's new permanent facility in Louis Armstrong Park. Busiest Oct. and Apr.; least crowded July and Aug.

FEES & HOURS

Free. Visitor center open Tues.–Sat. 9–5.

HOW TO GET THERE

In New Orleans via I–10 to Exit 236 Esplanade, south to Decatur St., and west to N. Peters St., or via I–10 to Exit 235 Canal, south to Decatur St., and east to N. Peters St.

CONTACTS

New Orleans Jazz National Historic Park (Attention: Superintendent, 419 Decatur, New Orleans, LA 70130, tel. 504/589–4806, fax 504/589–3865, www.nps.gov/neor). New Orleans Metropolitan Convention & Visitors Bureau (2020 St. Charles Ave., New Orleans, LA 70130, tel. 800/672–6124 or 504/566–5011, www.neworleanscvb.com).

Poverty Point National Monument/State Historic Site

In northeastern Louisiana, near Epps

Owned and funded by the Louisiana Office of State Parks, this 402-acre site interprets the culture of the peoples who constructed prehistoric earthworks here between 1700 and 700 BC. The observation tower offers views of much of their terrain, while a museum, an archeological laboratory, interpretive trails, and audiovisual programs tell the stories of these ancient local residents. Tram tours and craft workshops bring Native American cultural traditions to life. The site was designated a national monument on October 31, 1988.

WHAT TO SEE & DO

Touring museum and site. **Facilities:** Visitor center, museum, outdoor interpretive exhibits, movies, hiking trails. **Programs & Events:** Guided open-air tram tours (Mar.–Oct.), basket weaving workshops (Oct.–Feb.), Fall School Days (last Fri., Sept.), flintknapping workshop (3rd weekend, Feb.). **Tips & Hints:** Tour in morning during summer to avoid heat. Busiest Oct., Apr. and May; least crowded Jan. and Feb.

FOOD, LODGING & SUPPLIES

Camping: None in park. In Epps: Hale Campground (off Rte. 577, near park's northern boundary, tel. 318/926–5698; 15 sites; $10–$15; hook-ups). **Hotels:** None in park. In Delhi: Best Western Delhi Inn (135 Snider Rd., tel. 318/878–5126; 45 rooms; $49–$52), Days Inn of Delhi (113 Snider Rd., tel. 318/878–9000; 48 rooms; $55–$65). **Restaurants:** None in park. In Epps: Lil' Cafe (915 Rte. 17, tel. 318/926–2200; $7; no dinner Mon.). In Delhi: Hannah's Sideboard (1 Broadway Sq., tel. 318/878–9721; $7; no lunch Sat.). **Groceries:** In Epps: Bestway Grocery (910 Rte. 17, tel. 318/926–3902).

FEES & HOURS

Free. Park and visitor center open daily 9–5.

HOW TO GET THERE

Near Epps; from I–20 take Exit 153 (Rte. 17) north to Epps, make a right on Rte. 134 for 5 mi, then left on Rte. 577 for 1 mi. Closest airports: Monroe (55 mi), Jackson, MS (75 mi).

CONTACTS

Poverty Point National Monument (c/o Poverty Point State Historic Site, Box 276, Epps, LA 71237, tel. 318/926–5492 or 888/926–5492, www.nps.gov/popo or www.crt.state.la.us). Epps Town Hall (120 Maple St., Epps, LA 71237, tel. 318/926–5224).

See Also

Vicksburg National Military Park, Mississippi.

MAINE

Acadia National Park

On Mount Desert Island,
off the southeastern coast of Maine

Acadia's glaciated coastal and island landscape embraces towering mountains, shimmering lakes, and thick hardwood and evergreen forests. Its rich cultural history, provided by various indigenous peoples and successive waves of French and English immigrants, can be traced back 5,000 years. The Sieur de Monts Spring nature center near Bar Harbor and the Islesford Historical Museum on Little Cranberry Island explore the area's natural beauty and cultural ties. Walking trails and 45 mi of carriage roads cut through gorgeous countryside, and ranger-led programs explain the importance of the surrounding scenery. The park was proclaimed as Sieur de Monts National Monument on July 8, 1916, established as Lafayette National Park on February 26, 1919, and changed to Acadia National Park on January 19, 1929.

WHAT TO SEE & DO

Bicycling and boating (rentals in Bar Harbor, Northeast Harbor, Southwest Harbor), camping, cross-country skiing (rentals in Bar Harbor), fishing, hiking, rock climbing (permit required, *see below*), swimming. **Facilities:** Visitor center: Hulls Cove (3 mi north of Bar Harbor, off Rte. 3). Sieur de Monts Spring Nature Center (1½ mi south of Bar Harbor, off Rte. 3), Islesford Historical Museum (Little Cranberry Island). Beaches, museum, guided and self-guided tours, hiking trails. Book and map sales, picnic tables with fire grills. **Programs & Events:** Daily ranger-guided walks, hikes, talks, demonstrations, amphitheater programs, and boat cruises (late May–mid-Oct.). **Tips & Hints:** Avoid touring 10–2 in summer because of crowds. Visit late May–early June for wildflowers and migrating warblers, or first half of Oct. for fall foliage and raptor migration. Basic snacks are available, and a shuttle bus runs through the park. Busiest in July and Aug., least crowded Jan. and Feb.

FOOD & LODGING

Camping: 3 campgrounds in the park: Blackwoods (Mount Desert Island; 300 sites; $20; flush toilets May–Nov., pit toilets Dec.–Apr.; reservations required May–Oct.), Seawall (Mount Desert Island; 200 sites; $20; flush toilets; closed Oct.–mid-May), Isle de Haut (5 lean-tos; $25; pit toilet; closed mid-Oct.–mid-May; permit required, *see below*). In Bar Harbor: KOA (136 County Rd., tel. 207/288–3520; 200 sites; $30–$53; flush toilets, showers, hook-ups; closed Nov.–May). **Hotels:** None in park. In Bar Harbor: Quality Inn (40 Kebo St., tel. 207/288–5403 or 800/282–5403; 77 rooms; $149–$179), Cadillac Motor Inn (336 Main St., tel. 207/288–3831; 48 rooms, 5 apts; $79–$119; closed Oct.–mid-May), Ledgelawn Inn (66 Mount Desert St., tel. 207/288–

4596 or 800/274–5334; 33 rooms; $125–$275; closed mid-Oct.–Apr.).

✕ **Restaurants:** In the park: Jordan Pond House Restaurant (tel. 207/ 276–3316; $9–$15; closed late Oct.–mid-May); snacks at Cadillac Mountain, Thunder Hole. In Bar Harbor: Island Chowder House (38 Cottage St., tel. 207/288–4905; $5–$15; closed Nov.–Apr.), Terrace Grill (Newport Dr., tel. 207/288–3351; $7–$21).

FEES, HOURS & REGULATIONS

Entrance fee: $10 per vehicle. Permit ($25) required to camp at Isle de Haut. Write for lean-to reservations; written forms must be received after Apr. 1. Maine fishing license ($14 for one day, $24 for three, and $37 for seven) required for freshwater fishing. Rock climbing permit (free) required for groups of 6 or more at Otter Cliff. No hunting. No pets on beaches or ladder trails, leashed pets on the rest. No trail bikes. No bikes on hiking trails. No motorized vehicles on trails; only foot traffic, strollers, and electric wheelchairs on carriage roads. Park open daily but most scenic roads close in winter. Hulls Cove Visitor Center open mid-Apr.–June and Sept.–Oct., daily 8–4:30; July–Aug., daily 8–6. Park headquarters open mid-Apr.–Oct., daily 8–4:30, Nov.–mid-Apr., weekdays 8–4:30. Visitor center moved to park headquarters Nov.–mid-Apr. Sieur de Monts Nature Center open Mar., weekends 9–5; June–Sept., daily 9–5. Islesford Historical Museum open mid-June–Sept., daily 9–3:30.

HOW TO GET THERE

3 mi north of Bar Harbor via Rte. 3. Closest airports: Trenton (12 mi), Bangor (45).

CONTACTS

Acadia National Park (Box 177, Bar Harbor, ME 04609, tel. 207/288–3338; 800/365–2267 camping reservations; 207/ 288–3338 group camping and lean-to reservations, fax 207/288–8813, www.nps.gov/acad). Bar Harbor Chamber of Commerce (Box 158, Bar Harbor, ME 04609-0158, tel. 800/288–5103). Southwest Harbor–Tremont Chamber of Commerce (Box 1143, Southwest Harbor, ME 04679, tel. 800/423–9264 or 207/244–9264). Mount Desert Chamber of Commerce (Box 675, Northeast Harbor, ME 04662, tel. 207/276–5040). Acadia Information Center (Box 139, Mount Desert, ME 04660, tel. 800/358–8550 or 207/667–8550).

St. Croix Island International Historic Site

Northeast Maine, near Calais

Pierre Dugua Sieur de Mons and his company of 78 men attempted to establish a French settlement on St. Croix Island in 1604–05. Preceding Jamestown (1607) and Plymouth (1620), Sieur de Mons' outpost was one of the earliest European settlements on the North Atlantic coast of North America. The settlement was short-lived. In the summer of

1605, the French moved to a more favorable location where they established the Port Royal Habitation on the shores of the present-day Annapolis Basin, Nova Scotia. The first international historic site in the National Park System was authorized as a national monument in 1949 and redesignated in 1984.

WHAT TO SEE & DO

Picnicking, walking to interpretive shelter with view of island. **Facilities:** Interpretive sign, hiking trails. **Programs & Events:** 400th anniversary of settlement (summer, 2004). **Tips & Hints:** Plan to spend a half hour; dress warmly for constant breezes. Summer temperatures average around 80°F. No facilities, so bring snacks and drinking water.

FOOD & LODGING

Hotels: None in park. In Calais: Heslin's Motel (U.S. 1, tel. 207/454–3762; 11 rooms, 10 cottages; $55–$100; closed Nov.–Apr.). In Robbinston: Redclyffe Shore Motor Inn (U.S. 1, tel. 207/454–3270; 16 rooms; $62–$73; closed Nov.–Apr.). ✗ **Restaurants:** None in park. In Calais: Calais Motor Inn (633 Main St., tel. 207/454–7111; $7–$15; no lunch Mon., breakfast only Sat.), Wickachee (282 Main St., tel. 207/454–3400; $5–$24).

FEES, HOURS & REGULATIONS

Free. No fires. Site open daily dawn–dusk.

HOW TO GET THERE

120 mi north of Bar Harbor via U.S. 1; from Bangor, take Rte. 9 to Calais, then U.S. 1 south for 6 mi. Access to island by private boat only. Closest airport: Bangor (90 mi).

CONTACTS

Superintendent, Saint Croix Island International Historic Site (c/o Acadia National Park, Box 177, Bar Harbor, ME 04609, tel. 207/288–3338, www.nps.gov/sacr). Calais Regional Chamber of Commerce (30 Swan St., Calais, ME 04619, tel. 207/454–2308 or 888/422–3112, www.visitcalais.com).

See Also

Appalachian National Scenic Trail, West Virginia.

Antietam
National Battlefield

In northwestern Maryland, near Sharpsburg

Antietam is one of the best-preserved battlefields in the nation. On these fields on September 17, 1862, the Union army stopped the northern advance of Confederate forces in the bloodiest single-day battle of the American Civil War. Wayside exhibits and tablets describe the battle, and cannons line the 8½-mi auto tour. A stop along the route at a tower offers a view of the ¼-mi stretch known as "Bloody Lane," where 5,600 Union and Confederate soldiers were killed, wounded, or captured in three hours—more casualties than occurred during the entire eight years of the American Revolution. The site was established as a national battlefield in 1890 and transferred to the Park Service in 1933.

WHAT TO SEE & DO

Auto touring, cross-country skiing, hiking, horseback riding, picnicking, walking. **Facilities:** Visitor center, outdoor interpretive exhibits, guided and self-guided tours, museum, movies, hiking trail. Bookstore. **Programs & Events:** Self-guided auto tour, one-hour documentary *Antietam* (daily at noon), orientation film (daily, every half-hour except noon and 12:30), ranger programs. Concert and fireworks (1st Sat., July); battle anniversary hikes, tours, and programs (week of Sept. 17); Annual Memorial Illumination (1st Sat., Dec.). **Tips & Hints:** Auto-touring cassette available (fee). Horseback riding groups of five or more must sign in at visitor center. Busiest July and Aug., least crowded Jan. and Feb.

FOOD, LODGING & SUPPLIES

Camping: In the park: Rohrbach (10 sites; $25; closed early Nov.–Apr.). **Hotels:** In the park: Piper House B&B (tel. 301/797–1862; 3 rooms; $95). In Shepherdstown, WV: Days Inn (2001 Maddex Sq., tel. 304/876–3160; 51 rooms; $94). In Hagerstown, MD: Four Points by Sheraton (1910 Dual Hwy./U.S. 40, tel. 301/790–3010; 108 rooms; $69–$99). **Restaurants:** None in park. In Shepherdstown: Bavarian Inn & Lodge (Rte. 480, tel. 304/876–2551; $8–$16). In Hagerstown: Oliver's Pub & Restaurant (1565–67 Potomac Ave., tel. 301/790–0011; $5–$10; no lunch Sun.). **Groceries & Gear:** None in park. In Shepherdstown, WV: Food Lion (1009 Maddex Sq., tel. 304/876–0601), Shepherdstown Outback Basics (104 E. German St., tel. 304/876–1810).

FEES, HOURS & REGULATIONS

Entrance fee: $3 adults, free ages 16 and under, $5 per family. No open water for horses; spigots only. No firearms or edged weapons. No hunting, metal detecting, or relic hunting. Leashed pets only. Crop fields, pastures, reforested areas, barns, and other farm areas closed to public. No climbing on monuments or cannons. Bikes on roads only. No kite flying, ball games, sunbathing, model airplane or rocket flying, or Frisbees. Park open daily dawn–dusk. Visitor center open Sept.–May, daily 8:30–5, June–Aug., daily 8:30–6.

HOW TO GET THERE

1 mi north of Sharpsburg, MD, on Rte. 65.

CONTACTS

Antietam National Battlefield (Box 158, Sharpsburg, MD 21782, tel. 301/432–5124, fax 301/432–4590, www.nps.gov/anti). Hagerstown–Washington County Convention & Visitors Bureau (16 Public Sq., Hagerstown, MD 21740, tel. 301/791–3246 or 800/228–7829).

Assateague Island National Seashore

In eastern Virginia, near Chincoteague; also in southeastern Maryland, near Ocean City

The 37-mi-long shoreline is one of the few protected and undeveloped barrier islands on the East Coast. This dynamic seashore environment provides refuge to wild horses, as well as abundant and specialized flora, fauna, and marine life. It was authorized on September 21, 1965.

WHAT TO SEE & DO

Bicycling (rentals in park), canoeing (rentals in park), clamming, crabbing, fishing, hiking, hunting, off-road driving (permit required, *see below*), swimming, viewing aquariums. **Facilities:** 3 visitor centers: Barrier Island (Maryland district), Chincoteague National Wildlife Refuge, and Tom's Cove (Virginia district). Beaches, guided and self-guided tours, hiking trails. Bookstores, picnic tables with fire grills. **Programs & Events:** Ranger-led shellfishing and surf fishing demonstrations, beach walks, marsh walks, bay exploring, canoe trips (reservations required, *see below*), campfire programs and night walks (Easter–Oct.). Pony penning in Chincoteague, VA (last Wed. and Thurs., July). **Tips & Hints:** Bring insect repellent, screen tents, sunscreen, and sand stakes. Proper food storage strictly enforced. Bike and canoe rentals available June–Aug., daily; April, May, Sept., and Oct., weekends. No roads connect north and south entrances to Assateague Island. Busiest July and Aug., least crowded Jan. and Feb.

FOOD, LODGING & SUPPLIES

Camping: In the park: 153 sites scattered around the park ($16–$20; portable toilets, cold showers; closed mid-Oct.–mid.-Apr.). In Berlin, MD: Assateague State Park (7307 Stephen Decatur Hwy., tel. 888/432–2267 reservations; 410/641–2918 camp office; 350 sites; $25–$35; flush toilets, hook-ups). In Chincoteague: Maddox Family Campgrounds (6742 Maddox Blvd., tel. 757/336–3111; 340 sites; $27–$33; flush toilets, showers, hook-ups). **Hotels:** None in park. In Ocean City: Dunes Manor Hotel (28th St. at the ocean, tel. 410/289–1100; 170 rooms; $189–$325). In Berlin: Holland House (5 Bay St., tel. 410/641–1956; 6 rooms; $100–

$125; no room phones, TV in common area, no kids under 15, no smoking). **✕ Restaurants:** None in park. Concession stand at Maryland State Park (May–Sept.). In Ocean City: Waterman's Seafood Co. (U.S. 50, tel. 410/213–1020; $5–$8). **⌂ Groceries & Gear:** None in park. In Berlin, MD: Buck's Place (11848 Stephen Decatur Hwy., tel. 410/641–4177). In West Ocean City: Food Lion (Rte. 611 off U.S. 50, tel. 410/213–0166).

FEES, HOURS & REGULATIONS

Entrance fee: $10 per vehicle (includes entry to wildlife refuge in VA), $3 per person on foot or bicycle (MD). Ranger-led canoe trips: $20 per canoe (reservations required in person at Barrier Island Visitor Center). Backcountry camping permit ($5) required. Off Road Vehicle Permit ($70 annual, restrictions apply) required. Hunting permitted Sept.– Jan., Maryland state hunting license ($45 for three days) required. No stopping along park roads to view horses. No feeding or touching wild horses. Leashed pets only in limited areas at Assateague; no pets in Virginia areas. Maryland District: Seashore open daily. Barrier Island Visitor Center open daily 9–5. Virginia District: Refuge open Nov.–Mar., daily 6 AM–6 PM; Apr. and Oct., daily 6 AM–8 PM; May–Sept., daily 5 AM–10 PM. Visitor centers open daily 9–4.

HOW TO GET THERE

Offshore of Maryland and Virginia: Maryland district 8 mi south of Ocean City via Rte. 611; Virginia district entrance at Chincoteague via U.S. 13 and Rte. 175. Closest airport: Salisbury (40 mi west of Ocean City, 45 mi northwest of Chincoteague, VA).

CONTACTS

Assateague Island National Seashore (7206 National Seashore La., Berlin, MD 21811, tel. 410/641–1441 or 410/641–3030; 800/365–2267 camping reservations, fax 410/641–1099, www.nps.gov/asis). Ocean City Visitors Bureau (4001 Coastal Hwy., Ocean City, MD 21842, tel. 410/ 289–8181 or 800/626–2326). Chincoteague Chamber of Commerce (Box 258, Chincoteague, VA 23336, tel. 757/336–6161).

Catoctin Mountain Park

In northern Maryland, near Thurmont

The eastern hardwood forests of the Catoctin Mountains are rich with opportunities for camping, picnicking, fishing, and hiking. Created during the Great Depression, the park was built by the Works Progress Administration and the Civilian Conservation Corps as a set of neighborhood recreational areas and camps for federal employees. One of these camps eventually became Camp David, which is closed to the public. Catoctin Recreation Demonstration Area was transferred to the Park Service in 1936 and renamed in 1954.

WHAT TO SEE & DO

Cross-country skiing, fishing, hiking, horseback riding (rentals, Gettysburg), picnicking, rock climbing (permit required, *see below*), wildlife watching. **Facilities:** Visitor center, hiking trails. Bookstore. **Programs &**

Events: Interpretive programs. Campfire programs (weekends May–Sept.), Whiskey Still talks (weekends June and Sept.), Fall Color Walks (weekends mid-Oct.). **Tips & Hints:** Plan to spend 30 minutes in visitor center. Hikes vary from 30 minutes to 7 hours; average is 2–3 hours. Busiest July, Aug., and Oct. weekends, least crowded Jan. and Feb.

FOOD, LODGING & SUPPLIES

Camping: 3 campgrounds in the park: Adirondack Shelter (free; permit required, *see below*), Camp Greentop (12 cabins; $350; flush toilets, showers; closed mid-June–July and Nov.–Mar.), Camp Misty Mount (26 cabins, 3 lodges; $35–$45; $90–$120 lodges; flush toilets, showers; closed late Oct.–mid-Apr.), Camp Round Meadow (4 dormitories; $100; flush toilets, showers), Owens Creek (51 sites; $16; flush toilets, shower; closed late-Nov.–mid-Apr.), Poplar Grove (3 group sites; $30; pit toilets; reservations required; closed Mar.–mid-Apr.). **Hotels:** None in park. In Thurmont: Cozy Country Inn (103 Frederick Rd./Rte. 806, tel. 301/271–4301; 16 rooms, 5 cottages; $52–$150), Super 8 (300 Tippin Dr., tel. 301/271–7888; 46 rooms; $61–$70). **Restaurants:** None in park. In Thurmont: Cozy Country Inn (105 Frederick Rd./Rte. 806, tel. 301/271–7373; $6–$17), Little Creekside Café (210 N. Church St., tel. 301/271–3794; $5–$20; closed Sun.), Mountain Gate Family Restaurant (133 Frederick Rd., tel. 301/271–4373; $7). **Groceries & Gear:** None in park. In Thurmont: Food Lion (U.S. 15 and Tippin Dr., tel. 301/271–9949). In Frederick: Trail House (17 S. Market St., tel. 301/694–8448).

FEES, HOURS & REGULATIONS

Free. Park Central Rd. and part of Manahan Rd. closed in winter for cross-country skiing. Permits (free) required for Adirondack Shelters and rock climbing. Maryland State fishing license ($14) required. Park open daily. Visitor center open Mon.–Thurs. 10–4:30, Fri. 10–5, weekends 8:30–5.

HOW TO GET THERE

18 mi from Frederick via U.S. 15 north and Rte. 77 west. Closest airports: Washington, DC (60 mi), Baltimore (65 mi).

CONTACTS

Catoctin Mountain Park (6602 Foxville Rd., Thurmont, MD 21788, tel. 301/663–9388; 301/271–3140 cabin rentals; www.nps.gov/cato). Tourism Council of Frederick County, Inc. (19 E. Church St., Frederick, MD 21701, tel. 301/228–2888 or 800/999–3613).

Chesapeake & Ohio Canal National Historical Park

Parallels 185 mi of Potomac River from Georgetown, in Washington, DC, to Cumberland, Maryland

This waterway, built between 1828 and 1850 and used until 1924, preserves the history of the C&O Canal and its related structures. The river system's 74 lift locks raise the boats from near sea level to an elevation of

605 feet, providing quiet waters for several short and widely separated stretches perfect for canoeists, kayakers, and anglers. Its towpath offers a nearly level byway for hikers and bicyclists. The canal was established as a national historical park on January 8, 1971.

WHAT TO SEE & DO

Biking (rentals in Cumberland, MD, Harpers Ferry, and Washington, DC), boating and canoeing (rentals in Cumberland, Harpers Ferry, and Washington, DC), hiking, picnicking, viewing falls in Potomac, MD. **Facilities:** 6 visitor centers with interpretive displays: Georgetown (Washington, DC), Brunswick, Great Falls Tavern, Williamsport, Hancock, and Cumberland, MD; outdoor interpretive exhibits. Covered picnic tables. **Programs & Events:** Ranger walks and talks. Replica canal boats at Georgetown (late Apr.–early Nov.). C&O CanalFest in Cumberland, MD (July or Aug.), C&O Canal Days in Williamsport, MD (3rd weekend, Aug.), Canal–Apple Days in Hancock, MD (mid-Sept.), Brunswick Railroad Days (early Oct.). **Tips & Hints:** Avoid towpath after heavy rains. Busiest June–Aug., least crowded Jan. and Feb.

FOOD & LODGING

Camping: 6 campgrounds ($10; pit toilets) in the park: Antietam Creek (mile 69; 20 sites), Fifteen Mile Creek (mile 140.9; 10 sites), McCoys Ferry (mile 110.4; 14 sites), Paw Paw (mile 156.1; 8 sites), Spring Gap (mile 173.3; 21 sites), Marsden Tract (mile 11.5; group campsite; $20; permit required). 30 primitive campsites (free) located along the canal approximately every 5–7 mi from Swains Lock (mile 16.6) to Evitts Creek (mile 180.1). In Flintstone: Rocky Gap State Park (12500 Pleasant Valley Rd. NE, tel. 888/432–2267 reservations; 301/777–2138 campground; 278 sites; $23–$28; flush toilets, showers, hook-ups). **Hotels:** None in park. In Cumberland: Holiday Inn (100 S. George St., tel. 301/724–8800; 130 rooms; $109–$159). **Restaurants:** In the park: snack bar at Great Falls, MD. In Cumberland: Kramer's Deli (13 Canal St., tel. 301/722–8003; $7–$9; closed Sun.).

FEES, HOURS & REGULATIONS

Entrance fee: $5 per car (Great Falls only), $3 for bicyclists and hikers. Canal boat (tel. 202/653–5190): $8 adults, $6 ages 62 and over, $5 ages 4–14, free ages 3 and under. Reservations available for Carderock picnic pavilion. Maryland or Washington, DC, fishing license required. No gas-powered boats in park. Electric motors allowed in Big Pool, Little Pool, and canal waters from Lock 68 to Town Creek. No motorized vehicles, mopeds, or trail bikes on towpath. Bike riding on towpaths only. Leashed pets only. No hunting. Towpath open daily dawn–dusk. Georgetown Visitor Center open June–Aug., Wed.–Sun. 9:30–5. Great Falls Visitor Center open daily 9–4:45. Brunswick Visitor Center open Thurs.–Fri. 10–2, Sat. 10–4, Sun. 1–4. Williamsport Visitor Center open Wed.–Sun. 9–4:30. Hancock Visitor Center open Fri.–Tues. 9–4:30. Cumberland Visitor Center open daily 9–5.

HOW TO GET THERE

From Cumberland: I–68 to Hancock, then I–70 to Frederick, then I–270 to Capital Beltway (I–495). Take Exit 41, Clara Barton Pkwy. west, then left to onto MacArthur Blvd. The visitor center is at the intersection with Falls Rd. (Rte. 189).

CONTACTS

Chesapeake & Ohio Canal National Historical Park (Headquarters: 1850 Dual Hwy., Suite 100, Hagerstown, MD 21740, tel. 301/739–4200; 301/767–3731 for group camping at Marsden Tract and Carderock picnic pavilion, www.nps.gov/choh. Georgetown (tel. 202/653–5190). Great Falls Tavern (tel. 301/767–3714). Brunswick and Williamsport (tel. 301/582–0813). Hancock (tel. 301/678–5463). Cumberland (tel. 310/72–8226).

Clara Barton National Historic Site

Northwest of Washington, DC

Clara Barton, humanitarian and founder of the American Red Cross, lived in Glen Echo the last 15 years of her life. From 1897 to 1904, her 30-plus-room mansion also served as the Red Cross headquarters, and as a warehouse for disaster relief supplies. From here, she organized and directed relief efforts for victims of natural disasters and war. Today the home has numerous exhibits and audiovisual programs detailing her work, and the picnic grounds adjacent to Glen Echo Park makes a pleasant break after touring the grounds The site was authorized on October 26, 1974.

WHAT TO SEE & DO

Picnicking, touring house. **Facilities:** Indoor interpretive exhibits, guided tours, movies. Bookstore, picnic tables. **Programs & Events:** Guided tours (hourly 10–4). Evening Open House programs (spring and fall). **Tips & Hints:** Allow 30–45 minutes for tour. Busiest on weekend afternoons, least crowded mornings.

FEES, HOURS & REGULATIONS

Free. Guided tours only. Site open daily.

HOW TO GET THERE

9 mi northwest of Georgetown via MacArthur Blvd. and Oxford Rd. to Clara Barton Pkwy., and via I–495/I–95 (Beltway) to Clara Barton Pkwy. (watch for signs to Glen Echo Park). Public transportation via Montgomery County Transit Authority Ride-on-Bus 29 from Friendship Heights metro stations (Red line) or by taxi. Closest airports from the site: Washington, DC: Reagan Washington National (11 mi), Dulles (22 mi).

CONTACT

Clara Barton National Historic Site (5801 Oxford Rd., Glen Echo, MD 20812, tel. 301/492–6245, www.nps.gov/clba).

Fort McHenry National Monument & Historic Shrine

In Baltimore

The American resistance of a British naval attack against Fort McHenry on September 13–14, 1814, prevented the capture of Baltimore during the War of 1812. A large flag was raised over the fort after the 25-hour battle, and the victory inspired Francis Scott Key to write "The Star-Spangled Banner." Today—via electronic map, no less—you'll find the restored fort complete with renovated barracks and guardhouses. The fort was authorized as a national park under the War Department in 1925, transferred to the Park Service in 1933, and redesignated in 1939.

WHAT TO SEE & DO

Bicycling, jogging, picnicking, touring fort, watching film. **Facilities:** Visitor center, guided and self-guided tours, museum, movie. Book-and-gift shop, picnic tables. **Programs & Events:** Flag Change programs (twice daily, weather permitting). Ranger-guided interpretive programs (June–Labor Day), Fort McHenry Guard living-history programs (mid-June–Aug., weekend afternoons), bird walks (June–Sept.). Civil War Encampment (last weekend, Apr.), Flag Day Program (June 14), Defenders' Day Celebration (2nd weekend, Sept.), Veterans' Day program. **Tips & Hints:** Visit in spring and fall for best weather. Busiest May and June, least crowded Feb. and Mar.

FEES, HOURS & REGULATIONS

Entrance fee: $5 adults, free ages 17 and under. No pets in fort, leashed pets only elsewhere. No climbing on cannons or earthworks. No skates or skateboards. No fishing off seawall. No public docking. No food or drink in buildings. Visitor center and fort open June–Aug., daily 8–7:45, Sept.–May, daily 8–4:45.

HOW TO GET THERE

3 mi southeast of the Baltimore Inner Harbor via I–95 to Exit 55 Key Hwy. and Lawrence St.; turn left, then left on E. Fort Ave. and continue 1 mi (follow blue–green FORT MCHENRY signs along all major routes to the park). From the Inner Harbor, take Light St. south to Key Hwy., turn left, then follow Fort McHenry signs to Lawrence St. Closest airport: Baltimore, 10 mi from the fort.

CONTACT

Fort McHenry National Monument & Historic Shrine (End of E. Fort Ave., Baltimore, MD 21230-5393, tel. 410/962–4290, fax 410/962–2500, www.nps.gov/fomc).

Fort Washington Park

South of Washington, DC

Built between 1814 and 1824, the main garrison here actually replaced the original Fort Washington, which was destroyed during the War of 1812. Constructed to protect Union forces housed in Washington, DC, during the Civil War, the fort was obsolete by 1872, but still stands as the only permanent fortification to protect the nation's capital. It served various additional functions for the U.S. Coast Artillery and U.S. Army until the end of World War II. The transfer to the Park Service was authorized in 1930 and became effective in 1940.

WHAT TO SEE & DO

Bird-watching, hiking, picnicking, touring fort and grounds. **Facilities:** Visitor center, hiking trail. Bookstore, picnic tables with fire grills. **Programs & Events:** Fort tours (weekends at 2 and 3, weekdays by request). Artillery firings (Apr.–Oct., 1 Sun. monthly). Universal Soldier Military Timeline Events (1st weekend May, last weekend Sept.); living-history programs (schedules vary). **Tips & Hints:** Different parts of the fort are scheduled to be under restoration until 2008. Expect to spend 30–60 minutes on tour. Busiest May and June, least crowded Dec.–Mar.

FEES & HOURS

Entrance fee: $5 per vehicle or $3 per walk-in, bicyclist, or bus passenger. Fort and visitor center open Apr.–Sept., daily 9–noon and 2–5, Oct.–Mar., daily 9–noon and 2–4:30. Park grounds open daily 8–dark.

HOW TO GET THERE

In Fort Washington, MD via the Capital Beltway (I–495) to Exit 3A (Indian Head Hwy. or Rte. 210 south; continue to Fort Washington Rd., turn right, and follow to park entrance. Closest airport: Washington, DC (Reagan Washington National, 15 mi).

CONTACT

Fort Washington Park (13551 Fort Washington Rd., Fort Washington, MD 20744, tel. 301/763–4600, fax 301/763–1389, www.nps.gov/fowa).

Greenbelt Park

In central Maryland, in Greenbelt

This 1,176-acre park provides a green oasis between Washington, DC, and Baltimore, MD. A refuge for native plants and animals, it's a favorite local spot for camping, hiking, and picnicking. The park was transferred from the Public Housing Authority on August 3, 1950.

WHAT TO SEE & DO

Bicycling, hiking, jogging, picnicking, walking. **Facilities:** Information kiosk, 10 mi of trails. Picnic tables. **Programs & Events:** Natural, service, and cultural resource programs. National Trails Day events (1st Sat., June), Potomac River Watershed Cleanup (early Apr.), National

Park Week (late Apr.), Public Lands Day (Sept.). **Tips & Hints:** Busiest Memorial Day weekend, least crowded in Jan. and Feb.

LODGING

🏕 **Camping:** In the park: Greenbelt Campground (174 sites; $14; flush toilets, showers).

FEES & HOURS

Free. Rangers on duty Labor Day–Memorial Day, Fri.–Sun. 8–4; Memorial Day–Labor Day, weekdays 8–7. Headquarters open weekdays 8–4. Self-registration campground open daily.

HOW TO GET THERE

12 mi from Washington, DC, 38 mi from Baltimore via I–95 to Exit 23 (Kenilworth Ave. S); turn left on Greenbelt Rd. E, park is on right. Closest Metro subway stop is Greenbelt Station (2½ mi). Closest airport: Washington, DC (Reagan Washington National, 17 mi), Baltimore (21 mi).

CONTACT

Park Headquarters, Greenbelt Park (6565 Greenbelt Rd., Greenbelt, MD 20770, tel. 301/344–3948 picnic area reservations; 301/344–3944 ranger station; 800/365–2267 camping reservations, fax 301/344–1012, www.nps.gov/gree).

Hampton
National Historic Site

In central Maryland, in Towson

Hampton preserves and interprets what once was a vast agricultural and commercial estate owned by one family for more than 150 years, and which was supported by a large workforce (including indentured servants and slaves). The mansion was the centerpiece of the formerly 24,000-acre property, which also had an iron foundry, farm, formal grounds, and gardens. Today, some 20 buildings and 40,000 artifacts survive, including the mansion, slave quarters, family cemetery, farm, and outbuildings. The site was designated in 1948.

WHAT TO SEE & DO

Touring the mansion, outbuildings, grounds, and formal gardens. **Facilities:** Visitor center, guided and self-guided tours. Book-and-gift shop. **Programs & Events:** Guided mansion tours (daily 9–4, on the hour). Guided grounds tours (Memorial Day–Labor Day). History lectures and discussions (monthly). **Tips & Hints:** Mansion is not air-conditioned. Busiest Apr. and May, least crowded Jan. and Feb.

FEES & HOURS

Free. Park and visitor center open daily 9–5. Gift shop open Mar.–early Jan.

HOW TO GET THERE

Near the Baltimore Beltway (I–695) via Exit 27B. Closest airport: Baltimore (40 mi from estate).

CONTACTS

Hampton National Historic Site (535 Hampton La., Towson, MD 21286, tel. 410/823–1309, fax 410/823—8394, www.nps.gov/hamp). Baltimore County Conference and Visitors Bureau (825 Dulaney Valley Rd., Towson Town Center, Towson, MD 21204, tel. 800/570–2836 or 410/296–4886, www.visitbacomd.com).

Monocacy National Battlefield

In central Maryland, near Frederick

Known as the "Battle that Saved Washington," the Battle of Monocacy on July 9, 1864, was the last Confederate attempt to carry the Civil War into the north. Although Confederate General Jubal A. Early defeated the Union forces under Major General Lew Wallace, the latter commander's effort delayed Early long enough to marshal a successful defense of Washington, DC. The site was authorized as Monocacy National Military Park in 1934, with no land acquisition until 1976, when the name was changed to Monocacy National Battlefield.

WHAT TO SEE & DO

Auto touring battlefield, hiking, viewing electric map orientation program. **Facilities:** Visitor center, hiking trail. Bookstore. **Programs & Events:** Ranger-led programs (Memorial Day–Labor Day); living-history programs and special events (monthly, Apr.–Aug.). **Tips & Hints:** Busiest July and Aug., least crowded Dec. and Jan.

FEES, HOURS, & REGULATIONS

Free. Leashed pets only. No hunting or relic collecting. No bikes on trail. Visitor center open Labor Day–Memorial Day, daily 8–4:30, Memorial Day–Labor Day, daily 8:30–5.

HOW TO GET THERE

2½ mi south of Frederick via Rte. 355; from I–270, take Exit 26 at Urbana and follow Rte. 80 east to Rte. 355 north, then proceed about 4 mi to battlefield on right. From I–70, take Exit 54 (Market St., Rtes. 85 and 355) and follow Rte. 355 south about 4 mi to battlefield on left. Closest airports: Washington, DC (Dulles, 45 mi) and (Reagan, 50 mi).

CONTACTS

Monocacy National Battlefield (4801 Urbana Pike, Frederick, MD 21704, tel. 301/662–3515, fax 301/662—3420, www.nps.gov/mono). Tourism Council of Frederick County (19 E. Church St., Frederick, MD 21701, tel. 301/228–2888 or 800/999–3613).

Piscataway Park

In southern Maryland, near Accokeek

This attractive park stretches 6 mi along the Potomac River from Piscataway Creek to Marshall Hall, part of a plan to preserve the river view from Mount Vernon as it was in George Washington's day. The park also has serene spots to picnic, bird-watch, view the mansion across the Potomac, and tour the working 18th-century National Colonial Farm. Preservation efforts began in 1952, and the park was authorized on October 4, 1961.

WHAT TO SEE & DO

Backcountry hiking, bird-watching, fishing, picnicking, touring farm. **Facilities:** Picnic area. **Tips & Hints:** Farm tours run by separate, nonprofit organization; call for details. Busiest Apr.–Oct., least crowded Dec. and Jan.

FEES & HOURS

Free. Open daily dawn–dusk.

HOW TO GET THERE

14 mi south of Washington, DC, via I–95 (Capital Beltway) to Exit 3A to Rte. 210 south (Indian Head Hwy.); drive 10 mi to intersection in Accokeek, turn right on Bryan's Point Rd., park is 4 mi ahead on the Potomac River. Closest airport: Washington, DC (Reagan, 21 mi).

CONTACTS

Piscataway Park (c/o Fort Washington Park, 13551 Fort Washington Rd., Fort Washington, MD 20744, tel. 301/763–4600, www.nps.gov/pisc). National Colonial Farm tour reservations (tel. 301/283–2113).

Thomas Stone
National Historic Site

In southern Maryland, near Port Tobacco

Haberdeventure plantation was the home of Thomas Stone, one of Maryland's four signers of the Declaration of Independence. Stone was a delegate to the Continental Congress between 1775 and 1777 and again between 1783 and 1784. As a member of the Continental Congress, he served on the 13-member committee that drafted the country's first system of government under the Articles of Confederation. Today, the 322-acre site contains Stone's five-part tidewater plantation house and several outbuildings typical of an 18th- and 19th-century Maryland plantation. The site was authorized on November 10, 1978.

WHAT TO SEE & DO

Taking guided tour, viewing exhibits. **Facilities:** Visitor center, guided tours, movie. Bookstore. **Programs & Events:** Ranger-led tours (10–4), audiovisual programs. Seasonal activities and special events available.

Tips & Hints: Plan to spend an hour visiting site, 20 minutes on tour. Busiest June and July, least crowded Dec. and Jan.

FOOD & LODGING

🏨 **Hotels:** None at site. In La Plata: Best Western (6900 Crain Hwy. S [U.S. 301], tel. 301/934–4900; 65 rooms, 8 suites; $78–$92, $110–$130 suites). ✗ **Restaurants:** None at site. In La Plata: Casey Jones Pub (417 Charles St., tel. 301/932–6226; $7–$15; closed Sun.).

FEES & HOURS

Free. Site open mid-June–Aug., daily 9–5; Sept.–mid-June, Wed.– Sun. 9–5.

HOW TO GET THERE

30 mi south of Washington, DC, via U.S. 301 to Rte. 6, or via Rte. 225 to Rose Hill Rd., near Port Tobacco. Closest airport: Washington, DC (Reagan, 30 mi).

CONTACTS

Thomas Stone National Historic Site (6655 Rosehill Rd., Port Tobacco, MD 20677, tel. 301/392–1776, fax 301/934–8793, www.nps.gov/thst). Charles County Chamber of Commerce (6360 Crane Hwy., La Plata, MD 20646, tel. 301/932–6500).

See Also

Appalachian National Scenic Trail, West Virginia. *George Washington Memorial Parkway,* Virginia. *Harpers Ferry National Historical Park,* West Virginia. *Potomac Heritage National Scenic Trail,* District of Columbia.

Adams
National Historical Park

In eastern Massachusetts, in Quincy

The birthplace, home, and final resting place of presidents John Adams and John Quincy Adams—the nation's second and sixth presidents—are preserved in this park. A free trolley-bus service takes visitors to the 17th-century saltbox houses where these great men were born. The tour also includes a visit to the "Old House," which from 1788 to 1927 was the family home of four Adams generations. A visit to the United First Parish Church, final resting place of both presidents and first ladies, completes the tour. The site was designated on December 9, 1946, and redesignated by Congress in 1998.

WHAT TO SEE & DO

Touring the three homes, church, and grounds. **Facilities:** Main visitor center (1250 Hancock St.) and Carriage House visitor orientation center (135 Adams St.); guided tours. Bookstore (1250 Hancock St.). **Programs & Events:** Interpretive tours (Apr. 19–Nov. 10, daily). Special programs, reenactments, lecture series available. **Tips & Hints:** Parking free at President's Place garage with validation stamp from main visitor center. Go Apr.–Aug. for garden blooms, Sept.–Nov. for fall foliage. Busiest July and Aug.

FEES, HOURS & REGULATIONS

Park entrance fee and tour: $3 per adult. United First Parish Church: $3. No backpacks, strollers, flash photography, or video cameras in homes. No pets. Park open mid-Apr.–mid-Nov., daily 9–5. Main visitor center open mid-Apr.–mid-Nov., daily 9–5; mid-Nov.–mid-Apr., Tues.–Fri. 10–4. Carriage House visitor orientation center open mid-Apr.–mid-Nov., daily 9–5. Last full tour departs at 3:15; no tours mid-Nov.–mid-Apr.

HOW TO GET THERE

Via the Red Line to Quincy Center Station; cross to Hancock St. and Galleria for Visitor Center. Closest airport: Boston (8 mi).

CONTACTS

Adams National Historical Park (135 Adams St., Quincy, MA 02169, tel. 617/770–1175, fax 617/472–7562, www.nps.gov/adam).

Boston African-American National Historic Site

In Boston

Fifteen pre–Civil War structures here shelter the history of Boston's free 19th-century African-American community. Located in the Beacon Hill neighborhood and linked by the 1.6-mi Black Heritage Trail, the collection of buildings includes the African Meeting House, the oldest standing African-American church in the United States, and the Abiel Smith School. Also on site is Augustus Saint-Gaudens' memorial to Robert Gould Shaw, the white officer who led the 54th Regiment, the first African-American regiment recruited from the North by the U.S. government during the Civil War. The site was authorized on October 10, 1980.

WHAT TO SEE & DO

Taking Black Heritage Trail walking tour. **Facilities:** Indoor and outdoor interpretive exhibits and signs. Park office in Museum of Afro-American History (partner). **Programs & Events:** Guided walking tours. Living-history programs (mid-June–mid-July). **Tips & Hints:** Walking tour maps and guides free at the African Meeting House. Tour participants meet at the Shaw monument (Park and Beacon Sts.). Park busiest July and Aug., least crowded Dec. and Jan.

FEES, HOURS & REGULATIONS

Free. Donations support the Museum of Afro-American History, which is open Mon.–Sat. 10–4. Tours of site (Memorial Day–Labor Day, daily at 10, noon, and 2; Labor Day–Memorial Day, Tues.–Sat. at 10, 12, 2).

HOW TO GET THERE

In Boston via I–90 (Massachusetts Tpke.) to Copley Sq. exit and Stuart St., then left on Charles St. (Rte. 28) to Boston Common; or via I–93 to Storrow Dr. and Copley Sq. exit, then left on Beacon St., right on Arlington St., left on Boylston St., and left on Charles St. (Rte. 28). Several parking garages are close by. Closest MBTA subway stops are Park St. on the Red and Green lines and Bowdoin Sq. on the Blue Line. Closest airport: Boston.

CONTACTS

Boston African American National Historic Site (14 Beacon St., Suite 503, Boston, MA 02108, tel. 617/742–5415, fax 617/720–0848, www. nps.gov/boaf).

Boston Harbor Islands National Park Area

In Boston Harbor

The park encircles 34 islands that range in size from less than 1 acre to more than 200. As a system of islands, these glacial drumlins are unique in the United States. Interactive videos, exhibit boards, and the information kiosk at Long Wharf provide all the details. The area was authorized in 1996.

WHAT TO SEE & DO

Beachcombing, boat riding, fishing, hiking, kayaking, picnicking, sailing. **Facilities:** Fan Pier visitor center (U.S. Courthouse) and Spectacle Island visitor center; information booth, dock. Book-and-gift shop. **Programs & Events:** Nature walks, living-history programs, marine ecology programs (May–Oct.). Family Fun Days interactive performance, music, and historic activities on George's Island (Sat. July and Aug.); Civil War Encampment (mid-July); Halloween program (Oct.). **Tips & Hints:** Plan on 90-minute round-trip ferry ride to George's Island. Bring food and water for visit to park; sustenance is available only on George's Island.

LODGING

⚠ **Camping:** Primitive camping on Bumpkin, Grape, Lovells, and Peddocks islands (44 sites; $8–$15; pit toilets; closed mid-Oct.–Apr.; reservations and permit required, *see below*).

FEES, HOURS & REGULATIONS

Free. Ferry from Long Wharf: May–late June, every 2 hrs 10–4; late June–Labor Day, hourly 10–5; Labor Day–Columbus Day, every 2 hrs 10–2. Permit required ($6) for island camping. Reservation fee ($8) for camping on Bumpkin and Grape islands. No bikes except on Deer Island and World's End. No motorized equipment, pets, or alcohol. Islands open Mar.–Memorial Day, weekends 9–sunset; Memorial Day–Labor Day, daily 9–sunset; Labor Day–Nov., weekends 9–sunset. Visitor centers open Memorial Day–Columbus Day, weekends 10–5. Information kiosk open Memorial Day–Labor Day, daily 9–4:30.

HOW TO GET THERE

Via ferry from Long Wharf. Closest airport: Boston.

CONTACTS

Boston Harbor Islands National Park Area (408 Atlantic Ave., Suite 228, Boston, MA 02110-3350, tel. 617/223–8666, fax 617/223–8671, www.nps.gov/boha, www.bostonislands.com). Greater Boston Convention and Visitors Bureau (2 Copley Pl., Suite 105, Boston, MA 02116, tel. 617/536–4100 or 888/733–2678, fax 617/424–7664).

Boston
National Historical Park

In Boston

The 2.5-mi Freedom Trail stretches along the relics of the revolutionary generation of Bostonians who blazed a trail from colonialism to independence. On the way are the Old State House, Old South Meeting House, Faneuil Hall, Paul Revere House, Old North Church, Bunker

Hill Monument, and Charlestown Navy Yard, where the USS *Constitution* ("Old Ironsides") is berthed. The park was authorized on October 1, 1974.

WHAT TO SEE & DO

Touring historic sites, walking tour trail. **Facilities:** 3 visitor centers: Downtown (15 State St.), Charlestown Navy Yard, and Bunker Hill Lodge. Museum, book-and-gift shops. **Programs & Events:** Ranger-led historical talks at Faneuil Hall and Bunker Hill Monument, self-guided and guided (Labor Day–Memorial Day) tours of World War II destroyer USS *Cassin Young*, self-guided and U.S. Navy-led (year-round) tours of USS *Constitution*. Ranger-led walking tours of downtown section of Freedom Trail (mid-Apr.–Nov.), Charlestown Navy Yard, and Commandant's House (both Memorial Day–Labor Day). Boston's Harborfest (July 4 weekend), Charlestown Navy Yard international visiting ships program. **Tips & Hints:** Sites are accessible by public transport. The downtown visitor center is at the State St. stop of the Blue and Orange lines. Water transport connects downtown Boston (Long Wharf) and the Charlestown Navy Yard. Busiest July and Aug., least crowded Jan. and Feb. Tours fill up quickly in summer.

FEES & HOURS

Free admission to federally owned sites (Bunker Hill Monument, USS *Constitution,* Dorchester Heights Monument), and to ranger-led programs on the Freedom Trail and at Faneuil Hall. Fees collected at privately owned and operated sites: Old South Meeting House and Old State House ($5 adults, $4 ages 62 and over and per student with ID, $1 ages 6–17, free ages 5 and under), Paul Revere House ($3 adults, $2.50 ages 62 and over and per student with ID, $1 ages 5–17, free ages 4 and under). Downtown visitor center open daily 9–5. Charlestown Navy Yard open mid-June–Labor Day, daily 9–6; Labor Day–mid-June, daily 9–5. Most historic sites open mid-Apr.–Labor Day, daily 9:30–5; Labor Day–mid-Apr., daily 10–4. USS *Constitution* open Apr.–Oct., Tues.–Sun. 10–4; Nov.–Mar., Thurs.–Sun. 10–4; tours every half hour 10:30–3:30.

HOW TO GET THERE

Near downtown Boston via U.S. 1 and I–93 north or south; follow signs to Charlestown Navy Yard. Closest airport: Boston.

CONTACTS

Boston National Historical Park (Charlestown Navy Yard, Boston, MA 02129-4543, tel. 617/242–5601). Downtown visitor center (15 State St., tel. 617/242–5642). Charlestown Navy Yard Visitor Information Center (55 Constitution Rd., tel. 617/242–5601). Bunker Hill Monument (tel. 617/242–5641, fax 617/242–6006, www.nps.gov/bost).

Cape Cod National Seashore

On outer Cape Cod

More than 43,000 acres of pristine beaches and grassy, wind-swept uplands fill this gorgeous seaside park, which stretches from Chatham to

Provincetown on the state's Outer Cape. The main 40-mi band of shoreline draws many visitors to its mesmerizing ocean views, but further explorations uncover little embers of local history in statuesque lighthouses, charming Cape Cod–style dwellings, and weathered lifesaving stations. It's a wonderful walking area, with dozens of clear, deep, freshwater kettle ponds pocketing the land, and pleasant trails threaded throughout the fields and dunes. The site of the former Marconi Wireless Station, where in 1903 Guigelmo Marconi transmitted the first wireless message across the Atlantic, from President Theodore Roosevelt to King George of England, is also found here. The park was authorized in 1961 and established in 1966.

WHAT TO SEE & DO

Bicycling, boating (rentals, *see below*), fishing (MA license required, *see below*), hiking, picnicking, swimming, touring historic sites. **Facilities:** Salt Pond visitor center and Province Lands visitor center, 6 swimming beaches, movies, 11 self-guided nature trails, 3 bike trails. Bookstores. **Programs & Events:** Ranger-led hikes, canoe tours, beach walks, historic-house tours. Ranger-led interpretive programs (late May–early Nov.), campfire programs (Memorial Day–Labor Day). **Tips & Hints:** Plan on at least a half-day visit. Busiest July and Aug., least crowded Jan. and Feb.

FOOD, LODGING & SUPPLIES

Camping: None at site. In Brewster: Nickerson State Park (3488 Main St., Rte 6A, tel. 508/896–3491; 877/422–6762 reservations; 418 sites, 5 yurts; $12–$15, $25–$30 yurts; flush toilets, showers; closed Columbus Day–mid-Apr.). **Hotels:** None in park. In Provincetown: Best Western Tides Beachfront (837 Commercial St., tel. 508/487–1045 or 800/528–1234; 64 rooms; $159–$319; closed mid-Oct.–mid-May). In North Eastham: Captain's Quarters Motel & Conference Center (U.S. 6, tel. 508/255–5686 or 800/327–7769; 75 rooms; $135; closed Dec.–Mar.). **Restaurants:** None in park. In Provincetown: Lobster Pot (321 Commercial St., tel. 508/487–0842; $7–$20; closed Jan.–Mar.). **Groceries:** None in park. In Provincetown: Grand Union (28 Shank Painter Rd., tel. 508/487–4903).

FEES, HOURS & REGULATIONS

Entrance fee: $10 per vehicle, $3 per bicyclist or walk-in at lifeguard-protected swimming beaches (Memorial Day–late June, weekends; late June–Labor Day, daily; Labor Day–Columbus Day, weekends). Seasonal pass $30. Permits required for beach campfires and overnight parking while fishing. Seasonal permit ($65) required for dune-riding; weekly permit ($40) required for off-road vehicles. Seasonal RV permits ($110, mid-Apr.–mid-Nov.) required for overnight stays. Parking lots open daily 6–midnight. Salt Pond Visitor Center open June–mid-Oct., daily 9–5; mid-Oct.–June, daily 9–4:30. Province Lands Visitor Center open May–Oct., daily 9–5.

HOW TO GET THERE

Near Provincetown, via Rte. 3 south; from Boston via Sagamore Bridge in Bourne, then along U.S. 6 east to Eastham and Provincetown; from

Providence, RI, via I–95 north to I–195 east, then along U.S.. 6 east as above. Closest airports: Hyannis (35 mi), Boston (120 mi).

CONTACTS

Cape Cod National Seashore (99 Marconi Station Site Rd., Wellfleet, MA 02667, tel. 508/349–3785, fax 508/349–9052, www.nps.gov/caco). Salt Pond Visitor Center (U.S. 6, Eastham, MA 02642, tel. 508/255–3421). Province Lands Visitor Center (Race Point Rd., Provincetown, tel. 508/487-1256). Cape Cod Chamber of Commerce (Box 790, Hyannis, MA 02601, tel. 508/362–3225 or 888/332–2732, www.capecodchamber.org).

Frederick Law Olmsted National Historic Site

In eastern Massachusetts, in Brookline

The site preserves the home and office of America's leading landscape architect, Frederick Law Olmsted, who created some 5,000 public and private landscapes—including New York's Central Park and the U.S. Capitol grounds in Washington, DC. In 1883, Olmsted opened the Brookline office that would be inherited by his sons, associates, and successors, and which would eventually become a vital part of America's national heritage. More than 1 million landscape design documents were produced at Olmsted's home and office, and the grounds are now a living exhibit of the artist's design ideals. The site was established in 1979.

WHAT TO SEE & DO

Touring historic grounds, watching film. **Facilities:** Visitor center, guided tours. Bookstore. **Programs & Events:** Interpretive tours (Fri.–Sun. 10–4:30), ranger-led tours of Olmsted-designed landscapes in Boston area. Holiday Open House (Dec.). **Tips & Hints:** Parking is limited. Busiest May–June, least crowded Nov.–Jan.

FEES, HOURS & REGULATIONS

Free. No smoking or pets inside historic buildings. Site open Fri.–Sun. 10–4:30.

HOW TO GET THERE

Near Brookline, 3 mi from downtown Boston via MBTA Bus 60 (exit at intersection of Boylston and Warren Sts. in Brookline, then follow Warren St. ⅛ mi to Olmsted NHS), MBTA Riverside "D" Green Line subway (exit at Brookline Hills station, turn right, follow sidewalk to Cypress St. and across Boylston St. intersection, turn right on Walnut St., left on Warren St., and continue to intersection with Warren and Dudley Sts.). Closest airport: Boston (8 mi).

CONTACTS

Frederick Law Olmsted National Historic Site (99 Warren St., Brookline, MA 02445, tel. 617/566–1689, fax 617/232–4073, www.nps.gov/

frla). Brookline Chamber of Commerce (1101 Beacon St., Brookline, MA 02446, tel. 617/739–1330).

John Fitzgerald Kennedy National Historic Site

In eastern Massachusetts, in Brookline

The site preserves the house where the 35th president of the United States was born in 1917. This was the first home shared by the president's father and mother, Joseph P. and Rose Fitzgerald Kennedy, and represents the social and political beginnings of one of the world's most prominent political families. The nine-room house was restored in the 1960s, under the direction of Rose Kennedy as a memorial to her son. Included are household furnishings, photographs, and significant family mementos representing the Kennedy family lifestyle. The site was established in 1969.

WHAT TO SEE & DO

Touring the home. **Facilities:** Visitor center, guided tours. Bookstore. **Programs & Events:** Guided home tours (May–Oct., daily 10–4:30), walking tours of neighborhood (May–Oct.). Kennedy Birthday Weekend (last weekend in May). **Tips & Hints:** No on-site parking. Busiest in July and Aug.

FEES, HOURS & REGULATIONS

Entrance fee (with guided home tour): $3 adults, free ages 16 and under. No smoking or pets in building. Park and visitor center open May–Oct., Wed.–Sun. 10–4:30.

HOW TO GET THERE

In Brookline, 3 mi from Boston via MBTA Green Line ("C" – Cleveland Circle) train; exit at intersection of Beacon and Harvard Sts. (Coolidge Corner), walk 4 blocks north on Harvard St., turn right onto Beals St. and continue ¾ block. Closest airport: Boston (7 mi).

CONTACTS

John Fitzgerald Kennedy National Historic Site (83 Beals St., Brookline, MA 02446, tel. 617/566–7937, fax 617/730–9884, www.nps.gov/jofi). Brookline Chamber of Commerce (1101 Beacon St., Brookline, MA 02446, tel. 617/739–1330).

Longfellow National Historic Site

Near Boston, in Cambridge

Henry Wadsworth Longfellow raised a family and wrote many of his most beloved poems here between 1837 and his death in 1882. The house, built in 1759, also served as George Washington's headquarters early in the American Revolution. Handsomely furnished rooms exhibit an array of American and European decorative arts, paintings, and sculptures, as well as Longfellow's personal library of 12,000 books. The house is an outstanding example of mid-Georgian architecture, surrounded by formal gardens where the Longfellows entertained some of the world's famous writers and artists. The site was authorized in 1972.

WHAT TO SEE & DO

Touring the house and gardens. **Facilities:** Visitor center, museum, guided and self-guided tours. Bookstore. **Programs & Events:** Self-guided tours of grounds and neighborhood. Guided tours of house (May–Oct., Wed.–Sun. at 10:30, 11:30, 1, 2, 3, and 4), guided tours of neighborhood (May–Oct.), Longfellow Summer Festival of Music & Poetry (June–Sept.). **Tips & Hints:** No on-site parking. Busiest in July and Aug.

FEES & HOURS

Entrance fee: $3 adults, free ages 16 and under. House and visitor center open May–Oct., Wed.–Sun. 10–4:30. Museum open by appointment Tues. and Wed. 9–5. Garden and grounds open daily dawn–dusk.

HOW TO GET THERE

In Cambridge, 3 mi from Boston via MBTA Red Line (Alewife) train outbound; exit at Harvard Sq., follow signs for Church St., continue to Brattle St., turn right, and walk 7–10 minutes. Closest airport: Boston (7 mi).

CONTACTS

Longfellow National Historic Site (105 Brattle St., Cambridge, MA 02138, tel. 617/876–4491, fax 617/497–8718, www.nps.gov/long). Cambridge Chamber of Commerce (859 Massachusetts Ave., Cambridge, MA 02139, tel. 617/876–4100).

Lowell National Historical Park

In northeast Massachusetts, in Lowell

America's Industrial Revolution is commemorated at this park, which includes the Suffolk Mill turbine and authentic "mill girl" boarding houses. The main sight is the Boott Cotton Mills Museum, which encloses a weave room of 88 operating looms. Altogether, the informative exhibits document the Northeast's transition from farm to factory, as well as the history of immigrant labor. The site was authorized on June 5, 1978.

WHAT TO SEE & DO

Guided and self-guided tours. **Facilities:** Visitor center, museum, movie. **Programs & Events:** Exhibits, self-guided tours. Trolley tours (Mar.–

Nov.), boat and walking tours (weekends late May–late June, daily late June–mid-Oct.; reservations required), museum talks (late May–mid-Oct.). Kids Week (Feb., Apr.), Lowell Women's Week, (1st week, Mar.), Lowell Folk Festival (last full weekend, July), Lowell Summer Music Festival (July and Aug.), National Park Day (Aug. 25), Banjo and Fiddle Contests (Sept.). **Tips & Hints:** Tours go out rain or shine. Busiest May–July, least crowded Dec.–Feb.

FEES, HOURS & REGULATIONS

Free. Canal tours: $6 adults; $4 ages 6–16, $5 ages 62 and over, free ages 5 and under. Trolley tours free. Boott Cotton Mills Museum: $4 adults, $2 ages 6–16, $3 ages 62 and over, free ages 5 and under. No eating, drinking, or smoking in buildings. Visitor center open Sept.–late June, daily 9–5; late June–Aug., 9–5:45. Boott Cotton Mills Museum open daily 9–5.

HOW TO GET THERE

In Lowell, via the Lowell Connector from either I–495 or Rte. 3; exit on Thorndike St. north, turn right on Dutton St. to marked parking lot. Closest airport: Boston (25 mi).

CONTACTS

Lowell National Historical Park (67 Kirk St., Lowell, MA 01852, tel. 978/970–5000, fax 978/275–1762, www.nps.gov/lowe). Greater Lowell Chamber of Commerce (144 Merrimack St., Suite 403, Lowell, MA 01852, tel. 978/459–8154, fax 978/452–4145). Greater Merrimack Valley Convention & Visitors Bureau (9 Central St., Suite 201, Lowell, MA 01852, tel. 978/459–6150, fax 978/459–4595). Boott Cotton Mills Museum (400 Foot of John St.).

Minute Man National Historical Park

In eastern Massachusetts, in Concord, Lincoln, and Lexington

Preserved here are the historic sites, structures, and landscapes associated with the events of April 19, 1775, and the beginning of the American Revolution. The North Bridge, Minute Man Statue, and Battle Road are global symbols of man's universal struggle for freedom and independence. The park also celebrates the 19th-century literary Renaissance at the Wayside, home of Nathaniel Hawthorne, Louisa May Alcott, and Margaret Sidney. The Battle Road Trail winds through the area, while Hartwell Tavern explores the more raucous side of 18th-century life. The park was authorized on September 21, 1959.

WHAT TO SEE & DO

Biking, canoeing (rentals in Concord), cross-country skiing (Battle Road Trail), hiking, picnicking, touring historic buildings and sites. **Facilities:** 2 visitor centers: Minute Man (Lexington) and North Bridge

(Concord); interpretive signs, movie, self-guided tours, hiking trails. Bookstores, picnic tables. **Programs & Events:** Winter Lecture series (Feb.); Patriots' Day weekend (mid-Apr.); ranger-led programs, colonial reenactments, fife-and-drum demonstrations, military encampments, musket firings (late May–Oct.). **Tips & Hints:** Begin visit by watching multimedia presentation at Minute Man Visitor Center. Busiest July and Oct., least crowded Dec.–Feb.

FOOD, LODGING & SUPPLIES

Hotels: None in park. In Concord: Colonial Inn (48 Monument Sq., tel. 978/369–9200 or 800/370–9200; 48 rooms, 8 suites; $175–$225, $300–$525 suites). In Acton: Concordian Motel (71 Hosmer St., Rte. 2E, tel. 978/263–7765; 45 rooms; $65). ✗ **Restaurants:** None in park. In Concord: Colonial Inn (48 Monument Sq., tel. 978/369–2373; $8–$12), Papa Razzi (768 Elm St., tel. 978/371–0030; $8–$15), Walden Grille (24 Walden St., tel. 978/371–2233; $7–$10). ⚙ **Groceries:** None in park. In Concord: White Hen Pantry (1224 Main St., tel. 978/369–1434).

FEES, HOURS & REGULATIONS

Entrance fee (The Wayside only): $4 adults, free ages 16 and under. No campfires or hunting. No horses or recreational vehicles on Battle Road Trail. Leashed dogs only. North Bridge Visitor Center open Apr.–Oct., daily 9–5; Nov.–Mar., daily 9–4. Minute Man Visitor Center open Apr.–Oct., daily 9–5; Nov.–Mar., daily 9–4. The Wayside guided tours May–Oct., Thurs.–Tues. 9:30–5:30. Hartwell Tavern open May–Oct., daily 9:30–5:30. Battle Road Trail open daily sunrise–sunset.

HOW TO GET THERE

The park stretches between Lexington and Concord, along Rte. 2A and Lexington Rd. From I–95, take Exit 30B to Minute Man Visitor Center on Rte. 2A in Lexington. Closest airports: Boston (22 mi), Manchester, NH (40 mi).

CONTACTS

Minute Man National Historical Park (174 Liberty St., Concord, MA 01742, tel. 978/369–6993, fax 978/371–2483, www.nps.gov/mima). Concord Chamber of Commerce (100 Main St., Suite 310–2, Concord, MA 01742, tel. 978/369–3120, www.concordmachamber.org).

New Bedford Whaling National Historical Park

In southeast Massachusetts, in New Bedford

This site commemorating whaling and its impact on American history is unique in the National Park System. The enormous 13-block, 34-acre National Historic Landmark. District is home to such intriguing sights as the Working Waterfront, the Seamen's Bethel, and the schooner *Ernestina*. The New Bedford Whaling Museum brings northeastern whaling and seafaring traditions to life while showing their importance to the region's economy. The Garden Museum and Rotch-Jones-Duff House are also open for viewing. The park was authorized on November 12, 1996.

WHAT TO SEE & DO

Touring historic district. **Facilities:** Visitor center, guided and self-guided tours, museums, movie. **Programs & Events:** Art, History, and Architecture Gallery night (2nd Thurs. monthly, 5 PM–9 PM), walking tours of historic district (daily July and Aug.). **Tips & Hints:** Plan to stay a full day. Elm St. Garage 2 blocks from visitor center. Busiest in July and Aug., least crowded in Jan. and Feb.

FOOD, LODGING & SUPPLIES

Hotels: In Westport: Hampton Inn (53 Old Bedford Rd., tel. 508/675–8500; 133 rooms; $109–$139). **Restaurants:** In the park: Freestone's City Grill (41 William St., tel. 508/993–7477; $7–$10), No Problemos (813 Purchase St., tel. 508/984–1081; $6.50–$7; no dinner Sat., closed Sun.). In New Bedford: Davy's Locker (1480 E. Rodney French Blvd., tel. 508/992–7359; $6–$10).

FEES & HOURS

Free. Some partner institutions charge fees: Rotch-Jones-Duff House & Garden Museum ($5 adults, $4 ages 65 and over; $2 ages 4–12, free ages 3 and under), New Bedford Whaling Museum ($10 adults, $9 ages 59 and over and for students with ID, $8 ages 6–14, free ages 6 and under). Visitor center open daily 9–5, 9 AM–9 PM 2nd Thurs.

HOW TO GET THERE

In New Bedford, 30 mi east of Providence, RI, via I–195 (take Exit 15, drive 1 mi to the downtown exit, turn right on Elm St., and continue to Bethel St.); 20 mi west of Cape Cod via I–195; 50 mi south of Boston via I–93 to Rte. 24 to Rte. 140. Closest airports: In New Bedford (4 mi), in Boston (60 mi), and in Warwick, RI (40 mi).

CONTACTS

New Bedford Whaling National Historical Park (33 William St., New Bedford, MA 02740, tel. 508/996–4095, fax 508/984–1250, www.nps. gov/nebe). New Bedford Office of Tourism (Wharfinger Bldg., Pier #3, New Bedford, MA 02740, tel. 800/508–5353, www.ci.new-bedford.ma. us). Rotch-Jones-Duff House and Garden Museum (396 County St., New Bedford, MA 02740, tel. 508/997–1401). New Bedford Whaling Museum (Old Dartmouth Historical Society, 18 Johnny Cake Hill, New Bedford, MA 02740, tel. 508/997–0046, www.whalingmuseum.org). Seamen's Bethel (New Bedford Port Society, 15 Johnny Cake Hill, New Bedford, MA 02740, tel. 508/992–3295). *Ernestina* schooner (New Bedford State Pier, Box 2010, New Bedford, MA 02741-2010, tel. 508/992–4900, www.ernestina.org). New Bedford Chamber of Commerce (794 Purchase St., Box 8827, New Bedford, MA 02742, tel. 508/999–5231, www.newbedfordchamber.com).

Salem Maritime
National Historic Site

In northeast Massachusetts, in Salem

The port town of Salem was a major northeast trading point for early America, and this historic park restores the exciting days when creaky wooden schooners cruised into the docks beneath billowing sails. Bounding the water are authentic 18th- and 19th-century wharves, where such buildings as the Custom House, the West India Goods Store, and the 17th-century Narbonne-Hale House are open for exploration. The Public Stores are stocked with sundries of the times, and the home of 18th-century merchant E.H. Derby shows off the lavish tastes of the era's top traders. You can also tour the *Friendship*, the North Shore's tallest Tall Ship, a full-size replica of a 342-ton merchant ship built in Salem in 1797. The site was designated on March 17, 1938.

WHAT TO SEE & DO

Touring the wharves, historic buildings, neighborhoods, and 18th-century merchant sailing ship, viewing films, visiting 18th-century garden. **Facilities:** Visitor center, orientation center, guided and self-guided tours. Bookstores. **Programs & Events:** Tours year-round. Salem Maritime Festival (July), visiting Tall Ships. **Tips & Hints:** Allow a full day for Salem, and at least another to see historic and cultural attractions of Essex County. Parking is difficult, so take public transportation to site. Busiest July and Oct., least crowded Jan. and Feb.

FEES & HOURS

Free. Ranger-led historic tours: $5 adults, $3 ages 6–16 and 62 and over, free ages 5 and under. Site open daily 9–5.

HOW TO GET THERE

In Salem, 15 mi north of Boston via Rte. 128 north to Rte. 114 east; via Newburyport–Rockport Commuter Line train from Boston's North Station; via Bus 455 or 450 from Boston's Haymarket Square or South Station to Salem rail depot. From Boston's Logan International Airport take Bus 459 from Terminal C; if driving, take Rte. 1A north and follow signs once in Salem. Closest airport: Boston (17 mi).

CONTACTS

Salem Maritime National Historic Site (174 Derby St., Salem, MA 01970, tel. 978/740–1660 park headquarters, www.nps.gov/sama). Visitor center (193 Derby St., Salem, MA 01970, tel. 978/740–1650, fax 978/740–1665).

Saugus Iron Works National Historic Site

In eastern Massachusetts, in Saugus

This open-air park along the Saugus River is the site of the first integrated ironworks in North America. In use from 1646 to 1668, the iron works complex still houses the reconstructed blast furnace, a forge, a rolling mill, a blacksmith shop, and a restored 17th-century dwelling. The museum, which sits beside the river, has working waterwheels and machinery. The park was authorized on April 5, 1968.

WHAT TO SEE & DO

Touring museum, historic house, and site; viewing film; walking nature trail. **Facilities:** Visitor center, museum, movie, guided and self-guided tours, hiking trail. Book and map sales. **Programs & Events:** Ranger-led tours (Apr.–Oct.), evening concerts and movies (July–Aug.), Saugus Founder's Day (Sept.), Hammersmith Christmas Stroll (Dec.). **Tips & Hints:** Plan to spend two hours. Busiest June–Aug., least crowded Jan. and Feb.

FEES & HOURS

Free. Site open Apr.–Oct., daily 9–5, Nov.–Mar., daily 9–4.

HOW TO GET THERE

20 minutes (10 mi) south of Salem and 20 minutes (10 mi) north of Boston via I–95 or U.S. 1 to Exit 43–Walnut St. (drive east toward the town of Lynn and follow signs to park), or via U.S. 1 to Main St. Saugus exit. Closest airport: Boston (10 mi).

CONTACT

Saugus Iron Works National Historic Site (244 Central St., Saugus, MA 01906, tel. 781/233–0050, fax 781/231–7345, www.nps.gov/sair).

Springfield Armory National Historic Site

In western Massachusetts, in Springfield

The nation's first national armory, authorized by President George Washington, was created here in 1794. Fifty-five acres are dotted with original armory buildings, as well as a museum that maintains one of the world's most extensive and unique collections of small firearms. Also on exhibit are examples of the largest exhibit of experimental and standard military arms in the United States. Displays depict weapons manufacturing processes, with details about their inventors and the women who worked here. The site was authorized in 1974 and established in 1978.

WHAT TO SEE & DO

Touring the museum and grounds, watching film and videos. **Facilities:** Information booth, indoor interpretive exhibits, museum, self-guided tours. Bookstore. **Programs & Events:** Exhibits on display year-round. Ranger talks and blank firing demonstrations (Sat. 1:30), firearms storage tours (Tues, Fri., Sat.). National Park Week (late Apr.), Military Encampment (June). **Tips & Hints:** Go in fall to view the foliage. Busiest June–Aug., least crowded Dec. and Jan.

FEES, HOURS & REGULATIONS

Free. Firearms storage tours $12, maximum 10 people per tour. Leashed pets only. Site and museum open Tues.–Sun. 10–5:30.

HOW TO GET THERE

In Springfield via I–91, take Broad St. exit to Technical Community College campus on corner of State and Federal Sts. Closest airport: Windsor Locks, CT (17 mi).

CONTACTS

Springfield Armory National Historic Site (1 Armory Sq., Springfield, MA 01105, tel. 413/734–8551, fax 413/747–8062, www.nps.gov/spar). Greater Springfield Convention & Visitors Bureau (1441 Main St., Springfield, MA 01103, tel. 413/787–1548 or 800/723–1548, fax 413/781–4607).

See Also

Appalachian National Scenic Trail, West Virginia. *Blackstone River Valley National Heritage Corridor* and *Essex National Heritage Area,* in Other National Parklands.

MICHIGAN

Isle Royale National Park

In Lake Superior, near Minnesota

Isle Royale is actually an archipelago of more than 200 islands, all of which are clustered around one huge chunk of forested wilderness. Measuring 9 mi by 45 mi, this central island is the largest in Lake Superior, and it's home to a variety of wildlife. Moose may have found the island by swimming here in the early 1900s, while wolves probably arrived here by crossing a rare ice bridge from Canada in the late 1940s. Although sightings of these animals are special events, there are many other small mammals and birds commonly found along the park trails. Ranger stations at Amygdaloid and Malone Bay have informative staff, and the Edisen Fishery, Rock Harbor Lighthouse, and McCargoe Cove are also on site. The park was authorized in 1931 and designated a Biosphere Reserve in 1980.

WHAT TO SEE & DO

Backpacking, boat cruising, canoeing (rentals in park), diving (charters available), hiking, kayaking, powerboating (rentals in park), sailing. **Facilities:** 3 visitor centers: Houghton (800 E. Lakeshore Dr.), Rock Harbor (northeast section of park), and Windigo (southwest section of park); outdoor interpretive exhibits, guided tours, hiking trails. Book and map sales, covered picnic tables with fire grills. **Programs & Events:** Evening programs at Rock Harbor and Windigo, interpretive program at Daisy Farm (twice weekly), daily guided walks and dockside talks at Windigo and Rock Harbor, living-history fishing demonstration at Edisen Fishery (four times weekly): all available mid-June–Labor Day. **Tips & Hints:** Come prepared for variable weather, which tends to be cool and wet Apr.–early June and Sept.–Oct. Go June–Aug. for flowers, May and Sept. for migrating birds. Bring repellent, netting, long-sleeve shirts, and long pants to avoid bites from mosquitoes, flies, gnats, and other insects. Busiest July and Aug., least crowded in May and Oct.

FOOD & LODGING

⚠ **Camping:** In the park: 112 sites and 50 shelters scattered throughout the park (free; pit toilets; closed Nov.–mid-Apr.). Backcountry camping allowed (permit required, *see below*). Rock Harbor Marina has electrical hook-ups and boat pump-out. In Grand Portage, MN: Grand Portage Marina & Campground (Marina Rd., adjacent to Grand Portage Lodge, tel. 218/475–2476; 10 RV sites, tent camping area; $12–$20; flush toilets, showers, hook-ups; closed Nov.–Apr.). 🏨 **Hotels:** In the park: Rock Harbor Lodge (tel. 906/337–4993 or 270/773–2191 in winter; 52 rooms, 20 cabins; $178–$276; closed early Sept.–late May). In Copper Harbor: Keweenaw Mountain Lodge (U.S. 41, tel. 906/289–4403; 8

rooms, 34 cottages, $77–$103; closed mid-Oct.–mid-May). In Grand Portage, MN: Grand Portage Lodge & Casino (Off U.S. 61, tel. 218/475–2401 or 800/543–1384; 100 rooms; $67–$77). In Hancock: Ramada Inn (99 Navy St., tel. 906/482–8400; 51 rooms; $85). In Houghton: Best Western Franklin Square Inn (820 Shelden Ave., tel. 906/487–1700; 103 rooms; $99–$189). ✗ **Restaurants:** In the park: Rock Harbor Complex (tel. 906/337–4993 or 270/773–2191; $8–$12; closed early Sept.–late May). In Copper Harbor: Mariner North (245 Gratiot St., tel. 906/289–4637; $5–$16; closed weekdays Nov. and Apr.). In Houghton: Suomi Restaurant (54 Huron St., tel. 906/482–3220; $5–$7).

FEES, HOURS & REGULATIONS

User fee: $4 adults, free ages 11 and under. Park access summer only via ferry service, floatplane, or private boat. Personal vessels can access the island mid-Apr.–late Oct. Public transportation to island available mid-May–mid-Oct. from Grand Portage, MN (tel. 715/392–2100), Houghton (tel. 906/482–0984), and Copper Harbor (tel. 906/289–4437). Seaplane service available from Houghton (tel. 906/482–0984). Camping permits (free) required for all camping (available from Windigo and Rock Harbor visitor centers and for boaters from Gunflint Ranger District in Grand Marais, MN). Michigan state fishing license ($7 for one day) required when fishing in Lake Superior. Dive permits (free) required for all diving. No hunting, pets, bikes, motorized or mechanized equipment allowed. Wheelchairs allowed in developed areas only. Park open mid-Apr.–late Oct., daily. Houghton Visitor Center (off-island in Houghton, MI) open mid-June–late Aug., Mon.–Sat. 8–6; Sept.–mid-June, weekdays 8–4:30. Rock Harbor Visitor Center open June–Labor Day, daily 8–8; intermittently Apr.–May and Labor Day–Oct. Windigo Visitor Center open June–Labor Day, daily 8–6; intermittently Apr.–May and Labor Day–Oct.

HOW TO GET THERE

Via ferry: 22 mi east of Grand Portage, MN; 56 mi northwest of Copper Harbor; and 73 mi north of Houghton. Closest airport: Houghton–Hancock (10 mi from downtown).

CONTACTS

Isle Royale National Park (800 E. Lakeshore Dr., Houghton, MI 49931, tel. 906/482–0984, fax 906/487–7170, www.nps.gov/isro). Keweenaw Tourism Council (56638 Calumet Ave., Calumet, MI 49913, tel. 906/337–4579 or 800/338–7982, www.keweenaw.org.).

Keweenaw National Historical Park

Upper Peninsula of Michigan, in Calumet

Copper mining has taken place on the Keweenaw Peninsula for 7,000 years, and many of the processes developed within these parklands were fundamental to the success of mining in the United States. Here,

1,870 acres of private land are split in two units: Quincy, home of the world's largest steam hoist, and Calumet, home of one of the most productive copper mines in world history. In addition to self-guided historic tours, there are scenic drives, hiking trails, and ski and snowmobile tracks for exploring. A trackless trolley makes stops around the Calumet unit, while tour boats ply the Keweenaw waterway in summer. There are no federal facilities in either section, but the Keweenaw Tourism Council and cooperating sites do provide information. The park was established on October 27, 1992.

WHAT TO SEE & DO

Bicycling, cross-country skiing, hiking, mountain biking, snowmobiling, touring fort, mines, museums, and historic buildings. **Facilities:** No National Park Service facilities. Keweenaw Tourism Council (Houghton, Calumet), beach, outdoor interpretive exhibits, museum, hiking trails. **Tips & Hints:** Go early in day July and Aug. to buy tickets for Quincy mine tour. Plan to spend three days to visit all cooperating sites. Go late Sept.–early Oct. for fall foliage. Expect snow between Thanksgiving and Easter. Busiest July and Aug., least crowded Jan. and Feb.

FOOD, LODGING & SUPPLIES

⚠ **Camping**: None at site. In Hancock: Hancock Campground (Rte. 203, tel. 906/482–7413; 88 sites; $8–$14; flush toilets, showers, hookups; closed Nov.–Apr.). Backcountry camping in Porcupine Mountains (permit required, *see below*). 🛏 **Hotels:** None in park. In Calumet: AmericInn Lodge & Suites (56925 S. 6th St., tel. 906/337–6463; 68 rooms, 15 suites; $83, $113 suites), Arcadian Acres Motel (51950 U.S. 41, tel. 906/482–0288; 13 rooms; $35–$45), Oak Street Inn (808 Oak St., tel. 906/337–7337; 2 suites; $125). ✕ **Restaurants:** None in park. In Calumet: The Hut Inn (58540 U.S. 41, tel. 906/337–1133; $5–$10; closed Mon.), Jim's Pizza & Family Restaurant (117 6th St., tel. 906/337–4440; $2–$7), Michigan House (300 6th St., tel. 906/337–1910; $4–$14; closed Wed.). 🛒 **Groceries & Gear:** None in park. In Houghton: Down Wind Sports (308 Sheldon Ave., tel. 906/482–2500). In Hancock: Keweenaw Co-Op Natural Foods & Groceries (1035 Ethel Ave., tel. 906/482–2030).

FEES, HOURS & REGULATIONS

Entrance fees to cooperating sites vary. Quincy mine and hoist tour: $12.50 adults, $7 ages 6–12, free ages 5 and under. Permit required for backcountry camping at Porcupine Mountains Wilderness state Park ($9 per night). Motor vehicle pass ($4 daily, $20 annually) required for Fort Wilkins, Porcupine Mountains Wilderness, and McLain state parks.

HOW TO GET THERE

Quincy: 1 mi north of Hancock via U.S. 41; Calumet: 8 mi north of Quincy via U.S. 41. Directions available from Keweenaw Tourism Council. Closest airport: Houghton (6 mi).

CONTACTS

Keweenaw National Historical Park (25970 Red Jacket Rd., Box 471, Calumet, MI 49913, tel. 906/337–3168, fax 906/337–3169, www.nps.gov/kewe). Keweenaw Tourism Council (56638 Calumet Ave.,

Calumet, MI 49913, tel. 906/337–4579 or 800/338–7982). Upper
Peninsula Travel and Recreation Association (Box 400, Iron Mountain,
MI 49801, tel. 906/774–5480 or 800/562–7134).

Pictured Rocks
National Lakeshore

Upper Michigan, between Munising and Grand Marais

Only 5 mi across at its widest point, this 73,236-acre park hugs the Lake
Superior shoreline for 40 mi and shows off some of Michigan's most attractive landscapes. Multicolored sandstone cliffs, rocky beaches, and
gently sloping sand dunes decorate the park's fringes, while the inland
areas are filled out by thundering waterfalls, placid lakes, and northern
hardwood forests that shelter a multitude of animal species. The
lakeshore was authorized on October 15, 1966.

WHAT TO SEE & DO

Backpacking, boating, canoeing, cross-country skiing, fishing, ice fishing, kayaking, hiking, hunting, picnicking, snowmobiling, snowshoeing,
wildlife watching. **Facilities:** 5 visitor centers: Park Headquarters
(N8391 Sand Point Rd., Munising), Pictured Rocks National Lakeshore
(Hiawatha National Forest, 400 E. Munising Ave., junction of Rte. 28
and Rte. 58, Munising), Grand Sable Visitor Center (E21090 Rte. 58, 1
mi west of Grand Marais), Munising Falls Interpretive Center (1505
Sand Point Rd., Munising), and Miners Castle Information Station
(N9310 Miners Castle Rd., near Munising); information kiosk, interpretive exhibits, museum, guided and self-guided tours, hiking trails.
Bookstores, picnic tables with fire grills. **Programs & Events:** Au Sable
Light Station tours (July–Labor Day, Fri.–Tues.); Artist-in-Residence
public programs (generally two weeks in spring or fall); Michigan Great
Outdoors Culture Tour (6 times in July and Aug.). **Tips & Hints:** Expect
summer highs near 90°F, with much cooler evenings and below-freezing temperatures in winter. Watch for Lake Superior storms year-
round. Bring layered clothing and rain gear. Use caution when hiking
cliff trails and while swimming, wading, or boating. Bring insect repellent in late spring or early summer when black flies and mosquitoes are
out in force. Much of the main access road (Rte. 58) is unpaved and
uneven in sections. Busiest July and Aug., least crowded Oct.–May.

FOOD, LODGING & SUPPLIES

Camping: 3 campgrounds ($10; pit toilets) in the park: Hurricane
River (21 sites; closed Nov.–mid-May), Little Beaver Lake (8 sites;
closed mid-Oct.–Apr.), Twelvemile Beach (36 sites). Backcountry
camping allowed (reservations available, permit required, *see below*).
In Munising: Wandering Wheels Jellystone Campground (E10160 Rte.
28 E, tel. 906/387–1580; 215 sites; $20–$33; flush toilets, showers,
hook-ups). **Hotels:** None in park. In Munising: Best Western (Rte.
28 E, tel. 906/387–4864; 80 rooms; $89). In Grand Marais: North Shore
Lodge (Coastguard Point Rd., Rte. 77, tel. 906/494–2361; 41 rooms, 9

cottages; $77, $410–$470 per week for cottages). ✕ **Restaurants:** None in park. In Au Train: Brownstone Inn (E4635 Rte. 28, tel. 906/892–8332; $4–$9; closed 1st 2 wks in Nov. and Mon. from Labor Day to Memorial Day). In Grand Marais: West Bay Diner & Delicatessen (Corner of Veterans and Woodruff Sts., tel. 906/494–2607; $4–$12; closed 4–6 weeks in late fall and 4–6 weeks in early spring, no dinner in winter). ⚭ **Groceries & Gear:** None in park. In Munising: Bob's IGA (131 W. Superior St., Munising, tel. 906/387–4073).

FEES, HOURS & REGULATIONS

Free. Backcountry permit ($8 per person per night, $15 tent sites for up to 6, $30 group sites for 7–20) required for all backcountry camping. Reservations by fax or mail only (Box 40, Munising, MI 49862-0040, fax 906/387–4457). Michigan state hunting and fishing license ($7–$14 for one day) required. Daily summer boat tours of park (late May–mid-Oct., tel. 906/387–2379) depart from Munising. Altran runs summer backpacker shuttle service (reservation required, tel. 906/387–4845). No motorized or wheeled vehicles, pets, or domestic pack animals in backcountry. Leashed pets only in day-use areas and drive-in campgrounds. No hunting Apr.–Labor Day. No hunting in visitor-use areas. Park open daily. Park headquarters open weekdays 8–4:30. Munising Visitor Center open mid-May–early June and Labor Day–mid-Oct., daily 9–5; early June–Labor Day, daily 8–6; mid-Oct.–mid-May, Mon.–Sat. 9–4:30. Grand Sable Visitor Center open late May–Labor Day, daily 9–5:30. Miners Castle Information Station open Memorial Day–Labor Day, daily 9:30–5.

HOW TO GET THERE

Via Rte. 58 between Munising and Grand Marais; reach Munising via Rte. 28 and Grand Marais via Rte. 77. Closest airports: Marquette (55 mi), Escanaba (65 mi).

CONTACTS

Pictured Rocks National Lakeshore (Box 40, N8391 Sand Point Rd., Munising, MI 49862-0040, tel. 906/387–3700 information; 906/387–2607 headquarters, www.nps.gov/piro). Alger Chamber of Commerce (521 Rte. 28 E, Munising, MI 49862, tel. 906/387–2138). Grand Marais Chamber of Commerce (Box 139, Grand Marais, MI 49839, tel. 906/494–2447). Grand Marais Maritime Museum (Coast Guard Point, Grand Marais, E22030 Coast Guard Point Rd.).

Sleeping Bear Dunes National Lakeshore

Northwest lower Michigan, near Empire

Massive sand dunes rise like smooth mountains above the Lake Michigan coasts, protecting 35 mi of shoreline and edging acres of gorgeous inland terrain. Beech-maple forests shimmer with light in the summer, and months later their cheery autumn hues are reflected in dozens of clear lakes and quiet rivers. Grassy bluffs rise up to 460 feet, providing sweeping views of Lake Michigan's two offshore wilderness islands, as well as a wetland environment filled with birds and mammals. The area's history is rediscovered at the Boat Museum and the Maritime Museum in Glen Haven; a cannery is also open for touring. The park was authorized in 1970 and established in 1977.

WHAT TO SEE & DO

Apple and mushroom picking, auto touring, bicycling, bird-watching, canoeing (rentals in and near park), cross-country skiing (rentals in Traverse City), dune climbing, fishing, hang gliding (permit required, *see below*), hunting, picnicking, nonpowered-model flying, scuba diving (rentals in Traverse City), snowshoeing (rentals in Glen Arbor, Traverse City), swimming, touring museum, tubing (rentals in and near park), walking beaches. **Facilities:** 2 visitor centers: Empire (9922 Front St.) and South Manitou Island; 2 museums, outdoor interpretive exhibits, hiking trails. Covered picnic tables with fire grills. **Programs & Events:** Guided walks and campfire programs (late June–Labor Day), snowshoe hikes (Dec.–Mar., weekends), lyle-gun firing (Memorial Day–Labor Day, weekly). Special events (Apr–mid-Sept.). **Tips & Hints:** Expect summer highs near 90°F with much cooler evenings, and below-freezing temperatures in winter. Bring layered clothing and rain gear. Use caution when hiking trails near sand cliffs. Bring insect repellent in warmer months to combat black flies and mosquitoes. No food or lodging available on islands. Make ferry reservations in advance for travel to the Manitou Islands. Busiest July and Aug., least crowded Nov.–Apr.

FOOD, LODGING & SUPPLIES

Camping: In the park: D.H. Day (87 sites; $10; vault toilets; closed late Nov.–early Apr.), Platte River (179 sites; $12–$21; flush toilets, showers, hook-ups). Backcountry camping ($5–$12) available at Valley View, White Pine, and on North and South Manitou Islands. **Hotels:** None in park. In Thompsonville: Crystal Mountain (12500 Crystal Mountain Dr., tel. 231/378–2000 or 800/968–7686; 63 rooms, 29 suites, 136 condos; $289). In Frankfort: Harbor Lights Motel & Condos (15 2nd St., tel. 231/352–9614 or 800/346–9614; 29 rooms, 22 suites, 20 condos; $115–$135, $195–$225 suites). **Restaurants:** None in park. In Frankfort: Hotel Frankfort (231 Main St., tel. 231/352–4303; $5–$10). In Glen Arbor: Western Avenue Grill (6410 Western Ave., tel. 231/334–3362; $6–$10). **Groceries & Gear:** None in park. In Empire: Deering's Food Market (11033 Main St., tel. 231/326–5249).

FEES, HOURS & REGULATIONS

Park pass: $10 per car, $5 per person on foot, bicycles, or motorcycles. Permits required for all ($5–$20) backcountry campers. Obtain Valley View permit from D.H. Day; obtain White Pine permit from Platte River. Permit required (free) for hang gliding and nonpowered-model flying. Ferries $25 round-trip adults, $14 round-trip ages 12 and under. Michigan state fishing and hunting licenses ($7–$14 per day) required. Stay on established trails, especially on dunes. No pets on Dune Climb, islands, swim beaches, or ski trails. Leashed pets elsewhere. No boat motors on most inland lakes. No glass on beaches. Park open daily.

Philip A. Hart Visitor Center in Empire open Memorial Day–Labor Day, daily 9–6; Labor Day–Memorial Day, daily 9–4. Scenic drive open mid-Apr.–mid-Nov. Maritime Museum buildings open Memorial Day–Labor Day, daily 10:30–5, Labor Day–mid-Oct., weekends with varying hours. Manitou Islands ferry runs from Leland May–Oct.

HOW TO GET THERE

25 mi north of Frankfort via Rte. 22, and 25 mi west of Traverse City via Rte. 72. Closest airport: Traverse City (30 mi).

CONTACTS

Sleeping Bear Dunes National Lakeshore (9922 Front St., Empire, MI 49630, tel. 231/326–5134; 800/365–2267 camping reservations, fax 231/326–5382, www.nps.gov/slbe). Manitou Island Transit (tel. 231/256–9061 ferry reservations). Benzie County Chamber of Commerce & Visitors Bureau (Box 204, Benzonia, MI 49616, tel. 231/882–5801 or 800/882–5801, fax 231/882–9249). Traverse City Area Chamber of Commerce (202 E. Grandview Pkwy., Traverse City, MI 49684, tel. 231/947–5075, fax 231/946–2565). Leelanau Peninsula Chamber of Commerce (5046 S.W. Bay Shore Dr., Suite G, Suttons Bay, MI 49682, tel. 231/271–9895, fax 231/271–9896).

See Also

Automobile National Heritage Area and *North Country National Scenic Trail*, in Other National Parklands.

MINNESOTA

Grand Portage National Monument

In northeastern Minnesota

The partially reconstructed stockade area appears as it did in the 1790s, when it was the North West Company's fur-trading headquarters on Lake Superior's western shore. The 8½-mi portage was a vital link on one of the principal routes for Native Americans, explorers, missionaries, and fur trappers heading for the northwest. Daily boat service also runs to Isle Royale National Park in summer. The site was designated a national historic site in 1951 and became a national monument in 1958.

WHAT TO SEE & DO

Hiking, picnicking, snowshoeing, touring post. **Facilities:** Outdoor interpretive exhibits, movies, hiking trails. Bookstore, picnic tables, dock. **Programs & Events:** Interpretive talks, living-history demonstrations, cultural demonstrations, daily boat trips to Isle Royale National Park in Michigan (mid-June–Labor Day); *see separate entry*. Grand Portage Rendezvous and Grand Portage Pow Wow (both 2nd full weekend, Aug.). **Tips & Hints:** Visit mid-June–mid-Sept. for most activities and services. Busiest July and Aug., least crowded Jan. and Feb.

FOOD & LODGING

Camping: In the park: 2 backcountry sites (free; pit toilets; backcountry permit required, *see below*). In Grand Portage: Grand Portage Marina & Campground (Marina Rd., adjacent to Grand Portage Lodge & Casino, tel. 218/475–2476; 10 RV sites, tent camping area; $12–$20; flush toilets, showers, hook-ups; closed Nov.–Apr.). **Hotels:** None in park. In Grand Marais: Best Western Superior Inn & Suites (U.S. 61 E, tel. 218/387–2240 or 800/842–8439; 56 rooms, 10 suites; $89–$159££). In Grand Portage: Grand Portage Lodge & Casino (U.S. 61, tel. 218/475–2401 or 800/543–1384; 100 rooms; $67–$77), Ryden's Border Store, Cafe & Hotel (9301 Ryden Rd., tel. 218/475–2330; 4 rooms; $44; closed mid-Oct.–Apr.). **Restaurants:** None in park. In Grand Portage: Island View Dining (Grand Portage Lodge, U.S. 61, tel. 218/475–2401££; $6–$10), Ryden's Border Store, Cafe & Hotel (9301 Ryden Rd., tel. 218/475–2330; $4–$9; closed mid-Oct.–mid-Mar.).

FEES, HOURS & REGULATIONS

Entrance fee: $3 adults, free ages 16 and under, $6 per family. Parking fee: $3.50 to leave car while taking Isle Royale boats. Backcountry camping permits (free) required (pick up at Grand Portage ranger station and trailheads). No hunting. No motorized vehicles or bikes on trail. Leashed pets only on trail. No pets in buildings or within stockade. Grounds open daily, dawn–dusk. Park facilities open Memorial Day–mid-Oct., daily 9–5.

HOW TO GET THERE

36 mi northeast of Grand Marais via U.S. 61. Closest airports: Thunder Bay, Canada (45 mi), Duluth, MN (156 mi).

CONTACTS

Grand Portage National Monument (Headquarters: Box 668, 315 S. Broadway, Grand Marais, MN 55604, tel. 218/387–2788, fax 218/387–2790; Site: Box 426, 211 Mile Creek Rd., Grand Portage, MN 55605, www.nps.gov/grpo). Grand Marais Area Tourism Association (Box 1048, Grand Marais, MN 55604, tel. 218/387–2524).

Mississippi National River & Recreation Area

In southeastern Minnesota, from Dayton and Ramsey to Hastings

Museums, cultural centers, and natural and historical attractions stretch along 72 mi of the Mississippi River corridor, representing the dynamic history of the great, 2,350-mi waterway. Twenty-five communities are settled along this 54,000-acre section of river, each unique in its coastal attractions, which range from quiet rural parks to bustling metropolitan riverfronts. Numerous exhibits and museums are points of interest in each town, notably the Minnesota History Center and the Science Museum of Minnesota in St. Paul; the Sibley House Historic Site in Mendota; and the Mill City Museum in Minneapolis. The area was established on November 18, 1988.

WHAT TO SEE & DO

Bicycling, boating, boat touring, canoeing, cross-country skiing, fishing, guided and self-guided tours, hiking, picnicking, swimming. **Facilities:** 5 visitor centers: Mississippi River (lobby of Science Museum of Minnesota, St. Paul), Coon Rapids Dam East (9750 Egret Blvd., Coon Rapids), Coon Rapids Dam West (10360 W. River Rd., Brooklyn Park), Fort Snelling State Park (1 Post Rd., St. Paul), and North Mississippi Regional Park (4900 Mississippi Court, Minneapolis); museums, hiking trails. **Programs & Events:** Informational talks, museum events, interpretive centers, and stewardship programs. **Tips & Hints:** River may freeze Dec.–Mar.

FOOD & LODGING

🏕 **Camping:** None at site. In Andover: Anoka County Park (550 Bunker Lake Blvd. NW, tel. 763/757–3920; 48 sites; $14–$19; flush toilets, showers, hook-ups). 🏨 **Hotels:** None in the park. In Anoka: Anoka Super 8 (1129 W. U.S. 10, tel. 763/422–8000 or 800/800–8000; 56 rooms; $60–$85). In Hastings: Hastings Country Inn & Suites (300 33 St. W, tel. 651/437–8870; 50 rooms, 11 suites; $75, $89 suites). ✕ **Restaurant:** None in the park. In Prescott, WI: Steamboat Inn & River Charters (U.S. 10 at Bridge, tel. 651/480–8222; $7–$12; closed Mon. and Tues.).

FEES, HOURS & REGULATIONS

Free. Fees to enter some parks in corridor: Coon Rapids Dam East ($4), Coon Rapids Dam West ($4), Fort Snelling State Park ($7). Minnesota fishing and watercraft license ($9.50–$18 for one day) required. Area open daily 24 hours. Science Museum Visitor Center open mid-June–early-Sept., Mon.–Sat. 9:30–9, Sun. noon–5; early Sept.–mid-June, Mon.–Wed. 9:30–5, Thurs.–Sat. 9:30–9, Sun. noon–5. Closed one week in early Sept.; shorter hours on some holidays. Other visitor center hours vary by site.

HOW TO GET THERE

The park covers a 72-mi stretchof the Mississippi River from Dayton and Ramsey, through the Minneapolis–St. Paul metro region, to south of Hastings. Closest airport: Minneapolis–St. Paul.

CONTACTS

Mississippi National River & Recreation Area (111 E. Kellogg Blvd., Suite 105, St. Paul, MN 55101, tel. 651/290–4160, fax 651/290–3214, www.nps.gov/miss). Coon Rapids Dam Regional Park (9750 Egret Blvd., Coon Rapids, MN 55433, tel. 763/757–4700 east side, 763/757–8187 west side, www.co.anoka.mn.us). Fort Snelling State Park (1 Post Rd, St. Paul, MN 55111, tel. 612/725–2724, www.dnr.state.mn.us). North Mississippi Regional Park (4900 Mississippi Court, Minneapolis, MN 55430, tel. 612/370–4865). Science Museum Visitor Center (120 W. Kellogg Blvd., St. Paul, MN, 55102, tel. 651/293–0200). Minnesota Office of Tourism (100 Metro Sq., 121 7th Pl. E, St. Paul, MN, 55101, tel. 651/296–5029 or 800/657–3700).

Pipestone
National Monument

In southwestern Minnesota, near Pipestone

For centuries Native Americans obtained stone from these lands to make pipes for ceremonial and social uses, and today the 282-acre site preserves the noted Pipestone Quarries in their natural prairie setting. The Native American crafts center has locally made items on display and for sale. About 160 acres of the area are bluestem prairie, an important remnant of the once-abundant grasslands typical of the plains. The monument was established in 1937.

WHAT TO SEE & DO

Buying Native American crafts, hiking through prairie and quarries, picnicking, taking self-guided tour, touring museum, watching pipe-making and crafts demonstrations. **Facilities:** Visitor center, cultural center, interpretive exhibits, museum, movies, hiking trail. Picnic tables with fire grills. **Programs & Events:** Pipe-making, craft, and cultural demonstrations (Apr.–Oct.), ranger-led trail walks (June–Aug.), videos of craftwork and quarrying (Nov.–Mar.). Founders Day (Aug. 25). **Tips & Hints:** Busiest July and Aug., least crowded Dec. and Jan.

FOOD, LODGING & SUPPLIES

 Camping: None at site. In Pipestone: Pipestone Campground (919 N. Hiawatha Ave., tel. 507/825–2455; 89 sites; $16–$28; flush toilets, showers, hook-ups; closed Nov.–mid-Apr.). **Hotel:** None in park. In Pipestone: Historic Calumet Inn (104 W. Main St., tel. 507/825–5871 or 800/535–7610; 41 rooms; $80). **Restaurant:** None in park. In Pipestone: Historic Calumet Restaurant (104 W. Main St., tel. 507/825–5871; $6–$9; no dinner Sun.). **Groceries & Gear:** None in park. In Pipestone: Jubas Super Value (220 2nd Ave. NE, tel. 507/825–4201), M & M Distributing (120 2nd St. NW, tel. 507/825–4133).

FEES, HOURS & REGULATIONS

Entrance fee: $3 per person, $5 per family. No hunting or fishing. Leashed pets only on trail. No bikes, skateboards, or in-line skates on trail. Park and trail open daily. Visitor center open Memorial Day–Labor Day, Mon.–Thurs. 8–6, Fri.–Sun. 8–8; Labor Day–Memorial Day, daily 8–5.

HOW TO GET THERE

On the northern edge of Pipestone via U.S. 75 or Rtes. 23 or 30. Closest airport: Sioux Falls, SD (45 mi).

CONTACTS

Pipestone National Monument (36 Reservation Ave., Pipestone, MN 56164, tel. 507/825–5464, fax 507/825–5466, www.nps.gov/pipe). Pipestone Area Chamber of Commerce (Box 8, Pipestone, MN 56164, tel. 507/825–3316 or 800/336–6125, fax 507/825–3317, www.pipestoneminnesota.com).

Voyageurs National Park

In northeastern Minnesota, near International Falls

Water dominates the landscape of this 218,000-acre park, nearly half of which is covered with more than 30 glacier-carved lakes. French Canadian voyageurs once traveled these waters in birch-bark canoes on their way to trade for furs, food, medicine, and guide services with the resident Native American tribes, and the "voyageurs highway" along these waters now stretches from the Great Lakes into the interior of the Pacific Northwest. Although the birch-bark canoes have all but disappeared, today the most popular park activities still include sailing, kayaking, and houseboating on lakes Rainy, Kabetogama, Namakan, and Sand Point. Bears roam the fragrant pine forests while eagles soar over the meadows by day; after dark, listen for loons and wolves. It's a place to explore scenic nature, learn about local geology, and step back into the fascinating history of the region's fur-trading economy. The park was authorized in 1971 and established in 1975.

WHAT TO SEE & DO

Canoeing, cross-country skiing, fishing, hiking, houseboating, kayaking, motorboating, picnicking, sailing, snowmobiling, snowshoeing. **Facilities:** 3 visitor centers: Rainy Lake (11 mi east of International Falls),

Kabetogama Lake (9924 Gappa Rd./Rte. 123), and Ash River (9899 Meadwood Rd., off Rte. 129); beaches, outdoor interpretive displays. Book and map sales, picnic tables with fire grills, docks. **Programs & Events:** Ranger-led walks, canoe trips, boat tours (daily mid-June–Labor Day), Wild Winter Rendezvous (Jan.–Mar.), Ice Box Days (International Falls, 3rd week in Jan.), Spring Birding Rendezvous (June), Autumn Rendezvous (Kabetogama and Ash River visitor centers, Labor Day weekend). **Tips & Hints:** Primary access to park, campsites, and concession-run hotel–restaurant by watercraft in summer and snowmobile in winter. Visitor centers and boat tours accessible by car. Go Jan. and Feb. for snowmobiling, year-round for fishing, June for wildflowers, May–Sept. for eagles, and mid-Sept. for fall color. Busiest July and Aug., least crowded Nov.–Apr.

FOOD, LODGING & SUPPLIES

Camping: In the park: 215 tent and houseboat sites throughout the park (free; pit toilets; permit required, *see below*). In Soudan Underground Mine State Park: Woodenfrog Campground (Off U.S. 169, tel. 218/753–2245; 61 sites; $10; pit toilets). **Hotels:** In the park: Kettle Falls Hotel & Resort (tel. 218/374–4404, 218/875–2070, or 888/534–6835; 12 rooms, 4 suites; $70££; closed Oct.–Apr.). In International Falls: Days Inn (2331 U.S. 53 S, tel. 218/283–9441; 58 rooms; $79), Holiday Inn (1500 U.S. 71, tel. 218/283–4451; 119 rooms, 7 suites; $89–$105££). **Restaurant:** In the park: Kettle Falls Hotel & Resort (tel. 218/374–4404, 218/875–2070, or 888/534–6835; $5–$14; closed Oct.–Apr.). **Groceries & Gear:** None in park. In Ray: Gateway Store (9378 U.S. 53, tel. 218/875–2121). In International Falls: Loon's Nest (3587 Rte. 415, tel. 218/286–5850), Outdoorsman Headquarters (1100 3rd Ave., tel. 218/283–9337).

FEES, HOURS & REGULATIONS

Free. Concession tour boats (reservations recommended, tel. 888/381–2873): $12–$33 adults, $8–$21 ages 2–15, free ages 1 and under. Park-provided boats $10 per day. North Canoe program: $4 adults, $2 ages 5–16. Camping permit required (free). No personal watercraft. Minnesota state fishing license ($9.50–$18 for one day) required. No hunting or trapping. No mountain bikes on trails. No off-road vehicles. Leashed pets in front country only. No pets on trails. Snowmobiles on main lakes and designated safety portages only. Park open daily. Main park inaccessible mid-Nov.–Dec. due to thin ice, Apr.–early May due to thaws. Rainy Lake Visitor Center open early May–early Sept., daily 9–5; mid-Sept.–Apr., Wed.–Sun. 9–4:30. Kabetogama Lake and Ash River visitor centers open early May–early Sept., daily 9–5.

HOW TO GET THERE

11 mi east of International Falls via U.S. 53, 160 mi north of Duluth via U.S. 53., and 300 mi north of Minneapolis via I–35 and U.S. 53. Closest airport: International Falls (15 mi).

CONTACTS

Voyageurs National Park (3131 U.S. 53 S, International Falls, MN 56649, tel. 218/283–9821; 218/875-2111 boat use on interior lakes, fax

218/285–7407, www.nps.gov/voya). International Falls Convention and Visitors Bureau (301 2nd Ave., International Falls, 56649, tel. 218/283–9400 or 800/325–5766, www.rainylake.org). Kabetogama Tourism Bureau (9903 Gamma Rd., Lake Kabetogama, MN 56669, tel. 218/875–2621 or 800/524–9085, www.kabetogama.com). Crane Lake Visitor and Tourism Bureau (7238 Handberg Rd., Crane Lake, MN 55725, tel. 800/362–7405, www.visitcranelake.com). Ash River Information Center (Orr, MN 55771, tel. 800/950–2061, www.ashriver.com).

See Also

North Country National Scenic Trail, in Other National Parklands. *Saint Croix National Scenic Riverway,* Wisconsin.

MISSISSIPPI

Brices Cross Roads
National Battlefield Site

In northeastern Mississippi, near Baldwyn

Comprising just an acre of historic grounds, this memorial site commemorates a famous Civil War battle. On June 10, 1864, General William Tecumseh Sherman's northern forces defeated General Nathan Bedford Forrest's Confederate troops, who were trying to disrupt a key Union supply route. The site was established in 1929 and transferred to the Park Service in 1933.

WHAT TO SEE & DO

Reading interpretive panels and commemorative granite marker, viewing battlefield and cannons. **Facilities:** Visitor center (mile 266, Baldwyn), interpretive signs. **Programs & Events:** Visitor center and craft center programs (monthly). **Tips & Hints:** Informational folder available at site or from Natchez Trace Parkway Visitor Center. Busiest Oct.–Apr., least crowded Dec. and Jan.

FOOD, LODGING & SUPPLIES

Camping: None at site. In Tupelo: Bicycle Only Campground (on National Scenic Trail, Natchez Trace Pkwy., mile 266; 5 cabins, tent camping area; pit toilets; free). **Hotels:** None in park. In Tupelo: Comfort Inn (1190 N. Gloster St., tel. 662/842–5100 or 800/228–5150; 83 rooms; $75), Howard Johnson (923 N. Gloster St., tel. 662/842–8811; 124 rooms; $69). **Restaurants:** None in park. In Tupelo: Jefferson Place (823 Jefferson St., tel. 662/844–8696; $6–$8; closed Sun.). **Groceries & Gear:** None in park. In Tupelo: Ascent Outdoors (404 N. Gloster St., tel. 662/690–6620), Kroger (960 W. Main St., tel. 662/840–8448).

FEES & HOURS

Free. Visitor center open Tues.–Sat. 9–5.

HOW TO GET THERE

6 mi west of Baldwyn via Rte. 370. Closest airports: Memphis, TN (104 mi), Tupelo (20 mi).

CONTACTS

Superintendent, Natchez Trace Parkway (2680 Natchez Trace Pkwy., Tupelo, MS 38804, tel. 662/680–4025; 800/305–7417 camping reservations, fax 662/680–4034, www.nps.gov/brcr).

Natchez
National Historical Park

In southwestern Mississippi, in Natchez

One of the greatest collections of significant antebellum properties in the United States is found in Natchez, Mississippi. This park celebrates the history of the city, as well as its historic roles in the settlement of the old Southwest, the Cotton Kingdom, and the Antebellum South. Here, the 18th-century Fort Rosalie was built by the French and occupied by the British, Spanish, and Americans. The William Johnson House was a house owned by William Johnson, a free black man, whose diary tells the story of everyday life in antebellum Natchez. The Melrose estate once belonged to John T. McMurran, who rose from being a middle-class lawyer to a position of wealth and power in antebellum Natchez. Although Fort Rosalie is closed to the public, Melrose and the William Johnson House are open for touring. A slavery exhibit is also on site. The park was authorized on October 7, 1988.

WHAT TO SEE & DO

Touring historic buildings. **Facilities:** Visitor information center (Melrose), Natchez Visitor Reception Center, hiking trails. Bookstore. **Programs & Events:** Guided tours of Melrose (hourly 9–4). Walking tours of historic district (Memorial Day–Labor Day, Sat. AM). Spring and Fall Pilgrimages (Mar. and Oct.), Natchez Literary Celebration (1st week, June). **Tips & Hints:** Plan to spend about two hours touring the historic homes, grounds, and outbuildings. Pick up a Discovery Kit at Melrose for in-depth self-guided touring. Busiest Apr.–Oct., least crowded Jan. and Feb.

FOOD, LODGING & SUPPLIES

Camping: None at site. Near Stanton: Nachez State Park (40 Wickliff Rd., off U.S. 61, tel. 601/442–2658; 50 sites; $13–$14; flush toilets, showers, hook-ups). **Hotels:** None in park. In Natchez: Monmouth Plantation (36 Melrose Ave., tel. 601/442–5852 or 800/828–4531; 15 rooms, 15 suites; $195–$215), Natchez Eola Hotel (110 N. Pearl St., tel. 601/445–6000 or 866/445–3652; 132 rooms; $108), Ramada Inn Hilltop (130 John R. Junkin Dr., tel. 601/446–6311 or 800/256–6311; 160 rooms, 6 suites; $86). **Restaurants:** None in park. In Natchez: Biscuits & Blues (315 Main St., tel. 601/446–9922; $6–$9; closed Mon.), Magnolia Grill (49 Silver St., tel. 601/446–7670; $10–$15). **Groceries & Gear:** None in park. In Natchez: Natchez Market (280 John R. Junkin Dr., tel. 601/442–9156), Sports Center (305 Sgt. S. Prentiss Dr., tel. 601/442–4827).

FEES, HOURS & REGULATIONS

Outbuildings and grounds free. Melrose tour: $6 adults, $3 ages 63 and over, $3 ages 6–17, free ages 5 and under. No flash photography in mansion. Natchez Visitor Reception Center open Mon.–Sat. 8:30–5, Sun. 9–4. Melrose open daily 8:30–5. The William Johnson House is expected to open in spring 2004.

HOW TO GET THERE

80 mi north of Baton Rouge, LA, via U.S. 61 north; 70 mi south of Vicksburg via U.S. 61 south; and 100 mi southeast of Jackson via I–20, the Natchez Trace Pkwy., and U.S. 61 to Melrose Montebello Pkwy. Closest airport: Baton Rouge (70 mi).

CONTACTS

Natchez National Historical Park (640 S. Canal St., Box E, Natchez, MS 39120, tel. 601/442–7047 headquarters; 601/446–5790 Melrose, fax 601/442–8845, www.nps.gov/natc). Natchez Convention & Visitors Bureau (640 S. Canal St., Natchez, MS 39120, tel. 601/446–6345).

Natchez Trace National Scenic Trail

From southwestern Mississippi, in Natchez, through northwestern Alabama to north-central Tennessee, near Nashville

Four segments of the proposed 694-mi trail have been constructed within the boundaries of the Natchez Trace Parkway (*see below*), a 444-mi motor road commemorating the historic old Natchez Trace network of trails created by local Native American tribes and later used by explorers, missionaries, and settlers. A 20-mi segment in Tennessee is south of Franklin, near the community of Leipers Fork. In Mississippi a 6-mi segment near Tupelo, a 21-mi segment in Ridgeland near Jackson, and a 10-mi segment at the Rocky Springs camping area near Port Gibson, MS, are open to the public. The trail was established on March 28, 1983.

WHAT TO SEE & DO

Hiking, horseback riding. **Facilities:** Visitor center, hiking trails.

FOOD & LODGING

🏕 **Camping:** *See Natchez Trace Parkway.* 🏨 **Hotels:** *See Brices Cross Roads National Battlefield Site* for Tupelo area, *Natchez National Historical Park* for Natchez area. ✕ **Restaurants:** *See Brices Cross Roads National Battlefield Site* for Tupelo area, *Natchez National Historical Park* for Natchez area.

FEES & HOURS

Free. Trail open 24 hrs.

HOW TO GET THERE

Trail segments: between mileposts 50.8 and 59, north of Port Gibson; between mileposts 107.9 and 140.9 north of Jackson; between mileposts 260.8 and 266 north of Tupelo; and between mileposts 408 and 427.6 south of Franklin. Closest airports: Nashville, TN (38 mi north of Garrison Creek) and Jackson, MS.

CONTACT

Natchez Trace National Scenic Trail (c/o Natchez Trace Pkwy., 2680 Natchez Trace Pkwy., Tupelo, MS 38804, tel. 662/680–4025 or 800/ 305–7417, fax 662/680–4034, www.nps.gov/natt).

Natchez Trace Parkway

From southwestern Mississippi, in Natchez, through northwestern Alabama, to central Tennessee, in Nashville

The 444-mi parkway commemorates the historic Natchez Trace, a series of trails used by Natchez, Choctaw, Chickasaw, Creek, and Cherokee peoples. The Trace later served European explorers, boatmen, settlers, soldiers, outlaws, itinerant preachers, and missionaries as a trade and transportation route, helping to form the old Southwest. The unit was established as a National Park Service unit on May 18, 1938.

WHAT TO SEE & DO

Bicycling, driving, fishing, hiking, horseback riding. **Facilities:** Mount Locust Visitor Center (mile 15.5), Colbert Ferry Information Kiosk (mile 327.3), Kosciusko Information Center (mile 160). Jeff Busby Site (mile 193.1), Meriwether Lewis Site (mile 385.9), Rocky Springs Site (mile 54.8). Book and map sales. **Programs & Events:** 12-minute film. Ranger-led tours of Mount Locust (Feb.–Nov., daily); crafts demonstrations at Mississippi Crafts Center (weekends May–Oct.). Meriwether Lewis Crafts Fair (2nd weekend, Oct.), Pioneer and Indian Crafts Fair (Oct.). **Tips & Hints:** Pick up parkway map and guide at visitor center. Listing of local bicycle shops at visitor center. Check for parkway detours; last 15 mi on north end may close during inclement weather. Go Mar. and Apr. for wildflowers, Oct. and Nov. for fall colors. Busiest in Apr. and Oct., least crowded Dec. and Jan.

FOOD, LODGING & SUPPLIES

 Camping: 3 campgrounds (free; flush toilets) in the park: Jeff Busby (mile 193.1; 18 sites), Meriwether Lewis (mile 385.9 in Tennessee; 32 sites), Rocky Springs (mile 54.8; 22 sites). Federal, state, and private campgrounds available along length of parkway. **Hotels:** *See Brices Cross Roads National Battlefield Site* for Tupelo area, *Natchez National Historical Park* for Natchez area. **Restaurants:** *See Brices Cross Roads National Battlefield Site* for Tupelo area, *Natchez National Historical Park* for Natchez area. **Groceries & Gear:** Camp store at Jeff Busby (mile 193.1).

FEES, HOURS & REGULATIONS

Free. Mississippi, Alabama, or Tennessee state fishing license required. No hunting. Leashed pets only. No bicycling or motorized vehicles on trails. Speed limit 50 mph unless otherwise posted. No commercial vehicles. Parkway open daily. Visitor center open daily 8–5. Mount Locust Visitor Center open Feb.–Nov., daily 8–5. Colbert Ferry Information Kiosk open Apr.–Nov., daily 8–5.

HOW TO GET THERE

100 mi south of Memphis, TN, via U.S. 78. Closest airports: Nashville, TN, Jackson, MS.

CONTACTS

Natchez Trace Parkway (2680 Natchez Trace Pkwy., Tupelo, MS 38804, tel. 800/305–7417; 662/680–4025 headquarters; 800/305–7417 closures and detours, fax 662/680–4033, www.nps.gov/natr). Natchez Tourism (640 S. Canal St., Natchez, MS 39120, tel. 800/647–6724). Vicksburg Convention & Visitors Bureau (1221 Washington St., Vicksburg, MS 39183, tel. 800/221–3536). Jackson Convention & Visitors Bureau (921 N. President St., Box 1450, Jackson, MS 39215-1450, tel. 601/960–1891 or 800/354–7695). Tupelo Convention & Visitors Bureau (399 E. Main St., Tupelo, MS 38804, tel. 662/841–6521). Tennessee Department of Tourism (320 6th Ave. N, Rachel Jackson Bldg., 5th fl., Nashville, TN 37243, tel. 615/741–2158). Williamson County–Franklin Chamber of Commerce (Box 156, Franklin, TN 37065-0156, tel. 800/356–3445). Nashville Area Convention & Visitors Bureau (501 Broadway, Nashville, TN 37203, tel. 615/259–4747 or 800/657–6910). Mississippi Crafts Center (mile 102, tel. 662/856–7546).

Tupelo National Battlefield

In northeastern Mississippi, in Tupelo

The Battle of Tupelo, which was part of a larger strategy by General William Tecumseh Sherman to protect his railroad supply line, occurred on July 13 and 14, 1864, when Federal troops under General A. J. Smith fought Confederate soldiers under General Nathan Bedford Forrest. Both sides also battled the heat that ultimately forced the Federal retreat. A monument marks the event, and the park is dotted with old cannons and interpretive placards. The 1-acre Tupelo National Battlefield Site was established in 1929, transferred to the Park Service in 1933, and redesignated in 1961.

WHAT TO SEE & DO

Visiting site and monument. **Facilities:** Interpretive signs. **Tips & Hints:** Busiest in Apr. and Oct., least crowded Dec. and Jan.

FOOD, LODGING & SUPPLIES

See Brices Cross Roads National Battlefield Site.

FEES & HOURS

Free. Park open daily 24 hrs.

HOW TO GET THERE

In Tupelo via Rte. 6, 1.3 mi west of intersection with U.S. 45 and 1 mi east of Natchez Trace Pkwy. Closest airports: Tupelo (4 mi), Memphis, TN (100 mi).

CONTACTS

Tupelo National Battlefield (c/o Natchez Trace Parkway, 2680 Natchez Trace Pkwy., Tupelo, MS 38804, tel. 601/680–4025 or 800/305–7417, www.nps.gov/tupe). Tupelo Convention & Visitors Bureau (399 E. Main St., Tupelo, MS 38804, tel. 662/841–6521).

Vicksburg National Military Park

In western Mississippi, in Vicksburg

A key battle of the Civil War—including the campaign, siege, and defense of Vicksburg from March 29 to July 4, 1863—is commemorated at this park. Battles at Port Gibson, Raymond, Jackson, Champion Hill, and Big Black River were all part of the Vicksburg campaign, as was the 47-day Union siege against the city. Located high on the bluffs, Vicksburg was known as "The Gibraltar of the Confederacy" and guarded the Mississippi River; with its surrender, the Union regained control of the lower Mississippi River and split the Confederacy in two. Today, more than 1,300 monuments and markers are scattered throughout the grounds, as are reconstructed trenches and earthworks, an antebellum structure, more than 125 emplaced cannons, and the Vicksburg National Cemetery. The U.S.S. *Cairo* Museum and Gunboat is also on the grounds. A 16-mi auto-tour road winds past many of the significant historic sites. The park was established in 1899 and transferred to the Park Service in 1933.

WHAT TO SEE & DO

Auto touring, bird-watching, hiking, touring museum and cemetery, viewing restored Union gunboat, walking. **Facilities:** Visitor center, interpretive signs, U.S.S. *Cairo* Museum and Gunboat (mile 7.9). Bookstore, picnic tables. **Programs & Events:** Guided battlefield tours, self-guided driving tours. Ranger talks, black powder demonstration, living-history program, and cannon firing demonstrations (all mid-June–mid-Aug.). **Tips & Hints:** Wear comfortable clothing and walking or hiking shoes. Audiotapes available for driving tours. Best weather Mar.–May. Busiest Apr. and May, least crowded Nov. and Dec.

FOOD & LODGING

Hotels: None in park. In Vicksburg: Ameristar Casino Hotel (4155 Washington St., tel. 601/638–1000 or 800/700–7770; 149 rooms; $69–$189), Battlefield Inn (4137 I–20 N. Frontage Rd., tel. 601/638–5811 or 800/359–9363; 118 rooms; $50–$75), Hampton Inn (3332 Clay St., 601/636–6100 or 888/568–4044; 147 rooms; $75). **✗ Restaurants:** None in park. In Vicksburg: Eddie Monsour's (127 Country Club Dr., tel. 601/638–1571; $5–$10; no lunch Sat., no dinner Sun.), Walnut Hills Round Tables (1214 Adams St., tel. 601/638–4910; $7–$17; closed Sat., no dinner Sun.).

FEES, HOURS & REGULATIONS

Entrance fee: $5 per vehicle, $3 per bus passenger. Guided battlefield tour: $30 per car, $40 per van, $60 per bus; reservations available. No hunting. No metal detectors. No fires or cooking. Park open daily dawn–dusk. Visitor center open daily 8–5. Cairo Museum open Nov.–Mar., daily 8:30–5; Apr.–Oct., daily 9:30–6.

HOW TO GET THERE

In Vicksburg off I–20/U.S. 61 at Exit 4B; take Clay St. (U.S. 80) west for ¼ mi to park. Closest airport: Jackson (50 mi).

CONTACTS

Vicksburg National Military Park (3201 Clay St., Vicksburg, MS 39183, tel. 601/636–0583; 601/636–3827 battlefield tour, fax 601/636–9497, www.nps.gov/vick). Vicksburg Convention & Visitors Bureau (Box 110, Vicksburg, MS 39181, tel. 601/636–9421).

See Also

Gulf Islands National Seashore, Florida.

George Washington Carver National Monument

In southwestern Missouri, near Diamond

George Washington Carver, who was born here in 1864, ascended national prominence as a scientist, educator, and humanitarian. The park preserves the historic 1881 home where he lived and a cemetery (though George W. Carver is not buried there). Kids have fun at the hands-on discovery center, and talks on local history and nature are held year-round at the multipurpose classroom facility. The monument was authorized in 1943 and established in 1953.

WHAT TO SEE & DO

Hiking, picnicking, touring home and cemetery, watching film. **Facilities:** Visitor center, movie, outdoor interpretive exhibits. Book-and-gift shop, picnic tables. **Programs & Events:** Ranger-guided tours; interpretive, living-history, cultural, and nature programs; educational field trips. Black Heritage Month and 4th-grade Art & Essay Contest (Feb.), March for Parks (Apr.), Carver Day Celebration (July), Prairie Day Celebration (Sept.), Holiday Open House (Dec.). **Tips & Hints:** Busiest in May and July, least crowded Dec. and Jan.

FOOD, LODGING & SUPPLIES

⛺ **Camping:** None at site. In Carthage: Ballard's Campground (U.S. 71, tel. 417/359–0359; 30 sites; $11–$15; flush toilets, showers, hookups). 🛏 **Hotels:** None in park. In Carthage: Best Western Precious Moments Hotel (2701 Hazel Ave., tel. 417/359–5900 or 800/551–7676; 121 rooms; $71), Days Inn (2244 Grand Ave., tel. 417/358–2499 or 888/454–2499; 40 rooms; $51–$56). ✕ **Restaurants:** None in park. In Carthage: Ranch House (2937 S. Grand Ave., tel. 417/359–5200; $5–$8; closed Sun.). In Joplin: Undercliff Grill & Bar (6385 Old U.S. 71, tel. 417/623–8382; $5–$13; closed Mon. and Tues.; no dinner Sun.). 🛒 **Groceries & Gear:** None in park. In Diamond: Barb's One Stop (101 N. Washington St., tel. 417/325–7114).

FEES, HOURS & REGULATIONS

Free. No hunting or fishing. No motorized or mechanized equipment on trails. Leashed pets only. Monument and visitor center open daily 9–5.

HOW TO GET THERE

10 mi east of Joplin via I–44, take Exit 11A to U.S. 71 south, then the Diamond exit 4 mi east and travel ½ mi south. Closest airport: Joplin (15 mi).

CONTACTS

George Washington Carver National Monument (5646 Carver Rd., Diamond, MO 64840, tel. 417/325–4151, fax 417/325–4231, www.nps.gov/gwca). Joplin Convention & Visitors Bureau (222 W. 3rd St., Joplin, MO 64801, tel. 417/625–4789 or 800/657–2534). Carthage Chamber of Commerce (107 E. 3rd St., Carthage, MO 64836, tel. 417/358–2373, fax 417/358–7479). Neosho Chamber of Commerce (Box 605, Neosho, MO 64850, tel. 417/451–1925, fax 417/451–8097).

Harry S. Truman National Historic Site

In west-central Missouri, near Independence

Preserved at this historic site is a remarkably complete collection of structures and objects associated with the life of Harry S. Truman, 33rd president of the United States. Five properties and associated structures stand within it: the Truman Home (219 N. Delaware St.), Frank Wallace House (601 W. Truman Rd.), George Wallace House (605 W. Truman Rd.), Noland House (216 N. Delaware St.), and Truman Farm (Grandview, ½ mi west of U.S. 71 on Blue Ridge Blvd.). Truman lived on the farm for 11 years before moving to the 219 North Delaware house in 1919 after his marriage to Bess Wallace, whose family lived there. He returned to the Delaware Street home after his term ended in 1953. The Trumans lived there until his death in 1972 and her death in 1982. The 219 North Delaware Street site was authorized in 1983. The other three homes and the farm were acquired in 1991 and 1994.

WHAT TO SEE & DO

Touring the home, farm, and surrounding National Historic Landmark District, viewing slide program. **Facilities:** Visitor center, outdoor interpretive exhibit. Bookstore. **Programs & Events:** National Historic Landmark District Walking Tours (daily at 10), self-guided tours of Truman Farm. Guided tours of the Truman Home (Memorial Day–Labor Day, daily every 15 min 9–4:45; Labor Day–Memorial Day, Tues.–Sun. tickets required), Farm Home tours (Memorial Day–Labor Day, Fri.–Sun., every half-hour 9:30–4, tickets required). **Tips & Hints:** Same-day Truman Home tour tickets available at 8:30 from the visitor center; passes are first-come, first-served and groups are limited to eight people. Same-day Farm Home tour tickets, available on site at 9:30, are limited to groups of six people. Go Jan. and Feb. to avoid crowds. Busiest June and July, least crowded Jan. and Feb.

FEES, HOURS & REGULATIONS

Truman Home tour: $3 adults 16, free ages 15 and under, others free; tickets required for all. Truman Farm Home tour free; tickets also required. No advance tour reservations accepted. No purses, diaper bags, backpacks, cameras, camera bags, cell phones, or pagers permitted on either home tour. No pets in buildings. Leashed pets allowed on grounds of farm only. No smoking or picnicking. No vehicles off paved roads or parking lots. Visitor center open daily 8:30–5. Truman Farm grounds open daily dawn–dusk.

HOW TO GET THERE

From Independence via I–70, take Noland Rd. north to Truman Rd., turn left, drive two blocks to visitor center. Via I–435, take Truman Rd. exit east to corner of Truman Rd. and Main St.. Reach Truman Farm via U.S. 71 to Grandview, then exit west onto Blue Ridge Blvd. and drive ½ mi. Closest airport: Kansas City (31 mi).

CONTACTS

Harry S. Truman National Historic Site (223 N. Main St., Independence, MO 64050, tel. 816/254–9929, fax 816/254–4491, www.nps.gov/hstr). Independence Chamber of Commerce (210 W. Truman Rd., Independence, MO 64050, tel. 816/252–4745). Grandview Chamber of Commerce (12500 S. U.S. 71, No. 100, Grandview, MO 64030, tel. 816/761–6505).

Jefferson National Expansion Memorial

In east-central Missouri, in St. Louis

The memorial commemorates St. Louis's role in the westward growth of the United States from 1803 through 1890. Important buildings here include the city's Old Courthouse, built between 1839 and 1862, and the Gateway Arch, an internationally renowned 1965 structure designed by Eero Saarinen. The fascinating Museum of Westward Expansion chronicles the region's growth westward during the 19th century. The memorial was established on December 20, 1935.

WHAT TO SEE & DO

Riding to the top of the arch, touring museum and courthouse, viewing films. **Facilities:** Visitor center, information kiosks, museum, movies. Book-and-gift shops. **Programs & Events:** Ranger-guided tours. African-American Heritage Month (Feb.), St. Louis Storytelling Festival (1st weekend, May), Patriotic 4th of July, Victorian Christmas (Dec.). **Tips & Hints:** Park in garage at north end of grounds on Washington Ave. Lot on south end handles oversize vehicles (higher than 7 feet). Gateway Arch requires hiking up at least 96 nonstandard steps. Inform ranger beforehand about fear of heights or confined spaces. Arrive ½–1 hour ahead of reservation time for security check. Busiest July and Aug., least crowded Jan. and Feb.

FEES, HOURS & REGULATIONS

Entrance fee: $3 adults, free ages 16 and under; $6 per family. Separate charges for arch ride and films. Old Courthouse free. Leashed pets only on grounds. No in-line skating, skateboarding, and other recreational activities, except walking and jogging. Gateway Arch and visitor center open Memorial Day–Labor Day, daily 8 AM–10 PM; Labor Day–Memorial Day, daily 9–6. Old Courthouse open daily 8–4:30.

HOW TO GET THERE

In St. Louis, visitor center at base of Gateway Arch. Closest airport: St. Louis (8 mi).

CONTACTS

Jefferson National Expansion Memorial (11 N. 4th St., St. Louis, MO 63102, tel. 314/655–1700, fax 314/655–1642, www.nps.gov/jeff). St. Louis Convention & Visitors Commission (1 Metropolitan Sq., Suite 1100, St. Louis, MO 63102, tel. 314/421–1023 or 800/325–7962).

Ozark
National Scenic Riverways

In southeastern Missouri, near Van Buren

Around 134 mi of waterways along the Current and Jacks Fork rivers provide scenic settings for canoeing, tubing, fishing, and swimming. More than 300 springs pour thousands of gallons of clear, cold water into the streams, while forests and meadows fill in the surrounding hills and valleys. Ozark culture also is preserved throughout the 80,790-acre park. The park was authorized in 1964 and established in 1972.

WHAT TO SEE & DO

Boating, canoeing (rentals at campgrounds, and in Eminence and Van Buren), fishing, hunting, swimming, tubing. **Facilities:** 2 visitor centers: Alley Mill (Alley Spring, near Eminence) and park headquarters (Van Buren); outdoor interpretive exhibits. Covered picnic tables. **Programs & Events:** Evening programs (Memorial Day–Labor Day, weekends), Round Spring Cave tours (Memorial Day–Labor Day, daily at 10 and 2), concerts (June–Aug., weekends). **Tips & Hints:** Wear life jackets on river (required for children 12 and under). Canoeing possible any time of year. Busiest July and August, least crowded Jan. and Feb.

FOOD, LODGING & SUPPLIES

△ **Camping:** 5 campgrounds ($12; flush toilets, showers) in the park: Alley Spring (162 sites), Big Spring (123 sites), Pulltite (50 sites), Round Spring (60 sites), Two Rivers (19 sites). Near Salem: Montauk State Park (Rte. 5, tel. 573/548–2201; 877/422–6766 reservations; 156 sites; $14–$8; flush toilets, showers, hook-ups). 🏨 **Hotels:** In the park: Big Spring Cabins (Rtes. 103 and Z, off U.S. 60, near Van Buren, tel. 573/323–4332; 14 cabins; $55–$110; closed mid-Nov.– Mar.). In Van Buren: Smalley's Motel (702 Main St., tel. 573/323–4263 or 800/727–4263; 28 rooms; $45). ✕ **Restaurants:** In the park: Big Spring Historic Dining Lodge (Rtes. 103 and Z, off U.S. 60, tel. 573/323–4423; $4–$7; closed Labor Day–Memorial Day). In Van Buren: Float Stream Café (102 Main St., tel. 573/323–9606; $5–$16). In Eminence: Winfield's Restaurant (106 S. Main, tel. 573/226–3400; $5–$7). ⚲ **Groceries & Gear:** Camp stores at Akers Ferry, Alley Spring, Round Spring, Two Rivers.

FEES, HOURS & REGULATIONS

Free. Cave tours $5 adults, $2 ages 12 and under. Missouri state fishing and hunting licenses ($5–$10 for one day) required. No inboard motors. No Jet skis. Horsepower limits apply. Leashed pets only. Park open daily. Alley Mill Visitor Center open Memorial Day–Labor Day, daily 9–4; Labor Day–mid-Oct., weekends 9–4. Park Headquarters Visitor Center open weekdays 8–4:30.

HOW TO GET THERE

175 mi south of St. Louis and 250 mi southeast of Kansas City via Rte. 19 to Akers Ferry, Pulltite, and Round Spring; from Eminence via Hwy. 106 to Alley Spring and Two Rivers; and 4 mi from Van Buren via Rte. 103 to Big Spring. Closest airports: St. Louis and Springfield (140 mi).

CONTACT

Ozark National Scenic Riverways (404 Watercress Dr., Box 490, Van Buren, MO 63965, tel. 573/323–4236, fax 573/323–4140, www.nps. gov/ozar).

Ulysses S. Grant
National Historic Site

In east-central Missouri, in St. Louis

The 9.6-acre heart of the former 1,000-acre plantation owned by Ulysses and Julia Grant is preserved at this National Historic Landmark. The site is significant for its association with the apparently "average" man who led the army that saved the Union, served two terms as president, and wrote one of the most important military commentaries of modern times. The property also includes the main house, summer kitchen, chicken house, ice house, and barn. The site was authorized on October 2, 1989.

WHAT TO SEE & DO

Ranger-led and self-guided tours of buildings and grounds. **Facilities:** Visitor center, museum. Book-and-gift shop. **Programs & Events:** Daily ranger-led tours, daily Junior Ranger program, guest lectures, living-history demonstrations, children's programs. Night Walk into the Past program (Aug.), Holidays at White Haven (Dec.). **Tips & Hints:** Walking is required to fully experience the park. Watch for uneven ground and slippery surfaces. Busiest July and Aug., least crowded Jan. and Feb.

FEES, HOURS & REGULATIONS

Free. Reservations suggested for special events. Leashed pets only. Site open daily 9–5.

HOW TO GET THERE

In south St. Louis County via Gravois Rd. (Rte. 30) and Watson Rd. (Rte. 366). Closest airport: St. Louis (20 mi).

CONTACTS

Ulysses S. Grant National Historic Site (7400 Grant Rd., St. Louis, MO 63123, tel. 314/842–3298, fax 314/842–1659, www.nps.gov/ulsg). St. Louis Convention & Visitors Bureau (1 Metropolitan Sq., Suite 1100, St. Louis, MO 63102, tel. 314/421–1023). St. Louis Visitors Center (308 Washington Ave., St. Louis, MO 63102, tel. 314/241–1764). Missouri Tourism Information Center (Rest Area 270 and Riverview on Dunn Rd., Box 38182, St. Louis, MO 63138, tel. 314/869–7100).

Wilson's Creek National Battlefield

In southwestern Missouri, near Springfield

On August 10, 1861, the first major Civil War engagement west of the Mississippi River was fought at this site. It was a battle of more than 5,000 Union troops and 10,000 Confederates; the former lost General Nathanial Lyon, the first Union leader, while the latter emerged victorious. Today, with the exception of the vegetation, the 1,750-acre battlefield has changed little from its historic setting. Major sites include a 5-mi tour road, the restored 1852 Ray House, and "Bloody Hill," the scene of the major battle. The site was authorized as a national battlefield park in 1960 and redesignated in 1970.

WHAT TO SEE & DO

Hiking, touring battlefield and Ray House. **Facilities:** Visitor center, outdoor interpretive exhibits, guided and self-guided tours, hiking trails. Bookstore, covered picnic tables. **Programs & Events:** Self-guided auto tour, self-guided tours of Bloody Hill. Living-history programs and Ray House tours (weekends Memorial Day–Labor Day). Battle anniversary (Aug. 10). **Tips & Hints:** Plan to spend at least two hours. Busiest May–Aug., least crowded in Nov. and Jan.

FOOD, LODGING & SUPPLIES

Hotel: None in park. In Springfield: Clarion (3333 S. Glenstone St., tel. 417/883–6550; 195 rooms; $70–$90). **✕ Restaurants:** None in park. In Springfield: Hemingway's Restaurant (1935 S. Campbell Ave., 4th fl. Bass Pro Shop, tel. 417/891–5100; $5–$10; no dinner Sun.), Zio's Italian Kitchen (1249 E. Kingsley St., tel. 417/889–1919; $5–$10). **Groceries & Gear:** None in park. In Springfield: Bass Pro Shops (1935 S. Campbell Ave., tel. 417/887–7334). In Republic: Price Cutter (1013 U.S. 60 E, tel. 417/732–2828).

FEES & HOURS

Entrance fee: $3 adults, free ages 17 and under, $5 per vehicle. Park open daily 8–5; extended hours in summer. Visitor center open daily 8–5.

HOW TO GET THERE

18 mi southwest of Springfield via I–44 and Exit 70 (Rte. MM), Rte. ZZ south, and Farm Rd. 182; and via U.S. 60/65, Rte. 14, Rte. ZZ, and Farm Rd. 182. Closest airport: Springfield.

CONTACTS

Wilson's Creek National Battlefield (6424 W. Farm Rd. 182, Republic, MO 65738, tel. 417/732–2662, fax 417/732–1167, www.nps.gov/wicr). Springfield Convention & Visitors Bureau (3315 E. Battlefield Rd., Springfield, MO 65804, tel. 417/881–5300).

See Also

California National Historic Trail, Lewis & Clark National Historic Trail, Oregon National Historic Trail, Pony Express National Historic Trail, Santa Fe National Historic Trail, and *Trail of Tears National Historic Trail,* in Other National Parklands.

MONTANA

Big Hole National Battlefield

In southwestern Montana, near Wisdom

One of the West's most tragic stories played out on this battlefield. In 1877 the U.S. Army was charged with forcing resistant Nez Perce Indians onto a reservation in Idaho. In the same year, a few Nez Perce warriors killed several white settlers as retribution for Nez Perce deaths and mistreatment at the hands of white people. The bloodshed provoked a massive manhunt and the beginning of a 1,500-mi odyssey. The Nez Perce fled north from their homeland in central Idaho, pursued by the U.S. Army. The tribe engaged 10 separate U.S. commands in 13 battles and skirmishes. One of the fiercest of these took place at Big Hole Battlefield, where both sides suffered serious losses. The site was established as a national monument in 1910, transferred to the Park Service in 1933, and changed to a National Battlefield in 1963.

WHAT TO SEE & DO

Cross-country skiing, fishing, picnicking, snowshoeing, touring battlefield, watching introductory video. **Facilities:** Visitor center, museum, movie, guided tours, hiking trails. Book and map sales, picnic tables. **Programs & Events:** Guided hikes, interpretive talks (June–Aug.). Big Hole Battle Annual Commemoration (weekend near Aug. 9). **Tips & Hints:** Busiest July and Aug., least crowded Dec. and Jan.

FOOD, LODGING & SUPPLIES

Camping: None at site. In Beaverhead-Deerlodge National Forest: May Creek Campground (Rte. 43, 17 mi west of Wisdom, tel. 406/689–3243; 21 sites; $7; pit toilets; closed Labor Day–July). **Hotels:** None in park. In Jackson: Jackson Hot Springs Lodge (Rte. 278, tel. 406/834–3151; 20 rooms; $33–$75). In Wisdom: Nez Perce Motel (Rte. 43, tel. 406/689–3254; 8 rooms; $53). **Restaurants:** None in park. In Wisdom: Antler Saloon (Main St., tel. 406/689–9393; $9–$14), Big Hole Crossing Restaurant (105 Park St. tel. 406/689–3800; $5–$8; no dinner Tues. and Wed. Labor Day–June). **Groceries & Gear:** None in park. In Wisdom: Conover's Trading Post (Rte. 43, tel. 406/689–3272), Wisdom Market (Rte. 43, tel. 406/689–3271).

FEES, HOURS & REGULATIONS

Entrance fee (collected Memorial Day–late Sept.): $3 per person or $5 per car. Montana state fishing license required. Pets only in parking areas; must be leashed. No hunting. Trails open until dusk. Visitor center open daily 9–5, with extended, variable hours Memorial Day–Labor Day.

HOW TO GET THERE

10 mi west of Wisdom via Rte. 43. Closest airport: Missoula (100 mi).

CONTACT
Big Hole National Battlefield (Box 237, Wisdom, MT 59761, tel. 406/689–3155, fax 406/689–3151, www.nps.gov/biho).

Bighorn Canyon National Recreation Area

*South-central Montana, near Hardin,
to north-central Wyoming, near Lovell*

The most compelling attraction here is the geology of the canyon, which is several thousand feet deep in places. Naturally, Bighorn Canyon also has plenty of bighorn sheep, and it's the site of the nation's first wild horse range, the Bad Pass Trail. The Ok-A-Beh scenic road winds through the park and past several historic ranches. Look for the Bighorn River, located below the Yellowtail Dam. The area was established in 1966.

WHAT TO SEE & DO

Boating (rentals, lake marina), fishing, hiking, hunting, ice fishing, skiing, swimming, touring canyon. **Facilities:** 2 visitor centers: Yellowtail Dam (Fort Smith, MT) and Bighorn Canyon (Lovell, WY); outdoor interpretive exhibits, hiking trails. Bookstores, picnic tables with fire grills. **Programs & Events:** Canoe trips, interpretive talks, campfire programs (June–Aug.). Mustang Days fireworks at Horseshoe Bend (Sun. before July 4), Afterbay Dam, MT, fireworks (July 4). **Tips & Hints:** Watch for rattlesnakes and fragile edges near drop-offs. Be aware of and respect Crow Indian Reservation boundaries. Bighorn Canyon is relatively undiscovered treasure, with few visitors there at any time.

FOOD, LODGING & SUPPLIES

Camping: 5 campgrounds ($5) in the park: Afterbay Canyon (29 sites; vault toilets), Black Canyon (17 boat-in sites; vault toilets), Horseshoe Bend (54 sites; flush toilets), Medicine Creek (6 boat-in or hike-in sites; vault toilets), Trail Creek (12 sites; vault toilets). In Yellowtail, MT: Cottonwood Camp (3 mi north of Fort Smith, tel. 406/666–2391; 16 RV sites, tent-camping area, 19 cabins; $10–$65; flush toilets, showers, hook-ups). **Hotels:** None in park. In Hardin, MT: Super 8 (201 14th St. W, tel. 406/665–1700 or 800/800–8000; 63 rooms; $70), Lariat Motel (709 Center Ave., tel. 406/665–2683; 18 rooms; $44). In Lovell, WY: Super 8 (595 E. Main, tel. 307/548–2725 or 800/800–8000; 32 rooms; $63). **Restaurants:** In the park: grill and staples at Ok-A-Beh Marina. In Hardin, MT: Purple Cow (Rte. 1, off Rte. 47 at north end of town, tel. 406/665–3601; $6–$8), Lariat Country Kitchen, (721 Center Ave., tel. 406/665–1139; $5–$7; no dinner Sun.). **Groceries:** None in park. In Fort Smith, MT: Yellowtail Market (Parkdale Ct., tel. 406/666–2333). In Lovell, WY: Red Apple (9 E. Main St., tel. 307/548–2224).

FEES, HOURS & REGULATIONS

Entrance fee: $5 per vehicle. Montana or Wyoming state fishing license required. No hunting in restricted areas. Leashed pets only. No motorized or mechanical vehicles off paved or dirt roads. Park open daily. Yellowtail Dam Visitor Center open Memorial Day–Labor Day, daily 9–5. Bighorn Canyon Visitor Center open Memorial Day–Labor Day, daily 8–6; Labor Day–Memorial Day, daily 8:30–5.

HOW TO GET THERE

North Unit (Montana side) 1 mi west of Fort Smith; South Unit (Wyoming side) 14 mi northeast from Lovell. Closest airports: Billings (90 mi from North District), Cody, WY (50 mi).

CONTACTS

Bighorn Canyon National Recreation Area, North Unit (Box 7458, Fort Smith, MT 59035, tel. 406/666–2412, fax 406/666–2415, www.nps.gov/bica). Bighorn Canyon National Recreation Area, South Unit (20 U.S. 14A E, Lovell, WY 82431, tel. 307/548–2251, fax 307/548–7826). Hardin Area Chamber of Commerce (15 E. 4th St., Hardin, MT 59034, tel. 406/665–1672). Lovell Area Chamber of Commerce (287 E. Main St., Box 295, Lovell, WY 82431, tel. 307/548–7552).

Glacier National Park

In northwestern Montana, near West Glacier

This ruggedly beautiful park, considered one of the most ecologically intact temperate areas in the world, offers spectacular mountain scenery, and the chance for a true wilderness experience. Within the boundaries of the 1-million-acre park are nearly 50 glaciers, endless 10,000-foot peaks, and numerous lakes and waterways set amid expansive meadows and steep ravines. Grizzly bears, cougars, gray wolves, moose, and bighorn sheep are but a few of the creatures that can be seen in the vast forests, while swift, shallow rivers shelter beaver, otters, muskrats, raccoons, and a variety of other small mammals. Look overhead to spot bald eagles, hawks, falcons, and other birds of prey; the marshy lakeshores and riverbanks are also home to numerous waterfowl. The area has many Native American ties as well, and the visitor centers host summer programs by Blackfeet, Salish, and Kooterai tribal members. The park was established in 1910, authorized as part of the Waterton-Glacier International Peace Park in 1932, designated a Biosphere Reserve in 1976, and a World Heritage Site in 1995.

WHAT TO SEE & DO

Auto touring, backpacking (rentals in Columbia Falls and West Glacier), bicycling (rentals in East Glacier), boating and canoeing (rentals in Apgar, Lake McDonald, Many Glacier, Two Medicine), cross-country skiing (rentals in Essex), fishing, golfing (in East Glacier, Columbia Falls), hiking, horseback riding, kayaking (rentals in Apgar, Lake McDonald, Many Glacier, Two Medicine), picnicking, rafting (trips from West Glacier), snowshoeing, touring park in vintage buses (fee, *see below*), wildlife watching. **Facilities:** 3 visitor centers: Apgar (west side of park), Logan Pass (on Going-to-the-Sun Rd.), St. Mary (east side of park); Red Jammer tour buses, outdoor interpretive exhibits, movies, guided and self-guided tours, 700 mi of hiking trails. Book and map sales, book-and-gift shops, picnic tables. **Programs & Events:** Ranger talks (evenings), slide shows, boat tours, guided walks, and daylong hikes. Native America Speaks series by Blackfeet, Salish, and Kooterai tribal members (July and Aug.); Show Me Day (snow-removal day, May). **Tips & Hints:** Beware of water and snow hazards, altitude sickness, and hypothermia. Ticks are prevalent throughout the woods. *Do not bother or feed wild animals*, and know what to do when confronted by a bear or cougar. If camping, bring 25 feet of rope to hoist food up into trees; bear boxes also available. Go in Sept. to avoid crowds. Busiest July and Aug., least crowded Nov. and Dec.

FOOD, LODGING & SUPPLIES

🛖 **Camping:** 13 campgrounds in the park (1,000 sites; $12–$17; some flush toilets, some pit toilets, some showers). Backcountry camping available, permit required, *see below*). 🏨 **Hotels:** In the park: Apgar Village Lodge (tel. 406/888–5484; 48 rooms; $71–$110; closed early Oct.–early May), Granite Park Chalet (tel. 406/387–5555 or 800/521–7238; 12 rooms; $66; closed mid-Sept.–June), Sperry Chalet (tel. 406/387–5654 or 888/345–2649; 17 rooms; $255; closed mid-Sept.–mid-July), Lake McDonald Lodge (tel. 406/892–2525; 100 rooms; $96–$149; closed Oct.–May), Many Glacier Hotel (tel. 406/892–2525; 215 rooms, 8 suites; $135; closed mid-Sept.–mid-May), Rising Sun Motor Inn (tel. 406/892–2525; 72 rooms; $92; closed mid-Sept.–mid-June), Swiftcurrent Motor Inn (tel. 406/892–2525; 88 rooms; $92; closed mid-Sept.–mid-June), Village Inn (tel. 406/892–2525; 36 rooms; $109–$177; closed Oct.–May), Glacier Park Lodge (tel. 406/892–2525; 161 rooms; $155; closed Oct.–mid-May), Prince of Wales Hotel (Waterton, Canada, tel. 406/892–2525; 84 rooms; CAN$286; closed mid-Sept.–May). ✕ **Restaurants:** In the park: Great Northern Steak & Rib House (Glacier Park Lodge), Italian Gardens (Swiftcurrent Motor Inn), Jammer Joe's Grill & Pizzeria (Lake McDonald Lodge), Ptarmigan Dining Room (Many Glacier Hotel), Royal Stewart Dining Room (Prince of Wales Hotel), Russell's Fireside Dining Room (Lake McDonald Lodge), Two Dogs Flat Grill (Rising Sun Motor Inn). 🛒 **Groceries & Gear:** In the park: Swiftcurrent camp store (Many Glacier Valley), Rising Sun camp store (east part of the park), Two Medicine camp store (southeast part of the park), Lake MacDonald Lodge camp store. In St. Mary: Trail & Creek Outfitters and Country Market (Resort at Glacier, tel. 406/732–4431; closed early Oct.–early May).

FEES, HOURS & REGULATIONS

Entrance fee: $10 per vehicle, $5 per pedestrian, bicyclist, or motorcyclist. Backpacking permits ($4 per person per night, $20 additional fee for advance reservation). Backcountry camping permits required. Red Jammer tours $25–$77. Hiker shuttle $8–$24 ($8 per segment). No vehicles wider than 8 feet or longer than 21 feet allowed on Logan Pass between Avalanche and Sun Point. No backcountry campfires in summer. No hunting. No pets or bikes on trails. No personal watercraft or snowmobiles. Park open daily. Logan Pass open mid-June–mid-Oct. Apgar Visitor Center open Nov.–Apr., weekends 9–4; May–Oct., daily 8 AM–9 PM. Logan Pass Visitor Center open mid-June–mid.-Oct., daily 9–7. St. Mary Visitor Center open mid-May–mid-Oct., daily 8 AM–9 PM.

HOW TO GET THERE

West entrance, near West Glacier, 19 mi east of Columbia Falls via U.S. 2; east entrance, in St. Mary, 22 mi northwest of Browning via U.S. 89. Closest airport: Kalispell (25 mi from west entrance)

CONTACTS

Glacier National Park (West Glacier, MT 59936, tel. 406/888–7800; 800/365–2267 camping reservations, fax 406/888–7808, www.nps.gov/glac). Glacier Park, Inc., sightseeing buses (tel. 406/892–2525). Flathead Convention & Visitor Bureau (15 Depot Park, Kalispell, MT 59901, tel. 800/543–3105). Cut Bank Area Chamber of Commerce (725 E. Main St., Box 1243, Cut Bank, MT 59427, tel. 406/873–4041). Glacier Country (836 Holt Dr., Suite 320, Box 1035, Bigfork, MT 59911-1035, tel. 406/837–6211 or 800/338–5072). Columbia Falls Area Chamber of Commerce (Box 312, Columbia Falls, MT 59912, tel. 406/892–2072, www.columbiafallschamber.com).

Grant-Kohrs Ranch National Historic Site

In southwestern Montana, in Deer Lodge

Established by Canadian fur trader John Grant and expanded by cattle baron Conrad Kohrs, the site was the headquarters for one of the largest 19th-century range ranches in the country. The 1,500-acre park is maintained today as a working ranch, and the 90 historic structures serve as a living museum of the frontier cattle industry of the 1860s–1930s. The site was authorized in 1972.

WHAT TO SEE & DO

Bird-watching; observing cattle, poultry, and horses; touring ranch and outbuildings; walking nature trail. **Facilities:** Visitor center, guided and self-guided tours, hiking trails. Bookstore. **Programs & Events:** Ranger-led ranch house tours, self-guided walks of ranch outbuildings. Living-history programs on blacksmithing, chuck-wagon cooking, 1890s cowboy life (May–Sept.). Western Heritage Days (2nd full weekend, July). **Tips & Hints:** Plan two hours for visit. Busiest July and Aug., least crowded Jan. and Feb.

FOOD, LODGING & SUPPLIES

Camping: None at site. In Deer Lodge: Indian Creek RV Park (745 Maverick La., tel. 406/846–3848; 50 sites; $19; flush toilets, showers, hook-ups). **Hotels:** None in park. In Deer Lodge: Western Big Sky Inn (210 Main St., tel. 406/846–2590; 20 rooms; $50). **Restaurants:** None at site. In Deer Lodge: Four B's Restaurant (130 Sam Beck Rd., tel. 406/846–2620; $6–$12). ♿ **Groceries & Gear:** None in park. In Deer Lodge: Ace Hardware (506 2nd St., tel. 406/846–2461), Valley Foods IGA (711 Main St., tel. 406/846–2684).

FEES, HOURS & REGULATIONS

Free. No smoking or pets beyond parking lot or visitor center areas. Site open June–Aug., daily 8–5:30, Sept.–May, daily 9–4:30.

HOW TO GET THERE

Via I–90 to Deer Lodge exit; follow signs, park at north end of town. Closest airports: Butte (36 mi), Helena (60 mi), and Missoula (80 mi).

CONTACTS

Grant-Kohrs Ranch National Historic Site (266 Warren La., Deer Lodge, MT 59722, tel. 406/846–2070, fax 406/846–3962, www.nps.gov/ grko). Deer Lodge Chamber of Commerce (1171 Main St., Deer Lodge, MT 59722, tel. 406/846–2094).

Little Bighorn Battlefield National Monument

In southeastern Montana, near Hardin

One of the last armed efforts of the Northern Plains people to preserve their way of life is memorialized here. On June 25 and 26, 1876, in the valley of the Little Bighorn River, more than 260 soldiers and attached personnel of the U.S. Army met defeat and death at the hands of several thousand Lakota and Cheyenne warriors. Among the dead were Lieutenant Colonel George Armstrong Custer and every member of his immediate command. Although the Native Americans won the battle, they subsequently lost the war against the expansion of Euro-Americans into the Northern Plains. In 2003 a memorial dedicated to the Sioux and Cheyenne who died at the battle was erected. The monument was designated a national cemetery in 1879 and a national monument in 1946.

WHAT TO SEE & DO

Touring battlefield by car. **Facilities:** Visitor center, outdoor interpretive exhibits, museum, hiking trails. Bookstore. **Programs & Events:** Ranger talks (Memorial Day–Labor Day). Battle Anniversary (June 25). **Tips & Hints:** Cassette tapes ($12.95) available for auto tours. Research library open by appointment. Visit Sept.–May for good weather and fewer crowds. Busiest June–Aug., least crowded Dec. and Jan.

FOOD, LODGING & SUPPLIES

See Bighorn Canyon National Recreation Area.

FEES, HOURS & REGULATIONS

Entrance fee: $5 per person or $10 per vehicle. No pets. Park and visitor center open Memorial Day–July, daily 8 AM–9 PM; Aug.–Labor Day, daily 8–8; Labor Day–Sept., mid-Apr.–Memorial Day, daily 8–6; Oct.–mid-Apr., daily 8–4:30.

HOW TO GET THERE

18 mi southeast of Hardin, near junction of I–90 and U.S. 212. Closest airport: Billings (60 mi).

CONTACTS

Little Bighorn Battlefield National Monument (Box 39, Crow Agency, MT 59022, tel. 406/638–3204, fax 406/638–2623, www.nps.gov/libi). Bighorn County Museum and Visitor Center (Rte. 1, Box 1206A, Hardin, MT 59034, tel. 406/665–1671). Hardin Area Chamber of Commerce (10 E. Railway, Box 446, Hardin, MT 59034, tel. 406/665–1672).

See Also

Fort Union Trading Post National Historic Site, North Dakota. *Nez Perce National Historical Site,* Idaho. *Yellowstone National Park,* Wyoming. *Continental Divide National Scenic Trail, Flathead River, Lewis and Clark National Historic Trail,* and *Nez Perce National Historic Trail,* in Other National Parklands.

Agate Fossil Beds
National Monument

In northwestern Nebraska, north of Scottsbluff

Animal fossils in beds of sedimentary rock, formed about 19 million years ago by the compression of mud, clay, and eroded materials deposited by water and wind, are concentrated under the grass-covered hills at this monument along the Niobrara River. Native American artifacts document the visits of Lakota Chief Red Cloud and others to pioneer rancher James Cook's property from 1890 to 1940. The monument was authorized on June 5, 1965.

WHAT TO SEE & DO

Attending ranger talks, fishing, hiking, picnicking, touring historic quarry sites, viewing exhibits, watching film. **Facilities:** Visitor center, outdoor interpretive exhibits, museum, movie, hiking trails. Bookstore. **Programs & Events:** Ranger-guided tours. Guided walks, talks, and cultural demonstrations (Memorial Day–Labor Day). **Tips & Hints:** Go late May–Sept. for wildflowers. Busiest June and July, least crowded in Dec. and Feb.

FOOD & LODGING

Hotels: None in park. In Crawford: Fort Robinson Lodge (3200 U.S. 20, tel. 308/665–2900; 22 rooms, 34 cabins; $35–$90; closed Dec.–Mar.), Hilltop Motel (304 McPherson St., tel. 308/665–1144 or 800/504–1444; 13 rooms; $54). In Harrison: Sowbelly Bed & Breakfast Hideaway (407 Sowbelly Rd., tel. 308/668–2537; 2 rooms; $40). **Restaurants:** None in park. In Crawford: Frontier Restaurant (342 2nd St., tel. 308/665–1872; $6–$8). In Harrison: Sioux Sundries (201 Main St., tel. 308/668–2577; $3–$8; closed Sun.).

FEES, HOURS & REGULATIONS

Entrance fee: $3 adults, free ages 16 and under, $5 per vehicle. Nebraska state fishing license required. No hunting. Leashed pets only. No motorized or mechanized equipment except wheelchairs on trails or off roads. Monument open daily dawn–dusk. Visitor center open Memorial Day–Labor Day, daily 8–6; Labor Day–Memorial Day, daily 8–5.

HOW TO GET THERE

Between Harrison and Mitchell via Rte. 29. Closest airport: Scottsbluff (50 mi).

CONTACTS

Agate Fossil Beds National Monument (301 River Rd., Harrison, NE 69346-2734, tel. 308/668–2211, fax 308/668–2318, www.nps.gov/agfo). Scottsbluff-Gering United Chamber of Commerce (1517 Broadway,

Suite 104, Scottsbluff, NE 69361, tel. 308/632–2133 or 800/788–9475, fax 308/632–7128, www.visitscottsbluff.com).

Homestead National Monument of America

In southeastern Nebraska, near Beatrice

The monument memorializes the Homestead Act of 1862, which encouraged pioneers to settle the American West by granting 160 acres of land to any household head who would live, work, and build on the land. It encompasses the site of the Daniel Freeman homestead, one of the very first claimed on January 1, 1863—the first day the Act took effect. The Homestead Act remained in place through 1976 in the continental United States, and until 1986 in Alaska. The monument includes 100 acres of restored tallgrass prairie, the restored Palmer–Epard cabin, and the Freeman School, an original one-room prairie schoolhouse. The site was established in 1936.

WHAT TO SEE & DO

Cross-country skiing, hiking, picnicking, touring facilities, watching videos. **Facilities:** Visitor center, museum, guided and self-guided tours, hiking trails. Bookstore, picnic tables. **Programs & Events:** Ranger-led interpretive talks and walks. Homestead Days (2nd full weekend, June), American Indian History Month (Nov.), Winter Festival of Prairie Cultures (Thanksgiving–Jan. 1), Monumental Fiddling Championship (Sat., Memorial Day weekend), Heartland Storytelling Festival (2nd Fri., May). **Tips & Hints:** Go Aug. and Sept. to see tallgrass prairie at full height; May–Sept. for wildflowers; and Mar.–May, Sept. and Oct. for migrating birds. Busiest May and June, least crowded Jan. and Feb.

FOOD & LODGING

Hotels: None in park. In Beatrice: Super 8 (3721 N. 6th St., tel. 402/228–8808; 56 rooms; $59), Holiday Inn Express (U.S. 77 N, tel. 402/228–7000; 70 rooms; $55–$70). **Restaurant:** None in park. In Beatrice: Black Crow (405 Court St., tel. 402/228–7200; $4–$9; closed Sun. and Mon.).

FEES, HOURS & REGULATIONS

Free. No hunting. Nebraska state fishing license required. No bikes or motorized vehicles on trails. Leashed pets in picnic area only. Trails open daily sunrise–sunset. Visitor center open Memorial Day–Labor Day, daily 8:30–5; Labor Day–Memorial Day, weekdays 8:30–5, weekends 9–5.

HOW TO GET THERE

4 mi west of Beatrice via Rte. 4. Closest airport: Lincoln (49 mi).

CONTACTS

Homestead National Monument of America (8523 W. Rte. 4, Beatrice, NE 68310, tel. 402/223–3514, fax 402/228–4231, www.nps.gov/home).

Beatrice Chamber of Commerce (226 S. 6th St., Beatrice, NE 68310, tel. 402/223–2338 or 800/755–7745, www.beatricechamber.com).

Missouri
National Recreational River

From Niobrara, Nebraska to southeastern South Dakota, near Yankton, to northeastern Nebraska, near Ponca

The recreational waterway includes two reaches of the Missouri River, west and east of Lewis and Clark Lake along the Nebraska–South Dakota border, as well as 20 mi of the lower Niobrara River and 8 mi of its tributary, Verdigre Creek. The rivers represent the environment that existed when Lewis and Clark made their journey about 200 years ago. High chalk bluffs, stands of cottonwood, marshy areas, and wide plains dominate the area. Farming is practiced by landowners, and descendants of Czech, German, and Finnish immigrants maintain a rich cultural heritage. The park unit was authorized in 1978 and expanded in 1991.

WHAT TO SEE & DO

Bird-watching, boating, canoeing (rentals Yankton, SD), fishing, hiking, horseback riding, swimming at state parks. **Facilities:** No National Park Service facilities. Army Corps of Engineers visitor centers at Fort Randall and Gavins Point dams; Nebraska state visitor centers at Niobrara and Ponca state parks. **Programs & Events:** Ranger-led interpretive programs (Memorial Day–Labor Day); Army Corps of Engineers, state parks, and local communities sponsor activities in summer. **Tips & Hints:** Most surrounding land is private; respect owners' property rights. Visit May–Oct. for best on-river activities, although July and Aug. can be very hot and windy. Busiest July and Aug., least crowded in Dec. and Jan.

FOOD, LODGING & SUPPLIES

Camping: None at site. In Niobrara: Niobrara State Park (89261 522nd Ave., tel. 402/857–3373; 106 sites; $6–$13; flush and pit toilets, showers, hook-ups). In Ponca: Ponca State Park (88090 Rte. 26 E, tel. 402/755–2284; 72 sites; $9–$13; flush toilets, showers, hook-ups).
Hotels: None in park. In Niobrara: Blue Moon Resort (89702 518 Ave., tel. 402/229–3226; 7 cabins; $50). In Yankton, SD: Best Western Kelly Inn (1607 U.S. 50, tel. 605/665–2906; 123 rooms; $79).
Restaurants: None in park. In Niobrara: Custer's Country Cafe & Drive-In (89141 Rte. 14, tel. 402/857–3544; $5–$7; no dinner Tues.).
Groceries & Gear: None in park. In Pickstown, SD: Fort Randall Bait & Tackle (U.S. 281, tel. 605/487–7760). In Yankton, SD: EconoFood (2404 Broadway Ave., tel. 605/665–3081), Hy-Vee Food Store (2100 Broadway Ave., tel. 605/665–3412).

FEES, HOURS & REGULATIONS

Free. Facilities along corridor may charge fees. Nebraska or South Dakota state hunting and fishing licenses required. Landowner permission needed for hunting. No trespassing on private land. No rest rooms. Area open daily. Army Corps of Engineers Lewis and Clark Visitor Center open Memorial Day–Labor Day, Sun.–Thurs. 8–6, Fri.–Sat. 8 AM–9 PM; Labor Day–Memorial Day, weekdays 8–4:30, weekends 10–6. Ponca State Park Visitor Center open Memorial Day–Labor Day, daily 8–8; Labor Day–Memorial Day, daily 8–5.

HOW TO GET THERE

Along the Missouri River east and west of Yankton, SD. Closest airport: Sioux City, SD (95 mi east of Niobrara).

CONTACTS

Missouri National Recreational River (Box 591, O'Neill, NE 68763, tel. 402/667–2550 or 402/336–3970, fax 402/336–3981, www.nps.gov/mnrr). U.S. Army Corps of Engineers (Box 710, Yankton, SD 57078, tel. 402/667–2545). Yankton Area Chamber of Commerce (218 W. 4th St., Box 588), Yankton, SD 57078, tel. 605/665–3636 or 800/888–1460, www.yanktonsd.com). Ponca State Park Visitor Center (tel. 402/755–2284).

Niobrara
National Scenic River

In north-central Nebraska, near Valentine

Eastern deciduous, western pine, and northern boreal forest ecosystems merge with short and mixed-grass prairie in the beautiful Niobrara River valley. Free-grazing cattle, windmills, abandoned historic barns, and dilapidated ranch homes offset the natural landscape. The upper portion of the 76-mi stretch of waterway is excellent for canoeing. The scenic river was authorized on May 24, 1991.

WHAT TO SEE & DO

Canoeing and tubing (rentals in Valentine and along river). **Facilities:** Visitor center, hiking trails. **Programs & Events:** Niobrara Council River Cleanup and BBQ (May), Canoe Outfitters River Appreciation Day & Clean-up (Sept.). **Tips & Hints:** Go weekdays to avoid crowds; May–Oct. to run river; May, June, Oct. and Nov. for migrating waterfowl; June for wildflowers; and late Sept.–mid-Oct. for fall colors. Most common canoeing section of river begins east of Valentine and runs downstream 30 mi. Much of river frontage is privately owned; respect landowners' property rights. Busiest on July and Aug. weekends, least crowded Nov.–Mar.

FOOD, LODGING & SUPPLIES

🏕 **Camping:** None at site. Near Valentine: Smith Falls State Park (Rte. 12, 15 mi east of Valentine, tel. 402/376–1306; 16 sites; $3; flush and pit toilets, showers, hook-ups). 🏨 **Hotels:** None in park. In Valentine: Comfort Inn (101 Main St., tel. 402/376–3300 or 800/478–3307; 50

rooms, 6 suites; $75), Holiday Inn Express Hotel & Suites (803 U.S. 20 E, tel. 402/376–3000 or 877/376–3003; 41 rooms, 19 suites; $90). ✕ **Restaurants:** None in park. In Valentine: Hot Stuff (203 E. Rte. 20, tel. 402/376–2283; $3–$14), Peppermill (112 N. Main St., tel. 402/376–1440; $5–$10; no dinner Sun.). ⌂ **Groceries & Gear:** None in park. In Valentine: Henderson's IGA (710 E. U.S. 20, tel. 402/376–1144), Yucca Dune (148 E. 1st St., tel. 402/376–3330).

FEES & HOURS

Free. River access fee $2 per boat at wildlife refuge. Smith Falls State Park entrance fee ($2.50). River open daily, but may freeze in winter. Wildlife refuge visitor center open Memorial Day–Labor Day, daily 8–4:30; Labor Day–Memorial Day, weekdays 8–4:30.

HOW TO GET THERE

Valentine is off U.S. 83, 76 mi south of I–90 and 130 mi north of I–80. River access points are in Fort Niobrara Refuge, Smith Falls State Park, and the Middle Niobrara Natural Resource District. Nearest airport: Rapid City, SD (215 mi).

CONTACTS

Niobrara National Scenic River (Box 591, O'Neill, NE 68763, tel. 402/336–3970, fax 402/336–3981, www.nps.gov/niob). Valentine Ranger Station (146 S. Hall St., Valentine, NE 69201, tel. 402/376–1901). Valentine Chamber of Commerce (239 S. Main St., Valentine, NE 69201, tel. 402/376–2969). Fort Niobrara National Wildlife Refuge (5 mi east of Valentine on Rte. 12).

Scotts Bluff National Monument

In western Nebraska, near Gering

A prominent natural landmark for emigrants on the Oregon Trail, the 800-foot-high Scotts Bluff, along with Mitchell Pass and the adjacent prairie lands, are set aside in a 3,000-acre national monument. This site preserves the memory of the historic Oregon, California, and Mormon trails, remnants of which still can be seen. The monument museum contains exhibits about the area's natural and cultural history, as well as houses a unique collection of watercolor paintings by the frontier photographer and artist William Henry Jackson. The site was proclaimed on December 12, 1919.

WHAT TO SEE & DO

Driving or hiking to bluff summit, hiking to remnants of Oregon–California Trail, touring museum. **Facilities:** Visitor center, outdoor interpretive signs, museum, guided tours, hiking trails. Book-and-gift shop. **Programs & Events:** Local art show, Spring Up the Bluff relay race (mid-Apr.); summit shuttle, living-history programs, interpretive walks and talks (Memorial Day–Labor Day); amphitheater program (mid-June–mid Aug., Tues.). Christmas on the Prairie (1st Sat., Dec.). **Tips &**

Hints: Carry plenty of water when hiking in summer. Watch for rattlesnakes. Go in spring for prairie flowers, fall for cooler temperatures and fewer people. Busiest July and Aug., least crowded Dec. and Jan.

FOOD, LODGING & SUPPLIES

⚠ **Camping:** None at site. In Scottsbluff:

KOA Campground (180037 KOA Dr., tel. 308/635–3760; 45 sites, 1 cabin; $19–$35; flush toilets, showers, hook-ups). 🛏 **Hotels:** None in park. In Gerig: Microtel Inn & Suites (1130 M St., tel. 308/436–1950; 61 rooms; $60). In Scottsbluff: Holiday Inn Express (1821 Frontage Rd., tel. 308/632–1000 or 800/465–4329; 70 rooms, 15 suites; $69–$89). ✗ **Restaurant:** None in park. In Scottsbluff: El Charrito Restaurant & Lounge (802 21st Ave., tel. 308/632–3534; $4–$7; closed Mon.). ⛅ **Groceries:** None at site. In Gerig: Sun Mart (1270 10th St., tel. 308/436–3158).

FEES, HOURS & REGULATIONS

Entrance fee: $5 per car. Stay on trails. Leashed pets only. No hunting. No rock, plant, or animal gathering. No off-road usage. No vehicles longer than 25 feet or taller than 11 feet 7 inches on summit road. Monument open daily dawn–dusk. Visitor center open Memorial Day–Labor Day, daily 8–7; Labor Day–Memorial Day, daily 8–5.

HOW TO GET THERE

3 mi west of Gering on Rte. 92. Closest airport: Scottsbluff (10 mi).

CONTACTS

Scotts Bluff National Monument (Box 27, Gering, NE 69341, tel. 308/436–4340, fax 308/436–7611, www.nps.gov/scbl). Scottsbluff-Gering United Chamber of Commerce (1517 Broadway, Suite 104, Scottsbluff, NE 69361, tel. 308/632–2133 or 800/788–9475, fax 308/632–7128, www.visitscottsbluff.com).

See Also

California National Historic Trail, Chimney Rock National Historic Site, Lewis and Clark National Historic Trail, Mormon Pioneer National Historic Trail, and *Oregon National Scenic Trail, Pony Express National Historic Trail,* in Other National Parklands.

NEVADA

Great Basin National Park

In east-central Nevada, near Baker

High-desert terrain yields to hundreds of small pools and lakes in Great Basin, and these are interspersed with dramatic mountains, including 13,063-foot-high Wheeler Peak. Roads and trails lead to the rim of the peak's cirque, in which you can see Nevada's only glacier. The park also has an ancient bristlecone-pine forest; the 75-foot Lexington Arch; and Lehman Caves, harboring many unusual limestone formations. The park was established as Lehman Caves National Monument in 1922. In 1986, 77,000 acres of surrounding forest land was added to the monument to create Great Basin National Park.

WHAT TO SEE & DO

Auto touring, cave touring, caving (permit required, *see below*), fishing, hiking, picnicking. **Facilities:** Visitor center (Lehman Caves entrance), scenic drive, wayside exhibits, nature trails, amphitheaters. Bookstore, gift shop, mail drop, picnic area. **Programs & Events:** Year-round cave tours, slide show, and movie. Ranger-led hikes, walks, talks, and evening programs; scenic drive to Wheeler Peak (mid-June–mid-Aug.). **Tips & Hints:** Watch for altitude sickness. Wear good walking shoes or boots in cave. Leave pets at home. Visit year-round for caves, June–Sept. to explore landscape and bristlecone pines. Busiest in May and July, especially during holiday weekends; least crowded Dec. and Jan.

FOOD, LODGING & SUPPLIES

Camping: 4 campgrounds ($10; pit toilets) in the park: Baker Creek (32 sites; closed Sept.–mid-May), Lower Lehman Creek (11 sites); Upper Lehman Creek (24 sites; closed Sept.–mid-May), Wheeler Peak (37 sites; closed Sept.–May). Primitive campsites along Strawberry Creek Rd. and Snake Creek Rd. (free). Backcountry camping allowed. In Baker: Border Inn (U.S. 6/50, tel. 775/234–7300, 22 sites; $15; flush toilets, showers, hook-ups). **Hotel**: In Baker: Border Inn (U.S. 6/50, tel. 775/234–7300, 26 rooms; $37). **Restaurants**: In the park: Lehman Caves Gift & Café (tel. 775/234–7221; closed Nov.–Mar.). In Baker: Border Inn (U.S. 6/50, tel. 775/234–7300; $5–$7); T & D's Country Store, Restaurant & Lounge (1 Main St., tel. 775/234–7264; $5–$10; no lunch Nov.–Apr., Mon.–Thurs.). **Groceries:** None in park. In Baker: T & D's Country Store, Restaurant & Lounge (1 Main St, tel. 775/234–7264).

FEES, HOURS & REGULATIONS

Free. Cave tours $2–$8 adults, free–$4 ages 11 and under. Backcountry registration strongly recommended. Wild caving permits required two weeks in advance. Nevada state fishing license required. No bikes on trails. No fireworks. No guns. No pets on trails or in caves. Leashed pets elsewhere. Vehicles over 24 feet long not recommended on Scenic Dr. to Wheeler Peak. No watercraft on lakes. Park open daily. Visitor center open mid-June–Labor Day, daily 7:30–5:30; Labor Day–mid-June, daily 8–4:30.

HOW TO GET THERE

5 mi west of Baker on Rte. 488 and 68 mi east of Ely via U.S. 6/50. Closest airports: Ely (68 mi), Salt Lake City (234 mi), Las Vegas (300 mi).

CONTACTS

Great Basin National Park (Baker, NV 89311, tel. 775/234–7331 Ext. 242 cave tour reservations; Ext. 228 wild caving permits, fax 775/234–7269, www.nps.gov/grba). White Pine Chamber of Commerce (636 Aultman St., Ely, NV 89301, tel. 775/289–8877, www.whitepinechamber.com).

Lake Mead National Recreation Area

Near Las Vegas in southern Nevada and northwestern Arizona

The 1.5-million-acre national recreation area, the nation's first, draws nearly 10 million visitors a year. Boating, fishing, and swimming are available on the two huge lakes formed by the Hoover and Davis dams. Three of America's four desert ecosystems—the Mojave, Great Basin, and Sonoran deserts—meet at Lake Mead. Bighorn sheep, mule deer, coyotes, kit foxes, bobcats, ringtail cats, desert tortoise, numerous lizards, and snakes all can be found in the recreation area. The area is administered under agreements with the Bureau of Reclamation signed in 1936 and 1947. It was established as a national recreation area in 1964.

WHAT TO SEE & DO

Auto touring, boating (rentals), canoeing, diving, fishing, hiking, kayaking, picnicking, sailing, sunbathing, swimming, waterskiing. **Facilities:** Visitor center (4 mi northeast of Boulder City, NV, on U.S. 93), 8 contact stations (Lake Mead: Callville Bay, Echo Bay, Las Vegas Bay, and Overton Beach in NV; Temple Bar in AZ. Lake Mohave: Cottonwood Cove in NV, Katherine and Willow Beach in AZ), marinas, beaches, trails. Bookstore, fuel. **Programs & Events:** Ranger-led programs and hikes, paddle-wheel tour boats to Hoover Dam, rafting tours. Lecture series (Jan.–Apr.). **Tips & Hints:** Summer temperatures reach 120°F in the shade. Go Oct.–May for best hiking weather. Busiest June and July, least crowded Nov. and Dec.

FOOD, LODGING & SUPPLIES

⚠ **Camping:** 7 campgrounds ($10; flush toilets) in the park: Boulder Beach (154 sites), Callville Bay (80 sites), Las Vegas Bay (89 sites), Cottonwood Cove (149 sites), Katherine Landing (173 sites), Echo Bay

(166 sites), Temple Bar (153 sites). Backcountry camping allowed. ⏣ **Hotels:** In the park: Cottonwood Cove Resort & Marina (tel. 702/297–1464; 24 rooms; $108), Echo Bay Resort (tel. 702/394–4000; 52 rooms; $90–$105), Lake Mead Lodge (tel. 702/293–2074; 33 rooms; $75), Lake Mohave Resort (at Katherine Landing, tel. 928/754–3245; 49 rooms; $85), Temple Bar Marina (tel. 928/767–3211; 18 rooms, 4 cabins; $55–$115). ✗ **Restaurants:** In the park: Snack bars or restaurants at all marinas. ♿ **Groceries & Gear:** Grocery and supply stores at all marinas.

FEES & HOURS

Entrance fee (good for 5 days): $3 per person or $5 per vehicle; $10 per vessel for lake use. Recreation area open daily. Visitor center open daily 8:30–4:30.

HOW TO GET THERE

The visitor center is 27 mi east of Las Vegas via U.S. 93. Other lake access available via I–15 north of Las Vegas, U.S. 95 south of Las Vegas, and U.S. 93 in Arizona. Closest airports: Las Vegas, Bullhead City, AZ.

CONTACTS

Lake Mead National Recreation Area (601 Nevada Hwy., Boulder City, NV 89005, tel. 702/293–8907; 702/293–6180 paddle boat tours, fax 702/293–8936, www.nps.gov/lame or www.funonthelake.com for concessionaires).

See Also

Death Valley National Monument, California. *California National Historic Trail* and *Pony Express National Historic Trail,* in Other National Parklands.

NEW HAMPSHIRE

Saint-Gaudens National Historic Site

In western New Hampshire, in Cornish

This renowned artist's retreat in the New Hampshire hills was the home and studio of Augustus Saint-Gaudens (1848–1907), one of America's most popular and talented sculptors. Centered on Saint-Gaudens' 18th-century Federal-style house, "Aspet," combines secluded studios, galleries, and gardens where the artist's works are on display. A stable building houses a collection of antique carriages. The site was authorized in 1964 and established in 1977.

WHAT TO SEE & DO

Hiking, picnicking, touring gardens, house, and galleries, viewing orientation video. **Facilities:** Information booth, movie, guided and self-guided tours, hiking trails. Picnic tables. **Programs & Events:** Interpretive tours of house, art exhibits. Sunday concert series (July–mid-Aug.). **Tips & Hints:** Walking tours are one hour. Turning around is difficult for large RVs towing vehicles. Busiest July and Aug., least crowded May and June.

FOOD & LODGING

Camping: None at site. In Ascutney, VT: Running Bear Camping Area (6248 U.S. 5, tel. 802/674–6417; 159 sites; $20–$27; flush toilets, showers, hook-ups). **Hotels**: None in park. In West Lebanon, NH: Airport Economy Inn (45 Airport Rd., tel. 603/298–8888; 56 rooms; $110). In Newport, NH: Newport Motel (467 Sunapee St., tel. 603/863–1440 or 800/741–2619; 18 rooms; $60–$80). **Restaurants**: None in park. In Windsor, VT: Windsor Diner (135 Main St., tel. 802/674–5555; $7.50).

FEES, PERMITS & REGULATIONS

Entrance fee: $5 adults, free ages 16 and under. No snowmobiles or off-road vehicles. Buildings and grounds open late May–Oct., daily 9–4:30; grounds also open Nov.–late May, daily 8–dark.

HOW TO GET THERE

9 mi north of Claremont via Rte. 12A; 2 mi from Windsor, VT via I–91 to Exit 8 or 9; or via I–89 to Exit 20, heading 12 mi south. Closest airports: Lebanon, NH (11 mi), NH (80 mi), and Windsor Locks, CT (125 mi).

CONTACTS

Saint-Gaudens National Historic Site (139 Saint Gaudens Rd., Cornish, NH 03745, tel. 603/675–2175, fax 603/675–2701, www.nps.gov/saga). Greater Claremont Chamber of Commerce (Moody Bldg., Tremont Sq., Claremont, NH 03743, tel. 603/543–1296).

See Also

Appalachian National Scenic Trail, West Virginia. *Lamprey Wild & Scenic River*, in Other National Parklands.

NEW JERSEY

Edison National Historic Site

In northeastern New Jersey, in West Orange

Thomas Edison's lab and 29-room estate, Glenmont, were home to the inventor from 1887 until his death in 1931. At his "Invention Factory," he developed the phonograph, invented the movie camera, and the nickel-iron-alkaline battery, and was awarded more than half of his 1,093 patents. The complex includes his chemistry lab, machine shop, library, and a replica of the world's first picture studio. The graves of Thomas and Mina Edison are on the Glenmont grounds. The Edison Home National Historic Site was designated in 1955, the Edison Laboratory National Monument was proclaimed in 1956, and the sites were combined as Edison National Historic Site in 1962.

WHAT TO SEE & DO

Touring lab complex and 16-acre Glenmont estate. **Facilities:** Visitor center, movies. Bookstore. **Tips & Hints:** Parking is on Main St., across from the lab. The laboratory and home are closed for renovations through 2005.

HOW TO GET THERE

15 mi west of New York City, in West Orange, via the Garden State Pkwy. to Exit 145 or via the New Jersey Tpke. to Exit 15W; from either, take I–280 west to Exit 10, then the first right off the ramp, go to end of street and make a left onto Main St., and continue ¾ mi. From the west, take I–280 east to Exit 9 and make a left at end of ramp, then a left on Main St. at second light. Public transportation available via New Jersey Transit (800/772–2222). Closest airport: Newark (20 mi).

CONTACT

Edison National Historic Site (Main St. and Lakeside Ave., West Orange, NJ 07052, tel. 973/736–0550, fax 973/736–8496, www.nps.gov/edis).

Great Egg Harbor National Scenic & Recreational River

In southern New Jersey, near Atlantic City

The Great Egg Harbor River, a 129-mi waterway with 17 tributaries, drains 304 mi of pristine marshes into the heart of New Jersey's Pinelands National Reserve. Fallen leaves and cedar roots tint the water the color of tea, and the river's mix of freshwater and tidal wetlands draw waterfowl throughout the year. The Fox Nature Center reveals other creatures hidden amid the wetlands, as well as the park's cultural background. The cooperatively managed river (the National Park Service owns no land here) was designated in 1992.

WHAT TO SEE & DO

Bicycling, bird-watching, boating, camping, canoeing, fishing, hiking, visiting historic sites. **Tips & Hints:** River runs primarily through private property. There are no National Park Service Facilities, but you can go to the Fox Nature Center in Estell Manor County Park (tel. 609/625–1897) for visitor information.

FOOD & LODGING

⚠ **Camping:** None at site. In Belleplain: Belleplain State Forest (Rte. 550, Exit 17 off Garden State Pkwy., tel. 609/861–2404; 169 sites; $15; flush toilets, showers). 🛏 **Hotels:** None in park. In Ocean City: Days Inn (7th and Boardwalk, tel. 609/398–2200; 80 rooms; $150–$265; closed mid-Oct.–mid-Apr.). In Somers Point: Residence Inn (900 Mays Landing Rd., tel. 609/927–6400 or 800/331–3131; 120 suites; $209). ✗ **Restaurant:** None in park. In Somers Point: Crab Trap (2 Broadway, tel. 609/927–7377; $5–$13).

FEES, HOURS & REGULATIONS

Free. Corridor open daily. New Jersey state fishing and hunting licenses required.

HOW TO GET THERE

Take the Garden State Pkwy. to the Great Egg Harbor Bay near Somers Point.

CONTACTS

Great Egg Harbor National Scenic & Recreational River (National Park Service, Northeast Regional Office, Custom House, 3rd fl., 200 Chestnut St., Philadelphia, PA 19106, tel. 215/597–9175, fax 215/597–5747, www.nps.gov/greg). Fox Nature Center, Atlantic County Parks (Estell Manor Park, Rte. 50, Mays Landing, NJ 08330, tel. 609/645–5960). Atlantic County Chamber of Commerce (1337 Tilton Rd., Suite 201, Northfield, NJ 08225, tel. 609/646–2214, www.atlanticcountychamber.com).

Morristown National Historical Park

In northern New Jersey, near Morristown

During two winters, Morristown sheltered the main encampment of the Continental Army. General George Washington held his troops together and rebuilt his forces here through the winter of 1777 and encountered one of the greatest tests of his leadership during the winter of 1779–80, when starvation and cold drove his men to mutiny. Displays at the Jockey Hollow Visitor Center, Washington's Headquarters, the Ford Mansion, the Wick Farm House, and the park museum re-create the events and various settings from the era. The site was authorized in 1933.

WHAT TO SEE & DO

Attending programs, hiking, picnicking, touring museum and buildings. **Facilities:** Visitor center, museum, guided and self-guided tours, hiking trails. Book and map sales. **Programs & Events:** Guided tours of Ford Mansion, interpretive talks, soldier-life demonstrations, living-history demonstrations at Wick Farm House. National Trails Day (1st Sat., June), reading of the Declaration of Independence (July 4), Holly Walk (1st week, Dec.). **Tips & Hints:** Busiest Apr.–June, least crowded Dec. and Jan.

FEES, HOURS & REGULATIONS

Entrance fee: $4 adults, free ages 16 and under. No bikes on trails. No motorized or mechanized equipment on trails. No unleashed pets. Visitor center and museum open daily 9–5. Wick House open daily 9:30–4:30.

HOW TO GET THERE

Via I–287 to Exits 30 (Jockey Hollow) and 36 (Washington Headquarters and Museum). Closest airport: In Newark (18 mi).

CONTACTS

Morristown National Historical Park (30 Washington Pl., Morristown, NJ 07960, tel. 973/539–2016, fax 973/539–8361, www.nps.gov/morr). Chamber of Commerce of Morris County (25 Lindsley Dr., Suite 105, Morristown, NJ 07960, tel. 973/539–3882, fax 973/539–3960). Morris County Visitors Center (6 Court St., Morristown, NJ 07960, tel. 973/631–5151, www.morristourism.org).

See Also

Appalachian National Scenic Trail, West Virginia. *Delaware Water Gap National Recreation Area,* Pennsylvania. *Gateway National Recreation Area,* New York. *Middle Delaware National Scenic River,* Pennsylvania. *Statue of Liberty National Monument,* New York. *Maurice Scenic and Recreational River, Pinelands National Reserve,* in Other National Parklands.

Aztec Ruins
National Monument

In northwestern New Mexico, in Aztec

Numerous and varied structures of the Ancestral Pueblo people are preserved at this intriguing World Heritage Site. Recent evidence suggests that the settlement was planned sometime in the late 1000s, and that the community's design remained intact until the group moved away two centuries later. The enormous West Ruin, a pueblo of 400 rooms, is open to the public through an 800-yard, self-guided trail. The reconstructed Great Kiva is one of the walk's highlights. The site was proclaimed a national monument January 24, 1923, and designated a World Heritage Site in 1987.

WHAT TO SEE & DO

Hiking, watching video program. **Facilities:** Visitor center with museum and interpretive exhibits, movie, self-guided tours, hiking trails. Picnic area. **Programs & Events:** Interpretive talks (daily Memorial Day–Labor Day; less frequently May, Sept., and Oct.). **Tips & Hints:** Busiest July and Aug., least crowded Dec. and Jan. Visit in May for wildflowers and Oct. for fall colors.

FOOD, LODGING & SUPPLIES

⚠ **Camping:** None at site. In Farmington: Riverside Mobile Park (120 S. Gooding La., tel. 505/327–2566; 11 RV sites; $6–$17). 🛏 **Hotels:** None in park. In Farmington: Best Western Inn & Suites (700 Scott Ave., tel. 505/327–5221; 194 rooms; $99–$109). In Aztec: Step Back Inn (123 W. Aztec Blvd., tel. 505/334–1200 or 800/334–1255; 39 rooms; $98). ✕ **Restaurants:** None in park. In Aztec: Aztec Restaurant (107 E. Aztec Blvd., tel. 505/334–9586; $5–$7), Highway Grill (401 N.E. Aztec Blvd., tel. 505/334–6533; $6–$12; closed Sun.). 🛒 **Groceries & Gear:** None in park. In Aztec: Frontier Sports (300 N.E. Aztec Blvd., tel. 505/334–0009), Safeway (415 N. Main St., tel. 505/334–7334).

FEES, HOURS & REGULATIONS

Entrance fee: $4 adults, free ages 17 and under. Leashed pets in picnic area, no pets on trail. Monument and visitor center open Memorial Day–Labor Day, daily 8–6; Labor Day–Memorial Day, daily 8–5.

HOW TO GET THERE

10 mi east of Farmington and 35 mi south of Durango, CO, via U.S. 550, ½ mi south of Ruins Rd. Closest airports: Farmington (15 mi), Albuquerque (180 mi).

CONTACTS

Aztec Ruins National Monument (84 County Rd. 2900, Aztec, NM 87410, tel. 505/334–6174, fax 505/334–6372, www.nps.gov/azru). Aztec

Chamber of Commerce & Visitor's Center (110 N. Ash St., Aztec, NM 87410, tel. 505/334–9551, fax 505/334–7648, www.aztecnm.com).

Bandelier National Monument

In north-central New Mexico, near Los Alamos

Pajarito Plateau is rich with archeological sites, which were the homes of ancestral Pueblo people from the 12th through the 16th centuries. Trails afford access to crumbling beige cliffs, forested mesas, and deep gorges, all within a dramatic landscape formed by a huge volcanic eruption more than 1 million years ago. Two-thirds of the 32,737-acre park is wilderness. The park was proclaimed on February 11, 1916, and transferred from the Forest Service on February 25, 1932.

WHAT TO SEE & DO

Camping, cross-country skiing, fishing, hiking, picnicking, guided and self-guided walks, viewing evening slide programs. **Facilities:** Visitor center, museum, guided and self-guided tours, hiking trails. Book and map sales, book-and-gift shop, picnic tables. **Programs & Events:** Guided walks, interpretive talks, evening programs, cultural and craft demonstrations (all June–Sept.). **Tips & Hints:** Juniper Campground prone to weather closures in winter. Visit in Apr., May, Sept., and Oct. for moderate temperatures and less chance of snow. Busiest July and Aug., least crowded in Dec. and Jan.

FOOD, LODGING & SUPPLIES

Camping: 2 campgrounds in the park: Juniper (94 sites; $10; flush toilets), Ponderosa (2 group sites; $35; pit toilets; reservations required, *see below*). Backcountry camping available (permit required, *see below*). **Hotels:** None in park. In Los Alamos: Best Western Hilltop House Hotel (400 Trinity Dr., tel. 505/662–2441 or 800/462–0936; 92 rooms; $89), Los Alamos Inn (2201 Trinity Dr., tel. 505/662–7211 or 800/279–9279; 116 rooms; $90). **Restaurants:** In the park: snack bar. In Los Alamos: Hill Diner (1315 Trinity Dr., tel. 505/662–9745; $7–$10). **Groceries & Gear:** None in park. In White Rock: Smith's Food & Drug Centers (31 Sherwood Blvd., tel. 505/672–3811).

FEES, HOURS & REGULATIONS

Entrance fee: $10 per private vehicle for 7-day permit. Backcountry camping permit required (free, must obtain in person at visitor center). New Mexico state fishing license required. No bikes or motorized or mechanized equipment on trails. No firewood gathering. No hunting. No pets on trails or in backcountry. Leashed pets only in campground, picnic area, parking areas, along roadways. Park open dawn–dusk. Visitor center open Memorial Day–Labor Day, daily 8–6; Labor Day–mid-Oct. and mid-Apr.–Memorial Day, daily 9–5:30; mid-Oct.–mid-Apr, daily 8–4:30.

HOW TO GET THERE

10 mi south of Los Alamos via Rtes. 501 and 4; 8 mi southwest of White Rock via Rte. 4; 47 mi northwest of Santa Fe via U.S. 84/285 and Rtes. 502 and 4. Closest airports: Santa Fe (50 mi), Albuquerque (100 mi).

CONTACTS

Bandelier National Monument (HCR 1, Box 1, Suite 15, Los Alamos, NM 87544, tel. 505/672–3861 Ext. 517, fax 505/672–9607, www.nps. gov/band). Bandelier Visitor Center (Park Headquarters, Frijoles Canyon, 3 mi from entrance station). White Rock Tourist Information Center (125 Rte. 4, White Rock, NM 87544, tel. 505/672–3183). Los Alamos County Chamber of Commerce and Visitor Center (109 Central Park Sq., Box 460, Los Alamos, NM 87544, tel. 505/662–8105 or 800/444–0707, www.visit.losalamos.com).

Capulin Volcano National Monument

In northeastern New Mexico, east of Raton

Capulin Volcano, named for the *capulin* (chokecherry) plants that grow on its slopes, is a cinder cone formed by a volcanic eruption that occurred between 56,000 and 62,000 years ago. The 1,082-foot mountain that remains consists mostly of loose cinders and ash, and is one of the most accessible cinder cones in the United States. The pinyon-juniper woodland and brush-covered slopes in the High Plains ecosystem of the Raton-Clayton Volcanic Field provide habitat for a number of animal species. The monument was proclaimed August 9, 1916, as Capulin Mountain National Monument, then changed to Capulin Volcano National Monument on December 31, 1987.

WHAT TO SEE & DO

Driving, hiking, picnicking, watching movie. **Facilities:** Visitor center, movies, guided and self-guided tours, hiking trails. Book and map sales, picnic tables with fire grates. **Programs & Events:** Ranger-led volcano talks (daily June–Aug.). **Tips & Hints:** Avoid rim trail during threatening weather. Go in June and July for wildflower bloom peaks and ladybugs swarming on rim trail. Visit in May, late Aug., and Sept. for best weather with few visitors. Busiest June and July, least crowded Jan. and Feb.

FOOD

✗ **Restaurants:** None in park. In Capulin: Capulin Country Store (corner of U.S. 64/87 and Rte. 325, tel. 505/278–3900; $5–$8; no dinner, closed Nov.–Apr. on Mon.–Thurs.).

FEES, HOURS & REGULATIONS

Entrance fee: $5 per vehicle, $3 per person on motorcycle. No hunting. No off-trail hiking. No pets or strollers on trails. No trailers, towed vehicles, pedestrians, or bikes on volcano road. Park and visitor center open Memorial Day–Labor Day, Sun.–Thurs. 7:30–6:30, Fri. and Sat. dawn–dusk; Labor Day–Memorial Day, daily 8–4.

HOW TO GET THERE

3 mi north of Capulin via Rte. 325; 37 mi east of Raton or 61 mi west of Clayton via U.S. 64/87. Closest airport: Raton.

CONTACTS

Capulin Volcano National Monument (Box 40, Capulin, NM 88414, tel. 505/278–2201, fax 505/278–2211, www.nps.gov/cavo). Raton Chamber and Economic Development Council (100 Clayton Rd., Raton, NM 87740, tel. 505/445–3689).

Carlsbad Caverns
National Park

In southeastern New Mexico, near Carlsbad

The underground passageways of Carlsbad Cavern contain an incomparable realm of huge subterranean chambers, trickling icicle forests of stalactites and stalagmites, and beautiful cave formations. The main attractions aren't just the enormous caverns—which include the nation's deepest limestone cave (1,597 feet); this is also the haunt for thousands of Mexican free-tail bats, who stream out in black clouds from a crevasse at dusk. More than 70 smaller caves are also threaded beneath the desert and rocky cliff faces; there's even a theater and cafeteria inside the chambers. The park was proclaimed Carlsbad Cave National Monument on October 25, 1923, established as Carlsbad Caverns National Park on May 14, 1930, and became a World Heritage Site on December 6, 1995.

WHAT TO SEE & DO

Attending bat-flight programs, hiking, picnicking, touring caves. **Facilities:** Visitor center, guided tours, hiking trails. Book-and-gift shop. **Programs & Events:** Daily ranger-guided tours. Evening bat programs (May–Oct.). Bat Flight Breakfast Program (2nd Thurs., Aug.), Founders Day (Aug. 25). **Tips & Hints:** Go Mar.–late Oct. to see bats. It's damp and very chilly inside the caves; wear rubber-soled shoes and bring jacket or sweater. Be prepared for 75-story descent on Natural Entrance Route. Reservations recommended for cave tours; call the visitor center, which will direct inquiries to reservations service. Busiest June and July, least crowded in Nov. and Jan.

FOOD & LODGING

⛺ **Camping:** None at site. Backcountry camping available (permit required, *see below*). 🏨 **Hotels:** None in park. In White's City: Best Western Cavern Inn–Guadalupe Inn (17 Carlsbad Caverns Hwy., tel. 505/785–2291; 105 rooms; $65–$100). In Carlsbad: Holiday Inn (601 S. Canal St., tel. 505/885–8500; 100 rooms; $80). ✕ **Restaurants:** In the park: Restaurant in visitor center (tel. 505/785–2281), lunchroom in cave. In Carlsbad: Furr's Family Dining (901 S. Canal St., tel. 505/885–0430; $6), Red Chimney (817 N. Canal St., tel. 505/885–8744; $7–$9; closed weekends).

FEES, HOURS & REGULATIONS

Cave entry fee: $6 adults, $3 ages 6–15, free ages 6 and under. Fee includes two self-guided cave tours (Natural Entrance and Big Room routes, both 1 mi each). Audio-guide rental: $3. Ranger-guided King's Palace tour additional $8 adults, $4 ages 6–15. No children under 5. Ranger-guided Slaughter Canyon Cave tour (reservations recommended) $15 adults; $7.50 ages 6–15. No children under 6. Guided wild cave tours $7–$20. Permit required (free) for all backcountry camping. Visitor center open Memorial Day–Labor Day, daily 8–7; Labor Day–Memorial Day, daily 8–5. Self-guided tours Memorial Day–Labor Day, daily 8:30–5 (Natural Entrance closes at 3:30); Labor Day–Memorial Day, daily 8:30–3:30 (Natural Entrance closes at 2).

HOW TO GET THERE

20 mi south of Carlsbad via U.S. 62/180, 150 mi northeast of El Paso, TX; visitor center (near Carlsbad Cavern entrance) 7 mi from Whites City, NM. Closest airports: Carlsbad, El Paso, TX.

CONTACTS

Carlsbad Caverns National Park (3225 National Parks Hwy., Carlsbad, NM 88220, tel. 505/785–2232, Ext. 429 wild cave tours; 800/967–2283 Slaughter Canyon tour, fax 505/785–2302, www.nps.gov/cave). Carlsbad Convention and Visitors Bureau (Box 910, Carlsbad, 88220, tel. 800/221–1224 or 505/887–6516, www.caverns.com/~chamber). Whites City Chamber of Commerce & Visitor Information (17 Carlsbad Caverns Hwy., Whites City, NM 88268, tel. 505/785–2121).

Chaco Culture
National Historical Park

In northwestern New Mexico,
between Grants and Bloomfield

This World Heritage Site preserves the extraordinary architecture and cultural legacy of the Chaco Anasazi, the ancestral Pueblo people whose culture flourished in Chaco Canyon from the mid-9th century to the mid-13th century. The area was the cultural hub for an integrated system of villages linked by an elaborate road network running throughout the present Four Corners region. The site was proclaimed Chaco Canyon National Monument on March 11, 1907, redesignated and renamed in 1980, and designated a World Heritage Site on December 8, 1987.

WHAT TO SEE & DO

Attending video presentations and evening interpretive programs, biking and hiking 9-mi loop road and to backcountry archaeological sites, camping, picnicking, taking self-guided and ranger-led tours, touring visitor center museum. **Facilities:** Visitor center with interpretive displays, videos, and museum, outdoor interpretive signs, guided and self-guided tours, hiking trails. Bookstore, book and map sales, book-and-gift shop. **Programs & Events:** Daily video programs. Ranger-guided tours, evening astronomy programs (both Apr.–Oct.); guided hikes and campfire programs (both May–Sept.). **Tips & Hints:** Call ahead for road conditions in inclement weather. North access to park from U.S. 550 requires driving 16 mi on graded dirt road; south access requires 20 mi drive on dirt road and can be impassable in bad weather. The site is very remote, with no food or gas. Bring firewood and charcoal. Visit May–Sept. for wildflowers.

LODGING

🔥 **Camping:** In the park: Gallo Campground (49 sites; $10; flush toilets). 🏨 **Hotels:** None in park. In Cuba: Cuban Lodge (6332 Rte. 44/U.S. 550. tel. 505/289–3269; 23 rooms; $38–$45). ✘ **Restaurants:** None in park. In Cuba: El Bruno's (Rte. 44/U.S. 550 at Rt. 126, tel. 505/289–9429; $4–$7).

FEES, HOURS & REGULATIONS

Entrance fee: $8 per vehicle, $4 per person on bike or motorcycle. Backcountry hiking permit (free) required. No collecting, disturbing, or removing pottery or artifacts. No firearms or hunting. No motorized or mechanized equipment on trails. No touching, defacing, or chalking petroglyphs or rock paintings. Leashed pets permitted on backcountry trails. Mountain bikes on three designated trails only. Park open daily. Visitor center open daily 8–5. Loop drive closes at sunset.

HOW TO GET THERE

24 mi southeast of Nageezi via U.S. 550 to Rte. 7900, then follow signs 21 mi to park.

CONTACTS

Chaco Culture National Historical Park (Box 220, Nageezi, NM 87037, tel. 505/786–7014, fax 505/786–7061, www.nps.gov/chcu). Farmington Convention and Visitors Bureau (3041 E. Main St., Farmington, NM 87402, tel. 505/326–7602 or 800/448–1240).

El Malpais National Monument

In west-central New Mexico, near Grants

El Malpais means "the badlands" in Spanish, and here volcanic lava flows, cinder cones, pressure ridges, and complex lava-tube systems dominate the harsh landscape. Sandstone bluffs and mesas border the eastern side of the monument, providing access to vast wilderness. Historic and archaeological sites provide reminders of the 10,000 years of human habitation in the area, while cultural resources are kept alive by the spiritual and physical presence of contemporary Native Americans. Here, the Puebloan peoples of the Acoma, Laguna, and Zuni, and Ramah Navajo tribes continue their ancestral uses of El Malpais by gathering herbs and medicines, paying respect, and renewing ties. El Malpais is managed jointly by the National Park Service and the Bureau of Land Management. The site was established on December 31, 1987.

WHAT TO SEE & DO

Backpacking, bird-watching, caving, four-wheel-drive touring, hiking, mountain biking, picnicking. **Facilities:** Visitor center, movie, guided tours, hiking trails. Bookstores, picnic tables. **Programs & Events:** Ranger-led hikes, programs, cave explorations. Evening bat flights (June–Aug.). **Tips & Hints:** Weather can be unpredictable. Exploring lava tubes requires warm clothing, protective headgear, three sources of light, and leather gloves. Never go hiking or caving alone. Use extreme caution and wear sturdy boots when hiking on lava terrain. Carry a daypack with water, snacks, rain gear, first-aid kit, and sunscreen. Bring topographical maps and compass or global-positioning devices for backcountry exploration. Busiest July and Aug., least crowded in Dec. and Jan.

FOOD, LODGING & SUPPLIES

⚠ **Camping:** In the park: backcountry camping available (permit recommended, *see below*). In Grants: Grants–Cibola Sands KOA (Rte. 53, ½ mi south of I-40, tel. 505/287–4376; 888/562–5608 reservations; 48 sites, 2 cabins; $20–$36; flush toilets, showers, hook-ups). Campgrounds also at El Morro National Monument (*see below*). 🛏 **Hotels:** None in park. In Grants: Best Western Inn & Suites (1501 E. Santa Fe Ave., tel. 505/287–7901; 126 rooms; $71–$79), Holiday Inn Express (1496 E. Santa Fe Ave., tel. 505/285–4676; 58 rooms; $69–$99). ✗ **Restaurants:** None in park. In Grants: El Jardin Southwest Cuisine (319 W. Santa Fe Ave., tel. 505/285–5231; $4–$6; no lunch Sat.), La Ventana Steakhouse (110½ Geis St., tel. 505/287–9393; $6–$8; closed Sun.). 🛒 **Groceries:** Smith's Food & Drug Center (700 E. Roosevelt Ave., Grants, tel. 505/285–6336).

FEES, HOURS & REGULATIONS

Free. Backcountry camping permit (free) recommended for backcountry camping. Advance permit required for some cave exploring. High-clearance and four-wheel-drive vehicles only on backcountry dirt roads. No mechanized vehicles in wilderness areas. Monument open daily. Sandstone Bluffs Overlook closes at dusk. Visitor Center open daily 8–5. Information center open daily 8:30–4:30.

HOW TO GET THERE

Visitor center 23 mi south of Grants via Rte. 117 (I-40, Exit 89) and Rte. 53 (I-40, Exit 81); Northwest New Mexico Visitor Center 1 mi south of Grants via I-40 at Exit 85. Closest airport: Albuquerque (72 mi).

CONTACTS

El Malpais National Monument (123 E. Roosevelt Ave., Grants, NM 87020, tel. and fax 505/783–4774, www.nps.gov/elma). Northwest New Mexico Visitor Center (1900 E. Santa Fe Ave., Grants, NM 87020, tel. 505/876–2783). Grants–Cibola County Chamber of Commerce (100 Iron St., Box 297, Grants, NM 87020, tel. 505/287–4802).

El Morro
National Monument

In western New Mexico, near Grants

Rising some 200 feet above the valley floor, El Morro's massive sandstone mesa dominates the land. A natural basin at the foot of El Morro's held the area's only water for Native Americans, explorers, and travelers, who gathered here as early as the turn of the first millennium. Petroglyphs carved by the prehistoric Ancestral Puebloans are the oldest inscriptions on El Morro, probably dating from AD 1000 to AD 1400; the earliest known European inscription is that of Don Juan de Onate, in 1605. The monument's most significant prehistoric pueblo site, however, is the 13th–14th-century village of Atsinna atop El Morro, which is part of the Zuni Indian tradition and folklore. The monument was proclaimed on December 8, 1906.

WHAT TO SEE & DO

Hiking to inscriptions and ruins, picnicking, watching video. **Facilities:** Visitor center, self-guided tours, hiking trail. Book and map sales, picnic tables with fire grills. **Programs & Events:** Cultural fair with arts and crafts demonstrations (monthly in summer). **Tips & Hints:** Mesa Top trail may be closed during bad weather in winter. Visit in Nov. for better weather and fewer crowds. Busiest July and Aug., least crowded Dec. and Jan.

FOOD & LODGING

Camping: 1 primitive campground in the park (9 sites; $5 charged May–Oct.; pit toilets). In El Morro: Ancient Way RV Park (Rte. 53, tel. 505/783–4612; 38 sites, 4 cabins; $10–$18, $55–$65 cabins; flush toilets, showers, hook-ups). **Hotels:** None in park. Near Grants: Cimarron Rose B&B (689 Oso Ridge Rte., tel. 505/783–4770 or 800/856–5776; 2 rooms, 2 suites; $55–$70). In Zuni: Inn at Halona (Shalako Dr., tel. 505/782–4118; 8 rooms; $85). **Restaurants:** In El Morro: Ancient Way Café (Rte. 53, tel. 505/783–4612; $5–$8; closed Sun.), Tinaja Family Restaurant (Rte. 53, mile 50, tel. 505/783–4349; $4–$12; closed Mon.).

FEES, HOURS & REGULATIONS

Entrance fee: $3 adults, free ages 16 and under. Leashed pets only on trails. No mountain bikes, trail bikes, motorized equipment on trails. Entry to park trails open daily 9–4. Visitor center open daily 9–5.

HOW TO GET THERE

56 mi from Gallup via Rte. 602 south and Rte. 53 east through Ramah. Closest airport: Albuquerque (120 mi).

CONTACTS

El Morro National Monument (Rte. HC 61, Box 43, Ramah, NM 87321, tel. 505/783–4226, fax 505/783–4689, www.nps.gov/elmo). Gallup–McKinley Chamber of Commerce (103 Rte. 66, Gallup, NM

87301, tel. 505/722–2228). Grants–Cibola County Chamber of Commerce (100 Iron St., Box 297, Grants, NM 87020, tel. 505/287–4802).

Fort Union
National Monument

In northeastern New Mexico, near Watrous

Three forts, the first of which was constructed in 1851 on this site near the Santa Fe Trail, served as headquarters and supply depot for the Military Department of New Mexico. A 1.5-mi trail leads visitors past the ruins of the last two forts. Wagon ruts along the Santa Fe Trail are visible here. The monument was established on April 5, 1956.

WHAT TO SEE & DO

Picnicking, touring the ruins. **Facilities:** Visitor center, museum, guided and self-guided tours, hiking trails. Book and map sales, picnic tables. **Programs & Events:** Self-guided tours. Guided walks, talks (weekends spring and fall, daily June–Aug.). First Fort Site Tour (June), Cultural Encounters on the Santa Fe Trail (July), An Evening at Fort Union (Aug.), living-history demonstrations (during special events). **Tips & Hints:** Plan to spend two hours. Self-guided 1.5-mi walking tour takes 1½ hours. Busiest July and Aug., least crowded Dec. and Jan.

FOOD & LODGING

Hotels: None in park. In Las Vegas, NM: Comfort Inn (2500 N. Grand Ave., tel. 505/425–1100; 101 rooms; $60–$80), Inn on the Santa Fe Trail (1133 Grand Ave., tel. 505/425–6791 or 888/448–8438; 33 rooms, 2 suites, 2 casitas; $69–$74). **Restaurant:** None in park. In Las Vegas, NM: El Rialto Restaurant & Lounge (141 Bridge St., tel. 505/454–0037; $5–$20; closed Sun.).

FEES, HOURS & REGULATIONS

Entrance fee: $3 adults, free ages 17 and under. Don't climb on walls or foundations of ruins. Stay on trail to avoid rattlesnakes in the tall grass. First fort arsenal site closed to public. No pets in buildings, leashed pets permitted on trails only. Monument open mid-Apr.–Memorial Day, daily 8–5; Memorial Day–late Oct., daily 8–6; late Oct.–mid-Apr., daily 8–4.

HOW TO GET THERE

8 mi north of I–25 (Exit 366) at end of Rte. 161. Closest airport: Las Vegas, NM (20 mi), Albuquerque (153 mi).

CONTACTS

Fort Union National Monument (Box 127, Watrous, NM 87753, tel. 505/425–8025 or 505/454–1155, www.nps.gov/foun). Las Vegas–San Miguel County Chamber of Commerce (701 Grand Ave., Box 128, Las Vegas, NM 87701, tel. 505/425–8631, fax 505/425–3057, www. lasvegasnm.org).

Gila Cliff Dwellings National Monument

In southwestern New Mexico, north of Silver City

A glimpse of 13th-century Native American life can be seen at these well-preserved cliff dwellings. Homes rise up into the sheer, pale rock faces, looking much as they did when they were inhabited from around 1280 through the early 1300s. The Gila Wilderness surrounding the cliffs has numerous hiking trails, horseback riding paths, and back-country campsites. The monument was proclaimed in 1907 and transferred to the Park Service in 1933.

WHAT TO SEE & DO

Bird-watching, camping, fishing, hiking, horseback riding, touring cliff dwellings, watching video. **Facilities:** Visitor center, guided tours, hiking trail. Bookstore. **Programs & Events:** Daily guided tours (at 11, 2). **Tips & Hints:** Call ahead for winter hours and road hazards, and in summer for wilderness fire conditions. To reach park, U.S. 180 east option is 25 mi longer but in much better condition than Rte. 15. Busiest in Mar., July, summer holiday weekends; least crowded Dec. and Jan.

FOOD, LODGING & SUPPLIES

Camping: None at site: In Gila Hot Springs: Gila Hot Springs RV Park (Rte. 15, 4½ mi south of monument, tel. 505/536–9551; 34 sites; $12–$17; flush toilets, showers, hook-ups). **Hotel:** None in park. In Gila Hot Springs: Wilderness Lodge (Jackass La., tel. 505/536–9749; 7 rooms, 1 suite; $58). **Restaurant:** None in park. In Lake Roberts: Grey Feathers Lodge & Restaurant Rtes. 35 and 15, tel. 505/536–3206; $3–7; no dinner Sun.). **Groceries:** None in park. In Gila Hot Springs: Doc Campbell's Post (Rte. 15, 4½ mi south of monument, tel. 505/536–9551).

FEES, HOURS & REGULATIONS

User fee: $3 adults, free ages 13 and under, $10 per family. Trailers over 20 feet or large motor homes must take Rte. 35 to reach monument. Monument open Memorial Day–Labor Day, daily 8–6; Labor Day–Memorial Day, daily 9–4. Visitor center open Memorial Day–Labor Day, daily 8–5; Labor Day–Memorial Day, daily 8–4:30.

HOW TO GET THERE

44 mi north of Silver City on Rte. 15, or via U.S. 180 east to Rte. 152, then Rte. 35 to Rte. 15. Closest airport: Silver City (64 mi).

CONTACTS

Gila Cliff Dwellings National Monument (HC 68, Box 100, Silver City, NM 88061, tel./fax 505/536–9461, www.nps.gov/gicl). Silver City–Grant County Chamber of Commerce (201 N. Hudson Ave., Silver City, NM 88061, tel. 505/538–3785 or 800/548–9378, www.silvercity.org).

Pecos
National Historical Park

In northeastern New Mexico, near Pecos

Two separate historic areas are preserved in this important park: the ruins of the 15th-century Pueblo of Pecos, and the site of the Civil War battle at Glorieta Pass. Several old buildings are the attractions of Pecos, including the remains of two 17th- and 18th-century Spanish colonial missions. Sections of the Santa Fe Trail are threaded throughout the terrain, and the area also includes the former Forked Lightning cattle ranch and Kowlowski's Trading Post. Pecos National Monument was authorized in 1965 and redesignated in 1990.

WHAT TO SEE & DO

Hiking, picnicking, touring ranch, ruins, and battlefield. **Facilities:** Visitor center, guided and self-guided tours, 1.25-mi hiking trail. Bookstore, picnic area. **Programs & Events:** Tours of battlefield and ruins. Cultural demonstrations (Memorial Day–Labor Day, weekends), full-moon tours and ranch tours (both Memorial Day–Labor Day). Feast Day Mass (1st Sun., Aug.). **Tips & Hints:** Plan a one- to two-hour visit. Tours of ruins and battlefield must be booked in advance; ranch tours also require advance bookings after Labor Day. Busiest July and Aug., least crowded Jan. and Feb.

FOOD

✕ **Restaurants**: None in park. In Pecos: Casa de Herrera (Rte. 63, tel. 505/757–6740; $3–$9; no dinner Sun., closed Mon.), Frankie's (Rte. 63, tel. 505/757–3322; $6–$8; closed some Tues. in winter).

FEES & HOURS

Entrance fee: $3 per person. Park open Memorial Day–Labor Day, daily 8–6; Labor Day–Memorial Day, daily 8–5. Visitor center open daily 8–5.

HOW TO GET THERE

2 mi south of Pecos via Rte. 63, and 28 mi southeast of Santa Fe via I–25 to Exit 299 (if traveling north) or Exit 307 (if traveling south).

CONTACTS

Pecos National Historical Park (Box 418, Pecos, NM 87552, tel. 505/757–6414, fax 505/757–8460, www.nps.gov/peco).

Petroglyph
National Monument

West side of Albuquerque

Nearly 20,000 petroglyphs carved by ancestral Puebloans, Hispanic sheepherders, and early settlers stretch 17 mi along this volcanic escarpment. Hiking trails wind through the gorgeous Boca Negra Canyon, many to petroglyphs and associated archaeological sites relating the 12,000-year story of human habitation on Albuquerque's West Mesa. The park was authorized on June 27, 1990.

WHAT TO SEE & DO

Hiking, viewing petroglyphs. **Facilities:** Visitor center, guided and self-guided tours, hiking trails. Book and map sales, picnic tables. **Programs & Events:** Ranger-led tours (weekends Memorial Day–mid-Oct., otherwise by reservation), cultural demonstrations (weekends Memorial Day–Labor Day). Founders Day (around Aug. 25). **Tips & Hints:** Before hiking, get maps at visitor center. Come in spring for cactus and wildflower blooms, Sept. and Oct. for best weather. Watch for rattlesnakes. Busiest May–Oct., least crowded Dec. and Jan.

FEES, HOURS & REGULATIONS

Canyon parking fee: $1 per car weekdays, $2 weekends. No hunting. No motorized equipment. No pets at Boca Negra Canyon, leashed pets only on some backcountry trails. Stay on designated paths. Park and visitor center open daily 8–5.

HOW TO GET THERE

3 mi north of I–40, on Unser Blvd. NW at Western Trail. Closest airport: Albuquerque (12 mi).

CONTACTS

Petroglyph National Monument (6001 Unser Blvd. NW, Albuquerque, NM 87120, tel. 505/899–0205, fax 505/899—0207, www.nps.gov/petr).

Salinas Pueblo Missions National Monument

In central New Mexico, near Mountainair

This former major trade center, and once one of the most populous regions of the Pueblo world during the 17th century, is composed of three distinct sections of stone ruins. Built between 1622 and 1660 by the Tompiros and Tiwa people, the Abó, Quarai, and gran Quivira pueblos were abandoned in the 1670s after drought, famine, and attacks by hostile tribes. Gran Quivira was proclaimed a national monument in 1909, and Abó and Quarai became monuments in 1981, when Salinas was established.

WHAT TO SEE & DO

Picnicking, touring ruins and museum, watching video. **Facilities:** Visitor center, guided and self-guided tours, museum, movie, hiking trails. Picnic area. **Programs & Events:** Ranger-led tours (by request), self-guided tours. **Tips & Hints:** Busiest July–Sept., least crowded Dec. and Jan.

FOOD, LODGING & SUPPLIES

Camping: None at site. Near Mountainair: Manzano Mountain State Park (Rte. 55, 13 mi northwest of Mountainair, tel. 505/847–2820; 45

sites; $8–$14; flush toilets, hook-ups; closed Nov.–Mar.). **Hotels:** None in park. In Mountainair: El Rancho Motel (901 U.S. 60 W, tel. 505/847–2577; 17 rooms; $33), Tillie's Inn (303 U.S. 60 E, tel. 505/847–0248; 10 rooms; $49–$55). **✗ Restaurants:** None in park. In Mountainair: Ancient Cities (603 U.S. 60 W, tel. 505/847–2368; $3–$7), Kowboy Kafe (110 Broadway, tel. 505/847–0950; $5–$13). **Groceries:** None in park. In Mountainair: Mountainair Grocery (204 Broadway, tel. 505/847–2223).

FEES & HOURS

Free. Monument open Memorial Day–Labor Day, daily 9–6; Labor Day–Memorial Day, daily 9–5. Visitor center open Memorial Day–Labor Day, daily 8–6; Labor Day–Memorial Day, daily 8–5.

HOW TO GET THERE

Visitor center 1 block west of intersection of U.S. 60 and Rte. 55; to Abó, continue 9 mi west via U.S. 60 and ½ mi north on Rte. 513; to Quarai head 8 mi north on Rte. 55 and 1 mi west; to Gran Quivira head 25 mi south on Rte. 55. Closest airport: Albuquerque (70 mi).

CONTACTS

Salinas Pueblo Missions National Monument (Box 517, Mountainair, NM 87036, tel. 505/847–2585, fax 505/847–2441, www.nps.gov/sapu).

White Sands National Monument

In southern New Mexico, near Alamogordo

The glistening white sands of the world's largest gypsum dunefield are partially protected by this fascinating park. Spread over 176,000 acres, the hills rise to 60 feet in some places, providing a harsh environment for the hardy species of flora and fauna that survive here today. Glimpses of the desert's plants and creatures are at the Heart of the Sands Nature Center, or along the 8-mi scenic drive through the park. Full-moon shows at the amphitheater program offer spectacular starlight views over the dunes. The monument was proclaimed on January 18, 1933.

WHAT TO SEE & DO

Auto touring, hiking, picnicking, watching video. **Facilities:** Visitor center, hiking trails. Book-and-gift shop, picnic tables with grill fires. **Programs & Events:** Daily sunset nature walks, guided and self-guided tours, Lake Lucero tours (monthly). Evening campfire programs (Memorial Day–Labor Day), full-moon programs (June–Aug.). **Tips & Hints:** Bring water if hiking, and a compass and map if hiking off trails. Call ahead to see if park is closed for White Sands Missile Range testing. Go in fall and winter for best weather, spring for whitest dunes and dune movement because of winds, May for wildflowers, late May–mid-June for yucca blooms. Busiest July and Aug., least crowded in Nov. and Jan.

FOOD, LODGING & SUPPLIES

Camping: In the park: backcountry camping (permit required, *see below*) and group campsite. In Alamogordo: Desert Paradise (1090 U.S. 70 west, tel. 505/434–2266; 30 RV sites; $20; flush toilets, showers, hook-ups). **Hotels:** None in park. In Alamogordo: Best Western Desert Aire (1021 S. White Sands Blvd., tel. 505/437–2110; 99 rooms; $57), Holiday Inn Express (1401 S. White Sands Blvd., tel. 505/437–7100 or 800/465–4329; 108 rooms; $59). ✗ **Restaurants:** In the park: snacks at visitor center. In Alamogordo: Compass Rose (2203 E. 1st St., tel. 505/434–9633; $5–$9; closed Sun.), Margo's Mexican Food (504 1st St., tel. 505/434–0689; $5–$10). **Groceries:** None in park. In Alamogordo: J&J Mini Market (901 U.S. 70, tel. 505/434–4317).

FEES, HOURS & REGULATIONS

Entrance fee: $3 adults, free ages 17 and under. Backcountry camping permits ($3 per night) required. Lake Lucero tours: $3 adults, $1.50 ages 16 and under. No hunting. No vehicles or bikes on trails or off roads. Leashed pets on trails. Dunes Dr. open Memorial Day–Labor Day, daily 7 AM–9 PM; Labor Day–Memorial Day, daily 7–sunset. Closed during missile range testing. Visitor center open Memorial Day–Labor Day, daily 8–7; Labor Day–Memorial Day, daily 8–5.

HOW TO GET THERE

15 mi southwest of Alamogordo and 52 mi northeast of Las Cruces via U.S. 70. Closest airport: El Paso, TX (90 mi).

CONTACTS

White Sands National Monument (Box 1086, Holloman AFB, NM 88330-1086, tel. 505/679–2599, fax 505/479–4333, www.nps.gov/whsa). Alamogordo Chamber of Commerce (1301 N. White Sands Blvd., Alamogordo, NM 88310, tel. 505/437–6120 or 800/826–0294, www.alamogordo.com).

See Also

Continental Divide National Scenic Trail and *Santa Fe National Historic Trail,* in Other National Parklands.

Castle Clinton
National Monument

In New York City

The site preserves the fort built between 1807 and 1811 to defend New York City during the War of 1812. In 1815 the Southwest Battery, constructed on the rocks off the tip of Manhattan, was renamed Castle Clinton in honor of DeWitt Clinton, mayor of New York City. The fort later became a restaurant and entertainment center, opera house and theater, an immigrant-landing depot where 8 million people entered the United States, and finally the New York City Aquarium. It closed in 1941. The monument was authorized on August 12, 1946.

WHAT TO SEE & DO

Self- and ranger-guided tours of the site. **Facilities:** Museum, building. Bookstore, ticket booth for ferries to Liberty Island and Ellis Island. **Programs & Events:** Ranger-led programs and tours. Concert series (Thurs., July–1st Thurs. in Aug.). **Tips & Hints:** Use mass transit. Plan on 25 minutes to tour site. Busiest July and Aug. and late Nov.–late Dec., least crowded Jan. and Feb.

FEES & HOURS

Free. Monument open daily 8:30–5.

HOW TO GET THERE

The monument is in Battery Park at the southern tip of Manhattan. Public transportation is recommended. The west-side 1 and 9 subway trains stop at South Ferry station in Battery Park. The east-side 4 and 5 subway trains stop at Bowling Green station adjacent to Battery Park. The crosstown N and R subway trains stop at Whitehall St. station adjacent to Battery Park. Frequent bus service to South Ferry is provided by route M-6, which operates daily on Broadway; route M-1, which operates weekdays on 5th Ave., Park Ave., and Broadway; and by route M-15, which operates daily on 2nd Ave. Closest airports: JFK and LaGuardia (New York); Newark (New Jersey).

CONTACT

Castle Clinton National Monument (26 Wall St., New York, NY 10005, tel. 212/344–7220, www.nps.gov/cacl).

Eleanor Roosevelt National Historic Site

In southeastern New York, in Hyde Park

Eleanor Roosevelt used Val-Kill Cottage in her younger years as a retreat and in her later years as her home, where she entertained heads of state. It was built as a factory building for Val-Kill Industries before being converted to a house in 1937. The site was authorized on May 26, 1977.

WHAT TO SEE & DO

Touring home and grounds. **Facilities:** Playhouse with introductory film, furnished home, Rose Garden, Cutting Garden, The Stone Cottage conference center, walkways and trails. **Programs & Events:** Guided tours (reservations required July, Aug., and Oct.). **Tips & Hints:** Allow one hour for film and tour, more for viewing landscaped grounds and walking trail. Busiest in Aug. and Oct., least crowded Jan. and Feb.

FOOD & LODGING

Camping: None at site. In Rhinebeck: Interlake RV Park (428 Lake Dr., tel. 845/266–5387; 159 sites; $25–$32; flush toilets, showers, hook-ups). **Hotels:** None at site. In Hyde Park: Golden Manor (4100 Albany Post Rd./U.S. 9, tel. 845/229–2157; 40 rooms; $55–$65), Super 8 (4142 Albany Post Rd./U.S. 9, tel. 845/229–0088 or 800/800–8000; 61 rooms; $77–$81). **✕ Restaurants:** None at site. In Hyde Park: Eveready Diner (540 Albany Post Rd./U.S. 9, tel. 845/229–8100; $4–$10), Hyde Park Brewing Co. (4076 Albany Post Rd./U.S. 9, tel. 845/229–8277; $4–$7).

FEES & HOURS

Free. Guided tour $8 adults, free ages 16 and under. $22 for combination pass to FDR site and either Vanderbilt Mansion National Historic Site (*see separate listing*) or Top Cottage tour (*see Home of Franklin D. Roosevelt National Historic Site*). Site open May–Oct., daily 9–5; Nov.–Apr., Thurs.–Mon. 9–5. Grounds open daily until sunset.

HOW TO GET THERE

In Hyde Park, two hours north of New York City on Rte. 9G. From U.S. 9, make a right on St. Andrews Rd. (Rte. 40A). Turn left on Rte. 9G. Home is on the right. Closest airport: Newburgh (45 mi)should really give NYC distance - most people are going to fly in there.

CONTACTS

Eleanor Roosevelt National Historic Site (4097 Albany Post Rd., Hyde Park, NY 12538, tel. 845/229–9115; 800/967–2283 house tours, fax 845/229–0739, www.nps.gov/elro). Dutchess County Tourism Promotion Agency (3 Neptune Rd., Suite M17, Poughkeepsie, NY 12601, tel. 800/445–3131 or 845/46–4000, www.dutchesstourism.com).

Federal Hall
National Memorial

In New York City

This graceful building occupies the site of the original Federal Hall, where the trial of John Peter Zenger, involving freedom of the press, was held in 1735. The Stamp Act Congress convened here in 1765 and the Second Continental Congress met here in 1785. George Washington took the oath as first U.S. president and the Bill of Rights was adopted here in 1789. The present building was completed in 1842. The statue of Washington is by John Quincy Adams Ward. The site was designated as Federal Hall Memorial National Historic Site in 1939 and redesignated in 1955.

WHAT TO SEE & DO

Attending ranger program, self-guided tours of museum, viewing video. **Facilities:** Museum. Museum shop. **Programs & Events:** Self-guided tours, ranger-led programs and tours, orientation video (daily). Seasonal activities and special events available. **Tips & Hints:** Use mass transit to get to memorial. Busiest July and Aug., least crowded Jan. and Feb.

FEES & HOURS

Free. Memorial open weekdays 9–5.

HOW TO GET THERE

The 7th Ave. 2 and 3 subway trains stop at Wall and William Sts., one block east of Federal Hall. The Lexington Ave. 4 and 5 subway trains stop at Wall St. and Broadway, one block west of Federal Hall. On weekdays, the J, M, and Z subway trains stop at Wall and Broad Sts. Frequent bus service is provided by route M-6 on Broadway, one block to the west, and by route M-15 on Water St., three blocks to the east. Closest airports: JFK and LaGuardia (New York); Newark (New Jersey).

CONTACT

Federal Hall National Memorial (26 Wall St., New York, NY 10005, tel. 212/825–6888, fax 212/825–6874, www.nps.gov/feha).

Fire Island
National Seashore

*In southeastern New York,
on Long Island's south shore*

The seashore's 32-mi-long barrier island contains extensive salt marshes, a 300-year-old American holly forest, and the only federally protected wilderness in New York State. It includes the Fire Island Light Station; Sailors Haven; Watch Hill; the Wilderness Visitor Center at Smith Point; and the 612-acre estate of William Floyd, a signer of the Declaration of Independence, in Mastic Beach, Long Island. The seashore was authorized in 1964.

WHAT TO SEE & DO

Boating, canoeing, fishing, hiking, house and tower touring, kayaking, picnicking, swimming. **Facilities:** 3 visitor centers: Watch Hill, Sailors Haven, Wilderness. Fire Island Lighthouse; William Floyd Estate (Mastic Beach); beaches, marinas, trails. Book sale areas, gift shops, grills, picnic tables. **Programs & Events:** Tower tours (Fire Island Lighthouse). Guided nature walks (Sailors Haven and Watch Hill, July and Aug.), canoe program (Watch Hill, July and Aug.), house tours (William Floyd Estate, Memorial Day–Oct.). Cultural programs Fire Island Light Station, William Floyd Estate (occasional). **Tips & Hints:** Island has no roads and is accessible only by boat or passenger ferry, or by driving to Robert Moses State Park or Smith Point County Park and walking in. Bring adequate food, water, and supplies for day trips. Go in late Apr., May, Sept., or Oct. for songbird migration; Sept. and Oct. for hawk migration; June–Aug. for wildflower blooms. Busiest July and Aug., least crowded Jan. and Feb.

FOOD & LODGING

Camping: Campground: Watch Hill (26 sites; $28 minimum includes two nights, reservations required, closed mid-Oct.–mid-May; flush toilets, drinking water, grills, picnic tables, public phone). Backcountry camping available (permit required, *see below*). ✕ **Restaurants:** At the seashore: snack bar and convenience store at Watch Hill (tel. 631/597–6655), snack bar and gift shop at Sailors Haven (tel. 631/597–6171).

FEES, HOURS & REGULATIONS

Free. Ferry fees vary. Fee charged for parking at Robert Moses State Park and at Smith Point County Park. Fire Island Lighthouse fee: $5 adults, $4 ages 62 and over, $3.50 ages 11 and under. Backcountry permits required (free). Leashed pets only. No skating, bicycling, or skateboarding. No mechanical equipment or metal detectors. Sailors Haven Visitor Center open mid-May–late June, weekends 10–2; late June–Labor Day, daily 9:30–3:30; Labor Day–mid-Oct., weekends 10–2. Watch Hill Visitor Center open mid-May–late June, Sat. 1–5, Sun. 8–1; late June–Labor Day, daily 9–11 and 1–5; Labor Day–mid-Oct., Sat. 1–5, Sun. 8–1. William Floyd Estate open Jan.–Memorial Day, weekends 9–4:30; Memorial Day–Labor Day, Fri.–Sun. and holiday Mon., 11–4:30. Fire Island Lighthouse open daily 9:30–5. Wilderness Visitor Center open mid-May–Dec., Wed.–Sun. 9–4.

HOW TO GET THERE

The seashore is accessible by ferry or boat off the south shore of Long Island in Bayshore, Patchogue, Sayville. You can also drive to Robert Moses State Park (via Robert Moses Pkwy.) or Smith Point County Park (via William Floyd Pkwy.) and walk to the island. Closest airport: MacArthur (Islip).

CONTACTS

Fire Island National Seashore (120 Laurel St., Patchogue, NY 11772, tel. 631/289–4810; 631/289–9336 camping reservations, fax 631/289–4898, www.nps.gov/fiis). Watch Hill Visitor Center (tel. 631/475–1665). Sailors Haven Visitor Center (tel. 631/589–8980). Fire Island Tourism Bureau (40 Main St., Sayville, NY 11782, tel. 631/563–8448).

Fort Stanwix National Monument

In central New York, in Rome

The British built a fort at the site in 1758 to protect the Oneida Carry portage that linked the waterway between the Atlantic Ocean and Great Lakes. Fort Stanwix was rebuilt by Americans in 1776 and then, in 1777, attacked by the British from August 3 to 23 until British troops retreated to Canada. The fort has been almost entirely reconstructed to its 1777 appearance. The site was authorized in 1935. It became a National Historic Landmark in 1963 and was listed on the National Register of Historic Places in 1984.

WHAT TO SEE & DO

Touring the fort. **Facilities:** Visitor center, fort, museum, living-history quarters, trail. Bookstore. **Programs & Events:** Ranger-guided tours, interpretive programs, living-history demonstrations (June–Aug.). Syracuse Symphony Orchestra (last Sat., July), occasional reenactments. **Tips & Hints:** Busiest July and Aug., least crowded Nov., Dec. and Apr.

FOOD, LODGING & SUPPLIES

Camping: None in park. Near Rome: Delta Lake State Park (8797 Rte. 46, tel. 315/33–4670; 800/456–2267 reservations; 101 sites; $13–$19; flush toilets, showers; closed Columbus Day–early May). **Hotels:** None in park. In Rome: Beeches Paul Revere Lodge (7900 Turin Rd., tel. 315/336–1776 or 800/765–7251; 75 rooms; $85), Quality Inn (200 S. James St., tel. 315/336–4300; 104 rooms; $150). **Restaurant:** None in park. In Rome: Beeches Paul Revere Lodge (7900 Turin Rd., tel. 315/336–1700; $3–$15; closed Mon., no lunch Sat.). **Groceries & Gear:** None in park. In Rome: Herb Philipson's Army & Navy (300 W. Dominick St., tel. 315/336–1300), Price Chopper (1919 Black River Blvd., tel. 315/339–1919).

FEES, HOURS & REGULATIONS

Free. No pets in fort buildings. Leashed pets elsewhere. Fort open Apr.–Dec., daily 9–5. Monument grounds open daily, 24 hrs.

HOW TO GET THERE

The monument is in downtown Rome on Rte. 49 north. Closest airport: Syracuse (50 mi).

CONTACTS
Fort Stanwix National Monument (112 E. Park St., Rome, NY 13440, tel. 315/336–2090, fax 315/334–5051, www.nps.gov/fost). Rome Area Chamber of Commerce (139 W. Dominick St., Rome, NY 13440, tel. 315/337–1700).

Gateway
National Recreation Area

*In New York City, and in northeastern New Jersey,
on Sandy Hook peninsula*

Gateway, one of two major urban national parks in the country, offers residents of New York, New Jersey, Connecticut, and Pennsylvania a national-park experience with diverse cultural, historical, and recreational opportunities. It is the nation's fifth most visited national park site, with more than 7 million visitors each year. The recreation area includes Jamaica Bay in Queens and Brooklyn; Staten Island; and Sandy Hook in New Jersey. The park was authorized on October 17, 1972.

WHAT TO SEE & DO
Attending ethnic and special events, beach-going, bicycling, bird-watching, boating, fishing, hiking, jogging, participating in organized athletics, sunbathing, swimming, touring forts and lighthouses, walking. **Facilities:** 5 visitor centers: Floyd Bennett Field, Jamaica Bay Wildlife Refuge, Fort Tilden, Fort Wadsworth, Sandy Hook. Ecology Village (Jamaica Bay), Canarsie Pier, Great Kills Park Beach Center, Fort Hancock Museum, Fort Hancock History House, Sandy Hook Lighthouse, Battery Potter, beaches, trails, waysides, boardwalk, theater. At Jamaica Bay Unit: picnic areas, bookshop, marina, car-top boating ramp (Floyd Bennett Field). At Staten Island Unit: picnic areas, bookshop, marina and boat-launching ramp (Great Kills Park). At Sandy Hook Unit: picnic areas, bookshop and map sales area, beach concessions, and ferry service. **Programs & Events:** Ranger-led programs and walks (several times weekly, weekends). Outdoor programs (May–Oct.). At Jamaica Bay Unit: Canarsie Pier Concert Series (June–Aug.), Fort Tilden Concert Series (June–Aug.). At Staten Island Unit: New York City Five Borough Bike Tour (May), Metropolitan Opera Concert (June), New York Philharmonic Orchestra Concert (July), New York City Half Marathon (Oct.), New York City Marathon (Nov.). At Sandy Hook Unit: Clearwater Festival (Aug.), Beach Concert Series (June–Aug.). **Tips & Hints:** Watch for deer ticks. Get to Sandy Hook beach early on summer weekends. Access can be limited or closed between 10 and 3. Best weather: Apr.–Oct. Go in spring and fall to see migrating bird species, and Sept. and Oct. to see monarch butterflies. Busiest July and Aug., least crowded Jan. and Feb.

FOOD & LODGING
Camping: 2 campgrounds in the park: Floyd Bennett Field (tel. 718/338–4306); Sandy Hook (tel. 732/872–5970). Near Matawan, NJ:

Cheesequake State Park (300 Gordon Rd., tel. 732/566–2161; 53 sites; $15; flush toilets, showers). ✘ **Restaurants:** In Jamaica Bay Unit: restaurant at Canarsie Pier, snack bar at Riis Park Boardwalk (Memorial Day–Labor Day). In Staten Island Unit: snack bar and evening bar at Carriage House at Fort Wadsworth, seasonal snack bar and roving meal mobiles at Miller Field and Great Kills. In Sandy Hook Unit: Meals at Seagull's Nest Restaurant (tel. 732/872–0025; $6–$14), seasonal snack bars at beach houses.

FEES, HOURS & REGULATIONS

Free. Sandy Hook parking fee Memorial Day–Labor Day: $8 weekdays, $10 weekends. $25 annual fee for anglers to use designated parking lots. Leashed dogs only. No dogs on swimming beach Mar. 15–Labor Day at Sandy Hook or at Great Kills Park. Permit required to drive on beach at Breezy Point. No off-road bicycling in park. No horse trails. Park open daily sunrise–sunset except in designated fishing–beach areas that are covered under a permit. Visitor center hours: At Jamaica Bay, Fort Tilden Visitor Center open daily 8:30–5; Ryan Visitor Center at Floyd Bennett Field open daily 8:30–5; Canarsie Pier open daily 9–4:30; Jamaica Bay Wildlife Refuge open daily 8:30–5. At Staten Island Unit, Fort Wadsworth open Wed.–Sun. 10–5. Sandy Hook visitor center open daily 10–5.

HOW TO GET THERE

Breezy Point District is on Rockaway Peninsula in Queens. Take Flatbush Ave. (Exit 11S) off Belt Pkwy. over the Marine Park Bridge. The Jamaica Bay District is in Brooklyn. Take Flatbush Ave. (Exit 11S) off Belt Pkwy. The Jamaica Bay Wildlife Refuge is in Queens. Take Cross Bay Blvd. (Exit 17S) off Belt Pkwy. Closest airports: JFK and LaGuardia Airports. Staten Island Unit: Fort Wadsworth is on Staten Island. Take Verrazano Narrows Bridge–Staten Island Expressway to Bay St. exit and follow signs. Miller Field is on Staten Island. Take New Dorp La. off Hylan Blvd. Great Kills Park is on Staten Island off Hylan Blvd. south of New Dorp La. Closest airport: Newark, NJ (10 mi). The Sandy Hook Unit is on Sandy Hook Peninsula in NJ. Take the Garden State Pkwy. to Exit 117, then Rte. 36 east past Highlands, NJ. Closest airport: Newark, NJ (25 mi).

CONTACTS

Gateway National Recreation Area (Public Affairs Office, 210 New York Ave., Staten Island, NY 10305, tel. 718/354–4606, fax 718/338–6284, www.nps.gov/gate). Jamaica Bay Unit Visitor Center (Floyd Bennett Field, Bldg. 69, Brooklyn, NY 11234, tel. 718/338–3799). Staten Island Unit, Fort Wadsworth Visitor Center (210 New York Ave., Staten Island, NY 10305, tel. 718/354–4500). Sandy Hook Unit Visitor Center (Box 530, Highland, NJ 07732, tel. 732/872–5970). New York State Dept. of Economic Development, Division of Tourism (Box 2603, Albany, NY 12220-0603, tel. 800/225–5697). New Jersey Department of Tourism and Travel (Box 826, 20 W. State St., Trenton, NJ 08625, tel. 800/537–7397).

General Grant National Memorial

In New York City

The memorial, popularly known as Grant's Tomb, is the final resting place of Ulysses S. Grant and his wife, Julia Dent Grant. After serving as Union commander during the Civil War, Grant served two terms as president before entering business on Wall Street. As president, Grant signed an act on March 1, 1872, establishing Yellowstone as the nation's first national park. His tomb, designed by architect John Duncan, is constructed of 8,000 tons of granite and marble. The 150-foot-tall memorial is the largest mausoleum in North America. It was dedicated in 1897 and authorized to be transferred to federal ownership and Park Service administration in 1958.

WHAT TO SEE & DO

Touring memorial and museum. **Facilities:** Visitor center, memorial, museum. Museum shop. Bookstore. **Programs & Events:** Ranger-led programs and tours, costumed interpretations. **Tips & Hints:** Plan on 20–30 minutes for tours and programs. Busiest July and Aug., least crowded Jan. and Feb.

FEES & HOURS

Free. Memorial open daily 9–5.

HOW TO GET THERE

The memorial is at Riverside Dr. and 122nd St. in Manhattan in New York City. Subway trains 1 or 9, which run along 7th Ave. and Broadway, stop at the W. 116th St. Station at Broadway, two blocks east and six blocks south of Grant's Tomb. Bus service is provided on Riverside Dr. up to 120th St. by route M-5. Closest airports: JFK and LaGuardia (New York); Newark (New Jersey).

CONTACT

Superintendent, General Grant National Memorial (26 Wall St., New York, NY 10005, tel. 212/666–1640, www.nps.gov/gegr).

Governors Island National Monument

In New York Harbor, off the coast of Manhattan, in New York City

This 172-acre island was a U.S. Army base from 1783 to 1966, then a Coast Guard base from 1966 to 1996. The monument includes two early 19th-century fortifications: Castle Williams and Fort Jay. From the island, you can see views of Manhattan, the Statue of Liberty and New York Harbor. The island is being converted from military to public use and is open to the public by reservation. It's managed in partnership with the Governors Island Preservation and Education Corporation. A portion of the island (approximately 22 acres) was designated a National Monument in 2001 and transferred to the Park Service on January 31, 2003.

WHAT TO SEE & DO

Taking guided tour of forts and historical sections of island. **Facilities**: Forts. **Programs & Events**: Ranger-guided tours (Apr.–Oct., reservations required). **Tips & Hints**: Park is under development. Call park to make tour reservations and get transportation information. Expect to spend 10 minutes on the ferry and about 2 hours on the tour.

FEES & HOURS

Free. Park open by reservation only.

HOW TO GET THERE

Island accessible by ferry from lower Manhattan only. Closest airports: Newark, NJ; JFK and LaGuardia, NY.

CONTACTS

Governors Island National Monument (Federal Hall, 26 Wall St., New York, NY 10005, tel. 212/514–8296 information and tour reservations, fax 212/514–8302, www.nps.gov/gois).

Hamilton Grange National Memorial

In New York City

Alexander Hamilton, American patriot, co-author of the *Federalist Papers*, and first U.S. Treasury Secretary, built the Grange on Manhattan's Upper West Side in 1802. The Grange, named after the Hamilton family's ancestral home in Scotland, served as his home for two years. On July 11, 1804, Hamilton was fatally wounded in a duel with his political rival, Aaron Burr. The memorial was authorized on April 27, 1962.

WHAT TO SEE & DO

Touring renovated parts of house, viewing exterior of building. **Facilities:** Partially renovated house. **Programs & Events:** Ranger-guided tours (hourly), period music. Hamilton's Birthday (Sun. nearest Jan. 11). **Tips & Hints:** Busiest June and July, least crowded Jan. and Feb.

FEES & HOURS

Free. Visitor center and museum, Fri.–Sun. 9–5. Part of the house is open Fri.–Sun. 9–5.

HOW TO GET THERE

The house is at 287 Convent Ave., between W. 141st and W. 142nd Sts., in New York City. From I–87 (Major Deegan Expressway), take Exit 4 (E. 149th St). Go west on 149th St. across bridge onto W. 145th St.; west on 145th St. six blocks to Convent Ave.; south four blocks to house. The 1 or 9 subway trains, which run along 7th Ave./Broadway, stop at the W. 137th St. station on Broadway, two blocks west and five blocks south of Hamilton Grange. The A, B, C, and D subway trains stop at the W. 145th St. station on St. Nicholas Ave., four blocks north and two blocks east of Hamilton Grange. Frequent bus service is provided on Broadway two blocks to the west by routes M-4 and M-5, on Amsterdam Ave. one block to the west by routes M-100 and M-101, and by route BX-19 operating crosstown on 145th St. Half-hourly bus service on Convent Ave. is provided by route M-18. Closest airports: JFK and LaGuardia (New York); Newark (New Jersey).

CONTACT

Superintendent, Hamilton Grange National Memorial (26 Wall St., New York, NY 10005, tel. 212/666–1640, www.nps.gov/hagr).

Home of Franklin D. Roosevelt National Historic Site

In southeastern New York, in Hyde Park

Springwood was the birthplace and lifetime residence of the 32nd president. The gravesites of Franklin Delano Roosevelt and Eleanor Roosevelt are in the Rose Garden. Also on site is the FDR Presidential Library and Museum. Tours to Top Cottage, built in 1938, are available from here. The site was designated on January 15, 1944.

WHAT TO SEE & DO

Touring home and adjacent library and museum, viewing film. **Facilities:** Visitor center, introductory film, furnished home, memorial Rose Garden, icehouse, stables, grounds, trails. Bookstore, café. **Programs & Events:** Ranger-led tours of house, self-guided tours of grounds and museum. Driving tour to Top Cottage (May–Oct., fee). **Tips & Hints:** Allow one to two hours to see house and grounds, one to two more hours to see adjoining FDR Presidential Library and Museum, and two hours for Top Cottage tour and tour of Hyde Park. Busiest Aug. and Oct., least crowded Jan. and Feb.

FOOD & LODGING

See Eleanor Roosevelt National Historic Site.

FEES & HOURS

Grounds and garden: free. FDR Presidential Library and Museum (including tour): $14 adults, free ages 16 and under; $22 for combination pass to FDR site and either Eleanor Roosevelt National Historic Site, Vanderbilt Mansion National Historic sites (*see separate listings for both*), or Top Cottage tour. Visitor center open daily 9–5. Grounds open daily 7–sunset. Top Cottage open May–Oct., Thurs.–Mon. by guided tour only.

HOW TO GET THERE

The site is on U.S. 9 in Hyde Park, just north of Poughkeepsie and two hours north of New York City. Closest airport: Newburgh (45 mi).

CONTACTS

Home of Franklin D. Roosevelt National Historic Site (4097 Albany Post Rd., Hyde Park, NY 12538, tel. 845/229–9115; 800/967–2283 tour reservations, fax 845/229–0739, www.nps.gov/hofr). Dutchess County Tourism Promotion Agency (3 Neptune Rd., Suite M17, Poughkeepsie, NY 12601, tel. 800/445–3131 or 845/463–4000, www.dutchesstourism.com).

Martin Van Buren National Historic Site

In east-central New York, in Kinderhook

The 36-room mansion and retirement home of Martin Van Buren, the nation's eighth president, is at this 40-acre site. Van Buren bought the Federal-style home in 1839. He hired architect Richard Upjohn to remodel the home and build an Italianate addition. The mansion has been restored to the Van Buren period. The site was authorized on October 26, 1974.

WHAT TO SEE & DO

Touring home and grounds, watching video. **Facilities:** Visitor center, orientation video, home, grounds, wayside exhibits, nature trails. Bookstore. **Programs & Events:** Ranger-led tours of home. Interpretive talks, bike tours, hikes, living-history programs, crafts demonstrations. **Tips & Hints:** Plan to spend 1½ hours touring home and grounds. House isn't air-conditioned and some activities are outdoors. Busiest July and Aug., least crowded Sept. and Oct.

FOOD & LODGING

Hotels: None in park. In Hudson: St. Charles Hotel (16–18 Park Pl., tel. 518/822–9900; 34 rooms, 2 suites; $79–$109). In Valatie: Blue Spruce Inn & Suites (3093 U.S. 9, tel. 518/758–9711; 22 rooms, 4 suites; $75–$95). **Restaurants:** None in park. In Hudson: Cascades (407 Warren St., tel. 518/822–9146; $7; no dinner, closed Sun.). In Kinderhook: La Bella Brick Oven Pizza & Cafe (6 Broad St., tel. 518/758–6611; $5–$7). In Valatie: Kinderhook Diner (Rte. 9H, tel. 518/758–1399; $3–$13).

FEES, HOURS & REGULATIONS

Entrance fee: $3 adults, free ages 16 and under. No strollers or video cameras. Still photography with no flash only. Visitor center open Memorial Day–Oct., daily 9–4:30; Nov.–early Dec., weekends 9–4:30. House open by guided tour only with signup at ranger station.

HOW TO GET THERE

Site is on Rte. 9H in Kinderhook. From I–90 east, take Exit B1 to U.S. 9 south. Bear right on Rte. 9H to site 5 mi on right. From I–90 west, take Exit 12 onto U.S. 9 south and follow directions above. From I–87 south (New York State Thruway), take Exit 21 to Rte. 23 east. Cross Rip Van Winkle Bridge (toll), turn left on Rte. 9H north. Site is 15 mi north on left. Be careful not to confuse U.S. 9 and Rtes. 9J, 9G, and 9W, all of which are near site, with Rte. 9H, which is the location of the site.

CONTACTS

Martin Van Buren National Historic Site (1013 Old Post Rd., Kinderhook, NY 12106, tel. 518/758–9689, fax 518/758–6986, www.nps.gov/mava). Columbia County Chamber of Commerce (507 Warren St., Hudson, NY 12534, tel. 518/828–4417, www.columbiachamber-ny.com).

Sagamore Hill
National Historical Site

On Long Island, New York, near Oyster Bay

Sagamore Hill was the home of Theodore Roosevelt (1887–1919), 26th president of the United States from 1901 to 1909. The rambling 23-room, Queen Anne–style house reflects the many roles this man played: cowboy, conservationist, big-game hunter, scientist, politician, naval strategist, orator, soldier, family man, and Nobel Peace Prize winner. Also on the 83-acre site are the outbuildings of the Sagamore Hill Farm and Old Orchard Museum, the former home of Roosevelt's son, Congressional Medal of Honor winner Brigadier General Theodore Roosevelt Jr. The site was authorized in 1962.

WHAT TO SEE & DO

Touring home, grounds, and museum; watching film. **Facilities:** Visitor center, Theodore Roosevelt home, Old Orchard Museum. Bookstore. **Programs & Events:** Ranger-guided tours of home (daily, hourly, 10–4). Nature walks, grounds tours (Memorial Day–Labor Day, weekends). Navy Day (spring), July 4th Celebration, Neighborhood Night (summer). **Tips & Hints:** Go early to pick up house tour tickets for later in the day. House tours sell out by early afternoon on weekends and in summer. The best times to visit are early summer weekdays or weekday afternoons in spring and fall. Go mid-Oct.–mid-Nov. for fall foliage. Busiest July and Aug., least crowded Jan. and Feb.

FEES, HOURS & REGULATIONS

Free. Home tour fee: $5 adults, free ages 16 and under. Admission to home by guided tour only. No hunting. Leashed pets only. Bicycles and vehicles on entry road and parking area only. Grounds open daily dawn–dusk. Visitor center open Memorial Day–Labor Day, daily 9–4:50; Labor Day–Memorial Day, Wed.–Sun. 9–4:50. Theodore Roosevelt home open Memorial Day–Oct., daily 9:30–4; Nov.–Memorial Day, Wed.–Sun. 9:30–4.

HOW TO GET THERE

3 mi east of Oyster Bay via Cove Rd. and Cove Neck Rd. The Long Island Railroad connects with Amtrak from New York City's Pennsylvania Station at 7th Ave. and 33rd St. Get off at Oyster Bay Station (on the Oyster Bay Line) or Syosset Station (on the Port Jefferson Line). Take

taxi to site. By car, take either Exit 41N from I–495/Long Island Expressway or Exit 35N from the Northern State Pkwy. to Rte. 106 north. Follow Sagamore Hill signs. Closest airports: JFK (28 mi), LaGuardia (27 mi), MacArthur (30 mi).

CONTACTS

Sagamore Hill National Historic Site (20 Sagamore Hill Rd., Oyster Bay NY 11771, tel. 516/922–4788, fax 516/922–4792, www.nps.gov/sahi). Long Island Convention and Visitors Bureau (330 Motor Pkwy., Suite 203, Hauppauge NY 11788, tel. 800/441–4601, fax 516/951–3439, www.licvb.com). Oyster Bay Chamber of Commerce (Box 21, Oyster Bay, NY 11771, tel. 516/922–6464).

Saint Paul's Church National Historic Site

In southeastern New York, in Mount Vernon

Located on the former village green of Eastchester, the park contains a 5-acre burial ground dating to 1665, an 18th-century church associated with the American Revolution, and a site museum. The site was designated in 1943 and transferred to the Park Service in 1980.

WHAT TO SEE & DO

Touring church, burial ground, and museum. **Facilities:** Visitor center, church, burial ground, museum, 1833 organ, 1758 church bell. **Programs & Events:** Site tours (weekdays), burial-ground tours (occasional weekends). Tower walks (Apr.–Oct., Fri. 3 PM), living-history programs, costumed interpretation programs with special activities for children (July, Aug., Wed. at 12:15 PM), Black History Month (Feb.), Women's History Month (Mar.). Military encampment and reenactment commemorating 1776 Battle of Pell's Point (3rd Sat., Oct.). **Tips & Hints:** Visit Apr.–Oct.. Busiest June and July, least crowded Jan. and Feb.

FEES & HOURS

Free. Site and visitor center open weekdays 9–5.

HOW TO GET THERE

From the Hutchinson River Pkwy. Exit 7, turn left onto Boston Post Rd., take Boston Post Rd. to Pelham Pkwy., and make a right; 4 stoplights later make left on to S. Columbus Ave. Closest airport: LaGuardia (10 mi).

CONTACTS

Saint Paul's Church National Historic Site (897 S. Columbus Ave., Mount Vernon, NY 10550, tel. 914/667–4116, fax 914/667–3024, www.nps.gov/sapa). Mount Vernon Chamber of Commerce (53 Valentine Ave., Mount Vernon, NY 10550, tel. 914/667–7500).

Saratoga National Historical Park

In east-central New York, near Stillwater

The Battles of Saratoga, the first significant American military victory during the American Revolution, rank among the 15 most decisive battles in world history. Here in 1777 American forces met, defeated, and forced a major British army to surrender, an event that led France to recognize the independence of the United States and enter the war as a decisive military ally of the struggling Americans. The park comprises three units—the Battlefield in Stillwater, the General Philip Schuyler House in Schuylerville, and the Saratoga Monument, a 155-foot-tall obelisk in the village of Victory. The park was authorized on June 1, 1938.

WHAT TO SEE & DO

Auto or bike touring of battlefield, cross-country skiing, guided touring of Schuyler House, hiking, picnicking, viewing orientation film, visiting monument, walking. **Facilities:** Battlefield visitor center, tour road (audio tour rentals), 4.5-mi Wilkinson National Historic Trail, 6 mi of road trace trails, wayside exhibits, Neilson House (1777). Bookstore and sales area, picnic areas. **Programs & Events:** Guided tours of Schuyler House (mid-June–Labor Day), Frost Faire, March for Parks (Jan.–Apr.). July 4 Celebration, Battle Anniversary Commemoration (Sept.), Schuyler House Candlelight Tour (mid-Oct.). Military encampments and demonstrations (occasionally). **Tips & Hints:** Plan to stay overnight in area to visit battlefield and other sites. Some land is privately owned; respect rights of landowners. Make lodging and dining reservations early if you plan to visit during Saratoga horse racing season (end of July and Aug.). Busiest July and Aug., least crowded in Dec. and Feb.

FOOD & LODGING

⊞ **Hotels:** None in park. In Saratoga Springs: Holiday Inn (232 Broadway, tel. 518/584–4550; 168 rooms; $280), Inn at Saratoga (231 Broadway, tel. 518/583–1890 or 800/274–3573; 38 rooms; $259–$309). ✕ **Restaurants:** None in park. In Saratoga Springs: Parting Glass (40–42 Lake Ave., tel. 518/583–1916; $6–$10). In Malta: Ripe Tomato (2721 U.S. 9, tel. 518/581–1530; $5–$10).

FEES & HOURS

Entrance fee: $5 per vehicle or $3 per bicyclist or walk-in for touring battlefield (May–Oct.). General Philip Schuyler House or Saratoga Monument free. Visitor center open daily 9–5. Tour road usually open Apr.–mid-Nov. Schuyler House open for guided tours mid-June–Labor Day. Saratoga Monument and Neilson House open mid-June–Labor Day, hours vary.

HOW TO GET THERE

40 mi north of Albany and 15 mi southeast of Saratoga Springs on U.S. 4/Rte. 32. From I–87 (Northway), take Exit 12 (if heading north) right

to Rte. 67, left onto U.S. 9, right onto Rte. 9P, right onto Rte. 423, left on Rte. 32, right to battlefield; or Exit 14 (if headed south). Head east on Rte. 29 and south on U.S. 4 or Rte. 32 to park. Closest airport: Albany (29 mi).

CONTACTS

Saratoga National Historical Park (648 Rte. 32, Stillwater, NY 12170, tel. 518/664–9821, fax 518/664–9830, www.nps.gov/sara). Saratoga County Tourism Department and Chamber of Commerce (28 Clinton St., Saratoga Springs, NY 12866, tel. 800/526–8970 or 518/584–3255, www.saratoga.org).

Statue of Liberty National Monument

In New York Harbor and off Jersey City shoreline

The 152-foot copper statue bearing the torch of freedom was a gift from the French people to the United States in 1886 to commemorate the alliance of the two nations during the American Revolution. Designed by Frederic Bartholdi, the statue symbolized freedom for the nearly 12 million immigrants who arrived at nearby Ellis Island between 1892 and 1954. The main building on Ellis Island is now a museum dedicated to the history of immigration. The statue was proclaimed a national monument in 1924, transferred to the Park Service in 1933, and designated a World Heritage Site in 1984. Ellis Island was incorporated into the national monument in 1965.

WHAT TO SEE & DO

Taking ferry to Liberty and Ellis islands, touring museums, watching Ellis Island documentary. **Facilities:** Statue, Ellis Island Main Building, museums, Ellis Island library and oral-history collection. **Programs & Events:** Ranger-led tours (when staffing permits at Ellis and Liberty Islands). **Tips & Hints:** You may have to wait in line an hour or more for the ferry to the islands. Drink plenty of fluids in summer. Dress warmly in winter. Arrive early for shorter lines. The statue interior was closed on September 11, 2001, after the attacks on the World Trade Center. In late 2003, the Statue of Liberty–Ellis Island Foundation, Inc. announced plans to reopen the statue after improving security there. At this writing, a date for the reopening has not been set. Busiest July and Aug., least crowded Jan. and Feb.

FOOD

✕ **Restaurants:** In the park: cafeterias on Liberty Island and Ellis Island.

FEES & HOURS

Free. Round-trip ferry fee (includes both islands): $10 adults, $8 ages 62 and over, $8 ages 3–12, free age 2 and under. Monument open Sept.–May, daily 9–5:30; Memorial Day–Aug., weekdays 8:30–6:15, weekends 8:30–8:30.

HOW TO GET THERE

Islands accessible by ferry only. Ferries (tel. 212/269–5755) leave Battery Park in lower Manhattan and Liberty State Park in Jersey City, NJ. Closest airports: JFK and LaGuardia (New York); Newark (New Jersey).

CONTACT

Statue of Liberty National Monument (Liberty Island, New York, NY 10004, tel. 212/363–3200, fax 212/363–8347, www.nps.gov/stli).The Statue of Liberty–Ellis Island Foundation, Inc. (292 Madison Ave., New York, NY 10017-7769, tel. 212/561–4500, www.ellisisland.org).

Theodore Roosevelt Birthplace National Historic Site

In New York City

Theodore Roosevelt, apostle of the strenuous life, larger-than-life hero to millions of Americans, and 26th president of the United States, was born in a brownstone house on this site on October 27, 1858. His family lived here until he was 13. The house was demolished in 1916, reconstructed in 1923, and furnished by the Women's Roosevelt Memorial Association with the assistance of the president's widow and sisters. The site was authorized on July 25, 1962.

WHAT TO SEE & DO

Touring house, viewing video and museum exhibits. **Facilities:** Five rooms furnished and decorated as they were during Roosevelt's occupancy, museum. Museum shop. **Programs & Events:** Ranger-led programs and tours (throughout the day). **Tips & Hints:** Use mass transit to get to house. Plan to spend an hour at the site. House tours last 30 minutes and start on the hour; last tour at 4. Busiest in Mar. and Apr., least crowded in July and Jan.

FEES & HOURS

Entrance fee: $3 adults, free ages 17 and under. House open Tues.–Sat. 9–5.

HOW TO GET THERE

The reconstructed house is in Manhattan at 28 E. 20th St., between Broadway and Park Ave. S. Use mass transit to get to house because parking is scarce. The 6 subway, which runs along Lexington Ave., stops at the E. 23rd St. station on Park Ave. S. The N and R subway trains stop at the E. 23rd St. station on Broadway. Frequent bus service is provided by routes M-6 and M-7 on Broadway, by route M-1 on Park Ave. S, and by route M-23 operating crosstown on 23rd St. Closest airports: JFK and LaGuardia (New York); Newark (New Jersey).

CONTACT

Theodore Roosevelt Birthplace National Historic Site (28 E. 20th St., New York, NY 10003, tel. 212/260–1616, fax 212/677–3587, www.nps. gov/thrb).

Theodore Roosevelt Inaugural National Historic Site

In Buffalo

Theodore Roosevelt was sworn in here on September 14, 1901, to become the 26th president of the United States after William McKinley was assassinated. The house, which was built in the 1830s as officers' quarters for the Buffalo Barracks, is an outstanding example of Greek Revival architecture. The site was designated in 1966 and opened in 1971.

WHAT TO SEE & DO

Touring house, gardens, and neighborhood; watching audiovisual program. **Facilities:** Visitor center, house, grounds. Gift shop, research library. **Programs & Events:** Guided house tours, self-guided architectural walking tours. Victorian Days Children's Program (July and Aug.), guided architectural and historical walking tours (May–Sept., reservations required, fee for architectural tours). Mother-Daughter Tea (Apr. or May), Teddy Bear Picnic (Aug.), Inaugural Commemoration (Sept.), Victorian Christmas (Dec.). **Tips & Hints:** Park in lot behind site on Franklin St. Visit May–Sept. for garden blooms, in Dec. for Victorian holiday decorations. Busiest July, Aug. and Dec., least crowded in Jan. and Feb.

FEES & HOURS

Entrance fee: $3 adults, $2 ages 62 and older, $1 ages 6–14; $6.50 per family. Architectural tours: $5 adults, $2.50 ages 6–14. Site open weekdays 9–5, weekends noon–5.

HOW TO GET THERE

1 mi north of downtown Buffalo at 641 Delaware Ave. Closest airport: Buffalo (5 mi).

CONTACTS

Theodore Roosevelt Inaugural National Historic Site (641 Delaware Ave., Buffalo, NY 14202, tel. 716/884–0095, fax 716/884–0330, www. nps.gov/thri). Buffalo Niagara Convention and Visitors Bureau (617 Main St., Suite 400, Buffalo, NY 14203, tel. 716/852–0511, fax 716/852–0131).

Vanderbilt Mansion
National Historic Site

In southeastern New York, in Hyde Park

Once the country home of Frederick W. Vanderbilt, a grandson of Cornelius Vanderbilt who amassed the family fortune, the Vanderbilt Mansion is a magnificent example of the great estates built by wealthy financial and industrial leaders between 1880 and 1900. The site was designated on December 18, 1940.

WHAT TO SEE & DO

Taking guided tours of home, taking self-guided tours of formal garden and grounds. **Facilities:** Visitor center, furnished home of Frederick Vanderbilt, grounds and gardens, trails. Bookstore, gift shop. **Programs & Events:** Ranger-led mansion tours, talks on lifestyle of the Vanderbilts and their contemporaries, industrial expansion, turn-of-the-20th-century technology, and landscape architecture. **Tips & Hints:** Allow one to two hours to see house and grounds and four to eight hours to fully explore the house, grounds, and trails. Busiest June–Aug., least crowded Jan. and Feb.

FOOD & LODGING

See Eleanor Roosevelt National Historic Site.

FEES & HOURS

Entrance fee: $8 adults, free ages 16 and under; $22 for combination pass to FDR site and either Eleanor Roosevelt National Historic Site (*see separate listing*) or Top Cottage tour (*see Home of Franklin D. Roosevelt National Historic Site*). Site open daily 9–5; grounds open daily 7 AM–sunset.

HOW TO GET THERE

Two hours north of New York City on the east bank of the Hudson River on U.S. 9, 8 mi north of Poughkeepsie. Closest airport: Newburgh (45 mi).

CONTACTS

Vanderbilt Mansion National Historic Site (4097 Albany Post Rd., Hyde Park, NY 12538, tel. 845/229–9115; 800/967–2283 reservations, fax 845/229–0739, www.nps.gov/vama). Dutchess County Tourism Promotion Agency (3 Neptune Rd., Suite M17, Poughkeepsie, NY 12601, tel. 800/445–3131 recorded information; 845/463–4000, www. dutchesstourism.com).

Women's Rights National Historical Park

In central New York, in Seneca Falls and Waterloo

Seneca Falls is the birthplace of the women's rights movement in the United States. Park sites include the Wesleyan Methodist Chapel, the site of the first Women's Rights Convention in 1848; the Elizabeth Cady Stanton house, home of one of the founders of the women's rights movement; the Hunt House, where the convention organizers first met; the M'Clintock House, where the "Declaration of Rights and Sentiments" was written; and other sites related to notable early women's rights activists. The park was authorized on December 28, 1980.

WHAT TO SEE & DO

Touring museum, historic buildings, district, and homes; watching movie. **Facilities:** Visitor center (136 Fall St.), Elizabeth Cady Stanton home, Women's Education and Cultural Center (116 Fall St.). Bookstore. **Programs & Events:** Wesleyan Chapel talks and Stanton House programs (daily). Ranger-guided programs at Wesleyan Chapel, Stanton House, M'Clintock House, and Suffrage Press Workshop (May–Sept., twice daily). Women's History Month (Mar.), Canalfest (June), Convention Days (3rd weekend, July), Elizabeth Cady Stanton's Birthday (Nov. 12). **Tips & Hints:** Busiest July and Aug., least crowded Jan. and Feb.

FOOD & LODGING

Camping: None in park. Near Seneca Falls: Cayuga Lake State Park (2678 Lower Lake Rd., tel. 315/568–5163; 800/456–2267 reservations; 286 sites; $13–$19; flush toilets, showers, hook-ups). **Hotels:** None in park. In Waterloo: Holiday Inn (2468 Rte. 414, tel. 315/539–5011; 148 rooms; $125–$159). In Seneca Falls: Microtel Inn & Suites (1966 Rte. 5/U.S. 20, tel. 315/539–8438; 48 rooms, 21 suites; $55–$76). **Restaurant:** None in park. In Waterloo: Abigail's Restaurant (Waterloo–Seneca Falls Rd., tel. 315/539–9300; $7; no lunch Sat.).

FEES, HOURS & REGULATIONS

Entrance fee (includes visitor center and movie): $3 adults, free ages 16 and under, $1 each for historic homes. Tickets available at visitor center and M'Clintock House (14 E. Williams St., Waterloo). No pets in visitor center. Park open daily 9–5.

HOW TO GET THERE

Park visitor center is at 136 Fall St. (Rte. 5/U.S. 20), which is reached via Exit 41 off New York State Thruway (I–90), then Rte. 414 for 4 mi and Rte. 5/U.S. 20 east for 2 mi. Closest airports: Syracuse (48 mi), Rochester (55 mi).

CONTACTS

Women's Rights National Historical Park (136 Fall St., Seneca Falls, NY 13148, tel. 315/568–2991, fax 315/568–2141, www.nps.gov/wori). Seneca County Tourism Department (1 DiPronio Dr., Seneca Falls, NY 13165, tel. 315/539–1752 or 800/732–1848, www.visitsenecany.net).

See Also

Appalachian National Scenic Trail, West Virginia. *Upper Delaware Scenic and Recreational River,* Pennsylvania. *Hudson River Valley National Heritage Area,* and *North Country National Scenic Trail,* in Other National Parklands.

Blue Ridge Parkway

The parkway follows the Blue Ridge and Southern Appalachian mountains for 469 mi through western Virginia and North Carolina

The parkway provides recreational opportunities and scenic overlooks and preserves remnants of Appalachian culture from the late 19th and early 20th centuries. With elevations ranging from 650 feet to nearly 6,050 feet, the parkway protects a wide variety of plant and animal life. Within the park are 1,200 identified types of vascular plants and more than two dozen rare or endangered plants and animals. Parkway construction began on September 11, 1935, with funding from the National Industrial Recovery Act. The parkway was established on June 30, 1936.

WHAT TO SEE & DO

Bicycling, camping, canoeing (rentals Julian Price Park, mile 295), driving, fishing, hiking, picnicking. **Facilities:** 469-mi-long parkway and 12 visitor centers: Humpback Rocks (mile 6), James River (mile 63), Peaks of Otter (mile 86), Blue Ridge at Explore Park (mile 115), Rocky Knob (mile 169), Cumberland Knob (mile 217), Moses H. Cone Memorial Park (mile 294), Linn Cove (mile 304), Linville Falls (mile 316), Museum of North Carolina Minerals (mile 331), Craggy Gardens (mile 364), and Waterrock Knob (mile 451). The Northwest Trading (mile 258) sells crafts and foods produced in the northwestern North Carolina mountains, and the Folk Art Center (mile 382) sells products from the Southern Highlands Craft Guild. Trails, wayside exhibits, bulletin boards. Gift shops, picnic facilities, sales outlets. **Programs & Events:** Ranger-led crafts demonstrations and/or interpretive talks at all major parkway locations (June–Oct.). Brinegar Days at Brinegar Cabin (mile 238; Aug.), Mountain Music at Mabry Mill (mile 176; May–Oct., Sun.) and Roanoke Mountain Campground (mile 120; June–Sept., Sun.), outdoor concerts (Blue Ridge Music Center, mile 213; June–Sept., weekly). **Tips & Hints:** Speed limit is 45 mph. Go during the week to avoid traffic. Go Apr.–May for wildflowers, mid-Oct. for fall leaf color. Winter weather can close sections for long periods. Get gas at Peaks of Otter (mile 86), Doughton Park (mile 241), Mount Pisgah (mile 408). Busiest July–Oct., least crowded Jan. and Feb.

FOOD & LODGING

Camping: 9 campgrounds ($14; flush toilets; closed late Oct.–Mar. or Apr.) in the park: Otter Creek (mile 60, tel. 434/299–5125; 69 sites), Peaks of Otter (mile 86, tel. 540/586–4357; 141 sites), Roanoke Mountain (mile 120, tel. 540/767–2492; 104 sites), Rocky Knob (mile

167, tel. 540/745–9660; 109 sites), Doughton Park (mile 239, tel. 336/372–8568; 135 sites), Price Park (mile 297, tel. 828/963–5911; 197 sites), Linville Falls (mile 316, tel. 828/765–7818; 70 sites), Crabtree Meadows (mile 339, tel. 828/675–0941; 93 sites), and Mount Pisgah (mile 408, tel. 828/465–8829; 140 sites). Backcountry camping allowed at Rocky Knob area at Rockcastle Gorge and Doughton Park area at Basin Cove (permit required, *see below*). 🏨 **Hotels:** In the park: Peaks of Otter (mile 86, tel. 540/586–1081; 63 rooms; $93), Rocky Knob Cabins (mile 174, tel. 540/593–3503; 7 cabins; $54), Bluffs Lodge (mile 241, tel. 336/372–4499; 23 rooms; $78; closed Nov.–early May), and Pisgah Inn (mile 409, tel. 828/235–8228; 51 rooms; $80–$90; closed Nov.–Mar.). In Asheville: Holiday Inn Sunspree Resort (1 Holiday Inn Dr., off I–240 at Exit 3B, tel. 828/254–3211; 272 rooms; $109–$179). In Brevard: Sunset Motel (415 S. Broad St., tel. 828/884–9106; 20 rooms; $40–$60). In Waynesville: Waynesville Country Club Inn (176 Country Club Dr., tel. 828/456–3551 or 800/627–6250; 103 rooms, 9 cottages; $88–$178). ✕ **Restaurants:** 4 restaurants (closed Oct.–May) in the park: Peaks of Otter (mile 86, tel. 540/586–1081; $5–$10), Bluffs Lodge & Coffee Shop (mile 241, tel. 336/372–4499; $3–$7), Crabtree Meadows (mile 339, tel. 828/675–4236; $3–$6), Pisgah Inn (mile 409, tel. 828/235–8228; $6–$10). In Pisgah Forest: Pisgah Fish Camp (141 U.S. 64 E, tel. 828/877–3129; $3–$9).

FEES, HOURS & REGULATIONS

Free. Backcountry permits required (free; available from Basin Cove, tel. 336/372–8568). Virginia or North Carolina state fishing license required. No hunting. Trails for foot travel only, except designated horse trails. Park open daily except in bad weather. All visitor centers open generally May–Oct., except Peaks of Otter, open year-round. Visitor centers open daily 9–5.

HOW TO GET THERE

Major cities along the Blue Ridge Pkwy are Waynesboro (U.S. 250 and I–64) and Roanoke (U.S. 220, U.S. 460, and I–81) in Virginia and Boone (U.S. 321 and U.S. 421), Asheville (I–40 and I–26, and U.S. 70, U.S. 74, and U.S. 23), and Waynesville (U.S. 19/23 and I–40) in North Carolina. Closest regional airports: Roanoke, VA; Asheville, NC.

CONTACTS

Blue Ridge Parkway (199 Hemphill Knob Rd., Asheville, NC 28803, tel. 828/298–0398 recorded information; 828/271–4779 for headquarters, www.nps.gov/blri). Greater Augusta Regional Chamber of Commerce (732 Tinkling Spring Rd., Fishersville, VA 22939, tel. 540/949–8203). Roanoke Valley Convention & Visitors Bureau, VA (114 Market St., Roanoke, VA 24011, tel. 540/342–6025 or 800/635–5535). Boone Convention & Visitors Bureau (208 Howard St., Boone, NC 28607, tel. 800/852–9506 or 828/264–2225).

Cape Hatteras National Seashore

On Outer Banks

The nation's first national seashore, Cape Hatteras preserves significant portions of North Carolina's famed barrier islands—Bodie, Hatteras, and Ocracoke. Cape Hatteras Light, the tallest brick lighthouse in the world, harks back to the days when this stretch of ocean was known as the "Graveyard of the Atlantic" because of its treacherous currents and offshore shoals. The park was authorized in 1937.

WHAT TO SEE & DO

Beach-going, bird-watching, boardsailing, fishing, hiking, hunting, surfing, swimming, touring lighthouses. **Facilities:** 3 visitor centers: Bodie Island (8 mi south of U.S. 158/U.S. 64 intersection), Hatteras Island (Buxton, 45 mi south of U.S. 158/U.S. 64 intersection), and Ocracoke Island. Contact station at Whalebone Junction (U.S. 158/U.S. 64 intersection, Nags Head), lighthouses and restored keepers' homes, nature trails, wayside exhibits. Book sale areas, changing and shower facilities, picnic areas. **Programs & Events:** Guided beach walks, nature trail hikes, ecology demonstrations, lighthouse tours, ranger-led recreational demonstrations, campfire programs (Apr.–mid-Oct.). **Tips & Hints:** Guided lighthouse tours by timed ticket entry only with no advance reservations. Arrive early to be sure to get tickets. Plan for a wait in summer for free 40-minute ferry from Hatteras to Ocracoke Island. Go Mar. and Apr., and Oct. and Nov. for bird migrations. Busiest July and Aug., least crowded Jan. and Feb.

FOOD, LODGING & SUPPLIES

Camping: 4 campgrounds ($18; flush toilets, cold showers) in the park: Cape Point (202 sites; closed Aug.–late May), Frisco (127 sites; closed mid-Oct.–mid-Apr.), Ocracoke (tel. 800/365–2267; 136 sites; closed mid-Oct.–mid-Apr.), Oregon Inlet (120 sites; closed mid-Oct.–mid-Apr.). **Hotel:** None in park. In Hatteras: Seaside Inn (57303 Monitor Trail, tel. 252/986–2700; 10 rooms; $105–$140). **Restaurants:** None in park. In Waves: Down Under (25920 Rte. 12, tel. 252/987–2277; $5–$15; closed Dec.–Mar.). In Frisco: Quarterdeck (Rte. 12, tel. 252/986–2425; $2–$22; no lunch Sat., closed late Nov.–mid-Mar.). **Groceries:** None in park. In Avon: Food Lion (685 Rte. 12, tel. 252/995–4488).

FEES, HOURS & REGULATIONS

Free. Lighthouse tours $4 adults, $2 ages 13 and under and 62 and over. North Carolina state and U.S. federal migratory bird-hunting licenses required. North Carolina saltwater fishing license required. Group camping permit required. Leashed pets only. No all-terrain vehicles. Access to some areas barred because of habitat–nesting and endangered species. Seashore open daily. Visitor centers open Sept.–May, daily 9–5; June–Aug., daily 9–6. Closed Dec. 25.

HOW TO GET THERE

Via U.S. 168–158 from the north, U.S. 64 from the west, and U.S. 70 and Cedar Island ferry from the south. Closest major airport: Norfolk, VA (85 mi).

CONTACTS

Cape Hatteras National Seashore (1401 National Park Dr., Manteo, NC 27954, tel. 252/473–2111; 800/365–2267 camping at Ocracoke; 919/473–2111, fax 252/473–2595, www.nps.gov/caha). Outer Banks Chamber of Commerce (Box 1757, 101 Town Hall Dr., Kill Devil Hills, NC 27948, tel. 252/441–8144, fax 252/441–0338, www.outerbankschamber. com). Outer Banks Visitors Bureau (1 Visitors Center Circle, Manteo, NC 27954, tel. 252/473–2138, www.outerbanks.org).

Cape Lookout National Seashore

In eastern North Carolina, near Morehead City

The 56-mi-long barrier islands of Cape Lookout National Seashore run from Ocracoke Inlet to Beaufort Inlet. They consist mostly of wide, bare beaches with low dunes, flat grasslands, and large expanses of salt marsh along the Core Sound. Attractions include the Cape Lookout lighthouse, historic Portsmouth Village, Shackleford horses, and two lifesaving stations. The seashore was authorized in 1966.

WHAT TO SEE & DO

Beachcombing, boating, fishing, shelling, swimming. **Facilities:** 3 visitor centers: Cape Lookout (Harkers Island), Keepers' Quarters, Portsmouth Village. Bookstores. **Programs & Events:** Lighthouse talks, walks, and Portsmouth Village programs (June–Aug.). **Tips & Hints:** Bring everything you'll need with you, including water, sunscreen, and insect repellent. Visit in spring and fall for best weather and fewer crowds. Busiest Aug. and Nov., least crowded Feb. and Mar.

FOOD, LODGING & SUPPLIES

Camping: In the park: backcountry camping available on Core Banks and Shackleford Banks (permit required, *see below*). **Hotels:** In the park: Alger Willis Fishing Camps (tel. 252/729–2791; 25 cabins; $65–$150; closed early Dec.–Apr.), Morris Marina Kabin Kamps (tel. 252/225–4261; 20 units; $100–$110; closed early Dec.–Mar.). In Ocracoke: Pony Island Motel (785 Irvin Garrish Hwy., tel. 252/928–4411; 50 rooms; $87–$150). **Restaurants:** None in park. At Harker's Island: Captain's Choice (977 Island Rd., tel. 252/728–7122; $5–$8; closed late Dec.–early Jan. and Mon.), Island Restaurant & Dairyland Grill (1243 Island Rd., tel. 252/728-2247; $1–$11; closed Sun.). **Groceries & Gear:** None in park. At Harker's Island: Eastards Variety Store (1344 Island Rd., tel. 252/728–7149), Best Supermarket/Billy's (1016 Island Rd., tel. 252/728–4393).

FEES, HOURS & REGULATIONS

Free. Public ferries $14 per person. Parking $10. Permit required (free) for backcountry camping. Park open daily. Cape Lookout Visitor Center open daily 8–4:30. Keepers' Quarters, Portsmouth visitor centers open Memorial Day–Labor Day, daily 9–5.

HOW TO GET THERE

21 mi from Beaufort, NC. From U.S. 70 east, take right on Rte. 1333 (Harkers Island Rd.) to Harkers Island. Ferry services and visitor center on Harkers Island. Closest airport: New Bern (45 mi).

CONTACTS

Cape Lookout National Seashore (131 Charles St., Harkers Island, NC 28531, tel. 252/728–2250, fax 252/728–2160, www.nps.gov/calo). Carteret County Tourism Development Authority (3409 Arendell St., Morehead City, NC 28557, tel. 252/726–8148 or 800/786–6962, www.sunnync.com).

Carl Sandburg Home National Historic Site

In western North Carolina, in Flat Rock

The site preserves Connemara, the 245-acre farm where Pulitzer Prize–winning author and poet Carl Sandburg (1878–1967) and his family lived the last 22 years of his life. The farm consists of a 22-room house, barns, sheds, rolling pastures, mountainside woods, trails, two small lakes, a trout pond, flower and vegetable gardens, and an orchard. The site was authorized on October 17, 1968.

WHAT TO SEE & DO

Bird-watching, hiking, picnicking, touring house and grounds. **Facilities:** Visitor information station, historic home, trails, outdoor amphitheater. Bookstore. **Programs & Events:** Guided house tours, self-guided walking tours of grounds, barn, and Chikaming goat herd. Ranger-led programs and walks (June–Aug. and Oct.), plays (late June–mid-Aug.), Poetry Celebration (Apr.), Sandburg Folk Music Festival (Memorial Day), Christmas at Connemara (Dec.). Book signings, special presentations by noted authors and historians (dates vary). **Tips & Hints:** Plan to spend at least two hours. Be prepared for rain. Temperatures are moderate. Weather is unpredictable in spring and fall. Busiest July and Oct., least crowded Jan. and Feb.

FOOD & LODGING

Hotel: None at site. In Flat Rock: Holiday Inn Express (111 Commercial Blvd., tel. 828/698–8899 or 800/465–4328; 66 rooms; $75–$95). **Restaurant:** None at site. In Flat Rock: Dean's Deli (2770 U.S. 25 S, tel. 828/692–5770; $3–$6).

FEES, HOURS & PERMITS

Guided house tour $3 adults, free ages 16 and under. Site open daily 9–5.

HOW TO GET THERE

Take U.S. 25 south for 5 mi from Hendersonville, turn on Little River Rd. at the Flat Rock Playhouse. From Asheville, take I–26 south for 26 mi to Upward Rd. exit and follow park signs. Closest airport: Asheville.

CONTACTS

Carl Sandburg Home National Historic Site (81 Carl Sandburg La., Flat Rock, NC 28731, tel. 828/693–4178, fax 828/693–4179, www.nps. gov/carl). Hendersonville Visitor Information Center (201 S. Main St., Hendersonville, NC 28792, tel. 828/693–9708, www. historichendersonville.org).

Fort Raleigh National Historic Site

On Roanoke Island in northeastern North Carolina.

One of the first British colonies in the New World is commemorated here. Sir Walter Raleigh established a community of about 250 colonists on the island in 1585. Hard winters, insufficient supplies, and hostile relations with the native people, however, led to the abandonment of the settlement by 1587. The fate of the settlers remains a mystery. The park includes a reconstruction of an earthen fort built by the British, plus Elizabethan Gardens. The outdoor symphonic drama, *The Lost Colony,* has been performed here since 1937. The park's mission was altered in 1990 to include the memorialization, by way of exhibits and special programs, of Native American culture, the American Civil War, the Freedman's Colony, and the activities of radio pioneer Reginald Fessenden. The site was designated on April 5, 1941.

WHAT TO SEE & DO

Attending outdoor drama, touring fort and gardens, walking trails, watching video. **Facilities:** Visitor center, restored earthen fort, Waterside Theater, trails, gardens. Gift shop. **Programs & Events:** Video, ranger-led interpretive programs and trail walks. *The Lost Colony* drama (mid-June–Aug., Mon.–Sat. nights; tel. 252/473–3414 or 800/488–5012). Virginia Dare birthday commemoration (Aug. 18). Dare was the first child born to English parents (1587) in the New World. **Tips & Hints:** Plan to spend two hours to view the exhibits and video, and to tour the grounds. Evening productions of *The Lost Colony* drama run 2½ hours. Bring insect repellent if you plan to attend outdoor drama. Busiest June and July, least crowded Dec. and Jan.

FOOD & LODGING

None at site. *See Cape Hatteras National Seashore.*

FEES & HOURS

Free. *The Lost Colony* drama ($16–$20 adults, $15 °ages 62 and over, $8 ages 11 and under). Site open June–Aug., daily 9–6; Sept.–May, daily 9–5.

HOW TO GET THERE

On Roanoke Island, off U.S. 64/264 and about 3 mi north of Manteo, 92 mi southeast of Norfolk, VA, and 197 mi east of Raleigh. Closest airport: Dare County Municipal Airport (2 mi).

CONTACTS

Fort Raleigh National Historic Site (c/o Cape Hatteras National Seashore, 1401 National Park Dr., Manteo, NC 27954, tel. 252/473–5772, fax 252/473–2595, www.nps.gov/fora, www.thelostcolony.org). *See Cape Hatteras National Seashore* for additional contacts.

Guilford Courthouse National Military Park

Midstate, in Greensboro

The battle fought here on March 15, 1781, was the largest, most hotly contested action of the Revolutionary War's climactic Southern Campaign. The loss of British soldiers at Guilford Courthouse foreshadowed the final American victory at Yorktown seven months later. The site includes 28 monuments, including the graves of two signatories of the Declaration of Independence. The park was established in 1917 and transferred to the Park Service in 1933.

WHAT TO SEE & DO

Auto touring (audio guide available, fee), bicycling, hiking, watching film and animated battle map program. **Facilities:** Visitor center with museum exhibits, battlefield, animated map program, 30-minute orientation film, 2¼-mi tour road, bike and foot trails, interpretive displays, monuments. Bookstore. **Programs & Events:** Self-guided audio tours, ranger-led programs. Battle Anniversary (Mar. 15). **Tips & Hints:** Busiest May and July, least crowded Dec. and Jan.

FEES, HOURS & REGULATIONS

Free. Leashed pets only. Bicycling only in bike lanes. No motorized or mechanized equipment or bicycles on walking trails. No climbing on cannons or monuments. Park and visitor center open daily 8:30–5.

HOW TO GET THERE

In northwest Greensboro, from U.S. 220 (Battleground Ave.), turn east on New Garden Rd. to reach entrance. Closest airport: Piedmont Triad International (6 mi).

CONTACTS

Guilford Courthouse National Military Park (2332 New Garden Rd., Greensboro, NC 27410-2355, tel. 336/288–1776, fax 336/282–2296, www.nps.gov/guco). Greensboro Convention & Visitor Bureau (317 S. Greene St., Greensboro, NC 27401, tel. 336/274–2282 or 800/344–2282).

Moores Creek National Battlefield

In southeastern North Carolina, near Currie

The 88-acre park commemorates the decisive American Revolution victory by 1,000 Patriots over 1,600 Loyalists at the Battle of Moores Creek Bridge on February 27, 1776. The battle ended British Royal Governor Josiah Martin's hopes of regaining control of the colony. This first decisive Patriot victory of the war raised morale for Patriots throughout the colonies. The Loyalist defeat ended British plans for an invasionary force to land in Brunswick, North Carolina. The colony of North Carolina voted to declare independence from the British on April 12, 1776. The site was established as a national military park in 1926, transferred to the Park Service in 1933, and redesignated in 1980.

WHAT TO SEE & DO

Bird- and wildlife watching, picnicking, touring battlefield by walking trails. **Facilities:** Visitor center, video, trails. Bookstore, grills, picnic areas, shelter, tables. **Programs & Events:** Talks, walks, and demonstrations (Memorial Day–Labor Day, weekends). Battle anniversary commemoration (last full weekend, Feb.), Colonial Day with living-history programs (2nd Sat., Apr.), Scots Heritage Day (1st Sat., June), "Celebrating the Constitution" (Sept. 17). **Tips & Hints:** Plan to spend an hour touring visitor center, exhibits, and trails, and watching video. Busiest May and June, least crowded Dec. and Jan.

FOOD, LODGING & SUPPLIES

Hotels: None in park. In Wilmington: Best Western (2916 Market St., tel. 910/763–4653; 61 rooms; $79–$89), Hampton Inn and Suites–Landfall Park (1989 Eastwood Rd., tel. 910/256–9600; 90 rooms, 30 suites; $94–$129). **Restaurants:** None in park. In Wilmington: Annabelle's Restaurant & Pub (4106 Oleander Dr., tel. 910/791–4955; $8–$10), Rucker Johns (5511 Carolina Beach Rd., tel. 910/452–1212; $4–$7). **Groceries:** None in park. In Currie: Quick Stop (5703 Blueberry Rd., tel. 910/283–5674).

FEES & HOURS

Free. Site open daily 9–5.

HOW TO GET THERE

20 mi northwest of Wilmington via U.S. 421 and Rte. 210. From I–40, take Rte. 210 west for 15 mi to park. Closest airport: New Hanover International (25 mi).

CONTACTS

Moores Creek National Battlefield (40 Patriots Hall Dr., Currie, NC 28435, tel. 910/283–5591, fax 910/283–5351, www.nps.gov/mocr). Cape Fear Coast Convention & Visitors Bureau (24 N. 3rd St., Wilmington, NC 28401, tel. 910/341–4030).

Wright Brothers National Memorial

In Kill Devil Hills on Outer Banks

The first successful, sustained, controlled, powered flights in a heavier-than-air machine were made here by Wilbur and Orville Wright on December 17, 1903. The site includes a 60-foot-tall granite monument perched atop 90-foot-tall Kill Devil Hill, reconstructed living quarters and hangar, the first flight trail area, and a Centennial Pavilion. The site was authorized in 1927, transferred to the Park Service in 1933, and renamed in 1953.

WHAT TO SEE & DO

Air touring, touring visitor center, Centennial Pavilion, reconstructed living quarters and hangar building, viewing reproduction of Wright flyer and glider, walking first-flight grounds to monument. **Facilities:** Visitor center, Centennial Pavilion, wayside exhibits, monument. Bookstore. **Programs & Events:** Ranger talks (daily at 10, 11, noon, 2, 3, and 4). Ranger-led interpretive children's programs on kite building, flying objects, plane takeoffs, paper airplanes, and first-flight tours (mid-June–Aug.). First Flight Anniversary Celebration (Dec. 17), National Aviation Day and Orville Wright's Birthday (Aug. 19). **Tips & Hints:** Allow 1–2 hours to visit site. Watch for cacti and sandspurs. Stay on walkway. Busiest July and Aug., least crowded Jan. and Feb.

FOOD, LODGING & SUPPLIES

Camping: None at site. In Kill Devil Hills: Colington Park (1608 Colington Rd., tel. 252/441–6128; 150 sites; $25; flush toilets, showers, hook-ups). **Hotel:** None at site. In Kill Devil Hills: Quality Inn (2009 S. Virginia Dare Trail, tel. 252/441–7141; 107 rooms; $130–$230). **Groceries:** None at site. In Kill Devil Hills: Food Lion (1720 N. Croatan Hwy., tel. 252/480–1016).

FEES, HOURS & REGULATIONS

Entrance fee: $3 adults, free ages 16 and under; $4 per vehicle, free per person age 16 and under. Leashed pets only. No motorized vehicles or skateboards on trails. Airstrip daylight use only. 24-hour parking limit for planes. Park and visitor center open Labor Day–mid-June, daily 9–5; mid-June–Labor Day, daily 9–6.

HOW TO GET THERE

At mile 7.5 on U.S. 158. Closest airports: at Memorial; Dare County in Manteo (18 mi); Norfolk, VA (77 mi).

CONTACTS

Wright Brothers National Memorial (c/o Cape Hatteras National Seashore, 1401 National Park Dr., Manteo, NC 27954, tel. 252/441–7430, fax 252/441–7730, www.nps.gov/wrbr). *See Cape Hatteras National Seashore* for additional contacts.

See Also

Appalachian National Scenic Trail, West Virginia. *Great Smoky Mountains National Park,* Tennessee. *Overmountain Victory National Historic Trail* and *Trail of Tears National Historic Trail,* in Other National Parklands.

Fort Union Trading Post National Historic Site

In northwestern North Dakota, near Williston

The park is a reconstruction of the most significant fur-trading post on the upper Missouri River. John Jacob Astor's American Fur Company built Fort Union in 1828. In its heyday, the post employed up to 100 people to trade beaver furs and buffalo robes. In 1867, the fort was dismantled by the Army for materials to expand nearby Fort Buford. The site was authorized in 1966.

WHAT TO SEE & DO

Touring the fort, picnicking. **Facilities:** Visitor center, fort, wayside exhibits. Book sales area, picnic area, Trade House with reproduction trade goods for sale. **Programs & Events:** Ranger-guided tours (mid-May–mid-Sept. on request). Rendezvous (3rd weekend, June), Indian Arts Showcase (mid-Aug.), Living History Weekend (Labor Day), Winter Camp (Dec.). **Tips & Hints:** Busiest June and July, least crowded Dec. and Jan.

FOOD & LODGING

Camping: None at site. Nearby: Fort Buford State Historic Site (Rte. 23, 25 mi south of Williston, tel. 701/572–9034; 12 primitive sites; free; flush toilets; closed mid-Sept.–mid-May). **Hotel:** None at site. In Williston: El Rancho Motor Hotel (1623 2nd Ave. W, tel. 701/572–6321 or 800/433–8529; 92 rooms; $52). **Restaurant:** None at site. In Williston: Dakota Farms Family Restaurant (1906 2nd Ave. W, tel. 701/572–4480, $8–$15).

FEES, HOURS & REGULATIONS

Free. No hunting. Leashed pets only. Park and visitor center open Memorial Day–Labor Day, daily 8–8; Labor Day–Memorial Day, daily 9–5:30.

HOW TO GET THERE

On Rte. 1804, 25 mi southwest of Williston. Closest airport: Williston.

CONTACTS

Fort Union Trading Post National Historic Site (15550 Rte. 1804, Williston, ND 58801, tel. 701/572–9083, fax 701/572–7321, www.nps.gov/fous). Williston Area Chamber of Commerce (10 Main St., Williston, ND 58801, tel. 701/577–6000, www.willistonchamber.net).

Knife River Indian Villages National Historic Site

Midstate, near Stanton

Remnants of historic and prehistoric Native American villages are preserved at this 1,759-acre site, which was last occupied in 1845 by the Hidatsa and Mandan. An array of artifacts of the Plains Native American culture and a full-scale furnished earth lodge are on exhibit. The area also was the home of Sacagawea, who accompanied Lewis and Clark on their expedition to the Northwest. The site was authorized in 1974.

WHAT TO SEE & DO

Bird-watching, canoeing, cross-country skiing, fishing, hiking, picnicking, touring the site. **Facilities:** Visitor center, museum, trails, interpretive panels. Bookstore, picnic tables. **Programs & Events:** Guided tours of earth lodge (Memorial Day–Labor Day). Northern Plains Indian Culture Fest (last full weekend, July). **Tips & Hints:** Visit June–Aug. for programs. Busiest June–Aug., least crowded Nov. and Dec. Park is on Mountain Time.

FOOD, LODGING & SUPPLIES

Camping: None in park. In Lake Sakakawea State Park (Rte. 200, 1 mi north of Park City, tel. 701/487–3315 or 800/ 807–4723): Elbowoods (38 sites; $14; flush toilets, showers, hook-ups), Sanish (100 sites; $14; flush toilets, showers, hook-ups), Van Hook (30 primitive sites; $7; pit toilets). **Hotels:** None in park. In Stanton: Missouri River Lodge (140 42nd Ave. NW, tel. 701/748–2023; 7 rooms; $60–$85). In Hazen: Roughrider Motor Inn (Rte. 200, tel. 701/748-2209; 60 rooms; $44–$48). **Restaurants:** None in park. In Stanton: Glo's Kitchen (Rte. 31, tel. 701/745–3535; $6), Sweet Violets (Harmon Ave., tel. 701/745–3600; $5–$6; closed Sept.–Apr.). **Groceries & Gear:** None in park. In Stanton: Stanton Super Mart (418 Harmon Ave., tel. 701/745–3282).

FEES, HOURS & REGULATIONS

Free. North Dakota fishing license required. Leashed pets only on trails. No hunting. No mountain bikes, trail bikes, motorized or mechanized equipment on trails. Earth lodge unfurnished Nov.–Mar. Trails open daily 6 AM–10 PM. Park and visitor center open Labor Day–Memorial Day, daily 8–4:30; Memorial Day–Labor Day, daily 7:30–6.

HOW TO GET THERE

Rte. 37, ½ mi north of Stanton. Closest airport: Bismarck (50 mi).

CONTACTS

Knife River Indian Villages National Historic Site (Box 9, Stanton, ND 58571, tel. 701/745–3300, fax 701/745–3708, www.nps.gov/knri). Hazen Chamber of Commerce (146 E. Main St., Hazen, ND 58545, tel. 701/748–6848).

Theodore Roosevelt National Park

In western North Dakota, near Medora (South Unit) and Watford City (North Unit)

Theodore Roosevelt first came to Dakota Territory in September 1883 to hunt bison. Before returning home to New York, he became interested in the cattle business and established the Maltese Cross Ranch partnership. The next year he returned to the badlands and started a second open-range ranch, the Elkhorn. Roosevelt witnessed the decline in wildlife and saw the grasslands destroyed because of overgrazing. He became an avid conservationist and eventually established the U.S. Forest Service. In his lifetime, Roosevelt signed into law five national parks, 150 national forests, 51 bird reserves, and four game preserves, totaling about 360,000 square mi of protected land. Today the colorful North Dakota badlands provide the scenic backdrop to the park that memorializes the 26th president for his enduring contributions to the conservation of our nation's resources. The Little Missouri River winds through the 70,447-acre park, which was established as a memorial park in 1947 and became a national park in 1978.

WHAT TO SEE & DO

Auto touring, bird-watching, canoeing, hiking, horseback riding, picnicking, skiing, touring Maltese Cross Cabin, viewing wildlife. **Facilities:** 3 visitor centers: Medora (South Unit entrance), Painted Canyon (7 mi east of Medora on I–94), and North Unit (near entrance); Maltese Cross Cabin, wayside exhibits, trails, scenic drives. Book and map sales, picnic sites with fire grates. **Programs & Events:** Orientation films. Talks, evening campfire programs, nature walks and hikes, cultural demonstrations (June–mid-Sept.); tours of Maltese Cross Cabin (mid-June–early Sept.). Guided ski tours, winter walks (occasionally). **Tips & Hints:** Be prepared for variable weather in summer. Go May–Sept. for the best weather. Busiest July and Aug., least crowded Dec. and Jan.

FOOD, LODGING & SUPPLIES

Camping: 2 campgrounds in the park: Cottonwood (South Unit; 76 sites; $10; flush toilets), Juniper (North Unit; 50 sites; $10; flush toilets). In Medora: Medora Campground (195 3rd Ave., off Pacific Ave., tel. 701/623–4435; 191 sites; $16–$26; flush toilets, showers, hook-ups; closed Labor Day–Memorial Day), Red Trail Campgrounds (250 E. River Rd. S, off Pacific Ave., tel. 701/623–4317; 104 sites; $14–$24; flush toilets, showers, hook-ups; closed Sept.–Apr.). **Hotels:** None in park. In Medora: AmericInn Motel & Suites (75 E. River Rd. S, tel. 701/623–4800 or 800/634–3444; 56 rooms, 8 suites; $150–$196). In Watford City: Roosevelt Inn & Suites (600 2nd Ave. SW, tel. 701/842–3686; 42 rooms; $48–$51). **Restaurants:** None in park. In Medora: Chuck Wagon Buffet (3rd Ave. and Main St., tel. 701/623–4444; $7–$8; closed Oct.–Apr.), Little Missouri Saloon & Dining (440 3rd St., tel. 701/623–4404; $5–$7; closed Oct.–Mother's Day), Rough Rider Hotel Dining Room (301 3rd Ave., at Main St., tel. 701/623–4444; $7–$20;

closed Sun. and Labor Day–Memorial Day). ♿ **Groceries & Gear:** None in park. In Medora: Medora Convenience Store (220 Pacific Ave., tel. 701/623–4479).

FEES, HOURS & REGULATIONS

Entrance fee: $5 per person or $10 per vehicle. Backcountry permits (free) required for all backcountry camping. No hunting. No pets on trails or in backcountry. Leashed pets elsewhere. No bikes on trails. No horses in campground or on nature trails. Weed-free horse feed required. Park open daily. Scenic drives sometimes closed in winter. Medora Visitor Center open Labor Day–mid-June, daily 8–4:30 Mountain Time; mid-June–Labor Day, daily 8–8 Mountain Time. Painted Canyon Visitor Center open Apr.–mid-June and Labor Day–mid-Nov., daily 8:30–4:30 Mountain Time; mid-June–Labor Day, daily 8–6 Mountain Time. North Unit Visitor Center open Memorial Day–Sept., daily 9–5:30 Central Time; Oct.–Memorial Day, weekends 9–5:30 Central Time.

HOW TO GET THERE

South Unit: 1 mi north of Medora, off I–94. North Unit: 15 mi south of Watford City via U.S. 85. Closest airports: Dickinson (35 mi from Medora); Williston (60 mi from North Unit); Bismarck (167 mi from North Unit, 133 mi from South Unit).

CONTACTS

Theodore Roosevelt National Park (Box 7, Medora, ND 58645, tel. 701/623–4466 South Unit; tel. 701/842–2333 North Unit, fax 701/623–4840, www.nps.gov/thro). Medora Information (475 4th St., Medora, ND 58645, tel. 701/623–4829). Dickinson Convention & Visitors Bureau (72 E. Museum Dr., Dickinson, ND 58601, tel. 701/483–4988 or 800/279–7391). McKenzie County Tourism Bureau (Box 699, Watford City, ND 58854, tel. 701/842–2804 or 800/701–2804).

See Also

International Peace Garden, Lewis & Clark National Historic Trail, and *North Country National Scenic Trail,* in Other National Parklands.

OHIO

Cuyahoga Valley National Park

In northeastern Ohio, between Cleveland and Akron

The area preserves 33,000 acres of pastoral valley along 22 mi of the Cuyahoga River. It includes the river and its floodplain, steep and gentle valley walls forested by deciduous and evergreen woods, and numerous tributaries and their ravines. The area was authorized as a national recreation area on December 27, 1974, established on June 26, 1975, and redesignated as a national park on October 11, 2000.

WHAT TO SEE & DO

Attending performing arts and cultural and natural-history programs, bicycling (rentals), cross-country skiing (rentals), hiking, snowshoeing (rentals). **Facilities:** 6 visitor centers: Canal (Valley View), Happy Days (Rte. 303), Hunt Farm (Bolanz Rd. near Towpath Trail), Boston Store with canal boatbuilding museum (Boston), Frazee House with early settlement exhibits (Canal Rd.), Peninsula Depot with area orientation exhibits (Cuyahoga Valley Scenic Railroad); trails. Book-and-gift shops, meeting rooms, picnic shelters. **Programs & Events:** Interpretive programs year-round. Lecture series (Jan.–Mar., Fri. evenings); costumed Lock 38 demonstrations (Canal Visitor Center, Memorial Day–Labor Day, weekends. **Tips & Hints:** Busiest June–Aug. and Oct., least crowded Dec.–Feb.

LODGING

☎ **Hotels:** In the park: Inn at Brandywine Falls (8230 Brandywine Rd., Sagamore Hills, tel. 330/467–1812 or 888/306–3381; 3 rooms, 3 suites; $119–$150), Stanford Youth Hostel (tel. 330/467–8711; 30 dorm beds, 1 private room; $16.15 per person; closed Tues. and Wed. from Jan. to Mar.).

FEES, HOURS & REGULATIONS

Free. Some interpretive programs, picnic shelters, and meeting rooms have fees. Leashed pets only. No hunting. Bikes on designated trails only. Park open daily. Some areas close at dusk. Canal Visitor Center open daily 10–4. Happy Days Visitor Center, Peninsula Depot, Boston Store, Frazee House, and Hunt Farm Visitor Information Center hours all vary seasonally.

HOW TO GET THERE

The park is east of I–77, between Cleveland and Akron. Closest airports: Cleveland (15 mi), Akron (20 mi).

CONTACTS

Cuyahoga Valley National Park (15610 Vaughn Rd., Brecksville, OH 44141, tel. 216/524–1497, fax 440/546–5905, www.nps.gov/cuva). Ohio

Office of Travel & Tourism (77 S. High St., Box 1001, Columbus, OH 43216, tel. 800/282–5393).

Dayton Aviation Heritage National Historical Park

In western Ohio, in Dayton

The park preserves sites associated with Wilbur and Orville Wright and the early development of aviation. It also honors the life and work of African-American poet Paul Laurence Dunbar. The park, a cooperative effort between the National Park Service and three partners, includes four sites: Huffman Prairie Flying Field; the Wright-Dunbar Interpretive Center & Aviation Trail Visitor Center; the Wright Cycle Company Complex, which includes the Wright brothers' print shop building; the 1905 *Wright Flyer III* (in Carillon Historical Park); and the Paul Laurence Dunbar House State Memorial. The park was authorized on October 16, 1992.

WHAT TO SEE & DO

Touring four sites. **Facilities:** 2 visitor centers: Huffman Prairie Flying Field Interpretive Center and the Wright Cycle Company Complex, museum, exhibits at Paul Laurence Dunbar State Memorial, and Carillon Historical Park. Bookstores. **Programs & Events:** Interpretive talks on aviation, early transportation history, African-American lifestyles, and accomplishments of Paul Laurence Dunbar and Wilbur and Orville Wright. **Tips & Hints:** Plan to spend at least 45 minutes touring the Wright Cycle Company Complex, an hour at the Paul Laurence Dunbar State Memorial, an hour at the Huffman Prairie Flying Field, and 30 minutes at Wright Hall in Carillon Historical Park. Exploring all of Carillon Historical Park takes 2–3 hours. Travel time between park units can take 20–30 minutes. Busiest June and July, least crowded Jan. and Feb.

FEES &HOURS

Entrance fees: The Wright Cycle Company Complex, and the Huffman Prairie Flying Field are free. Paul Laurence Dunbar State Memorial $5 adults, $2 ages 6–12 and members; free ages 5 and under. Wright Hall–Carillon Historical Park $5 adults, $4 ages 60 and older, $3 ages 3–17, free for members and ages 2 and under. Huffman Prairie visitor center open daily 8:30–5:30. Wright Cycle Company Complex open daily 8:30–5. Paul Laurence Dunbar State Memorial open Memorial Day–Labor Day, Wed.–Sat. 9:30–4:30, Sun. and holidays noon–4:30; Labor Day–Oct., Sat. 9:30–4:30, Sun. 12:30–4:30; Nov.–Memorial Day, weekdays 9:30–4:30. Huffman Prairie Flying Field open Tues.–Sat., sunrise–sunset, when the Wright-Patterson Air Force Base is open. Wright Hall–Carillon Historical Park open Apr.–Oct., Tues.–Sat. 9:30–5, Sun. and holidays noon–5.

HOW TO GET THERE

To reach the Wright Cycle Company Complex, exit I–75 at 3rd St. in downtown Dayton. Cross the Miami River and turn left at the third stoplight on west side of river on S. Williams St. The building is on the left. From I–70 or U.S. 35, exit onto I–75 and follow above directions. Closest airport: Dayton (10 mi).

CONTACTS

Dayton Aviation Heritage National Historical Park (22 S. Williams St., Box 9280, Wright Brothers Station, Dayton, OH 45409, tel. 937/225–7705, fax 937/222–4512, www.nps.gov/daav). Paul Laurence Dunbar State Memorial (tel. 937/224–7061). Carillon Historical Park (tel. 937/293–2841). Huffman Prairie Flying Field (tel. 937/425–0008). Greene County Convention & Visitors Bureau (1221 Meadowbridge Dr., Suite A, Beaver Creek, OH 45434, tel. 937/429–9100). Dayton-Montgomery County Convention & Visitors Bureau (1 Chamber Plaza, Suite A, Dayton, OH 45402, tel. 937/226–8211 or 800/221–8235).

First Ladies National Historic Site

In Canton, in northeastern Ohio

Two properties, the home of First Lady Ida Saxton McKinley and the City National Bank Building, are preserved in this park, which commemorates the role of first lady in American history. The site, managed in cooperation with the National First Ladies' Library, was authorized on October 11, 2000.

WHAT TO SEE & DO

Touring house and library. **Facilities:** Saxton McKinley House (331 Market Ave. S), City National Bank Building (205 Market Ave. S). **Tips & Hints:** At this writing, the City National Bank Building is closed for renovations.

FEES & HOURS

Saxton-McKinley House open for guided tours ($7 per person) only; reservations required.

HOW TO GET THERE

Take I–77 to the Tuscarawas St. exit. Drive east to the corner of Market Ave. and 4th St. Nearest airport: Akron-Canton Regional Airport.

CONTACTS

First Ladies National Historic Site (331 Market Ave. S, Canton, OH 44702, tel. 330/452–0876, fax 330/456–3414, www.nps.gov/fila).

Hopewell Culture
National Historical Park

In south-central Ohio, near Chillicothe

Archaeological remnants of earthwork and mound complexes built by the Hopewell, who inhabited the Ohio River valley between 200 BC and AD 500, are preserved in this park. The Mound City Group, a 13-acre rectangular earth enclosure with at least 23 mounds, provides insight into the social, ceremonial, political, and economic life of the Hopewell people. The site was proclaimed the Mound City Group National Monument in 1923 and renamed in 1992.

WHAT TO SEE & DO

Touring earthworks, picnicking. **Facilities:** Visitor center, interactive computer program with in-depth cultural and archaeological information, museum, trails, video. Book sales area, picnic area. **Programs & Events:** Crafts demonstrations, nature and archaeology walks. Ranger-guided tours (Memorial Day–Labor Day, daily). National Parks week (3rd week, May), Ohio Archaeology week (3rd. week, June). **Tips & Hints:** Busiest July and Aug., least crowded Dec. and Jan.

FEES, HOURS & REGULATIONS

Entrance fee: $3 adults, free ages 16 and younger, $5 per vehicle. Leashed pets only. No bicycles on trails. Park open daily sunrise–sunset. Visitor center open Sept.–May, daily 8:30–5; June–Aug., daily 8:30–6.

HOW TO GET THERE

3 mi north of Chillicothe on Rte. 104. Closest airport: Columbus (50 mi).

CONTACTS

Hopewell Culture National Historical Park (16062 Rte. 104, Chillicothe, OH 45601, tel. 740/774–1125, fax 740/774–1140, www.nps.gov/hocu). Ross–Chillicothe Convention & Visitors Bureau (Box 353, Chillicothe, OH 45601, tel. 740/702–7677 or 800/413–4118).

James A. Garfield
National Historic Site

In northeast Ohio, in Mentor

#The Victorian-era home of the 20th president of the United States is preserved at this site. The estate, called Lawnfield, was where Garfield was shot less than seven months after becoming president. The site was authorized in 1980.

WHAT TO SEE & DO

Touring visitor center (a restored carriage barn), home, and grounds of Lawnfield; viewing interpretive displays and artifacts. **Facilities:** Visitor center, family home, grounds, wayside exhibits, video. Gift shop. **Programs & Events:** Interpretive talks, lectures, and home tours. **Tips & Hints:** Busiest July and Aug., least crowded Jan. and Feb.

FEES & HOURS

Free. Guided tours of home: $7 adults, $6 ages 60 and older, $5 ages 6–12, free ages 5 and under. National Park pass holders $4. AAA members receive $1 discount off list price for tours. Park and visitor center open May–Oct., Mon.–Sat. 10–5, Sun. noon–5, Nov.–Apr., Sat. 10–5 and Sun. noon–5. Last tour of home at 4:15 PM.

HOW TO GET THERE

25 mi east of Cleveland, off I–90 on Mentor Ave. (U.S. 20). Closest airport: Cleveland–Hopkins International (35 mi).

CONTACTS

James A. Garfield National Historic Site (8095 Mentor Ave., Mentor, OH 44060, tel. 440/255–8722, fax 440/255–8545, www.nps.gov/jaga or www.wrhs.org). Lake County Visitors Bureau (35300 Vine St., Suite A, Eastlake, OH 44095, tel. 800/368–5253 or 440/975–1234). Mentor Area Chamber of Commerce (7547 Mentor Ave., Suite 302, Mentor OH 44060, tel. 440/946–2625).

Perry's Victory & International Peace Memorial

On South Bass Island in Lake Erie

The memorial column that rises 352 feet above Lake Erie commemorates war and peace. Oliver Hazard Perry's victory over a British fleet in the Battle of Lake Erie served as a turning point in the War of 1812. The monument was built between 1912 and 1915, established as a national monument in 1936, and redesignated in 1972.

WHAT TO SEE & DO

Fishing, kite flying, sunbathing, touring memorial, rotunda, and observation deck. **Facilities:** Visitor center, interpretive exhibits, video. Bookstore. **Programs & Events:** Ranger talks (mid-June–Aug.), costumed presentations and musket firings (mid-June–Aug.). Battle Anniversary (weekend after Labor Day), concerts, and ceremonies. **Tips & Hints:** Plan to spend two hours visiting the memorial. In summer, expect to wait in line for the elevator to the observation deck. Spring in Lake Erie is cool and windy into June. Busiest July and Aug., least crowded Dec.–Mar.

FOOD, LODGING & SUPPLIES

⚠ **Camping:** None at memorial. In Put-in-Bay: South Bass Island State Park (Box 326, tel. 419/285–2112; 135 sites, 10 with hook-ups; $22–$27; flush toilets, showers). 🏨 **Hotels:** None at memorial. In Put-in-Bay: Park Hotel (234 Delaware Ave., tel. 419/285–3581; 25 rooms;

$116; closed Nov.–Apr.). ✗ **Restaurant:** None at memorial. In Put-in-Bay: The Boardwalk (Bay View Ave., tel. 419/285–3695; $6–$25; closed Oct.–Apr.). ♿ **Groceries:** None at memorial. In Put-in-Bay: Press House Corner Market (1400 Catawba Ave., tel. 419/285–2716).

FEES & HOURS

Entrance fee: $3 adults, free ages 16 and under. Memorial open late Apr.–mid-May and Sept.–mid-Oct., daily 10–5; mid-May–mid-June and Sept., daily 10–6; mid-June–Aug., daily 10–7; mid-Oct.–late Apr., by appointment.

HOW TO GET THERE

On South Bass Island in the village of Put-in-Bay. Access to the island by boat or plane only. Miller Boat Line (no reservations, tel. 800/500–2421) provides ferry service Mar.–Nov. from Catawba Point, near Port Clinton. Put-in-Bay Boat Lines–Jet Express (tel. 800/245–1538) provides ferry service seasonally from Port Clinton to Put-in-Bay. Closest airports: Cleveland (85 mi), Toledo, OH (50 mi); and Detroit, MI (75 mi).

CONTACTS

Perry's Victory and International Peace Memorial (93 Delaware Ave., Box 549, Put-in-Bay, OH 43456, tel. 419/285–2184, fax 419/285–2516, www.nps.gov/pevi). Put-in-Bay Chamber of Commerce (Box 250, Put-in-Bay, OH 43456, tel. 419/285–2832, www.put-in-bay.com).

William Howard Taft National Historic Site

In Cincinnati

William Howard Taft is the only person in U.S. history to have served as both president (1909–13) and Chief Justice of the United States (1921–30). He was born and raised in this 1840s Greek Revival–style home. Four furnished rooms have been restored to depict the lifestyle of Taft and his family during the 1860s. The site was authorized on December 2, 1969.

WHAT TO SEE & DO

Taking ranger-guided and self-guided tours of home. **Facilities:** Home, Taft Education Center with interactive displays, orientation film. Bookstore, gift shop. **Programs & Events:** Year-round: ranger-guided and self-guided tours. New Year's Open House (Jan.), Constitution Day and Taft's Birthday (Sept.), Father Christmas (Dec.), Christmas Decoration Workshop (Dec.). **Tips & Hints:** Busiest Apr. and May, least crowded Nov. and Jan.

FEES, HOURS & REGULATIONS

Free. No smoking, pets, food, or drink in house. House open daily 8–4.

HOW TO GET THERE

The Taft House is at 2038 Auburn Ave., in the Mount Auburn section of Cincinnati. From I–71 north, take Exit 2 (Reading Rd.). Make a left onto Dorchester St. Turn right on Auburn and drive 1½ blocks to the home. From I–71 south, take Exit 3 (Taft Rd.) to Auburn Ave. Turn left to home. Closest airport: Greater Cincinnati International (10 mi).

CONTACTS

William Howard Taft National Historic Site (2038 Auburn Ave., Cincinnati, OH 45219, tel. 513/684–3262, fax 513/684–3627, www.nps.gov/wiho). Cincinnati Convention & Visitors Bureau (300 W. 6th St., Cincinnati, OH 45202, tel. 513/621–2142).

See Also

David Berger National Memorial, North Country National Scenic Trail, and *Ohio & Erie Canal National Heritage Corridors,* in Other National Parklands.

OKLAHOMA

Chickasaw National Recreation Area

In south-central Oklahoma, near Sulphur

This recreation area was named in honor of the Chickasaw, the land's longtime inhabitants. Numerous springs, streams, and lakes attract nature lovers and adventure seekers from all over the state. Sulphur Springs Reservation was authorized in 1902, renamed and redesignated Platt National Park in 1906, combined with Arbuckle National Recreation Area, and renamed and redesignated in 1976.

WHAT TO SEE & DO

Auto touring, boating (permit required, *see below*), fishing, hiking, hunting, picnicking, swimming, watching film, waterskiing. **Facilities:** Information and nature center with live exhibits, 20 mi of trails, scenic roads. Bookstore, picnic pavilions (reservations required). New visitor expected to open late 2004. **Programs & Events:** Ranger-led nature walks, campfire programs (weekends). Creek Walks (Memorial Day–Labor Day), Bald Eagle Watch (Jan. and Feb.), Historic Candlelight Tour (late Nov. or early Dec.). **Tips & Hints:** Busiest June and July, least crowded Jan. and Feb.

FOOD, LODGING & SUPPLIES

Camping: 5 campgrounds in the park: Buckhorn (135 sites; $8–$14; flush toilets, showers, hook-ups), Cold Springs (63 sites; $8–$14; flush toilets; closed early Oct.–early May), Guy Sandy (40 sites; $8; portable toilets; closed Sept.–Apr.), Rock Creek (106 sites; flush toilets), the Point (55 sites; $8–$14; flush toilets, showers). **Hotels:** None in park. In Sulphur: Chickasaw Lodge & Artesian Restaurant (W. 1st St., tel. 580/622–2156; 68 rooms; $45). **Restaurants:** None in park. In Sulphur: The Bricks (2118 W. Broadway, tel. 580/622—3125; $4–$6). **Groceries:** None in park. In Sulphur: Sooner Foods (815 W. Broadway, tel. 580/622–3656).

FEES, HOURS & REGULATIONS

Free. Boat launching permit ($4 per day) required. Picnic pavilion reservation fee ($30). Boat launch and camping fees taken through automated machines; cash and credit cards accepted. Park open daily. Travertine Information and Nature Center open daily 8–5.

HOW TO GET THERE

On U.S. 177, south of Sulphur, 90 mi south of Oklahoma City, and 120 mi north of Dallas, TX. From I–35 south, take Exit 55 to Rte. 7. From I–35 north, take Exit 51 to Rte. 7. After Sulphur (10 mi), turn south on Rte. 177. Closest airports: Oklahoma City, Dallas.

CONTACTS

Chickasaw National Recreation Area (1008 W. 2nd St., Sulphur, OK 73086, tel. 580/622–3165; 580/622–3161 headquarters; www.nps.gov/chic). Sulphur Chamber of Commerce (717 W. Broadway, Sulphur, OK 73086, tel. 580/622–2824). Davis Chamber of Commerce (300 E. Main St., Davis, OK 73030, tel. 580/369–2402).

Oklahoma City National Memorial

In Oklahoma City

The memorial is on the site of the former Alfred P. Murrah Federal Building, where a bomb detonated on April 19, 1995 killed 168 people. It was, at the time, the deadliest terrorist attack ever on American soil. The memorial is composed of 168 bronze-and-glass chairs arranged in nine rows, representing the number of victims and the number of floors of the Murrah Building when the explosion occurred. The site includes the Outdoor Symbolic Memorial, the Memorial Museum Center, and the Oklahoma City National Memorial Institute for the Prevention of Terrorism. The memorial was authorized on October 9, 1997 and dedicated on April 19, 2000.

WHAT TO SEE & DO

Facilities: Memorial site and museum. **Programs & Events**: Ranger-led programs (daily 10–4, hourly). **Tips & Hints:** Expect to spend at least one hour at the site.

FEES & HOURS

Outdoor Memorial free. Memorial Center Museum $7 adults, $6 ages 62 and over, $5 ages 6–17 and college students with ID, free ages 5 and under. Outdoor Symbolic Memorial open daily 24 hours, Memorial Center open Mon.–Sat. 9–6, Sun. 1–6.

HOW TO GET THERE

Take the downtown Oklahoma City exit off I–40 or I–235. The site is on 5th St. between Robinson and Harvey Aves. Closest airport: Oklahoma City (10 mi).

CONTACTS

Oklahoma City National Memorial (Box 676, Oklahoma City, OK 73102, tel. 405/231–4422, fax 405/231–4633, www.nps.gov/okci). Oklahoma City National Memorial Trust (Box 323, Oklahoma City, OK 73101, tel. 405/235–3313, fax 405/235–3315, www.oklahomacitynationalmemorial.org).

Washita Battlefield National Historic Site

In western Oklahoma, near Cheyenne

The park preserves the site of the Battle of the Washita (November 27, 1868), one of the most controversial engagements between Plains tribes and the U.S. Army. Lieutenant Colonel George A. Custer attacked a sleeping Cheyenne village and killed about 50 men, women, and children, including tribe leader Chief Black Kettle. The events symbolize the struggle of the southern Great Plains tribes to maintain their traditional way of life and not to submit to reservation confinement. The park was authorized on November 12, 1996.

WHAT TO SEE & DO

Viewing battlefield from overlook, walking on trails. **Facilities:** Overlook with historical plaque, commemorative monument, panel indicating approximate route, approach, and attack of Custer, 1.5 mi of trails. Visitor center scheduled for construction in 2004. Black Kettle Museum in Cheyenne, operated by the Oklahoma Historical Society, contains battle exhibits and information. Bookstore in Black Kettle Museum. **Programs & Events:** Ranger-led walks and talks (Memorial day–Labor Day). Battle anniversary symposium (Nov., in even-numbered years). **Tips & Hints:** Visit in spring and fall, summers are very hot.

FOOD, LODGING & SUPPLIES

Camping: None at site. In Black Kettle Recreation Area: 2 campgrounds with primitive sites (10 mi northwest of Cheyenne on U.S. 283, tel. 580/497–2143; free; pit toilets). **Hotels:** None at site. In Cheyenne: Cheyenne Motel (U.S. 283 N, tel. 580/497–3383; 63 rooms; $45), Coyote Hills Guest Ranch (4 mi northwest of Rte. 47, tel. 580/497–3931; 20 rooms; $65). **Restaurants:** None at site. In Cheyenne: 1 Okie (U.S. 283 N, tel. 580/497–2584; $6), Odes Drive-In (1st and Broadway, tel. 580/497–2393; $2.50–$6.50; closed Sun., no lunch Sat.) **Groceries & Gear:** None at site. In Cheyenne: Hanawalt's Variety (127 Broadway, tel. 580/497–2242), Market Square Thriftway (300 S. L. L. Males, tel. 580/497–2600).

FEES, HOURS & REGULATIONS

Free. No hunting. No pets on trail. Site open daily dawn–dusk. Headquarters open weekdays 8–noon and 1–5. Black Kettle Museum in Cheyenne open daily 9–5.

HOW TO GET THERE

2 mi west of Cheyenne on Rte. 47A and 30 mi north of I–40 via Exit 20 (U.S. 283 north). Closest airports: Oklahoma City and Amarillo, TX (both 140 mi).

CONTACTS

Washita Battlefield National Historic Site (Rte. 47A, Cheyenne, OK 73628, tel. 580/497–2742, fax 580/497–2712, www.nps.gov/waba). Headquarters (426 E. Broadway, Rte. 47 and U.S. 283, same tel. as site). Black Kettle Museum (Rte. 47 and U.S. 283, tel. 580/497–3929). Cheyenne Chamber of Commerce (Box 57, Cheyenne, OK 73628, tel. 580/497–3318 or 877/497–3318, www.cheyenneokchamber.com).

See Also

Fort Smith National Historic Site, AR. *Santa Fe National Historic Trail* and *Trail of Tears National Historic Trail*, in Other National Parklands.

OREGON

Crater Lake National Park

In southern Oregon,
60 mi northwest of Klamath Falls

Crater Lake is one of the most famous lakes on Earth, principally because of its unusual blue color and its mountain setting. At a depth of 1,943 feet, Crater Lake is the deepest lake in the United States and the seventh deepest in the world, and it holds the world record for natural water clarity. The mature forests that surround Crater Lake are largely untouched. The park was established on May 22, 1902.

WHAT TO SEE & DO

Auto and boat touring, cross-country skiing (rentals, Klamath Falls, Medford), hiking. **Facilities:** 2 visitor centers: Steel and Rim Village (summer only), wayside exhibits, film. Map sale areas, picnic areas, post office. **Programs & Events:** Campfire programs, geology and natural-history walks (late June–Labor Day, daily), boat tours (late June–mid-Sept.), snowshoe walks (late Nov.–Mar.). **Tips & Hints:** Go early July–late Sept. to avoid snow, mid-July–early Aug. for wildflowers. Busiest July and Aug., least crowded Dec.–Feb.

FOOD, LODGING & SUPPLIES

Camping: 2 campgrounds in the park: Lost Creek (16 tent sites; $10; pit toilets; closed Oct.–June), Mazama (211 sites; $16–$21; flush toilets, showers, hook-ups; closed early Oct.–mid-June,). Backcountry camping allowed (permit required, *see below*). In Fort Klamath: Crater Lake Resort (50711 Rte. 62, tel. 541/381–2349; 26 sites; $20; flush toilets, showers, hook-ups). **Hotels:** In the park: Crater Lake Lodge (tel. 541/830–8700; 71 rooms; $123–$170; closed mid-Oct.–mid-May), Mazama Village Motor Inn (tel. 541/830–8700; 40 rooms; $101; closed early Oct.–early June). **Restaurants:** In the park: Dining Room at Crater Lake Lodge (tel. 541/594–2255; $6–$13; closed mid-Oct.–mid-May). **Groceries & Gear**: In the park: Mazama Village (tel. 541/594–2255 Ext. 3703). In Fort Klamath: Fort Klamath General Store (52620 Rte. 62, tel. 541/381–2263).

FEES, HOURS & REGULATIONS

Entrance fee: $10 per car, $5 for cyclists and walk-ins. Backcountry permits required (free). No bicycles or off-road vehicles allowed off paved roads. Leashed pets allowed in front country only. No private boats. No wildlife feeding or hunting. No climbing or hiking inner caldera walls except on Cleetwood Cove Trail. Park open daily. Steel Visitor Center open early Apr.–early Nov., daily 9–5; early Nov.–early Apr., daily 10–4. Rim Village Visitor Center open June–Sept., daily 9:30–5.

HOW TO GET THERE

Take Rte. 62, 60 mi northwest of Klamath Falls and 80 mi northeast of Medford. Closest airports: Medford, Klamath Falls.

CONTACT

Crater Lake National Park (Box 7, Crater Lake, OR 97604, tel. 541/594–3100, fax 541/594–3010, ww.nps.gov/crla).

Fort Clatsop National Memorial

In northwestern Oregon, near Astoria

After their epic journey across the West, the 33-member Lewis and Clark Expedition spent the winter of 1805–06 at Fort Clatsop. In 1955 local citizens built a replica of the explorers' fort in a lush spruce and hemlock forest that is the focal point of the memorial. The Salt Works site in nearby Seaside commemorates where the explorers set up a camp to boil seawater to produce salt for use at the fort and on the return trip. The memorial was authorized on May 29, 1958.

WHAT TO SEE & DO

Touring fort replica, canoe landing, and saltworks, walking trails, picnicking. **Facilities:** Visitor center, trails, trailside interpretive panels, replica of stone oven (Seaside). Bookstore, covered picnic tables. **Programs & Events:** Audiovisual programs. Interactive living-history programs (mid-June–Labor Day). Newfoundland Dog Day (July), National Park Service Founders Day (Aug. 25), Explorers' Christmas at Fort Clatsop (Dec. 26–Jan. 1). Numerous special events commemorating the bicentennial of the Lewis and Clark Expedition are in thr works for November 2005–March 2006. **Tips & Hints:** Fort replica floors are slippery and uneven. Go in winter for more authentic expedition weather, in Sept. and Oct. for good weather and few visitors. Busiest July and Aug., least crowded Jan. and Feb.

FOOD, LODGING & SUPPLIES

Camping: None in park. In Hammond: Fort Stevens State Park (100 Peter Iredale Rd., tel. 503/861–1671 park; 800/452–5687 reservations; 519 sites; $17–$21; flush toilets, showers, hook-ups). **Hotels:** None in park. In Astoria: Astoria Dunes (288 W. Marine Dr., tel. 503/325–7111 or 800/441–3319; 58 rooms; $55–$110), Red Lion Inn (400 Industry St., tel. 503/325–7373; 124 rooms; $99–$119). **Restaurants:** None in park. In Astoria: Columbian Café (1114 Marine Dr., tel. 503/325–2233; $5–$10; no dinner Sun.–Tues.), Pig 'N' Pancake (146 W. Bond St., tel. 503/325–3144; $4–$10), Ship Inn (1 2nd St., tel. 503/325–0033; $7–$15). **Groceries & Gear:** None in park. In Warrenton: Fred Meyer (695 S. U.S. 101, tel. 503/861–3000).

FEES, HOURS & REGULATIONS

Entrance fee: $3 adults, free ages 16 and under, $5 per car. No hunting or fishing. No bikes on trails. No skateboards. No pets in fort rooms or visitor center. Leashed pets elsewhere. Park and visitor center open Labor Day–mid-June, daily 9–5; mid-June–Labor Day, daily 8–6.

HOW TO GET THERE

6 mi southwest of Astoria, off U.S. 101. Closest airport: Portland (100 mi).

CONTACTS

Fort Clatsop National Memorial (92343 Fort Clatsop Rd., Astoria, OR 97103, tel. 503/861–2471, fax 503/861–2585, www.nps.gov/focl). Astoria–Warrenton Chamber of Commerce (111 W. Marine Dr., Astoria, OR 97103, tel. 503/325–6311). Seaside Chamber of Commerce (7 N. Roosevelt Dr., Seaside, OR 97138, tel. 503/738–6391).

John Day Fossil Beds National Monument

In north-central Oregon,
near Dayville, Mitchell, and Clarno

The heavily eroded volcanic deposits of the scenic John Day River basin house a well-preserved fossil record of plants and animals that spans more than 40 of the 65 million years of the Cenozoic Era, or Age of Mammals. The monument is composed of three widely separated units: Sheep Rock, Painted Hills, and Clarno. The monument was authorized in 1974 and established in 1975.

WHAT TO SEE & DO

Auto touring, self-guided trail tours, visiting fossil museum at Sheep Rock Unit. **Facilities:** Paleontology Center with fossil museum, visitor center, Cant Ranch sheep-ranching cultural museum, theater. Bookstore. Exhibits at Painted Hills and Clarno, scenic roads, trails, picnic tables with fire grills. **Programs & Events:** Self-guided tours, ranger-led talks in fossil museum, ranger-led trail hikes. Campfire programs (Apr.–Oct., monthly) in nearby state campgrounds, ranger-led auto tours and hikes (Apr.–Oct.). **Tips & Hints:** Go to Clarno in morning, Sheep Rock in early afternoon, and Painted Hills in late afternoon for best light for scenic views and photography. Go mid-Apr.–mid-May for wildflowers at Painted Hills. Busiest July and Aug., least crowded Jan. and Feb.

FOOD & LODGING

Camping: None in park. Near Mitchell: Ochoco Divide (U.S. 26, 15 mi west of Mitchell, tel. 541/416–6500 or 877/444–6777; 28 sites; $10; vault toilets). **Hotels:** None in park. In John Day: Best Western Inn (315 W. Main St., tel. 541/575–1700; 39 rooms; $72), Sunset Inn (390 W. Main St., tel. 541/575–1462 or 800/452–4899; 43 rooms; $60). **✕ Restaurants:** None in park. In John Day: Grub Steak Mining Company (149 E. Main St., tel. 541/575–1970; $4–$10), Outpost Pizza Pub & Grill (201 W. Main St., tel. 541/ 575–0250; $4–$10).

FEES, HOURS & REGULATIONS

Free. No collecting or disturbing fossils or geologic or biological resources. No public telephones at sites. Park trails, overlooks, and grounds open sunrise–sunset. Paleontology Center, Cant Ranch, and visitor center at Sheep Rock open Mar.–Memorial Day and Labor Day–Thanksgiving, daily 9–5; Memorial Day–Labor Day, daily 9–6; and Thanksgiving–Feb., weekdays 9–5.

HOW TO GET THERE

Paleontology center with fossil museum, and Cant Ranch center, at Sheep Rock Unit are 9 mi west of Dayville, near intersection of U.S. 26 and Rte. 19. Painted Hills Unit is 10 mi west of Mitchell off U.S. 26. Clarno Unit is 18 mi west of Fossil on Rte. 218. Closest airports to Sheep Rock Unit: Redmond (80 mi), Portland (250 mi), and Boise, ID (240 mi).

CONTACTS

John Day Fossil Beds National Monument (32651 Rte. 19, Kimberly, OR 97848-9701, tel. 541/987–2333, fax 541/987–2336, www.nps.gov/joda). Grant County Chamber of Commerce (281 W. Main St., John Day, OR 97845, tel. 541/575–0547 or 800/769–5664, www.grantcounty.cc). Prineville–Crook County Chamber of Commerce (390 N.E. Fairview, Prineville, OR 97754, tel. 541/447–6304).

Oregon Caves National Monument

In southwestern Oregon, near Cave Junction

Below ground at this monument is a marble cave created by natural forces over hundreds of thousands of years in one of the world's most diverse geologic realms. Above ground is 480 acres of wilderness, including a remnant of old-growth coniferous forest, crisscrossed with hiking trails. In addition to its unique geologic setting, Oregon Caves has Pleistocene mammal fossils and a large assortment of endemic cave life. The monument was proclaimed in 1909 and transferred to the National Park Service in 1933.

WHAT TO SEE & DO

Cave touring, hiking. **Facilities:** Visitor center with interpretive displays, trails. Book sales area. **Programs & Events:** Ranger-guided walks, day programs (Memorial Day–Labor Day). **Tips & Hints:** Entrance to caves by guided tour only. No reservations. Come early to avoid crowds. Wear tennis shoes or boots and a jacket for cave tours. Temperature is 42°F in cave. Don't take tour if you have breathing or heart problems. Cave trail is 1 mi with ascent of 250 feet; there are more than 500 stairs. Tour takes about 1½ hours. Large RVs not recommended on road to park, shuttles available from Cave Junction (*see below*). Go late Apr. or May for wildflowers in valleys, June for meadow flowers. Busiest July and Aug., least crowded Labor Day–Memorial Day.

FOOD, LODGING & SUPPLIES

⚠ **Camping:** None in park. In Siskiyou National Forest: Cave Creek (Rte. 46, 16 mi east of Cave Junction, tel. 541/592–2166; 17 sites; $10; pit toilets; closed mid-Sept.–mid-May), Grayback (Rte. 46, 12 mi east of Cave Junction, tel. 541/592–2166; 35 sites; $10; flush toilets; closed Sept.–mid-May). In Cave Junction: Country Hills Resort (7901 Caves Hwy., tel. 541/592–3406; 25 sites; $14–$18; flush toilets, showers, hook-ups). 🏨 **Hotels:** In the park: Oregon Caves Chateau (20000 Caves Hwy., tel. 541/592–3400; 22 rooms, 3 suites; $75–$125; closed Nov.–Apr.). In Cave Junction: Out N' About (300 Page Creek Rd., tel. 541/592–2208; 1 cabin, 9 tree houses; $85–$160). ✗ **Restaurant:** In the park: Oregon Caves Chateau (20000 Caves Hwy., tel. 541/592–3400; $7; closed Nov.–Apr.). ⚕ **Groceries:** None in park. In Cave Junction: Shop Smart (205 Watkins St., tel. 541/592–3333).

FEES, HOURS & REGULATIONS

Free. Cave tour $7.50 adults, $5 ages 16 and under. Free tour to first room for families with small children. Cave restrictions: children must be at least 42 inches tall and able to climb a set of test stairs unassisted. No infants. No child care available. Canes allowed in first cave room only. First room (only) wheelchair accessible. No pets on trails, leashed pets elsewhere. Mountain bikes on existing roads only. No motor vehicles on trails. Monument open daily. Visitor center open mid-Mar.–Memorial Day and mid-Oct.–Nov., daily 9:30–4, Memorial Day–late June and Labor Day–mid-Oct., daily 8:30–5; late June–Labor Day, daily 8:30–7. Cave tours run mid-June–Labor day, daily every 15 mins; Labor Day–mid.-Oct., daily on the hour.

HOW TO GET THERE

20 mi southeast of Cave Junction via Rte. 46. Closest airport: Medford (80 mi). Shuttles (tel. 541/659–5103 or 888/203–8502) from Cave Junction cost $20 for the first person in the group and $2 for each additional person.

CONTACTS

Oregon Caves National Monument (19000 Caves Hwy., Cave Junction, OR 97523, tel. 541/592–2100, fax 541/592–3981, www.nps.gov/orca or www.cavejunction.com).

See Also

Nez Perce National Historical Park, Idaho. *California National Historic Trail, Lewis and Clark National Historic Trail, McLoughlin House National Historic Site, Nez Perce National Historic Trail, Oregon National Historic Trail,* and *Pacific Crest National Scenic Trail,* in Other National Parklands.

Allegheny Portage Railroad National Historic Site

In central Pennsylvania, 10 mi west of Altoona

Preserved here are the remains of the first railroad to cross the Allegheny Mountains, including the first railroad tunnel built in the United States. The 36-mi-long Portage Railroad, completed in 1834, used a series of 10 inclined planes to lift canal boats loaded on railroad-type flatcars across the mountains between Hollidaysburg and Johnstown. The railroad, in conjunction with the Pennsylvania Main Line Canal, reduced the time to travel the 390 mi between Philadelphia and Pittsburgh to four or five days from three weeks. The site was authorized on August 31, 1964.

WHAT TO SEE & DO

Cross-country skiing (rentals in Altoona), hiking, picnicking, viewing the historic area of the park, walking. **Facilities:** Visitor center, film, interpretive displays at Engine House No. 6, Historic Lemon House Tavern, wayside exhibits. Book sale area, picnic pavilion with grills, tables. **Programs & Events:** Interpretive tours of Lemon House. Costumed demonstrations including log hewing, stonecutting, and lifestyles of the past (June–Aug.). Evening on the Summit outdoor concert ($2) and guest lectures (concerts and lectures, Sat. nights in summer), guided Heritage Hikes and bus tours to lesser-known areas of the railroad (June–Aug., Sun.; reservations required, tel. 814/886–6150). **Tips & Hints:** Go Apr. and May for wildflowers, Oct. for fall colors. Busiest July and Aug., least crowded Dec. and Jan.

FOOD, LODGING & SUPPLIES

Camping: None in park. In Duncansville: Wrights Orchard Station (2381 Old Rte. 220, tel. 814/695–2628; 40 sites; $18–$28; flush toilets, hook-ups). **Hotels:** None in park. In Altoona: Hampton Inn (180 Charlotte Dr., tel. 814/941–3500; 110 rooms; $79–$92). In Ebensburg: Comfort Inn (111 Cook Rd., tel. 814/472–6100 or 800/228–5150; 78 rooms; $59–$68). **Restaurants:** None in park. In Altoona: Jethro's (417 Parkview La., tel. 814/942–2178; $7–$16; no lunch Sun.). In Ebensburg: Noon-Collins Restaurant (114 E. High St., tel. 814/472–4311; $12–$20). **Groceries & Gear:** None in park. In Altoona: Wal-Mart Supercenter (2600 Plank Rd. Commons, tel. 814/949–8980).

FEES, HOURS & REGULATIONS

Entrance fee: $3 per person. Bikes restricted to hard-surface roads. No hunting. Leashed pets only. Visitor center open daily 9–5.

HOW TO GET THERE

10 mi west of Altoona, 15 mi east of Ebensburg on U.S. 22 (Gallitzin exit). Nearest airports: Johnstown (30 mi), Martinsburg (20 mi), Pittsburgh (80 mi).

CONTACTS

Allegheny Portage Railroad National Historic Site (110 Federal Park Rd., Gallitzin, PA 16641, tel. 814/886–6150, fax 814/884–0206, www.nps.gov/alpo). Allegheny Mountains Convention & Visitors Bureau (tel. 814/943–4183 or 800/842–5866, fax 814/943–8094, www.alleghenymountains.com). Greater Johnstown–Cambria Convention & Visitors Bureau (111 Market St., Johnstown, PA 15901, tel. 814/536–7993 or 800/237–8590, www.visitjohnstownpa.com).

Delaware Water Gap National Recreation Area

The Delaware River on the Pennsylvania–New Jersey border, from East Stroudsburg to Milford

The recreation area contains 70,000 acres of forest along a 40-mi stretch of the Delaware River; the geologically significant "water gap," a mile-wide cut in the Kittatinny Ridge created by the Delaware River; and thousands of acres of woodland open to hiking and other recreational activities. One of the last free-flowing rivers on the East Coast, the river is home to threatened and endangered plants and animals. Significant prehistoric and historic sites are located throughout the park. The park was authorized on September 1, 1965.

WHAT TO SEE & DO

Boating, canoeing (rentals), cross-country skiing, fishing, hiking, hunting, picnicking, snowshoeing, swimming. **Facilities:** 3 visitor centers: Kittatinny Point (off Exit 1, I–80 in New Jersey), Bushkill (U.S. 209), Dingman's Falls (U.S. 209); Millbrook Village (Old Mine Rd., NJ side); beaches, trails, roadside radio interpretation, bulletin boards. Picnic areas with tables but no fire rings or pits. **Programs & Events:** Nature study programs (weekends, Pocono Environmental Education Center, 5 mi south of Dingman's Visitor Center). Guided hikes, children's programs, waterfall walks, campfire programs (June–Sept., weekends); cultural history demonstrations (May–Oct., weekends; Millbrook Village). Delaware River Sojourn (mid- to late June); Peter's Valley Craft Fair (last weekend, Sept.); Millbrook Days Folk Life Festival (1st full weekend, Oct.); Van Campen Day (3rd Sun., Oct.). **Tips & Hints:** Bring your own cookstove. Go in fall for hawk-watching, winter for eagles. Busiest July and Aug., least crowded Jan. and Feb.

FOOD, LODGING & SUPPLIES

Camping: In the park: Worthington State Forest Campground (Old Mine Rd., tel. 908/841–9575; 69 sites; $15; flush toilets, showers; closed Jan.–Mar.). Backcountry camping for Appalachian Trail users only.

🛏 **Hotels:** None in park. In Stroudsburg: Echo Valley Cottages (1 Lower Lakeview Dr., tel. 570/223–0662; 9 cottages; $150–$250 weekly). ✗ **Restaurants:** None in park. In Stroudsburg: Arlington Diner (834 N. 9th St., tel. 570/421–2329; $6–$12). ⛄ **Groceries & Gear:** None in park. In Delaware Water Gap: Pack Shack Adventures (88 Broad St., tel. 570/424–8522). In West Hazleton: Weis Market (100 Weis La., tel. 570/455–0612).

FEES, HOURS & REGULATIONS

Free. Smithfield and Milford beaches: $7 weekends, $5 weekdays per vehicle. No pets in Worthington State Forest Campground, leashed pets only elsewhere. Bicycling in designated areas only. Pedestrian traffic only on trails. No ground fires. Kittatinny Point Visitor Center open May–Oct., daily 9–5; Nov.–Apr., weekends 9–4:30. Dingman's Falls Visitor Center closed until mid-2004. Bushkill Visitor Center open May–Oct., daily 9–5. Millbrook Village open May–Oct., Fri.–Sun. 9–5.

HOW TO GET THERE

The recreation area is on the Pennsylvania–New Jersey border from I–80 (Delaware Water Gap) to I–84 (just north of Milford). Closest airport: Lehigh Valley International Airport near Allentown (44 mi from town of Delaware Water Gap).

CONTACTS

Delaware Water Gap National Recreation Area (River Rd., Bushkill, PA 18324, tel. 570/588–2451, fax 570/588–2780, www.nps.gov/dewa). Kittatinny Point Visitor Center (tel. 908/496–4458). Dingman's Falls Visitor Center (tel. 570/828–7802). Bushkill Visitor Center (tel. 570/588–7044).

Edgar Allan Poe National Historic Site

In Philadelphia

The life and work of Edgar Allan Poe, one of America's most gifted authors, are explored in a three-building complex at 532 N. 7th Street, where he lived from 1843 to 1844. The site was authorized on November 10, 1978.

WHAT TO SEE & DO

Touring unfurnished home, viewing exhibits, watching slide presentation. **Facilities:** Sales area. **Programs & Events:** Ranger-guided and self-guided home tours. Edgar Allan Poe's literary legacy tours, Poetry Month (Apr.). **Tips & Hints:** Busiest Aug. and Oct., least crowded Jan. and Feb.

FEES & HOURS

Free. Site open Wed.–Sun. 9–5.

HOW TO GET THERE

At 532 N. 7th St., 2 mi from the visitor center at the Independence National Historical Park (*see separate entry*). Closest airport: Philadelphia.

CONTACTS

Edgar Allan Poe National Historic Site (532 N. 7th St., Philadelphia, PA 19123, tel. 215/597–8780, fax 215/597–1901, www.nps.gov/edal). Independence Visitors Center (6th and Market Sts., tel. 215/965–7676).

Eisenhower National Historic Site

In Gettysburg, in south-central Pennsylvania

The 230-acre site preserves the former home and farm of Dwight D. Eisenhower, the 34th president of the United State, and his wife Mamie. The farm served as a weekend retreat, a refuge in time of illness, and a gathering place for political groups and the Eisenhower family. Premier Khrushchev, Chancellor Adenauer, President de Gaulle, and other VIPs trooped over its fields and toured the cattle barns during Eisenhower's terms as president, when he used the farm for his personal style of diplomacy. From 1961 to 1969, the farm served as the couple's retirement home. The site was designated on November 27, 1967.

WHAT TO SEE & DO

Touring home, farm, and cattle barns. **Facilities:** Visitor center, home, barns, farm. Bookstore. **Programs & Events:** Tours of grounds and home, Junior Secret Service Program (daily). Tours and interpretive talks, living-history programs (Apr.–Oct.), cattle show barn (Apr.–Oct.). Fabulous Fifties Weekend (June), World War II Weekend (Sept.), Eisenhower Seminar (Oct.), Christmas with the Eisenhowers (Dec.). **Tips & Hints:** Go Apr.–Oct., when all facilities are open and tours and programs scheduled. Busiest July and Oct., least crowded Jan. and Feb.

FOOD & LODGING

⚠ **Camping:** None in park. In Gettysburg: Artillery Ridge Campground (610 Taneytown Rd., tel. 717/334–1288; 104 sites, 3 cabins; $19–$22, $40 cabins; flush toilets, showers, hook-ups). 🏨 **Hotels:** None in park. In Gettysburg: Battlefield B&B (2264 Emmittsburg Rd., tel. 717/334–8804; 8 rooms; $135–$185), Comfort Inn (871 York Rd., tel., 717/337–2400; 81 rooms, 3 suites; $95–$105). ✗ **Restaurants:** None in park. In Gettysburg: Dobbin House (89 Steinwehr Ave., tel. 717/334–2100; $16–$34; no lunch), Farnsworth House Inn (401 Baltimore St., tel. 717/334–8838; $8–$15).

FEES, HOURS & REGULATIONS

Entrance fee: $7 adults, $4 ages 13–16, $3 ages 6–12, free ages 5 and under. All visits by shuttle bus. No on-site parking. No pets. Park open daily.

HOW TO GET THERE

Via shuttle bus from Gettysburg National Park Visitor Center, 1 mi south of Gettysburg, PA, off U.S. 15 Bus. Closest airport: Harrisburg (60 mi).

CONTACTS

Eisenhower National Historic Site (97 Eisenhower Farm La., Gettysburg, PA 17325, tel. 717/338–9114, fax 717/338–0821, www.nps.gov/eise). Gettysburg Convention & Visitors Bureau (35 Carlisle St., Gettysburg, PA 17325, tel. 717/334–6274, fax 717/334–1166).

Flight 93 National Memorial

In southwestern Pennsylvania, north of Shanksville.

A memorial to commemorate the passengers and crew of United Airlines Flight 93 is planned for this site. On the morning of September 11, 2001, Flight 93 took off from Newark International Airport bound for San Francisco. When it neared Cleveland, hijackers on board commandeered the plane and piloted it into an about turn, heading in the direction of Washington, DC. Passengers and crew members on board are believed to have acted together to crash-land the plane in a remote field in rural Pennsylvania before it reached the capital. The crash site was established as a national memorial on September 24, 2002.

WHAT TO SEE & DO

Viewing crash site and temporary memorial. At this writing, park development is in the planning stage and there are no facilities. The crash site and a temporary, informal memorial are both on private land. The crash site is closed to the public; the temporary memorial consists of a chain-link fence and objects, signs, and flowers left there by visitors.

FEES, HOURS & REGULATIONS

Free. Crash site is closed to the public but can be viewed from parking area behind chain-link fence. A Flight 93 National Memorial ambassador is generally on hand weekdays 9–5 to answer questions. Memorial open daily 24 hours.

HOW TO GET THERE

From U.S. 219, take the Stoystown–Jennerstown exit onto U.S. 30 east. Continue 7.2 mi on U.S.. 30, then turn right onto Lambertsville Rd. Drive 1.7 mi, then turn left onto Skyline Dr. and continue 0.8 mi to the temporary memorial.

CONTACTS

Joanne Hanley, Director of Southwestern Pennsylvania National Parks, (109 W. Main St., Suite 104, Somerset, PA 15501, tel. 724/329–5512, www.nps.gov/flni). Somerset County Chamber of Commerce (601 N. Center Ave., Somerset, PA 15501, tel. 814/445–6431, www.somersetcountychamber.com).

Fort Necessity National Battlefield

In southwestern Pennsylvania, southeast of Uniontown

On July 3, 1754, the opening battle of the French and Indian War took place at a palisade fort built here by a 22-year-old George Washington. He was forced to surrender to an enemy for the first and only time in his military career. The fort has been reconstructed on the site. The site was established as a national battlefield in 1931, transferred to the Park Service in 1933, and redesignated in 1961.

WHAT TO SEE & DO

Cross-country skiing, hiking, picnicking, touring fort, historic tavern, grave site, and glen. **Facilities:** Visitor center, historic tavern, trails, wayside exhibits, grave. Bookstore, grills, pavilions, picnic area. **Programs & Events:** Ranger-guided walks, soldier-life programs (mid-June–mid-Aug.). National Road Festival (3rd weekend, May), Battle Anniversary Memorial Program (July 3). **Tips & Hints:** Go in summer for interpretive programs, fall for foliage. Busiest July and Aug., least crowded Dec. and Jan.

FOOD, LODGING & SUPPLIES

Camping: None in park. In Ohiopyle: Ohiopyle State Park (400 Kentuck Rd., off Rte. 381, tel. 724/329–8591; 226 tent sites, 4 cottages; $14–$36 cottages; flush toilets, showers, hook-ups). **Hotels:** None in park. In Chalk Hill: Lodge at Chalk Hill (U.S. 40, tel. 724/438–8880 or 800/833–4283; 60 rooms, 6 suites; $78–$84). **Restaurants:** None in park. In Hopwood: Sun Porch (U.S. 40, tel. 724/439–5734; $8–$12; closed Mon., no lunch Sat.). In Uniontown: Caileigh's (105 E. Fayette St., tel. 724/437–9436; $14–$23; closed Mon.). **Groceries & Gear:** None in park. In Hopwood: Adrians Market (1776 National Pike E, tel. 724/438–4304). In Ohiopyle: Falls Market (69 Main St., tel. 724/329–4973).

FEES, HOURS & REGULATIONS

Entrance fee: $3 adults, free ages 16 and under. No hunting. Leashed pets only. No motorized or mechanized equipment on trails. Visitor center open daily 9–5. Fort open daily 8–sunset. Mount Washington Tavern open daily for guided tours only. Jumonville Glen open mid-Apr.–Oct., daily. Braddock Grave site open daily.

HOW TO GET THERE

On U.S. 40, 11 mi east of Uniontown. Closest airports: Connellsville (16 mi); Morgantown, WV (37 mi); Pittsburgh (75 mi).

CONTACTS

Fort Necessity National Battlefield (1 Washington Pkwy., Farmington, PA 15437, tel. 724/329–5512, fax 724/329–8682, www.nps.gov/fone). Fayette County Chamber of Commerce (Box 2124, Uniontown, PA 15401, tel. 724/437–4571). Laurel Highland Convention & Visitors Bureau (120 E. Main St., Ligonier, PA 15658, tel. 724/238–5661).

Friendship Hill
National Historic Site

In southwestern Pennsylvania, near Point Marion

This site, on the Monongahela River, preserves the brick, frame, and stone home that belonged to Albert Gallatin, Secretary of the Treasury from 1801 to 1814 under presidents Jefferson and Madison. It was authorized in 1978.

WHAT TO SEE & DO

Cross-country skiing, hiking, picnicking, touring the mansion. **Facilities:** Visitor center, mansion, trail, wayside exhibits. Bookstore, picnic area, and pavilion. **Programs & Events:** Self-guided audio tour of mansion. Ranger-guided tours, special talks (Memorial Day–Labor Day). Festi-Fall (last Sun., Sept.). **Tips & Hints:** Busiest May–Sept., least crowded Jan. and Feb.

FOOD, LODGING & SUPPLIES

None in park. *See Fort Necessity National Battlefield.*

FEES, HOURS & REGULATIONS

Free. No hunting. Leashed pets only. No cars or bikes on trails. No off-trail hiking. Park and visitor center open daily 9–5.

HOW TO GET THERE

On Rte. 166, 3 mi north of Point Marion. Closest airports: Morgantown, WV (10 mi); Pittsburgh (60 mi).

CONTACTS

Friendship Hill National Historic Site (1 Washington Pkwy., Farmington, PA 15437, tel. 724/725–9190, fax 724/725–1999, www.nps.gov/frhi). Fayette County Chamber of Commerce (65 W. Main St., Uniontown, PA 15401, tel. 724/437–4571 or 800/916–9365). Laurel Highland Convention & Visitors Bureau (120 E. Main St., Ligonier, PA 15658, tel. 800/333–5661).

Gettysburg
National Military Park

Near Gettysburg, in south-central Pennsylvania

The Civil War battle fought here on July 1–3, 1863, resulted in a Union victory that repelled the second Confederate invasion of the North, a major turning point in the war. More than 51,000 soldiers were killed, wounded, or captured in this battle, making it the bloodiest of the war. The Soldiers' National Cemetery at Gettysburg contains more than 7,000 interments, of which 3,500 are from the Civil War. President Abraham Lincoln delivered his immortal Gettysburg Address here on November 19, 1863. The park was established in 1895 and transferred to the Park Service in 1933.

WHAT TO SEE & DO

Auto touring, bicycling, horseback riding, viewing electric map, cyclorama, museum, battlefield, cemetery, and monuments. **Facilities:** Visitor center (between Taneytown Rd./Rte. 134 and Steinwehr Ave./U.S. 15 Bus. 1 mi south of Gettysburg), electric battlefield map, Cyclorama Center, auditorium, film, battlefield, cemetery, tour roads, hiking trails, horse trail, and 1,600 monuments, markers, and memorials. Bookstores. **Programs & Events:** Interpretive programs on battle, national cemetery, and Gettysburg Address (Apr.–Oct.); walking tours (mid-June–mid-Aug., several times daily; as staffing permits at other times), campfire programs (mid-June–mid-Aug.), living-history demonstrations (Apr.–Oct., weekends). Memorial Day Ceremony, Battle Anniversary (July 1–3), Gettysburg Address Anniversary (Nov. 19), Remembrance Day (closest Sat. to Nov. 19). **Tips & Hints:** Plan to spend at least four hours. Busiest July and Aug., least crowded Jan. and Feb.

FOOD & LODGING

Camping: In the park: group campground for organized youth groups only (tel. 717/334–1124 Ext. 423; reservations required). **Hotels:** *See Eisenhower National Historic Site.* **Restaurants:** *See Eisenhower National Historic Site.*

FEES, HOURS & REGULATIONS

Free. Electric Map and Cyclorama fees: $4 adults, $3 ages 62 and over, $3 ages 7–16, free ages 6 and under. Reservations recommended for licensed battlefield guides (tel. 717/334–4474 or 877/438–8929). Off-road biking not allowed. Park grounds and roads open daily 6 AM–10 PM. Visitor center open mid-June–mid-Aug., daily 8–6; mid-Aug.–mid-June, daily 8–5. Cyclorama Center open daily 9–5.

HOW TO GET THERE

From U.S. 15, follow signs to park. For visitors traveling west on U.S. 30, exit onto U.S. 15 south and follow park signs. From Rte. 30 east, proceed into town, turn right on Washington St. Go 1 mi to visitor center on right. Closest airport: Harrisburg (60 mi).

CONTACTS

Gettysburg National Military Park (97 Taneytown Rd., Gettysburg, PA 17325, tel. 717/334–1124, www.nps.gov/gett). Gettysburg Convention & Visitors Bureau (35 Carlisle St., Gettysburg, PA 17325, tel. 717/334–6274, www.gettysburg.com).

Hopewell Furnace National Historic Site

In southeastern Pennsylvania, near Elverson

This rural American 19th-century iron plantation is home to a blast furnace, the ironmaster's mansion, and auxiliary structures. Hopewell Furnace was founded in 1771 by Ironmaster Mark Bird and operated until 1883. The site was designated in 1938 and renamed in 1985.

WHAT TO SEE & DO

Touring site. **Facilities:** Visitor center, furnace complex and buildings, charcoal hearth, tour trail, wayside exhibits, audio stations. Bookstore. **Programs & Events:** Self-guided tours. Living-history programs, molding and casting demonstrations (June–Labor Day), apple sales (Sept. and Oct.). Sheep shearing (May), Establishment Day (1st weekend, Aug.), Apple Harvest Day (Sept.), "Women's Work" (Oct.), Iron Plantation Christmas (Dec.). **Tips & Hints:** Plan to stay two to four hours. Busiest Aug. and Sept., least crowded Jan. and Feb.

FOOD, LODGING & SUPPLIES

⚠ **Camping:** None in park. In Elverson: French Creek State Park (843 Park Rd., tel. 610/582–9680; 201 sites; $12–$19; flush toilets, showers, hook-ups). ▥ **Hotels:** None in park. In Pottstown: Comfort Inn (Rte. 100 and Shoemaker Rd., tel. 610/970–7230; 151 rooms; $89–$119). ✕ **Restaurants:** None in park. In Phoenixville: Sly Fox Brewing Co. (Rte. 113, tel., 610/935–4540; $9–$17). ⛂ **Groceries & Gear:** None in park. In Birdsboro: Birdsboro Market (1st and Chestnut Sts., tel. 610/582-2273).

FEES & HOURS

Entrance fee: $4 adults, free ages 16 and under. Fees also charged for interpretive programs. Site open daily 9–5.

HOW TO GET THERE

5 mi south of Birdsboro on Rte. 345 and 10 mi from the Morgantown interchange on the PA Tpke. (I–76) via Rtes. 23 east and 345 north. Closest airports: Reading (21 mi); Allentown (41 mi); Philadelphia (53 mi); Harrisburg (79 mi).

CONTACT

Park Superintendent, Hopewell Furnace National Historic Site (2 Mark Bird La., Elverson, PA 19520, tel 610/582–8773, fax 610/582–2768, www.nps.gov/hofu).

Independence National Historical Park

In Philadelphia

Here are the Liberty Bell, an international symbol of freedom, and Independence Hall, where the nation's founders drafted both the Declaration of Independence and the U.S. Constitution. The park, which spans 45 acres in downtown Philadelphia, includes Carpenter's Hall, Christ Church, and 17 other buildings open to the public. The park was authorized in 1948. Independence Hall was designated a World Heritage Site in 1979.

WHAT TO SEE & DO

Touring historic buildings, using interactive exhibits, viewing films, 18th-century artifacts, paintings, and furnishings. **Facilities:** Visitor center (6th and Market Sts.), buildings. Museum shops. **Programs & Events:** Guided tours of Independence Hall (every 15 min), tours of Todd House and Bishop White House, ranger programs at other sites. Seasonal activities available. **Tips & Hints:** Visit Dec.–early Mar. to avoid crowds. Busiest June and July, least crowded Jan. and Feb.

FEES, HOURS & REGULATIONS

Entrance to the park and all tours are free. For tour reservations ($1.50) call 800/967–2283. Buildings generally are open daily 9–5; some are open later June–Aug. Visitor center open daily 9–5.

HOW TO GET THERE

The visitor center is at 6th and Market Sts., in Philadelphia's downtown. From I–95, follow signs for the Central Philadelphia/I–676/Independence Hall exit. Stay to the right and follow the signs to Callowhill St. Continue straight to 6th St. Turn left onto 6th St; the garage entrance is on the left side, just past Arch St. Closest airport: Philadelphia.

CONTACTS

Park visitor center (6th and Market Sts, tel. 215/965–2305). Visitor Information, Independence National Historic Park (313 Walnut St., Philadelphia, PA 19106, tel. 215/597–8974, www.nps.gov/inde). Philadelphia Convention and Visitors Bureau (1515 Market St., Suite 2020, Philadelphia, PA 19102, tel. 215/636–1666).

Johnstown Flood National Memorial

In southwestern Pennsylvania, in St. Michael

Johnstown, a steel company town with a population of 30,000 in 1889, was built on a floodplain at the fork of the Little Conemaugh and Stony Creek rivers. When an old dam broke on May 31, 1889, after a night of heavy rains, 20 million tons of water devastated the town and killed more than 2,200 people. The memorial was authorized on August 31, 1964.

WHAT TO SEE & DO

Hiking, touring house and visitor center, watching film. **Facilities:** Visitor center (Lake Rd.), Historic Unger House, trails. Bookstore, picnic area. **Programs & Events:** Film (hourly year-round). Memorial program, luminaria commemorating flood victims (May 31), ranger presentations (summer). **Tips & Hints:** Busiest July and Aug., least crowded Jan. and Feb.

FOOD, LODGING & SUPPLIES

Camping: None in park. In Patton: Prince Gallitzin State Park (966 Morin Rd., tel. 814/674–1000; 430 sites; $19; flush toilets, showers, hook-ups). **Hotels:** None in park. In Johnstown: Holiday Inn (250 Market St., tel. 814/535–7777; 159 rooms; $94–$159). **Restaurants:** None in park. In Johnstown: Em's Original Subs (345 Main St., tel. 814/

535–5959; $4–$8). ♿ **Groceries & Gear:** None in park. In Johnstown: Ideal Market (Centertown Mall, Walnut St., tel. 814/539–4680).

FEES & HOURS

Entrance fee: $3 adults, free ages 16 and under. Visitor center open daily 9–5.

HOW TO GET THERE

10 mi northeast of Johnstown. Take U.S. 219 to the St. Michael–Sidman exit. Head east on Rte. 869 for 1½ mi. Turn left on Lake Rd. at the memorial sign. Follow Lake Rd. 1½ mi to visitor center on the right. Closest airport: Johnstown.

CONTACTS

Superintendent, Johnstown Flood National Memorial (733 Lake Rd., South Fork, PA 15956, tel. 814/495–4643, www.nps.gov/jofl). Greater Johnstown Cambria County Convention & Visitors Bureau (416 Main St., Suite 100, Johnstown, PA 15901, tel. 814/536–7993 or 800/237–8590, fax 814/539–3370 or 800/237–8590, www.visitjohnstownpa.com).

Middle Delaware National Scenic River

In northeastern Pennsylvania and northwestern New Jersey

The river flows 40 mi through the Delaware Water Gap National Recreation Area (*see separate listing*). The scenic river was established Nov. 10, 1978.

WHAT TO SEE & DO

Boating, fishing, swimming. *See Delaware Water Gap National Recreation Area.*)

CONTACT

Middle Delaware National Scenic River (c/o Delaware Water Gap National Recreation Area, River Rd., Bushkill, PA 18324, tel. 570/588–2451, www.nps.gov/dewa).

Steamtown National Historic Site

In northeastern Pennsylvania, in Scranton

In the former Scranton Yards of the Delaware, Lackawanna & Western Railroad, this site interprets the story of main-line steam railroading and its effect on the country. Included are an operating roundhouse, locomotive shop, museum, train tours, and excursions. The park was authorized in 1986.

WHAT TO SEE & DO

Picnicking; riding steam railroad train; touring museum, train, and lo-comotive shop; watching film. **Facilities:** Visitor center, trains, museum, locomotive shop, roundhouse, theater. Museum store, picnic tables. **Programs & Events:** Ranger tours, walking tours. Two-hour steam train excursion to Moscow, PA (Memorial Day–1st weekend in Nov., week-ends; reservations recommended, tel. 570/340–5203, 570/340–5204, or 888/693–9391), train tours on site (late Apr.–Dec.). National Park Week (3rd week, Apr.); Memorial Day Celebration; Rail Expo (Labor Day weekend); Toys for Tots (Fri. and Sat. after Thanksgiving); Polar Ex-press (mid-Dec.); Festival of Trees (3rd week Dec.–1st week Jan.). **Tips & Hints:** Visitor center and museums are climate controlled. The rest of the site is outdoors. Trains have heat but no air-conditioning. Busiest July and Aug., least crowded Jan. and Feb.

FEES, HOURS & REGULATIONS

Free. Museum interpretive fee: $6 adults, $5 ages 62 and over, $3 ages 6–12, free ages 5 and under. Golden Age, Golden Eagle, Golden Access passports not honored. Excursion fee: $12 adults, $10 ages 62 and over, $6 ages 12 and under. Discount on combination museum–excursion fee. No pets, food, drink, or tobacco in any building. Food and drink al-lowed on excursion, but no pets or tobacco. Leashed pets only else-where. No alcohol. Bicycles on park roads only. Site open daily 9–5.

HOW TO GET THERE

In downtown Scranton via Exit 53 (Central Scranton Expressway) off I–81.

CONTACTS

Steamtown National Historic Site (150 S. Washington Ave., Scranton, PA 18503, tel. 570/340–5200 or 888/693–9391, fax 570/340–5235, www.nps.gov/stea). Northeast Pennsylvania Convention & Visitors Bureau (99 Glenmaura National Blvd., Moosic, PA 18507, tel. 800/229–3526).

Thaddeus Kosciuszko National Memorial

In Philadelphia

Thaddeus Kosciuszko, Polish-born patriot and hero of the American Revolution, is commemorated at 301 Pine Street, Philadelphia. His ef-forts on behalf of the American fight for independence are remem-bered at the small town house where he rented a room during the winter of 1797–98. The memorial was authorized on October 21, 1972.

WHAT TO SEE & DO

Viewing exhibits and slide program (in English and Polish). **Facilities:** House. Sales area. **Programs & Events:** Exhibits and slide program (June–Oct., daily; Nov.–May, Wed.–Sun.). Thaddeus Kosciuszko Birthday (Feb. 4). **Tips & Hints:** Busiest July and Aug., least crowded Dec. and Jan.

FEES & HOURS

Free. Memorial open Wed.–Sun. 10–5.

HOW TO GET THERE

At 301 Pine St., five blocks from the Independence National Historical Park Visitor Center (*see separate entry*). Closest airport: Philadelphia (10 mi).

CONTACTS

Superintendent, Thaddeus Kosciuszko National Memorial (313 Walnut St., Philadelphia, PA 19106, tel. 215/597–9618, fax 215/597–1416, www. nps.gov/thko). Philadelphia Convention & Visitors Bureau (1515 Market St., Philadelphia, PA 19102, tel. 215/636–1666, fax 215/636–3327).

Upper Delaware Scenic & Recreational River

In southeastern New York and northeastern Pennsylvania, along the states' borders

The 73-mi stretch of free-flowing river between Hancock and Port Jervis, New York, includes the Roebling Bridge, believed to be the oldest existing wire-cable suspension bridge, and the Zane Grey home and museum. The park was authorized on November 10, 1978.

WHAT TO SEE & DO

Boating, eagle watching, fishing, kayaking. **Facilities:** Narrowsburg Information Center (NY), park headquarters (near Narrowsburg, NY), Zane Grey Museum (Lackawaxen, PA), Roebling's Delaware Aqueduct and Tollhouse (Minisink Ford, NY), Barryville Office (Barryville, NY), Milanville Office (Milanville, PA), bulletin boards at river accesses; traveler's information radio station (1610 AM) at Sparrowbush, NY. **Programs & Events:** Seasonal activities available. River festivals (July and Aug.). Shad fests (May), Delaware River Sojourn (June), Annual River Clean-up (July), Fall Foliage Train Tours, Oktoberfests (Oct.). **Tips & Hints:** Respect rights of private property owners who own most of the land along the river. Busiest July and Aug., least crowded Dec. and Jan.

FOOD, LODGING & SUPPLIES

⛺ **Camping:** In the park: Buckhorn Natural Area (at Stairstep Rapids, tel. 845/557–0222; 10 canoe-in sites; free; no water; permit required). In Barryville, NY: Kittatinny Campground (3854 Rte. 97, tel. 845/557–8611; 350 sites; $19–$25; flush toilets, showers, hook-ups). ☗ **Hotels:** None in park. In Barryville, NY: Hickory Haven Lodge (25 Rte. 55, tel. 888/557–8077; 15 rooms; $80–$110). In Eldred, NY: Eldred Preserve (1040 Rte. 55, tel. 845/557–8316 or 800/557–3474; 26 rooms; $75–$95). ✕ **Restaurants:** In Eldred, NY: Eldred Preserve (1040 Rte. 55, tel. 845/557–8316; $13–$23). In Lackawaxen: Lackawaxen House (188 Scenic Dr., tel. 570/685–7061; $10–$29). ⛴ **Groceries & Gear:** None in park. In Lackawaxen: T.C.'s General Store (1 Scenic Dr., 1-C, tel. 570/685–1350).

FEES, HOURS & REGULATIONS

Free. New York or Pennsylvania state hunting and fishing license required. Permit required (free) for backcountry camping at Stairway Rapids (tel. 845/557–0222). Zane Grey Museum and tour free. Public river access open daily 5 AM–10 PM. Visitor contact facilities open Memorial Day–Labor Day. Zane Grey Museum hours vary.

HOW TO GET THERE

From New York, take I–84 to Port Jervis (Exit 1), then U.S. 6 west to Rte. 97 north, which parallels most of the river. Northern sections may be reached off Rte. 17. From Pennsylvania, take I–84 east to U.S. 6 west (Exit 10), then follow signs to Lackawaxen, Zane Grey Museum, and Roebling Bridge. Closest airports: Stewart International, Newburgh, NY (85 mi); Wilkes-Barre–Scranton International (45 mi).

CONTACTS

Upper Delaware Scenic & Recreational River (R.R. 2, Box 2428, Beach Lake, PA 18405-9737, tel. 570/729–8565, fax 570/685–4874, www.nps.gov/upde). Zane Grey Museum (Scenic Dr., Lackawaxen, PA, tel. 570/685–4871).

Valley Forge National Historical Park

In southeastern Pennsylvania, in Valley Forge

Protected here is the site of the third winter encampment of George Washington's Continental Army. The army lived here from December 19, 1777, to June 19, 1778, during the American Revolution, and 2,000 soldiers died here from disease caused by shortages of food, blankets, and clothing needed to protect them from the bitter cold. Local residents now use the park for recreation and visitors tour the park for its history. On display are part of Washington's tent and one of the largest collections of 18th-century military equipment in the nation. The park was authorized on July 4, 1976.

WHAT TO SEE & DO

Auto tour, bicycling, cross-country skiing, fishing, hiking, horseback riding, jogging, picnicking, watching 18-minute film. **Facilities:** Visitor center, museum, historic buildings, 10-mi driving tour, 6-mi trail, interpretive waysides. Bookstore, picnic areas. **Programs & Events:** Interpretive programs (monthly). Walking tours and commander-in-chief talks (Memorial Day–Labor Day). George Washington's Birthday (Presidents Day weekend, Feb.), French Alliance Day (weekend closest to May 6), March-Out of the Continental Army (weekend closest to June 19), March-In of Washington's Army (Dec. 19, 6:30–9:00 PM). **Tips & Hints:** Visit Valley Forge Historical Society's museum and Washington Memorial Chapel, privately owned facilities within the park. Be careful during driving tours when crossing three busy state roads. Go Apr. and May for dogwood blooms, late Sept. and Oct. for fall foliage. Busiest July and Aug., least crowded Dec. and Jan.

FOOD, LODGING & SUPPLIES

🛏 **Camping:** None in park. In Elverson: French Creek State Park (843 Park Rd., tel. 610/582–9680; 201 sites; $12–$19; flush toilets, showers, hook-ups). 🏨 **Hotels:** None in park. In King of Prussia: Best Western (127 S. Gulph Rd., tel. 610/265–4500; 168 rooms; $89–$115), Comfort Inn–Valley Forge (550 W. DeKalb Pike at U.S. 202 N, tel. 610/962–0700; 121 rooms; $95–$149). ✕ **Restaurants:** None in park. In King of Prussia: Bertolli's Authentic Trattoria (160 N. Gulph Rd., tel. 610/265–2965; $9–$19). In Malvern: General Warren Inn (Old Lancaster Hwy., tel. 610/296–3637; $20–$26). 🛒 **Groceries & Gear:** None in park. In King of Prussia: Acme Supermarket (320 W. De Kalb Pike, tel. 610/768–4100).

FEES, HOURS & REGULATIONS

Entrance fee: $3 adults and free ages 16 and under to visit Washington's Headquarters. Summer bus tour Fri.–Mon. (tel. 610/768–0281). Pennsylvania state fishing license required. No hunting. Leashed pets only. Bikes and horseback riding on designated paths and areas only. No motorized vehicles off tour road. No in-line skating or skateboarding. Park open daily dawn–dusk (some areas remain open until 10 PM). Visitor center and Washington Headquarters open daily 9–5. Varnum's Quarters open May–Sept., weekends noon–4.

HOW TO GET THERE

20 mi west of Philadelphia, at the intersection of Rte. 23 and N. Gulph Rd. Closest airport: Philadelphia.

CONTACTS

Valley Forge National Historical Park (Box 953, Valley Forge, PA 19482, tel. 610/783–1077, fax 610/783–1053, www.nps.gov/vafo). Valley Forge Convention & Visitors Bureau (600 W. Germantown Pike, Plymouth Meeting, PA 19462, tel. 610/834–1550 or 800/441–3549, fax 610/834–0202).

See Also

Potomac Heritage National Scenic Trail, District of Columbia. *Appalachian National Scenic Trail*, West Virginia. *Benjamin Franklin National Memorial, Delaware & Lehigh Navigation Canal National Heritage Corridor, Gloria Dei (Old Swedes') Church National Historic Site, North Country National Scenic Trail, Southwestern Pennsylvania Industrial Heritage Route, Steel Industry American Heritage Area,* and *White Clay Creek*, in Other National Parklands.

RHODE ISLAND

Roger Williams National Memorial

In northeastern Rhode Island, in Providence

The memorial commemorates the life of Roger Williams, the founder of Rhode Island. A champion of religious freedom, Williams was banished from Massachusetts and founded Providence in 1636. This colony served as a refuge where all could come to worship freely. The memorial is on a common lot of the original settlement and includes 4½ acres of landscaped park. The memorial was designated on October 22, 1965.

WHAT TO SEE & DO

Picnicking, viewing exhibits and video, walking. **Facilities:** Visitor center (N. Main and Smith Sts.), wayside exhibits. Bookstore. **Programs & Events:** Junior Ranger program. **Tips & Hints:** Combine visit with trips to Rhode Island State House, Historic Benefit St., and other sites along Providence Banner Trail. Go in June and Sept. for the best weather, Sept. and Oct. for fall foliage. Busiest May and Oct., least crowded Jan. and Feb.

FEES, HOURS & REGULATIONS

Free. Leashed pets only. Memorial and visitor center open daily 9–4:30.

HOW TO GET THERE

From I–95 take the downtown Providence exit. Turn left onto Francis St., right at Gaspee St, right onto Smith St, right onto Canal St. Entrance to parking lot is on the left. Closest airport: Warwick (10 mi).

CONTACTS

Roger Williams National Memorial (282 N. Main St., Providence, RI 02903, tel. 401/521–7266, fax 401/521–7239, www.nps.gov/rowi). Rhode Island Economic Development Corp. (1 W. Exchange St., Providence, RI 02903, tel. 800/556–2484, fax 401/273–8270, www.visitrhodeisland. com). Providence and Warwick Convention & Visitors Bureau (1 W. Exchange St., 3rd fl., Providence, RI 02903, tel. 800/233–1636).

See Also

Blackstone River Valley National Heritage Corridor and *Touro Synagogue National Historic Site,* in Other National Parklands.

Charles Pinckney National Historic Site

In southeastern South Carolina, north of Charleston

Charles Pinckney (1754–1824) was a statesman, officer in the American Revolution, and a principal framer of the U.S. Constitution. He served four terms as governor of South Carolina and in the State Assembly. He also served in the U.S. Senate, House of Representatives, and as President Jefferson's minister to Spain. His ancestral home, Snee Farm, once consisted of 715 acres, 28 of which are today preserved at this site. Archaeological remains of brick foundations from the Pinckney era and an 1820s tidewater cottage also are maintained. The site was authorized on September 8, 1988.

WHAT TO SEE & DO

Touring facility and grounds. **Facilities:** Visitor center, wayside exhibits. Bookstore. **Programs & Events:** Self-guided walking tours through the house and grounds. Constitution Week (3rd week, Sept.), Archaeology Week (last week, Sept.). **Tips & Hints:** Go late Mar.–mid-Apr. for azalea and camellia blooms.

FEES, HOURS & REGULATIONS

Free. No hunting. No mountain or trail bikes. Leashed pets only. Park and visitor center open daily 9–5.

HOW TO GET THERE

The park is at 1254 Longpoint Rd., off U.S. 17 in Mount Pleasant, north of Charleston. Closest airport: Charleston (10 mi).

CONTACTS

Charles Pinckney National Historic Site (c/o Fort Sumter National Monument, 1214 Middle St., Sullivan's Island, SC 29482, tel. 843/881–5516, fax 843/881–7070, www.nps.gov/chpi). Mount Pleasant Visitors Information Center (291 Johnnie Dodds Blvd., Mount Pleasant, SC 29464, tel. 843/849–6154). Charleston Convention & Visitors Bureau (81 Mary St., Charleston, SC 29403, tel. 843/853–8000).

Congaree Swamp National Monument

In central South Carolina, near Hopkins

The 22,200-acre monument contains the last significant tract of old-growth bottomland hardwood forest in the United States. The swamp, most of which is managed as wilderness, is home to more than 75 tree species, including state and national champion trees, and abundant wildlife that includes the endangered red-cockaded woodpecker. The monument was authorized in 1976 and designated an International Biosphere Reserve in 1983.

WHAT TO SEE & DO

Bird-watching, camping, canoeing, fishing, hiking, kayaking, picnicking. **Facilities:** Visitor center, film, 25 mi of hiking trails, 10-mi canoe trail, 2½-mi boardwalk. Bookstore, picnic tables. **Programs & Events:** Self-guided walks, guided canoe trips. Owl prowls (Mar.–May and Sept.–Nov., every other Fri. evening). Naturefest (1 week, Apr.), American Rivers Month Programs (June), Public Lands Day, River Sweep (both in Sept.), Harry Hampton Memorial Walk (Nov.). **Tips & Hints:** Plan to stay at least two to four hours. Longer trails can take eight hours to explore. Canoe trips can vary in duration from four hours to overnight. Busiest Mar. and Apr., least crowded Dec. and Jan.

FOOD & LODGING

Camping: Backcountry camping allowed (permit required, *see below*). Near Columbia: Sesquicentennial State Park (9574 Two Notch Rd., off I–20, tel. 803/788-2706; 87 sites; $16; flush toilets, showers, hook-ups). **Hotels:** None in park. In Columbia: Adam's Mark (1200 Hampton St., tel. 803/771–7000 or 800/444–2326; 301 rooms; $79–$154), Best Western Governor's House Hotel & Suites (1301 Main St., tel. 803/779–7790; 100 rooms, 15 suites; $59–$119). ✕ **Restaurants:** None in park. In Columbia: Mr. Friendly's New Southern Café (2001-A Greene St., tel. 803/254–7828; $9–$22), Motor Supply Co. Bistro (920 Gervais St., tel. 803/256–6687; $13–$25; closed Mon.).

FEES, HOURS & REGULATIONS

Free, donations accepted. Reservations for guided programs should be made two weeks in advance, six weeks in advance in spring and fall. Backcountry permits required (free from visitor center). South Carolina state fishing license required. Monument open daily dawn–dusk. Visitor center open daily 8:30–5.

HOW TO GET THERE

From I–77, take Exit 5 onto Rte. 48 (Bluff Rd.), and follow signs. Closest airport: Columbia (25 mi).

CONTACTS

Superintendent, Congaree Swamp National Monument (100 National Park Rd., Hopkins, SC 29061, tel. 803/776–4396, fax 803/783–4241, www.nps.gov/cosw). Columbia Convention & Visitors Center (900 Assembly St., Columbia, SC 29201, tel. 803/545–0000 or 800/264–4884, fax 803/545–0013, www.columbiacvb.com).

Cowpens
National Battlefield

In northwestern South Carolina, near Chesnee

The battlefield commemorates a decisive Revolutionary War battle that helped turn the tide of war in the South. On this field on January 17, 1781, Daniel Morgan led his army of tough Continentals, militia, and cavalry to a brilliant victory over Banastre Tarleton's larger force of British regulars. Walking trails, auto tour road, monuments, and an 1828 log cabin are available. Cowpens was established as a national battlefield site in 1929, transferred to the Park Service in 1933, and redesignated in 1972.

WHAT TO SEE & DO

Auto touring, biking, bird- and wildlife watching, hiking, jogging, picnicking, walking. **Facilities:** Visitor center, fiber-optic battle program, tour roads and trails, wayside exhibits, overlooks, circa 1828 log cabin, monuments. Bookstore, picnic area. **Programs & Events:** "Daybreak at the Cowpens" presentation (daily 9–4, hourly). Battle anniversary (weekend nearest Jan. 17). Seasonal activities available. **Tips & Hints:** Plan to stay at least two hours. Busiest June and July, least crowded Nov. and Dec.

FOOD & LODGING

Camping: None in park. In Gaffney: Pine Cone Campground (160 Saratt School Rd., tel. 864/489–2022; 121 sites; $15–$27; flush toilets, showers, hook-ups). **Hotels:** None in park. In Gaffney: Comfort Inn (143 Corona Dr., tel. 864/487–4200; 83 rooms; $49–$68). In Spartanburg: Jameson Inn (115 Rogers Commerce Blvd., tel. 864/814–0560 or 800/526–3766; 42 rooms; $56). **Restaurants:** None in park. In Chesnee: Bantam Chef (418 S. Alabama Ave., tel. 864/461–8403; $5–$10). In Gaffney: Ruby Tuesday's (1513 W. Floyd Baker Blvd., tel. 864/488–9889; $6–$13). In Spartanburg: Stefano's (1560 Union St., tel. 864/591–1941; $7–$18; closed Sun., no lunch).

FEES, HOURS & REGULATIONS

Free. "Daybreak at the Cowpens" fee: $adults, 50¢ ages 6–12. Battlefield open daily 9–5.

HOW TO GET THERE

At the intersection of Rtes. 11 and 110, 2 mi east of Chesnee, 10 mi west of Gaffney and I–85 via Exit 92, and 17 mi northeast of Spartanburg via U.S. 221. From I–26, take Exit 5 to Rte. 11 east. Closest airports: Greenville–Spartanburg (45 mi), Charlotte, NC (60 mi).

CONTACTS

Cowpens National Battlefield (Box 308, Chesnee, SC 29323, tel. 864/461–2828, fax 864/461–7077 or 864/461–7795, www.nps.gov/cowp). Spartanburg Convention & Visitors Bureau (298 Magnolia St., Spartanburg, SC 29306, tel. 864/594–5050 or 800/374–8326, fax 864/594–5052, www.spartanburgchamber.com).

Fort Sumter National Monument

*In southeastern South Carolina,
in Charleston Harbor (and on Sullivan's Island).*

Fort Sumter was one of many coastal fortifications built by the United States after the War of 1812. The first shots of the Civil War were fired here on April 12, 1861, during a Confederate two-day bombardment that ended with the Union troops' withdrawal. Fort Moultrie, administered with Fort Sumter, is the site of the first Patriot victory over the British Navy in the American Revolution, a victory that contributed to British reluctance to invade the South. The fort served as the Charleston operational headquarters of the Confederate Army during the opening battle of the Civil War and the siege of Charleston. The monument was authorized in 1948. Fort Moultrie was transferred to the Park Service in 1961.

WHAT TO SEE & DO

Touring the forts. **Facilities:** Fort Sumter: museum, wayside exhibits. Fort Moultrie: visitor center, wayside exhibits. A tour boat facility with interpretive exhibits (downtown Charleston) is under development. Bookstores. **Programs & Events:** Fort Sumter: ranger orientation and history talks, battle anniversary and living-history programs (Apr. 12). Fort Moultrie: self-guided walking tours, interpretive talks (June–Aug.), battle anniversary and living-history programs (June 28). **Tips & Hints:** Fort Sumter: Get to boat departure area at least 15 min early. Go Sept. and Oct. for best weather and smaller crowds. Fort Moultrie: Allow two hours for tour. Busiest Apr. and July, least crowded Dec. and Jan.

FEES, HOURS & REGULATIONS

Fort Sumter: free. Tour boat fees apply. (tel. 843/722–2628). No pets. Fort open Mar. and Sept.–Nov., daily 10–4; Apr.–Labor Day, daily 10–5:30; hours vary rest of year. Fort Moultrie: $2 adults, $1 ages 15 and under and age 62 and over, $5 per family. No pets. Fort open daily 9–5.

HOW TO GET THERE

Fort Sumter is in Charleston Harbor and accessible only by boat. Departures at City Marina (Lockwood Dr., downtown Charleston) and Patriots Point (Patriots Point Naval and Maritime Museum, Mount Pleasant). Fort Moultrie is on Sullivan's Island. From Mount Pleasant, take Rte. 703 to Middle St. Closest airport: Charleston (20 mi).

CONTACTS

Fort Sumter National Monument (1214 Middle St., Sullivan's Island, SC 29482, tel. 843/883–3123, fax 843/883–3910, www.nps.gov/fosu). Charleston Convention & Visitors Bureau (Box 975, Charleston SC 29402, tel. 843/853–8000). Fort Moultrie (1214 Middle St., Sullivan's Island, SC 29482, tel. 843/883–3123, fax 843/883–3910, www.nps.gov/fomo).

Kings Mountain National Military Park

In north-central part of the state, near Gaffney

Preserved in this park is the site of a pivotal American Revolution battle, which was fought here on October 7, 1780. After a series of British victories, patriots from Virginia, the Carolinas, and Georgia defeated British Major Patrick Ferguson at Kings Mountain. The U.S. victory forced British General Charles Cornwallis to retreat back into South Carolina for the winter and helped turn the tide of the war against the British. The park was established in 1931.

WHAT TO SEE & DO

Hiking, touring battlefield, viewing film. **Facilities:** Visitor center, trail, wayside exhibits, amphitheater. Bookstore. **Programs & Events:** Living-history encampments (occasionally). Evening programs and concerts (May–Oct.), musket and rifle demonstrations (May–Oct., weekends). Battle anniversary (Oct. 7). **Tips & Hints:** Best times to visit are spring and fall. Go in spring and summer for wildflowers. Busiest May and June, least crowded Dec. and Jan.

FOOD, LODGING & SUPPLIES

Camping: In the park: Backcountry camping allowed (check-in at visitor center required). In Blacksburg: Kings Mountain State Park (1277 Park Rd., tel. 803/222–3209; 126 sites; $12–$16; flush toilets, showers, hook-ups). **Hotels:** *See Cowpens National Battlefield.* **Restaurants:** *See Cowpens National Battlefield.* **Groceries & Gear:** In Kings Mountain, NC: Harris Teeter (610 E. King St., tel. 704/739–7458).

FEES, HOURS & REGULATIONS

Free. No hunting, mountain biking, or ATV use. No metal detecting. Leashed pets only. Park open daily 9–5.

HOW TO GET THERE

On Rte. 216, 4 mi southeast of I–85 via Exit 2 (just over the border in NC). Closest airports: Greenville, SC (70 mi), Charlotte, NC (40 mi).

CONTACT

Kings Mountain National Military Park (2625 Park Rd., Blacksburg, SC 29702, tel. 864/936–7921, fax 864/936–9897, www.nps.gov/kimo).

Ninety Six National Historic Site

In southern South Carolina, near Greenwood

Ninety Six was named by traders who thought the stopping place was 96 mi from the Cherokee village of Keowee. The park commemorates the role the settlement played during British settlement of the frontier and the southern campaign of the American Revolution. It also offers historic roads and paths, the earthen British-built Star Fort (circa 1781), and the partially reconstructed Stockade Fort. Archaeological complexes abound, including the underground remains of two villages, plantations, houses, and forts. The site was authorized on August 16, 1976.

WHAT TO SEE & DO

Fishing, hiking interpretive trail, picnicking, viewing museum exhibits and video. **Facilities:** Visitor center, auditorium, trail, wayside exhibits. Book sales area, picnic tables. **Programs & Events:** "Lifeways of the Cherokee Indians and Colonial Settlers," Revolutionary War Days Encampment (Apr.). Annual Autumn Candlelight Tour (2nd Sat., Oct.). **Tips & Hints:** Visit in spring and fall when temperatures are cooler. Busiest in May and Oct., least crowded Jan. and Feb.

FOOD, LODGING & SUPPLIES

⚠ **Camping:** None in park. In Ninety Six: Lake Greenwood State Recreation Area (302 State Park Rd., tel. 864/543–3535; 130 sites; $12–$19; flush toilets, showers, hook-ups). 🏨 **Hotels:** None in park. In Greenwood: Inn on the Square (104 Court St., tel. 864/223–4488; 46 rooms; $80). ✗ **Restaurants:** None in park. In Greenwood: Regan's (328 Main St., tel. 864/388–0565; $8–$19; closed Sun., no lunch Sat.). ⛽ **Groceries & Gear:** None in park. In Ninety Six: Piggly Wiggly (Rte. 246, tel. 864/543–3918).

FEES, HOURS & REGULATIONS

Free. Donations accepted. South Carolina state fishing license required. Leashed pets only. No hunting. No mechanized equipment on trails. No bicycles on walking trail; no skateboards. Park is open daily dawn–dusk. Visitor center open daily 8–5.

HOW TO GET THERE

2 mi south of the town of Ninety Six, which is on Rte. 34, 10 mi east of Greenwood. Closest airport: Greenville (65 mi).

CONTACTS

Ninety Six National Historic Site (Box 496, Ninety Six, SC 29666, tel. 864/543–4068, fax 864/543–2058, www.nps.gov/nisi). Ninety Six Chamber of Commerce (Box 8, Ninety Six, SC 29666, tel. 864/543–2200).

See Also

Historic Camden, Overmountain Victory National Historic Trail, and *South Carolina National Heritage Corridor,* in Other National Parklands.

Badlands National Park

In southwestern South Dakota, near Wall

The 244,000-acre park is well known for its outstanding geological features—steep canyons, sharp ridges, gullies, spires, and knobs—and its rich paleontological resources, especially Oligocene-era mammal fossils. But it also contains the largest protected mixed-grass prairie in the National Park Service, 64,000 acres of wilderness, and the site of the reintroduction of the black-footed ferret, one of the most endangered land mammals in North America. The Stronghold Unit, which is managed under an agreement with the Oglala Sioux Tribe, includes the sites of the 1890s Ghost Dances. The site was authorized as a national monument in 1939 and redesignated a national park in 1978.

WHAT TO SEE & DO

Auto touring, hiking, horseback riding. **Facilities:** 2 visitor centers: Ben Reifel (Cedar Pass, Rte. 240 northeast of Interior) and White River (Stronghold Unit); loop roads, trails. Book and map sale areas, gift shop, picnic tables. **Programs & Events:** Guided walks, talks, and slide programs (mid-June–Labor Day). **Tips & Hints:** Bring hats and sunglasses to protect against bright sun. Watch for cactus. Give bison plenty of room. Busiest July and Aug., least crowded Dec. and Jan.

FOOD, LODGING & SUPPLIES

Camping: 2 campgrounds in the park: Cedar Pass (100 sites; $10; flush toilets, pit toilets), Sage Creek (primitive camping area; free; pit toilets). Backcountry camping allowed. In Interior: Badlands KOA (Rte. 44, 4 mi south of Interior, tel. 605/342–7365; 144 sites; $18–$28; flush toilets, showers, hook-ups; closed mid-Oct.–Apr.). In Wall: Arrow Camp (515 Crown St., tel. 605/279–2112; 100 sites; $12–$18; flush toilets, showers, hook-ups). **Hotels:** In the park: Cedar Pass Lodge (1 Cedar St./Rte. 240, tel. 605/433–5460; 24 cabins; $47–$70; closed Oct.–Mar.). In Interior: Badlands Ranch & Resort (Rte. 44, tel. 605/433–5599; 4 rooms, 7 cabins; $52–$56, $62–$100 cabins). **Restaurants:** In the park: Cedar Pass Lodge Restaurant (1 Cedar St./Rte. 240, tel. 605/433–5460; $8–$16; closed Oct.–Mar.). In Wall: Western Art Gallery Restaurant (Wall Drug Store, 510 Main St., tel. 605/279–2175; $5–$15). **Groceries & Gear:** None in park. In Interior: Badlands Grocery (10 Main St., tel. 605/433–5445). In Wall: Wall Drug Store (510 Main St., tel. 605/279–2175).

FEES, HOURS & REGULATIONS

Entrance fee: $5 per person or $10 per vehicle. No hunting, collecting, open campfires, off-road travel. Backcountry campers must be at least a half-mile away from roads and trails, not visible, and leave no trace. Bicycling on established roads only. Pets allowed on roads and established campgrounds only and must be on a leash. Park open daily. Ben Reifel Visitor Center open daily 9–4, extended hrs in summer. White River Visitor Center open early June–late Aug., daily 9–4.

HOW TO GET THERE

The park loop road (Rte. 240) can be accessed from I–90 via Exits 110 or 131. Follow signs to visitor center. Closest airport: Rapid City (80 mi).

CONTACTS

Badlands National Park (Box 6, Interior, SD 57750, tel. 605/433–5361, fax 605/433–5404, www.nps.gov/badl). South Dakota Tourism (711 E. Wells Ave., Pierre, SD 57501, tel. 605/773–3301 or800/732–5682).

Jewel Cave National Monument

In southwestern South Dakota, near Custer

With more than 122 mi surveyed, Jewel Cave is recognized as the third-longest cave in the world. Air flow inside the cave's passages indicates a vast area yet to be explored. Cave tours provide opportunities for viewing this pristine cave system and its wide variety of speleothems, including stalactites, stalagmites, draperies, flowstone, frostwork, boxwork, and hydromagnesite balloons. The cave is an important hibernaculum for several species of bats. Above ground the monument protects Hell and Lithograph canyons, a ranger cabin listed on the National Register of Historic Structures, and some of the last unlogged ponderosa pine forest in the Black Hills. The monument was established in 1908 and transferred to the Park Service in 1933.

WHAT TO SEE & DO

Hiking surface trails, picnicking, touring caves. **Facilities:** Visitor center, video, Historic Area Ranger Station, trails. Book sales areas, picnic tables. **Programs & Events:** Ranger-led scenic cave tours (daily). Ranger-led Lantern Tours (June–Labor Day, daily; reservations required), Spelunking cave tours (June–Aug., daily; reservations required). **Tips & Hints:** Arrive early in the day, especially July and Aug., to avoid a wait for cave tours. Cave is 49°F year-round. Busiest July and Aug., least crowded Dec. and Jan.

FOOD, LODGING & SUPPLIES

Camping: None in park. In Custer: Beaver Lake Campground (12005 U.S. 16, tel. 605/673–2464; 92 sites; $20–$24; flush toilets, showers, hook-ups), Comanche Park (U.S. 16, 6 mi west of Custer, tel. 605/574–4402; 877/444–6777 reservations; 32 sites; $13; vault toilets; closed mid-Sept.–mid-May). **Hotels:** None in park. In Custer: Dakota Cowboy Hotel (208 W. Mt. Rushmore Rd., tel. 605/673–4659; 48 rooms; $48–$75; closed mid-Oct.–Apr.). In Custer State Park: Blue Bell Lodge & Resort (Rte. 87, tel. 605/255–4531 or 800/658–3530; 29

cabins; $87–$170), State Game Lodge & Resort (U.S. 16A, tel. 605/255–4541 or 800/658–3530; 47 rooms, 33 cabins; $89–$215, $75–$315 cabins). ✕ **Restaurants:** None in park. In Custer: Chief Restaurant (140 W. Mt. Rushmore Rd., tel. 605/673-4402; $5–$10; closed mid-Oct.–May). In Custer State Park: State Game Lodge & Resort (U.S 16A, tel. 605/255–4541; $15–$28). ♨ **Groceries & Gear:** None in park. In Custer: Lynn's Dakota Mart (800 Mt. Rushmore Rd., tel. 605/673–4463), True Value Hardware (529 Mt. Rushmore Rd., tel. 605/673–2227).

FEES, HOURS & REGULATIONS

Free. Scenic cave tour fees: $8 adults, $4 ages 6–16, free ages 5 and under. No children under 6 on some tours. Spelunking tour fees: $20 per person; no children under 16. No pets, tripods, or walking sticks in cave. Leashed pets only on trails. No mountain or trail bikes, motorized or mechanized equipment on trails. No hunting or open fires. Park open Memorial Day–Labor Day, daily 8–7:30; Labor Day–Memorial Day, daily 8–4:30.

HOW TO GET THERE

13 mi west of Custer and 24 mi east of Newcastle, WY, via U.S. 16. Closest airport: Rapid City (53 mi).

CONTACTS

Jewel Cave National Monument (R.R. 1, Box 60AA, Custer, SD 57730, tel. 605/673–2288, fax 605/673–3294, www.nps.gov/jeca). Custer County Chamber of Commerce (615 Washington St., Custer, SD 57730, tel. 605/673–2244 or 800/922–9818, fax 605/673–3726). Newcastle Chamber of Commerce (6 W. Warwick St., Newcastle, WY 82701, tel. 307/746–2739).

Minuteman Missile National Historic Site

In southwestern South Dakota, in Interior

The history of the Cold War is the focus of this park unit. The site consists of a launch control center, an aboveground facility attached to a subterranean capsule; and a launch facility, known as a missile silo. The site was established on December 2, 1999.

WHAT TO SEE & DO

This is a new site under development and not yet open to the public. *See Badlands National Park* for information on nearby facilities.

CONTACT

Minuteman Missile National Historic Site (c/o Badlands National Park, Box 6, Interior, SD 57750, tel. 605/433–5361, fax 605/433–5248, www.nps.gov/mimi).

Mount Rushmore National Memorial

In southwestern South Dakota, near Keystone

The faces of four U.S. presidents—George Washington, Thomas Jefferson, Abraham Lincoln, and Theodore Roosevelt—are carved into the southeast side of the granite mountain. Sculptor Gutzon Borglum and 400 workers spent 14 years (1927–41) carving the images that collectively represent the birth, growth, development, and expansion of the first 150 years of the United States. The memorial was authorized in 1925.

WHAT TO SEE & DO

Climbing, hiking, viewing the memorial. **Facilities:** Information center, Lincoln Borglum Museum, Sculptors Studio, amphitheater, theaters, trails. Bookstore, religious services (June–Aug.). **Programs & Events:** Guided talks, guided walks to Sculptors Studio, evening lighting ceremony (mid-May–Sept.). July 4 Celebration. **Tips & Hints:** Visit in the early morning for the best light. Busiest July and August, least crowded Dec. and Jan.

FOOD & LODGING

Camping: None in park. In Hill City: Mount Rushmore KOA (Rte. 244, tel. 605/574–2525; 500 sites, 85 cabins; $22–$30; flush toilets, showers, hook-ups; closed Oct.–Apr.). *See also Jewel Cave National Monument.* **Hotels:** None in park. In Hill City: Lodge at Palmer Gulch (12620 Rte. 244, tel. 605/574–2525 or 800/562–8503; 62 rooms, 30 cabins; $113). *See also Jewel Cave National Monument and Wind Cave National Park.* **Restaurants:** In Hill City: Alpine Inn (225 Main St., tel. 605/574–2749; $6–$12; closed Sun.). In Keystone: Buffalo Dining Room (Rte. 244, tel. 605/574–2515; $7–$13). *See also Jewel Cave National Monument.*

FEES, HOURS & REGULATIONS

Free. Parking fees: $8 (good for one year). Leashed pets only. Trails for walking only. No off-road travel. Park open daily. Information center and museum open Memorial Day–Labor Day, daily 8 AM–10 PM; Labor Day–Memorial Day, daily 8–5.

HOW TO GET THERE

The memorial, which is surrounded by the Black Hills National Forest, is 25 mi southwest of Rapid City via U.S. 16 and 3 mi from Keystone via U.S. 16A and Rte. 244. Closest airport: Rapid City.

CONTACTS

Superintendent, Mount Rushmore National Memorial (Box 268, Keystone, SD 57751, tel. 605/574–2523, fax 605/574–2307, www.nps.gov/moru). Keystone Chamber of Commerce (Box 653, Keystone, SD 57751, tel. 605/666–4896). Rapid City Chamber of Commerce (Box 747, Rapid City, SD 57709, tel. 605/343–1744). South Dakota Department of Tourism (711 E. Wells Ave., Pierre, SD 57501, tel. 605/773–3301 or 800/732–5682).

Wind Cave National Park

In southwestern South Dakota, near Hot Springs

Wind Cave, in the scenic Black Hills, is one of the longest and most complex caves in the world. It contains beautiful boxwork—a rare cave formation—in greater variety and profusion than any other cave in the world. The 28,295-acre park's rolling mixed-grass prairie, pine-covered hills, and woodland ravines also are home to a diverse mix of eastern and western plant and wildlife species, including bison, elk, pronghorn, mule deer, coyotes, and prairie dogs. The park was established on January 9, 1903.

WHAT TO SEE & DO

Cave touring, fishing, hiking, picnicking, wildlife watching. **Facilities:** Visitor center, Cave Elevator Building with exhibits, amphitheater, self-guided nature trails, wayside exhibits, fire lookout tower. Bookstore, fire grates, picnic tables. **Programs & Events:** Cave tours (daily). Guided prairie hikes, interpretive talks, campfire programs (all June–Aug.). **Tips & Hints:** Wear walking shoes and sweater or jacket in cave. Cave temperature is 53°F. Stay away from bison and prairie dogs and their burrows, which harbor rattlesnakes. Go in spring or fall to avoid crowds. Busiest July and Aug., least crowded Dec. and Jan.

FOOD, LODGING & SUPPLIES

Camping: In the park: Elk Mountain (75 sites; $12; flush toilets; closed late Oct.–Apr.). *See also Jewel Cave National Monument.* **Hotels:** None in park. In Hot Springs: Best Western Inn (602 W. River St., tel. 605/745–4292 or 888/605–4292; 32 rooms; $49–$104), Comfort Inn (737 S. 6th St., tel. 605/745–7378 or 800/228–5150; 51 rooms, 9 suites; $109). *See also Jewel Cave National Monument.* **Restaurants:** None in park. In Hot Springs: Seven Sisters Steakhouse & Lounge (U.S. 18, near Mammoth Site, tel. 605/745–6666; $9–$18), Elk Horn Cafe (310 S. Chicago St., tel. 605/745–6556; $5–$10). *See also Jewel Cave National Monument.* **Groceries & Gear:** In Hot Springs: Family Thrift (505 S. 6th St., tel. 605/745–3203).

FEES, HOURS & REGULATIONS

Free. Cave tour fees: $6–$9 adults, free ages 5 and under. Spelunking (Wild) tour: $20, no children under 16. Reservations available for Candlelight and Wild cave tours (tel. 605/745–4600). South Dakota state fishing license required. Backcountry permits (free from visitor center or Centennial Trail trailheads) required for all backcountry camping. No hunting. No pets on trails or in backcountry. Leashed pets elsewhere. No bikes off road. Fires in campground fire grates and picnic area only. No food, drink, or camera tripods in caves. Park open daily. Visitor center open May and Sept., daily 8–6; June–Aug., daily 8–7:30; Oct.–Apr., daily 8–4:30.

HOW TO GET THERE

7 mi north of Hot Springs and 20 mi south of Custer via U.S. 385. Closest airport: Rapid City (60 mi).

CONTACTS

Wind Cave National Park (R.R. 1, Box 190 WCNP, Hot Springs, SD 57747, tel. 605/745–4600, fax 605/745–4207, www.nps.gov/wica). Hot Springs Area Chamber of Commerce (801 S. 6th St., Hot Springs, SD 57747, tel. 800/325–6991). Custer County Chamber of Commerce (615 Washington St., Custer, SD 57730, tel. 605/673–2244 or 800/922–9818).

See Also

Missouri National Recreational River and *Niobrara National Scenic Riverway*, Nebraska. *Lewis and Clark National Historic Trail*, in Other National Parklands.

Andrew Johnson National Historic Site

In northeastern Tennessee, in Greeneville

At this site are two homes, the tailor shop, and the burial site of Andrew Johnson, who became president in 1865 after Abraham Lincoln was assassinated. Guided tours explore the presidential homestead, which belonged to Johnson from 1851 until his death in 1875. The site was authorized as a national monument August 29, 1935; established April 27, 1942; and redesignated a national historic site December 11, 1963.

WHAT TO SEE & DO

Touring the facilities. **Facilities:** Visitor center with museum and tailor shop, early Johnson home with museum, president's homestead, national cemetery where Johnson is buried. Book sales area. **Programs & Events:** Ranger-guided tours (daily at 9:30, 10:30, 11:30, 1:30, 2:30, 3:30, and 4:30). Memorial Day program (May 30). **Tips & Hints:** Busiest May and Oct., least crowded Jan. and Feb.

FOOD, LODGING & SUPPLIES

Camping: None in park. Near Greenville: Horse Creek (Horse Creek Rd., off Rte. 107, tel. 423/638–4109; 15 sites; $8; flush toilets, showers), Old Forge (Old Forge Rd., off Horse Creek Rd., tel. 423/638–4109; 10 sites; $8; flush toilets, showers), Paint Creek (off Rte. 70, tel. 423/638–4109; 19 sites; $10; flush toilets, showers, hook-ups). **Hotels:** None in park. In Greeneville: Big Spring Inn (315 N. Main St., tel. 423/638–2917; 4 rooms, 1 suite; $70–$86; closed Nov.–Mar.), Jameson Inn (3160 E. Andrew Johnson Hwy., tel. 423/638–7511; 55 rooms; $64). **Restaurants:** None in park. In Greeneville: Deidra's Cafe (140 W. Depot St., tel. 423/636–8806; $15–$20; closed Sun., no dinner Mon.), Olde Tusculum Eatery (905 Erwin Hwy., tel. 423/638–9210; $4–$11; closed weekends, no dinner). **Groceries & Gear:** None in park. In Greeneville: Food City (905 Snapps Ferry Rd., tel. 423/638–5345).

FEES, HOURS & REGULATIONS

Free. Leashed pets only. Site open daily 9–5.

HOW TO GET THERE

In downtown Greeneville, at the corner of College and Depot Sts. Closest airport: Kingsport (40 mi).

CONTACTS

Andrew Johnson National Historic Site (Box 1088, Greeneville, TN 37744-1088, tel. 423/639–3711, fax 423/798–0754, www.nps.gov/anjo). Greene County Partnership–Chamber of Commerce (115 Academy St., Greenville, TN 37743, tel. 423/638–4111, fax 423/638–5345).

Big South Fork National River & Recreation Area

In northeastern Tennessee and south-central Kentucky

The free-flowing Big South Fork of the Cumberland River and its tributaries pass through 90 mi of scenic gorges and valleys containing a range of natural and historic features. Recreational opportunities abound. Planning and development by the U.S. Army Corps of Engineers was authorized in 1974, Park Service management was authorized in 1976, and transfer to Park Service was settled in 1991.

WHAT TO SEE & DO

Biking, canoeing (rentals in Whitley City), fishing, hiking, horseback riding, hunting, kayaking, rafting (rentals in Whitley City), swimming. **Facilities:** 2 visitor centers: Bandy Creek (15 mi west of Oneida, TN, off Rte. 297); Kentucky center (Rte. 92 in Stearns), outdoor museum (Blue Heron Mining Community, KY), hiking and horse trails, overlooks, pool. Bookstores. **Programs & Events:** Astronomy programs, dulcimer concerts. Evening programs (Memorial Day–Sept., Sat.), Storytelling and Craft Festival (Sept.), Pioneer Encampments (Oct.). **Tips & Hints:** Use caution when crossing rivers on foot or horseback. Be careful when swimming in rivers, approaching overlooks, and in weather when hypothermia is risk. Busiest Sept. and Oct., least crowded Jan. and Feb.

FOOD, LODGING & SUPPLIES

Camping: 3 campgrounds in the park: Alum Ford (end of Rte. 700; 8 sites; $5; pit toilets), Bandy Creek (off Rte. 297; 146 sites; $20; flush toilets, showers, hook-ups), Blue Heron (off Rte. 742; 45; $20; flush toilets, showers, hook-ups). Backcountry camping and horse campsites available (permit required, *see below*). **Hotels:** In the park: Charit Creek Lodge (tel. 865/429–5704; 2 cabins, 2 lodge rooms; $110; hike or ride in only). In Jamestown: Big South Fork Lodge & Stables (3607 Leatherwood Ford Rd., tel. 931/879–4230; 6 rooms, 1 cabin; $49–$85). In Oneida: Tobe's Motel & Restaurant (20151 Alberta St., tel. 423/569–8581; 48 rooms; $48–$54). **Restaurants:** None in park. In Oneida: Tobe's Motel & Restaurant (20151 Alberta St., tel. 423/565–4689; $6–$11). **Groceries & Gear:** None in park. In Jamestown: Willy Lee's General Store (Rte. 297, tel. 931/879–6987). In Whitley City, KY: Sheltowee Trace Outfitters (Rte. 90, tel. 800/541–7238).

FEES, HOURS & REGULATIONS

Free. Guided horseback rides available (tel. 423/286–7433). Big South Fork Scenic Railway offers train excursions from Stearns, KY, to the Blue Heron Mining Community (tel. 800/462–5664). Backcountry permit required ($5). Hunting allowed in recreation area only. Tennessee or Kentucky state hunting and fishing licenses required. Park open daily. Bandy Creek Visitor Center open Nov.–May, daily 8–4:30; June–Oct., daily 8–6. Kentucky Visitor Center open Apr.–Nov., daily 9–5:30; Dec.–Mar., weekends 9–5:30.

HOW TO GET THERE

The Tennessee visitor center is 15 mi west of Oneida, off Rte. 297. The Kentucky visitor center is on Rte. 92 in Stearns. Park headquarters is 9 mi west of Oneida on Rte. 297. Closest airports: Knoxville (80 mi) and Nashville (150 mi); and Lexington, KY (261 mi).

CONTACTS

Big South Fork National River & Recreation Area (Park Headquarters, 4564 Leatherwood Rd., Oneida, TN 37841, tel. 423/569–9778 or 423/286–7275; 606/376–5073 in KY, www.nps.gov/biso).

Fort Donelson National Battlefield

In northwestern Tennessee, near Dover

Fort Donelson was created to preserve and interpret the remains of the Battle of Fort Donelson, the 1862 Civil War conflict. The park includes the fort, river batteries, outer defense earthworks, Surrender House (Dover Hotel), and a national cemetery. The historical significance of the park centers on three major themes: Union commander Ulysses S. Grant ("Unconditional Surrender" Grant) and his capture of the fort and 13,000 Confederate prisoners; the use of ironclad gunboats on inland rivers; and the beginning of the Union Army's control of the north-to-south inland waters of the Tennessee and Cumberland rivers. The park was established as a national military park on March 26, 1928, transferred to the Park Service in 1933, and redesignated in 1985.

WHAT TO SEE & DO

Auto touring, hiking, picnicking, visiting museum, watching slide program. **Facilities:** Visitor center, Surrender House (Dover Hotel), museum, wayside exhibits, trails, interpretive tour tapes. Book and map sale area, picnic tables. **Programs & Events:** Slide program. Surrender House (Dover Hotel) open June–Sept., daily noon–4. Costume interpretive programs (occasionally, Feb.–Oct.). **Tips & Hints:** Go Apr.–June for flowers, Sept.–Mar. for smaller crowds. Busiest June and July, least crowded Jan. and Feb.

FOOD, LODGING & SUPPLIES

Camping: None in park. Near Dover: Piney Campground (Land Between the Lakes National Forest, 621 Fort Henry Rd., tel. 931/232–5556; 383 sites, 9 cabins; $16–$29; flush toilets, showers, hookups). **Hotels:** None in park. In Clarksville: Hachland Hill Inn (1601 Madison St., tel. 931/647–4084; 7 rooms, 3 cottages; $95), Riverview Inn (50 College St., tel. 931/552–3331; 154 rooms, 11 suites; $54–$85). **Restaurants:** None in park. In Dover: Cindy's Catfish Kitchen (2148 Donelson Pkwy., tel. 931/232–4817; $4–$6) **Groceries & Gear:** None in park. In Dover: Piggly Wiggly (1536 Donelson Pkwy, tel. 931/232–7024).

FEES, HOURS & REGULATIONS

Free. Leashed pets only. No metal detectors, skating, skateboards, vehicles on trails, hunting. Park open daily sunrise–sunset. Visitor center open daily 8–4:30.

HOW TO GET THERE

1 mi west of Dover, off U.S. 79. Closest airport: Nashville (90 mi).

CONTACTS

Fort Donelson National Battlefield (Box 434, Dover, TN 37058, tel. 931/232–5706, fax 931/232–6331, www.nps.gov/fodo). Dover–Stuart County Chamber of Commerce (Box 147, Dover, TN 37058, tel. 931/232–8290).

Great Smoky Mountains National Park

In eastern Tennessee, near Gatlinburg; and western North Carolina, near Cherokee

The 521,621-acre forested park is world renowned for the diversity of its plants and animals, the beauty of its ancient mountains, the quality of its remnants of American pioneer culture, and the depth and integrity of the wilderness sanctuary within its boundaries. It's one of the largest protected areas in the East. The park was authorized in 1926 and designated a Biosphere Reserve in 1976 and a World Heritage Site in 1983.

WHAT TO SEE & DO

Auto touring, bicycling (rentals in Cades Cove), fishing, hiking, horseback riding, picnicking, swimming, tubing. **Facilities:** 3 visitor centers: Sugarlands (2 mi south of Gatlinburg, TN, on U.S. 441), Oconaluftee (1 mi north of Cherokee, NC), and Cades Cove (near Townsend, TN); Mountain Farm Museum, scenic drives, 850 mi of trails. Bookstores, picnic areas, orientation film at Sugarlands. **Programs & Events:** Ranger-led interpretive walks and talks, slide presentations, and campfire programs (June–Sept.). Old Timers' Day, storytelling, Quilt Show, Women's Work, Mountain Life Festival, Sorghum Molasses and Apple Butter Making, and living-history programs (all May–Oct.). **Tips & Hints:** Expect temperatures to be 10–20 degrees cooler on mountaintops (up to 6,643 feet). Summers are hot and humid at lower elevations; frost begins in late Sept.; the driest weather is in fall. Busiest July and Aug., least crowded Jan. and Feb.

FOOD, LODGING & SUPPLIES

🏕 **Camping:** 10 campgrounds in the park (all with flush toilets): Abrams Creek (16 sites; $12; closed Nov.–mid-Mar.), Balsam Mountain (46 sites; $14; closed mid-Oct.–mid-May), Big Creek (12 tent sites; $12; closed Nov.–mid-Mar.), Cades Cove (161 sites; $14–$17), Cataloochee (27 sites; $12; closed Nov.–mid-Mar.), Cosby (157 sites; $14; closed Nov.–mid-Mar.), Deep Creek (108 sites; $14; closed Nov.–mid-

Apr.), Elkmont (220 sites; $14–$20; closed Dec.–mid-Mar.), Look Rock (92 sites; $14; closed Nov.–mid-May), Smokemount (140 sites; $14–$16). Backcountry camping in designated sites only (permit required, *see below*). 🏨 **Hotels:** In the park: LeConte Lodge (tel. 865/429–5704; 50 beds; $55.50 per person; closed mid-Nov.–Apr.). In Gatlinburg: Brookside Resort (463 E. Parkway, tel. 865/436–5611 or 800/251–9597; 240 rooms, 60 suites, 8 cottages; $55). ✕ **Restaurants:** None in park. In Gatlinburg: Atrium (432 Parkway, tel. 865/430–3684; $5–$8), Greenbrier Restaurant (370 Newman Rd., tel. 865/436–6318; $14–$22). 🛒 **Groceries & Gear:** None in park. In Gatlinburg: Food City (1219 E. Parkway, tel. 865/430–3116), Happy Hiker (905 River Rd., tel. 800/445–3701).

FEES, HOURS & REGULATIONS

Free. Fees charged at developed campgrounds. Permit required (free) for backcountry camping. Great Smoky Mountains Institute at Tremont offers workshop (tel. 865/448–6709). Smoky Mountain Field School offers weekend workshops (tel. 800/284–8885). Reservations available for five horse camps (tel. 800/365–2267). Call park for private stables within park. Tennessee or North Carolina fishing license required. No pets on most trails. Leashed pets elsewhere. Park, Sugarlands, and Oconaluftee open daily 9–4, longer hours in summer. Cades Cove open daily.

HOW TO GET THERE

The park has three main entrances. From I–40 east in TN, take Exit 407 (Sevierville) to Rte. 66 south, continue to U.S. 441 south, follow U.S. 441 to park. From I–40 west in TN, take Exit 386B in Knoxville to U.S. 129 south to Alcoa–Maryville. At Maryville proceed on U.S. 321 east through Townsend. Continue straight on Rte. 73 into park. From I–40 in NC, take U.S. 19 west through Maggie Valley. Proceed to U.S. 441 north at Cherokee into the park. From Atlanta and points south, follow U.S. 23 north to U.S. 441 north. Closest airports: Knoxville, TN (50 mi), Asheville, NC (60 mi).

CONTACT

Great Smoky Mountains National Park (107 Park Headquarters Rd., Gatlinburg, TN 37738, tel. 865/436–1200, fax 865/436–1220, www.nps.gov/grsm).

Obed Wild & Scenic River

In east-central Tennessee, near Wartburg

Clear and Daddy's creeks, about 45 mi of free-flowing streams on the Obed and Emory rivers, are protected in this park. The river provides some of the most rugged scenery in the Southeast and has spectacular gorges 500 feet deep. The river was authorized on October 12, 1976.

WHAT TO SEE & DO

Fishing, hiking, hunting, picnicking, rock climbing, swimming, whitewater boating. **Facilities:** Visitor center (Wartburg), trails. Bookstore. **Programs & Events:** Slide presentations (on request). Ranger-led talks and walks (Apr.–Oct., most weekends). **Tips & Hints:** Be aware of changing weather conditions if boating or climbing. Expect white-water conditions suitable for experienced boaters only. Go Jan.–Apr. for best white-water boating. Call park for water levels and float information.

FOOD, LODGING & SUPPLIES

⚠ **Camping:** In the park: Rock Creek (Off Catoosa Rd., near Nemo Bridge; 12 sites; $7; no water). Near Wartburg: Frozen Head State Park (964 Flat Fork Rd., tel. 423/346–7732; 19 sites; $11; pit toilets). ⊞ **Hotels:** None in park. In Crossville: Ramada Inn (4083 U.S. 127, tel. 931/484–7581 or 800/228–2828; 130 rooms; $84). In Wartburg: Yesterday's Inn Bed & Breakfast (3579 Morgan County Hwy., tel. 423/346–5188; 3 rooms; $50). ✕ **Restaurants:** None in park. In Wartburg: Angie's (721 Main St., tel. 423/346–2504; $5–$7). ⛁ **Groceries & Gear:** None in park. In Wartburg: Darnell's Food Market (1014 Main St., tel. 423/346–3344).

FEES, HOURS & REGULATIONS

Free. No glass bottles at river access points. No alcohol. Tennessee hunting and fishing licenses required. Visitor center open daily 8–4:30.

HOW TO GET THERE

From I–40, follow U.S. 27 north or U.S. 127 north. From the south, follow I–75 north to I–40 west. From the north, take I–75 to Rte. 63 west to U.S. 27 south. Closest airport: Knoxville (50 mi).

CONTACTS

Obed Wild and Scenic River (Box 429, Wartburg, TN 37887, tel. 423/346–6294, www.nps.gov/obed).

Shiloh National Military Park

In southwestern Tennessee, near Savannah

The largest battle of the 1862 Civil War campaign for possession of the railroads of the western Confederacy and military control of the lower Mississippi River occurred on this site. The park includes 4,000 acres of preserved battlefield, with more than 150 monuments, 217 cannons, 450 iron interpretive tablets, and the historic Peach Orchard, Hornets Nest, and Bloody Pond. Shiloh also protects an extensive Native American mound complex. The park was established in 1894 and transferred to the Park Service in 1933.

WHAT TO SEE & DO

Auto or bike tours, genealogy and military research, hiking, touring museum, walking, watching film. **Facilities:** 2 visitor centers: Pittsburg Landing and Battery Robinett (Corinth, MS; due to open in spring 2004); museum and film, 450 tablets, 151 monuments, 14 wayside panels, and 5 audio boxes. Bookstore, fire pits and grates, pavilion, picnic tables. **Programs & Events:** Film, *Shiloh: Portrait of a Battle* (daily, every half hour), ranger-guided tours and talks (occasionally). Guided hikes, interpretive talks, cultural demonstrations (May–Aug.). Shiloh anniversary (closest weekend to Apr. 6–7), Memorial Day Service (May), living-history demonstrations (occasionally). **Tips & Hints:** Observe 25-mph speed limit. Watch for pedestrians, bicyclists, and wildlife. Face traffic when hiking on road. Watch for snakes. Go in early spring when crowds are smaller and historic Peach Orchard is blooming, fall for foliage. Busiest Apr. and May, least crowded Dec. and Jan.

FOOD, LODGING & SUPPLIES

Camping: None in park. In Pickwick Dam: Pickwick Landing State Park (Rte. 57 S, tel. 731/689–3129 or 800/250–8615; 48 sites; $14–$17; flush toilets, showers, hook-ups). **Hotels:** None in park. In Pickwick Dam: Pickwick Landing (Rte. 57 S, tel. 731/689–3135 or 800/250–8615; 78 rooms, 3 suites, 10 cabins; $46–$150). **Restaurants:** None in park. In Savannah: Woodys (705 Main St., tel. 901/925–0104; $6–$13). **Groceries & Gear:** None in park. In Counce: Ray & Sandy's Store (Rte. 57, tel. 731/689–3292).

FEES, HOURS & REGULATIONS

$3 per person or $5 per family. No hunting, metal detecting, or removing archaeological resources. Leashed pets only. Bicycles on pavement only. No in-line skating or skateboarding. Visitor center open daily 8–5. Grounds open until sunset.

HOW TO GET THERE

12 mi south of Savannah via U.S. 64 and Rte. 22 and 22 mi north of Corinth, MS, via U.S. 45 and Rte. 22. Closest airports: Hardin County (15 mi), Memphis (115 mi).

CONTACTS

Superintendent, Shiloh National Military Park (1055 Pittsburgh-Landing Rd., Shiloh, TN 38376, tel. 731/689–5696, fax 731/689–5450, www.nps.gov/shil). Team Hardin County, Department of Tourism (507 Main St., Savannah, TN 38372, tel. 731/925–2364 or 800/552–3866, www.hardincountytn.com).

Stones River National Battlefield

Midstate, in Murfreesboro

Between December 31, 1862, and January 2, 1863, the Union Army of the Cumberland and the Confederate Army of the Tennessee fought here in a battle that cost each side nearly 30% in casualties. The battle was a key Union victory that marked the start of the campaign to take Chattanooga and Atlanta. Stones River National Cemetery, with 6,831 interments, of which 2,562 are unidentified, adjoins the battlefield. The cemetery was established in 1865 and the park was established in 1927.

WHAT TO SEE & DO

Self-guided or audiotape-guided auto touring; self-guided bicycle or walking tours of the battlefield. **Facilities:** Visitor center (3501 Old Nashville Hwy., Murfreesboro), interpretive waysides and exhibits along tour route and trail, Fortress Rosecrans (Old Fort Park, off Rte. 96), trails. Bookstore, connections to Stones River Greenway, picnic tables. **Programs & Events:** 18-minute slide program (year-round). Interpretive walks and talks (June–Sept.), living-history demonstrations (mid-June–Aug.), "Hallowed Ground" cemetery tour by lantern (mid-June–Aug.). Battle Anniversary (Dec. 31–Jan. 2). **Tips & Hints:** Go to visitor center first. Go in early to mid-spring and most of fall for best weather. Busiest July and Oct., least crowded Dec. and Jan.

FOOD, LODGING & SUPPLIES

Camping: None in park. In Lebanon: Cedars of Lebanon State Park (328 Cedar Forest Rd., tel. 615/443–2769; 117 sites; $14–$17; flush toilets, showers, hook-ups). **Hotels:** None in park. In Murfreesboro: Best Value Inn (1954 S. Church St., 615/896–6030; 125 rooms; $51–$75). **Restaurants:** None in park. In Murfreesboro: Luby's Cafeteria (1720 Old Fort Pkwy., tel. 615/890–4188; $4–$10), Slick Pig Bar-B-Que (1920 E. Main St., tel. 615/890–3583; $5–$7). **Groceries & Gear:** None in park. In Lebanon: Bi-Lo (1313 Main St., tel. 615/453–3986).

FEES, HOURS & REGULATIONS

Free. Stay on trails. No hunting. Leashed pets only. No metal detectors. No removing artifacts. No in-line skating, rollerblading, or skateboarding. Bikes on park roads only. Battlefield open daily 8–5, grounds open until dark for visitors on foot.

HOW TO GET THERE

On Old Nashville Hwy. (U.S. 41/70) in Murfreesboro, 27 mi south of Nashville via I–24. Closest airport: Nashville.

CONTACTS

Stones River National Battlefield (3501 Old Nashville Hwy., Murfreesboro, TN 37129, tel. 615/893–9501, fax 615/893–9508, www.nps.gov/stri). Lebanon-Wilson County Chamber of Commerce (149 Public Sq., Lebanon, TN   37087, tel. 615/444–5503 or 800/789–1327, fax 615/443–0596, www.wilsoncounty.com/lebanonchamber). Rutherford County Chamber of Commerce (501 Memorial Blvd., Murfreesboro, TN 37129, tel. 615/893–6565, fax 615/890–7600).

See Also

Appalachian National Scenic Trail, West Virginia. *Chickamauga and Chattanooga National Military Park*, Georgia. *Cumberland Gap National Historical Park*, Kentucky. *Natchez Trace National Scenic Trail*, Mississippi. *Natchez Trace Parkway*, Mississippi. *Overmountain Victory National Historic Trail, Tennessee Civil War Heritage Area, Trail of Tears National Historic Trail,* in Other National Parklands.

Alibates Flint Quarries
National Monument

Texas Panhandle, north of Amarillo

Few prehistoric Native American archaeological sites in the Canadian River region of the Texas Panhandle are as dramatic as Alibates Flint Quarries. People quarried flint for tools here for 12,000 years, since the time of the Ice Age Clovis culture, when Native Americans used Alibates flint for spear points to hunt the Imperial Mammoth. The monument was authorized as Alibates Flint Quarries and Texas Panhandle Pueblo Culture National Monument on August 21, 1965, and redesignated on November 10, 1978.

WHAT TO SEE & DO

Flint-chipping demonstrations, guided tours. **Facilities:** Contact station. Picnic tables. **Programs & Events:** Guided tours by reservation. Flint-chipping demonstrations, school tours. **Tips & Hints:** You are not allowed entry without a guide. Call several days in advance Labor Day–Memorial Day for tour reservations. Busiest May and June, least crowded Dec. and Jan.

FOOD, LODGING & SUPPLIES

Camping: *See Lake Meredith National Recreation Area.* **Hotels:** None in park. In Fritch: Lake Town Inn (205 E. Broadway, tel. 806/857–3191; 20 rooms; $40). **Restaurants:** None in park. In Fritch: Carolyn's (805 W. Broadway, tel. 806/857–2055; $2–$6). **Groceries & Gear:** None in park. In Fritch: B&R Thriftway (316 E. Broadway, tel. 806/857–2976).

FEES, HOURS & REGULATIONS

Free. No entrance to monument except with ranger. Tour reservations required (tel. 806/857–3151). Boating permit $4 per day, $12 for 3 days, $40 per year. Park Headquarters at 419 E. Broadway open weekdays 8–4:30.

HOW TO GET THERE

12 mi southwest of Fritch. Closest airport: Amarillo (40 mi).

CONTACTS

Alibates Flint Quarries National Monument (Box 1460, Fritch, TX 79036, tel. 806/857–3151, www.nps.gov/alfl). Amarillo Convention & Visitor Council (1000 S. Polk St., Amarillo, TX 79101, tel. 800/692–1338 or 806/374–1497, www.amarillo-cvb.org).

Amistad National Recreation Area

On the Rio Grande, north of Del Rio

Amistad—the name means "friendship"—is a 58,000-acre international recreation area on the United States–Mexico border. The Amistad Reservoir offers outstanding water sports and was created by the 6-mi-long Amistad Dam on the Rio Grande, a joint U.S.–Mexico project. Archaeological research shows that Native Americans lived in this area continuously for 10,000 years before the arrival of Europeans. The rock paintings they left are considered to be as significant as sites in Europe, Australia, and Baja California. The region also contains some of the oldest and best-preserved archaeological deposits in North America. The park is administered under a November 11, 1965, cooperative agreement with the International Boundary and Water Commission as Amistad Recreation Area and was authorized as Amistad National Recreation Area on November 28, 1990.

WHAT TO SEE & DO

Boating (rentals), camping, fishing, hunting, picnicking, scuba diving, swimming, visiting rock art sites, waterskiing. **Facilities:** Headquarters (U.S. 90, west of Del Rio) with visitor information and bookstore, 2 unstaffed visitor centers with exhibits (Amistad Dam, Rough Canyon); nature trails, beaches, fishing docks, boat ramps, amphitheater, interpretive panels, park information on radio (1540 AM). Book and map sales, picnic areas with grills, tables and shade shelters, group picnicking (reservations required, tel. 830/775–7491). **Programs & Events:** 25-minute video on rock art (on request) at park headquarters. Evening interpretive programs (Nov.–Mar.), ranger-led guided bird walks (Sept.–June, 3rd Sat. of the month), other interpretive programs (Dec.–Apr., periodically). Seminars on rock art, archaeology, and other natural history topics several times a year. **Tips & Hints:** Get drinking water at Diablo East and Park Headquarters. Watch for strong lake winds. Go in spring for wildflower blooms. Busiest Apr. and May, least crowded Nov. and Dec.

FOOD, LODGING & SUPPLIES

Camping: 4 campgrounds in the park: Governor's Landing (15 sites; $8; vault toilets), San Pedro (35 sites; $4; vault toilets, no water), Spur 406 (8 sites; $4; vault toilets, no water), 277 North (17 sites; $4; vault toilets, no water). Backcountry camping allowed. In Comstock: Seminole Canyon State Historical Park (Park Rd. 67, off U.S. 90, tel. 915/292–4464; 31 sites; $9–$13, plus $2 park entry fee; flush toilets, showers, hook-ups). **Hotels:** None in park. In Del Rio: Best Western Inn (810 Ave. F, tel. 830/775–7511; 62 rooms; $69), Laguna Diablo Resort, (1 Sanders Point Rd., tel. 830/774–2422 or 866/227–7082; 10 apartments; $69–$79). **Restaurants:** None in park. In Ciudad Acuña, Mexico: Crosby's (195 Hidalgo, tel. 877/2–2020; $5–$16). In Del Rio: Memo's (804 E. Losoya, tel. 830/774–8104; $5–$12; closed Sun.). **Groceries & Gear:** None in park. In Del Rio: HEB Grocery (500 Pecan St., tel. 830/774–2596).

FEES, HOURS & REGULATIONS

Free. Lake-use permits required on U.S. side of Lake Amistad ($4 per day or $40 per year; Golden Age and Access Passport holders get 50% discount). Permits are available from automated fee machines at Diablo East and Rough Canyon or at Park Headquarters. Texas state and Mexico fishing license required in respective waters. Texas state hunting license and free park hunting license required. Hunting allowed in designated areas in certain seasons only. Leashed pets only. No off-road travel. Vehicle access to reservoir and boat launch sites restricted. Park open daily. Park Headquarters open weekdays 8–5.

HOW TO GET THERE

Closest lake access: 8 mi west of Del Rio on U.S. 90 or 277. Closest airport: Del Rio.

CONTACTS

Amistad National Recreation Area (HCR 3, Box 5 J, Del Rio, TX 78840, tel. 830/775–7491, fax 830/775–7299, www.nps.gov/amis). Del Rio Chamber of Commerce (1915 Ave. F, Del Rio, TX 78840, tel. 830/775–3551).

Big Bend National Park

In southwest Texas, near Marathon

The 801,163-acre park is a land of borders. Situated on the U.S.–Mexico border on the Rio Grande, it's a place where countries and cultures meet. It's also a place that merges natural environments from desert to mountains while offering a great diversity of plants and animals. The park was authorized in 1935, established in 1944, and designated an International Biosphere Reserve in 1976.

WHAT TO SEE & DO

Auto touring, biking (rentals, Study Butte–Terlingua), bird- and wildlife watching, hiking, rafting (rentals, Study Butte–Terlingua). **Facilities:** 4 visitor centers: Panther Junction, Persimmon Gap, Chisos Basin, and Rio Grande Village; visitor contact station (Castolon); trails; paved and primitive roads. Bookstore, gas station, laundry. **Programs & Events:** Nature walks, workshops, and evening slide programs. **Tips & Hints:** The park is very large and remote. Come prepared with food, water, and a full tank of gas. Plan to spend two days to see most of the park from the main roads or a week if hiking. Always carry drinking water. Busiest Mar. and Apr., least crowded Dec. and Jan.

FOOD, LODGING & SUPPLIES

Camping: 4 campgrounds in the park: Chisos Basin (65 sites; $10; flush toilets), Cottonwood (31 sites; $10; pit toilets), Rio Grande Village (100 sites; $10; flush toilets, showers), Rio Grande RV Park (25 sites; $18; flush toilets, showers, hook-ups). Backcountry camping available throughout park (116 sites; permit required, *see below*). **Hotels:** In the park: Chisos Mountain Lodge (tel. 432/477–2291; 72 rooms; $70–$100). In Terlingua: Lajitas on the Rio Grande (Rte. 170, tel. 432/

424–3471; 81 rooms; $60–$195). ✗ **Restaurants:** In the park: Chisos Mountain Lodge (tel. 432/477–2291; $5–$15). In Lajitas: The Badlands (Lajitas on the Rio Grande, Rte. 170, tel. 915/424–3471; $3–$9). ⚇ **Groceries:** Rio Grande Village, Chisos Basin, and Cottonwood campgrounds.

FEES, HOURS & REGULATIONS

Entrance fee: $15 per vehicle, $5 per cyclist, bus passenger, or walk-in. Permit required (free) for backcountry camping. Trailers over 20 feet or RVs over 24 feet not recommended on Ross Maxwell Scenic Drive to Castolon and the road to the Chisos Mountains Basin. High-clearance vehicles only on dirt roads. Leashed pets in backcountry campsites; none on trails. Leashed pets only on roads and in drive-in campground. Park open daily. Panther Junction Visitor Center open daily 8–6. Chisos Visitor Center open daily 9–4:30. Persimmon Gap Visitor Center generally open Oct.–May, daily 9–5. Rio Grande Village generally open Nov.–Apr., daily 8:30–4:30.

HOW TO GET THERE

Park headquarters is 70 mi south of Marathon via U.S. 385 and 108 mi from Alpine via Rte. 118. Closest airports: Midland-Odessa (230 mi), El Paso (325 mi).

CONTACT

Big Bend National Park (Box 129, Big Bend National Park, TX 79834, tel. 432/477–2251, www.nps.gov/bibe).

Big Thicket National Preserve

In southeast Texas, near Beaumont

The preserve protects an area of rich biological diversity where the eastern hardwood forests, the southern coastal wetlands, the western prairies, and the arid southwest converge. It consists of eight land units and four water corridors encompassing 86,000 acres. The preserve was authorized in 1974 and designated a Biosphere Reserve in 1981.

WHAT TO SEE & DO

Bicycling, bird-watching, boating, canoeing, fishing, hiking, horseback riding, hunting, picnicking, powerboating. **Facilities:** Visitor center, films, trails. Bookstore, picnic sites. **Programs & Events:** Guided walks, tours, off-site talks, and environmental education programs (all by reservation, tel. 409/246–2337). **Tips & Hints:** Allow two hours to see the visitor center and hike the inside loop of the Kirby Nature Trail. Watch for flooded trails after rains and heavy releases from Steinhagen Reservoir that can flood popular campsites along the Neches River. Go in spring and fall for best weather. Wear comfortable sportswear and walking shoes and carry rain gear. Rain, heat, and humidity are typical. Temperatures typically reach 85°F–95°F in summer, and 55°F in winter. Go Sept.–May for best hiking; Mar. and Oct. for wildflower identification; mid-Apr.–mid-May for bird-watching; Apr. and Oct. for boating, fishing, and canoeing; Oct. and mid-Jan. for hunting. Busiest Apr. and Oct., least crowded Jan. and Feb.

FOOD, LODGING & SUPPLIES

Camping: In the park: Backcountry camping allowed (permit required, *see below*). In Lumberton: Village Creek State Park (off Alma Dr., tel. 409/755–7322; 41 sites; $6–$12, plus $2 park entry fee; flush toilets, showers, hook-ups). **Hotels:** None in park. In Beaumont: Best Western–Beaumont Inn (2155 N. 11th St., tel. 409/898–8150; 152 rooms; $54–$72), Holiday Inn–Beaumont Plaza (3950 I–10, tel. 409/842–0315; 253 rooms, 80 suites; $90). **Restaurants:** In Beaumont: Chula Vista (1135 N. 11th St., tel. 409/898–8855; $5–$15), Sartin's (6725 Eastex Fwy., Beaumont, tel. 409/892–6771; $10–$18). **Groceries & Gear:** In Kountze: Brookshire Brothers (U.S. 69 at Rte. 326, tel. 409/246–3804).

FEES, HOURS & REGULATIONS

Free. Backcountry camping permit required (free, tel. 409/246–2337). Texas state fishing, hunting, and trapping licenses required. Hunting and trapping by permit (free) only. No vehicles on trails. Leashed pets on trails. All-terrain bicycles and horses on Big Sandy Trail only. Visitor center open daily 9–5.

HOW TO GET THERE

Visitor center is at junction of U.S. 69 and Rte. 420. Major north–south access is via U.S. 69/287; major east–west access is via U.S. 190, U.S. 90, or I–10. Closest airports: Beaumont–Port Arthur (10 mi), Houston (90 mi).

CONTACTS

Superintendent, Big Thicket National Preserve (3785 Milam, Beaumont, TX 77701, tel. 409/839–2689, www.nps.gov/bith). Beaumont Convention & Visitors Bureau (801 Main St., Beaumont, tel. 409/880–3749 or 800/392–4401, www.beaumontcvb.com).

Chamizal National Memorial

In west Texas, in El Paso

Chamizal National Memorial commemorates the peaceful settlement of a century-old boundary dispute between Mexico and the United States. The Chamizal Treaty of 1963 was a milestone in the diplomatic relations between the two countries and is celebrated in parks across the river from each other. The memorial focuses on the arts and provides an avenue for cross-cultural understanding and enrichment that transcends barriers of race, ethnicity, and language. The park was authorized in 1966 and established in 1974.

WHAT TO SEE & DO

Attending indoor theater and outdoor amphitheater events, bicycling, jogging, picnicking, touring facility. **Facilities:** Visitor center (800 S. San

Marcial St., between Paisano St. and Delta Dr.), indoor theater, trail. Art gallery, bookstore, grills, outdoor amphitheater, picnic tables. **Programs & Events:** Plays, musicals, recitals, ballet (weekly). Siglo de Oro Spanish Drama Festival (1st week, Mar.), Music Under the Stars (June–Aug., Sunday evening). July 4 evening concert, Mexican Independence Day Celebration (Sept. 15), Chamizal Festival (1st weekend, Oct.). **Tips & Hints:** Go May–Sept. for best weather. Busiest June and July, least crowded Jan. and Feb.

FEES, HOURS & REGULATIONS

Free. Leashed pets only. No motorized vehicles on trail. Park grounds open daily 5 AM–10 PM. Visitor center open daily 8–5.

HOW TO GET THERE

In downtown El Paso at 800 S. San Marcial St., between Paisano and Delta Sts. Closest airport: El Paso International.

CONTACTS

Chamizal National Memorial (800 S. San Marcial St., El Paso, TX 79905, tel. 915/532–7273, fax 915/532–7240, www.nps.gov/cham). El Paso Convention & Visitor Bureau (1 Civic Center Plaza, El Paso, TX 79901, tel. 915/534–0653, fax 915/532–2963). El Paso Hispanic Chamber of Commerce (2829 Montana Ave., Suite B-100, El Paso, TX 79903, tel. 915/566–4066). The Greater El Paso Chamber of Commerce (10 Civic Center Plaza, El Paso, TX 79901, tel. 915/534–0500).

Fort Davis
National Historic Site

In west Texas, in Fort Davis

Soldiers from Fort Davis helped open the area to settlement and protected travelers, freight wagons and mail carriers along the San Antonio–El Paso Road from 1854 to 1891. Today the fort is regarded as one of the best preserved in the Southwest. The 474-acre site was authorized in 1961 and established in 1963 as a unit of the National Park Service.

WHAT TO SEE & DO

Hiking, picnicking, self-guided tours of five restored fort buildings and ruins. **Facilities:** Visitor center, museum, fort buildings, video, ruins, and trails. Bookstore, picnic area. **Programs & Events:** Interpretive programs (Memorial Day–Labor Day). Friends of Fort Davis Festival (Sat. of Columbus Day weekend), special evening tours (Nov.). Junior Ranger Program. **Tips & Hints:** Plan to stay about three hours. Busiest Mar. and July, least crowded Dec. and Jan.

FOOD & LODGING

Camping: None in park. Near Fort Davis: Davis Mountains State Park (Rte. 118 off Rte. 17, 4 mi northwest of Fort Davis, tel. 432/426–3337; 100 sites; $8–$18, plus $3 park entry fee; flush toilets, showers, hook-ups). ☷ **Hotels:** None in park. In Fort Davis: Indian Lodge (Park Rd. 3, tel. 432/426–3254; 39 rooms; $55–$85), Hotel Limpia (Main St., tel. 432/426–3237 or 800/662–5517; 36 rooms; $79–$190). ✗ **Restaurants:** None in park. In Fort Davis: Cueva de Leon Café (100 W. 2nd St., tel. 432/426–3801; $2–$9), Reata Restaurant (203 N. 5th St., tel. 915/837–9232; $13–$27).

FEES & HOURS

Entrance fee: $3 adults, free ages 16 and under. Fort and facilities open daily 8–5.

HOW TO GET THERE

On the north edge of the town of Fort Davis on Rtes. 17 and 118. The site can be reached from the north via I–10, from the south via U.S. 90. The town of Marfa is 21 mi to the south. Closest airport: Midland-Odessa (165 mi).

CONTACTS

Fort Davis National Historic Site (Box 1379, Ft. Davis, TX 79734, tel. 432/426–3224, fax 432/426–3122, www.nps.gov/foda). Fort Davis Chamber of Commerce (Box 378, Fort Davis, TX 79734, tel. 800/524–3015, www.fortdavis.com).

Guadalupe Mountains National Park

In west Texas, near Pine Springs

The 86,416-acre park includes part of the Capitan Reef, one of the most extensive and significant noncoral Permian-period fossil reefs in the world. Guadalupe contains more than 1,000 identified plant species, 296 bird species, 58 mammal species, 56 reptile and amphibian species, and numerous archaeological sites. The park is also home to Guadalupe Peak, the highest point in Texas (8,749 feet), and McKittrick Canyon, which contains the park's only perennial stream. Also on view are relic forest and riparian areas, spectacular scenery, historic structures such as the Pinery, a remnant of the Butterfield overland mail route, and various cultural resources from prehistoric to pioneer ranching. The park was authorized in 1966 and established in 1972.

WHAT TO SEE & DO

Backpacking, bird-watching, hiking, observing wildlife, picnicking. **Facilities:** Visitor center (Pine Springs), visitor contact station (McKittrick Canyon), ranger station (Dog Canyon), museum (Frijole Ranch), trails, amphitheater. Bookstore, picnic tables. **Programs & Events:** Slide show. Interpretive programs (Memorial Day–Labor Day). **Tips & Hints:** Watch for high winds and rapid weather changes. Prepare for steep, rocky trails. Carry plenty of water. Go in spring for birds, May–Sept. for wildflowers, Oct. for fall colors. Busiest Mar. and Oct., least crowded Jan. and Feb.

FOOD, LODGING & SUPPLIES

🏕 **Camping:** 2 campgrounds in the park: Dog Canyon (off Rte. 137; 13 sites; $8; flush toilets), Pine Springs (behind visitor center; 39 sites; $8; flush toilets). 10 backcountry campsites available (permit required, *see below*). In Cornudas: Cornudas High Desert RV Park (U.S. 62/180, tel. 915/964–2409; 6 RV sites; $16; flush toilets, hook-ups). 🏨 **Hotels:** Cornudas High Desert Motel (U.S. 62/180, tel. 915/964–2409; 6 cabins, 3 trailers; $40). ✕ **Restaurants:** None in park. In Cornudas: Cornudas Café (U.S. 62/180, 17 mi southwest of junction with Rte. 54, tel. 915/964–2409; $4–$7). In Pine Springs: Nickel Creek Café (U.S. 62/180, 15 mi northeast of junction with Rte. 54, tel. 915/828–3295; $4–$7; closed Sun.). ⛽ **Groceries & Gear:** In Carlsbad, NM: Wal-Mart (2401 S. Canal St., tel. 505/885–0727).

FEES, HOURS & REGULATIONS

$3 per person entrance fee. Backcountry permits (free) required for all backcountry camping. No fishing or hunting. No open fires in park (including charcoal). No pets outside campgrounds, leashed pets only in campgrounds. No mountain bikes or trail bikes except on Williams Ranch Rd. No motorized or wheeled vehicles on trails. No pack and riding stock except on designated trails. No overnight use of stock in backcountry. No swimming, bathing, or wading. Park open daily. Visitor center open Labor Day–Memorial Day, daily 8–4:30; Memorial Day–Labor Day, daily 8–6. Highway gate to McKittrick Canyon open Apr.–Oct., daily 8–6; Nov.–Mar., daily 8–4:30.

HOW TO GET THERE

110 mi east of El Paso via U.S. 62/180, 65 mi north of Van Horn via Rte. 54, and 55 mi southwest of Carlsbad, NM, via U.S. 62/180. Closest airports Carlsbad, NM, El Paso, TX.

CONTACTS

Guadalupe Mountains National Park (HC 60 Box 400, Salt Flat, TX 79847, tel. 915/828–3251, fax 915/828–3269, www.nps.gov/gumo). Carlsbad Chamber of Commerce (Box 910, Carlsbad, NM 88220, tel. 505/887–6516).

Lake Meredith National Recreation Area

Texas Panhandle, near Amarillo

Each year more than 1.5 million visitors come to this lake, which is the prime recreation area in the Texas Panhandle and was created by the Sanford Dam on the Canadian River. The 12-mi-long lake is bordered by the red beds of the Permian formations and the white dolomite of the Alibates formation. The lake has been administered in cooperation with the Bureau of Reclamation since 1965.

WHAT TO SEE & DO

Bird-watching, boating, fishing, horseback riding, hunting, motorcycle and off-road vehicle riding, parasailing, picnicking, scuba diving, swimming. **Facilities:** Park headquarters, Alibates contact station, lake. Picnic areas, sales areas. **Tips & Hints:** Go Feb.–May or Oct.–Dec. for bird migrations. Busiest July and Aug., least crowded Jan. and Feb.

FOOD, LODGING & SUPPLIES

⚠ **Camping:** 13 campgrounds in the park: (about 1,000 sites; $10–$18; flush toilets, some showers, some hook-ups). Backcountry camping allowed. 🛏 **Hotels:** None in park. In Fritch: Lake Town Inn (205 E. Broadway, tel. 806/857–3191; 20 rooms; $40). ✗ **Restaurants:** In Fritch: Carolyn's (805 W. Broadway, tel. 806/857–2055; $2–$5). 🛒 **Groceries & Gear:** None in park. In Fritch: B&R Thriftway (316 E. Broadway, tel. 806/857–2976). In Borger: Wal-Mart (1404 W. Wilson St., tel. 806/274–7257).

FEES, HOURS & REGULATIONS

Free. Boating fee: $4 per day. Texas state hunting and fishing licenses required. Permits required for parasailing. Leashed pets only. Horses restricted to Plum Creek, McBride Creek, and while hunting. Park open daily. Park headquarters open weekdays 8–4:30.

HOW TO GET THERE

Park headquarters is on Rte. 136 in Fritch. Closest airports: Borger (20 mi), Amarillo (35 mi).

CONTACTS

Lake Meredith National Recreation Area (Box 1460, 419 E. Broadway, Fritch, TX 79036, tel. 806/857–3151, fax 806/857–2319, www.nps.gov/lamr). Amarillo Chamber of Commerce (Box 9480, Amarillo, TX 79105, tel. 806/373–7800). Texas Travel Information Center (9400 E. I–40, Amarillo, TX 79118, tel. 806/335–1441).

Lyndon B. Johnson National Historical Park

In south-central Texas, in Johnson City and Stonewall

Historically significant properties associated with Lyndon B. Johnson, the 36th president of the United States, are preserved here. In the Johnson City District are the President's Boyhood Home and the Johnson Settlement, a complex of restored historic structures that traces the evolution of the Texas Hill Country from the open-range cattle kingdom of President Johnson's grandfather, Sam E. Johnson Sr., to the local ranching and farming of more recent times. At the LBJ Ranch, visitors can view the one-room schoolhouse attended by Johnson, his Reconstructed Birthplace, the Johnson Family Cemetery, where the president is buried, the Texas White House, and the ranching operation that continues today. The park was authorized in 1969 as a national historic site and enlarged and redesignated as a national historical park in 1980.

WHAT TO SEE & DO

Touring LBJ Ranch, Boyhood Home, Johnson Settlement; viewing exhibits and films. **Facilities:** 2 visitor centers: (100 Ladybird La., Johnson City; LBJ State Historical Park, U.S. 290, near Stonewall), ranch, home, settlement. Bookstores (both sites), education center (at National Historical Park), amphitheater, fishing, picnic tables with grills, pool, softball field, tennis courts (all at LBJ State Historical Park). **Programs & Events:** Guided bus tour of LBJ Ranch (daily from LBJ State Historical Park), ranger-guided tours of Boyhood Home (daily). Guided tours begin at 9 AM and are offered every half hour, last tour at 4:30. Costumed interpretive programs (Mar.–June and Oct.–Dec.). Night Skies (spring and fall). LBJ Ranch Roundup (Apr.). Wreath laying at Johnson Family Cemetery (Aug. 27), Hill Country Heritage Day (Oct.), Christmas Tour of the Boyhood Home and Johnson Settlement, Tree Lighting and Tour of LBJ Ranch (Dec.). **Tips & Hints:** Dress casually. Summers can be very hot. Don't approach longhorn cattle or wildlife. Go in Mar., Apr., and Oct. for best weather. Go Mar. and Apr. for migratory birds and wildflowers. Busiest Mar. and Apr., least crowded Dec. and Jan.

FOOD, LODGING & SUPPLIES

Camping: None in park. In Blanco: Blanco State Park (101 Park Rd. 23, tel. 830/833–4331; 31 sites, 7 shelters; $14–$21, plus $3 park entry fee; flush toilets, showers, hook-ups). In Johnson City: Padernales Falls State Park (Rte. 2766 and Rte. 3232, tel. 830/868–7304; 86 sites; $18, plus $2 park entry fee; flush toilets, showers, hook-ups). **Hotels:** None in park. In Fredericksburg: Best Western Sunday House (501 E. Main St., tel. 830/997–4484; 124 rooms; $65–$130). In Johnson City: Save Inn Motel (107 U.S. 281, tel. 830/868–4044; 53 rooms; $36–$46). **Restaurants:** None in park. In Fredericksburg: Altdorf German Biergarten & Dining Room (301 W. Main St., tel. 830/997–7865; $10–$14), Mamacita's (506 E. Main St., tel. 830/997–9546; $6–$13). **Groceries & Gear:** None in park. In Blanco: Super S (111 Blanco Ave., U.S. 281, tel. 830/833–4521).

FEES, HOURS & REGULATIONS

Free. Bus tours of the LBJ Ranch: $3 adults, free ages 6 and under. No pets allowed on LBJ Ranch Bus Tour, inside park buildings, or at Johnson Settlement. Leashed pets elsewhere. Access to the LBJ Ranch is by tour bus only. Johnson Settlement open daily sunrise–sunset. LBJ Ranch Bus Tours available 10–4. Private vehicles allowed on part of LBJ Ranch 5 PM–sunset. LBJ State Historical Park open daily until 10 PM. Johnson City visitor center open daily 8:45–5. LBJ State Historical Park visitor center open daily 8–5.

HOW TO GET THERE

The Johnson City District is at 100 Ladybird La., in Johnson City, 48 mi west of Austin on U.S. 290 and 65 mi north of San Antonio on U.S. 281. The LBJ Ranch and LBJ State Historical Park are on U.S. 290, 14 mi west of Johnson City and 16 mi east of Fredericksburg. Closest airports: Austin, San Antonio.

Lyndon B. Johnson National Historical Park (Box 329, Johnson City, TX 78636, tel. 830/868–7128 Ext. 244, fax 830/868–0810, www.nps.gov/ lyjo). Johnson City Chamber of Commerce (Box 485, Johnson City, TX 78636, tel. 830/868–7684, fax 830/868–7830). Stonewall Chamber of Commerce (Box 1, Stonewall, TX 78671, tel. 830/644–2735). Lyndon B. Johnson State Historical Park (Box 238, Stonewall, TX 78671, tel. 830/644–2252, fax 830/644–2430). Fredericksburg Convention & Visitor Bureau (106 N. Adams St., Fredericksburg, TX 78624, tel. 830/997–6523, fax 830/997–8588).

Padre Island
National Seashore

In southeast Texas, near Corpus Christi

The seashore provides a rare opportunity for primitive beach recreation on 80 mi of the longest barrier island in the world. Padre Island is well known for its wide sandy beaches, excellent fishing, and abundant bird and marine life. The seashore was authorized in 1962 and established in 1968.

WHAT TO SEE & DO

Beachcombing, bird-watching, boating, fishing, picnicking, swimming, windsurfing (rentals, Bird Island Basin). **Facilities:** Visitor center (Malaquite, Park Rd. 22), orientation video, swim beach, boat launch ramp, nature trail. Book and map sale areas, gift shop. **Programs & Events:** Ranger-led campfire programs, beach walks, deck talks, and Junior Ranger program. Sea-turtle hatchling releases (June–Aug.), Adopt-A-Beach Cleanup (Apr. and Sept.), Center for Marine Conservation Cleanup (Apr. and Sept.). **Tips & Hints:** Go in spring for wildflowers, spring and fall for neo-tropical migratory birds. Go to Bird Island Basin in spring for windsurfing. Go May–Aug. to view nesting sea turtles. Go in winter to see winter waterfowl and fish for black drum and bull redfish. Watch for rattlesnakes. Busiest July and Aug., least crowded Sept. and Oct.

FOOD, LODGING & SUPPLIES

Ⓐ **Camping:** 5 campgrounds in the park: Bird Island Basin (primitive camping area; $5; pit toilets; permit required), Malaquite Beach (42 sites; $8; flush toilets, cold showers), North Beach (primitive camping area; free; no water; permit required, *see below*), South Beach (primitive camping area; free; no water; permit required, *see below*), Yarborough Pass (primitive camping area; free; no water; permit required, *see below*). 🏨 **Hotels:** None in park. In Corpus Christi: Days Inn (4302 Surfside Blvd., tel. 361/882–3297; 56 rooms; $39–$90). In Corpus Christi: Fortuna Bay B&B (15405 Fortuna Bay Dr., tel. 361/949–7554; 5 suites; $110). ✕ **Restaurants:** In Corpus Christi: Black-Eyed Pea (4801 S. Padre Island Dr., tel. 361/993–4588; $6–$10), Crawdaddy's (414 Starr St., tel. 361/883–5432; $10–$12). ⏛ **Groceries &**

Gear: In Corpus Christi: HEB Grocery (10241 S. Padre Island Dr., tel. 361/937–2653).

FEES, PERMITS & REGULATIONS

Entrance fee: $10 per vehicle. Bird Island day-use fee: $5 per day or $10 per year. Texas state fishing license and saltwater stamp required. Camping in designated areas only; permit ($5) required. No hunting, loaded firearms, large boat launching into gulf, vehicles in dunes. Leashed pets only. Park open daily. Visitor center open Labor Day–Memorial Day, daily 8:30–4:30; Memorial Day–Labor Day, daily 8:30–6.

HOW TO GET THERE

On North Padre Island, 10 mi southeast of Corpus Christi via South Padre Island Dr., which turns into Park Rd. 22. Closest airport: Corpus Christi.

CONTACTS

National Park Service, Padre Island National Seashore (Box 181300, Corpus Christi, TX 78480, tel. 361/949–8068, fax 361/949–9951, www. nps.gov/pais). Corpus Christi Chamber of Commerce (1201 N. Shoreline Blvd., Corpus Christi, TX 78401, tel. 800/766–2322).

Palo Alto Battlefield National Historic Site

In south Texas, near Brownsville

On May 8, 1846, the Battle of Palo Alto took place—the first major battle of the Mexican-American War (1846–48). General Zachary Taylor's 2,300-man U.S. Army of Occupation used its superior cannon and innovative artillery methods to outduel General Mariano Arista's 3,600-man force. At war's end, Mexico ceded claims to what are now Texas, New Mexico, Arizona, Utah, Nevada, and California to the United States. The site was authorized in 1978 and dedicated in 1993.

WHAT TO SEE & DO

Viewing exhibits, watching video. **Facilities:** Visitor center (7200 Paredes Line Rd., Brownsville), video, walking trail with interpretive markers leading to overlook. Book sales area. **Programs & Events:** Interpretive talks (periodically). **Tips & Hints:** South Texas summer weather is generally hot and humid. Wear lightweight cotton clothing. Winter weather is generally mild, but expect cool mornings. Busiest June–Aug.

FOOD, LODGING & SUPPLIES

⚠ **Camping:** None in park. In Rio Hondo: Adolph Thomae Park (37844 Marshall Hutts Rd., tel. 956/748–2044; 85 sites; $12–$20; flush toilets, showers, hook-ups). On South Padre Island: Isla Blanca Park (½ Park Rd. 100, tel. 956/761–5494; 725 sites; $12–$20; flush toilets, showers, hook-ups). ⊞ **Hotels:** None in park. In Brownsville: Comfort Inn

(825 N. Expressway Dr., tel. 956/504–3331; 52 rooms, 1 suite; $55–$60). In Rancho Viejo: Rancho Viejo Resort (1 Rancho Viejo Dr., tel. 956/350–4000 or 800/531–7400; 32 rooms, 23 suites; $103). ✕ **Restaurants:** None in park. In Matamoros, MX: Mi Pueblito (Calle 5a y Constitucion, tel. 956/793–7716; $6–$16), Los Comparos (1442 International Blvd., tel. 956/546–8172; $9–$16). ♿ **Groceries & Gear:** None in park. In Brownsville: HEB Market (2155 Paredes Line Rd., tel. 956/574–9701).

FEES & HOURS

Free. Visitor center open daily 8–4:30.

HOW TO GET THERE

In Brownsville on Rte. 1847, 0.2 mi north of the intersection with Rte. 511. Closest airport: Brownsville.

CONTACTS

Palo Alto Battlefield National Historic Site (1623 Central Blvd., Suite 213, Brownsville, TX 78520, tel. 956/541–2785, fax 956/541–6356, www.nps.gov/paal). Brownsville Convention & Visitors Bureau (Box 4697, Brownsville TX 78523, tel. 956/546–3721, fax 956/546–3972).

Rio Grande Wild & Scenic River

In south Texas, along the Rio Grande

This remote, undeveloped 191-mi strip on the American shore of the Rio Grande in the Chihuahuan Desert protects the river. It begins in Big Bend National Park and continues downstream to the Terrell–Val Verde county line. There are no Park Service facilities outside of Big Bend National Park (*see separate entry*). The wild and scenic river was authorized on November 10, 1978.

WHAT TO SEE & DO

See Big Bend National Park.

CONTACT

Rio Grande Wild & Scenic River (c/o Big Bend National Park, Box 129, Big Bend National Park, TX 79834, tel. 915/477–2251, www.nps.gov/rigr).

San Antonio Missions National Historical Park

In south-central Texas, in San Antonio

Preserved here are four 18th-century Spanish missions—Concepcion, San Jose, San Juan, and Espada—that were built along the San Antonio River to introduce Coahuiltecan Native Americans to Spanish society and Catholicism. These missions, along with their presidio and settlement, were the foundation of the city of San Antonio. The missions still serve as active parishes and represent a virtually unbroken link with the past. The park was authorized in 1978 and established in 1983.

WHAT TO SEE & DO

Picnicking, touring missions, viewing museum exhibits, watching film. **Facilities:** Visitor center (San Jose), 3 park contact stations (Concepcion, San Juan, Espada), trail. Picnic tables, sales outlets. **Programs & Events:** Ranger-guided walks and talks (daily), ranger-guided walk of Rancho de Las Cabras (1st Sat. each month). **Tips & Hints:** Prepare for summer heat. Watch for fire ants. Busiest July and Oct., least crowded Jan. and Feb.

FEES, HOURS & REGULATIONS

Free. No hunting. Leashed pets only. No bicycles in mission compounds. No motorized equipment on trails. Park and visitor center open daily 9–5.

HOW TO GET THERE

From I–37, exit on West Southcross, then turn left on Roosevelt to Mission San Jose. From I–10, exit south on Probandt and follow Park Service signs to Concepcion. Closest airport: San Antonio (15 mi).

CONTACTS

San Antonio Missions National Historical Park (2202 Roosevelt Ave., San Antonio, TX 78210-4919, tel. 210/534–8833, fax 210/534–1106, www.nps.gov/saan). South San Antonio Chamber of Commerce (908 McCreless Mall, San Antonio, TX 78223, tel. 210/533–5867, fax 210/532–7788). Greater San Antonio Visitor Information Center (317 Alamo Plaza, San Antonio, TX 78205, tel. 210/270–8748 or 800/447–3372, fax 210/207–6842).

Arches National Park

In east-central Utah, near Moab

The 76,519-acre park contains one of the largest concentrations of natural sandstone arches in the world. The arches and numerous other extraordinary geologic features, including spires, pinnacles, pedestals, and balanced rocks, are highlighted in striking foreground and background views created by contrasting colors, land forms, and textures. The site was proclaimed a national monument in 1929 and redesignated in 1971.

WHAT TO SEE & DO

Auto touring, biking, hiking, picnicking. **Facilities:** Visitor center, scenic road, overlooks, trails. Book and map sale area, picnic areas. **Programs & Events:** Ranger-led walks, guided hikes, evening campfire programs (mid-Mar.–Oct.). Easter Sunrise Service. **Tips & Hints:** Plan on a half-day visit for basic road tour and stops at overlooks; add more time for hiking. Conditions are hot and dry in summer. Carry drinking water. Go early in day to register for campsite. Register up to seven days ahead for popular Fiery Furnace guided hike. Hikes fill up quickly. Busiest July and Aug., least crowded Dec. and Jan.

FOOD, LODGING & SUPPLIES

Camping: In the park: Devil's Garden (52 sites; $10; flush toilets, pit toilets). **Hotels:** None in park. In Moab: Archway Inn (1551 N. U.S. 191, tel. 435/259–2599 or 800/341–9359; 80 rooms, 15 suites, 2 apartments; $94), Holiday Inn Express (1653 U.S. 191, tel. 435/259–1150 or 877/531–5084; 79 rooms; $89). **Restaurants:** None in park. In Moab: Jail House Café (101 N. Main St., tel. 435/259–3900; $5–$10). **Groceries & Gear:** None in park. In Moab: Boomer's Market (702 S. Main St., tel. 435/259–1105), City Market (425 S. Main St., tel. 435/259–5181).

FEES, HOURS & REGULATIONS

Entrance fee: $10 per vehicle. Fiery Furnace backcountry permit $2 adults, $1 ages 6–12. Fiery Furnace guided walks $8 adults, $4 ages 6–12. Walks are limited to 25 people each and usually fill a day ahead. Concessionaire offers four-wheel-drive tours. Park open daily. Visitor center open Nov.–Mar., daily 8–4:30; Apr.–Oct., daily 8–5 (hrs vary).

HOW TO GET THERE

5 mi north of Moab on U.S. 191. Closest airports: Canyonlands (15 mi) and Salt Lake City (250 mi); Grand Junction, CO (120 mi).

CONTACTS

Arches National Park (Box 907, Moab, UT 84532, tel. 435/719–2299, fax 435/719–2305, www.nps.gov/arch). Grand County Travel Council (Box 550, Moab, UT 84532 or 40 N. 100 E, Moab, UT 84532, tel. 800/635–6622).

Bryce Canyon National Park

In south-central Utah, near Tropic

The park is named for one of a series of horseshoe-shape amphitheaters carved from the eastern edge of the Paunsaugunt Plateau. Erosion has shaped colorful Claron limestone, sandstones, and mudstones into thousands of spires, fins, pinnacles, and mazes. These unique formations, called "hoodoos," are whimsically arranged and tinted with many colors. Ponderosa pines, high-elevation meadows, and spruce-fir forests border the rim of the plateau, and panoramic views of three states spread beyond the park's boundaries. The park was proclaimed a national monument on June 8, 1923; provisionally authorized as Utah National Park on June 7, 1924; renamed on February 25, 1928; and established in September 1928.

WHAT TO SEE & DO

Camping, cross-country skiing (rentals, Ruby's Inn), guided trail rides (tel. 435/679–8665), hiking, picnicking, snowshoeing, stargazing, van touring. **Facilities:** Visitor center with amphitheater, slide program, overlooks, trails, picnic areas. Gift shop, publication sales. **Programs & Events:** Hikes, walks, geology talks, evening slide programs, night sky programs, star parties, moonlight walks (all late May–Sept.). **Tips & Hints:** Use caution if unaccustomed to altitude. Busiest Aug. and Sept., least crowded Jan. and Feb.

FOOD, LODGING & SUPPLIES

Camping: 3 campgrounds in the park: North (102 sites; $10; flush toilets, showers), South (102 sites; $10; flush toilets, showers), Sunset (tel. 435/834–4801; group site; $30; flush toilets, showers; reservations required). Backcountry camping allowed (permit required, *see below*). In Bryce: Bryce Canyon Pines (Rte. 12, 9 mi east of U.S. 89, tel. 800/892–7923; 44 sites; $15–$25; flush toilets, showers, hook-ups; closed Nov.–Mar.). **Hotels:** In the park: Bryce Canyon Lodge (tel. 435/834–5361; 888/297–2757 reservations; 70 rooms, 40 cabins, 3 suites; $110, $130 cabins and suites; closed Nov.–mid-Apr.). In Ruby's Inn: Best Western (Rte. 63, tel. 435/834–5341 or 800/468–8660; 368 rooms; $49–$160). **Restaurants:** In the park: Bryce Canyon Lodge (tel. 435/834–5361; $8–$20; closed Nov.–Mar.), Bryce Canyon Pines Restaurant (Rte. 12, tel. 435/834–5441; $5–$16). **Groceries & Gear:** In the park: Sunrise Point General Store (tel. 435/834–5361 Ext. 167). In Panguitch: Joe's Main St. Market (10 S. Main St., tel. 435/676–2361).

FEES, HOURS & REGULATIONS

Entrance fee: $20 per vehicle. Backcountry permits required ($5; visitor center). Shuttle bus service (free) available along roads in park. No bikes on trails. No trailers beyond Sunset Campground. No hunting. No pets on trails, leashed pets only otherwise. Park open daily. Visitor center open May–Sept., daily 8–8; Oct.–Apr., daily 8–4:30.

HOW TO GET THERE

From north or south on U.S. 89, turn east on Rte. 12 (7 mi south of Panguitch, Utah). Turn south on Rte. 63 and travel 3 mi to reach the park entrance. From the east, travel west on Rte. 12. Turn south on Rte. 63 to reach the park entrance. Closest airport: Bryce Canyon Airport.

CONTACTS

Bryce Canyon National Park (Box 170001, Bryce Canyon, UT 84717-0001, tel. 435/834–5322, fax 435/834–4102, www.nps.gov/brca). Garfield County Travel Council (Box 200, Panguitch, UT 84759, tel. 800/444–6689).

Canyonlands National Park

In east-central Utah, near Moab

At the intersection of the Green River and the Colorado River, this park preserves 527 square mi of colorful canyons, mesas, buttes, fins, arches, and spires. Prehistoric American Indian rock art and ruins dot the red-rock landscape. The mighty river canyons divide the park into three districts, each offering spectacular sightseeing and exploration opportunities. The park was established on September 12, 1964.

WHAT TO SEE & DO

Four-wheel-drive touring, hiking, mountain biking, river running, rock climbing. **Facilities:** 2 visitor centers: Island in the Sky (Rte. 313 off U.S. 191) and Needles (Rte. 211 off U.S. 191); information center (Maze, Hans Flat Ranger Station, dirt road off Rte. 24), trails, backcountry roads. Bookstores. **Programs & Events:** Junior Ranger program (ages 6–12). Evening programs, overlook talks and other programs (Mar.–Oct.). **Tips & Hints:** Canyonlands is primarily a backcountry destination. Summer temperatures average at 92°F, and winter temperatures average at 39°F. Busiest Apr.–Oct., least crowded Dec. and Jan.

FOOD, LODGING & SUPPLIES

⚠ **Camping:** 2 campgrounds in the park: Squaw Flat (Needles district; 26 sites; $10; vault toilets), Willow Flat (Island in the Sky district; 12 sites; $5; vault toilets). Backcountry camping allowed (permit required, *see below*). 🛏 **Hotels:** None in park. *See Arches National Park.* ✕ **Restaurants:** None in park. In Monticello: Houston's (296 N. Main St., tel. 435/587–2531; $10–$15). *See Arches National Park.* 🛒 **Groceries & Gear:** None in park. *See Arches National Park.*

FEES, HOURS & REGULATIONS

Entrance fee (Mar.–Oct.): $10 per vehicle, $5 per person, free rest of the year. Backcountry permit required ($5–$30, tel. 435/259–4351). No pets on trails or in backcountry, even in vehicles. No ATVs. No mountain bikes on hiking trails or off designated roads. Park open daily. Island in the Sky Visitor Center open Mar.–Oct., daily 8–6; Nov.–Feb., daily 8–5. Needles Visitor Center open Mar.–May, daily 8–5:30; June–Oct., daily 8–5; Nov.–Feb., daily 8–4:30.

HOW TO GET THERE

Canyonlands is divided into three districts that are two to six hours apart by car. To reach Needles District from Moab, take U.S. 191 south and Rte. 211 west. To reach Island in the Sky District from Moab, take U.S. 191 north and Rte. 313 west. To reach the Maze District from Moab, take U.S. 191 north to I–70 west. Take Exit 147 off I–70 to Rte. 24 south, and then a graded dirt road east to the Hans Flat Ranger Station. Closest airports: Canyonlands (18 mi) and Salt Lake City (240 mi); Grand Junction, CO (115 mi).

CONTACTS

Canyonlands National Park (2282 S.W. Resource Blvd., Moab, UT 84532, tel. 435/719–2313, www.nps.gov/cany). San Juan Visitor's Center (117 S. Main St., or Box 490, Monticello, UT 84535, tel. 800/574–4386).

Capitol Reef National Park

In south-central Utah, near Torrey

The park's Waterpocket Fold, a giant, sinuous wrinkle in the Earth's crust created 65 million years ago, stretches for 100 mi with colorful cliffs, massive domes, soaring spires, and stark monoliths. The park also protects a section of the free-flowing Fremont River, the site of the prehistoric Fremont culture, remains of a Mormon pioneer settlement, and orchards of Fruita. The site was proclaimed a national monument in 1937 and redesignated in 1971.

WHAT TO SEE & DO

Bicycling (rentals), fishing, hiking, horseback riding (rentals), Jeep touring (rentals), picking fruit (in season), picnicking. **Facilities:** Visitor center with pioneer buildings and homes, trails, wayside panels, amphitheater, remains of uranium mine. Bookstore, sales outlet. **Programs & Events:** Geology talks, ranger presentations, evening programs (June–Sept., daily as staffing allows). **Tips & Hints:** Go in spring or fall for best hiking weather and wildflowers, summer and fall for fruit harvest. Watch for thunderstorms and flash floods July–Sept. Busiest July–Sept., least crowded in Dec. and Jan.

FOOD, LODGING & SUPPLIES

Camping: 3 campgrounds in the park: Cathedral Valley (6 sites; free; pit toilets, no water), Cedar Mesa (6 sites; pit toilets, no water), Fruita (71 sites; $10; flush toilets). Backcountry camping allowed (permit required, *see below*). **Hotels:** None in park. In Torrey: Best Western

Capitol Reef Resort (2600 E. Rte. 24, tel. 435/425–3300; 100 rooms; $99–$139), Boulder View Inn (385 W. Main St., tel. 435/425–3800; 12 rooms; $50–$65). ✗ **Restaurants:** None in park. In Torrey: Café Diablo (599 W. Main St., tel. 435/425–3070; $10–$19; closed mid-Oct.–mid-Apr.; no lunch), Capitol Reef Café (360 W. Main St., tel. 435/425–3271; $9–$24). ⛺ **Groceries & Gear:** None in park. In Torrey: Chuck Wagon Store (12 W. Main St., tel. 435/425–3288).

FEES, HOURS & REGULATIONS

Entrance fee: $5 for Scenic Drive. Backcountry permits (free) required for all backcountry camping. Utah state fishing license required. No hunting. No pets on trails, in buildings, or off roads. Carry water on hikes. No rock, plant, animal, or artifact collecting. No mountain bikes off roads. Park open daily. Visitor center open Oct.–Apr., daily 8–4:30; May–Sept., daily 8–6.

HOW TO GET THERE

37 mi west of Hanksville and 10 mi east on Torrey on Rte. 24. Closest airports: Hanksville, Bicknell (18 mi), Salt Lake City (195 mi); Grand Junction, CO (180 mi).

CONTACTS

Capitol Reef National Park (HC 70, Box 15, Torrey, UT 84775, tel. 435/425–3791, fax 435/425–3026, www.nps.gov/care). Wayne County Travel Council (Box 7, Teasdale, UT 84773, tel. 435/425–3365 or 800/858–7951, www.capitolreef.org).

Cedar Breaks National Monument

In southwestern Utah, near Cedar City

The monument preserves a large, multicolored geologic amphitheater that is 2,500 feet deep and 3 mi across. The rim of the amphitheater sits at 10,500 feet above sea level and is lined with forests of spruce and fir and subalpine meadows full of wildflowers that are brilliant with color in the summer. The monument was proclaimed on August 22, 1933.

WHAT TO SEE & DO

Camping, car touring, cross-country skiing, hiking, picnicking, snowmobiling, snowshoeing. **Facilities:** Cedar Breaks Visitor Center, amphitheater, 6-mi scenic drive, scenic overlooks, trails. Book sale area, fire grates, picnic tables. **Programs & Events:** Interpretive programs (Memorial Day–Columbus Day, daily 10–5, hourly), evening campfire programs (June 15–Sept. 1, nightly at 9), guided hikes (June 15–Sept. 1, weekends 10 AM). **Tips & Hints:** Come prepared for cool weather and high elevation (summertime high: 60°F, rim elevation: 10,000 feet). Visit in late June–late Sept. Busiest July and Aug., least crowded Jan. and Feb.

FOOD, LODGING & SUPPLIES

Camping: In the park: Point Supreme (30 sites; $12; flush toilets; closed Oct.–mid-June). In Dixie National Forest: Duck Creek (Rte. 14, tel. 877/444–6777; 97 sites; $10; flush toilets). **Hotels:** None in park. In Cedar City: Abbey Inn (940 W. 200 N, tel. 435/586–9966 or 800/325–5411; 81 rooms; $60–$85). **Restaurants:** None in park. In Cedar City: Market Grill (2290 W. 400 N, tel. 435/586–9325; $6–$13). **Groceries & Gear:** None in park. In Cedar City: Smith's (633 S. Main St., tel. 435/586–1203).

FEES, HOURS & REGULATIONS

Entrance fee: $3 per person. Utah state fishing license required. No hunting. Leashed pets only on roadsides, paved walkways, campground. No mountain bikes on trails. No motorized vehicles off paved roads. Park open mid-May–mid-Nov., daily. Visitor center open Memorial Day–Columbus Day, daily 8–6. Scenic drive open mid-May–mid-Nov.

HOW TO GET THERE

Cedar Breaks National Monument is along Rte. 148, between Rtes. 143 and 14. The visitor center is 23 mi from Cedar City via Rtes. 148 and 14, 8 mi from Brian Head via Rtes. 148 and 143, and 25 mi from Parowan via Rtes. 148 and 143. Closest airports: Cedar City, St. George.

CONTACTS

Cedar Breaks National Monument (2390 W. Rte. 56, Suite 11, Cedar City, UT 84720, tel. 435/586–9451, fax 435/586–3813, www.nps.gov/cebr). Cedar City Chamber of Commerce (581 N. Main St., Cedar City, UT 84720, tel. 435/586–4484).

Golden Spike National Historic Site

In northwestern Utah, in Promontory

The site commemorates the completion of the first transcontinental railroad on May 10, 1869, at Promontory Summit. On that day, a golden spike was symbolically tapped into a polished laurel-wood tie and then a final iron spike was driven to complete the railroad, thus linking East and West for the first time. The site was established in 1965.

WHAT TO SEE & DO

Auto touring, hiking, viewing golden spike reenactment ceremony and last spike site. **Facilities:** Visitor center, 1869 steam locomotive replica, museum, auto tours. Bookstore. **Programs & Events:** Ranger talks (Memorial Day–Labor Day, daily. Engine house tours (Columbus Day–Apr.) golden spike reenactment (mid-May–Labor Day, Sat.). Golden Spike Anniversary Celebration (May 10), Railroader's Festival (2nd Sat., Aug.), Winter Film Festival and Steam Demonstration (last weekend, Dec.). **Tips & Hints:** Plan to spend two to three hours. Go anytime to see locomotives, but go May–early Oct. to see them operate. Busiest May–Aug., least crowded Dec. and Jan.

FOOD, LODGING & SUPPLIES

⚠ **Camping:** None in park. Near Brigham City: Willard Bay State Park: (Exit 356 off I–15, tel. 435/734–9494; 39 sites; $14–$20; flush toilets, vault toilets, showers, hook-ups). 🛏 **Hotels:** None in park. In Brigham City: Crystal Inn (480 Westland Dr., tel. 435/723–0440 or 800/408–0440; 52 rooms; $55–$79), Galaxie Motel (740 S. Main St., tel. 435/723–3439 or 800/577–4315; 29 rooms; $34). ✕ **Restaurants:** None in park. In Brigham City: Maddox Ranch House (1900 S. U.S. 89, tel. 435/723–8545; $9–$23; closed Sun. and Mon.). ⛁ **Groceries & Gear:** None in park. In Brigham City: Smith's (156 S. Main St., tel. 435/734–2500). In Willard: Country Market (600 W. 750 N, tel. 435/723–5022).

FEES, HOURS & REGULATIONS

Entrance fee: May–Columbus Day, $4 per person or $7 per vehicle; rest of the year, $3 per person or $5 per vehicle. Steam locomotive runs May–Labor Day, daily 10:30–4:30. No hunting. Leashed pets only. No mechanized recreational vehicles on trails. Park and visitor center open May–Sept., daily 9–5:30; Oct.–Apr., Wed.–Sat., 9–5:30.

HOW TO GET THERE

In Promontory, 32 mi west of Brigham City via Rtes. 13 and 83. Closest airport: Salt Lake City (95 mi).

CONTACTS

Golden Spike National Historic Site (Box 897, Brigham City, UT 84302, tel. 435/471–2209, fax 435/471–2341, www.nps.gov/gosp). Brigham City Chamber of Commerce (6 N. Main St., Brigham City, UT 84302, tel. 435/723–3931). Bear River Chamber of Commerce (718 E. Main St., Tremonton, UT 84337, tel. 435/257–5968). Box Elder County Economic Development, Tourism Council (102 W. Forest St., Brigham City, UT 84302, tel. 435/734–2634).

Natural Bridges National Monument

In southeastern Utah, near Blanding

Owachomo Bridge, Sipapu Bridge, and Kachina Bridge depict the three phases in a natural bridge's history, as running water forms and then ultimately destroys these perforated rock walls. Utah's first national monument also offers outstanding examples of geological and erosion processes and preserves numerous ancestral Puebloan archaeological sites. The site was proclaimed on April 16, 1908.

WHAT TO SEE & DO

Auto and bicycle touring, hiking. **Facilities:** Visitor center (Rte. 275 off Rte. 95), 9-mi drive, solar photovoltaic array, trails, overlooks. Book and map sales area. **Programs & Events:** Campfire programs (May–mid-Oct.). **Tips & Hints:** Get drinking water at visitor center and carry plenty of water on hikes. Watch for flash floods and severe lightning July–Sept.

Avoid midget prairie rattlesnakes. Respect cultural sites. Visit late Apr.–
Oct. Busiest May–Sept., least crowded Dec. and Jan.

FOOD, LODGING & SUPPLIES

Camping: In the park: Natural Bridges (13 sites; $10; pit toilets). In
Blanding: Gopher Kamp Park (861 S. Main St., tel. 435/678–2770; 68
sites; $11–$16; flush toilets, showers, hook-ups). **Hotels:** None in
park. In Blanding: Best Western Gateway Inn (86 E. Center St., tel. 435/
678–2278; 57 rooms; $60–$80), Super 8 (755 S. Main St., tel. 435/678–
3880 or 800/800–8000; 47 rooms, 2 suites; $60–$67, $87 suites).
✕ Restaurants: None in park. In Blanding: Old Tymer (733 S. Main St.,
tel. 435/678–2122; $4–$16). In Fry Canyon: Fry Canyon Lodge Café
(Rte. 95, tel. 435/259–5334; $11–$23). **Groceries & Gear:** None in
park. In Blanding: Clark's Market (820 S. Main St., tel. 435/678–2721).

FEES, HOURS & REGULATIONS

Entrance fee: $6 per vehicle or $3 per person traveling by bicycle or
motorcycle. No climbing on bridges. No pets on trails or in canyons.
Leashed pets elsewhere. Bikes on paved roads only. No hunting or
gathering of flora or fauna. Bridge View Dr. open daily 8–1 hour after
sunset. Visitor center open May–Sept., daily 8–6; Oct.–Apr., daily 8–5.

HOW TO GET THERE

The visitor center is 38½ mi west of Blanding via Rtes. 95 and 275; 44
mi north of Mexican Hat via Rte. 261; and 50 mi east of Hite Marina on
Lake Powell via Rte. 95. Closest airports: Salt Lake City (353 mi);
Cortez, CO (120 mi); Denver, CO (480 mi); Phoenix, AZ (389 mi).

CONTACTS

Natural Bridges National Monument (HC 60 Box 1, Lake Powell, UT
84533, tel. 435/692–1234, fax 435/692–1111, www.nps.gov/nabr). Monticello Chamber of Commerce (Box 490, Monticello, UT 84535, tel.
435/587–2992).

Rainbow Bridge
National Monument

In south-central Utah, near Lake Powell

Rainbow Bridge is the world's largest natural bridge. The 275-foot-
wide, 290-foot-tall bridge has inspired people throughout time—from
the neighboring Native American tribes, who consider Rainbow Bridge
sacred, to the 300,000 people from around the world who visit it each
year. The monument was proclaimed on May 30, 1910.

WHAT TO SEE & DO

Boating (rentals), boat touring, hiking. **Facilities:** Ranger station with
bulletin board (Dangling Rope Marina, 10 mi from bridge), outdoor
exhibits, 0.5-mi trail. **Programs & Events:** Boat tours (May–Sept., daily;
Oct.–Apr., intermittently). Ranger-led natural- and cultural-history programs (mostly Memorial Day–Sept.). **Tips & Hints:** Plan on at least a

four-hour round trip to travel by boat to bridge (six hours from Hite). Wear lightweight, light-color clothing and a hat in summer, layers of clothing rest of year. Be prepared for summer temperatures up to 110°F with little, if any, shade; winter temperatures to 0°F; and windy springs. Respect the religious significance of Rainbow Bridge to neighboring tribes. View Rainbow Bridge from the viewing area. Busiest June and Sept., least crowded Jan. and Feb.

FOOD, LODGING & SUPPLIES

None in park. *See Glen Canyon National Recreation Area,* Arizona.

FEES, HOURS & REGULATIONS

Free. Fee is charged at Glen Canyon National Recreation Area. ARA-MARK (tel. 800/528–6154) provides boat tours to Rainbow Bridge May–Sept., daily, and intermittently rest of year. Half-day and full-day tours available at Wahweap. Full-day tours only available from Bullfrog and Halls Crossing. Hiking permit required (tel. 520/871–6647 or 520/698–2808) from Navajo Nation to backpack around Navajo Mountain to Rainbow Bridge. No water-based recreation activities (swimming, fishing, waterskiing, and so forth) allowed within monument. Ranger station at Dangling Rope Marina staffed intermittently year-round.

HOW TO GET THERE

The bridge is in San Juan County, UT, immediately adjacent to Navajo Mountain and the Navajo Reservation. Public access by boat across Lake Powell, through Arizona. Trips to the bridge may be made in private, rental, or tour boats. Courtesy dock available for short-term docking while people make the 0.5-mi walk to the bridge. By boat, 50 mi from Wahweap, Bullfrog, or Halls Crossing to Rainbow Bridge. Closest airport: Page, AZ (7 mi from Wahweap Marina).

CONTACTS

Rainbow Bridge National Monument (Box 1507, Page, AZ 86040, tel. 520/608–6404, www.nps.gov/rabr). Glen Canyon National Recreation Area (Box 1507, Page, AZ 86040, tel. 520/608–6404, www.nps.gov/glca).

Timpanogos Cave National Monument

In north-central Utah, near American Fork

Hansen Cave, Middle Cave, and Timpanogos Cave, three small but wonderfully decorated limestone caves, are the attractions at this monument. These exquisitely beautiful caverns are decorated with a dazzling display of helictites and anthodites in a variety of fantastic shapes. The monument was proclaimed in 1922 and transferred to the Park Service in 1933.

WHAT TO SEE & DO

Fishing, hiking, picnicking, touring caves, watching video. **Facilities:** Visitor center, video of cave tour, ¼-mi nature trail. Bookstore, fire grills, gift shop, picnic area. **Programs & Events:** Cave tours (mid-May–Oct., daily), weekend evening programs. **Tips & Hints:** Buy cave tour tickets in advance or arrive early in the day. Ticket reservations can be made with a credit card (tel. 801/756–5238). Bring a jacket or sweater. Cave temperature is 45°F. Bring water on three-hour cave hike. The 1.5-mi trail rises 1,065 feet. Visit early in the morning or on weekdays. Busiest July–Aug., least crowded May, Sept. and Oct.

FOOD, LODGING & SUPPLIES

Camping: None in park. In American Fork: Granite Flat (Rte. 92, tel. 877/444–6777; 44 sites; $13; flush and vault toilets), Little Mill (Rte. 92, tel. 877/444–6777; 78 sites; $12; vault toilets). **Hotels:** None in park. In Lehi: Best Western Timpanogos (195 S. 850 E, tel. 801/768–1400; 59 rooms; $69–$115), Motel 6 (210 S. 1200 E, tel. 801/768–2668; 112 rooms; $29–$89). **Restaurants:** None in park. In American Fork: JCW (580 E. State Rd., tel. 801/492–1762; $4–$8; closed Sun.). In Linden: Los Hermanos (395 N. State St., tel. 801/785–1715; $6–$15; closed Sun.). **Groceries & Gear:** None in park. In American Fork: Albertson's (135 E. Main St., tel. 801/756–1440).

FEES, HOURS & REGULATIONS

Entrance fee: $3 per vehicle. Cave tour tickets: $6 adults, $5 per ages 6–15, $3 ages 3–5 or ages 62 and over. Utah state fishing license required. No cave tours in winter. No pets, strollers, or other wheeled vehicles on cave trail. Tours run 7–4:30. Picnic areas open dawn–dusk. Visitor center open May–Sept., daily 7–5:30; late Sept.–Oct., daily 8–5.

HOW TO GET THERE

24 mi south of Salt Lake City via Exit 287 (Alpine Highland) off I–15. Turn east on Rte. 92 for 10 mi to monument. Closest airport: Salt Lake City.

CONTACTS

Timpanogos Cave National Monument (R.R. 3, Box 200, American Fork, UT 84003, tel. 801/756–5238, fax 801/756–5661, www.nps.gov/tica). Uinta National Forest (88 W. 100 N, Provo, UT 84601, tel. 801/377–5780). Utah Tourism & Recreation Information Center (300 N. State St., Salt Lake City, UT 84114, tel. 801/538–1030 or 800/200–1160). Provo–Orem Chamber of Commerce (51 S. University Ave., Suite 215, Provo, UT 84601, tel. 801/379–2555). Utah County Visitors Center (51 S. University Ave., Suite 111, Provo, UT 84601, tel. 801/370–8393).

Zion National Park

In southwestern Utah, near Springdale

Protected within Zion's 229 square mi are a spectacular landscape of cliffs and canyons and a wilderness full of the unexpected. Colorful canyon and mesa scenery includes erosion and rock-fault patterns that create phenomenal shapes and landscapes. The park is home to Kolob

Arch, the world's largest arch, with a span that measures 310 feet. Mule deer, golden eagles, and mountain lions also call Zion home. Mukuntuweap National Monument was proclaimed in 1909 and established as Zion National Park in 1919.

WHAT TO SEE & DO

Auto touring, bicycling, bird- and wildlife watching, hiking, horseback riding, picnicking, wading. **Facilities:** 2 visitor centers: Kolob Canyons (off I–15) and Zion Canyon (east of Springdale off Rte. 9); nature center, trails. Fire grates, picnic sites and tables, religious services (May–Sept.). **Programs & Events:** Guided walks, evening programs, talks, and horseback rides (late Mar.–early Oct.); Nature Center for kids (Memorial Day–Labor Day). **Tips & Hints:** Don't hike alone. Stay on trails and stay out of drainage areas during thunderstorms. Watch for rockfalls and landslides. Shuttle system (Apr.–Oct., free) operates along the 6 mi Zion Scenic Drive; access to this part of the park by shuttle only. All other park roads are open to private vehicles. Parking lot at visitor center is often full 10–3; park in Springdale and ride the town loop bus to the park. Busiest July and Aug., least crowded Dec. and Jan.

FOOD, LODGING & SUPPLIES

Camping: 3 campgrounds in the park: Lava Point (6 sites; free; no water; closed mid-Oct.–May), South (126 sites; $15–$18; flush toilets; closed Nov.–Mar.), Watchman (160 sites; $14–$20; flush toilets, hookups). Backcountry camping allowed (permit required, *see below*). **Hotels:** In the park: Zion Lodge (tel. 303/297–2757 or 435/772–3213; 121 rooms; $120–$143). In Springdale: Canyon Ranch Motel (668 Zion Park Blvd., tel. 435/772–3357; 22 rooms; $58–$88), Cliffrose Lodge & Gardens (281 Zion Park Blvd., tel. 435/772–3234 or 800/243–8824; 36 rooms; $109–$145). **Restaurants:** In the park: Zion Lodge (tel. 435/772–3213; $12–$20). In Springdale: Pioneer Lodge & Restaurant (828 Zion Park Blvd., tel. 435/772–3009; $8–$20), Switchback Grille & Trading Co. (1149 S. Zion Park Blvd., tel. 435/772–3777; $15–$30). **Groceries & Gear:** In Springdale: Zion Park Market (855 Zion Park Blvd., tel. 435/772-3251), Sole Foods Market (95 Zion Park Blvd., tel. 435/772–0277).

FEES, HOURS & REGULATIONS

Entrance fee: $20 per vehicle or $10 per walk-in, bicyclist, or motorcyclist with $20 maximum per family. No vehicles over 11 feet, 4 inches in Zion–Mt. Carmel Hwy. Tunnel. Permit required for hikes through Virgin River Narrows. Backcountry permits ($10) required; restrictions apply, inquire at visitor center or park headquarters for details.

HOW TO GET THERE

The Kolob Canyons visitor center can be reached via Exit 40 off I–15. The Zion Canyon visitor center is east of Springdale off Rte. 9. Closest airport: St. George (46 mi).

CONTACT

Superintendent, Zion National Park (Springdale, UT 84767-1099, tel. 435/772–3256, www.nps.gov/zion).

See Also

Glen Canyon National Recreation Area, Arizona. *Dinosaur National Monument* and *Hovenweep National Monument,* Colorado. *California National Historic Trail, Mormon Pioneer National Historic Trail, Oregon National Historic Trail,* and *Pony Express National Historic Trail,* in Other National Parklands.

Marsh-Billings-Rockefeller National Historical Park

In east-central Vermont, in Woodstock

The park, the first in the system to focus on conservation history, protects the home of some of America's most distinguished conservationists. George Perkins Marsh, who grew up here, wrote *Man and Nature*, which was published in 1864. Frederick Billings created a progressive dairy farm and forest on the estate here in the late 1800s. His granddaughter, Mary French Rockefeller and her husband Laurance, who have made enormous contributions to the national parks, lived here and donated the site to the National Park Service. The park contains one of the oldest professionally managed woodlands in the United States, and the mansion includes hundreds of artworks from influential 19th-century landscape painters. The site, which opened to the public in June 1998, is managed as a partnership between the National Park Service and the Woodstock Foundation, which operates the Billings Farm & Museum, located on private land within the park. The adjoining museum manages the farm as both a historic site and a working dairy farm. The park was established on August 26, 1992.

WHAT TO SEE & DO

Touring mansion, grounds, farm, and museum. **Facilities:** Visitor center (Billings Farm & Museum), mansion and grounds, 1890 farmhouse, museum, carriage roads, trails. **Programs & Events:** Guided tours of mansion, gardens, and grounds; conservation stewardship programs; cross-country skiing tours in winter (Woodstock Ski Touring Center, tel. 802/457–6674). **Tips & Hints:** Expect to spend up to a full day at park. Busiest June–Aug., least crowded Oct.–Feb.

FOOD, LODGING & SUPPLIES

Camping: None in park. In Barnard: Silver Lake State Park (North Rd. off Rte. 12, tel. 802/234–9451; 39 sites, 7 lean-tos; $16–$23; flush toilets, showers). **Hotels:** None in park. In Woodstock: The Shire Motel (46 Pleasant St., tel. 802/457–2211; 42 rooms; $68–$178), Woodstock Inn (14 The Green, tel. 802/457–1100; 134 rooms, 7 suites, 1 house; $199–$389). **Restaurants:** None in park. In Woodstock: Bentley's (3 Elm St., tel. 802/457–3232; $11–$20), Woodstock Inn (14 The Green, tel. 802/457–1100; $16–$32). **Groceries & Gear:** None in park. In Woodstock: F.H. Gillingham & Sons (16 Elm St., tel. 802/457–2100), Woodstock Farmers Market (16 U.S. 4, tel. 802/457–3658).

FEES & HOURS

Billings–Rockefeller Mansion and gardens: $6 adults, $3 ages 5–15 or ages 62 and over. Billings Farm & Museum: $8 adults, $7 ages 65 and over, $6 ages 13–17, $4 ages 5–12, $1 ages 3–4. Park open May–Oct., daily 10–4. Farm and museum open May–Oct., daily 10–5; Thanksgiving weekend, daily 10–3; Dec., weekends and Dec. 26–31, 10–3. Sleigh Ride Weekends: Martin Luther King Day and Presidents' Day weekends, 10–3.

HOW TO GET THERE

Off Rte. 12 in Woodstock, next to the Billings Farm & Museum. Closest airports: Lebanon, NH (17 mi); Burlington (85 mi).

CONTACTS

Marsh-Billings-Rockefeller National Historical Park (Box 178, 54 Elm St., Woodstock, VT 05091, tel. 802/457–3368, fax 802/457–3405, www.nps.gov/mabi). Billings Farm & Museum (Box 489, Woodstock, VT 05091, tel. 802/457–2355, fax 802/457–4663). Woodstock Area Chamber of Commerce (18 Central St., Box 486, Woodstock, VT 05091, tel. 802/457–3555 or 888/496–6378, www.woostockvt.com).

See Also

Appalachian National Scenic Trail, West Virginia.

VIRGINIA

Appomattox Court House National Historical Park

In south-central Virginia, 25 mi east of Lynchburg

General Robert E. Lee surrendered the Confederate Army of Northern Virginia to Lieutenant General Ulysses S. Grant at this historic village and battleground, bringing an end to the Civil War, which killed approximately 618,000 people. The site was authorized as a national historic monument on August 13, 1935, and designated a national historic park on April 15, 1954.

WHAT TO SEE & DO

Touring historic village, walking tours of the battlefield. **Facilities:** Visitor center and museum in reconstructed courthouse building, furnished room exhibits throughout the historic village, wayside exhibits in battlefield areas. Bookstore. **Programs & Events:** Audiovisual programs every half hour in visitor center. Ranger-guided tours, living-history and other programs (Memorial Day–Labor Day). **Tips & Hints:** Plan a two-hour stay to see the park. Spend another six hours driving the associated Lee's Retreat Route, which covers 100 mi and has 26 wayside stops with radio messages. Go mid-Apr.–mid-May, Sept. and Oct. Busiest June and July, least crowded Jan. and Feb.

FOOD, LODGING & SUPPLIES

Camping: None in park. Near Appomattox: Holliday Lake State Park (Rte. 24 off U.S. 460, tel. 434/248–6308; 30 sites; $20; flush toilets, showers, hook-ups). **Hotels:** None in park. In Appomattox: Babcock House B&B (106 Oakleigh Ave., tel. 434/352–7532; 5 rooms; $80–$100). **Restaurants:** None in park. In Lynchburg: Big Lick Publick House (4001 Murray Pl., tel. 434/528–3604; $6–$12), Merriwether's (4925 Boonsboro Rd., tel. 434/384–3311; $10–$22; reservations essential). **Groceries & Gear:** In Appomattox: Kroeger's (U.S. 460, tel. 434/352–0817), Wilbun's Supermarket (720 Confederate Blvd., tel. 434/352-5165).

FEES, HOURS & REGULATIONS

Entrance fee: $4 per person or $10 per car (Memorial Day–Labor Day), $3 per person or $5 per car (Labor Day–Memorial Day), under 17 free. No pets in buildings, leashed pets otherwise. No vehicles, bikes, or horses on trails or historic roads. Park and visitor center open daily 8:30–5.

HOW TO GET THERE

25 mi east of Lynchburg and 2 mi north of Appomattox on Rte. 24. Closest airport: Lynchburg.

CONTACTS

Appomattox Court House National Historical Park (Box 218, Appomattox, VA 24522-0218, tel. 434/352–8987, fax 434/352–8330, www.nps.gov/apco). Appomattox County Chamber of Commerce (Box 704, Appomattox, VA 24522, tel 434/352–2621).

Arlington House, the Robert E. Lee Memorial

In northern Virginia, in Arlington

The house that Robert E. Lee lived in for 30 years today is a memorial to Lee, who gained the respect of northerners and southerners through his service in the Civil War. The antebellum home overlooks the Potomac River and Washington, DC. The memorial was authorized in 1925, transferred to the Park Service in 1933, designated the Custis-Lee Mansion in 1955, and renamed in 1972.

WHAT TO SEE & DO

Touring the house. **Facilities:** House and museum. **Programs & Events:** Self-guided tours. Guided tours (Sept.–May). Lee's Birthday (Jan.), Lee's wedding anniversary (June 30). **Tips & Hints:** Busiest Apr. and July, least crowded Jan. and Feb.

HOW TO GET THERE

The memorial is accessible by shuttle bus or by a 10-minute walk from the Arlington National Cemetery Visitor Center parking area. Access from Washington, DC, is via the Memorial Bridge. Access from Virginia is from the George Washington Memorial Pkwy. The memorial is also accessible by the blue line of the Metro subway system. Closest airport: Reagan.

FEES, HOURS & REGULATIONS

Free. Tickets distributed at site beginning at 9:15 in summer. Arrive early to reserve tickets. Tickets are stamped with entry time. Ticket system in place Memorial Day to Labor Day only. Memorial open daily 9:30–4:30.

CONTACT

Arlington House, the Robert E. Lee Memorial (c/o National Park Service, George Washington Memorial Pkwy., Turkey Run Park, McLean, VA 22101, tel. 703/235–1530, www.nps.gov/arho).

Booker T. Washington National Monument

In southwestern Virginia, 22 mi southeast of Roanoke

Booker T. Washington, educator, orator, and presidential advisor, was born into slavery, reared, and emancipated at this former plantation site. The park is one of the few places where visitors can see how slavery and the plantation system worked on a smaller scale. It provides a focal point for discussions about one of the most powerful African-Americans in history and the evolving context of race in American society. It was authorized on April 2, 1956.

WHAT TO SEE & DO

Attending interpretive tours, viewing exhibits and audiovisual programs, walking historic and nature trails. **Facilities:** Visitor center, wayside exhibits. Bookstore, picnic area. **Programs & Events:** Ranger-guided tours (daily). Living-history program and demonstrations (periodically). Christmas program and open house (1st weekend, Dec.). **Tips & Hints:** Busiest July and Aug., least crowded Dec. and Jan.

FOOD, LODGING & SUPPLIES

⚠ **Camping:** None in park. In Vinton: Roanoke Mountain (Blue Ridge Pkwy., mile 120.4; 104 sites; $14; flush toilets). In Bedford: Peaks of Otter (Blue Ridge Pkwy., milepost 86; 131 sites; $14; flush toilets). 🛏 **Hotels:** None in park. In Bedford: Peaks of Otter Lodge (Blue Ridge Pkwy., mile 86; tel. 540/586–1081; 63 rooms; $80). ✕ **Restaurants:** None in park. In Bedford: Peaks of Otter Lodge (Blue Ridge Pkwy., mile 86, tel. 540/586–9263; $9–$18). 🛒 **Groceries & Gear:** None in park. In Moneta: Shop Rite (Rte. 655, tel. 540/297–6000).

FEES, HOURS & REGULATIONS

Free. Group tours and education programs (reservations required, tel. 540/721–2094). No hunting or bike riding. Leashed pets only. Park open daily 9–5.

HOW TO GET THERE

On Rte. 122, 16 mi northeast of Rocky Mount, 22 mi southeast of Roanoke via Rte. 116 south and Rte. 122 north, and 21 mi south of Bedford via Rte. 122 south. Closest airport: Roanoke.

CONTACTS

Booker T. Washington National Monument (12130 Booker T. Washington Hwy., Hardy, VA 24101, tel. 540/721–2094, fax 540/721–8311, www.nps.gov/bowa). Smith Mountain Lake Chamber of Commerce (16430 Booker T. Washington Hwy., 2, Moneta, VA 24121, tel. 800/676–8203).

Cedar Creek & Belle Grove National Historical Park

In the northern Shenandoah Valley, near Middletown and Strasburg

This park, together with several on-site nonprofit preservation organizations, strives to commemorate the history of the land and structures within its boundaries. Most of the property within the park is closed to visitors, except two partner sites: Belle Grove Plantation, an 18th-century farm and limestone farmhouse, and the Cedar Creek Battlefield Foundation Visitor Center, a memorial to the 1864 Civil War battle. The national historical park encompasses approximately 3,500 acres within Shenandoah Valley Battlefields National Historic District. The park was established on December 19, 2002.

WHAT TO SEE & DO

Touring plantation farm and house, touring battlefield and visitor center. **Facilities:** Belle Grove Plantation and Cedar Creek Foundation Visitor Center. **Programs & Events:** Guided and self-guided tours. Battle reenactments at Cedar Creek ($15; Oct.). **Tips & Hints:** There are no park service facilities in the park. Direct inquiries to Belle Grove Plantation and Cedar Creek Foundation.

FOOD, LODGING & SUPPLIES

⚠ **Camping:** In the park: Battle of Cedar Creek Campground (8950 Valley Pl., tel. 540/869–1888; 61 sites; $14–$42; toilets, showers, hookups). 🏨 **Hotels:** None in park. In Middletown: Wayside Inn (7783 Main St., tel. 540/869–1797; 16 rooms, 6 suites; $99). In Strasburg: Hotel Strasburg (213 S. Holliday St., tel. 540/465–9191 or 800/348–8327; 29 rooms; $79–$175). ✕ **Restaurants:** None in park. In Middletown: Wayside Inn (7783 Main St., tel. 540/869–1797; $7–$10). In Strasburg: Hotel Strasburg (213 S. Holliday St., tel. 540/465–9191; $15–$23). In Strasburg: Old Mill Restaurant (886 East King St., tel. 540/465–5590, $8–$15). ⛁ **Groceries & Gear:** None in park. In Strasburg: Food Lion (794 Shopping Center Rd., off U.S. 11, tel. 540/465–5335).

FEES, HOURS & REGULATIONS

Belle Grove Plantation Manor House daily tours: $6–$8 adults, $3 ages 6–12, free ages 5 and under. Cedar Creek Battlefield Visitor Center entrance fee and film: $2. Guided tours available by appointment. Belle Grove Plantation open Apr.–Oct., Mon.–Sat. 10–3:15, Sun. 1–4:15. Cedar Creek Battlefield Foundation Visitor Center open Apr.–Oct., Mon.–Sat. 10–4, Sun. 1–4; Nov.–Mar., by appointment.

HOW TO GET THERE

At the junction of I–81 and I–66 in the northern Shenandoah Valley, exit onto the historic Valley Turnpike (U.S. 11), which runs through the park. Closest airports: Dulles, Reagan, and Baltimore, all within 90 mi.

CONTACTS

Cedar Creek & Belle Grove National Historical Park (7718½ Main St., Middletown, VA 22645, tel. 540/868–9176, www.nps.gov/cebe). Belle Grove Plantation (336 Belle Grove Road, Middletown, VA 22645, tel. 540/869–2028, www.bellegrove.org). Cedar Creek Battlefield Foundation (8437 Valley Pike, Middletown, VA 22645, tel. 540/869–2064 or 888/628–1864, www.cedarcreekbattlefield.org).

Colonial National Historical Park

In southeastern Virginia, near Williamsburg

The park includes most of Jamestown Island, the site of the first permanent British settlement in North America; Yorktown, the site of the last major battle of the American Revolution; and the 23-mi-long scenic Colonial Parkway that connects the two. Also included is the Cape Henry Memorial, which marks the approximate site of the first landing of Jamestown's colonists in 1607. The park was authorized as Colonial National Monument on July 3, 1930; proclaimed on December 30, 1930; and redesignated Colonial National Historical Park on June 5, 1936.

WHAT TO SEE & DO

Auto touring, bicycling, learning area history, walking. **Facilities:** 2 visitor centers: Jamestown and Yorktown; wayside exhibits. At Jamestown: Glasshouse, Jamestown Archaeology Lab, Memorial Church. At Yorktown: Gov. Thomas Nelson House; Moore House, site of surrender negotiations; Surrender Field, interpretive pavilion at actual surrender site. Bookstore. **Programs & Events:** Ranger-guided tours. Living-history tours (Jamestown: daily), historical drama (Nelson House: mid-June–mid-Aug., daily). Lamb's Artillery Firing Program (Yorktown: periodically Mar.–Sept.); Jamestown Weekend (mid-May); Memorial Day Weekend–Civil War Weekend (Yorktown: end of May); Independence Day Celebration (Yorktown: July 4); First Assembly Day Commemoration (Jamestown: late July); Yorktown Victory Celebration (Yorktown: Oct. 19). **Tips & Hints:** Allow two to three hours to visit each site. Go in winter to avoid crowds. Busiest July and Aug., least crowded Jan. and Feb.

FEES, HOURS & REGULATIONS

Entrance fees: Jamestown, $6 adults; Yorktown, $5 adults; combination ticket, $9 adults. Jamestown open daily 8:30–dusk. Jamestown Visitor Center open daily 9–5. Grounds open daily dawn–dusk, last entry at 4:30. Yorktown Visitor Center open daily 9–5.

HOW TO GET THERE

Off I–64, near Williamsburg, with sections in Jamestown and Yorktown and a parkway connecting the two. Closest airports: Newport News–Williamsburg (11 mi), Richmond (56 mi), Norfolk (37 mi).

CONTACTS

Colonial National Historical Park (Box 210, Yorktown, VA 23690, tel. 757/898–2410, fax 757/898–6346, www.nps.gov/colo). Williamsburg Area Convention & Visitors Bureau (421 N. Boundary St., Williamsburg, VA 23187, tel. 757/253–0192, fax 757/229–2047).

Fredericksburg & Spotsylvania County Battlefields Memorial National Military Park

In eastern Virginia, in Fredericksburg area

One hundred thousand men became Civil War casualties in the four major battles fought in the vicinity of Fredericksburg—Fredericksburg, Chancellorsville, Wilderness, and Spotsylvania Court House. The park also includes the historic structures of Chatham, Salem Church, and the "Stonewall" Jackson Shrine and encompasses 9,000 acres, making it the largest military park in the world. The Fredericksburg National Cemetery, with 15,333 interments, 12,746 of them unidentified, is within the park. The park was established in 1927 and transferred to the Park Service in 1933.

WHAT TO SEE & DO

Touring battlefields by car and on foot. **Facilities:** 2 visitor centers: Fredericksburg and Chancellorsville; 2 exhibit centers (Wilderness, Spotsylvania Court House), Chatman, Salem Church, "Stonewall" Jackson Shrine, tour roads, trails. Bookstores. **Programs & Events:** Guided tours. National Cemetery Luminaria (Memorial Day weekend), Battle of Fredericksburg Commemoration Ceremony (Dec.). **Tips & Hints:** Allow two days to tour all four battlefields. Busiest June and July, least crowded Jan. and Feb.

FOOD, LODGING & SUPPLIES

Camping: None in park. In Fredericksburg: KOA (6400 Brookside La, tel. 540/898–7252; 117 sites; $27–$46; flush toilets, showers, hookups). **Hotels:** None in park. In Fredericksburg: Best Western (2205 William St., tel. 540/371–5050 or 800/937–8376; 107 rooms; $75), Dunning Mills Inn (2305C Jefferson Davis Hwy., tel. 540/373–1256; 54 rooms; $118). **Restaurants:** None in park. In Fredericksburg: Goolrick's Pharmacy (901 Caroline St., tel. 540/373–9878; $3–$6; closed Sun.). **Groceries & Gear:** None in park. In Fredericksburg: Giant (3501 Plank Rd., tel. 540/786–6145).

FEES & HOURS

Entrance fee: $4 adults, free ages 16 and under. Visitor centers open daily 9–5, extended hours in spring and summer. Park open daily.

HOW TO GET THERE

Fredericksburg is 50 mi south of Washington, DC; 50 mi north of Richmond; and 3 mi east of I–95. Fredericksburg Battlefield Visitor Center is at 1013 Lafayette Blvd. in Fredericksburg. Chancellorsville Battlefield Visitor Center is on Rte. 3, 8 mi west of I–95. Closest airport: Reagan (55 mi), Richmond (55 mi).

CONTACT

Fredericksburg and Spotsylvania County Battlefields Memorial National Military Park (120 Chatham La., Fredericksburg, VA 22405, tel. 540/371–0802, www.nps.gov/frsp).

George Washington Birthplace National Monument

In northeastern Virginia, near Colonial Beach

The park evokes the spirit of the 18th-century tobacco farm where Washington was born and includes a memorial mansion and gardens and the tombs of several generations of Washingtons. The historic buildings, groves of trees, livestock, gardens, rivers, and creeks were the earliest scenes of Washington's childhood. The site was established on January 23, 1930.

WHAT TO SEE & DO

Hiking, picnicking, touring site, viewing film and exhibits, watching wildlife. **Facilities:** Visitor center, home site, Colonial farm area, burial grounds, trails, beach. Bookstore. **Programs & Events:** Guided tours with costumed interpreters. George Washington's Birthday (Presidents Day and Feb. 22), Christmas at Pope's Creek. **Tips & Hints:** Plan one to two hours for the visit. Busiest June and July, least crowded Dec. and Jan.

FOOD, LODGING & SUPPLIES

Camping: None in park. Near Montross: Westmoreland State Park (Rte. 347, tel. 804/493–8821; 128 sites; $18–$23; flush toilets, showers, hook-ups). **Hotels:** None in park. In Colonial Beach: Days Inn on the Potomac (30 Colonial Ave., tel. 804/224–0404; 60 rooms; $67–$87). In Montross: Inn at Montross (21 Polk St., tel. 804/493–0573; 5 rooms; $95–$115). **Restaurants:** None in park. In Montross: John Minors Pub (21 Polk St., tel. 804/493–0573; $10–$25). **Grocieries & Gear:** None in park. In Montross: Food Lion (18044 Kings Hwy., tel. 804/493–7367).

FEES & HOURS

Entrance fee: $3 adults. Visitor center and monument open daily 9–5.

HOW TO GET THERE

On the Potomac River, 38 mi east of Fredericksburg, and accessible via Rte. 3 to Rte. 204. Closest airport: Richmond (75 mi).

CONTACT

George Washington Birthplace National Monument (1732 Popes Creek Rd., Washington's Birthplace, VA 22443, tel. 804/224–1732, www.nps.gov/gewa).

George Washington Memorial Parkway

In northeastern Virginia, near McLean

Natural scenery along the Potomac River, across the water from Washington, DC, is preserved along this parkway. It connects the historic sites from Mount Vernon, where Washington lived, past the nation's capital, which he founded, to the Great Falls of the Potomac, where the president demonstrated his skill as an engineer. The parkway was authorized in 1930 and transferred to the Park Service in 1933.

WHAT TO SEE & DO

Bicycling, hiking, scenic driving, touring sites. **Facilities:** The 7,200-acre parkway includes 15 sites: Arlington House; Clara Barton National Historic Site; Lyndon Baines Johnson Memorial Grove on the Potomac, and Theodore Roosevelt Island (*see separate entries for all four*); the Arlington Memorial Bridge; Claude Moore Farm; Dyke Marsh; Fort Hunt Park; Fort Marcy; Glen Echo Park; Great Falls Park; Netherlands Carillon; Turkey Run Park; U.S. Marine Corps Memorial (Iwo Jima); and the Women in Military Service to America Memorial—and trails. Boat ramps, marinas, picnic areas. **Programs & Events:** Interpretive programs, guided walks, concerts, children's camps, marathons. Sunset Parade (U.S. Marine Corps War Memorial, Memorial Day–Aug., Tues. evenings). **Tips & Hints:** Busiest June and July, least crowded Jan. and Feb.

FEES, HOURS & REGULATIONS

Reservations required for many interpretive programs offered at sites that are not regularly staffed. Permit required for group picnicking at Fort Hunt Park Thurs.–Sun. and holidays Apr.–Oct. Permit required to consume alcohol. No weapons.

HOW TO GET THERE

The parkway runs parallel to the Potomac River north and south of Washington, DC, and is accessible from all major travel routes from the south and west, including I–495, I–95, and I–66. Closest airport: Reagan.

CONTACT

Superintendent, George Washington Memorial Parkway (700 George Washington Memorial Pkwy., McLean, VA 22101, tel. 703/289–2500, fax 703/289–2598, www.nps.gov/gwmp).

Maggie L. Walker National Historic Site

In southeastern Virginia, in Richmond

This row house, at 110½ East Leigh Street, was the home of Maggie Lena Walker (1867–1934), a prominent African-American civic and fraternal leader who rose to prominence in post–Civil War Richmond. She is best known as the first woman bank president, serving from 1903 to 1931, in the United States. The site was authorized in 1978.

WHAT TO SEE & DO

Touring house, watching film. **Facilities:** Visitor center, home. Bookstore. **Programs & Events:** Ranger-guided tours (year-round, Mon.–Sat.). 2nd St. Festival (1st weekend, Oct.), Maggie Walker Birthday Celebration, mid-July, call for celebration date. **Tips & Hints:** Busiest Feb. and July, least crowded Sept. and Jan.

FEES, HOURS & REGULATIONS

Free. No pets. Site and visitor center open Mon.–Sat. 9–5.

HOW TO GET THERE

In Richmond, at 110½ E. Leigh St. via Exits 76A or B off I–95/I–64. Closest airport: Richmond (5 mi).

CONTACTS

Maggie L. Walker National Historic Site (600 N. 2nd St., Richmond, VA 23223, tel. 804/771–2017, fax 804/771–2226, www.nps.gov/malw). Metro Richmond Convention & Visitors Bureau (5550 E. Marshall St., Richmond, VA 23219, tel. 804/782–2777).

Manassas
National Battlefield Park

In northeastern Virginia, in Manassas

Two battles between Union and Confederate troops during the Civil War are commemorated here. Nearly 900 men lost their lives in July 1861, and another 3,300 died during a three-day battle in August 1862, which brought the Confederacy to the height of its power. The park was designated on May 10, 1940.

WHAT TO SEE & DO

Auto touring, hiking, picnicking. **Facilities:** Visitor center (Henry Hill, Rte. 234); contact station (Stuart's Hill, U.S. 29), interpretive trails, auto tours. Bookstore, picnic area. **Programs & Events:** Ranger-guided tours and programs, living-history demonstrations (mid-June–Aug.). Battlefield Hike (Apr. and Oct.). **Tips & Hints:** Use caution while driving heavily traveled roads that divide the park. Visit June–Oct. Busiest June and July, least crowded Dec.–Feb.

FOOD & LODGING

Camping: None in park. In Centreville: Bull Run Regional Park (7700 Bull Run Dr., tel. 703/631–0550; 150 sites; $17–$20; flush toilets, showers, hook-ups). In Haymarket: Greenville Farm Family Campground (14004 Shelter La., tel. 703/743–7944; 150 sites; $22–$28; flush toilets, showers). **Hotels:** None in park. In Manassas: Best Western Battlefield Inn (10820 Balls Ford Rd., tel. 703/361–8000; 121 rooms; $89), Courtyard Manassas (10701 Battleview Pkwy., tel. 703/

335–1300; 149 rooms; $84–$109). ✕ **Restaurants:** None in park. In Manassas: Carmello's & Little Portugal (9108 Center St., tel. 703/368–5522; $11–$20; no lunch weekends), Chez Marc (7607 Centerville Rd., tel. 703/369–6526; $27–$40; closed Sun., no lunch Mon.–Wed.).

FEES, HOURS & REGULATIONS

Entrance fee: $3 adults. No hunting. No bikes, motorized or mechanized equipment on trails. Leashed pets only. Park open daily dawn–dusk. Visitor center open daily 8:30–5. Contact station open weekends 1–4, mid-June–Labor Day.

HOW TO GET THERE

The park is 26 mi west of Washington, DC. Henry Hill Visitor Center is 1 mi north of I–66, via Exit 47B and Rte. 234. Closest airports: Dulles (25 mi), Reagan (30 mi).

CONTACTS

Manassas National Battlefield Park (6511 Sudley Rd., Manassas, VA 20109, tel. 703/361–1339, fax 703/361–7106, www.nps.gov/mana). Manassas City Visitor Center (9431 West St., Manassas, VA 20110, tel. 703/361–6599).

Petersburg National Battlefield

In southeastern Virginia, near Petersburg

Preserved in this park are three tracts associated with General Ulysses S. Grant's attack and siege of Petersburg during the Civil War. In the spring of 1864, after failing to defeat General Robert E. Lee's army and capture Richmond, the Confederate capital, Grant moved his army across the James River and attacked Petersburg. A 10-month siege resulted, ending when the last supply lines to Lee's army and Richmond were cut. The site was established as a national military park in 1926, transferred to the Park Service in 1933, and changed to a national battlefield in 1962.

WHAT TO SEE & DO

Auto touring, bicycling, hiking, horseback riding, picnicking, watching 17-minute map show. **Facilities:** 3 visitor centers: Eastern Front (Rte. 36 east of Petersburg); Five Forks (Courthouse Rd./SR 627, Dinwiddie County); Grant's Headquarters at City Point (Cedar La., Hopewell); interpretive signs, waysides. Gift shops, picnic area (Eastern Front). **Programs & Events:** 17-minute map show. Ranger-guided walks (mid-June–mid-Aug., daily). **Tips & Hints:** Visit in spring and fall. Go in Apr. for dogwood blooms, late Oct. for fall foliage. Busiest June and July, least crowded Jan. and Feb.

FOOD & LODGING

⛺ **Camping:** None in park. Near Chesterfield: Pocahontas State Park (10301 State Park Rd., tel. 804/796–4255; 65 sites; $20; flush toilets, showers, hook-ups). 🛏 **Hotels:** None in park. In Hopewell: Holiday Inn Express (4911 Oaklawn Blvd., tel. 804/458–1500; 115 rooms, 50 suites; $60–$95). In Petersburg: Comfort Inn (11974 S. Crater Rd., tel. 804/732–2900; 96 rooms; $75–$80). ✗ **Restaurants:** None in park. In Hopewell: Papa Granny's (224 N. Main St., tel. 804/541–0910; $4–$10; closed Sun., no dinner Tues. and Thurs.). In Petersburg: Alexander's (101 W. Bank St., tel. 804/733–7134; $11–$15; closed Sun., no dinner Mon. and Tues.).

FEES, HOURS & REGULATIONS

Entrance fee: $5 per vehicle. Stay off earthworks and on trails. No metal detectors or artifact hunting. No hunting. Leashed pets only. No mechanized equipment on trails. No horseback riding on paved trails. Park open daily sunrise–half hour before sunset. Visitor center hours: all are open daily 9–5.

HOW TO GET THERE

Eastern Front visitor center is 2½ mi east of central Petersburg on Rte. 36. Grant's Headquarters is in Appomattox Manor on Cedar La. in Hopewell. From I–95 or I–295, take Rte. 10, then make a left on Appomattox St., and a left on Cedar La. Five Forks is on Courthouse Rd., off I–85 in Dinwiddie County. Closest airport: Richmond (30 mi).

CONTACTS

Superintendent, Petersburg National Battlefield (1539 Hickory Hill Rd., Petersburg, VA 23803, tel. 804/732–3531, fax 804/732–0835, www. nps.gov/pete).

Prince William Forest Park

In northeastern Virginia, near Triangle

The 18,572-acre park contains the largest example of an eastern piedmont forest in the National Park System and is a sanctuary for native plants and animals in a rapidly developing region. The park encompasses the Quantico Creek watershed and a heritage of land usage that includes Colonial tobacco production, subsistence farming, iron pyrite mining, the Civilian Conservation Corps, and a World War II U.S. Army spy-training base. Congress created the Chopawamsic Recreational Demonstration Area in 1933. It was transferred to the Park Service in 1936 and renamed in 1948.

WHAT TO SEE & DO

Bird- and wildlife watching, fishing, hiking, on- and off-road biking, picnicking. **Facilities:** Visitor center, 11-mi scenic drive, 3-mi paved bike trail, 18 mi of fire roads for mountain biking, 35 mi of hiking trails. Map sale area. **Programs & Events:** Ranger-led tours and talks (weekends). **Tips & Hints:** Busiest May and June, least crowded Nov. and Jan.

FOOD, LODGING & SUPPLIES

⚠ **Camping:** 4 campgrounds in the park: Chopawamsic (8 hike-in sites; free; pit toilet; permit required, *see below*), Oak Ridge (100 sites; $10;

flush toilets), Travel Trailer Village (tel. 703/221–2474; 77 sites; $22–$25; flush toilets, showers, hook-ups), Turkey Run Ridge (tel. 703/221–7181; 6 group sites; $40; flush toilets). 5 cabin camps (tel. 703/221–5843; $30–$50; flush toilets, showers; reservations required). 🏨 **Hotels:** In Triangle: Ramada Inn Quantico (4316 Inn St., tel. 703/221–1181 or 800/272–6232; 145 rooms; $50–$72). ✘ **Restaurants:** None in park. In Triangle: Globe & Laurel (18418 Jefferson Davis Hwy., tel. 703/221–5763; $15–$20; closed Sun.). ⛺ **Groceries & Gear:** None in park. In Dumfries: Food Lion (5050 Waterway Dr., Dumfries, tel. 703/897–9220).

FEES, HOURS & REGULATIONS

Entrance fee: $5 per vehicle or $3 per bicyclist or walk-in. Backcountry permit (free) required for all backcountry camping. Park open daily dawn–dusk. Registered campers and cabin campers have access 24 hours. Visitor center open daily 8:30–5.

HOW TO GET THERE

32 mi south of Washington, DC, and 20 mi north of Fredericksburg, VA, via I–95 and Exit 150 (Rte. 619) west. Closest airports: Reagan, Dulles.

CONTACT

Prince William Forest Park (18100 Park Headquarters Rd., Triangle, VA 22172, tel. 703/221–7181, www.nps.gov/prwi).

Richmond
National Battlefield Park

In southeastern Virginia, in Richmond

Between 1861 and 1865, Union armies repeatedly tried to capture Richmond, capital of the Confederacy, to end the Civil War. Three of those campaigns came within a few miles of the city. The 763-acre park commemorates 11 different sites associated with those campaigns, including the battlefields at Gaines' Mill, Malvern Hill, and Cold Harbor. The park was authorized on March 2, 1936.

WHAT TO SEE & DO

Picnicking at Fort Harrison, touring battlefield sites. **Facilities:** Visitor center with audiovisual programs and film (5th and Tredegar Sts.); 4 contact stations: Chimborazo Medical Museum, Cold Harbor, Glendale Cemetery, and Fort Harrison; interpretive walking trails at Gaines Mill, Cold Harbor, Malvern Hill, Fort Harrison, and Drewry's Bluff; tour roads at Cold Harbor and Fort Harrison; audio stations. Bookstores. **Programs & Events:** Self-guided driving tours (audio cassette available). Ranger-led walking tours, talks, living history (June–Aug.). Battle anniversary commemorations: Drewry's Bluff (May 15), Memorial Day, Cold Harbor (June 3), Seven Days' Battle (June 26–July 1), and Fort Harrison (Sept. 29). **Tips & Hints:** Plan to spend at least a day visiting all 11 sites. Busiest June and July, least crowded Jan. and Feb.

FEES & HOURS

Free. Parking fee at Tredegar St. visitor center $4 per day. Battlefield sites open daily dawn–dusk. Visitor center, Chimborazo Park, Glendale and Fort Harrison contact stations open June–Aug., daily 9–5; Sept.–May, hours vary. Cold Harbor open June–Aug., daily 9–6; Sept.–May, hours vary.

HOW TO GET THERE

The visitor center (5th and Tredegar Sts.) is accessed via I–95. Southbound use Exit 75, northbound use Exit 74C west and then follow signs. From I–64 westbound, Exit 5th St. Closest airport: Richmond (7 mi).

CONTACT

Park Headquarters, Richmond National Battlefield Park (3215 E. Broad St., Richmond, VA 23223, tel. 804/226–1981, fax 804/771–8522, www.nps.gov/rich).

Shenandoah National Park

In northwestern Virginia, near Luray

Skyline Drive, which winds along the crest of the Blue Ridge Mountains between Front Royal and Waynesboro, is the central feature of the park. Along the 105-mi drive are 75 pullouts that overlook mountain peaks, gorges, and hollows. The heavily forested park also has 500 mi of trails, including a section of the Appalachian Trail, along which are streams, waterfalls, black bear, and deer. The 196,466-acre park was authorized in 1926 and established in 1935.

WHAT TO SEE & DO

Auto touring, bird-watching, fishing, hiking, horseback riding (guided rides, Skyland), picnicking, taking field study seminars. **Facilities:** 3 visitor centers: Dickey Ridge (mile 4.6), Harry F. Byrd (mile 51), and Loft Mountain (mile 79.5). Overlooks, wayside exhibits, amphitheaters, 500 mi of hiking trails. Book and map sales areas, fire pits and grates, gas, gift shops, laundries, picnic tables, showers. **Programs & Events:** Ranger-led nature and night walks, talks, evening programs (mostly late May–Oct.). Wildflower Weekend (mid-May), Butterfly Count (early July), Civilian Conservation Corps Reunion (late Sept.), Christmas Bird Count (late Dec.). **Tips & Hints:** Plan to spend one to two days for visit. Go in spring for wildflowers, migratory birds, and full streams leading to waterfalls; summer for more deer and bear sightings; fall for foliage; and winter for clearest views. Stay off rocks above waterfalls. Avoid fall weekends when the park is crowded with leaf-peepers. Park is usually 10 degrees cooler than valley below. Busiest July and Oct., least crowded Jan. and Feb.

FOOD, LODGING & SUPPLIES

Camping: 5 campgrounds in the park: Big Meadow (mile 51.3, tel. 800/365–3267; 217 sites; $19; flush toilets, showers; reservations required; closed Dec.–Apr.), Dundo (mile 83.7, tel. 800/365–3267; group site; $32; pit toilets; reservations required.), Lewis Mountain (mile 57.5; 32 sites; $16; flush toilets, showers; closed Nov.–Mar.), Loft Mountain (mile 79.5; 219 sites; $16; flush toilets, showers; closed Nov.–Apr.), Mathews Arm (mile 22.1; 179 sites; $16; flush toilets; closed Nov.–Apr.). Potomac Appalachian Trail Cabins (tel. 703/242–0693; 28 cabins; $25–$60; pit toilets). Backcountry camping allowed (permit required, *see below*). 🏨 **Hotels:** In the park: Big Meadows Lodge (mile 51.3, tel. 800/999–4714; 69 rooms, 11 cabins, 17 suites; $75–$123; closed Nov.–mid-Apr.), Lewis Mountain (mile 57.5, tel. 800/999–4714; 10 cabins; $64–$99), Skyland (mile 41.7, tel. 800/999–4714; 177 rooms, 20 cabins, 6 suites; $62–$100; closed Dec.–Mar.). ✗ **Restaurants:** In the park: Big Meadows Lodge (mile 51.3; $4–$7), Big Meadows Wayside (mile 51.2; $4–$8; closed Nov.–Mar), Elkwallow (mile 24.1; $4–$7; closed Nov.–Mar.), Loft Mountain Wayside (mile 79.5; $4–$7; closed Nov.–mid-Apr.), Skyland (mile 41.7; $4–$7; closed Dec.–Mar.). ⛽ **Groceries & Gear:** Elkwallow (mile 24.1), Big Meadows (mile 51.3), Lewis Mountain (mile 57.5), and Loft Mountain (mile 79.5).

FEES, HOURS & REGULATIONS

Entrance fee: $10 per vehicle or $5 per individual. Backcountry permit (free) required. Virginia fishing license required. Reservation required for horseback rides (tel. 540/999–2210). Reservation required for one- to two-day field-study seminars (June–Sept., tel. 540/999–3489). No hunting or feeding wild animals. Leashed pets only. No pets on some trails. No bicycles or motorized vehicles on trails. No open fires except in campgrounds and picnic areas. Park open daily. Park headquarters (on U.S. 211 east of Luray) open weekdays 8–4:30. Visitor centers open Apr.–Nov., daily 8:30–5. Skyline Dr. closes during bad weather and at night during hunting season.

HOW TO GET THERE

The park is between Front Royal and Waynesboro. The north entrance is on U.S. 340 in Front Royal. The south entrance is just east of Waynesboro on U.S. 250 and I-64. Closest airports: Charlottesville-Albemarle (45 mi), Staunton (20 mi), Dulles (80 mi).

CONTACTS

Shenandoah National Park (3655 U.S. 211 E, Luray, VA 22835-9036, tel. 540/999–3500, fax 540/999–3601, www.nps.gov/shen). ARAMARK–Shenandoah National Park (Box 727, Luray VA 22835, tel. 800/778–2851, www.visitshenandoah.com). Front Royal Chamber of Commerce (414 E. Main St., Front Royal, VA 22630, tel. 540/635–3185 or 800/338–2576). Harrisonburg Chamber of Commerce (10 E. Gay St., Harrisonburg, VA 22802, tel. 540/434–2319). Madison County Chamber of Commerce (R.R. 8 Box 40, Madison VA 22727, tel. 540/948–4455). Waynesboro Chamber of Commerce (301 W. Main St., Waynesboro, VA 22980, tel. 540/949–8203). Shenandoah Valley Travel Association (Box 1040, New Market, VA 22844, tel. 540/740–3132).

Wolf Trap National Park for the Performing Arts

In northeastern Virginia, near Vienna

Wolf Trap is the only national park dedicated to the performing arts. Within the boundaries of the park are 130 acres of rolling hills and woods. The Filene Center is an open-air performing arts pavilion that accommodates 7,000 people, including 3,100 on the lawn, from May to September. Along with the Barns of Wolf Trap, a 352-seat indoor theater in a rebuilt 18th-century barn just outside the park boundary, it hosts performances ranging from opera to dance to rock. The park was authorized on October 15, 1966.

WHAT TO SEE & DO

Attending performances, picnicking. **Facilities:** Performing arts pavilion, indoor theater, lawn, restaurant. Picnic area. **Programs & Events:** Performances (the Barns, year-round). Filene Center performances (May–Sept.), Theatre-in-the-Woods performances for children (July–Aug., tel. 703/255–1893), backstage tour of the Filene Center (winter, tel. 703/255–1890). **Tips & Hints:** Arrive early for best lawn seats. Filene Center gates open about 1½ hours before performance. Bring a picnic. Busiest July and Aug., least crowded Jan.

FOOD & LODGING

Camping: None in park. In Fairfax Station: Burke Lake Park (Ox Rd. off Burke Lake Rd., tel. 703/323–6601; 200 sites; $15; flush toilets, showers; closed late Oct.–mid-Apr.). In Reston: Lake Fairfax Park (Lake Fairfax Dr. off Baron Cameron Ave., tel. 703/471–5415; 136 sites; $17–$18.50; flush toilets, showers, hook-ups; closed Dec.–Feb.). **Hotels:** None in park. In Tysons Corner: Comfort Inn (1587 Spring Hill Rd., tel. 703/448–8020; 250 rooms; $90–$190), Tysons Corner Marriott (8028 Leesburg Pike, tel. 703/734–3200; 376 rooms, 14 suites; $189, $240–$429 suites). **✗ Restaurants:** In the park: Ovations (tel. 703/255–4017; $4–$12). In Vienna: Café Renaissance (163 Glyndon St., tel. 703/938–3311; $11–$27; no lunch weekends), Clyde's (8332 Leesburg Pike, tel. 703/734–1901; $6–$20).

FEES & HOURS

Entrance free, performance fees vary. Tickets available by phone (tel. 703/218–6500 or 800/955–5566), online (www.wolftrap.org or www.tickets.com), or in person at the Barns (weekdays 10–6, weekends noon–5, performance nights until 9).

HOW TO GET THERE

Take Exit 67 off I–66 and Exit 12 off Capital Beltway to reach Rte. 267 west (Dulles Toll Rd.). Follow signs to local exits, pay toll, and exit at the Wolf Trap ramp. The Filene Center is on the right. From Rte. 7 west, turn left on Towlston Rd., go 1 mi to Filene Center on left. From West Falls Church Metro station (Orange line), take Wolf Trap Shuttle (tel. 202/637–7000). Closest airports: Dulles (14 mi), Reagan (14 mi).

CONTACTS

Wolf Trap Farm Park for the Performing Arts (1551 Trap Rd., Vienna, VA 22182, tel. 703/255–1800, www.nps.gov/wotr). Wolf Trap Foundation (1624 Trap Rd., Vienna, VA 22182, tel. 703/938–2404).

See Also

Appalachian National Scenic Trail, West Virginia. *Assateague Island National Seashore*, Maryland. *Blue Ridge Parkway*, North Carolina. *Cumberland Gap National Historical Park*, Kentucky. *Harpers Ferry National Historical Park*, West Virginia. *Potomac Heritage National Scenic Trail*, District of Columbia. *Green Springs National Historic Landmark District, Jamestown National Historic Site, Red Hill Patrick Henry National Memorial,* and *Shenandoah Valley Battlefields*, in Other National Parklands.

Ebey's Landing
National Historical Reserve

On Whidbey Island

This rural historic district preserves an unbroken historical record of Puget Sound exploration and settlement from the 19th century to the present. Historic farms, still under cultivation in the prairies of Whidbey Island, reveal land-use patterns unchanged since settlers claimed the land in the 1850s under the Donation Land Claim Act. Two state parks and the Victorian seaport community of Coupeville are also in the reserve. The prairies, seaport, and dramatic coastal beaches and cliffs create a cultural landscape of national significance. The 19,000-acre reserve was authorized on November 10, 1978.

WHAT TO SEE & DO

Bird-watching, boating, hiking, picnicking, scuba diving, self-guided touring of Coupeville and surroundings on foot or by bike or car. **Facilities:** Island County Historical Museum (downtown Coupeville), scenic vistas and pullouts, wayside exhibits, historic homes and farmsteads, trails. Boat launch area. **Programs & Events:** Self-guided tours. Interpretive walks (June–Sept.). **Tips & Hints:** Stop at museum to pick up brochure for self-guided tours of Coupeville and surrounding reserve. Use caution on beach to avoid being caught on headlands during high tides. Busiest July and Aug., least crowded Dec. and Jan.

FOOD, LODGING & SUPPLIES

⚠ **Camping:** In the park: Fort Casey State Park (1280 Engle Rd., Coupeville, tel. 360/678–4519; 35 sites; $16; flush toilets, showers), Fort Ebey State Park (400 Hill Valley Dr., Coupeville, tel. 360/678–4636; 50 sites; $16–$21; flush toilets, showers, hook-ups; reservations required). ⌂ **Hotels:** In the park: Captain Whidbey Inn (2072 Captain Whidbey Inn Rd., Coupeville, tel. 360/678–4097; 32 rooms, 3 cottages; $85–$170), Inn at Penn Cove (702 N. Main St., Coupeville, tel. 360/678–8000 or 800/688–2683; 6 rooms; $60–$125). ✗ **Restaurants:** In the park: Christopher's (23 Front St., Coupeville, tel. 360/678–5480; $15–$20), Rosi's (602 N. Main St., Coupeville, tel. 360/678–3989; $17–$22; no lunch). ⌂ **Groceries & Gear:** In the park: Prairie Center Red Apple Market (408 S. Main St., Coupeville, tel. 360/678–5611).

FEES, HOURS & REGULATIONS

Free. No beach fires. Respect property rights of landowners. Hike on designated trails only. Leashed pets only. No collecting driftwood, plants, rocks, or other natural features. State parks open 8–dusk. Island County Historical Museum open May–Sept., daily 10–5; Oct.–Apr., daily 10–4.

HOW TO GET THERE

The reserve, on central Whidbey Island, can be reached by car via Rte. 20 or by the Washington State Ferry system (tel. 206/464–6400; 888/808–7977 in Washington), which provides year-round car and passenger service from Port Townsend and Mukilteo. Closest airports: Oak Harbor (8 mi), Seattle (90 mi).

CONTACTS

Ebey's Landing National Historical Reserve (Box 774, Coupeville, WA 98239, tel. 360/678–6084, www.nps.gov/ebla). Oak Harbor Chamber of Commerce (32630 Rte. 20, Oak Harbor, WA 98277, tel. 360/675–3535).

Fort Vancouver National Historic Site

In southwestern Washington, in Vancouver

This Columbia River site displays rebuilt structures from the 19th-century fort that was a key fur-trading post in North America. More than 20 Hudson's Bay Company posts in the Northwest shipped their furs here between 1825 and 1860 for shipment overseas. The fort attracted American emigrants newly arrived in the Oregon country and played a significant role in the settlement of the Northwest. The fort was established as a Park Service unit in 1947.

WHAT TO SEE & DO

Picnicking, touring fort and blacksmith shop. **Facilities:** Visitor center (Evergreen Blvd.), reconstructed fort, blacksmith shop, carpenter shop. Gift shop, picnic shelter and tables. **Programs & Events:** Guided tours or costumed interpreters in buildings. Special presentations (June–Sept., weekends). Queen Victoria's Birthday (late May); Brigade Encampment (June); "Founder's Day" (Aug. 25); Candlelight Tour (Sept.); Christmas at the Fort (early Dec.). **Tips & Hints:** Go during special events to see the fort at its most vibrant. Go May–Oct. for best weather. Winter is rainy season, spring is school-group season. Busiest May–July, least crowded Dec. and Jan.

FEES, HOURS & REGULATIONS

Entrance fee: $3 per person or $5 per family (June–Sept.); free (Oct.–May). No dogs. No smoking. No food or drink inside fort. Park and visitor center open June–Oct., Mon.–Thurs. 10–6, Fri.–Sun. 10–8; Sept.–Memorial Day, weekends 10–4.

HOW TO GET THERE

From I–5, exit on Mill Plain Blvd. Go east. Turn right on Fort Vancouver Way and left on Evergreen Blvd. to reach visitor center. Closest airport: Portland, OR (6 mi).

CONTACTS

Fort Vancouver National Historic Site (612 E. Reserve St., Vancouver, WA 98661, tel. 360/696–7655 or 800/832–3599, www.nps.gov/fova).

Greater Vancouver Chamber of Commerce (404 E. 15th St., Suite 11, Vancouver, WA 98663, tel. 360/694–2588, www.vancouverusa.com).

Lake Chelan
National Recreation Area

In north-central Washington, near Stehekin

Lake Chelan rests in a trough carved by glaciers in the Cascades Range. The recreation area is part of North Cascades National Park. With a depth of 1,500 feet, it's one of the nation's deepest lakes. Although the lake's average width is less than 2 mi, it extends almost 55 mi into the Cascade Mountains. At its deepest point, Lake Chelan drops to 400 feet below sea level. The Stehekin River drainage area and the upper 4 mi of the lake are protected by the recreation area. The area was established on October 2, 1968.

WHAT TO SEE & DO

Boating (rentals), bicycling (rentals), cross-country skiing, fishing, hiking, horseback riding and pack trips (rentals), hunting, mountain climbing, picnicking, river rafting, snowshoeing (rentals). **Facilities:** Golden West Visitor Center (Stehekin Landing), wayside exhibits, self-guided interpretive trails. Book and map sales areas, post office. **Programs & Events:** Junior Explorer Activity (June–Sept.), naturalist talks (June–Sept., daily at 1:30); evening programs (July–Aug., nightly at 8), Buckner Orchard Ride & Hike (June–Sept., Fri. at 11), Voices of the Mountain Series (occasionally), Earth Week (mid-Apr.). **Tips & Hints:** Be prepared for rapid weather changes. The North Cascades Complex is primarily a wilderness park with few frontcountry activities. Hang all food out of the reach of bears in backcountry. Beware of hazardous stream crossings. Check conditions before starting trips. Crossing snowfields may require special equipment. Busiest July and Aug., least crowded Dec. and Jan.

FOOD, LODGING & SUPPLIES

Camping: 5 campgrounds in the park: Bullion (2 walk-in sites; free; pit toilets), Harlequinn (6 walk-in sites; free; pit toilets), High Bridge (2 walk-in sites; free; pit toilets), Purple Point (7 walk-in sites; free; flush toilets), Tumwater (2 walk-in sites; free; pit toilets). Camping permits are required for all sites and can be obtained at Lake Chelan or Stehekin. Backcountry and boat-in sites available along Stehekin Valley Road and along Lake Chelan (permit required, *see below*). *See also North Cascades National Park and Ross Lake National Recreation Area.* **Hotels:** In the park: North Cascades Stehekin Lodge (tel. 509/682–4494; 28 rooms; $90–$165; hike in or boat in only). In Stehekin: Stehekin Valley Ranch (Stehekin Valley Rd., tel. 509/682–4677 or 800/536–0745; 5 cabins; $75–$85; closed Oct.–May), Silver Bay Inn & Cabins (Silver Bay Rd., tel. 509/682–2212; 4 units; $145–$295). **Restaurants:** None in park. In Stehekin: Stehekin Valley Ranch (Stehekin Valley Rd., tel. 509/682–4677 or 800/536–0745; $11–$20; closed Oct.–

mid-June). & **Groceries & Gear:** None in park. In Chelan: Safeway (106 W. Rte. 150, tel. 509/682–2615), Lake Chelan Sports Inc. (932 E. Woodin Ave., tel. 509/682–2629).

FEES, HOURS & REGULATIONS

Free. Shuttle bus fee: $6 per zone each way on bus in the Stehekin Valley. Reservations recommended (tel. 360/856–5700 Ext. 340, then Ext. 14). The bus operates May 15–Oct. 15. No dogs on shuttle. Backcountry permit (free) required for all backcountry camping (tel. 360/873–4590 Ext. 39). Permits issued in person only. Permits required for Stehekin Valley road campsites. Use of federal docks on lake requires Forest Service dock permit ($5 per day or $40 annual). Washington state fishing and hunting licenses required. Hunting permitted in recreation area only. Leashed pets only. Recreation area open daily. Heavy winter snows restrict travel and close roads. Golden West Visitor Center open Mar. 15–May 15, daily 12:30–2; May 16–Sept. 30, daily 8:30–5; Oct. 1–15, daily 10:30–2.

HOW TO GET THERE

The main access to Stehekin is by boat (tel. 509/682–2224) or floatplane (tel. 509/682–5555) from the town of Chelan on U.S. 97. Area can be reached by hiking trail in summer. Closest airport: Seattle–Tacoma (177 mi).

CONTACTS

North Cascades National Park Service Complex (810 Rte. 20, Sedro-Woolley, WA 98284, tel. 360/856–5700, fax 360/856–1934, www.nps/gov/noca). Lake Chelan Tourist Information (102 E. Johnson St., Lake Chelan, WA 98816, tel. 800/424–3526).

Lake Roosevelt National Recreation Area

In northeastern Washington, near Grand Coulee

The 1941 damming of the Columbia River, which was part of the Columbia River Basin project, created a 130-mi lake. Named for President Franklin D. Roosevelt, the lake is the largest recreation feature in the recreation area. Boating, fishing, swimming, camping, and hiking are all available, as are tours of Fort Spokane and the dam. Coulee Dam Recreation Area was administered under a cooperative agreement signed in 1946 with the Bureau of Reclamation, Bureau of Indian Affairs, and the U.S. Department of Interior; revised and renegotiated in 1990 by the Bureau of Reclamation, Bureau of Indian Affairs, National Park Service, Colville Confederated Tribes, and the Spokane Tribe of Indians; renamed in 1997.

WHAT TO SEE & DO

Bird-watching, boating (rentals in Keller Ferr, Fort Spokane, and Kettle Falls), fishing, hiking, hunting, picnicking, swimming, touring Fort Spokane and Grand Coulee Dam, waterskiing. **Facilities:** Visitor center, bathhouse. Boat dump stations, boat ramps, picnic areas. **Programs**

& Events: Canoeing, kayaking, and windsurfing lessons (mid-June–Labor Day). Interpretive talks, guided hikes. **Tips & Hints:** Busiest July and Aug., least crowded Dec. and Jan.

FOOD, LODGING & SUPPLIES

⚠ **Camping:** 27 campgrounds in the park (640 sites; $10; some flush toilets, some vault toilets). ⛺ **Hotels:** None in park. In Grand Coulee: Columbia River Inn (10 Lincoln St., tel. 509/633–2100 or 800/633–6421; 35 rooms; $49–$95), Coulee House (110 Roosevelt Way, tel. 509/633–1101 or 800/715–7767; 61 rooms; $64–$120). ✕ **Restaurants:** None in park. In Coulee Dam: Melody Restaurant (512 River Dr., tel. 509/633–1151; $8–$15). In Grand Coulee: Flo's Café (316 Spokane Way, tel. 509/633–3216; $4–$7). ⛀ **Groceries & Gear:** In the park: Seven Bays Marina (tel. 509/725–1676). In Grand Coulee: Safeway (101 Grand Coulee Ave., tel. 509/633–2411).

FEES, HOURS & REGULATIONS

Free. Boat launch permit ($6) required. Washington fishing and hunting permits required. No off-road vehicle use. Recreation area open daily. Visitor center open Memorial Day–Labor Day, daily 10–5; Labor Day–Memorial Day, intermittently.

HOW TO GET THERE

From I-90, the recreation area headquarters in Coulee Dam can be reached via Exit 179, then north on Rte. 17 east, and Rte. 155 north to Coulee Dam. From Spokane, take U.S. 2 west to Rte. 174 to Coulee Dam. Closest airport: Spokane (80 mi).

CONTACTS

Lake Roosevelt National Recreation Area (1008 Crest Dr., Coulee Dam, WA 99116, tel. 509/633–9441, www.nps.gov/laro). Grand Coulee Dam Area Chamber of Commerce (Box 760, 306 Midway, Grand Coulee, 99133-0760, tel. 800/268–5332 or 509/633–3074, www.grandcouleedam.org).

Mount Rainier National Park

In the west-central part of the state, near Ashford

This majestic 14,410-foot volcanic mountain, now glacier capped, sports rain forests with 1,000-year-old trees at its base, waterfalls, and subalpine flowering meadows. Native Americans called it "Tahoma," the snowy mountain. The 235,613-acre park is nearly all wilderness. The park was established on March 2, 1899.

WHAT TO SEE & DO

Auto touring, backpacking, bird-watching, cross-country skiing (rentals, Longmire), fishing, hiking, horseback riding, mountain climbing, picnicking, snowshoeing, wildflower and wildlife viewing. **Facilities:** 4 visitor centers: Paradise, Ohanapecosh, Sunrise, Longmire; White River information center, Longmire museum, trails. Gift shops, picnic areas. **Programs & Events:** Ranger-led interpretive programs and walks, campfire programs, movies and slide programs (June–early Sept.), guided snowshoe walks (Paradise). **Tips & Hints:** Bring rain gear. Get gas before entering park. Go on weekdays Sept.–early Oct. to avoid crowds, late June–early Sept. for wildflowers in subalpine meadows, Sept.–early Oct. for elk-mating season, Dec.–Apr. for cross-country ski season. Busiest July and Aug., least crowded Dec.–Feb.

FOOD, LODGING & SUPPLIES

Camping: 6 campgrounds in the park: Cougar Rock (173 sites; $15; flush toilets; closed mid-Oct.–May), Ipsut Creek (32 sites; free; vault toilets; closed mid-Oct.–May), Mowich Lake (tent-camping area; free; vault toilets; closed mid-Oct.–mid-June), Ohanapecosh (189 sites; $15; flush toilets; closed late June–Labor Day), Sunshine Point (18 sites; $10; vault toilets), White River (112 sites; $10; flush toilets; closed late June–mid-Sept.). Backcountry camping allowed (permit required, *see below*). **Hotels:** In the park: National Park Inn (Rte. 706, 10 mi east of Nisqually entrance, tel. 360/569–2275; 25 rooms; $77–$107), Paradise Inn (Rte. 706, 11 mi east of Longmire, tel. 360/569–2275; 127 rooms; $$77–$107; closed Nov.–mid-May.) **Restaurants:** In the park: National Park Inn (Rte. 706, tel. 360/569–2411; $10–$24), Paradise Inn (Rte. 706, tel. 360/569–2413; $12–$25). In Ashford: Alexander's Country Inn (37515 Rte. 706, tel. 360/569–2300; $11–$25; closed Mon.–Thurs. from Nov. to Mar.). **Groceries & Gear:** In the park: General Store at National Park Inn (Rte. 706, Longmire Visitor Complex, tel. 360/569–2411). In Eatonville: Eatonville Market (210 Center St., tel. 360/832–4551).

FEES, HOURS & REGULATIONS

Entrance fee: $10 per vehicle or $5 per bicyclist, motorcyclist, pedestrian, or bus passenger. Backcountry permit (free) required. Climbers must register with park and pay $30 fee. No bikes on trails. Longmire Visitor Center open daily 9–4. Jackson Visitor Center (Paradise) open May–Sept., daily 10–6; Oct.–Apr., intermittently. Ohanapecosh Visitor Center open late May–Oct., daily 9–6. Sunrise Visitor Center open July–late Sept., daily 9–6.

HOW TO GET THERE

The park can be reached from I–5, U.S. 12, and Rtes. 7, 706, 123, 410, and 165. The park's southwest Nisqually entrance, on Rte. 706, is open daily. Closest airport: Seattle–Tacoma (70 mi).

CONTACT

Mount Rainier National Park (Tahoma Woods, Star Route, Ashford, WA 98304-9751, tel. 360/569–2211, www.nps.gov/mora).

North Cascades National Park

In northwestern Washington, near Marblemount

Nearly all wilderness, the 505,000-acre North Cascades National Park contains some of America's most breathtakingly beautiful scenery. Attractions include more than 300 glaciers, waterfalls, rivers, lakes; lush forests; and diverse flora and fauna. The park was established on October 2, 1968.

WHAT TO SEE & DO

Bird- and wildlife watching, boating, fishing, hiking, horseback riding (rentals at Stehekin Valley Ranch), mountain climbing (rentals in Stehekin), river running (rentals at Stehekin Valley Ranch). **Facilities:** Visitor center (North Cascades, milepost 120 on Rte. 20 in Newhalem), Wilderness Information Center (Marblemount, milepost 105 on Rte. 20), Glacier Public Service Center (Glacier, Rte. 542), trails, wayside exhibits. Bookstore. **Programs & Events:** Art exhibits (June–Sept.), talks, demonstrations, guided nature walks, children's programs, evening presentations (mostly July–Sept. and winter holidays). Earth Day and Week (Apr.). **Tips & Hints:** Visit mid-June–late Sept. for best weather. Heavy snow and rain, depending on elevation, characterize the North Cascades from fall into spring. Snow is usually off all but the highest trails by July. Summer storms are common. Be prepared for rain and wind. Take good, light rain gear and tent if you are going into high and remote areas. Warm, waterproof clothing and a tent are virtually mandatory for spring, fall, and winter trips into the backcountry. Hang food and other items with fragrance at least 15 feet up and 5 feet out from tree trunk, away from animals, in backcountry. Be cautious crossing streams. Crossing snowfields and glaciers may require special equipment. Fragile vegetation, such as heather, particularly in subalpine areas, is easily damaged by foot traffic. Practice "Leave No Trace" hiking and camping techniques to minimize your impact on wilderness. Busiest July and Aug., least crowded Nov. and Jan.

FOOD, LODGING & SUPPLIES

⚠ **Camping:** Approximately 20 campgrounds in and near the park. *See Lake Chelan* and *Ross Lake national recreation areas.* Backcountry camping allowed (permit required, *see below*). 🛏 **Hotels:** In the park: *see Lake Chelan* and *Ross Lake national recreation areas.* In Winthrop: Chewuch Inn (223 White Ave., tel. 509/996–3107 or 800/747–3107; 8 rooms, 6 cabins; $75–$125). In Mazama: Freestone Inn (17798 Rte. 20, tel. 509/996–3906 or 800/639–3809; 21 rooms, 15 cabins; $100–$260). ✕ **Restaurants:** In the park: *see Lake Chelan National Recreation Area.* In Marblemount: Buffalo Run Restaurant (60084 Rte. 20, tel. 360/873–2461; $12–$15). In Winthrop: Duck Brand Cantina, Baker & Hotel (248 Riverside Ave., tel. 509/996–2192; $8–$17). 🛒 **Groceries & Gear:** None in park. In Newhalem: Skagit General Store (Rte. 20, ½ mi east of turnoff to the North Cascades Visitor Center, tel. 206/386–4489).

FEES, HOURS & REGULATIONS

Free. Northwest Forest Pass ($5 per day or $30 annual) required for parking along the Cascade River and at some trailheads within Ross Lake National Recreation Area. Permit required (free) for backcountry camping (Wilderness Information Center, tel. 360/873–4500 Ext. 39, May–Oct. in Marblemount for any backcountry area; National Park Headquarters, tel. 360/856–5700 Ext. 515, Oct.–May). Permits issued in person only, up to one day before trip. Reservations required (tel.

360/856–5700 Ext. 340, then Ext. 14, after May 14) for park shuttle buses in Stehekin Valley that serve the south end of the park. No pets on shuttle. Leashed dogs only on Pacific Crest Trail. No pets in any other backcountry. No wood fires except in forested, low-elevation areas with iron fire grates. No grazing of horses; bring feed. Washington state fishing license required. Hunting by permit only in Ross Lake National Recreation Area and Lake Chelan National Recreation Area (*see separate entries*). No mountain or trail bikes or mechanized or motorized equipment on trails. Park open daily. Access limited by snow in winter.

HOW TO GET THERE
The park is divided by Rte. 20, which runs from Burlington (I–5) on the west side to Okanogan on the east side, with branch routes to Baker Lake (at Concrete) and the Cascade River (at Marblemount). Hiking access and roadside views of the northwest corner of the park are available from Rte. 542, east from Bellingham. Two gravel roads enter the park: the Cascade River Rd. from Marblemount and the Stehekin Valley Rd. The latter does not connect to any roads outside the Stehekin Valley. Closest airport: Seattle–Tacoma (140 mi).

CONTACTS
North Cascades NPS Complex (810 Rte. 20, Sedro-Woolley, WA 98284, tel. 360/856–5700, fax 360/856–1934, www.nps.gov/noca). Mount Vernon Chamber of Commerce (Box 1007, Mount Vernon, WA 98273, tel. 360/428–8547). Sedro-Woolley Chamber of Commerce (714 B Metcalf St., Sedro-Woolley, WA 98284, tel. 360/855–1841). Concrete Chamber of Commerce (Box 743, Concrete, WA 98237, tel. 360/853–7042). Winthrop Chamber of Commerce (202 Riverside St., Winthrop, WA 98862, tel. 509/996–2125). Methow Valley Central Reservations (Box 505, Winthrop, WA 98862, tel. 509/996–2148 or 800/422–3048). Chelan Chamber of Commerce (Box 216, Chelan, WA 98816, tel. 509/ 682–2022 or 800/424–3526). Wenatchee Chamber of Commerce (116 N. Wenatchee Ave., Wenatchee, WA 98801, tel. 509/663–3723 or 800/ 572–7753).

Olympic National Park

In northwestern Washington, near Port Angeles

Olympic encompasses three distinctly different ecosystems—rugged glacier-capped mountains, more than 60 mi of wild Pacific coast, and magnificent stands of old-growth and temperate rain forest. About 95% of the park is designated wilderness, so these diverse ecosystems are largely pristine in character. Isolated for eons by glacial ice, the waters of Puget Sound, and the Strait of Juan de Fuca, the Olympic Peninsula has developed its own distinct array of plants and animals. Eight kinds of plants and 15 kinds of animals are found on the peninsula and live nowhere else in the world. Mount Olympus National Monument was proclaimed in 1909, transferred to the Park Service in 1933, renamed and redesignated in 1938, and designated a Biosphere Reserve in 1976 and a World Heritage Site in 1981.

WHAT TO SEE & DO

Auto touring, backpacking, bird- and wildlife watching, fishing, hiking, mountain climbing, picnicking, skiing, snowshoeing, swimming. **Facilities:** 3 visitor centers: Port Angeles, Hurricane Ridge, and Hoh Rain Forest. 11 ranger stations, 168 mi of roads, 600 mi of trails. **Programs & Events:** Ranger-led programs and activities (July and Aug.); ranger-led snowshoe walks (Dec.–Mar., weekends); Olympic Park Institute one- to three-day field seminars on natural history; nature photography; and kayak, canoe, and backpacking outings (Apr.–Oct., tel. 360/928–3720 or www.yni.org/opi). **Tips & Hints:** Drive to Hurricane Ridge for high country and mountain vistas, Hoh Rain Forest where 12 feet of rain a year creates huge trees and greenery, and Rialto or Ruby Beach for view of Pacific beaches. Come prepared for a variety of weather. Bring rain gear and layered clothing. Buy topographic maps for most hikes (tel. 360/452–0339). Busiest Aug. and Sept., least crowded Jan. and Feb.

FOOD, LODGING & SUPPLIES

Camping: 17 campgrounds in the park (tel. 360/452–0330; about 925 sites; $8–$15; some flush toilets, some pit toilets). Backcountry camping allowed (permit required, *see below*). **Hotels:** In the park: Kalaloch Lodge (U.S. 101, Forks, tel. 360/962–2271; 15 rooms, 44 cabins; $200–$300), Lake Crescent Lodge (416 Lake Crescent Rd., tel. 360/928–3211; 35 rooms, 17 cabins; $56–$180; closed Nov.–Apr.), Log Cabin Resort (3183 E. Beach Rd., tel. 360/928–3325; 28 rooms, 4 cabins; $58–$115; closed Oct.–Mar.). In Quinault: Lake Quinault Lodge (South Shore Rd., tel. 360/288–2900 or 800/562–6672; 92 rooms, 1 suite; $68–$195). **Restaurants:** In the park: Kalaloch Lodge (U.S. 101, tel. 360/962–2271; $15–$25), Lake Crescent Lodge (416 Lake Crescent Rd., tel. 360/928–3211; $15–$25). In Sequim: Three Crabs (11 Three Crabs Rd., tel. 360/683–4264; $10–$22). **Groceries & Gear:** In Fairholm: Fairholm General Store (U.S. 101 at west end of Lake Crescent, tel. 360/928–3020).

FEES, HOURS & REGULATIONS

Entrance fee: $10 per vehicle or $5 per bicyclist or bus passenger. RV sewage dump station fee: $3 per use. Ozette parking fee: $1 per day. Backcountry permit ($5–$7, tel. 360/565–3100) required. Stay on trails and use existing wilderness campsites. Park open daily. Visitor center in Port Angeles open daily 9–6. Hours vary at Hurricane Ridge and Hoh River Rain Forest visitor centers.

HOW TO GET THERE

The park, which occupies the center of the Olympic Peninsula and a 63-mi strip along the Pacific Coast, can be reached from the Seattle–Tacoma area via U.S. 101 or by ferry (www.wsdot.wa.gov/ferries). For car and passenger ferry service between Victoria, British Columbia, and Port Angeles, call 360/457–4491. For passenger ferry service in summer between Victoria and Port Angeles, call 360/452–8088. Closest airport: Fairchild International in Port Angeles (20 mi).

CONTACTS

Olympic National Park (600 E. Park Ave., Port Angeles, WA 98362-6798, tel. 360/565–3131, www.nps.gov/olym). North Olympic Peninsula Visitor & Convention Bureau (Box 670, Port Angeles, WA 98362, tel. 360/452–8552 or 800/942–4042, www.olympicpeninsula.org).

Ross Lake
National Recreation Area

In northwestern Washington, near Diablo

The 118,000-acre recreation area provides the corridor for the popular North Cascades Highway (Rte. 20). Its three lakes—12,000-acre Ross Lake, 910-acre Diablo Lake, and 210-acre Gorge Lake—afford water access to the more remote areas in the North Cascades National Park and Mount Baker–Snoqualmie National Forest. The area was established on October 2, 1968.

WHAT TO SEE & DO

Auto touring, bird- and wildlife watching, boating (rentals, Ross Lake Resort), canoeing, fishing, hiking, hunting, picnicking, river rafting, rock climbing. **Facilities:** North Cascades Visitor Center (Rte. 20 in Newhalem), amphitheaters, trails, wayside exhibits. Book and map sales area, boat-launching ramps. **Programs & Events:** Interpretive programs, guided and self-guided walks (mostly July–Sept.). Earth Day (mid-Apr.). **Tips & Hints:** Be prepared for rapid changes in weather. The surrounding area is primarily a wilderness park with few frontcountry activities. Hang all food out of the reach of bears. Check stream conditions before starting trips. Crossing snowfields may require special equipment. Go Memorial Day–Sept. for best weather. Busiest July and Aug., least crowded Dec. and Jan.

FOOD, LODGING & SUPPLIES

Camping: 4 campgrounds in the park: Colonial Creek (Rte. 20 at Diablo Lake; 152 sites; $12; flush toilets; closed Oct.–mid-May), Goodell Creek (Rte. 20, 10½ mi west of park visitor center turnoff; 21 tent sites; $10), Hozomeen (Hozomeen Trail; 152 walk-in tent sites; free; vault toilets; closed Nov.–Apr.), Newhalem Creek (Rte. 20 near Newhalem Visitor Center; 111 RV sites; $12; flush toilets; closed mid-Oct.–mid-May). Backcountry camping allowed (permit required, *see below*). **Hotels:** In the park: Ross Lake Resort (tel. 206/386–4437; 15 cabins; $92–$197; walk in or boat in only). **Restaurants:** None in park. *See Lake Chelan National Recreation Area* and *North Cascades National Park.* **Groceries & Gear:** None in park. *See Lake Chelan National Recreation Area* and *North Cascades National Park.*

FEES, HOURS & REGULATIONS

Free. Northwest Forest Pass ($5 per day or $30 annual) required for parking along the Cascade River and at some trailheads within Ross Lake. Permits required (free) for all backcountry and boat-in camping

(Wilderness Information Center, tel. 360/873–4500 Ext. 39, May–Oct. in Marblemount; National Park Headquarters, tel. 360/856–5700 Ext. 515, winter). Permits issued in person only, up to one day before trip. Washington state fishing and hunting licenses required. Leashed pets only on trails. Recreation area open daily. Visitor center (Newhalem) open mid-Apr.–early Nov., daily; early Nov.–mid-Apr., weekends. Part of Rte. 20 closes in winter. Exact opening and closing dates of highway depend on snow and avalanche conditions.

HOW TO GET THERE

Access to the area is via Rte. 20 from Burlington to the west and Winthrop to the east. The north end of Ross Lake is reached by a 39-mi gravel road exiting from Trans-Canada Rte. 1 near Hope, BC. There is no road access from Rte. 20 to the south end of Ross Lake. Closest airport: Seattle–Tacoma (140 mi).

CONTACTS

North Cascades National Park Service Complex (810 Rte. 20, Sedro Woolley, WA 98284, tel. 360/856–5700, fax 360/856–1934, www.nps. gov/rola). Sedro-Woolley Chamber of Commerce (714 B Metcalf St., Sedro-Woolley, WA 98284, tel. 360/855–1841). Concrete Chamber of Commerce (Box 743, Concrete, WA 98237, tel. 360/853–7042).

San Juan Island National Historical Park

On San Juan Island

Commemorated in this park are the 1853–72 events relating to the settlement of the Oregon boundary dispute between the United States and Great Britain. In 1859, military forces from both countries confronted each other in a crisis precipitated by the nations' dual claims to the island and the death of a Hudson's Bay Company pig at the hands of an American farmer. On view are remains of American and British camps. The island is also home to glacial landscapes with grasslands, forests, beaches, tide pools, and lagoons. The park was authorized in 1966.

WHAT TO SEE & DO

Beachcombing, hiking, picnicking, walking. **Facilities:** Information center (125 Spring St., Friday Harbor), 2 contact stations with interpretive exhibits (American Camp, 6 mi from Friday Harbor; and English Camp, 9 mi from Friday Harbor), beaches, trails. Picnic areas with tables, fire pits and grates, sales outlets. **Programs & Events:** Guided walks (June–Aug.), historical reenactments (June–Aug., Sat.), cultural and natural-history programs (June–Aug., Fri.–Sun.). **Tips & Hints:** Go in late spring for wildflowers, summer for whale-watching and good weather, winter for migrating birds. Busiest July and Aug., least crowded Nov. and Dec.

FOOD, LODGING & SUPPLIES

Camping: None in park. In Friday Harbor: San Juan County Park (50 San Juan Park Dr., tel. 360/378–1842; 20 sites; $23–$32; flush toilets, showers), Snug Harbor Resort (1997 Mitchell Bay Rd., tel. 360/378–4762; 11 sites; $15–$25; flush toilets, showers). **Hotels:** None in park. In Friday Harbor: Friday Harbor House (130 West St., tel. 360/378–8455; 20 rooms; $200–$300), Friday's Historical Inn (35 1st St., tel. 360/378–5848 or 800/352–2632; 14 rooms; $90–$215). **Restaurants:** None in park. In Friday Harbor: Duck Soup Inn (50 Duck Soup La., tel. 360/378–4878; $18–$27), Friday Harbor House Restaurant (130 West St., tel. 360/378–8453; $14–$23). **Groceries & Gear:** None in park. In Friday Harbor: King's Market (175 West St., tel. 360/367–4505).

FEES, HOURS & REGULATIONS

Free. Permits required (free) for horseback riding. Washington state fishing license required. Shellfish–seaweed license required for clamming. No hunting or collecting. Leashed pets only. Bikes and motorized vehicles restricted to roads and parking areas. Park grounds open daily dawn–11 PM. Friday Harbor information center open Memorial Day–Labor Day, daily 8:30–5; Labor Day–Memorial Day, weekdays 8:30–4:30. American Camp contact station open Memorial Day–Labor Day, daily 8:30–5; Labor Day–Memorial Day, Thurs.–Sun. 8:30–4:30. English Camp contact station open Memorial Day–Labor Day, daily 8:30–5.

HOW TO GET THERE

The island is accessible by Washington State Ferries from Anacortes (83 mi north of Seattle) or from Sidney, BC (15 mi north of Victoria). Closest airport: Friday Harbor.

CONTACTS

San Juan Island National Historical Park (Box 429, Friday Harbor, WA 98250, tel. 360/378–2240, www.nps.gov/sajh). San Juan Island Chamber of Commerce (Box 98, Friday Harbor, WA 98250–0098, tel. 360/378–5240, www.sanjuanisland.org).

Whitman Mission National Historic Site

In southeastern Washinton, near Walla Walla

Marcus and Narcissa Whitman founded a Protestant mission here in 1836 to convert the Cayuse people to Christianity and provide a way station for Oregon Trail pioneers. In 1847, a measles epidemic killed half the Cayuse. The survivors blamed Marcus Whitman for his inability to cure the measles and killed him, his wife, and 11 others on November 29, 1847. Another 50 hostages were ransomed a month later by agents from the Hudson's Bay Company. The site was authorized in 1936 and renamed in 1963.

WHAT TO SEE & DO

Fishing, picnicking, touring original building sites, a section of the Oregon Trail, and a mass grave of Whitman and others. Book sales area, picnic area with tables. **Facilities:** Visitor center, trails, wayside exhibits. **Programs & Events:** Slide program. Cultural demonstrations (June–Aug., weekends). **Tips & Hints:** Wear walking shoes. The best times to visit are early summer and fall. Busiest May and June, least crowded Dec. and Jan.

FOOD, LODGING & SUPPLIES

🏕 **Camping:** None in park. In College Place: the Country Estate (938 Scenic View Dr., tel. 509/529–5442; 4 sites; $18; showers, toilets, hookups). Near Touchet: Pierce's Green Valley RV Park (24672 W. U.S. 12, tel. 509/394–2387; 30 sites; $13–$22; vault toilets, hook-ups). 🛏 **Hotels:** None in park. In Walla Walla: La Quinta Inn & Suites (520 N. 2nd Ave., tel. 509/525–2522; 61 rooms, 5 suites; $69–$139). In Walla Walla: Marcus Whitman Hotel (6 W. Rose St., tel. 509/525–2200; 75 rooms, 16 suites; $75–$139). ✕ **Restaurants:** In Walla Walla: Paisano's (26 E. Main St., tel. 509/527–3511; $13–$20; closed Sun.), Red Apple (57 E. Main St., tel. 509/525–5113, $10–$20). 🛒 **Groceries & Gear:** None in park. In College Place: Wal-Mart Superstore (1700 S. E. Meadowbrook Rd., tel. 509/525–3468).

FEES, HOURS & REGULATIONS

Entrance fee: $3 adults, free ages 16 and under, $5 per family. Washington state fishing license required. No hunting. Leashed pets only. Walk bicycles on trails. Park open daily dawn–dusk. Visitor center open Memorial Day–Labor Day, daily 8–6; Labor Day–Memorial Day, daily 8–4:30.

HOW TO GET THERE

7 mi west of Walla Walla, off U.S. 12. Closest airport: Walla Walla.

CONTACTS

Whitman Mission National Historic Site (328 Whitman Mission Rd., Walla Walla, WA 99362, tel. 509/522–6360, fax 509/522–6355, www.nps.gov/whmi). Walla Walla Area Chamber of Commerce (Box 644, Walla Walla, WA 99362, tel. 509/525–0850, www.wwchamber.com).

See Also

Klondike Gold Rush National Historical Park, Alaska. *Nez Perce National Historical Park,* Idaho. *Lewis and Clark National Historic Trail, Oregon National Scenic Trail,* and *Pacific Crest National Scenic Trail,* in Other National Parklands.

WEST VIRGINIA

Appalachian National Scenic Trail

In the Appalachian Mountains, from Katahdin, ME, to Springer Mountain, GA

The 2,167-mi trail was the nation's first designated national scenic trail. The federally protected trail corridor protects the habitats of hundreds of rare, threatened, and endangered species and preserves some of the East Coast's finest remaining wildlands. Topography along the trail ranges from the rugged White Mountains in New Hampshire to the rolling farmlands of Pennsylvania's Cumberland Valley to the high-elevation grassy balds of Roan Mountain, Tennessee. The trail was built by volunteers and completed in 1937. It's maintained and managed primarily by volunteers, whose efforts are coordinated by the nonprofit Appalachian Trail Conference. It became a national scenic trail in 1968.

WHAT TO SEE & DO

Backpacking, hiking. **Facilities:** Visitor center: the Appalachian Trail Conference's national office in Harpers Ferry, WV; trail, shelters, huts. Map and guidebook sales area (Harpers Ferry, WV). **Tips & Hints:** Carry map, compass, whistle (3 blasts are an international call for help), flashlight (with extra batteries), sharp knife, fire starter (a candle, for instance), waterproof matches, first-aid kit, extra food, water (and some means to treat naturally occurring water), warm clothing and rain gear, and a heavy-duty garbage bag (to serve as an emergency shelter). Busiest June–Aug., least crowded Nov.–Apr.

LODGING

⚠ **Camping:** In the park: 260 three-sided shelters available about a day's hike apart along the trail; backcountry camping allowed. 🏨 **Hotels:** In the park: Appalachian Mountain Club Cabins (Gorham, NH, between Franconia Notch and Wildcat Ridge, tel. 603/466–2727; 8 huts; $23 self-service, $82 full service; full-service cabins closed Nov.–Feb.).

FEES, HOURS & REGULATIONS

Free. Overnight camping permits or user registration required at Great Smoky Mountains and Shenandoah national parks (*see separate entries*) and parts of the White Mountain National Forest in New Hampshire and Baxter State Park in Maine. No motor vehicles, bicycles, or mountain bikes on off-road sections. No horses or pack animals except in part of Great Smoky Mountains National Park. Leashed dogs only. Hunting is allowed on many of the lands through which the trail passes. No rest rooms. Trail open year-round. Visitor center open mid-May–mid-Sept., weekdays 9–5, weekends 9–4; mid-Sept.–mid-May, weekdays 9–5.

HOW TO GET THERE

The trail has 500 access points along its 2,167-mi length from Katahdin, Maine, to Springer Mountain, Georgia. It passes through Maine, New Hampshire, Vermont, Massachusetts, Connecticut, New York, New Jersey, Pennsylvania, Maryland, West Virginia, Virginia, Tennessee, North Carolina, and Georgia.

CONTACTS

Appalachian National Scenic Trail (Harpers Ferry Center, Harpers Ferry, WV 25425, tel. 304/535–6278, fax 304/535–6270, www.nps.gov/appa). Appalachian Trail Conference (Box 807, Harpers Ferry, WV 25425, tel. 304/535–6331, fax 304/535–2667, www.appalachiantrail.org).

Bluestone
National Scenic River

In southern West Virginia,
between Hinton and Princeton

This scenic river preserves relatively unspoiled land in southern West Virginia, contains natural and historic features of the Appalachian plateau, and offers excellent warm-water fishing, hiking, boating, and scenery in its lower 11 mi. The river was authorized on October 26, 1988.

WHAT TO SEE & DO

Bicycling, canoeing, fishing, hiking, horseback riding, hunting, white-water boating. **Facilities:** Bluestone Trail, 8 mi. **Programs & Events:** Guided hikes, interpretive programs (June–Nov.). **Tips & Hints:** Intermediate skill required for Class I and II white water. Busiest July and Aug., least crowded Jan. and Feb.

FOOD, LODGING & SUPPLIES

Camping: None in park. In Bluestone State Park: Meador Campground (off Rte. 20, at mouth of Bluestone River, tel. 304/466–2895; 32 sites; $7–$19; flush toilets, showers, hook-ups). In Pipestem Resort State Park: Pipestem Resort Campground (off Rte. 20, 12 mi south of Hinton, tel. 304/466–1800; 82 sites; $15–$21; flush toilets, showers, hook-ups). **Hotels:** None in park. In Pipestem Resort State Park: McKeever Lodge (off Rte. 20, tel. 304/466–1800; 112 rooms; $77–$160), Mountain Creek Lodge (off Rte. 20, tel. 304/466–1800; 30 rooms; $77–$160; accessible by tramway only). **Restaurants:** None in park. In Pipestem Resort State Park: Bluestone Dining Room (McKeever Lodge, tel. 304/466–1800 Ext. 368; $5–$25), Mountain Creek Dining Room (Mountain Creek Lodge, tel. 304/466–1800 Ext. 387; $11–$30). **Groceries & Gear:** None in park. In Hinton: Kroger's (308 Stokes Dr., tel. 304/466–4888). In Fayetteville: Ultimate Rafting (Gateway Rd., tel. 800/470–7238).

FEES, HOURS & REGULATIONS

Free. No hunting or trapping on upper river. Open 24 hours.

HOW TO GET THERE

The scenic river is south of Hinton and northeast of Princeton. Access is through the Bluestone and Pipestem Resort state parks on Rte. 20. A tram that can transport boats provides access to the river from Pipestem Resort State Park. Closest airport: Charleston (95 mi).

CONTACTS

Bluestone National Scenic River (Box 246, Glen Jean, WV 25846, tel. 304/465–0508, www.nps.gov/blue). West Virginia State Chamber of Commerce (90 McCorkle Ave. SW, South Charleston, WV 25303, tel. 800/225–5982, www.callwva.com).

Gauley River
National Recreation Area

In southern West Virginia, near Summersville

Twenty-five miles of free-flowing Gauley River and 6 mi of the Meadow River have Class V+ rapids and are some of the most challenging white-water boating sites in the East. The area was authorized on October 26, 1988.

WHAT TO SEE & DO

Fishing, hunting, kayaking, trapping, white-water rafting. **Facilities:** Visitor information available at Canyon Rim Visitor Center; *see New River Gorge National River.* U.S. Army Corps of Engineers visitor center at Summerville Dam. **Programs & Events:** Ranger-led hikes (Sept. and Oct.). Civil War battle reenacts (Sept., at Carnifex Ferry Battlefield State Park). **Tips & Hints:** Most land along the Gauley River is privately owned. Go to Carnifex Ferry Battlefield State Park for scenic overlook and to access hiking trails. Go weekends mid-Sept.–mid-Oct. for rafting season, which depends on releases from Summerville Dam. Only those skilled enough to handle Class V+ rapids should raft. Busiest Sept. and Oct., least crowded Dec. and Jan.

FOOD, LODGING & SUPPLIES

Camping: In the park: Gauley Tailwaters (18 sites; free; vault toilets, no water). In Clifftop: Babcock State Park (Rte. 41, tel. 304/438–3004; 52 sites; $15–$19; flush toilets, showers, hook-ups). In Mount Nebo: Battle Run Campground (Rte. 129 off U.S. 19, tel. 304/872–3459; 117 sites; $14–$18; flush toilets, showers, hook-ups; closed mid-Oct.–Apr.). **Hotels:** None in park. In Clifftop: Babcock State Park (Rte. 41, tel. 304/438–3004; 25 cabins; $52–$130). In Ansted: Hawk's Nest (U.S. 60, tel. 304/658–5212; 31 rooms; $75–$80). **Restaurants:** None in park. In Ansted: Hawk's Nest (U.S. 60, tel. 304/658–5212; $5–$15). In Canvas: Feed Box Saloon (Grove's Rd./Rte. 30, tel. 304/872–1603; $14–$23). **Groceries & Gear:** None in park. In Oak Hill: Kroger's (Fayette Sq., tel. 304/469–2921).

FEES, HOURS & REGULATIONS

Free. West Virginia state permit required for fishing and hunting. Open 24 hrs.

HOW TO GET THERE

The recreation area is between Summersville Dam and the town of Swiss. Access is via Rte. 129 at the Summersville Dam, off U.S. 19. Other access points include Carnifex Ferry Battlefield State Park, off Rte. 129, and Swiss Rd., off Rte. 39. Closest airport: Charleston (75 mi).

CONTACTS

Gauley River National Recreation Area (Box 246, Glen Jean, WV 25846, tel. 304/465–0508, www.nps.gov/gari). West Virginia State Chamber of Commerce (90 McCorkle Ave. SW, South Charleston, WV 25303, tel. 800/225–5982, www.callwva.com).

Harpers Ferry
National Historical Park

In eastern West Virginia, in Harpers Ferry

John Brown's raid on Harpers Ferry in 1859 thrust this small West Virginia town into national prominence. Located at the scenic confluence of the Shenandoah and Potomac rivers, the park includes 2,500 acres in the states of West Virginia, Virginia, and Maryland. A variety of museums, exhibits, and trails illustrate the six nationally significant themes interpreted here—natural environment, industry, the Brown raid, the Civil War, African-American history, and transportation—and how they are connected. Harpers Ferry was designated as a national monument in 1944 and changed to a national historical park in 1968.

WHAT TO SEE & DO

Fishing, hiking, picnicking, rock climbing, visiting museums and exhibits. **Facilities:** Visitor center (Cavalier Heights District) and visitor information center (Lower Town District); museums, exhibits, trails with wayside exhibits. Bookstore, picnic area. **Programs & Events:** Ranger-guided tours (Memorial Day–Labor Day), concerts (June–Sept.), living-history programs (June–Oct.). Independence Celebration, Christmas Celebration. **Tips & Hints:** Stay on trails. Go in fall for foliage. Busiest July and Aug., least crowded Jan. and Feb.

FOOD, LODGING & SUPPLIES

⚠ **Camping:** None in park. In Harpers Ferry: KOA (near park entrance, U.S. 340, tel. 304/535–6895; 250 sites, 36 cabins, 4 lodges; $30–$42, $50–$135 cabins, $110 lodges; flush toilets, showers, hookups). ⛺ **Hotels:** None in park. In Harpers Ferry: Cliffside Inn (U.S. 340, tel. 304/535–6302; 100 rooms; $79–$115). ✗ **Restaurants:** None in park. In Harpers Ferry: Anvil (1270 Washington St., tel. 304/535–2582; $5–$20). ⛄ **Groceries & Gear:** None in park. In Charles Town: Wal-Mart Superstore (96 Patrick Henry Way, tel. 304/728–2720).

FEES, HOURS & REGULATIONS

Entrance fee: $3 per person for walk-ins and cyclists, $5 per vehicle. Rock-climbing registration required at ranger station. West Virginia, Maryland, or Virginia state fishing license required. No hunting. No bikes or motorized or mechanized equipment on trails. Leashed pets only. Park open daily. Visitor center open daily 8–5.

HOW TO GET THERE

In the eastern panhandle of West Virginia, 65 mi northwest of Washington, DC, and 20 mi southwest of Frederick, Maryland, via U.S. 340. Closest airport: Dulles (50 mi).

CONTACTS

Harpers Ferry National Historical Park (Box 65, Harpers Ferry, WV 25425, tel. 304/535–6223, fax 304/535–6244, www.nps.gov/hafe). Jefferson County Chamber of Commerce (Box 426, Charles Town, WV 25414, tel. 304/725–2055).

New River Gorge National River

In southern West Virginia, from Hinton to Fayetteville

New River protects 53 mi of free-flowing waterway. The 71,000-acre park and surroundings are rich in cultural and natural history and contain an abundance of scenic and recreational opportunities. The New River is one of the most renowned fishing streams in the state and offers premier white-water boating. The river, one of the oldest on the continent, has cut a deep gorge that exposes rocks 330 million years old and harbors rare plants. The site was authorized on November 10, 1978.

WHAT TO SEE & DO

Fishing, hiking, horseback riding, hunting, mountain biking (rentals in Fayetteville), picnicking, recreational climbing, white-water canoeing (rentals in Hinton). **Facilities:** 4 visitor centers: Canyon Rim (U.S. 19, 2 mi north of Fayetteville), Thurmond Depot (Rte. 25, 7 mi from the Glen Jean exit of U.S. 19), Grandview (Rte. 9, 6 mi north of I–64 Exit 129B), Sandstone (at I–64 Exit 139); amphitheater, boardwalk, hiking trails. Bookstores, picnic shelters, tables, and fire grates. **Programs & Events:** Ranger-led walks, hikes, bike rides, and slide shows. Guided walks, hikes, and mountain bikes (all May–Oct.). New River Train (Oct., tel. 304/453–1451), New River Gorge Bridge Pedestrian Day (3rd Sat., Oct.). **Tips & Hints:** The park is very long and narrow, with several access points into the gorge, rather than one main entrance. Book white-water rafting trips on Sundays or weekdays to get discounts and avoid Saturday crowds. Narrow, winding, one-lane roads require driving with passenger-side wheels on the shoulder when meeting oncoming traffic. Some park roads are unsuitable for large recreational vehicles. Stay off CSX railroad property that runs through park. Go Apr., May, Sept. and Oct. for cool, crisp weather; mid-May for Grandview rhododendron blooms; late June–early July for wild rhododendron blooms; Apr.–Sept. for peak bird migrations; mid-Oct. for peak fall foliage. Busiest July and Aug., least crowded Jan. and Feb.

LODGING

🏕 **Camping:** 4 campgrounds in the park: Army Camp (11 sites; free; pit toilets, no water), Glade Creek (5 sites; free; pit toilets, no water), Grandview Sandbar (16 sites; free; pit toilets, no water), Stone Cliff (10 sites; free; pit toilets, no water). Backcountry camping allowed. *See Bluestone National Scenic River.*

FEES, HOURS & REGULATIONS

Free. Picnic shelter and group camping area reservation and fees (tel. 304/465–6517 Burnwood and Dunglen; tel. 304/465–8064 Grandview). West Virginia state fishing license required. Hunting on federally owned lands within the park only, except at Grandview and Burnwood. No trapping. No recreational climbing at Grandview. Leashed pets only. Horses or pack animals on designated trails only. Swimming and wading not recommended because of strong currents and undercut rocks. No alcohol at park headquarters, Dunglen, Grandview, and Stonecliff. Bikes on designated trails only. Park open daily. Canyon Rim Visitor Center open daily 9–5. Thurmond Depot Visitor Center open Memorial Day–Labor Day, daily 9–5; intermittent weekend hours in spring and fall. Grandview Visitor Center open Memorial Day–Labor Day, daily 9–5. Sandstone Visitor Center open daily 9–5.

HOW TO GET THERE

The river is one hour (65 mi) east of Charleston and 20 minutes (30 mi) from Beckley. It's accessible from the West Virginia Tpke., I–64 and 77, and U.S. 19 and 60. Closest airports: Beckley (30 mi), Charleston (65 mi).

CONTACTS

New River Gorge National River (Box 246, Glen Jean, WV 25846, tel. 304/465–0508, fax 304/465–0591, www.nps.gov/neri). Southern West Virginia Convention & Visitor Bureau, (200 Main St., Beckley, WV 25801, tel. 800/847–4898, fax 304/252–2252, www.visitwv.com or www. visitwv.org). West Virginia State Chamber of Commerce (90 McCorkle Ave. SW, South Charleston, WV 25303, tel. 800/225–5982, www. callwva.com). Fayette County Chamber of Commerce (310 Oyler Ave., Oak Hill, WV 25901, tel. 800/927–0263). West Virginia Travel Council (Box 50312, 2101 Washington St. E, Charleston, WV 25305-0317, tel. 800/225–5982).

See Also

Chesapeake & Ohio Canal National Historical Park, Maryland. *National Coal Heritage Area*, in Other National Parklands.

WISCONSIN

Apostle Islands National Lakeshore

*On the south shore of Lake Superior,
90 mi east of Duluth, MN*

Twenty-one sheltered islands in the world's largest freshwater lake, plus 12 mi of mainland shoreline, comprise this park. There are pristine beaches, sandstone cliffs, sea caves, wetlands, and dense forests to explore. Native Americans, loggers, quarrymen, farmers, and commercial fishermen left their marks on the island—today you can see their old quarries, barns, and log skid trails. Six historic light stations host exhibits about the region's maritime history. Waterside campsites throughout the islands, some accessible only by kayak or canoe, make for a true back-to-nature experience. The park was established on September 26, 1970.

WHAT TO SEE & DO

Beachcombing, boating, camping, cross-country skiing, fishing, hiking, hunting, kayaking (rentals in Bayfield), picnicking, riding excursion boats, sailing (rentals in Bayfield), scuba diving, swimming, touring lighthouses. **Facilities:** 2 visitor centers: Bayfield Visitor Center (Washington Ave., Bayfield) and Little Sand Bay Visitor Center (13 mi north of Bayfield); interpretive exhibits, movies, guided and self-guided tours, hiking trails. Book and map sales, docks. **Programs & Events:** Daily lighthouse lens talks (on request) at Bayfield Visitor Center. Guest lectures (Mon. nights mid-June–Aug.), guided hikes, campfire programs (mid-June–Labor Day); guided lighthouse tours (mid-June–Sept.). **Tips & Hints:** Monitor shoreside marine forecasts; weather can change dramatically on short notice. Water is available from wells on seven islands. Go May and June for best flowers, July and August for moderate waves, May and Sept. for bird migrations, Feb. and Mar. for over-ice travel to islands. Take insect repellent, especially June and July. Busiest July and Aug., least crowded Dec. and Jan.

FOOD, LODGING & SUPPLIES

Camping: In the park: 65 backcountry and group sites on 14 islands (permit required, *see below*). On Madeleine Island: Big Bay State Park (tel. 888/947–2757; 60 sites; $8–$10; flush toilets, showers). **Hotels:** None in Park. In Bayfield: Bayfield Inn (20 Rittenhouse Ave., tel. 715/779–3363; 21 rooms; $85–$95), Seagull Bay Motel (325 S. 7th St., 715/779–5558; 24 rooms, 1 cottage; $50–$70). **Restaurants:** None in park. In Bayfield: Maggie's Restaurant (41 Manypenny Ave., tel. 715/779–5181; $5–$7; no dinner), Old Rittenhouse Inn (314 Rittenhouse Ave., tel. 715/779–5111; $10; no lunch Nov.–Apr.). **Groceries & Gear:** None in park. In Bayfield: Andy's IGA (213 Rittenhouse Ave., tel. 715/779–5641), Wild by Nature (100 Rittenhouse Ave., tel. 715/779–5075), Track and Trail Adventure Outfitters (7 Washington Ave., tel. 800/354–8735).

FEES, HOURS & REGULATIONS

Camping permits ($15; tel. 715/779–3397) required. Wisconsin state hunting license and fishing license with Great Lakes trout stamp required. Scuba permit (free) required. Leashed pets only. No bikes on trails. No motorized vehicles on islands. No metal detectors. No personal watercraft or floatplanes. No snowmobiles. No hunting May 15–Sept. 30 except for bear hunting on Stockton, Sand, and Oak islands. Park open daily. Bayfield Visitor Center open daily 8–5. Little Sand Bay Visitor Center open early June–Sept., daily 9–5.

HOW TO GET THERE

The visitor center is one block from Rte. 13 in Bayfield, WI; 23 mi north of Ashland, WI; and 90 mi east of Duluth, MN. Closest airport: Duluth.

CONTACTS

Apostle Islands National Lakeshore (Rte. 1, Box 4, Old County Courthouse Bldg., Bayfield, WI 54814, tel. 715/779–3397, fax 715/779–3049, www.nps.gov/apis). Bayfield Chamber of Commerce (42 S. Broad St., Bayfield, WI 54814, tel. 800/447–4094, fax 715/779–5080).

St. Croix National Scenic Riverway

On the Minnesota–Wisconsin border, northeast of St. Paul, MN

Free-flowing and unpolluted, beautiful St. Croix River and its Namekagon tributary flow through some of the most scenic and least developed country in the upper Midwest. The 252-mi stretch of protected river is lined with forestland and is gentle enough for canoeing. The park was authorized on October 2, 1968.

WHAT TO SEE & DO

Bird- and wildlife watching, boating, canoeing (rentals in St. Croix Falls), cross-country skiing, fishing, hiking, hunting, snowshoeing. **Facilities:** 3 visitor centers: Headquarters (St. Croix Falls, WI), Namekagon (Trego, WI), and Marshland (Pine City, MN; groups only); guided and self-guided tours, hiking trails. Bookstores, covered picnic tables. **Programs & Events:** Campfire programs at state parks, ranger-guided tourboat cruises (both June–Aug.). **Tips & Hints:** Watch for deer ticks. Wear life preservers. Bring extra paddle, insect repellent, small gas stove, and drinking water if canoeing. Expect challenging canoeing for beginners. Go Apr.–Oct. for ice-free river, in May for migrating birds, May and June for wildflowers, late Sept.–early Oct. for fall colors, and in Oct. for waterfowl. Busiest July and Aug., least crowded Jan. and Feb.

FOOD, LODGING & SUPPLIES

🏕 **Camping:** In the park: backcountry sites along river. In St. Croix Falls: Wisconsin Interstate State Park (Rte. 35 near U.S. 8, tel. 715/483–3747; 85 sites; $8–$12). 🏨 **Hotels:** None in park. In St. Croix Falls: Dalles House Motel (726 Vincent St. S, tel. 715/483–3206 or 800/341–8000; 50 rooms; $43–$85), Wild River Bay Motel (517 N. Hamilton St., tel. 715/483–9343; 4 rooms; $61). ✕ **Restaurants:** None in park. In St. Croix Falls: St. Croix Café (103 S. Washington St., tel. 715/483–9079; $8–$10), Wayne's Restaurant (1961 U.S. 8, tel. 715/483–3121; $3–$10). 🛒 **Groceries & Gear:** In St. Croix Falls: St. Croix Outdoors (1298 198th St., tel. 715/483-9515), Wal-Mart (2179 U.S. 8, tel. 715/483–1399).

FEES, HOURS & REGULATIONS

Free. Make picnic shelter reservations at Osceola Landing. Minnesota or Wisconsin state fishing license required. Leashed pets only. No bicycles or motorized vehicles on trails. Obey slow speed and no-wake zones on river. No trapping. Park open daily. Headquarters open Memorial Day–Labor Day, Mon.–Thurs. 8:30–5, Fri.–Sun. 8:30–6; rest of May and Sept., daily 8:30–4:30; Oct.–Apr., weekdays 8–4:30. Namekagon Visitor Center open May and Sept., weekends 8–4:30; Memorial Day–Labor Day, daily 8–4:30. Marshland Visitor Center open for groups by request; call tel. 320/629–2148.

HOW TO GET THERE

Entrance in St. Croix Falls, at corner of Massachusetts and Hamilton Sts. Closest airport: Minneapolis–St. Paul (55 mi).

CONTACTS

St. Croix National Scenic Riverway (Box 708, St. Croix Falls, WI 54024, tel. 715/483–3284, fax 715/483–3288, www.nps.gov/sacn). Polk County Information Center (710 Rte. 35 S, St. Croix Falls, WI 54024, tel. 715/483–1410). Minnesota Office of Tourism (121 7th Pl. E, 100 Metro Sq., St. Paul 55101-2112, tel. 800/657–3700). Wisconsin Division of Tourism (201 W. Washington Ave., Madison, WI 53703, tel. 800/372–2737). State park information: Minnesota Department of Natural Resources Information Center (500 Lafayette Rd., St. Paul, MN 55101, tel. 651/296–6157). Wisconsin Department of Natural Resources Bureau of Parks and Recreation (Dept. of Natural Resources, Box 7921 Madison, WI 53707-7921, tel. 608/266–2181).

See Also

Ice Age National Scenic Trail, Ice Age National Scientific Reserve, Lewis and Clark National Historic Trail, and *North Country National Scenic Trail,* in Other National Parklands.

WYOMING

Devils Tower National Monument

In northeastern Wyoming, near Devils Tower

Devils Tower was the nation's first national monument. An igneous intrusion exposed by erosion, Devils Tower rises 867 feet from its base and is a magnet for rock climbers. Today, it's surrounded by pine forests of the Black Hills and the grasslands of the rolling plains. A healthy prairie dog town thrives on the property. The tower remains sacred to numerous Plains Indian tribes. The monument was proclaimed in 1906.

WHAT TO SEE & DO

Fishing, hiking, picnicking, rock climbing. **Facilities:** Visitor center, wayside exhibits, trails. Bookstore, picnic area with pavilion and fire grates. **Programs & Events:** Guided walking tours, special cultural programs, and evening campfire programs (Memorial Day–Labor Day). Cowboy Poetry Festival (Labor Day weekend). **Tips & Hints:** Plan to spend at least two hours visiting the monument. Prepare for summer heat of 95°F or higher. Voluntary climbing closure during June. Busiest July and Aug., least crowded Dec.–Feb.

FOOD, LODGING & SUPPLIES

Camping: In the park: Belle Fourche Campground (55 sites; $12; flush toilets). Nearby: Devil's Tower KOA (Rtes. 110 and 24, tel. 307/467–5395 or 800/562–5785; 156 sites, 11 cabins; $16–$65; flush toilets, showers, hook-ups; closed Oct.–Apr.). **Hotels:** None in park. In Sundance: Bear Lodge Motel (218 Cleveland St., tel. 307/283–1611; 33 rooms; $64), Sundance Mountain Inn (26 Rte. 585, tel. 307/283–3737 or 888/347–2794; 42 rooms; $79–$89). **Restaurants:** None in park. In Sundance: Aro Restaurant & Lounge (205 Cleveland St., tel. 307/283–2000; $6–$15), Log Cabin Café (U.S. 14, tel. 307/283–3393; $4–$12). **Groceries:** In Sundance: Decker's Grocery (106 North St., tel. 307/283–3155).

FEES, HOURS & REGULATIONS

Entrance fee: $3 per person (walk-ins, bicycles, or motorcycles) or $8 per vehicle. Wyoming state fishing license required. Climbers must register with park. No backcountry camping. No hunting or collecting park resource materials. No pets on tower or on trails. Leashed pets elsewhere. No vehicles, including bicycles, off maintained roadways. Park open daily. Visitor center open Memorial Day–Labor Day, daily 8–8; Mar.–Memorial Day and Labor Day–Oct., daily 8:30–5.

HOW TO GET THERE

From I–90, the monument can be reached via U.S. 14 north and Rte. 24. Closest airport: Gillette (60 mi).

CONTACTS

Devils Tower National Monument (Box 10, Devils Tower, WY 82714, tel. 307/467–5283, fax 307/467–5350, www.nps.gov/deto). Sundance Chamber of Commerce (Box 1004, Sundance, WY 82729, tel. 307/283–1000).

Fort Laramie
National Historic Site

In southeastern Wyoming part of the state, near Fort Laramie

The 12 restored historic buildings on the site interpret life at this "Queen Outpost of the Frontier Army." During the 1800s, the Wyoming wilderness fort on the Laramie River, near the river's confluence with the Platte, played a crucial role in the West's transformation. First serving as a fur-trading center, the fort later became a military garrison along the Oregon Trail. The military post played an essential role in western Army operations during the Indian wars. After 41 years of service, the post closed in 1890. The site was proclaimed a national monument in 1938 and redesignated a national historic site in 1960.

WHAT TO SEE & DO

Touring the fort, watching audiovisual program. **Facilities:** Visitor center with interpretive exhibits, fort. Bookstore. **Programs & Events:** Self-guided and audio tours. Interpretive programs, guided tours, living-history demonstrations (June–Aug.). **Tips & Hints:** Busiest July and Aug., least crowded Dec. and Jan.

FOOD, LODGING & SUPPLIES

Camping: None in park. In Fort Laramie: Carnahan Guest Ranch (935 Gray Rocks Rd., tel. 800/837–6730; tent camping area; $15–$20; flush toilets, showers, hook-ups). In Lingle: Pony Soldier RV Park (2302A U.S. 26, tel. 307/837–3078; 65 sites; $19–$20; flush toilets, showers, hook-ups). **Hotels:** None in park. In Torrington: Kings Inn (1555 S. Main St., tel. 307/532–4011; 54 rooms; $50–$100), Maverick Hotel (U.S. 26 W, tel. 307/532–4064; 10 rooms, 3 suites; $36). **Restaurants:** None in park. In Torrington: Little Moon Lake Supper Club (316 E. U.S. 26, Torrington, tel. 307/532–5750; $10–$20; closed Sun.). Liras (Connelly St. and U.S. 26 N, tel. 307/837–2826; $12–$17; closed Mon.). **Groceries & Gear:** None in park. In Guernsey: B&F Foods (452 W. Whalen St., tel. 307/836–2266).

FEES & HOURS

Entrance fee: $3 adults, free ages 16 and under. Fort grounds open daily 8–dusk. Visitor center open mid-May–Sept., daily 8–dusk; Oct.–mid-May, daily 8–dusk.

HOW TO GET THERE

3 mi southwest of the town of Fort Laramie, on Rte. 160. Closest airport: Torrington (20 mi).

CONTACTS

Fort Laramie National Historic Site (965 Gray Rocks Rd., Fort Laramie, WY 82212, tel. 307/837–2221, fax 307/837B-2120, www.nps. gov/fola).

Fossil Butte National Monument

In southwestern Wyoming, near Kemmerer

The 8,198-acre site contains one of the best-preserved and most complete paleoecosystems of fossilized plants, fish, insects, mammals, birds, and reptiles. The fossilized remnants of this freshwater lake date to a period of warmer climate that existed 50 million years ago. The monument was established in 1972.

WHAT TO SEE & DO

Hiking, picnicking, road touring. **Facilities:** Visitor center, trails. Bookstore, picnic area. **Programs & Events:** Porch programs and guided nature hikes (June–Sept.). **Tips & Hints:** Hiking trails are 7,000 feet to 8,000 feet above sea level and considered moderately strenuous. Go in late summer for best weather. Busiest July and Aug., least crowded Dec. and Jan.

FOOD, LODGING & SUPPLIES

Camping: None in park. In Kemmerer: Foothills RV Park (U.S. 189 N, Kemmerer, tel. 307/877–6634; 39 sites; $22; flush toilets, showers, hook-ups), Kemmerer Community Campground (Rte. 233 near city hall; 5 tent sites; $5; pit toilet). **Hotels:** None in park. In Diamondville: Energy Inn (3 U.S. 30, tel. 307/877–6901; 42 rooms; $48). In Kemmerer: Fairview Motel (61 U.S. 30, tel. 307/877–3938 or 800/247–3938; 61 rooms; $44–$50). **Restaurants:** None in park. In Kemmerer: Busy Bee (919 Pine St., tel. 307/877–6820; $5–$10). **Groceries & Gear:** None in park. In Kemmerer: Kemmerer Jubilee (625 Pine Ave., tel. 307/877–3698).

FEES, HOURS & REGULATIONS

Free. No hunting. Leashed pets only. Park open daily. Visitor center open Labor Day–Memorial Day, daily 8–4:30; Memorial Day–Labor Day, daily 8–7.

HOW TO GET THERE

13 mi west of Kemmerer, on U.S. 30. Closest airports: Salt Lake City, UT (145 mi), Rock Springs, WY (100 mi).

CONTACTS

Fossil Butte National Monument (864 Chicken Creek Rd., Box 592, Kemmerer, WY 83101, tel. 307/877–4455, fax 307/877–4457, www.nps. gov/fobu). Kemmerer Chamber of Commerce (800 Pine Ave., Kemmerer, WY 83101-2907, tel. 307/877–9761).

Grand Teton National Park

In northwestern Wyoming, near Jackson

Towering more than a mile above the valley known as Jackson Hole, the Grand Teton rises 13,770 feet above sea level. Twelve Teton peaks reach above 12,000 feet, high enough to support a dozen mountain glaciers. The park offers ribbons of green riparian plants bordering the Snake River and other streams, sagebrush flats, lodgepole pine and spruce forests, subalpine meadows, and alpine stone fields. Adjacent to the park is the National Elk Refuge, a winter feeding ground for the largest migrating elk herd in North America. Moose, buffalo, pronghorn antelope, bears, eagles, and trumpeter swans also inhabit the park. The park was initially established on February 26, 1929. Through the 1930s, John D. Rockefeller, Jr. purchased 35,000 acres of valley land from local ranchers and donated 33,000 acres to the National Park Service in 1949. In 1950 the current boundaries of the park were established with the inclusion of the valley land.

WHAT TO SEE & DO

Auto touring, backpacking, bicycling (rentals, Dornan's and in Jackson), boating, canoeing, fishing (rentals, in park and in Jackson), floating (rentals, in park and in Jackson), hiking, horseback riding (rentals, Colter Bay and Jackson Lake Lodge), mountaineering (rentals), skiing, snowmobiling (rentals, Flagg Ranch), snowshoeing, swimming, wildlife viewing. **Facilities:** 3 visitor centers: Moose (12 mi north of Jackson on U.S. 89/191/26), Jenny Lake (20 mi north of Jackson on Teton Park Rd.), and Colter Bay (42 mi north of Jackson on U.S. 89/191/26), Flagg Ranch Information Station (16 mi north of Colter Bay on U.S. 89/191/26). Auditorium, Indian Arts Museum, amphitheater at Colter Bay; 100 mi of scenic roads; 200 mi of trails. Bookstores, gas, gift shops, marina. **Programs & Events:** Ranger-led walks, talks, museum tours, evening slide presentations, and campfire programs (early June–late Sept.). **Tips & Hints:** Plan ahead or make reservations in summer for lodging, camping, and dining. Summer highs are near 85°F, lows near 45°F; winters are long and cold, with heavy snows Dec.–Feb. and daytime temperatures at or below freezing. Bring rain gear spring–fall. Busiest July and Aug., least crowded Oct., Nov., Jan., and Apr.

FOOD, LODGING & SUPPLIES

Camping: 6 campgrounds in the park: Colter Bay (350 sites; $12; flush toilets, showers), Colter Bay RV Park (tel. 307/543–2811; 112 sites; $39; flush toilets, showers, hook-ups), Flagg Ranch (175 sites; $22–$40; flush toilets, showers, hook-ups), Gros Ventre (360 sites; $12; flush toilets), Jenny Lake (49 tent sites; $12; flush toilets), Lizard Creek (60 sites; $12; flush toilets), Signal Mountain (86 sites; $12; flush toilets). Backcountry camping allowed (permit required; *see below*). **Hotels:** In the park: American Alpine Club Climber's Ranch dormitory (tel. 307/733–7271; 60 beds; $8; closed Oct.–May), Colter Bay Village (tel. 307/733–2522 or 800/628–9988; 166 cabins; $129; closed late Sept.–May), Dornan's Spur Ranch Cabins (tel. 307/733–2522; 12 cabins; $155–$230), Flagg Ranch (tel. 800/443–2311; 92 cabins; $135; closed mid-Oct.–mid-Dec. and mid-Mar.–mid-May), Jackson Lake Lodge (tel. 307/543–3100 or 800/628–9988; 385 rooms; $124–$225; closed late Oct.–mid-May), Jenny Lake Lodge (tel 307/733–3100 or 800/628–9988; 37 cabins; $429; closed mid-Oct.–late May), Moulton Ranch Cabins (tel. 307/733–3749 or 208/529–2354; 5 cabins; $85–$120; closed Sept.–May), Signal Mountain Lodge (tel. 800/672–6012; 47 rooms, 32 cabins; $95–$182; closed mid-Oct.–mid-May), Triangle X Ranch (tel. 307/733–2183; 22 cabins; $1,200–$1,700 per person per week; closed Nov.–Dec. 26 and Mar.–late May). ✕ **Restaurants:** In the park: Dornan's (tel. 307/733–2415; $14–$18), Flagg Ranch (tel. 800/443–2311; $10–$25), Jackson Lake Lodge (tel. 307/543–3100; $9–$22, Jenny Lake Lodge Dining Room (tel. 307/733–4647 or 800/628–9988; $45.50 prix-fixe; closed Oct.–May), Signal Mountain Lodge (tel. 800/672–6012; $10–$25). ⛄ **Groceries & Gear:** Colter Bay Village, Dornan's, South Jenny Lake, Signal Mountain, Colter Bay, and Flagg Ranch.

FEES, HOURS & REGULATIONS

Entrance fee: $20 per car, good for seven days in Yellowstone and Grand Teton national parks. Backcountry permit required (free). Backcountry campsite reservations ($15) available Jan.–May 15 and up to 24 hrs before first night's stay. Permit required (fee varies depending on boat type) for all watercraft. Wyoming state fishing license required. Park open daily. Moose Visitor Center open Memorial Day–Labor Day, daily 8–7; Labor Day–Memorial Day, daily 8–5. Jenny Lake Visitor Center open June–Labor Day, daily 8–7. Colter Bay Visitor Center open mid-May–June and Labor Day–Sept. 30, daily 8–5; June–Labor Day, daily 8–8. Flagg Ranch Information Station open June–Labor Day, daily 9–5:30.

HOW TO GET THERE

The Moose Visitor Center is 12 mi north of Jackson on U.S. 26, 89, and 191. Closest airport: Jackson Hole (8 mi).

CONTACTS

Grand Teton National Park (Drawer 170, Moose, WY 83012, tel. 307/739–3300, fax 307/739–3438, www.nps.gov/grte). Jackson Chamber of Commerce (Box 550 or 990 W. Broadway, Jackson, WY 83001, tel. 307/733–3316).

John D. Rockefeller Jr. Memorial Parkway

In northwestern Wyoming, near Jackson

This scenic 82-mi corridor commemorates Rockefeller's role in aiding the establishment of many parks, including Grand Teton. The parkway connects West Thumb in Yellowstone with the south entrance of Grand Teton National Park. The 23,777-acre parkway was authorized on August 25, 1972.

WHAT TO SEE & DO

See Grand Teton National Park.

FOOD, LODGING & SUPPLIES

None in park. *See Grand Teton National Park.*

CONTACTS

John D. Rockefeller Jr. Memorial Parkway (c/o Grand Teton National Park, Drawer 170, Moose, WY 83012, tel. 307/733-2880, www.nps. gov/jodr).

Yellowstone National Park

In northwestern Wyoming, southeast Montana, and northeast Idaho

Yellowstone, the world's oldest national park, is a true wilderness, one of the few large natural areas (2.2 million acres) remaining in the lower 48 states. Led by the fabled Old Faithful, the park has approximately 10,000 geysers and hot springs, the greatest number on the planet. Human history in the park is evidenced by cultural sites dating back at least 10,000 years. The park's 1,000 mi of trails allow visitors to see bison, bighorn sheep, elk, grizzly bears, moose, pronghorn, and trumpeter swans. The park was established in 1872 and designated a Biosphere Reserve in 1976 and a World Heritage Site in 1978.

WHAT TO SEE & DO

Backpacking, bicycling, bird- and wildlife watching, boating, bus touring, canoeing, cross-country skiing, fishing, hiking, horseback riding, photography touring, picnicking, snow-coach touring, snowmobiling, wildlife and nature touring. **Facilities:** 5 visitor centers: Albright (Mammoth Hot Springs), Old Faithful, Canyon, Fishing Bridge, and Grant Village. Norris Geyser Basin Museum and Bookstore; Museum of the National Park Ranger (Norris); Madison and West Thumb information stations; scenic roads; overlooks; 8 self-guided nature trails; 1,000 mi of trails. Bookstores, gasoline, gift shops, marina, religious services. **Programs & Events:** Exhibits at Albright Visitor Center at Mammoth Hot Springs. Ranger-led talks, demonstrations, walks, and hikes (mostly June–Aug.). **Tips & Hints:** Make lodging and camping reservations as early as possible. Limit your travels to one or two areas if you have one day or less to spend in the park. Allow two days or more to see major park attractions. Expect slow traveling July and Aug. because of crowds. Busiest July and Aug., least crowded Nov. and Dec.

FOOD, LODGING & SUPPLIES

Camping: 12 campgrounds in the park (2,202 sites; $10–$31; some flush toilets, some vault toilets, some showers, some hook-ups). Backcountry camping allowed (permit required, *see below*). **Hotels:** In the park: Canyon Lodge Cabins (tel. 307/344–7901; 532 cabins; $42–$111; closed mid-Sept.–May), Grant Village (tel. 307/344–7901; 300 rooms; $89–$101; closed mid-Sept.–mid-June), Lake Lodge (tel. 307/344–7901; 36 rooms; $100; closed mid-Sept.–mid-June), Lake Yellowstone Hotel

(tel. 307/344–7311; 158 rooms, 102 cabins; $100–$160; closed late Sept.–mid-May), Mammoth Hot Springs Hotel (tel. 307/344–7311; 97 rooms, 115 cabins; $52–$89; closed mid-Sept.–mid-Dec.), Old Faithful Inn (tel. 307/344–7311; 327 rooms, 6 suites; $68–$198; closed late Oct.– early May), Old Faithful Lodge (tel. 307/344–7311; tel. 307/344–7901, 99 cabins; $42–$65; closed mid-Sept.–mid-May), Old Faithful Snow Lodge (tel. 307/344–7901; 100 rooms; $131; closed mid-Oct.–mid-Dec. and mid-Mar.–mid-May), Roosevelt Lodge (tel. 307/344–7901; 80 cabins; $46–$64; closed early Sept.–early June). ✗ **Restaurants:** In the park: snack bars, cafeterias ($5–$10), and/or full-service restaurants ($12–$31) at all park lodgings. ⌂ **Groceries & Gear:** In the park: general stores at Bridge Bay, Canyon, Fishing Bridge, Grant Village, Lake, Mammoth Hot Springs, Old Faithful, and Tower Fall.

FEES, HOURS & REGULATIONS

Entrance fee: $20 per vehicle, $15 per snowmobile or motorcycle, $10 per bicyclist, walk-in, or skier 16 and up. Fee valid for seven days in Yellowstone and Grand Teton national parks. Bus and snow-coach tours (tel. 307/344–7311). Backcountry permit required ($15; reservations available: Backcountry Office, Box 168, Yellowstone National Park, WY 82190). No commercial hauling or travel through park. Permit required for fishing and boating. Summer season is mid-Apr.–late Oct. All park roads close at 8 AM after first Sun. in Nov. except North Entrance road to Northeast entrance. Only over-snow vehicles are allowed on other park roads. Winter season begins mid-Dec. and runs through mid-Mar. Only the road from the north entrance at Gardiner, Montana, to northeast entrance at Cooke City, Montana, is open to cars year-round. Over-snow vehicles only on other park roads. Albright Visitor Center open daily, hours vary. Old Faithful Visitor Center open mid-Apr.–late Oct., daily, hours vary; mid-Dec.–mid-Mar., daily, hours vary. Fishing Bridge, Grant Village, West Thumb Information Station, and Museum of the National Park Ranger open late May–late Sept., daily 9–5. Canyon Visitor Center, Madison Information Station, and Norris Geyser Basin Museum open late May–early Oct., daily, hours vary.

HOW TO GET THERE

There are five park entrances. To reach the north entrance, take U.S. 89 from I–90 at Livingston, MT; northeast entrance, take U.S. 212 from I–90 at Billings, MT, or Rte. 296 from Cody, WY; west entrance, take U.S. 191 from Bozeman, MT, or U.S. 20 from Idaho Falls, ID; east entrance, take U.S. 16 from Cody, WY; south entrance, take U.S. 89 from Jackson, WY. Closest airports: Cody (90 mi) and Jackson, WY (115 mi); Bozeman (105 mi), Billings (195 mi), and West Yellowstone (June–early Sept.; 5 mi), MT; and Idaho Falls, ID (135 mi).

CONTACTS

Yellowstone National Park (Box 168, Yellowstone National Park, WY 82190-0168, tel. 307/344–7381; 307/344–7311 reservations, www.nps. gov/yell). Big Sky Chamber of Commerce (Box 160100, Big Sky, MT 59716, tel. 800/943–4111), Billings Chamber of Commerce (Box 31177 or 815 S. 27th St., Billings, MT 59107, tel. 406/245–4111). Bozeman Chamber of Commerce (Box B, Bozeman, MT 59771 or 2000 Commerce Way, Bozeman, MT 59715, tel. 406/586–5421). Cooke City–Silver Gate Chamber of Commerce (Box 1071, Cooke City, MT 59020, tel. 406/838–2336). Gardiner Chamber of Commerce (Box 81, Gardiner, MT 59030, tel. 406/848–7971). Livingston Chamber of Commerce (303 E. Park St., Livingston, MT 59047, tel. 406/222–0850). Red Lodge Chamber of Commerce (Box 988, Red Lodge, MT 59068, tel. 406/446–1718). West Yellowstone Chamber of Commerce (Box 458, West Yellowstone, WY 59758, tel. 406/646–7701). Cody Chamber of Commerce (836 Sheridan Ave., Cody, WY 82414, tel. 307/587–2297). Dubois Chamber of Commerce (Box 632, Dubois, WY 82513, tel. 307/455–2556). Jackson Chamber of Commerce (Box 550 or 990 W. Broadway, Jackson, WY 83001, tel. 307/733–3316). Idaho Falls Chamber of Commerce and Eastern Idaho Visitor Information Center (Box 50498 or 505 Lindsay Blvd., Idaho Falls, ID 83405-0498, tel. 208/523–1010 or 800/634–3246).

See Also

Bighorn Canyon National Recreation Area, Montana. *California National Historic Trail, Continental Divide National Scenic Trail, Mormon Pioneer National Historic Trail, Nez Perce National Historic Trail, Oregon National Scenic Trail, Pony Express National Historic Trail,* in Other National Parklands.

National Park of American Samoa

In the South Pacific

An oceanic rain forest, the Indo-Pacific coral reef, and 3,000-year-old Samoan culture are protected in this park. It's located on three tropical volcanic islands—the main island of Tutuila and the Manua Islands of Ofu and Tau—separated by 60 mi of water. The park, which also protects the habitat of two species of flying fox (fruit bats), was authorized in 1988 and established in 1993.

WHAT TO SEE & DO

Auto touring on Tutuila, bat and bird-watching, hiking on shore, hiking to the summit of Mt. Alava (1,610 feet) on Tutuila, snorkeling on Ofu. **Facilities:** Pago Plaza Visitor Center (Pago Pago). **Tips & Hints:** Come prepared to experience Samoa on Samoan terms. Be open to new cultural experiences, and don't expect the same standards for visitor services that can be found on the mainland. The weather is hot and humid all year. Bring binoculars and snorkel gear. Always hike and snorkel with a partner. Stay away from breaking waves and steep areas. Don't touch corals, especially fire coral, which produces a nasty sting. Don't swim near an "ava"—a crevice in the reef face where water drains out as the tide goes out. Carry plenty of water. Visit May–Sept. (winter in the Southern Hemisphere), when the temperature is about 80°F with southeast trade winds and less rain, but expect rain almost every day.

FOOD, LODGING & SUPPLIES

Hotels: None in park. In Pago Pago: Motu-o-Fiafiaga B&B (on the main road from the airport, tel. 684/633–7777; 12 rooms, 1 penthouse; $50–$100, $125 penthouse). In Utulei: Rainmaker Hotel (across from the Executive Office Building, on the main road from the airport, tel. 684/633–4241; 181 rooms; $72–$85). ✕ **Restaurants:** None in park. In Pago Pago: Don't Drink the Water (Pago Plaza Bldg., tel. 684/633–5485; $3–$10). In Pago Pago: Evalani (Motu-o-fiafiaga B&B, on the main road from the airport, tel. 684/633–7777; $6–$17). ⛁ **Groceries & Gear:** None in park. In Tafuna: Cost-You-Less (airport road, tel. 684/699–5975), K-S Mart (airport road, tel. 684/699–5241).

FEES, HOURS & REGULATIONS

Free. No fishing. No rest rooms in park. Park open daily. Visitor center open weekdays 8–4:30, Sat. 8–noon.

HOW TO GET THERE

Park headquarters is in Pago Pago, American Samoa. Closest airport: Pago Pago International (10 mi).

CONTACTS

National Park of American Samoa (Pago Pago, American Samoa 96799, tel. 684/633–7082, 684/633–7083, or 684/633–7084, fax 684/633–7085, www.nps.gov/npsa). Tourism Office (Dept. of Commerce, American Samoa Government, Pago Pago, American Samoa 96799, tel. 684/633–1092).

GUAM

War in the Pacific National Historical Park

In the Pacific Ocean, on Guam

This park has seven sites, including the summit of Mt. Tenjo (1,033 feet), underwater relics on the offshore coral reefs (132 feet), former battlegrounds, and aging gun emplacements and trenches. The sites commemorate the battles that were fought there in the last months of World War II. The park was authorized on August 18, 1978.

WHAT TO SEE & DO

Hiking, picnicking, scuba diving, touring historic battle sites. **Facilities:** Trails, beaches. **Programs & Events:** Ranger-led walks and talks by appointment. **Tips & Hints:** The visitor center was destroyed by super-typhoon Pongsona in Dec. 2002, and remains closed. The park's trails and beaches sustained severe erosion, and are open on a limited basis. Live ordnance still may be found in the park. Report any ammunition or military explosives you find on- or offshore. Some open caves still may contain booby traps. Some areas of the park are privately owned; observe NO TRESPASSING signs. Busiest Feb. and Mar., least crowded Aug.–Oct.

FOOD, LODGING & SUPPLIES

Camping: None in park. In Yona: Tagachang Beach Park (tel. 671/475–6288; backcountry camping; $2; permit required). **Hotels:** None in park. In Tumon: Holiday Inn Resort (871 Pale San Vitores, tel. 671/647–7272; 252 rooms; $110–$195), Guam Hotel Okura (185 Gun Beach Rd., Tumon, tel. 671/646–1403; 366 rooms; $160–$295). **Restaurants:** None in park. In Tamuning: Lone Star Steak House (615 S. Marine Dr., tel. 671/646–6061; $10–$16). **Groceries & Gear:** None in park. In Tamuning: Payless Super Market (Airport Rd. and Marine Dr., tel. 671/646–1005).

FEES, HOURS & REGULATIONS

Free. All park units are open daily 8–3. Overlook is limited to walk-in visits.

HOW TO GET THERE

Guam, the southernmost island of the Mariana Islands, is in the West Pacific, 1,500 mi south of Tokyo and 6,100 mi west of San Francisco. Guam is 15 hours ahead of Eastern Standard Time and doesn't observe daylight saving time. The park consists of seven units, all on the Philippine Sea (west) side of island. The visitor center at 115 Marine Dr. is closed.

CONTACTS

Superintendent, War in the Pacific National Historical Park (115 Haloda Bldg., Marine Dr., Asan, Guam 96922, tel. 671/477–9362 or 671/472–7240, fax 671/472–7241, www.nps.gov/wapa). Guam Department of Parks and Recreation (Box 2950, Hagatna, Guam 96932, tel. 671/472–2887 or 671/477–8280). Guam Hotel & Restaurant Association (Box 8565, Tamuning, Guam 96931, tel. 671/649–1447, fax 671/649–8565, www.ghra.org.gu).

See Also

American Memorial Park, in Other National Parklands.

San Juan
National Historic Site

In San Juan

The site preserves the Spanish colonial forts of San Felipe del Morro, San Cristobal, El Cañuelo, and the city walls and gate of San Juan. These ancient stone fortifications built along the Atlantic Coast protected Spain's possessions and its trade monopoly in the New World. Begun by Spanish troops in the 16th century, the massive masonry defenses are the oldest European-style fortifications within the territory of the United States. The site was established in 1949 and designated a World Heritage Site in 1983.

WHAT TO SEE & DO

Jogging, picnicking, touring forts, watching video. **Facilities:** 2 visitor centers: El Morro and San Cristobal; museum (El Morro), wayside exhibits in forts, furnished troop quarters (San Cristobal). Bookstores. **Programs & Events:** Ranger-guided tours (San Cristobal: daily at 10 and 2 in English, 11 and 3 in Spanish; El Morro: daily at 10 and 2 in Spanish, 11 and 3 in English), video (daily, every 15 min, alternating English and Spanish). Living-history programs (occasionally). **Tips & Hints:** Surfaces are uneven in forts; wear appropriate walking shoes. Inside forts, surfaces are slippery during rain. Avoid metal sentry boxes during lightning. Busiest in Jan. and Feb., least crowded Aug. and Sept.

FEES, HOURS & REGULATIONS

Entrance fee: $3 adults, $2 ages 62 and over, $1 ages 13–17, free for children age 12 and under. Fort El Canuelo closed to public. Puerto Rico fishing permit required. No pets in forts, leashed pets only on Fort El Morro grounds. Shirts and shoes required in forts. No smoking in forts. No disturbing of plants and wildlife. No food or drinks in forts. Minors must be with adults. No climbing on walls. For campers in all Puerto Rico forests, permits must be obtained from the Department of Natural and Environmental Resources (Box 9066600, Pta. de Tierra, San Juan, Puerto Rico, 00906-6600, tel. 787/724–3647, fax 787/721–5984). The office is in San Juan next to Club Nautico marina by the bridges. Park open daily 9–5.

HOW TO GET THERE

Fort San Felipe del Morro and Fort San Cristobal are on Norzagaray St. in Old San Juan. Closest airport: San Juan (5 mi).

CONTACTS

San Juan National Historic Site (501 Norzagaray St., Old San Juan, PR 00901-2094, tel. 787/729–6777, fax 787/289–7972, www.nps.gov/saju). Puerto Rico Tourism Co. (Box 902, 3960 Old San Juan Station, San Juan, PR 00962-3960, tel. 800/866–7827, fax 787/722–5208).

VIRGIN ISLANDS

Buck Island Reef National Monument

On St. Croix

A magnificent elkhorn coral barrier reef, shallow-water lagoon, and marine garden encircle this uninhabited 180-acre tropical dry-forest island that rises 328 feet above the Caribbean waters. The island is a habitat for the endangered brown pelican, hawksbill and leatherback turtles, and the threatened green turtle. Charter boats take visitors to the beach and for a snorkel tour of the underwater interpretive trail. The monument was established December 28, 1961.

WHAT TO SEE & DO

Boating, hiking, picnicking, sailing, scuba diving, snorkeling, swimming. **Facilities:** Beaches, underwater interpretive trail, picnic areas, island trail, dock. Interpretive display boards. **Tips & Hints:** Don't touch the coral because it's easily damaged and it can injure the toucher. Go Dec. or Apr. for blooms. Take into account rainy seasons in Nov. and Mar. and hurricane season July–Sept. Busiest Feb.–June, least crowded Sept. and Oct.

FOOD, LODGING & SUPPLIES

None on island. *See Christiansted National Historic Site.*

FEES, HOURS & REGULATIONS

Free. Concession trips: $40 for a half day, $70 for a full day. Reservations recommended. Big Beard Adventures (tel. 340/773–4482); Charis (tel. 340/773–9027); Clyde, Inc. (tel. 340/773–8520); Diva (tel. 340/778–4675); MileMark Water Sports (tel. 340/773–2628); and Terero Charters (tel. 340/773–3161). No spearfishing or pets. No fishing or collecting in marine garden. Island and underwater trail closed at night. Vessels can anchor up to two weeks off West Beach. Pit toilets only on island. Park is open daily sunrise–sunset. Information is available from Christiansted National Historic Site (*see separate entry*). Visitor Center in downtown Christiansted, St. Croix, Virgin Islands. Open daily 8–5, weekends and federal holidays, 9–5.

HOW TO GET THERE

1½ mi off the northeast side of St. Croix, Virgin Islands. Closest airport: Henry Rohlsen Airport (8 mi west of Christiansted).

CONTACTS

Buck Island Reef National Monument, National Park Service (Danish Customs House, Kings Wharf 100, Christiansted, St. Croix, VI 00820-4611, tel. 340/773–1460, fax 340/773–5995, www.nps.gov/buis). Virgin Islands Department of Tourism (Box 6400, St. Thomas, VI 00804, tel.

800/372–8784). Christiansted Visitors Bureau (Box 4538, Christiansted, St. Croix, VI 00822, tel. 340/773–0495).

Christiansted National Historic Site

In Christiansted, St. Croix

The site protects 18th- and 19th-century buildings in the heart of the historic area of Christiansted, the capital of the former Danish West Indies. Attractions include museums at Fort Christiansvaern and the Steeple Building, and other historic buildings are being renovated. The site was designated Virgin Islands National Historic Site in 1952 and renamed in 1961.

WHAT TO SEE & DO

Self-guided walking tours of historic area, touring museums at fort and steeple. **Facilities:** Visitor contact station at Fort Christiansvaern, Steeple Building Museum. **Programs & Events:** Ranger-led group tours (by reservation only). **Tips & Hints:** Begin tour at fort. Busiest Feb. and Mar., least crowded Sept.–Dec.

FOOD & LODGING

Hotels: None in park. In Christiansted: Caravelle Hotel (44A Queen Cross St., tel. 340/773–0687; 44 rooms; $95–$160), Danish Manor (2 Company St., tel. 340/773–1377 or 800-524-2069; 34 rooms; $69–$175), Holger Danske Best Western (1200 King Cross St., tel. 340/773–3600; 30 rooms; $79–$125), Hotel on the Cay (Protestant Cay, tel. 340/773–2035; 55 rooms; $78–$106). **Restaurants:** None in park. In Christiansted: A Boardwalk Inn by Antoine (end of boardwalk, tel. 340/773–5762; $3–$10), Harbormaster Restaurant (at Hotel on the Cay, tel. 340/773–2035; $9–$35), Roadrunner Restaurant (Caravelle Hotel, 44A Queen Cross St., tel. 340/773–6585; $6–$25).

FEES & HOURS

Entrance fee: $3 adults for Fort and Steeple Building Museum. Site open daily 8–5. Museum open weekdays 8–5, weekends 9–5.

HOW TO GET THERE

The site is in the heart of Christiansted, surrounded by the Christiansted Historic District. The visitor contact station is at Fort Christiansvaern. Park headquarters is in the Danish Customs House. Closest airport: Henry Rohlsen on St. Croix (8 mi west of Christiansted).

CONTACTS

Christiansted National Historic Site (Box 160, Christiansted, VI 00821, tel. 340/773–1460, www.nps.gov/chri). Virgin Islands Department of Tourism (Box 6400, St. Thomas, VI 00804, tel. 800/372–8784). Christiansted Visitors Bureau (Box 4538, Christiansted, St. Croix, VI 00822, tel. 340/773–0495).

Salt River Bay National Historical Park & Ecological Preserve

On St. Croix

All major cultural periods in the history of the U.S. Virgin Islands are included in this park. It's the only known site where members of the Columbus expedition set foot on what is now U.S. territory. The park contains the only ceremonial prehistoric ball court ever discovered in the lesser Antilles, village middens, and burial grounds. Various European groups, including the Spaniards, French, Dutch, English, and Danish, attempted to colonize the area during the post-Columbian period. The site is marked by Fort Sale, a remaining earthworks fortification from the Dutch period of occupation. The site was authorized on February 24, 1992.

WHAT TO SEE & DO

Scuba diving (rentals, Anchor Dive Center), swimming, touring historic and prehistoric sites. Facilities: Visitor center (on wharf in Christiansted), beaches, overviews. **Programs & Events:** Ranger talks (year-round, on request).

FOOD & LODGING

None in park. *See Christiansted National Historic Site).*

FEES & HOURS

Free. Visitor center open daily 8–5.

HOW TO GET THERE

Visitor center is on the wharf in downtown Christiansted. Closest airport: Henry Rohlsen on St. Croix (8 mi west of Christiansted).

CONTACTS

Salt River Bay National Historical Park & Ecological Preserve (c/o Christiansted National Historic Site, Danish Custom House, Kings Wharf, 2100 Church St., 100, Christiansted, VI 00820-4611, tel. 340/773–1460, www.nps.gov/sari). Virgin Islands Department of Tourism (Box 6400, St. Thomas, VI 00804, tel. 800/372–8784). Christiansted Visitors Bureau (Box 4538, Christiansted, St. Croix, VI 00822, tel. 340/773–0495).

Virgin Islands Coral Reef National Monument

Submerged lands in the Atlantic ocean and Caribbean Sea off St. John

The park preserves 12,708 acres of submerged lands off St. John in the U.S. Virgin Islands and is part of an underwater platform that extends several miles from shore to the deepest part of the Atlantic. Many species, including migrating whales, dolphins, brown pelicans, terns, and sea turtles, live in a delicate balance here, interlinked through complex relationships developed over tens of thousands of years. The monument was created by presidential proclamation in 2001.

WHAT TO SEE & DO

Scuba diving, snorkeling. **Facilities:** *See Virgin Islands National Park.* **Tips & Hints:** Entire park is submerged. Diving and snorkeling is permitted from Hurricane Hole. No off-shore moorings available for private boats. Monument is designated a "no-take zone" but hardnose fishing and bait fishing is allowed at Hurricane Hole (permit required; *see below*), where some moorings are planned.

FEES, HOURS & REGULATIONS

Free. Permit required for fishing in Hurricane Hole; inquire at visitor center. Land access from Hurricane Hole only. Park open daily.

HOW TO GET THERE

A portion of the National Monument off St. John, Hurricane Hole, can be reached via Centerline Rd. Monument is approximately 3 mi east of Coral Bay. Hourly ferry service from Red Hook, St. Thomas, is available to St. John and operates 6 AM–midnight. Less frequent ferries make the trip from Charlotte Amalie. Closest airport: St. Thomas.

CONTACTS

Park Headquarters, Virgin Islands Coral Reef National Monument (1300 Cruz Bay Creek, St. John, VI 00830, tel. 340/776–6201, www.nps.gov/viis). Virgin Islands Department of Tourism (Box 6400, St. Thomas, VI 00804, tel. 800/372–8784).

Virgin Islands National Park

*On St. John and on Hassel Island
in Charlotte Amalie Harbor, St. Thomas*

The park covers about one half of St. John Island as well as Hassel Island in St. Thomas harbor and includes quiet coves, white-sand beaches, tropical forests, wildlife, wildflowers, breathtaking views, and offshore coral reefs. Also protected are early Carib Indian relics and the remains of Danish colonial sugar plantations. The park was authorized on August 2, 1956.

WHAT TO SEE & DO

Auto and safari bus touring, bird-watching, boating, fishing, hiking, picnicking, sailing, scuba diving, snorkeling (rentals), swimming, windsurfing. **Facilities:** Visitor center (Cruz Bay, 5-min walk from public ferry dock), information kiosk (Trunk Bay), bulletin boards, beaches, self-guided underwater trail, trails. Book and map sales area, picnic areas. **Programs & Events:** Guided island hikes, snorkeling trips, cultural crafts demonstrations, evening programs. Advance registration and transportation fees required in some cases. Black History Month Commemoration (late Feb., Annaberg Sugar Plantation), St. John's Carnival (week of July 4). Puppet shows, theater companies. **Tips & Hints:** Wear light cotton clothes and lightweight trousers to help protect against insect bites. Casual clothes are sufficient for most restaurants. Busiest Mar.–Dec., least crowded Sept. and Oct.

FOOD, LODGING & SUPPLIES

Camping: In the park: Cinnamon Bay Campground (North Shore Rd., Cruz Bay, tel. 800/539–9998; 31 tent sites, 50 tent-cabins; $27–$58; flush toilets, showers). **Hotels:** In the park: Cinnamon Bay Cabins (North Shore Rd., Cruz Bay, tel. 800/539–9998; 40 cabins; $70–$140). **Restaurants:** In the park: Tree Lizard Restaurant (Cinnamon Bay; $5–$15). Snack bars at Cruz Bay, Maho Bay, and Trunk Bay. **Groceries & Gear:** In the park: Camp store and water-sports shop at Cinnamon Bay (tel. 800/539–9998).

FEES, HOURS & REGULATIONS

Free except at Annaberg and Trunk Bay ($4 adults, free ages 16 and under). Make campground reservations for winter four to six months in advance. Most popular park areas are easily accessed by taxi, otherwise known as safari buses. Rental vehicles are needed to travel to more remote parts of the island. Boat rentals and charters are necessary to visit some of the park bays that do not have road access. Park open daily. Visitor center open daily 8–4:30.

HOW TO GET THERE

The park on St. John is reached via North Shore or Centerline Rds. Hourly ferry service from Red Hook, St. Thomas, is available to St. John and operates 6 AM–midnight. Less frequent ferries make the trip from Charlotte Amalie. Closest airport: St. Thomas.

CONTACTS

Park Headquarters, Virgin Islands National Park (1300 Cruz Bay Creek, St. John, VI 00830, tel. 340/776–6201, www.nps.gov/viis). Virgin Islands Department of Tourism (Box 6400, St. Thomas, VI 00804, tel. 800/372–8784).

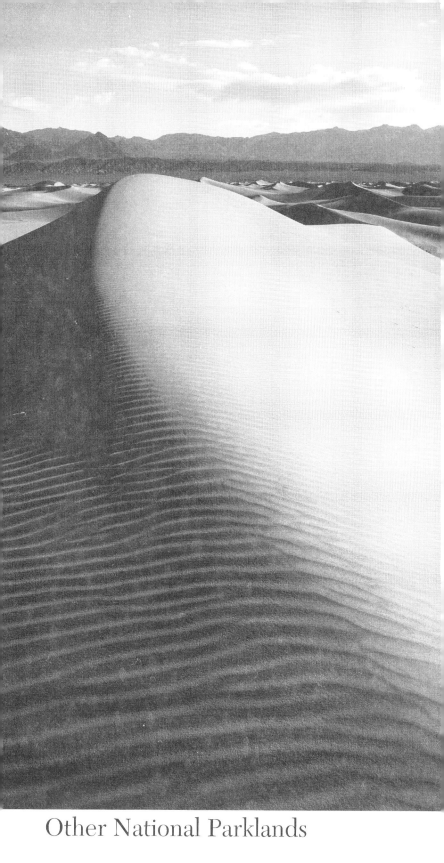

Other National Parklands

SPECIAL-INTEREST PARKS

The categories below are included to help you find the parks that relate to your interest in a specific aspect of our country's history and culture.

African-American History Sites

Booker T. Washington National Monument, Virginia.

Boston African American National Historic Site, Massachusetts.

Brown v. Board of Education National Historic Site, Kansas.

Central High School National Historic Site, Arkansas.

Cumberland Island National Seashore, Georgia.

Dayton Aviation Heritage National Historical Park, Ohio.

Frederick Douglass National Historic Site, District of Columbia.

George Washington Carver National Monument, Missouri.

Harpers Ferry National Historic Park, West Virginia.

Jefferson National Expansion Memorial, Missouri.

Maggie L. Walker National Historic Site, Virginia.

Martin Luther King Jr. National Historic Site, Georgia.

Mary McLeod Bethune Council House National Historic Site, District of Columbia.

Natchez National Historic Park, Mississippi.

New Orleans Jazz National Historical Park, Louisiana.

Nicodemus National Historic Site, Kansas.

Tuskegee Airmen National Historic Site, Alabama.

Tuskegee Institute National Historic Site, Alabama.

Archaeological & Paleontological Sites

Agate Fossil Beds National Monument, Nebraska.

Alibates Flint Quarries National Monument, Texas.

Aztec Ruins National Monument, New Mexico.

Badlands National Park, South Dakota.

Bandelier National Monument, New Mexico.

Canyon de Chelly National Monument, Arizona.

Casa Grande National Monument, Arizona.

Chaco Culture National Historical Park, New Mexico.

Dinosaur National Monument, Colorado.

Effigy Mounds National Monument, Iowa.

Florissant Fossil Beds National Monument, Colorado.

Fossil Butte National Monument, Wyoming.

Gila Cliff Dwellings National Monument, New Mexico.
Hagerman Fossil Beds National Monument, Idaho.
Hopewell Culture National Historical Park, Ohio.
Hovenweep National Monument, Colorado.
John Day Fossil Beds National Monument, Oregon.
Kaloko-Honokohau National Historical Park, Hawaii.
Mesa Verde National Park, Colorado.
Montezuma Castle National Monument, Arizona.
Navajo National Monument, Arizona.
Ocmulgee National Monument, Georgia.
Petroglyph National Monument, New Mexico.
Pipestone National Monument, Minnesota.
Poverty Point National Monument, Louisiana.
Pu'ukohola Heiau National Historic Site, Hawaii.
Theodore Roosevelt National Park, North Dakota.
Tonto National Monument, Arizona.
Tuzigoot National Monument, Arizona.
Walnut Canyon National Monument, Arizona.
Wupatki National Monument, Arizona.
Yucca House National Monument, Colorado.

Battlefields

Big Hole National Battlefield, Montana.
Colonial National Historical Park, Virginia.
Cowpens National Battlefield, South Carolina.
Fort Necessity National Battlefield, Pennsylvania.
Guilford Courthouse National Military Park, North Carolina.
Horseshoe Bend National Military Park, Alabama.
Jean Lafitte National Historical Park, Louisiana.
Kings Mountain National Military Park, South Carolina.
Little Bighorn Battlefield National Monument, Montana.
Minute Man National Historical Park, Massachusetts.
Moores Creek National Battlefield, North Carolina.
Palo Alto Battlefield National Historic Site, Texas.
Rock Creek Park, District of Columbia.
Saratoga National Historical Park, New York.
War in the Pacific National Historical Park, Guam.
Washita Battlefield National Historic Site, Oklahoma.

Civil War Sites

Andersonville National Historic Site, Georgia.
Antietam National Battlefield, Maryland.
Appomattox Court House National Historical Park, Virginia.

Arkansas Post National Memorial, Arkansas.

Brices Cross Roads National Battlefield Site, Mississippi.

Cedar Creek & Belle Grove National Historical Park, Virginia.

Chickamauga & Chattanooga National Military Park, Georgia.

Fort Donelson National Battlefield, Tennessee.

Fort Pulaski National Monument, Georgia.

Fort Sumter National Monument, South Carolina.

Fredericksburg & Spotsylvania County Battlefields Memorial National Military Park, Virginia.

Gettysburg National Military Park, Pennsylvania.

Harpers Ferry National Historical Park, West Virginia.

Kennesaw Mountain National Battlefield Park, Georgia.

Manassas National Battlefield Park, Virginia.

Monocacy National Battlefield, Maryland.

Pea Ridge National Military Park, Arkansas.

Pecos National Historical Park, New Mexico.

Petersburg National Battlefield, Virginia.

Richmond National Battlefield Park, Virginia.

Shiloh National Military Park, Tennessee.

Stones River National Battlefield, Tennessee.

Tupelo National Battlefield, Mississippi.

Vicksburg National Military Park, Mississippi.

Wilson's Creek National Battlefield, Missouri.

Hispanic Heritage Sites & Sites that Relate to America's Discovery

Amistad National Recreation Area, Texas.

Arkansas Post National Memorial, Arkansas.

Big Bend National Park, Texas.

Biscayne National Park, Florida.

Cabrillo National Monument, California.

Canyon de Chelly National Monument, Arizona.

Castillo de San Marcos National Monument, Florida.

Chamizal National Memorial, Texas.

Channel Islands National Park, California.

Christiansted National Historic Site, Virgin Islands.

Coronado National Memorial, Arizona.

Cumberland Island National Seashore, Georgia.

De Soto National Memorial, Florida.

Dry Tortugas National Park, Florida.

El Morro National Monument, New Mexico.

Fort Caroline National Memorial, Florida.

Fort Clatsop National Memorial, Oregon.
Fort Frederica National Monument, Georgia
Fort Matanzas National Monument, Florida.
Fort Point National Historic Site, California.
Golden Gate National Recreation Area, California.
Grand Portage National Monument, Minnesota.
Gulf Islands National Seashore, Florida and Mississippi.
Knife River Indian Villages National Historic Site, North Dakota.
Padre Island National Seashore, Texas.
Palo Alto Battlefield National Historic Site, Texas.
Pecos National Historical Park, New Mexico.
Point Reyes National Seashore, California.
Salinas Pueblo Missions National Monument, New Mexico.
Salt River Bay National Historical Park & Ecological Preserve, Virgin Islands.
San Antonio Missions National Historical Park, Texas.
San Juan National Historic Site, Puerto Rico.
Santa Monica Mountains National Recreation Area, California.
Timucuan Ecological & Historic Preserve, Florida.
Tumacacori National Monument, Arizona.
Wrangell–St. Elias National Park & Preserve, Alaska.

Presidential History Sites

Abraham Lincoln Birthplace National Historic Site, Kentucky.
Adams National Historic Site, Massachusetts.
Andrew Johnson National Historic Site, Tennessee.
Eisenhower National Historic Site, Pennsylvania.
Eleanor Roosevelt National Historic Site, New York.
Ford's Theatre National Historic Site, District of Columbia.
Franklin Delano Roosevelt Memorial, District of Columbia.
General Grant National Memorial, New York.
George Washington Birthplace National Monument, Virginia.
Harry S. Truman National Historic Site, Missouri.
Herbert Hoover National Historic Site, Iowa.
Home of Franklin D. Roosevelt National Historic Site, New York.
James A. Garfield National Historic Site, Ohio.
Jefferson National Expansion Memorial, Missouri.
Jimmy Carter National Historic Site, Georgia.
John Fitzgerald Kennedy National Historic Site, Massachusetts.

Lincoln Boyhood Home National Monument, Indiana.

Lincoln Home National Historic Site, Illinois.

Lincoln Memorial, District of Columbia.

Lyndon Baines Johnson Memorial Grove on the Potomac, District of Columbia.

Lyndon Baines Johnson National Historical Park, Texas.

Martin Van Buren National Historic Site, New York.

Mount Rushmore National Memorial, South Dakota.

Sagamore Hill National Historic Site, New York.

Shenandoah National Park, Virginia.

Theodore Roosevelt Birthplace National Historic Site, New York.

Theodore Roosevelt Inaugural National Historic Site, New York.

Theodore Roosevelt Island National Memorial, District of Columbia.

Theodore Roosevelt National Park, North Dakota.

Thomas Jefferson Memorial, District of Columbia.

Ulysses S. Grant National Historic Site, Missouri.

Washington Monument, District of Columbia.

White House, District of Columbia.

William Howard Taft National Historic Site, Ohio.

Volcanoes, Caves, & Hot Springs

Capulin Volcano National Monument, New Mexico.

Carlsbad Caverns National Park, New Mexico.

Crater Lake National Park, Oregon.

Craters of the Moon National Monument & Preserve, Idaho.

Devils Postpile National Monument, California.

Devils Tower National Monument, Wyoming.

El Malpais National Monument, New Mexico.

Great Basin National Park, Nevada.

Haleakala National Park, Hawaii.

Hawaii Volcanoes National Park, Hawaii.

Hot Springs National Park, Arkansas

Jewel Cave National Monument, South Dakota.

Lassen Volcanic National Park, California.

Lava Beds National Monument, California.

Mammoth Cave National Park, Kentucky.

Oregon Caves National Monument, Oregon.

Pinnacles National Monument, California.

Russell Cave National Monument, Alabama.

Sequoia National Park, California.

Sunset Crater Volcano National Monument, Arizona.

Timpanogos Cave National Monument, Utah.
Wind Cave National Park, South Dakota.
Yellowstone National Park, Wyoming.

Women's History Sites

Clara Barton National Historic Site, Maryland.
Eleanor Roosevelt National Historic Site, New York.
Lowell National Historical Park, Massachusetts.
Maggie L. Walker National Historic Site, Virginia.
Mary McLeod Bethune Council House National Historic Site, District of Columbia.
Sewall-Belmont House National Historic Site, District of Columbia.
Whitman Mission National Historic Site, Washington.
Women's Rights National Historical Park, New York.

World Heritage Sites

Carlsbad Caverns National Park, New Mexico.
Chaco Culture National Historical Park, New Mexico.
Everglades National Park, Florida.
Glacier Bay National Park and Preserve, Alaska.
Glacier National Park, Montana.
Grand Canyon National Park, Arizona.
Great Smoky Mountains National Park, Tennessee.
Hawaii Volcanoes National Park, Hawaii.
Independence National Historical Park, Pennsylvania.
Mammoth Cave National Park, Kentucky.
Mesa Verde National Park, Colorado.
Olympic National Park, Washington.
Redwood National Park, California.
San Juan National Historic Site, Puerto Rico.
Statue of Liberty National Monument, New York.
Wrangell–St. Elias National Park & Preserve, Alaska.
Yellowstone National Park, Wyoming.
Yosemite National Park, California.

AFFILIATED AREAS

AIDS Memorial Grove National Memorial

This memorial in Golden Gate Park in San Francisco is dedicated to individuals who have died as a result of acquired immune deficiency syndrome (AIDS). It's also in support of those who are living with AIDS and their loved ones and caregivers. The memorial was authorized on November 12, 1996.

CONTACT
AIDS Memorial Grove National Memorial (c/o San Francisco Park and Recreation Department, McLaren Lodge, Golden Gate Park, CA 94117, tel. 415/750–8340 or 888/294–7683, www.aidsmemorial.org or).

Aleutian World War II National Historic Area

Preserved here are lands owned by the Ounalaska Corporation on the island of Amaknak. The site interprets the history of the Aleut people and the role they and the Aleutian Islands played in the defense of the United States in World War II. It was authorized on November 12, 1996.

CONTACT
Aleutian World War II National Historic Area (Box 149, 400 Salmon Way, Unalaska, AK 99685, tel. 907/581–1276, www.ounalashka.com).

American Memorial Park

This site on the island of Saipan in the Northern Mariana Islands honors the sacrifices made during the Mariana Campaign of World War II. Recreational facilities, a World War II museum, and flag monument keep alive the memory of more than 4,000 U.S. military personnel and local islanders who died in June 1944. The park was authorized on August 18, 1978.

CONTACT
American Memorial Park (Box 5189 CHRB, Saipan, MP 96950).

Benjamin Franklin National Memorial

In the Rotunda of the Franklin Institute, a 20-foot, 30-ton seated statue of Franklin, sculpted by James Earle Fraser, honors the inventor-statesman. The memorial was designated on October 25, 1972, and is owned and administered by the Franklin Institute.

CONTACT
Benjamin Franklin National Memorial (Franklin Institute, 20th St. and Benjamin Franklin Pkwy., Philadelphia, PA 19103, tel. 215/448–1329).

Chicago Portage National Historic Site

A portion of the portage between the Great Lakes and the Mississippi, discovered by French explorers Jacques Marquette and Louis Joliet, is preserved here. The site was designated on January 3, 1952, and is administered by the Forest Preserve District of Cook County.

CONTACT

Chicago Portage National Historic Site (c/o Forest Preserve District of Cook County, 536 N. Harlem Ave., River Forest, IL 60305).

Chimney Rock National Historic Site

Pioneers traveling west along the Oregon Trail often camped near this famous landmark, which stands 500 feet above the Platte River. The site was designated on August 2, 1956, is owned by Nebraska, and administered by the city of Bayard, the Nebraska State Historical Society, and the National Park Service under a cooperative agreement of June 21, 1956.

CONTACT

Chimney Rock National Historic Site (Scotts Bluff National Monument, Box 27, Gering, NE 69341).

David A. Berger National Memorial

This monument serves as a reminder of violence that took place in Munich at the 1972 Olympic Games.

CONTACT

David A. Berger National Memorial (Mayfield Jewish Community Center, 3505 Mayfield Rd., Cleveland Heights, OH 44118, tel. 216/382–4000).

Delaware & Lehigh National Heritage Corridor

The corridor showcases the Delaware, Lehigh, and Wyoming valleys where anthracite coal was discovered, canals were built, and iron was first poured. During the Industrial Revolution, these canals and their associated early railroads gave access to the coalfields of eastern Pennsylvania. The corridor includes museums with displays about the region's cultural and industrial history and two state parks. It's administered by a federal commission appointed by the Secretary of the Interior and the Governor of Pennsylvania working with a consortium of state, county, local, and private landowners. It was designated on November 18, 1988 and reauthorized in 1998.

CONTACT

Delaware & Lehigh National Heritage Corridor (10 E. Church St., A-208, Bethlehem, PA 18018).

Father Marquette National Memorial

The life and work of Father Jacques Marquette, French priest and explorer, is memorialized here. The site is in Michigan Straits State Park, near St. Ignace, Michigan, where he founded a Jesuit mission in 1671 and was buried in 1678. The memorial was authorized on December 20, 1975.

CONTACT

Father Marquette National Memorial (Parks Division, Dept. of Natural Resources, Box 30028, Lansing, MI 48900).

Gloria Dei (Old Swedes') Church National Historic Site

This, the second oldest Swedish church in the United States, was founded in 1677. The present structure, a splendid example of 17th-century Swedish church architecture, was erected about 1700. The site was designated on November 17, 1942, and is owned and administered by Corporation of Gloria Dei (Old Swedes') Church.

CONTACT

Gloria Dei (Old Swedes') Church National Historic Site (Columbus Blvd. and Christian St., Philadelphia, PA 19106).

Green Springs
National Historic Landmark District

This portion of Louisa County in Virginia's Piedmont has fine rural manor houses and related buildings (none of which are open to the public) in an unmarred landscape. In 1974 the district was declared a national historic landmark by the Secretary of the Interior.

CONTACT

Green Springs National Historic Landmark District (c/o Shenandoah National Park, 3655 U.S. 211 E, Luray, VA 22835).

Historic Camden

Camden was established in 1732 and at that time was known as Fredericksburg Township. In 1768 the village was named Camden in honor of Charles Pratt, Lord Camden, a British Parliamentary champion of colonial rights. The town was occupied by the British under Lord Cornwallis from June 1, 1780, until May 9, 1781. It was one of the few frontier settlements to have hosted two battles during the American Revolution: the first on August 16, 1780, and the second on April 25, 1781. The Historic Camden Revolutionary War Site was authorized on May 24, 1982.

CONTACT

Historic Camden (Box 710, Camden, SC 29020, tel. 803/432–9841, www.hfistoric-camden.org).

Ice Age National Scientific Reserve

This country's first national scientific reserve is home to nationally significant features of continental glaciation. State parks in the area are open to the public. The reserve was authorized on October 13, 1964.

CONTACT

Ice Age National Scientific Reserve (Wisconsin Dept. of Natural Resources, Box 7921, Madison, WI 53707).

Illinois & Michigan Canal National Heritage Corridor

This canal was built in the 1830s and 1840s along the portage between Lake Michigan and the Illinois River, which had long been used as a Native American trade route. The canal rapidly transformed Chicago from an isolated crossroads into a critical transportation hub between the East and the developing Midwest. A 61-mi recreational trail follows the canal towpath. The corridor was designated on August 24, 1984.

CONTACT

Illinois & Michigan Canal National Heritage Corridor (15701 S. Independence Blvd., Lockport, IL 60441).

International Peace Garden

This 2,300-acre park, with its exquisite garden, is located on the North Dakota–Manitoba border. It serves as a unique tribute to the peace and friendship between the people of Canada and the United States.

CONTACT

International Peace Garden (R.R. 1, Box 116, Dunseith, ND 58329).

Inupiat Heritage Center

This center is affiliated with New Bedford Whaling National Historical Park to commemorate more than 2,000 19th-century whaling trips from New Bedford to the western Arctic. The center collects, preserves, and exhibits historical material, art objects, and scientific displays. The center was designated Feb. 3, 1999.

CONTACT

Inupiat Heritage Center (Box 749, Barrow, AK 99723, tel. 907/852–5494, www.nps.gov/inup).

Jamestown National Historic Site

Part of the site of the first permanent British settlement in North America (1607) is on the upper end of Jamestown Island, scene of the first representative legislative government on this continent, July 30, 1619. The site was designated on December 18, 1940, and is owned and administered by Association for the Preservation of Virginia Antiquities. The remainder of Jamestown site and island is part of Colonial National Historical Park.

CONTACT

Jamestown National Historic Site (c/o Association for the Preservation of Virginia Antiquities, John Marshall House, 2705 Park Ave., Richmond, VA 23220).

John H. Chafee Blackstone River Valley National Heritage Corridor

The American Industrial Revolution began in the mills (including Slater Mill), villages, and associated transportation networks in the Blackstone Valley, which runs along some 46 mi of river and canals from Worcester, Massachusetts, to Providence, Rhode Island. The corridor was established on November 10, 1986.

CONTACT

John H. Chafee Blackstone River Valley National Heritage Corridor (1 Depot Sq., Woonsocket, RI 02895, tel. 401/762–0250, www.nps.gov/blac).

Lower East Side Tenement National Historic District

The heart of the Lower East Side Tenement Museum is its landmark tenement building, home to more than 7,000 people from 20 nations between 1863 and 1935. The museum promotes tolerance and historical perspective at this gateway to America. The district was designated on November 12, 1998.

CONTACT

Lower East Side Tenement Museum National Historic Site (66 Allen St., New York, NY 10002, tel. 212/431–0233, www.nps.gov/loea or www.tenement.org).

McLoughlin House National Historic Site

Dr. John McLoughlin, often called the "Father of Oregon," was prominent in the development of the Pacific Northwest as chief factor of Fort Vancouver. He lived in this house between 1847 and 1857. The site was designated a national historic site on June 27, 1945. It is owned and administered by McLoughlin Memorial Association.

CONTACT
McLoughlin House National Historic Site (713 Center St., Oregon City, OR 97045, tel. 503/656–5146, www.nps.gov/mcho).

New Jersey Coastal Heritage Trail

From the Raritan Bay near New York City south to Cape May and along the Delaware River and Bay, this scenic vehicular trail explores the diverse resources along New Jersey's coast through a series of interpretive themes. Lighthouses, boardwalks, historic communities, wildlife habitats, and migratory flyways are part of the trail. There are fees for some activities sponsored by private and public institutions. Still under development, the trail was authorized on October 20, 1988.

CONTACT
New Jersey Coastal Heritage Trail Route (389 Fortescue Rd., Box 568, Newport, NJ 08385, tel. 856/447–0103, www.nps.gov/neje).

Pinelands National Reserve

The area is a sandy coastal plain of more than 1.1 million acres of low, dense pine and oak forests, streams, wetlands, cranberry bogs and blueberry fields, historic iron and glass factories, and small towns. Most facilities are provided within state forests, parks and wildlife management areas. The reserve was authorized on November 10, 1978, and designated a Biosphere Reserve in 1983.

CONTACT
Pinelands National Reserve (c/o Northeast Regional Office, National Park Service, 200 Chestnut St., Philadelphia, PA 19106-2818).

Port Chicago National Memorial

This memorial, located at the former Concord Naval Weapons Station in Concord, California, recognizes the critical role Port Chicago Naval Magazine played as an important facility for the Pacific Theater in World War II. It also commemorates the July 17, 1944, explosion that occurred at the site, which resulted in the largest stateside disaster of World War II. Open to the public by reservation only. It was authorized on October 8, 1992.

CONTACT

Port Chicago National Memorial (c/o Eugene O'Neill National Historic Site, Box 280, Danville, CA 94526, tel. 925/943–1531).

Quinebaug & Shetucket Rivers Valley National Heritage Corridor

The Quinebaug and Shetucket rivers valley in Connecticut is one of the last unspoiled and undeveloped areas in the northeastern United States. It has remained largely intact, including important aboriginal archaeological sites, excellent water quality, beautiful rural landscapes, architecturally significant mill structures and mill villages, and a large acreage of parks and other permanent open space. The corridor encompasses 850 square mi and includes 25 towns. It was authorized on November 2, 1994.

CONTACT

Quinebaug & Shetucket Rivers Valley National Heritage Corridor (Quinebaug-Shetucket Heritage Corridor, Inc., Box 161, Putnam, CT 06260).

Red Hill Patrick Henry National Memorial

The law office and grave of the fiery Virginia legislator and orator are preserved at this small plantation along with a reconstruction of Patrick Henry's last home, several dependencies, and a museum. The memorial was authorized on May 13, 1986.

CONTACT

Red Hill Patrick Henry National Memorial (Patrick Henry Memorial Foundation, Brookneal, VA 24528, tel. 804/376–2044, www.redhill.org).

Roosevelt Campobello International Park

President Franklin D. Roosevelt spent many vacations at his 34-room summer home on Campobello Island in New Brunswick's Bay of Fundy. The house and grounds include a visitor center, flower gardens, and historic furnishings. The park was established on July 7, 1964, and is owned and administered by the United States–Canadian Commission.

CONTACT

Roosevelt Campobello International Park (c/o Executive Secretary Roosevelt Campobello International Park Commission, Box 129, Lubec, ME 04652, tel. 506/752–2922, www.fdr.net).

Sewall-Belmont House National Historic Site

Rebuilt after fire damage from the War of 1812, this redbrick house is one of the oldest on Capitol Hill. It has been the National Woman's

Party Headquarters since 1929 and commemorates the party's founder and woman's suffrage leader, Alice Paul, and associates. It's open on a limited basis. The site was authorized on October 26, 1974.

CONTACT

Sewall-Belmont House National Historic Site (144 Constitution Ave. NE, Washington, DC 20002).

Touro Synagogue National Historic Site

This is the oldest synagogue in the United States. Designed by colonial architect Peter Harrison and dedicated in 1763, it is a fine example of 18th-century Georgian architecture. It was designated on March 5, 1940.

CONTACT

Touro Synagogue National Historic Site (85 Touro St., Newport, RI 02840, tel. 401/847–4794, www.tourosynagogue.org).

Thomas Cole National Historic Site

This is the Hudson River home of the eminent British-American landscape painter Thomas Cole (1801–48). He is recognized as the founder of the Hudson River School, America's first indigenous school of landscape painting. Cole created some of his great paintings, including the "Voyage of Life" series, in the small studio on the property. He lived in the 1815 Federal-style house. The site is owned and operated by the Greene County Historical Society, and it was authorized on December 9, 1999.

CONTACT

Thomas Cole National Historic Site (218 Spring St., Catskill, NY 12414, tel. 519/943–7465).

NATIONAL HERITAGE AREAS

America's Agricultural Heritage Partnership

Sites in this 37-county region of northeastern Iowa illustrate the transformation that took place as mechanization paved the way for a distinctly American system of industrialized agriculture. Tractor design and manufacture, mechanized farming, corn-hog production, dairying, beef cattle feeding, and meatpacking continue to characterize this region. The cultural histories of family farming and agribusiness are equally well represented. Primary federal assistance is being provided by the U.S. Department of Agriculture. It was authorized on November 12, 1996.

CONTACT

America's Agricultural Heritage Partnership (Box 2845, Waterloo, IA 50704).

Augusta Canal National Heritage Area

This 7-mi corridor follows the full length of the best preserved canal of its kind remaining in the southern United States. The canal transformed Augusta into an important regional industrial area on the eve of the Civil War, and was instrumental in the post–Civil War relocation of much of the nation's textile industry to the south. The area was authorized on November 12, 1996.

CONTACT

Augusta Canal National Heritage Area (Box 2367, Augusta, GA 30903).

Automobile National Heritage Area

Southeast Michigan, which includes the "Motor Cities" of Detroit, Lansing and Flint, is the region that put the world on wheels. The heritage area consists of six significant corridors. This collection of auto-related museums, attractions, activities, and events exists to preserve and interpret the story of the automobile and was authorized November 6, 1998.

CONTACT

Automobile National Heritage Area Partnership, Inc. (University of Michigan–Dearborn Office of Government Relations, 4901 Evergreen Rd., 1130 AB, Dearborn, MI 48128-1491, tel. 313/593–5140).

Cache La Poudre Corridor

The Cache La Poudre River Corridor is in north-central Colorado, beginning at the eastern end of the Arapahoe-Roosevelt National Forest and extending east through Fort Collins and Larimer County to Greeley and Weld County. The boundary of the 40-mi corridor is the river's 100-year floodplain. It commemorates the role of water development and management in the American West. The area was authorized on October 19, 2000.

CONTACTS

City of Greeley (1100 10th St., Suite 101, Greeley, CO 80631). Larimer County (Box 1190, Fort Collins, CO 80522).

Cane River National Heritage Area

Before becoming part of the United States, this area at the intersection of the Spanish and French realms in the New World gave rise to the unique Creole culture in a rural setting. The area supports the oldest community in the territory encompassed by the Louisiana Purchase. Historic plantations, Cane River Creole National Historical Park, and three state commemorative areas keep the region's Creole heritage alive. The area was authorized on November 2, 1994.

CONTACT

Cane River National Heritage Area (c/o Cane River Creole National Historic Park, Box 536, Natchitoches, LA 71457).

Delaware & Lehigh National Heritage Corridor

See Affiliated Areas.

Erie Canalway National Heritage Corridor

The 524-mi canal system, opened in 1825, is an engineering marvel that knitted together New England, New York, and the west, spreading commerce and ideas. The area was authorized on December 21, 2000.

CONTACT

Fort Stanwix National Monument (112 E. Park St., Rome, NY 13440-5816).

Essex National Heritage Area

Essex County is a 500-square-mi area north of Boston along the Atlantic Coast and the Merrimack River. It includes thousands of historic sites that illuminate colonial settlement, the development of the shoe and textile industries, and the growth and decline of the maritime industries—including fishing, privateering, and the China trade. It was authorized on November 12, 1996.

CONTACT

Essex National Heritage Commission, Inc. (140 Washington St., Salem, MA 01910, tel. 978/740–1650, www.essexheritage.org).

Hudson River Valley National Heritage Area

From Troy to New York City, the Hudson River valley contains a rich assemblage of natural features and nationally significant cultural and historical sites. The valley has maintained the scenic, rural character that inspired the Hudson Valley School of landscape painting and the Knickerbocker writers. Recreational opportunities are found on the river, in the mountains, parklands, and on greenway trails. The area was authorized on November 12, 1996.

CONTACT

Hudson River Valley National Heritage Area (Hudson River Valley Greenway and Conservancy, Capitol Bldg., Capitol Station, Room 254, Albany, NY 12224, tel. 518/473–3835, www.hudsongreenway.state.ny.us).

Illinois & Michigan Canal National Heritage Corridor

See Affiliated Areas.

John H. Chafee Blackstone River Valley National Heritage Corridor

See Affiliated Areas.

Lackawanna Valley National Heritage Area

The 40-mi-long Lackawanna Heritage Valley is at the center of what was once the world's most productive anthracite field. Located in Pennsylvania, the heritage area commemorates the history and culture of the anthracite coal mining industry, a cornerstone of the American industrial legacy. A combination of trails, museums, and other attractions help tell the story of anthracite. The area was authorized on October 6, 2000.

CONTACT

Lackawanna Heritage Valley Authority (1300 Old Plank Rd., Mayfield, PA 18433).

National Coal Heritage Area

The cultural geography here has been profoundly influenced over the last 125 years by the pervasive role of the coalmines. The communities in these 11 counties in southern West Virginia reflect their origins as "company towns" formed by local traditions, waves of immigrant workers, and the dominance of the mining companies. Ethnic neighborhoods and the physical infrastructure of the mines are still clearly seen throughout the region. The area was authorized on November 12, 1996.

CONTACT

National Coal Heritage Area (Cultural Center Capitol Complex, 1900 Kanawha Blvd. E, Charleston, WV 25305, tel. 304/558–0220, www.coalheritage.org).

Ohio & Erie Canal
National Heritage Corridor

This area of northeast Ohio celebrates the canal that enabled shipping between Lake Erie and the Ohio River and vaulted Ohio into commercial prominence in the early 1830s. The canal and towpath trail pass through agricultural lands and rural villages into industrial communities such as Akron, Canton, and Cleveland that trace their prosperity to the coming of the canal. (*See also Cuyahoga Valley National Recreation Area.*) The area was authorized on November 12, 1996.

CONTACT

Ohio & Erie Canal National Heritage Corridor (Ohio and Erie Canal Association, 1556 Boston Mills Rd., Boston, OH 44268).

Quinebaug & Shetucket Rivers Valley
National Heritage Corridor

See Affiliated Areas.

Rivers of Steel National Heritage Area

Steel made a great imprint on the Pittsburgh region in the late 19th and early 20th centuries. The industry made possible railroads, skyscrapers, and shipbuilding while altering corporate practice and labor organization. There are remnants of numerous mills as well as communities founded by mill workers, many of which are linked by hiking trails and riverboat tours. The area was authorized on November 12, 1996.

CONTACT

Steel Industry Heritage Corporation (338 E. 9th Ave., 1st fl., Homestead, PA 15120).

Schuylkill River Valley
National Heritage Area

Encompassing the 128-mi Schuylkill River Valley as it passes through five counties, the heritage area includes three national park areas, the city of Philadelphia, and many early communities and canal towns. The area has pre-Revolutionary mills, late-19th-century factories, and numerous historic districts and cultural attractions. The area was authorized on October 6, 2000.

CONTACT

Schuylkill River Greenway Association (960 Old Mill Rd., Wyomissing, PA 19610).

Shenandoah Valley Battlefields National Historic District

This fertile agricultural valley was of strategic value to both sides in the Civil War with the result that it became the site for 15 battles in the conflict. Authorized November 12, 1996.

CONTACT

Shenandoah Valley Battlefields Commission (Box 897, New Market, VA 22844, tel. 540/740–4543).

South Carolina Heritage Corridor

Two routes through 14 counties in western South Carolina begin in the mill villages, waterfalls, and mountains of the Up Country; run through historic courthouse towns and military sites and along the Savannah River; and follow the Edisto River and the South Carolina Railroad to the Low Country's wealth of African-American and antebellum history, centered in and around historic Charleston. The area was authorized on November 12, 1996.

CONTACT

South Carolina Heritage Corridor (Heritage Tourism Development Office, South Carolina Dept. of Parks, Recreation, and Tourism, 1205 Pendleton St., Columbia, SC 29201, tel. 803/734–1217).

Southwestern Pennsylvania Industrial Heritage Route

This 500-mi route travels through nine counties of southwestern Pennsylvania and features hundreds of sites relating to the nation's industrial story. Included are the Altoona Railyards, the Johnstown Flood National Memorial and Museum, the steel mills of Johnstown, and Horseshoe Curve, a 19th-century engineering marvel built by the Pennsylvania Railroad. Also called the Path of Progress National Heritage Route. The site was authorized on November 19, 1988.

CONTACT

Southwestern Pennsylvania Industrial Heritage Route (Southwestern Pennsylvania Heritage Preservation Commission, Box 565, 105 Zee Plaza, Hollidaysburg, PA 16648).

Tennessee Civil War Heritage Area

A number of areas throughout Tennessee preserve and interpret the legacy of the Civil War there. Heritage resources are focused on important events, geographic factors, decisive battles, engagements, and strategic maneuvers of the war; and the impact of the war on Tennessee's residents. The area was authorized on November 12, 1996.

CONTACT

Tennessee Civil War Heritage Area (Center for Historic Preservation, Middle Tennessee State University, Box 80, Murfreesboro, TN 37132).

Wheeling National Heritage Area

Once the capital of West Virginia, Wheeling marked the northernmost navigable port on the Ohio River. It became a thriving commercial, industrial, and cultural center, and by 1818 was the terminus of the National Road, our nation's first highway. The area was authorized on October 11, 2000.

CONTACT

Wheeling National Heritage Area Corporation (1400 Main St., Wheeling, WV 26003).

Yuma Crossing National Heritage Area

This natural ford on the mighty Colorado River has been a gathering spot for people for more than 500 years. It was an important 19th-century landmark during the westward expansion of our nation. The area was authorized on October 19, 2000.

CONTACT

Riverfront Development Office (200 W. 1st St., Yuma, AZ 85364, tel. 520/343–8744).

NATIONAL TRAILS SYSTEM

Appalachian National Scenic Trail

See the West Virginia chapter for a full description.

CONTACT

Appalachian National Scenic Trail (Appalachian Trail Conference, Box 807, Harpers Ferry, WV 25425-0807).

California National Historic Trail

The California Trail is a system of overland routes, starting at numerous points along the Missouri River and ending at many locations in California and Oregon. Over these trails passed one of America's great mass migrations, seeking the promise of gold and a new life in California in the late 1840s and 1850s. Traces of their struggles and triumphs are still evident at many trail sites. The trail was established on August 3, 1992.

CONTACT

California National Historic Trail (National Park Service, Box 45155, 324 S. State St., Salt Lake City, UT 84145-0155).

Continental Divide National Scenic Trail

Running the length of the Rocky Mountains near the Continental Divide, this trail extends from Canada's Waterton Lake into Montana, along the Idaho border, and on to Wyoming, Colorado, and New Mexico, ending at the U.S.–Mexico border. It was established on November 10, 1978.

CONTACT

Continental Divide National Scenic Trail (Forest Service, Region 2, 240 Simms St., Golden, CO 80401).

El Camino Real de Tierra Adentro

From 1598 to 1882, the 1,600-mi Camino Real de Tierra Adentro provided an important link between Mexico City and Santa Fe. As such it aided exploration, colonization, economic development, and subsequent culture interaction among Spanish, Anglo, and native people. Only the 404-mi portion of the trail in the United States is designated as a National Historic Trail. The trail was established on October 13, 2000.

CONTACT

Long Distance Trails Group (Box 728, Santa Fe, NM 87504-0728).

Florida National Scenic Trail

The trail runs the length of Florida from Big Cypress National Preserve near Miami to Gulf Islands National Seashore near Pensacola Beach. It's the only national scenic trail that explores tropical and subtropical regions. More than 600 mi have been developed for public use. The trail was established on March 28, 1983.

CONTACT

Florida National Scenic Trail (USDA Forest Service, National Forests in Florida, 325 John Knox Rd., F-100, Tallahassee, FL 32303, tel. 850/942-9300).

Ice Age National Scenic Trail

Winding over Wisconsin's glacial moraines, the trail links six of the nine units of the Ice Age National Scientific Reserve. It traverses significant features of Wisconsin's glacial heritage. Approximately 500 mi are open to public use; additional miles are being developed. It was authorized on October 3, 1980.

CONTACT

Ice Age National Scenic Trail (National Park Service, 700 Rayovac Dr., Suite 100, Madison, WI 53711).

Iditarod National Historic Trail

One of Alaska's preeminent Gold Rush Trails, the 2,350-mi Iditarod extends from Seward to Nome and is composed of a network of trails and side trails developed at the turn of the 20th century. It was established on November 20, 1978.

CONTACT

Iditarod National Historic Trail (Bureau of Land Management, 6881 Abbott Loop Rd., Anchorage, AK 99507).

Juan Bautista de Anza National Historic Trail

This trail commemorates the route of a party of Spanish soldier-settlers and their families, led by Lieutenant-Colonel Juan Bautista de Anza, from Sonora, Mexico, to found a presidio and mission at the port of San Francisco. The trail includes an autoroute linking more than 100 sites and 150 mi of trails in Arizona and California for recreational hiking. The 1,200-mi trail was established on August 15, 1990.

CONTACT

Juan Bautista de Anza National Historic Trail (600 Harrison St., Suite 600, San Francisco, CA 94107-1372, www.nps.gov/juba).

Lewis & Clark National Historic Trail

The route of the 1804–06 Lewis and Clark Expedition extends 3,700 mi, from the Mississippi River in Illinois to the Pacific Ocean at the mouth of the Columbia River in Oregon. Water routes, hiking trails, and marked highways follow the explorer's out-bound and return routes. The trail was established on November 10, 1978.

CONTACT

Lewis and Clark National Historic Trail (National Park Service, 1709 Jackson St., Omaha, NE 68102–2571, tel. 402/221–3471, www.nps.gov/lecl).

Mormon Pioneer National Historic Trail

This 1,300-mi trail follows the route over which Brigham Young led the Mormons from Nauvoo, Illinois, to the site of modern Salt Lake City, Utah, in 1846–47. An auto tour route has been marked near the trail corridor. It was established on November 10, 1978.

CONTACT

Mormon Pioneer National Historic Trail (National Park Service, Box 45155, 324 S. State St., Salt Lake City, UT 84154-0155).

Natchez Trace National Scenic Trail

See the Mississippi chapter for a full description.

CONTACT

Natchez Trace National Scenic Trail (c/o Natchez Trace Parkway, R.R. 1. NT-143, Tupelo, MS 38801-9718).

Nez Perce National Historic Trail

The 1,170-mi Nez Perce trail commemorates the flight of five bands of Nez Perce Indians in 1877. It begins in northeastern Oregon, extends across Idaho and western and central Montana, bisecting Yellowstone National Park in Wyoming and ending near the Bear Paw Mountains. It was established on October 6, 1986.

CONTACT

Nez Perce National Historic Trail (Forest Service Region 1, Box 7662, Missoula, MT 59807).

North Country National Scenic Trail

The trail connects seven northern tier states extending from Crown Point, New York, to Lake Sakakawea in North Dakota, where it connects with the Lewis and Clark National Historic Trail. Approximately 1,650 mi are open to public use. Additional miles are being developed. The trail was established on March 5, 1980.

North Country National Scenic Trail (National Park Service, 700 Rayovac Dr., Suite 100, Madison, WI 53711).

Oregon National Historic Trail

Tens of thousands of pioneers followed this 2,170-mi trail west from Independence, Missouri to Oregon City, Oregon, between 1841 and 1860. The trail was established on November 10, 1978.

CONTACT

Oregon National Historic Trail (National Park Service, Box 45155, 324 S. State St., Salt Lake City, UT 84145-0155).

Overmountain Victory National Historic Trail

This 300-mi route follows the path of American Revolution patriots who mustered in western Virginia and eastern Tennessee and came across the mountains of North Carolina to Kings Mountain, South Carolina, where they defeated British-led Loyalist militia in 1780. The trail was established on September 8, 1980.

CONTACT

Overmountain Victory National Historic Trail (Southeast Region National Park Service, 1924 Bldg., 100 Alabama St. SW, Atlanta, GA 30303).

Pacific Crest National Scenic Trail

Extending from the Mexican border northward along the Sierra and Cascade peaks of California, Oregon, and Washington, the 2,650-mi trail reaches the Canadian border near Ross Lake, Washington. The trail, which is one of the two initial components of the National Trails System, was established on October 2, 1968.

CONTACT

Pacific Crest National Scenic Trail (U.S. Forest Service, Nature of the Northwest Information Center, 800 N.E. Oregon St., Rm 177, Portland, OR 97232).

Pony Express National Historic Trail

For 18 months, 1860–61, riders on horseback carried mail 1,800 mi between St. Joseph, Missouri, and Sacramento, California, in less than 10 days, proving that a regular communications link to the Pacific coast was possible. Most of the 150 relay stations no longer exist. The trail was established on August 3, 1992.

CONTACT

Pony Express National Historic Trail (National Park Service, Box 45155, 324 S. State St., Salt Lake City, UT 84145-0155).

Potomac Heritage National Scenic Trail

See the District of Columbia chapter for a full description.

CONTACT

Potomac Heritage National Scenic Trail (National Capital Region, National Park Service, 1100 Ohio Dr. SW, Washington, DC 20242-0001).

Santa Fe National Historic Trail

This route of the Santa Fe Trail extends from a point near Arrow Rock, Missouri, through Kansas, Oklahoma, and Colorado to Santa Fe, New Mexico. To date, 20 certified sites and segments are open for public use.

CONTACT

Santa Fe National Historic Trail (National Park Service, Long Distance Trails Group, Box 728, Santa Fe, NM 57504-0728).

Selma to Montgomery National Historic Trail

This trail commemorates a 1965 voting rights march led by Dr. Martin Luther King Jr. The marchers walked along U.S. 80 from Brown Chapel A.M.E. Church in Selma, Alabama, to the state capitol in Montgomery. The marched helped inspire passage of voting rights legislation signed by President Johnson on August 6, 1965. The trail was established on November 12, 1965.

CONTACT

Selma to Montgomery National Historic Trail (National Park Service, Southeast Region, 1924 Bldg., 100 Alabama St. SW, Atlanta, GA 30303).

Trail of Tears National Historic Trail

The Trail of Tears commemorates two of the land and water routes used for the forced removal of more than 15,000 Cherokees from their ancestral lands in North Carolina, Tennessee, Georgia, and Alabama to the Indian Territories of Oklahoma and Arkansas. The journey lasted from June 1838 to March 1839. The trail was established on December 16, 1987.

CONTACT

Trail of Tears National Historic Trail (National Park Service, Long Distance Trails Group, Box 728, Santa Fe, NM 87504-0728).

WILD & SCENIC RIVERS SYSTEM

Alagnak Wild River

See the Alaska chapter for a full description.

CONTACT

Alagnak Wild River (Katmai National Park and Preserve, Box 7, King Salmon, AK 99613-0007).

Alatna Wild River

The stream lies wholly within Gates of the Arctic National Park & Preserve, Alaska, in the Central Brooks Range. Wildlife, scenery, and interesting geologic features abound in the river corridor. The river was authorized on December 2, 1980.

CONTACT

Alatna Wild River (Gates of the Arctic National Park & Preserve, 201 1st Ave., Fairbanks, AK 99701).

Aniakchak Wild River

The river, which lies within Aniakchak National Monument & Preserve, Alaska, flows out of Surprise Lake and plunges spectacularly through "The Gates."

CONTACT

Aniakchak Wild River (Katmai National Park & Preserve, Box 7, King Salmon, AK 99613-0007).

Bluestone National Scenic River

See the West Virginia chapter for a full description.

CONTACT

Bluestone National Scenic River (c/o New River Gorge National River, Box 246, Glen Jean, WV 25846-0246).

Charley Wild River

Lying within Yukon-Charley Rivers National Preserve, Alaska, this stream is known for the exceptional clarity of its water. For the experienced canoer or kayaker, it offers many miles of whitewater challenges. The river was authorized on December 2, 1980.

CONTACT

Charley Wild River (Yukon-Charley Rivers National Preserve, Box 167, Eagle, AK 99738-0167, tel. 907/547–2234, www.nps.gov/yuch).

Chilikadrotna Wild River

The river lies within Lake Clark National Park & Preserve, Alaska. Long stretches of swift water and outstanding fishing are exceptional features. The river was authorized on December 2, 1980.

CONTACT

Chilikadrotna Wild River (Lake Clark National Park & Preserve, 4230 University Dr., Suite 311, Anchorage, AK 99508-4626).

Farmington River (West Branch)

The river is an important habitat for wildlife, and the Farmington River Valley is currently one of the few places in Connecticut with nesting bald eagles. Atlantic salmon may soon return to the river after an absence of decades. Recreational value, rare wildlife, outstanding fisheries, and a rich history are some of the features of the Farmington.

CONTACT

Farmington River (National Park Service, 15 State St., Boston, MA 02109).

Flathead River

Branches of the Flathead River border the western and southern boundaries of Glacier National Park, Montana. These areas are popular for fishing, floating and recreation.

CONTACT

Flathead River (Glacier National Park, West Glacier, MT 59936-0128).

Great Egg Harbor Scenic & Recreational River

See the New Jersey chapter for a full description.

CONTACT

Great Egg Harbor Scenic & Recreational River (c/o Northeast Region National Park Service, 200 Chestnut St., Philadelphia, PA 19106-2818).

John Wild River

The river flows south through the Anaktuvuk Pass of Alaska's Brooks Range, and its valley is an important migration route for the Arctic Caribou herd. Gates of the Arctic National Park & Preserve contains the wild river. The river was authorized on December 2, 1980.

CONTACT
John Wild River (Gates of the Arctic National Park & Preserve, 201 1st Ave., Fairbanks, AK 99701).

Kern River

This river includes both the North and South forks of the Kern. The South Fork is totally free-flowing. It descends through deep gorges with large granite outcroppings and domes interspersed with open meadows. The upper 48 mi of the North Fork flow through Sequoia National Park & Golden Trout Wilderness. The river was authorized on November 24, 1987.

CONTACT
Kern River (Sequoia National Park, 47050 Generals Hwy., Three Rivers, CA 93271-9651, or Sequoia National Forest, 900 W. Grand Ave., Porterville, CA 93257).

Kings River

The river includes the entire Middle and South forks, which are largely in Kings Canyon National Park. Beginning in glacial lakes above timberline, the rivers flow through deep, steepsided canyons, over falls and cataracts, eventually becoming an outstanding whitewater rafting river in its lower reaches in Sequoia National Forest. Geology, scenery, recreation, fish, wildlife, and history are all significant aspects. It was authorized on November 3, 1987.

CONTACT
Kings River (Kings Canyon National Park, 47050 Generals Hwy., Three Rivers, CA 93271-9651).

Kobuk Wild River

Kobuk Wild River is contained within Gates of the Arctic National Park & Preserve, Alaska. From its headwaters in the Endicott Mountains, the stream courses south through a wide valley and passes through two scenic canyons. It was authorized on December 2, 1980.

CONTACT
Kobuk Wild River (Gates of the Arctic National Park & Preserve, 201 1st Ave., Fairbanks, AK 99701).

Lamprey Wild & Scenic River

This segment of the Lamprey River, extending from the Bunker Pond Dam in Epping downstream 24 mi to the confluence with the Picassic river in Newmarket, provides conservation opportunities for associated shore lands, floodplains, and wetlands. The Lamprey is considered the most important anadromous fish resource in New Hampshire. It was authorized on November 12, 1996.

CONTACT

Lamprey Wild & Scenic River (Boston System Support Office, Rivers and Trails Dept., 15 State St., Boston, MA 02109).

Lower Delaware Wild & Scenic River

The corridor contains the site of Washington's famous crossing of the Delaware River. Sheer cliffs that rise 400 feet above the river are home to rare flora and fauna in this region, including the prickly pear cactus. It was authorized on November 1, 2000.

CONTACT

Philadelphia Support Office, Stewardship and Partnership Team, Rivers and Trails Group (200 Chestnut St., Philadelphia, PA 19106-2818).

Maurice National Scenic & Recreational River

Portions of the Maurice River and three of its main tributaries, the Manumuskim River and the Menantico and Muskee creeks, were designated to protect critical habitat on the Atlantic Flyway. It was authorized on December 1, 1993.

CONTACT

Maurice National Scenic & Recreational River (c/o Northeast Region, National Park Service, 200 Chestnut St., Philadelphia, PA 19106-2818).

Merced River

Including the main stem and the South Fork, the Merced flows 81 mi in alternating pools, cascades, and waterfalls through Yosemite's superlative scenery—from glaciated peaks to lakes, alpine and subalpine meadows, glacially carved valleys and gorges of spectacular proportions. It was authorized on November 2, 1987.

CONTACT

Merced River (Yosemite National Park, Box 577, Yosemite National Park, CA 95389-0577).

Middle Delaware River

See the Pennsylvania chapter for a full description.

CONTACT

Middle Delaware River (Delaware Water Gap National Recreation Area, Bushkill, PA 18324-9410).

Missouri National Recreational River

See the Nebraska chapter for a full description.

CONTACT

Missouri National Recreational River (Box 591, O'Neill, NE 68763).

Mulchatna Wild River

Mulchatna Wild River, which lies within Lake Clark National Park & Preserve, Alaska, is exceptionally scenic as it flows out of the Turquoise Lake with the glacier-clad Chigmit Mountains to the east. Moose and caribou inhabit the area. The river was authorized on December 2, 1980.

CONTACT

Mulchatna Wild River (Lake Clark National Park & Preserve, 4230 University Dr., Suite 311, Anchorage, AK 99508-4626).

Niobrara National Scenic Riverway

See the Nebraska chapter for a full description.

CONTACT

Niobrara National Scenic Riverway (Box 591, O'Neill, NE 68763).

Noatak Wild River

Noatak Wild River is situated in Gates of the Arctic National Park & Preserve and Noatak National Preserve in Alaska. The Noatak drains the largest mountain-ringed river basin in America that is still virtually unaffected by human activities. It was authorized on December 2, 1980.

CONTACT

Noatak Wild River (Gates of the Arctic National Park & Preserve, 201 1st Ave., Fairbanks, AK 99701).

North Fork of the Koyukuk Wild River

The river flows from the south flank of the Arctic Divide through broad, glacially carved valleys beside the rugged Endicott Mountains in Alaska's Central Brooks Range. It was authorized on December 2, 1980.

CONTACT

North Fork of the Koyukuk Wild River (Gates of the Arctic National Park & Preserve, 201 1st Ave., Fairbanks, AK 99701).

Obed Wild & Scenic River

See the Tennessee chapter for a full description.

CONTACT

Obed Wild & Scenic River (Box 429, Wartburg, TN 37887-0429).

Rio Grande Wild & Scenic River

See the Texas chapter for a full description.

CONTACT

Rio Grande Wild & Scenic River (Big Bend National Park, Big Bend National Park, TX 79834-0129).

St. Croix National Scenic Riverway

See the Wisconsin chapter for a full description.

CONTACT

St. Croix National Scenic Riverway (Box 708, St. Croix Falls, WI 54024-0708).

Salmon Wild River

Salmon Wild River, located within Kobuk Valley National Park, Alaska, is small but exceptionally beautiful, with deep blue-green pools and many rock outcroppings. It was authorized December 2, 1980.

CONTACT

Salmon Wild River (Kobuk Valley National Park, Box 1029, Kotzebue, AK 99752-1029).

Sudbury, Assabet & Concord Rivers

Located about 25 mi west of Boston, the rivers are remarkably undeveloped and provide recreational opportunities in a natural setting. Ten of the river miles lie within the boundary of the Great Meadows National Wildlife Refuge. Historic sites of national importance, including many in the Minute Man National Historical Park, are located near the rivers in Concord.

CONTACT

Sudbury, Assabet & Concord Rivers (Sudbury Valley Trustees, Box 7, Wayland, MA 01778).

Tinayguk Wild River

Alaska's 44-mi Tinayguk River is the largest tributary of the North Fork of the Koyukuk. Both lie entirely within the pristine environment of Gates of the Arctic National Park. It was authorized on December 2, 1980.

CONTACT

Tinayguk Wild River (Gates of the Arctic National Park & Preserve, 201 1st Ave., Fairbanks, AK 99701).

Tlikakila Wild River

Located about 100 air miles west of Anchorage in Lake Clark National Park, Alaska, the 51-mi Tlikakila Wild River is closely flanked by glaciers, 10,000-foot-high rock-and-snow-capped mountains, and perpendicular cliffs. It was authorized on December 2, 1980.

CONTACT

Tlikakila Wild River (Lake Clark National Park & Preserve, 4230 University Dr., Suite 311, Anchorage, AK 99508-4626).

Tuolumne River

The Tuolumne originates from snowmelt off Mounts Dana and Lydell in Yosemite National Park and courses 54 mi before crossing into Stanislaus National Forest. The national forest segment contains some of the most noted whitewater in the high Sierras and is an extremely popular rafting stream. It was authorized on September 28, 1981.

CONTACT

Tuolumne River (Yosemite National Park, Box 577, Yosemite, CA 95389-0577).

Upper Delaware River

See the Pennsylvania chapter for a full description.

CONTACT

Upper Delaware River (Box C, Narrowsburg, NY 12764-0159).

White Clay Creek

CONTACT

White Clay Creek (National Park Service, 260 U.S. Custom House, 2nd and Chestnut Sts., Philadelphia, PA 19106, tel. 215/597–1655).

LODGING CONTACT INFORMATION

Adam's Mark	tel. 800/444–2326	www.adamsmark.com
Baymont Inns	tel. 800/428–3438	www.baymontinns.com
Best Western	tel. 800/528–1234	www.bestwestern.com
Budget Hosts Inns	tel. 800/283–4678	www.budgethost.com
Choice	tel. 800/424–6423	www.choicehotels.com
Clarion	tel. 800/424–6423	www.choicehotels.com
Colony Resorts	tel. 800/777–1700	
Comfort Inn	tel. 800/424–6423	www.choicehotels.com
Days Inn	tel. 800/325–2525	www.daysinn.com
Doubletree	tel. 800/222–8733	www.hilton.com
Econo Lodge	tel. 800/553–2666	www.econolodge.com
Embassy Suites	tel. 800/362–2779	www.embassysuites.com
Fairfield Inn	tel. 800/236–2427	www.marriott.com
Four Seasons	tel. 800/332–3442	www.fourseasons.com
Friendship Inns	tel. 800/453–4511	www.hotelchoice.com
Hilton	tel. 800/445–8667	www.hilton.com
Holiday Inn	tel. 800/465–4329	www.sixcontinentshotels.com
Howard Johnson	tel. 800/654–4656	www.hojo.com
Hyatt Hotels & Resorts	tel. 800/233–1234	www.hyatt.com
Inter-Continental	tel. 800/327–0200	www.intercontinental.com
La Quinta	tel. 800/531–5900	www.laquinta.com
Marriott	tel. 800/228–9290	www.marriott.com
Le Meridien	tel. 800/543–4300	www.lemeridien-hotels.com
Motel 6	tel. 800/466–8356	www.motel6.com
Nikko Hotels International	tel. 800/645–5687	www.nikkohotels.com
Omni	tel. 800/843–6664	www.omnihotels.com
Quality Inn	tel. 800/424–6423	www.choicehotels.com
Radisson	tel. 800/333–3333	www.radisson.com
Ramada	tel. 800/228–2828	www.ramada.com
Red Lion Hotels	tel. 800/222–8733	www.hilton.com
Renaissance Hotels & Resorts	tel. 800/468–3571	www.renaissancehotels.com
Ritz-Carlton	tel. 800/241–3333	www.ritzcarlton.com
Rodeway	tel. 800/228–2000	www.choicehotels.com
Sheraton	tel. 800/325–3535	www.starwood.com/sheraton
Sleep Inn	tel. 800/424–6423	www.choicehotels.com
Super 8	tel. 800/848–8888	www.super8.com.
Westin Hotels & Resorts	tel. 800/228–3000	www.starwood.com/westin
Wyndham Hotels & Resorts	tel. 800/822–4200	www.wyndham.com

Index

INDEX

NOTES

NOTES

_____

_____

_____

_____

_____

_____

_____

_____

_____

_____

_____

_____

_____

_____

_____

_____

_____

_____

_____

NOTES

NOTES

NOTES